Implementing Dietary Guidelines for Healthy Eating

Implementing Dietary Guidelines for Healthy Eating

Edited by

VERNER WHEELOCK
Verner Wheelock Associates Ltd
Bradford, UK

BLACKIE ACADEMIC & PROFESSIONAL
An Imprint of Chapman & Hall
London · Weinheim · New York · Tokyo · Melbourne · Madras

Published by Blackie Academic and Professional, an imprint of Chapman & Hall, 2–6 Boundary Row, London SE1 8HN, UK

Chapman & Hall, 2–6 Boundary Row, London SE1 8HN, UK

Chapman & Hall GmbH, Pappelallee 3, 69469 Weinheim, Germany

Chapman & Hall USA, 115 Fifth Avenue, New York NY 10003, USA

Chapman & Hall Japan, ITP-Japan, Kyowa Building, 3F,
2-2-1 Hirakawacho, Chiyoda-ku, Tokyo 102, Japan

DA Book (Aust.) Pty Ltd, 648 Whitehorse Road, Mitcham 3132, Victoria, Australia

Chapman & Hall India, R. Seshadri, 32 Second Main Road, CIT East, Madras 600 035, India

First edition 1997

Typeset in 10/12 pt Times by Mews Photosetting, Beckenham, Kent

Printed in Great Britain by St Edmundsbury Press Ltd, Bury St Edmunds, Suffolk

ISBN 0 7514 0304 0

A catalogue record for this book is available from the British Library

∞ Printed on acid-free text paper, manufactured in accordance with ANSI/NISO Z39.48-1992 (Permanence of Paper).

Contents

List of contributors

Annie S. Anderson	University of Glasgow, Department of Human Nutrition, Glasgow Royal Infirmary, Alexandra Parade, Glasgow G31 2ER, UK Now at Department of Management and Consumer Studies, University of Dundee, Dundee DD1 5HT, UK
Javier Aranceta	Programme of Nutrition, Department of Health, Basque Government, 48001 Bilbao, Spain
Alexander Baturin	Institute of Nutrition, Russian Academy of Medical Sciences, Moscow, Russia
Gunn-Elin Aa. Bjørneboe	National Nutrition Council, Calmeyers gate 1, Boks 8139 Dep., 0033 Oslo, Norway
Grete Botten	National Nutrition Council, Calmeyers gate 1, Boks 8139 Dep., 0033 Oslo, Norway
H.A.M. Brants	Department of Consumer Research and Epidemiology, TNO Nutrition and Food Research Institute, PO Box 360, 3700 AJ Zeist, The Netherlands
Åke Bruce	National Food Administration, PO Box 622, S-751 26 Uppsala, Sweden
Anne Cogdon	Heart Health Nova Scotia, Community Health and Epidemiology, Clinical Research Centre, Dalhousie University, 5849 University Avenue, Halifax, Nova Scotia, Canada.

Nigel Dickie — Holmes & Marchant Counsel, 15–17 Huntsworth Mews, London NW1 6DD, UK

Lorelei K. DiSogra — Dole Foods, 155 Bovet Street Suite 476, San Mateo, CA 94402, USA

Jane Farquharson — Community Health and Epidemiology, Clinical Research Center, Dalhousie University, 5849 University Avenue, Halifax, Nova Scotia, Canada.

Anna Ferro-Luzzi — National Institute of Nutrition, Via Ardeatina, 546-00178 Rome, Italy

Peter W.F. Fischer — Nutrition Research Division, Food Directories, Health Protection Branch, Health Canada, Ottawa, Ontario K1A 0L2, Canada

Susan B. Foerster — Nutrition and Cancer Prevention Program, California Department of Health Services, 601 North 7th Street, MS-65, PO Box 942732, Sacramento CA 94234-7320, USA

Jerianne Heimendinger — AMC Cancer Research Center, 1600 Pierce Street, Denver, CO 80214, USA

Sally Herne — Lambeth, Southwark and Lewisham Health Commission, 1 Lower Marsh, London SE1 7NT, UK

Johanna M. Hignett — Nestlé UK Ltd, St Georges House, Croydon, Surrey, UK

Rob Hood — Heart Health Nova Scotia, Community Health and Epidemiology, Clinical Research Center, Dalhousie University, 5849 University Avenue, Halifax, Nova Scotia, Canada

K.F.A.M. Hulshof — Department of Consumer Research and Epidemiology, TNO Nutrition and Food Research Institute, PO Box 360, 3700 AJ Zeist, The Netherlands

Lars Johansson — National Nutrition Council, Calmeyers gate 1, Boks 8139 Dep., 0033 Oslo, Norway

Lenore Kohlmeier	Department of Nutrition, University of North Carolina at Chapel Hill, School of Public Health, CB 7400, Chapel Hill, NC 27599
Areti Lagiou	National Nutrition Centre, National School of Public Health, 196 Alexandras Ave, 115 21 Athens, Greece
Michael E.J. Lean	University of Glasgow, Department of Human Nutrition, Glasgow Royal Infirmary, Alexandra Parade, Glasgow G31 2ER, UK
Catherine Leclercq	National Institute of Nutrition, Via Ardeatina, 546-00178 Rome, Italy
Gonçal Lloveras	Programme of Food and Nutrition, Department of Health and Social Security, Autonomous Government of Catalonia, 08028 Barcelona, Spain
M.R.H. Löwik	Department of Consumer Research and Epidemiology, TNO Nutrition and Food Research Institute, PO Box 360, 3700 AJ Zeist, The Netherlands
David R. MacLean	Heart Health Nova Scotia, Community Health and Epidemiology, Clinical Research Center, Dalhousie University, 5849 University Avenue, Halifax, Nova Scotia, Canada
Laura Martino	National Institute of Nutrition, Via Ardeatina, 546-00178 Rome, Italy
Kaare R. Norum	National Nutrition Council, Calmeyers gate 1, Boks 8139 Dep., 0033 Oslo, Norway
Ursula O'Dwyer	Health Promotion Unit, Department of Health, Hawkins House, Hawkins Street, Dublin 2, Ireland
Lars Ovesen	The National Food Agency of Denmark, Mørkhøj Bygade 19, DK-2860 Søborg, Denmark

Andres Petrasovits	Preventive Health Services Division, Health Promotion and Programs Branch, Health Canada, Ottawa, Canada
Stefka Petrova	Department of Nutrition, National Centre of Hygiene, Medical Ecology and Nutrition, 15 Dimitar Nestorov Str, 1431 Sofia, Bulgaria
Elizabeth Pivonka	Produce for Better Health Foundation, 1500 Casho Mill Road, PO Box 6035, Newark, DE 19714-6035, USA
Barry M. Popkin	Department of Nutrition, University of North Carolina at Chapel Hill, School of Public Health, Chapel Hill, NC 27599
Lourdes Ribas	Institute of Public Health, University of Barcelona, Pavelló Central, Campus de Bellvitge, Ctra de la Feixa Llanga s/n, 08907 L'Hospitalet, Spain
M. Riedstra	Department of Consumer Research and Epidemiology, TNO Nutrition and Food Research Institute, PO Box 360, 3700 AJ Zeist, The Netherlands
Lluís Salleras	General Directorate of Public Health, Department of Health and Social Security, Autonomous Government of Catalonia, 08028 Barcelona, Spain
Lluís Serra-Majem	School of Health Sciences, University of Las Palmas de Gran Canaria, P.O. Box 550, 35080 Las Palmas de Gran Canaria, Spain
Terry Sharp	Campden and Chorleywood Food Research Association, Chipping Campden, Gloucestershire GL55 6LD, UK
G.D. Spriegel	J Sainsbury Plc, Stamford House, Stamford Street, London SE1 9LL, UK
Kim Travers	Mount St Vincent University, Halifax, Nova Scotia, Canada

Antonia Trichopoulou National Nutrition Centre, National School of Public Health, 196 Alexandras Ave, 115 21 Athens, Greece

S.N. van Wechem Department of Consumer Research and Epidemiology, TNO Nutrition and Food Research Institute, PO Box 360, 3700 AJ Zeist, The Netherlands and Department of Health Education, State University Limburg, The Netherlands

M.J. Watson Department of Perinatal Medicine, Royal Women's Hospital, 132 Grattan Street, Carlton, Vic 3053, Australia

Janet Weber Department of Food Technology, Massey University, Palmerston North, New Zealand

Verner Wheelock Verner Wheelock Associates Ltd., Albert Mill, 10 Hey Street, Bradford, West Yorkshire BD7 1DQ, UK

Juliet Wiseman Department of Food Technology, Massey University, Palmerston North, New Zealand

Namvar Zohoori Department of Nutrition, University of North Carolina at Chapel Hill, School of Public Health, CB 7400, NC 27599

Preface

It is self-evident that the quality of nutrition is a critical factor determining a high standard of public health. However, there are major problems to be overcome if optimum nutrition is to be achieved. Some or all of the following steps may be involved:

1. research, which can cover a range of approaches and disciplines;
2. evaluation of the research and the formulation of nutritional requirements and dietary guidelines for different sectors of society;
3. putting the recommendations into practice, which is the main focus in this book.

The complexities are enormous. First, it is necessary to find out what people are eating in order to determine whether any nutritional issues need to be addressed. Invariably, this means that surveys have to be conducted, with the inevitable constraint that there has to be a trade-off between the extent and quality of the information obtained versus the number of people involved. The first section deals with this aspect.

It is virtually essential for governments to be key players in the formulation of programmes designed to improve the quality of the national diet. The second part of the book consists of a series of chapters explaining and describing the national policies in a variety of different countries. No attempt has been made to force these into a standard pattern because there are genuine differences between countries in history and in culture.

The actual nutritional issues do vary, as seen, for example, by comparing some of the northern European countries with those in the Mediterranean. Even within a country, the perspective of one group may well differ from that of others, equally qualified to describe the national policy.

Nevertheless, it will be clear that certain features are characteristic of most countries. The importance of sending out clear messages, which are readily understood and easy to apply, is identified time and time again. The need to avoid conflict, which leads to confusion, is paramount. Hence there is a definite responsibility on governments to ensure that there are authoritative sources of information, which can send out signals to consumers, health professionals, food industry, and the media.

The last two parts of the book draw together a number of initiatives that have been taken by health professionals and by companies in the food business.

Taking the book as a whole, it contains a wealth of knowledge based on extensive contributions from many different countries. Hopefully, it will be of value to anyone interested in improving nutritional standards.

V.W.
January 1997
Bradford, UK

Part One

Nutritional Surveillance

1 Nutritional surveillance systems: theoretical framework and management of secondary data

ANNA FERRO-LUZZI and LAURA MARTINO

1.1 Introduction

A nutritional surveillance system (NSS) is a decision-supporting system consisting of integrated activities of data collection, analysis and reporting which generates an overall picture of the nutritional situation of a population and of the factors influencing it (Kelly and Becker, 1991). The ultimate goal of the system is the prevention or control of dietary-related nutritional conditions and the reduction of their cost to society, by reducing the prevalence of unhealthy dietary habits. Its main intermediate purpose is to support the design and evaluation of public health programmes. As for this task, the system works as a decision-support tool that identifies the main problems, detects changes in the nutritional status over the medium and long term, identifies the dietary factors and the related conditions that explain these trends and develops indicators that are useful to policy-makers for monitoring the situation (Mason *et al.*, 1987). Another purpose of the system is to provide the basis for updating dietary guidelines in response to the varying needs of a country, and for formulating realistic national nutrient goals (Campbell, 1989). Such a task requires the evaluation and interpretation of current values and trends in the prevalence of dietary-related diseases and of the dietary risk factors that influence them.

The basic concepts in surveillance activity are displayed in Fig. 1.1. The first basic concept is that of **risk factors**. Risk factors are all the variables capable of significantly affecting health. In the specific case of dietary-related conditions, the risk factor is the specific pattern of food and nutrient consumption. Risk factors have **cut-off points** – often based on stated reference values – that mark the boundaries within which a given level of that factor must be maintained (WHO, 1976). The combination of risk factors and cut-off points generates **indicators**, key elements of the surveillance system as they concentrate the entire information relevant to a specified problem. There are three types of indicators, describing respectively:

Implementing Dietary Guidelines for Healthy Eating. Edited by Verner Wheelock. Published in 1997 by Blackie A&P, an imprint of Chapman & Hall, London. ISBN 0 7514 0304 0

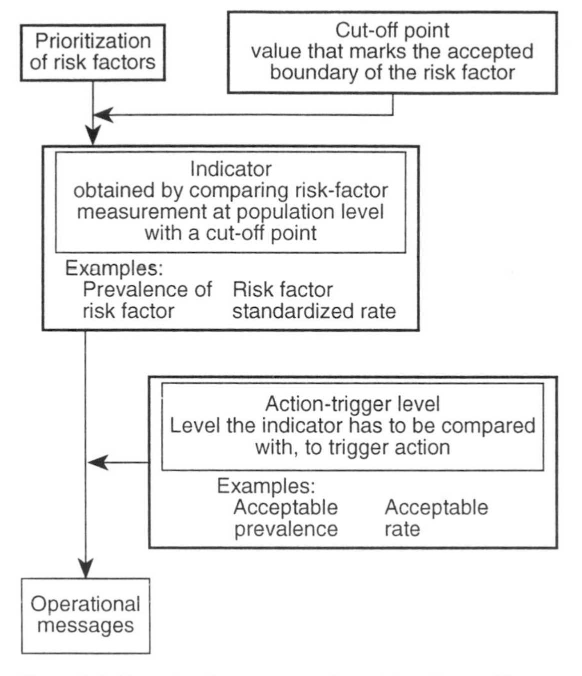

Figure 1.1 Some basic concepts of nutritional surveillance.

1. the outcome indicators, which are those that can be derived from morbidity and mortality statistics of nutrition-related diseases;
2. the non-dietary risk indicators that describe various life-style/behavioural parameters and health conditions; and
3. the dietary risk indicators that are derived from analysis of the eating patterns of the population.

Indicators need to be sensitive enough to be capable of revealing critical changes in the population and of triggering interventions when appropriate (Eylenbosch and Noah, 1988). When changes take place the indicators should be able to indicate both the occurrence of a new trend and its rate. **Action-trigger levels** are levels of presence of an indicator that identify the emergence of a public health problem and at which corrective action is deemed necessary. A trigger level usually consists of the proportion of the population above or below the cut-off point. The definition of action-trigger levels is of a political nature; they should detect or predict real emergencies and avoid false alarms, yet also take into account policy considerations and opportunities (WHO, 1976; Mason *et al.*, 1987).

The design of an NSS involves three main sequential steps (Ferro-Luzzi and Leclercq, 1991). As a first step, working hypotheses are stated for each of the nutritional conditions of interest, describing the likely causal relationship between food consumption variables and the nutritional problems. Indicators are then built from these variables and suitable sources of data are identified. Finally, a decision-support system is created, which receives information from the periphery, transforms it into relevant indicators, then integrates these various indicators into a picture that delivers outgoing messages. These should convey concise, understandable and meaningful policy-making information (Kelly and Becker, 1991).

1.2 Approaches to setting up a nutritional surveillance system

The information flowing into an NSS may be specifically collected (primary data), derive from existing databanks (secondary data) or be a mixture of the two.

The collection of primary data requires dietary and health surveys specifically designed within the framework of nutritional surveillance. These usually provide valuable and detailed information on food consumption and nutrient intake and often also data on health status and nutrition-related conditions, such as obesity, high blood cholesterol, triglycerides, etc. The main advantage of primary data is the high specificity of the information collected and the documentation of the distribution of the risk factors in the population. However, this approach, has a high cost that few governments are prepared to meet on a regular basis. Its high cost often hampers the coverage of suitably large population samples to ensure representativity at the tail ends of the distributions (Buss, 1991).

The second approach is based on the use of existing information. The basic concept of this approach is that a large amount of underexploited information, collected for purposes other than nutritional surveillance, is often available and could be usefully employed to develop nutritional status indicators. Secondary data sets, such as health statistics and food disappearance, are routinely collected in all or most industrialized countries. Although sometimes of a dubious quality and often requiring enhancement procedures, these data can nevertheless be retrieved with relative ease and reorganized for the specific purposes of nutrition policy. In any case, a nutritional surveillance system based on secondary data might represent the only low-cost solution in circumstances where financial resources are limited. Recourse to secondary data might also be conceived as a first step leading to the development of a highly targeted primary data collection, if the need and the feasibility are demonstrated. Such an approach based on secondary data has been adopted in Italy, where a prototypal nutritional surveillance system has been developed by the National Institute of Nutrition by request of the Ministry of Health. This will be described in more detail in section 1.3.

1.2.1 Nutritional surveillance systems based on primary data

Examples of nutritional surveillance activities that are based on *ad hoc* surveys and primary data are offered by several industrialized countries. In the

United States, the government has approved two national bills (the Farm Bill and the National Nutrition Monitoring and Related Research Act) to stimulate the formulation of a comprehensive monitoring system of the nutritional status of the US population by the secretariats of the Department of Agriculture (USDA) and the Department of Health and Human Services (US DHHS) (Moses and Dodds, 1987; US DHHS, 1992). The US nutritional monitoring programme provides information relating to five main areas: nutrition and related conditions; dietary consumption and nutrient intake; people knowledge, attitudes and behaviour; food composition; food market and supply (US DHHS, 1992). The main data sources on which the nutritional programme is based are the National Health and Nutritional Examination Survey (NHANES), consisting of a series of national probability samples of children and adults, and the Nationwide Food Consumption Survey (NFCS), consisting of a household survey of food use and a survey of food consumption by individuals. Special attention is given to higher-risk groups; such as, for example, pregnant women and children (Pregnancy Nutrition Surveillance System and Pediatric Nutrition Surveillance System: Kim *et al.*, 1992; Yip *et al.*, 1992).

Another example of an NSS based on primary data comes from the UK, where the need for monitoring activities on priority health problems was stressed in 1991 in a document, published by the government, entitled *The Health of the Nation* (Waldegrave, 1991). Following the successful completion of the *Dietary and Nutritional Survey of British Adults* (Gregory *et al.*, 1990) and evaluation of its benefits, new action has quickly followed. The Ministry of Agriculture, Fisheries and Food and the Ministry of Health jointly planned and implemented a programme called 'Dietary and Nutritional Survey of British Population', consisting of four successive rounds of surveys – cyclically repeated – of nationally representative samples drawn from different population subgroups: children aged 1½–4½ years, children aged 4–18 years, adults aged 16–64 years and the elderly. The younger children and the elderly have been monitored in 1992–93 and 1994–95, respectively (Gregory *et al.*, 1995). Children aged 4–18 years will be monitored in 1996–97 and adults in 1998–99. For each survey group, dietary habits, health conditions and biochemical indicators are assessed. The cost is approximately £2 million for each survey (A. Mills, personal communication).

In The Netherlands, the first Dutch National Food Consumption Survey (DNFCS) was undertaken in 1987–88, following the official request by the Food and Nutrition Council who required it in order to formulate recommendations on dietary patterns that would improve public health (Löwik and Hermus, 1988). The nutrition survey, repeated in 1992 to evaluate 5-year changes, represented the first step in developing a nutritional surveillance system. It was aimed at giving a systematic evaluation of prevailing dietary habits and nutritional status; identifying at-risk groups and studying the impact of life style and socio-demographic factors on dietary intake (Hulshof, 1993). Data collection was undertaken under the auspices of the Ministry of Health, Welfare and Sports and the Ministry of Agriculture and Fisheries. The TNO Nutrition and Food Research Institute co-ordinated the data analysis. The cost of the survey was approximately Dfl.2 millions (M.R.H. Löwik, personal communication).

A similar initiative was undertaken in Catalonia (Spain) (Chapter 16) when the local government stressed the need to support dietary recommendations with detailed information on the prevalence of dietary risk factors. As a result, in 1986 a Catalan nutrition survey was carried out and repeated in 1992–93. The latter gave an estimate of nutritional status of the population by evaluating food consumption and measuring biochemical and clinical–anthropometrical indicators (for example obesity, hypertension and blood cholesterol) (Serra-Majem *et al.*, 1994).

In Sweden it is the responsibility of the National Food Administration to monitor the food and nutrient intake of the population – as stated in policy documents (Chapter 14). The only national dietary survey was performed in 1989 on about 500 foods. It was an individual survey which recorded the food consumption of a national sample of 2047 individuals aged between 1 and 74 years (W. Becker, personal communication).

Finally, in the early nineties, the Danish Parliament passed a nutritional policy stating the need for a national food consumption survey (Chapter 6) even though a nutritional monitoring plan for nutrients and contaminants had already been incorporated in the Food Monitoring System in 1983, following the advice of a working group of the National Food Agency (National Food Agency of Denmark, 1990). In 1985 and 1995 the same agency performed the two major food consumption surveys in Denmark (Haralddsdottin *et al.*, 1986 and 1987). The more recent survey also included children. Its cost was estimated to be approximately kr.7.5 million (A. Møller, personal communication).

Since all the systems described above were set up in response to official recommendations and were designed to give support to the formulation of adequate programmes and interventions, they are truly part of a nutritional policy. Their findings are reliable and precise. However, their cost has been high (between £0.8 and 2 million on average).

1.2.2. Nutritional surveillance systems based on secondary data

As mentioned earlier, an NSS can be developed with exclusive recourse to secondary data. Also in this approach, a clear definition of the purpose of the exercise is required and the nature and quality of the data to be used must be defined precisely (Kelly, 1988). The preliminary steps therefore consist in the screening of the relevant databanks available in the country and the critical analysis of their quality and appropriateness. More specifically, several technical attributes of the data must be known, such as the periodicity of the collection of information (whether spot, periodic, continuous, occasional), the frequency of the collection (whether weekly, monthly, yearly, etc.), the level of aggregation of the information (individual, household, national average), the sampling design. Other important aspects that need to be established are the format in which the data are stored (in a computer, on paper, etc.) and their availability (often special permits are needed to retrieve databanks at a disaggregate level). The intrinsic value of the identified and available information needs to be established, such as its specificity, sensitivity, representativity, accuracy, predictive power, etc. Most often, the utilization of secondary data for deriving meaningful and reliable indicators will require that they be submitted to enhancement procedures. These procedures cannot be generalized and will have to be specifically designed, often relying on *ad hoc* combinations of different databanks (Declich and Carter, 1994). Developing enhancement procedures requires the setting up of realistic hypotheses on data links and of suitable algorithms to combine different information.

Secondary databanks also require standardization of the information on the basis of the age and sex composition of the population, to ensure better comparability between regions and countries and to allow for the evaluation of time trends and for making comparisons.

Three categories of information are needed: the first relates to the dietary habits of the population, the second to the prevalence of nutrition-related diseases and the third to life-style factors and nutrition-related conditions.

Food data. Information on dietary consumption in industrialized countries can be derived by a number of diverse sources. These include food balance sheets, household budget surveys, market share data and dietary surveys.

Food balance sheets (FBS) provide information on the food that is available at the national level for human consumption. They are based on food production, with allowance made for imports and exports, changes in stocks, agricultural and industrial uses. Per-capita supply is then calculated by dividing total food availability by the population size. Useful information on trends can be obtained as series are available from 1960 onward; for a few countries the information reaches back as far as 1934 (Kelly, Becker and Helsing, 1991). Since 1949, the Food and Agriculture Organization (FAO) has standardized and presented FBSs on a common basis across countries. In addition, since 1971 FBS data have entered a statistical data system called Interlink Computer Storage and Processing System of Food and Agricultural Commodity Data (ICS) (FAO, 1991). This provides information on primary crop, fishery commodities and 380 processed products –

grouped into 16 categories – along with rough estimates of supply of energy and macronutrients intake in 146 countries.

Despite the positive features of being standardized and widely available, there are problems in the use of FBSs for nutritional surveillance purposes. They only provide a rough estimate of per capita food availability, rather than a true measure of actual food consumption. For this reason they are referred to as food disappearance data. Furthermore, they tend to overestimate the intake of foods and nutrients, this error being different for the various countries and for the different food commodities. A major limitation of their use for surveillance purposes is that they do not provide an estimate of population distribution patterns, which makes it impossible to detect and monitor population subgroups and typologies of food consumption at risk. Thus, while occasionally used in nutritional surveillance, considerable caution needs to be exercised in the interpretation of the results (Kelley, Becker and Helsing, 1991).

Another important source of secondary dietary data is represented by the household budget survey (HHBS). These surveys are carried out regularly by National Statistical Offices in most Western countries. In Europe HHBSs are conducted regularly in Austria, Belgium, Cyprus, Denmark, Finland, France, Germany, Greece, Hungary, Ireland, Ireland, Italy, The Netherlands, Norway, Poland, Portugal, Spain, Sweden and the United Kingdom (Vassilakou and Trichopoulou, 1992), with a frequency ranging from every year (in Italy, Netherlands, Poland and UK) to every 7 years (as in Portugal). Although sharing a common purpose, the way the HHBSs are conducted in the various countries is not standardized and there are serious impediments to the possibility of comparing the findings of the national HHBSs directly across countries. An ongoing project of the European Union (DAFNE, Data Food Networking) is now attempting to harmonize at the international level dietary exposure data derived from HHBSs (Trichopoulou, 1995, unpublished report).

HHBSs are not primarily intended for nutritional purposes; they are designed to address the socio-economic connotation of household expenditures, inclusive of the costs for food purchase. Nevertheless, the latter information lends itself to be used to estimate food and nutrient consumption. However, the results suffer from a number of limitations. Thus, for example, in many countries household food stocks and their variation at the end of the survey period are not taken into account; losses and wastages of edible food are not considered and information on meals consumed outside the home is not usually available. All this may introduce errors and systematic biases that need to be corrected wherever possible or simply taken into account (Vassilakou and Trichopoulou, 1992). Another serious limitation in the use of HHBS data for surveillance purposes stems from the fact that in most countries the data relative to food commodities are recorded at a very high level of aggregation. The rationale of the aggregation is one of expedience, and the principles governing the way foods are aggregated in large groups are of an economic nature. This leads to the formation of food groups that are not easily converted in appropriate indicators of dietary risk. Finally, HHBSs provide information at the household level and individual exposures cannot be properly assessed.

Having touched briefly upon the various limitations of the HHBS data for surveillance purposes, it must be recognized that there are also several positive aspects. The main advantage is represented by the fact that these surveys are conducted on truly nationally representative samples of households. Moreover, the sample has multiple stratifications, thus allowing the analysis of the distribution of dietary risk factors on a socio-economic (level of education and occupational status of household membership) or geographical (level of urbanization, residence area) basis.

In conclusion, despite their several limitations, HHBSs appear to be a valuable, widely available source of secondary dietary data in industrialized countries, which can be retrieved with relative ease, be subjected to enhancement procedures and may be therefore incorporated in any NSS based on secondary data (Vassilakou and Trichopoulou, 1992).

Another valuable source of secondary data suitable for assessing dietary risk exposure is gathered by the private sector in its analysis of market share of selected food commodities. These surveys are usually conducted on well-stratified samples of households, representative of the local or national population. They provide frequently updated information at a very detailed level (food items are recorded at the brand level). However, as for HHBSs, these data also concern food purchases rather than actual consumption of food, and the survey accounts only for household, not for individual expenditure. Moreover, these surveys mainly address selected processed foods rather than the diet in its entirety, thus making it difficult to obtain a complete picture of the dietary patterns. Last but not least, access to these data is not free, and their cost may be very high. In Italy, for example, the cost of a series of 10 years' data, including the yearly average purchases at the national level of about 110 processed foods (ham, salami and industrial cheeses included) recorded on a representative sample of 4000 households and the same purchases at the regional level of the last year available, is about 42.000 Lst (L. Guadagnino, personal communication). Recourse to these types of data is being practised in France by the national demographic statistics institute, CREDOC (J.-L. Volatier, personal communication).

Finally, some food consumption data are also available as a secondary source, being collected for scientific purposes by research institutes. An example is provided by the information on food consumption collected within targeted projects such as MONICA (WHO, 1988) and SENECA (Euronut SENECA investigators, 1991) among others. However, these surveys tend to be sporadic, often only cover age- and/or sex-specific subgroups and, therefore, are rarely representative of the overall population.

They are generally not nationally representative, being conducted on numerically limited samples. On the other hand, the information provided by this type of survey can be very useful for nutritional surveillance purposes because, besides dietary data, biochemical indicators of nutritional status are also often available. This source of secondary data is also characterized by a high level of reliability and accuracy and pertains to the individual rather than representing household averages. The best use of these data within the context of nutritional surveillance is in combination with other sources of nationally representative data collected on a continuous basis.

Vital statistics. Data on health are obtained through mortality and morbidity registers (hospital discharge, cancer incidence, diabetes and cardiovascular events registers, etc.) or other information systems. The routine collection and analysis of death certificates is carried out on a nationwide basis in all Western countries. The coding system of causes of death is well standardized both within and between countries (WHO, 1978). The counting of cases is fairly accurate, since notification is compulsory. However, information on cause of death is somewhat less reliable because the certifying doctors often only report the immediate cause, rather than the underlying disease (De Becker, Laaser and Wenzel, 1988; Parkin, 1988). Misuse of coding represents another potential source of error. Despite these problems, when a fairly constant ratio between deaths and cases is observed, as frequently occurs when dealing with highly lethal diseases (such as infectious diseases, stroke, myocardial infarction), mortality statistics provide a fair approximation of the disease prevalence (Declich and Carter, 1994). In all other diseases, the trends highlighted by mortality data provide an imprecise and delayed response, because people may have been ill for many years before dying. Thus, a change in prevalence would be reflected in the mortality only after a period of time (Eylenbosch and Noah, 1988; Test, 1991).

Morbidity statistics complement the picture of the health status of the population, provided by the mortality statistics, offering additional information on non-lethal or mildly lethal diseases. The main limitation for their use is their poor availability. At a local level, prevalence and incidence data are available through registers only for a few diseases, such as cancers (Smans, Muir and Boyle, 1992) and cardiovascular diseases (by MONICA projects; WHO, 1988). At national level, hospital discharge registers can provide a fairly reliable indication of the prevalence and incidence of diseases, although there is some question on their representativity (Lambert and Roger, 1982). In Italy, for example, hospital discharges are collected in a non-random way, since only data derived from the first week of each month are recorded and only one discharge out of four is retained. Such data include information on diagnosis, length of stay and other factors such as disease severity. An example of a surveillance system based on hospital data is provided by Scotland. Here a hospital morbidity-recording system has been developed, which is capable of highlighting the changes in frequency and distribution of diseases in relation to some socio-economic factors (Paterson, 1988).

The main problems with hospital discharge registers are multiple counting (for patients admitted and discharged more than once in a year) and insufficient standardization of diagnostic criteria (Kelly, 1988). Such problems, more frequent in the presence of chronic conditions, particularly affect diseases such as ischaemic heart disease (De Becker, Laaser and Wenzel, 1988).

In section 1.3.2 we shall propose simple methods to improve low-quality data derived from mortality and morbidity registers.

Data on obesity. Obesity is a well-recognized risk factor for several pathologies, it is thus important for nutritional surveillance purposes to gain access to information relative to its prevalence and to its time and geographical trends. A certain amount of secondary information on obesity has been generated by epidemiological surveys on the prevalence and trend of cardiovascular disease risk factors. One of the earliest and more detailed monitoring activities of cardiovascular risk factors was undertaken as part of the Seven Countries Study. Even though it is now dated, the study has provided a large amount of data, covering a 20-year follow-up (from the beginning of the 1960s to the 1980s), including anthropometric measurements (Menotti *et al.*, 1989). Another example is that of the European Atherosclerosis Research Study (EARS; EARS Group, 1994) which, when addressing the contribution of environmental factors to the risk of cardiovascular diseases in young people with a paternal history of premature acute myocardial infarction, collected also data on the prevalence of overweight in 11 Western countries. The same risk factor is periodically monitored by the MONICA project (WHO, 1988) with standardized methodologies and protocols to ensure comparability within and between countries.

In addition to the studies described above, information on height and weight is also collected, during the draft board examination performed yearly by the Ministry of Defence, in those European countries where military service is compulsory. This means that all 18-year-old men undergo such an examination, thus creating a formidable and continuously updated databank. Such a databank has already been used in Denmark to monitor the prevalence of obesity (Sørensen and Price, 1990) and in The Netherlands to detect the existence of a relationship between nutritional status, dietary habits and socio-economic factors (Hulshof, Wedel and Ockhuizen, 1988). Draft board data have been also used in the Italian NSS (see below).

1.3 Case study: the Italian pilot NSS and the use of secondary data

In Italy, a low-budget pilot NSS has been developed by the National Institute of Nutrition (INN), upon request of the Ministry of Health, to monitor cardiovascular diseases and cancers. Upon express specification of the Ministry, and following a previous analysis that established the existence of sufficient secondary information (Ferro-Luzzi *et al.*, 1994b), the NSS was to make exclusive recourse to secondary data sets. Given the less than desirable quality of these data, the process of validating, improving and adapting these data represented the core of the activity. To this end, *ad hoc* mathematical algorithms were developed to combine various data sets and to improve their reliability and representativity through iterative processes of enhancement, standardization and normalization.

An example of these procedures of enhancement of secondary data is given below.

1.3.1 Upgrading the quality of dietary risk data

The dietary information required by the system was provided by the HHBSs. The general limitations of this source of information have been discussed above. The reliability of the Italian HHBS data has been evaluated in comparison with other data sources by Cialfa, Turrini and Lintas (1991) and the need to improve it by combining it with other data has been stressed (Turrini, 1993). In Italy, yearly HHBSs provide data on the food purchases of a representative sample of the entire population, stratified by altitude, by categories of dimension of the living conglomerate and by the economic activity prevalent in the area. About 39 000 households are studied; the recording does not correct for the food consumed by guests and does not include either the meals or foods consumed outside the home by the household members, nor the correction for wastage and proportion of edible part. Furthermore, the information on the individual food item is collected in a highly aggregated way, with only 51 broad food categories. The basis of the aggregation is not particularly relevant for anything other than socio-economic purposes and is, as such, poorly suitable for an analysis of dietary risk factors.

A first step for HHBS data enhancement therefore consisted of splitting the larger and more heterogeneous food categories into smaller, more homogeneous ones (Leclercq, Martino and Ferro-Luzzi, 1996). This was possible using the detailed findings of a food consumption survey conducted nationally by the National Institute of Nutrition (INN) in 1980–84 (Saba *et al.*, 1990). The procedure is shown in Fig. 1.2 and consists of several steps. First, the food consumption data of the INN survey were combined in 51 food aggregates comparable to those of the HHBS. This step was carried out on a regional basis in order to preserve any persisting geographical difference in dietary patterns (Ferro-Luzzi and Branca, 1995); four diverse sets were thus created, one for each of the main areas of Italy: north-east, north-west, centre and south (Ferro-Luzzi *et al.*, 1994a). This provided a guideline on the basis of which each of the 51 food categories of the HHBS could be further subdivided into the same 137 individual food items of the INN survey. For example, knowledge from the INN survey that respectively 7.6, 13.2, 29 and 30.2% of the cheese consumed in the north-west, the north-east, the centre and south of Italy are low fat (less than 20% of fat), allowed a split in the aggregated classification of the HHBS that only records all types of cheese without any nutritional distinction under the same denomination. Appropriate correction factors were then applied to obtain the edible proportion of food commodities such as fruit, vegetables, poultry, etc. (Carnovale and Miuccio, 1989). The net disaggregated values were used as such or after conversion into nutrients (applying the Italian Food Composition Table; Carnovale and Miuccio, 1989) for the creation of the appropriate dietary indicators.

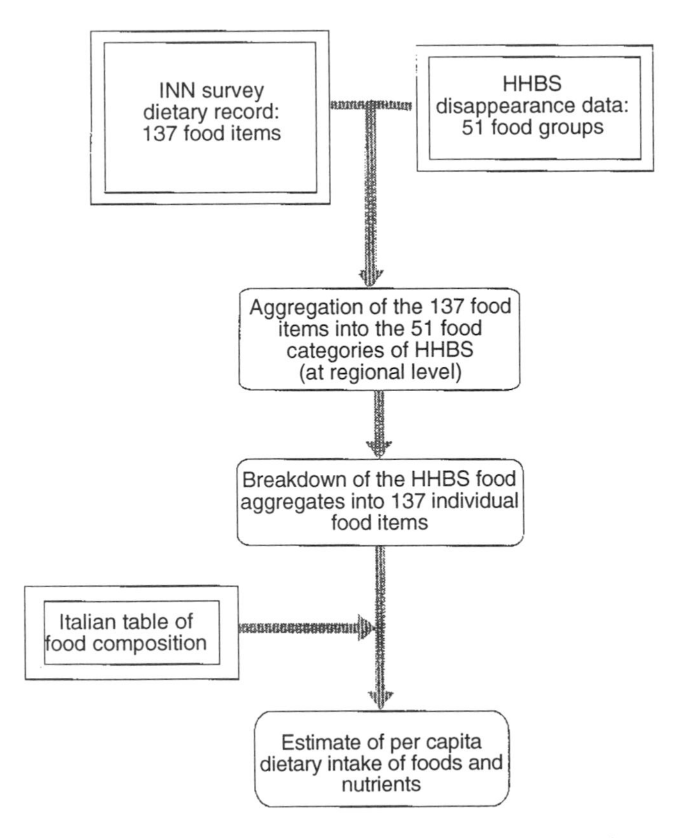

Figure 1.2 Enhancement of secondary data: HHBS and INN data.

1.3.2 Enhancing hospital discharge and mortality registers data

Data on patients discharged from hospitals, as well as data from mortality registers, have been used in the Italian NSS to approximate the prevalence and incidence of cardiovascular diseases. Given the problems of the quality of the morbidity data, discussed above, the data were submitted to a process of enhancement, based on the simplified MONICA method (Giampaoli and Menotti, 1991). According to this method the frequency of fatal and non-fatal cardiovascular events can be derived from mortality and morbidity registers on the basis of a set of ICD codes, that differs from the classical codes. Indeed, the use of the classical ICD codes 410–414 (ischaemic heart disease) produces a large bias in the calculation of the actual prevalence and incidence of the disease. The MONICA method identifies fatal cardiovascular events from the mortality register, by a set of ICD codes that includes ischaemic heart disease (410–414), disturbances of the rhythm (427), cardiac failure (428) and sudden death of unknown origin (798). The incidence of non-fatal ischaemic heart events is estimated by adding hospitalization cases which have a discharge diagnosis coded as acute myocardial infarction (410) and other forms of acute or sub-acute ischaemic heart disease (411). The simplified MONICA method was tested by comparing the frequency of cardiovascular events as recorded directly in the field by the MONICA study in 1983–85 in a specified Italian area, with that derived from mortality and morbidity registers according to the classical set of ICD codes and when applying the simplified MONICA approach. Table 1.1 shows the performance of the method for men. As can be seen, the classical method highly underestimates the number of fatal events (–22%) and grossly overestimates the number of non-fatal events (+144%). The MONICA method, although imprecise for single age classes, is much more accurate than the classical one. For fatal events the MONICA method appears to be pretty valid with –0.2% difference, while for non-fatal events, the percentage gap equals +9%. For

Table 1.1 Comparison between the number of fatal and non-fatal ischaemic heart disease events as estimated by the MONICA study, the MONICA method and the classical method – Men (modified from Giampaoli and Menotti, 1991).

	Fatal events		Non-fatal events	
Age (years)	% difference (MONICA method – MONICA study)	% difference (classical method – MONICA study)	% difference (MONICA method – MONICA study)	% difference (classical method – MONICA study)
35–44	+25.9%	–14.8%	+19.1%	+168.1%
45–54	–0.9%	–23.0%	+10.5%	+143.0%
55–64	–2.7%	–22.8%	+6.3%	+141.6%
Total	–0.2%	–22.4%	+8.8%	+144.4%

females such percentages are: for fatal events –4.8% (MONICA method) as compared to –38% (classical method) and for non-fatal events +31% as compared to +507%.

From these findings, we can conclude that there is scope in using the MONICA method to enhance the secondary data on mortality and morbidity.

1.3.3 Obesity among recruits and in the general population

In Italy every year, about 400 000 18-year-old men – representing the totality of the male population of that age – undergo draft board examinations. Data on place of birth and residence, socio-economic class, educational level and work are recorded; weight, height and chest circumference are measured. This creates a large volume of data which could be exploited for nutritional surveillance purposes. The advantage of such a database is that it is collected on a continuous basis, making this data set particularly adaptable for monitoring activities. To estimate from these data on 18-year-old men the prevalence of obesity in the entire population requires the hypothesis that a relationship exists between prevalence of overweight at different ages and between men and women, and that such a relationship is neither modified across the various Italian regions, nor over a relatively short lapse of time.

A model was thus developed to predict the prevalence of overweight in male and female Italian adults from the prevalence of overweight in young men. The findings of the Nine Communities Study (Research Group ATS-RF2-OB43 of the Italian National Research Council, 1987) were used. This study collected anthropometric data on nine independent population samples of 20–59-year-olds. The prevalence of overweight in the 5 decades between 20 and 60 years and in the age class 20–22 was calculated for men and women in these samples. A body mass index (BMI) greater than 25 kg/m^2 was set up as the cut-off point for overweight in both sexes (WHO, 1995). The relationship between the prevalence of obesity at 20–22 years (used as a proxy for the 18-year-old male group) and at later ages was found to be well described by a linear model (the adjusted determination coefficient ranging between 0.69 and 0.82 in men and between 0.75 and 0.96 in women) within each decade of age. A log-transformation (for men) and an exponential transformation (for women) of the obesity prevalence rate in the 20–22 years male group was therefore related to the obesity prevalence in each age group. Applying this linear model to the overweight prevalence observed in young males who underwent the draft board examination, the overweight prevalence in all adult age classes was obtained. The prevalence was calculated separately for each Italian region. Thus regional estimates were obtained.

1.3.4 Evaluation of the population at dietary risk

The evaluation of the prevalence of exposure to dietary risk is based on the comparison with population nutrient goals assumed to guarantee the maintenance of health in the whole population (WHO, 1990); this detects the existence of a risk, but does not estimate the percentage of population at risk. To quantify the proportion of the population at a given risk, we adopted the approach suggested by Mora (1989). This consists of adopting a cut-off curve rather than one specific cut-off point. The curve was assumed to have a normal distribution, with a mean value equal to the population dietary factor goal (as stated by WHO, 1990). The distribution of the intakes of all dietary factors was also assumed to be normal with the same shape (standard deviation) of the theoretical curve. Thus, for a population mean intake of the specified dietary factor equal to the recommended level, the observed and the theoretical reference curves completely overlap. In such a case, the prevalence of population at risk is zero. In all other situations, the probability of a risk is given by the portion of the observed curve that does not overlap the cut-off curve. Figure 1.3 shows the comparison between the theoretical distribution of desirable intakes of dietary fibre and the actual distribution of the intakes in the region of Piemonte. The latter had a mean intake of 17 g/capita/day in 1990, as compared to the mean desirable value of 27 g/capita/day, as stated by the WHO working group (WHO, 1990). On this basis, 28% of the population, shown as the hatched portion of the curve, is considered to be at risk.

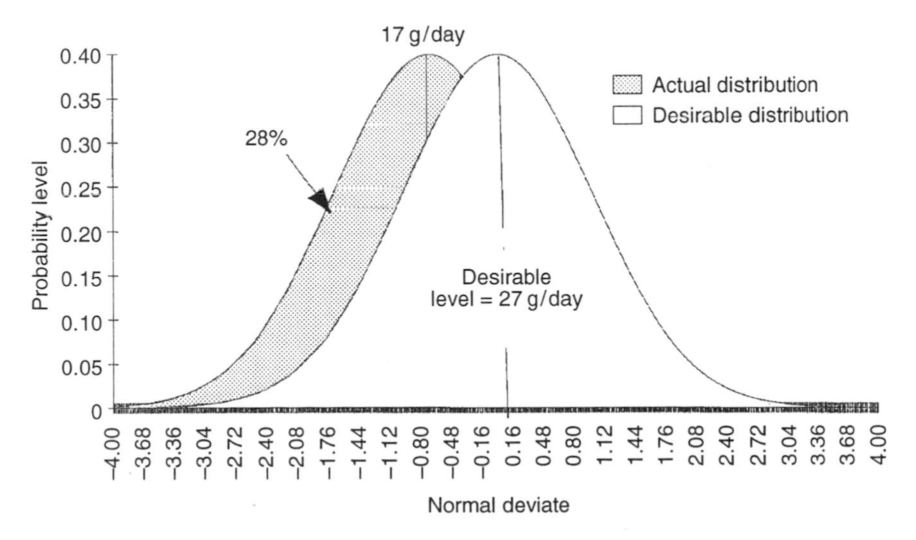

Figure 1.3 Estimation of dietary risk prevalence: fibre intake, Piemonte, 1990 (modified from a print-out of the PC software 'Computerized Italian Nutritional Surveillance System').

1.3.5 Theoretical framework and computerization of the system

The theoretical framework of the Italian NSS consists of a centrally located technical body that collates the information arriving from the peripheries and transforms it into appropriate indicators. A loop is then activated that uses the indicators to diagnose a situation, to identify trends, to specify needs and to provide a final explicit message. Risk priorities are defined according to the existence and direction of trends, the slope of the trends, i.e. the velocity in years that it will take for a condition to enter the high-risk stage, and the total number of people at risk. Outgoing channels deliver the information as simple action-oriented messages to the relevant governmental bodies.

The pilot Italian Nutritional Surveillance System has been developed in three steps, as described in Fig. 1.4 (Leclercq *et al.*, 1993). The first consisted of the identification, acquisition, validation, standardization and enhancement of relevant secondary databanks. The second step consisted of the process of transformation of the raw secondary information into indicators. The third step used the indicators to appraise the situation and to draw simple and operational messages.

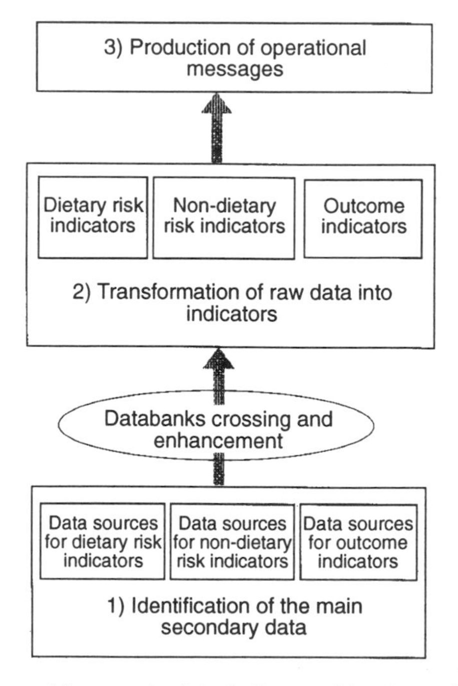

Figure 1.4 General framework of the Italian nutritional surveillance system.

All the above procedures and processes have been computerized to provide replicable information and to allow an easier processing of raw data

(Martino, Leclercq and Ferro-Luzzi, 1994). The system is composed of three modules. The first consists of the raw data banks and can be updated when new information becomes available. The second module allows the production and modification of the relationships between databases and the reference parameters. The last module displays the information in the form of colourful and attractive graphs. These describe the nutritional problems of Italian population, their trends, the groups of population at risk and the nature of the risk. Comparisons between geographical areas are available to detect the most critical situation. The software allows the operator to change trigger levels, thus, different risk scenarios can be developed according to different trigger-level selections. Didactic tools are also available on-line that explain the theoretical and practical features of the system. Information on data sources and explanations of the mathematical algorithms developed to enhance the quality of indicators are displayed in the form of technical comments. Explanatory comments on the conceptual framework of the system as well as references can be found in a specific section presented in the form of a book subdivided in chapters. A glossary gives a simple explanation of all technical words. The system therefore provides a practical example of how to develop a nutritional surveillance system by matching secondary data of different quality.

1.4 Conclusion

In conclusion, a general overview has been given of the nutritional surveillance activities set up in Europe. Even though primary data based activities may provide more precise and targeted information on the nutritional situation of the population, they are time and money consuming and not all countries would be prepared to support them. In addition, a large amount of secondary data seems to be available in Europe that allows description of the prevalence of risk factors associated with nutrition-related diseases. Suitably enhanced secondary data could easily be used for nutritional surveillance purposes. The Italian operational approach for the development of a nutritional surveillance system, which uses secondary data and improves the quality of databanks, has been described here as a practical example of how the process may be set up. It is country-specific, as the nature of databanks varies from one country to another. However, the process used here can be adopted by other industrialized countries which are, like Italy, taking their first steps toward developing an integrated food and nutrition policy, and by countries with limited budgets and large available secondary databanks. Possible solutions to some of the problems faced when using secondary data have been illustrated.

Acknowledgements

The authors thank Dr C. Leclercq, Dr F. Branca, Dr A. Albertini and Dr A. Turrini for their valuable suggestions and comments and Dr M. Loteryman for the English revision of the paper.

References

Buss, D.H. (1991) Food patterns in the British Isles. *Annals of Nutrition and Metabolism*, **35**, (Suppl. 1).

Campbell, C.C. (1989) Community-based nutrition monitoring. *Journal of the Canadian Dietetic Association*, **50**, (2), 93–7.

Carnovale, E. and Miuccio, F. (eds) (1989) *Tabelle di composizione degli alimenti*, edizione 1989, Istituto Nazionale della Nutrizione, Roma.

Cialfa, E., Turrini, A. and Lintas, C. (1991) A national food survey. Food balance sheets and other methodologies: a critical overview, in *Monitoring Dietary Intakes*, (ed. I. Macdonald), ILSI Monographs, Springer-Verlag, Berlin, pp. 24–44.

De Becker, G., Laaser U. and Wenzel H. (1988) Cardiovascular disease surveillance, in *Surveillance in Health and Disease*, (eds W.J. Eylenbosch and N.D. Noah), Oxford University Press, Oxford, pp. 115–24.

Declich, S. and Carter, A.O. (1994) Public health surveillance: historical origins, methods and evaluation. *Bulletin of the World Health Organization*, **72**, 285–304.

EARS Group (1994) The European atherosclerosis research study (EARS): design and objectives. *International Journal of Epidemiology*, **23**, (3), 465–71.

Euronut SENECA investigators (1991) Design, methods and participation. *European Journal of Clinical Nutrition*, **45**, (Suppl. 3), 5–22.

Eylenbosch, W.J. and Noah, N.D. (1988) The surveillance of disease. Part 1: General aspects, in *Surveillance in Health and Disease*, (eds W.J. Eylenbosch and N.D. Noah), Oxford University Press, Oxford, pp. 9–24.

FAO (Food and Agriculture Organization of the United Nations) (1991) *Food Balance Sheets. 1984–86 average*, FAO, Rome.

Ferro-Luzzi, A. and Branca, F. (1995) Mediterranean diet, Italian-style: prototype of a healthy diet. *American Journal of Clinical Nutrition*, **61**, (suppl.), 1338S–45S.

Ferro-Luzzi, A. and Leclercq, C. (1991) The decision-making process in nutritional surveillance in Europe. *Proceedings of the Nutrition Society*, **50**, 661–72.

Ferro-Luzzi, A. Martino, L., Leclercq, C. and Branca, F. (1994a) *Relazione scientifica del Progetto Pilota di Sorveglianza Nutrizionale elaborata peril Ministero della Sanità*, Istituto Nazionale della Nutritione, Rome.

Ferro-Luzzi, A., Leclercq, C., Martino, L. and Silano, V. (1994b) SIN: Sistema Informativo Nutrizionale. *Monografie dei Quaderni della Nutrizione*, Istituto Nazionale della Nutrizione, Rome.

Giampaoli, S. and Menotti, A. (1991) *Sorveglianza degli Eventi Coronarici Maggiori: Messa a Punto di una Meetodologia Semplificata Derivata dall'esperienza del Progetto MONICA – Area Latina,* Rapporti Istisan, Istituto Superiore di Sanità, Rome.

Gregory, J., Foster, K., Tyler, H. and Wiseman, M. (1990) *The Dietary and Nutritional Survey of British Adults*, HMSO, London.

Gregory, J.R., Collins, D.L., Davies, P.S.W. *et al.* (1995) *National Diet and Nutrition Survey: Children Aged 1½–4½ Years. Volume 1: Report of the Diet and the Nutrition Survey*, HMSO, London.

Haraldsdottir, J., Holm, L., Højmark Jensen, J. and Møller, A. (1986) *Danskernes Kost Vaner 1985: 1. Hovedresultater*, Publikation n. 136, MiljÆministeriet Levnedsmiddelstyrelsen, Soborg.

Haraldsdottir, J., Holm L., Højmark Jensen,J. and Møller,A. (1987) *Danskernes Kost Vaner 1985: 2. Hvem spiser hvad?*, Publikation n. 154, MiljÆministeriet Levnedsmiddelstyrelsen, Soborg.

Hulshof, K.F.A.M. (1993) Assessment of variety, clustering and adequacy of eating pattern. Dutch nutritional food consumption survey, PhD thesis, Rijksuniversiteit Limburg, Maastricht, The Netherlands.

Hulshof, K.F.A.M., Wedel, M. and Ockhuizen,T.H. (1988) Dietary intake, life-style and anthropometry of 18-year-old men in the Netherlands. *Nutrition Reports International*, **37**, (4), 755–65.

Kelly, A. (1988) Nutritional surveillance in Europe: an operational approach, in *Surveillance in Health and Disease*, (eds W.J. Eylenbosch and N.D. Noah), Oxford University Press, Oxford, pp. 125–42.

Kelly, A. and Becker, W. (1991) Nutrition information systems and data quality requirements, in *Food and Health Data. Their Use in Nutrition Policy-Making* (eds W. Becker and E. Helsing), WHO Regional Office for Europe, Copenhagen, pp. 15–24.

Kelly, A., Becker, W. and Helsing, E. (1991) Food balance sheets, in *Food and Health Data. Their Use in Nutrition Policy-making*, (eds W. Becker and E. Helsing), WHO Regional Office for Europe, Copenhagen, pp. 39–48.

Kim, I., Hungerford, D.W., Yip, R., Kuester, S.A., Zyrkowski, C. and Trowbridge, F.L. (1992) Pregnancy nutrition surveillance system – United States. *MMWR CDC Surveillance Summary*, **41**, (7), 25–41.

Lambert, P.M. and Roger, F.H. (1982) *Hospital Statistics in Europe*, North Holland Publishing, Amsterdam.

Leclercq, C., Martino, L., Silano, V. and Ferro-Luzzi, A. (1993) *Nutritional Surveillance System Based on Secondary Data: The Italian Model.* Symposium on Regional Approach to global objectives in nutrition, 26 September–1 October, 1993, Adelaide.

Leclercq, C., Martino, L. and Ferro-Luzzi, A. (1996) La sorveglianza nutrizionale: come e perchè. *Gionale Italiano di Chimica Clinica*, **20** (2), 87–97.

Löwik, M.R.H. and Hermus, R.J.J. (1988) The Dutch nutritional surveillance system. *Food Policy*, **13**, 359–65.

Martino, L., Leclercq, C. and Ferro-Luzzi, A. (1994) *Sistema Informatizzato di Sorveglianza Nutrizionale.* VIII Congresso Nazionale di Informatica Medica. 18–21 September 1994, Rome. Associazione italiana di Informatica Medica.

Mason, J.B., Habicht, J.P., Tabatabai, H. and Valverde, V. (1987) *La Surveillance Nutritionnelle*, WHO, Geneva.

Menotti, A., Keys, A., Aravanis, C. *et al.* (1989) Seven Countries study. First 20-year mortality data in 12 cohorts of six countries. *Annals of Medicine*, **21**, (3), 175–9.

Mora, J.O. (1989) A new method for estimating a standardized prevalence of child malnutrition from anthropometric indicators. *Bulletin of the World Health Organization*, **67**, 133–42.

Moses, E. and Dodds, J.M. (1987) Nutrition surveillance and monitoring. *Journal of Nutrition Education*, **19**, (3), 125–7.

National Food Agency of Denmark (1990) *Food Monitoring in Denmark, Nutrients and Contaminants 1983–87,* Publikation n. 195, Levnedsmiddelstyrelsen, Søborg.

Parkin, D. (1988) Surveillance of cancer, in *Surveillance in Health and Disease*, (eds W.J. Eylenbosch and N.D. Noah), Oxford University Press, Oxford, pp. 143–65.

Paterson, J.G. (1988) Surveillance systems from hospital data, in *Surveillance in Health and Disease*, (eds W.J. Eylenbosch and N.D. Noah), Oxford University Press, Oxford, pp. 49–61.

Research Group ATS-RF2-OB43 of the Italian National Research Council (1987) Time trends of some cardiovascular risk factors in Italy. *American Journal of Epidemiology*, **126**, 95.

Saba, A., Turrini, A., Mistura, G. *et al.* (1990) Indagine nazionale sui consumi alimentari delle famiglie 1980–84: alcuni principali risultati. *Rivista Società Italiana Scienza dell'Alimentazione*, **4**, 53–65.

Serrra-Majem, L., Ribas, L., Gracía-Closas, R. *et al.* (1994) *Hàbits Alimentaris, Consum*

d'Aliments i Nutrients i Estat Nutricional de la Població Catalana (1992–93), Departament de Sanitat i Seguretat Social, Barcelona.
Smans, M., Muir, C.S. and Boyle, P. (1992) *Atlas of Cancer Mortality in the European Economic Community*, IARC Scientific Publication n. 107, Lyons.
Sørensen, T.I.A. and Price, R.A. (1990) Secular trends in body mass index among Danish young men. *International Journal of Obesity*, **14**, 411–19.
Test, K. (1991) Health impact monitoring, in *Food and health data. Their use in nutrition policy-making*, (eds W. Becker and E. Helsing), WHO Regional Office for Europe, Copenhagen, pp. 25–38.
Trichopoulou, A. (1995) Network for the pan-European food data bank based on household budget survey data. Rationale for the exploitation of household budget data. Unpublished report for the Scientific Committee for Food of the European Communities.
Turrini, A. (1993) Indagini alimentari su scala nazionale: metodologia e possibilità di utilizzazione. *Giornale Europeo di Nutrizione Clinica*, **II**, (Suppl. 2), 61–9.
US DHSS (US Department of Health and Human Services) (1992) *United States Country Paper*. International Conference for Nutrition, December 1992, Rome. US Government Printing Office, Washington.
Vassilakou, T. and Trichopoulou, A. (1992) Overview of household budget surveys in 18 European countries, in Methodology and public health aspects of dietary surveillance in Europe: the use of household budget surveys. *European Journal of Clinical Nutrition*, **46** (Suppl. 5), S137–S153.
Waldegrave, W. (1991) *The Health of the Nation. A Consultative Document for Health in England,* HMSO, London.
WHO (1976) Methodology of nutrition surveillance. *WHO Technical Report Series 593*.
WHO (1978) *Manual for the International Statistical Classification of Diseases, Injuries, and Causes of Death*, WHO, Geneva.
WHO (1988) The World Health Organization MONICA project (monitoring trends and determinants in cardiovascular diseases): a major international collaboration. *Journal of Clinical Epidemiology*, **41**, (2), 105–14.
WHO (1990) Diet, nutrition and prevention of chronic diseases. *WHO Technical Report Series.*
WHO (1995) Physical status: the use and interpretation of anthropometry. *WHO Technical Report Series*, *854*.
Yip, R., Parvanta, I., Scanlon, K. *et al.* (1992) Pediatric nutrition surveillance system – United States. *MMWR CDC Surveillance Summary*, **41**, (7), 1–24.

2 Russia: monitoring nutritional change during the reform period

BARRY M. POPKIN, ALEXANDER BATURIN, LENORE KOHLMEIER and NAMVAR ZOHOORI

2.1 Background

Until 1992, the Russian Federation did not have a systematic method of monitoring dietary and nutritional status changes in its population. Before this time extensive efforts were made to collect food expenditure data for Russian households and food supply information. Unfortunately, apart from a small non-random survey of selected subpopulation groups, no dietary intake or anthropometric information was collected on the Russian population. This situation has changed significantly since the middle of 1992. Partially because of the concern in the country that the economic and political reforms could lead to problems of dietary deficit and partially related to the need to monitor a wide range of other social and economic factors, a monitoring survey system was established as a collaboration of the Russian Federation, the University of North Carolina at Chapel Hill (UNC-CH) and the World Bank. (The World Bank was only involved in funding of the first year of the Russian Longitudinal Monitoring System (RLMS) and partial funding of the second year. Subsequent funding has come from the US National Science Foundation, National Institutes of Health, and the Agency for International Development in separate grants to the University of North Carolina at Chapel Hill. These survey data will be available by the file transfer protocol (FTP) procedure through the worldwide web. For further information on the survey and procedures for obtaining the data, see the home page for the RLMS: http://www.cpc.unc.edu/projects/rlms/rlms_home.html.)

Beginning in 1992, the Russian Federation introduced sweeping reforms in the structure of its urban and rural economy, social-sector programmes and the financial accountability of state and service-sector organizations. In general, the use of market prices and the privatization of state enterprises have been cornerstones of reforms under way and planned. At the same time, currency exchange rates were allowed to fluctuate and the Russian

Implementing Dietary Guidelines for Healthy Eating. Edited by Verner Wheelock. Published in 1997 by Blackie A&P, an imprint of Chapman & Hall, London. ISBN 0 7514 0304 0

Federation began to undertake the complex and difficult process of attempting to completely reform the structure of the economy. Given the decentralized nature of the political process and the complex nature of this undertaking, tremendous variability over time and space in the implementation of the reforms is occurring.

This project was designed as a household-based survey to monitor systematically the effects of the Russian reforms on the economic well-being of households and individuals. In particular, measurement of the impact on consumption and nutritional status and health service utilization patterns are essential parts of the project. Most of the subsidies provided to protect food production and health care have been eliminated, or at least drastically changed. A cornerstone of the RLMS was to be careful monitoring of indicators of nutritional status, health service use, expenditure and food intake at the individual and household level, including sources of consumption from enterprises and other facilities and services.

In the early 1990s, at the beginning of the RLMS, it was clear that a breakdown in the systems for collecting statistical data in the Russian Federation and other republics was imminent. Also, the existing system did not collect household-based data needed to provide a representative profile of economic and social dimensions of the population, particularly of the poor. Therefore, in the initial 2 years of this effort, a central goal of the RLMS was to set up, in collaboration with the Russian State Statistical Bureau (Goskomstat) and the All-Russia Center for Preventive Medicine, an upgraded system for monitoring these topics in the Russian Federation, and also to develop data for more thorough analysis of the relevant issues. This goal was accomplished and the Goskomstat is now in a position to continue independently, and, in fact, has continued this expanded survey system. A further accomplishment of the RLMS was the creation of the first nationally representative sampling frame in Russia. More recently, assistance has been provided to the Goskomstat to develop representative samples at the regional and oblast levels (the equivalent, in political terms, of a state or province).

The thrust of the RLMS changed in 1994. The collaborators in Russia were changed and the emphasis has switched from institution-building to the provision of timely high-quality information. The new RLMS sample is smaller but the number of primary sampling units was doubled to enhance representativeness of the survey. The Institute of Nutrition, Russian Academy of Medical Sciences (RIN), became the lead agency for collecting and handling the dietary and body composition data. The Institute of Sociology, Russian Academy of Sciences (ISRosAN), assumed overall direction of the work in Russia and handles all field work and co-ordinates all data processing.

The RLMS survey instruments were designed by an interdisciplinary group of Russian and United States-based social science and biomedical researchers with extensive experience in survey research on these topics, in collaboration with the Institute of Sociology group. The senior author of this chapter led this effort. Particular care was taken to collect data that would allow us to answer policy-relevant questions concerning the design and impact of programmes and policies affecting a wide range of social sector outcomes.

2.2 Methods

2.2.1 *Russian Longitudinal Monitoring Survey (RLMS)*

The RLMS is a household-based survey to monitor systematically the effects of the Russian reforms on the economic well-being of households and individuals. The survey had two phases – the first four surveys were collected between August 1992 and January 1994 and were based on one longitudinal sample. These are termed Rounds 1–4. A second independent sample was surveyed between November 1994 and January 1995. This same sample was resurveyed from October through December, 1995 (Rounds 5 and 6). These two samples represent the first nationally representative samples of the Russian Federation. Greater detail on the design of Rounds 1–4 can be found elsewhere (Mroz and Popkin, 1995).

2.2.2 *Sampling design*

The survey covers the eight regions of the Russian Republic, which vary substantially in geography, economic development, public resources and health indicators. The initial sample of households for Phase 1 of the RLMS was identified from a stratified three-stage cluster sample of residential addresses. Cities as well as urban and rural portions of rayons (political and geographic units about the size of US counties) were the area units selected in the first stage. Probability proportionate to size (PPS) simple sampling was used to select the rayons. The rayons were stratified by the eight regions and by the percentage of urban population within each rayon.

Within each of the areas chosen in the first stage, a sample of 10 voting districts was chosen randomly, again by PPS systematic selection, from a geographically ordered list of voting districts falling in that area. Finally, within each selected voting district a list of households was updated using individual voter lists. These full lists of households, obtained from the 1989 census and updated with the use of voting lists, were then used to draw random samples of actual addresses (households). Each selected address was visited, and the household in residence at that address was selected to be part of the sample. In the event that more than one household lived at a sample address, only one was chosen randomly for participation.

Overall, 7200 households were targeted for interview in Round 1 of this survey. The final sample providing data for Round 1 was of 6485 households and 17 179 individuals for an initial response rate of 90.1%. In Round 3 there were 6163 households which provided data on 15 783 individuals. By Round 3, 728 households were lost to follow-up, and 363 new households responded to the Round 3 questionnaire that had not provided data in Round 1.

The Round 5 of the RLMS and all subsequent rounds use a sampling scheme which is different from that of Rounds 1–4. Rounds 1–4, while representative at the national level, were limited in the number of primary sampling points. The high degree of clustering of these first four rounds was required by the Goskomstat to allow them to manage the logistics of this new effort.

In general, the new national sample follows a similar multistage design but is not considered to be clustered. The first stage included three self-represented urban regions and 35 other primary sampling units. According to the sampling researchers involved in these designs, the second phase has effectively about 65 primary sampling units (PSUs) while the first phase had only 20. Thus, there was considerably more clustering in the first phase. The second phase collected representative samples of local living units based on population proportion to sample statistical techniques. Census lists were used as a first step in which much more detailed mapping and detailed checks were implemented at the local level to collect the final lists of households. (The sample design for the first phase was organized by Professor William Kalsbeek, Professor of Biostatistics, UNC-CH School of Public Health. The second-phase sampling was led by Professors Leslie Kish and Steve Heeringa, University of Michigan. In both surveys, Drs Michael Swafford, US, and Michael Kosolopov (ISRosAN) played major roles in the finalization of the design and its implementation.)

2.2.3 Instruments

Household survey questionnaires were separated into sections that focused on detailed socio-demographic and economic data. Separate sections collected information from each individual on time use, economic activities, demographics, dietary patterns and anthropometric and other health data.

The health component of the survey is designed to capture changes in health service use and nutritional status. Dietary and anthropometric data are the cornerstone of this effort. Trained interviewers who followed standard procedures outlined by the Nutrition Surveillance Section of the Centers for Disease Control collected weight and height data. For each survey, trained interviewers conducted a standard 24-hour dietary recall in the household for each member, using colour photos of foods to assist in assessing portion sizes. Data were reviewed in the field. The 1992 dietary data were processed by the staff of the Russian Research Center for

Preventive Medicine (RCPM). The 1993 and 1994 data were edited and processed by the Russian Institute of Nutrition (RIN).

During all rounds of data collection, interviewers obtain the detailed Russian name of each food and use food model photos as guidelines for selecting portion sizes. During Rounds 1–2 data entry used a menu-driven computer programme for selecting the appropriate food group and then the actual food. During all subsequent rounds, the trained staff of the RIN coded the food data and then entered the precoded food information. By the end of Round 1 over 1000 foods and recipes were collected and documented, which allowed us to begin to develop what will subsequently be a revised and expanded food list for Russia. Interviewers have been trained to provide documentation of foods previously not coded.

The first two rounds of dietary data used the food composition table of the Russian Academy of Preventive Medicine. All subsequent rounds used the RIN Food Composition Table (FCT). A linkage between the two FCTs has been developed so that all results presented here use the RIN FCT. Work is under way in preparation of a precise and detailed recipe file for Round 6 that will ultimately allow complete disaggregation of composite foods into basic foods and food groups.

2.2.4 Nutritional outcome measures

For this study, we use the body mass index (BMI), calculated as BMI = weight (kg)/height^2 (m^2).

BMI values are categorized in four ranges as suggested by international experts: <18.6, 18.6–25, 25.1–30 and >30 (Joint FAO/WHO/UNC, 1985; James, Ferro-Luzzi and Waterlow, 1988). BMI values under 18.6 are considered indicative of chronic energy deficiency. A BMI of 18.6–25 is considered normal, one of 25.1–30 represents overweight, and more than 30 indicates obesity. The cut-off of 30 for obesity has been used in other European nutritional studies of body composition.

Wasting and stunting measures are used. In both cases, the NCHS/WHO international standards for weight-for-height and height-for-age are used. Children who are below –2 Z-scores on the weight-for-height and height-for-age standards are classified as being wasted and stunted, respectively.

2.3 Dietary patterns in the pre-reform period

The basis data available for understanding dietary patterns for Russia during the period after the Second World War are food balance sheets and food expenditure surveys. The State Committee on Statistics, called Goskomstat, collected its own series of household food expenditure data annually. The sample is based on lists of public enterprises from the 1950s which have been only updated. This list of companies or enterprises was not representative of Russian enterprises. Within the enterprises, individuals willing to be interviewed provided very detailed income and food expenditure data on a weekly basis throughout the year. The food consumption data are based on a conversion of these expenditures into quantities of food and then into nutrient values for food as purchased. These nutrient values are based on complex conversion ratios. The results are useful for understanding consumption patterns and trends. They provide a better picture of food available to households than does the food balance data but they are from a sample which is clearly unrepresentative of the Russian population.

The pattern of change in the former Soviet Union during the 1950–70 period appears to be one that other countries have followed often during the past century (Popkin, 1994). Sugar intake increased rapidly, cereals and starchy tubers (mainly potatoes) declined greatly, and consumption of red meat and dairy products rose considerably (Fig. 2.1).

This figure shows that a dramatic shift in consumption patterns occurred in the 1960s. The largest increase in red meat consumption began in 1965 and continued until 1975. The increase in sugar and milk and milk product consumption was much more gradual and continuous throughout this period.

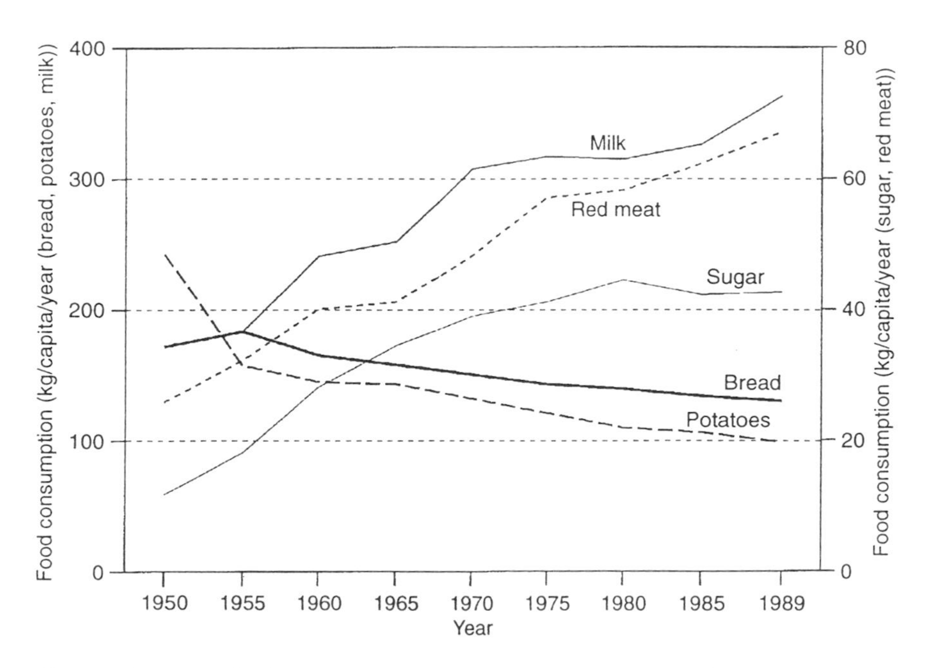

Figure 2.1 Changes in food consumption: annual intake of selected foods, Soviet Union, 1950–89. (Reprinted with permission from *Mortality patterns and Adult Health Interventions in the Newly Independent States*. Copyright 1995 by the National Academy of Sciences. Courtesy of the National Academy Press, Washington DC.)

Table 2.1 Food available for consumption, The Russian Federation 1965–92 (source: the State Statistical Bureau and Ministry of Agriculture, the Russian Federation)

	Annual food consumption (kg/capita)							
Food groups	1965	1970	1975	1980	1985	1990	1991	1992
Bread products	164	156	144	126	119	119	120	125
Potatoes	147	153	139	118	109	106	112	118
Vegetables and melon	69	70	82	94	98	89	86	77
Fruit and berries	17	30	36	30	40	35	35	33
Sugar	31	37	42	47	45	47	38	34
Meat products	41	42	50	59	62	69	63	55
Fish products	12	15	19	23	23	20	16	13
Milk products	255	271	331	328	344	386	347	281
Vegetable oil	6	8	7	9	10	10	8	7
Eggs	128	141	182	279	299	297	288	263
Daily protein intake	83	82	87	85	84	88	81	81
Daily fat intake	78	81	98	106	105	125	111	87
Daily calories intake	2844	2902	3045	3005	2923	3141	2906	2649
Energy from fat	0.25	0.25	0.28	0.31	0.32	0.36	0.35	0.30

These patterns occurred in the former Soviet Union (FSU) and the Russian Federation. Table 2.1 provides per capita food balance data for the 1965–92 period for the Russian Federation. The trends in the FSU and the Russian Federation were comparable. For instance, meat consumption increased by 63% from 1965 to 1989 in both the FSU and the Russian Federation. From 1950 to 1989, consumption of meat and milk products increased about 2.5 times for the USSR and there was a similar large increase in egg, sugar, vegetable oil, fruits, vegetables and fish products consumption. At the same time there were large decreases in the consumption of bread products and potatoes, the staples of the traditional Russian diet.

Energy intake increased considerably until the 1980s and thereafter did not change greatly. However, the structure of the diet continued to change and by 1990 over 36% of the Russian food supply was in energy from fat, making it one of the richest diets in the world in terms of meat and dairy consumption. Food expenditure and food supply data provide a comparable picture of food intake trends for this period. The consumer budget survey data from Goskomstat (Table 2.2) show a lower level of food intake, as is usually the case. The proportion of energy from animal products is also lower. None the less the two sets of results combine to provide some sense of a country which experienced a marked transformation of its diet after the Second World War.

Table 2.2 Goskomstat consumer budget survey: household food available (Russia only) (source: State Statistical Office (Goskomstat), Consumer Budget Survey)

	1970	1975	1980	1985	1990	1993
Energy (kcal)	2939	2946	2831	2739	2478	2617
Protein (g)	86.0	88.6	79.4	77.8	71.1	70.7
% Energy from fat	29.8	32.6	33.4	34.8	32.4	31.3
Cereals and products	125	115	112	105	97	110
Meat products (kg/capita/yr)	66	77	70	70	70	61
Milk products (kg/capita/yr)	371	413	391	378	378	318

The sample size was about 49 000 each year.

These dietary patterns have an important set of historic roots. Following the Organization of Petroleum Exporting Countries (OPEC) agreement and the increase in the world price of oil, incomes increased considerably in Russia during the 1970s. Depending on adjustments for inflation, income per capita at least doubled during this decade. In addition, the Russian government placed extensive emphasis on competing with the West and with achieving levels of production and consumption comparable with the West, particularly in the meat and dairy sectors. No nutritional standard was mentioned in speeches but if one divided the national production levels noted in speeches of Brezhnev or Kruschev by total population, 84 kg/capita/year was the result.

Russian nutritionists felt that the ideal diet should be based on a ratio of 1 g of protein to 1 g of fat to 4 g of carbohydrate. They recommended that an average person should consume daily 120 g of protein, 120 g of fat, and about 480 g of carbohydrate. Russian nutritionists did not set strict guidelines for animal and vegetable fat proportions but did recommend that one-third of fat should be from vegetables.

Table 2.3 Russian recommended daily allowances (RDA) for an active adult male, 1951–91

	Year of creation of the RDA				
Nutrients per day	1951[a]	1968[b]	1982[c]	1991[d]	WHO 1985[e]
Protein (g)	110	99	90	80	52.5
Fat (g)	100	97	110	93	–
Fat (% energy)	27–30	30	33	30	≤30
Carbohydrates	450	413	412	411	–
Energy (kcal)	3150	3100	3000	2800	2700

[a]Gabovich (1960); [b]Ministry of Health, USSR (1968); [c]Ministry of Health, USSR (1982); [d]Ministry of Health, USSR (1991); [e]Joint FAO/WHO/UNU (1985).

The recommended daily allowances (RDAs) are called in Russia norms of physiological requirements in nutrient and energy. Table 2.3 summarizes these RDAs for the average active man. The shift in RDAs for Russia was comparable with changes that have occurred in other countrics. However, there are large differences between the values of the Russian RDAs and those of the FAO and WHO. Table 2.1 highlights the large differences for macronutrients. Russian nutritionists have required that 55% of protein comes from animal sources and has not set similar levels for animal fat. However, they do recommend that one-third of the fat should be from vegetable sources (Ministry of Health, USSR, 1982) and not less than 4–6% of energy from linoleic acid (Ministry of Health, USSR, 1991). Similar differences are found between the FAO/WHO/UNI and Russian RDAs for children, women and the elderly. It is important to note that the Russian Institute of Nutrition is considering a revision of the RDAs to a level that would approximate those of the international nutrition community (Joint FAO/WHO/UNU, 1985).

State agriculture policy was built on increasing production of animal products. Speeches of two general secretaries of the Communist Party, as well as heads of state, are illuminating: 'we plan the following increases in the consumption per capita: meat and meat products – 2.5 times, milk and milk products – 2 times ... and some reduction in potato and bread consumption' (Kruschev, 1961).

'The nature of the goals that must be achieved in the next five-year period determines the increasing responsibility of agricultural committees, rural party branches, collective ... farms ... The average annual production of meat in the next 5 years must exceed 14 million tons, the production of milk must exceed 92 million tons, the production of eggs – 46 billion pieces' (Brezhnev, 1967).

2.4 Nutrition in the reform period

This section summarizes some of the key issues related to dietary consumption patterns of various age–gender groups.

2.4.1 Inflation

The Russian Federation experienced rapid inflation throughout the period covered by these surveys. Relative prices also moved considerably during this 26-month period, making it difficult to construct reliable cost-of-living price indices. To deflate nominal incomes and specify poverty lines, this report uses Goskomstat's consumer price index and the monthly, official government poverty lines. As developed by Russian officials and researchers and UNC-CH researchers, this poverty line is based solely on changes in the cost of food items in the Russian food basket for low-income adults, while the consumer price index reflects changes in the overall cost of living for all Russians. Figure 2.2 shows the trends in the price level and the poverty line for working-aged adult males, both normalized to 100 in June 1992. Such rapid changes in the rate of inflation make it difficult for salaries and transfer payments to adjust, and this can have significant effects on income levels and poverty rates.

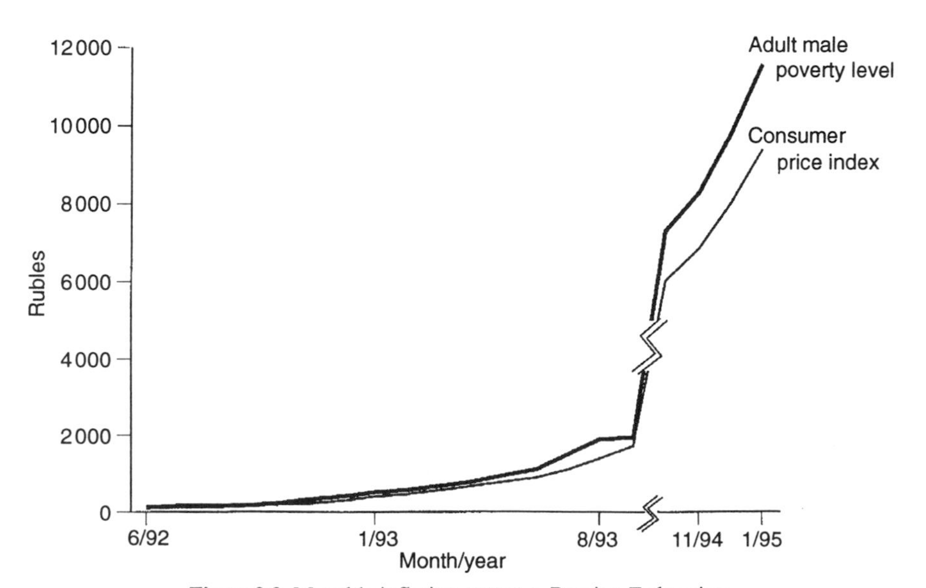

Figure 2.2 Monthly inflation patterns, Russian Federation.

2.4.2 Dietary intake

Data on fat and protein intake are presented to show the changes in the structure of the diet that has occurred in Russia during this period. Fat intake in Russia has been known to be much higher than the recommended level of 30% of energy intake. These high levels are of great concern because of implications for heart disease. However, it is heartening to note the trend shown in Figs 2.3 and 2.4. For all age groups, there was a steady decline in the percentage of energy from fats during the 2-year period from September 1992 to December 1994. Among the elderly (those 60 years and older) fat intake declined from 37% to the desired level of 31%. Although children and non-elderly adults were still consuming more than 30%, there were steady declines in these groups also. It is important to note that the dietary intake data used in Figs 2.3 and 2.4 are based on 24-hour recall measures of Russian individuals. These data, based on the nationally representative surveys of the Russian Longitudinal Monitoring Survey, report fat intake levels

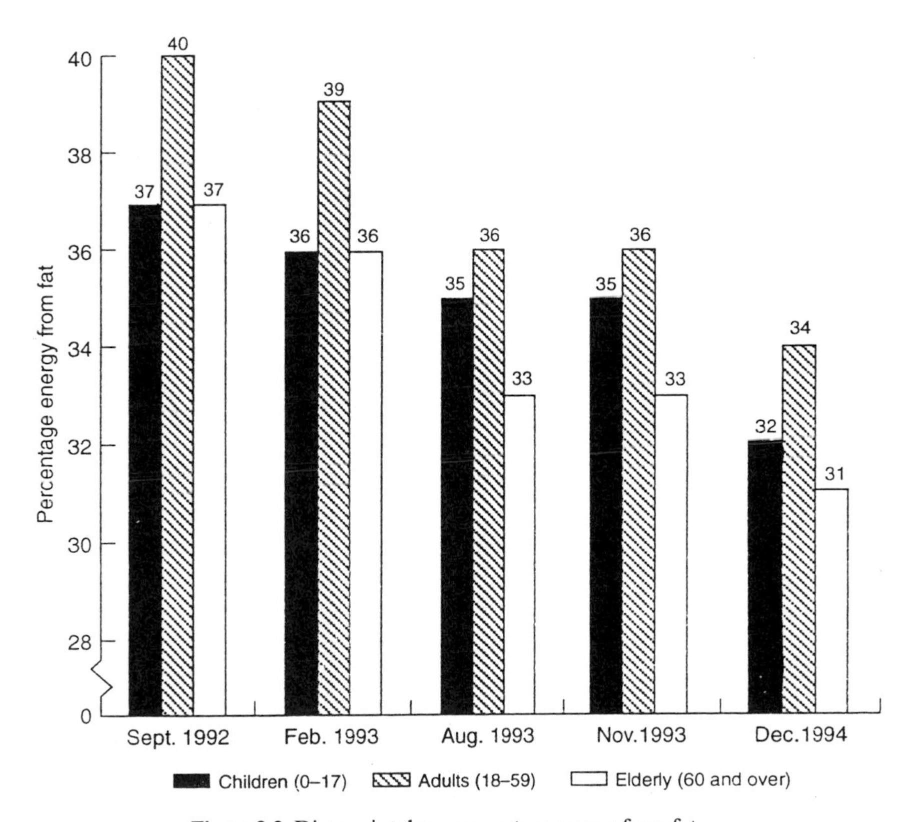

Figure 2.3 Dietary intake – percentage energy from fat.

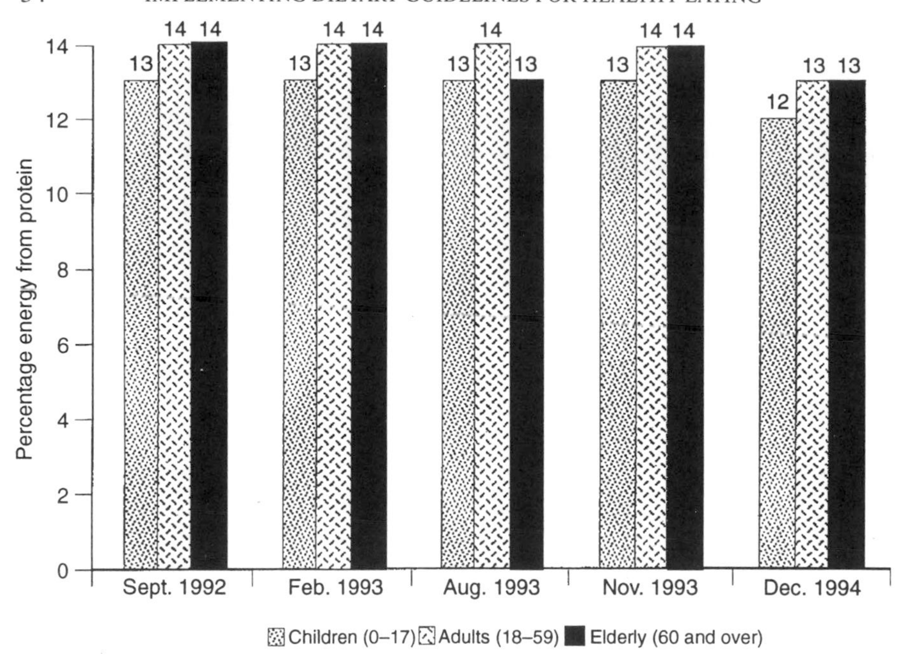

Figure 2.4 Dietary intake – percentage energy from protein.

higher than those based on the results presented in Table 2.1, which come from the Family Budget Survey of Goskomstat's food expenditure data. As noted by many researchers, the sample from this survey is a quota-based unrepresentative one (Mroz and Popkin, 1995).

Declines in the percentage of energy from protein during these 2 years bring this figure closer to a more desirable level. In general, a proportion of energy from protein of about 12% is adequate.

2.4.3 *Nutritional status*

Figures 2.5 and 2.6 present data on the nutritional status of children and adults, respectively. Of particular importance is the increase in the prevalence of stunting (an indicator of chronic malnutrition) among 2-year-olds and younger children – there was an increase from 6.9% to over 12%, with a figure of 12.8% in December 1994. These figures indicate that between September 1992 and August 1993 (a 1-year period) there was almost a doubling of the level of stunting among children of this age group, and that a year later, in December 1994, the figure remained at the higher level. Elsewhere, we show that these increases in stunting are statistically significant (Mroz and Popkin, 1995).

Among adults and the elderly, the situation is reversed. Here, there is no indication of an increase in the underweight group. Rather, for all age

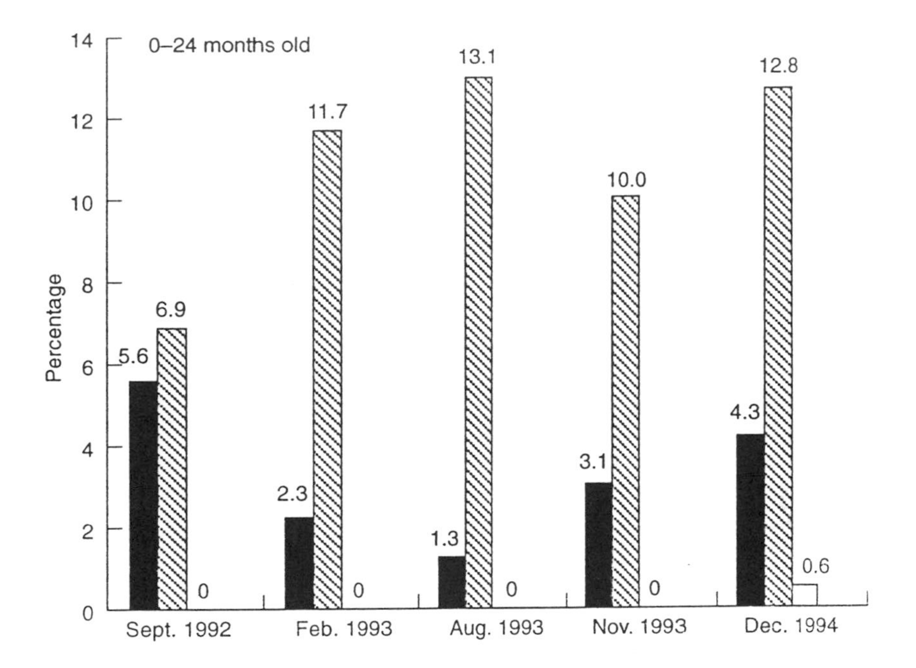

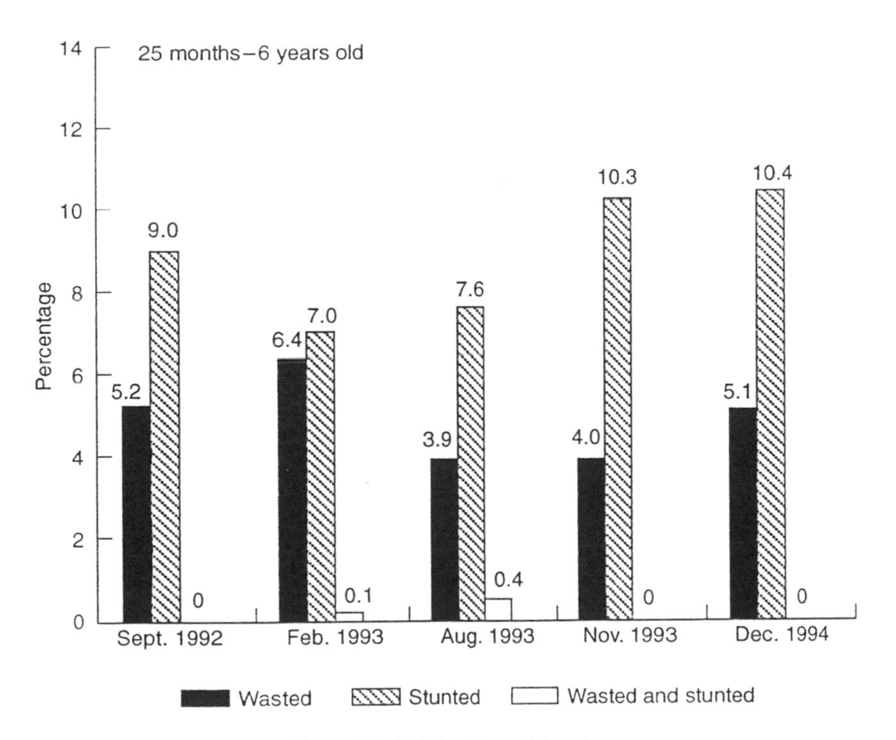

Figure 2.5 Children's nutritional status.

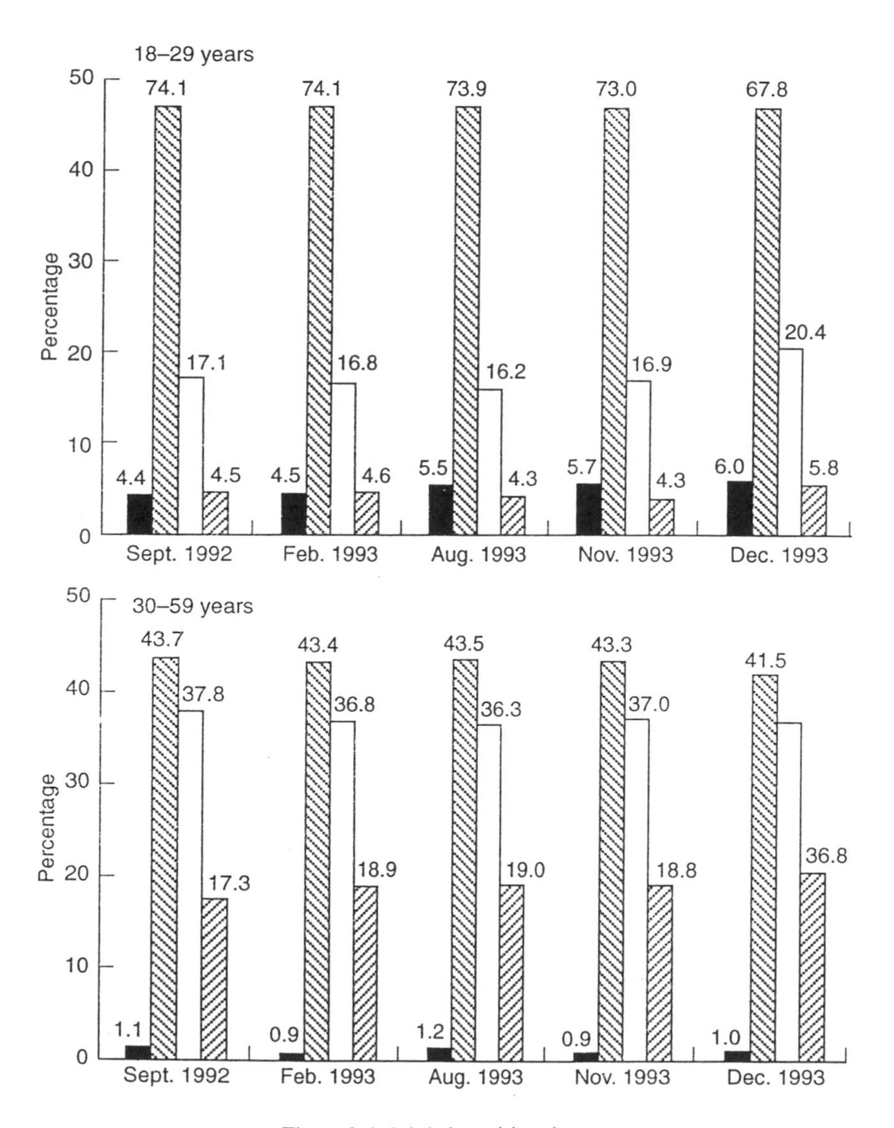

Figure 2.6 Adults' nutritional status.

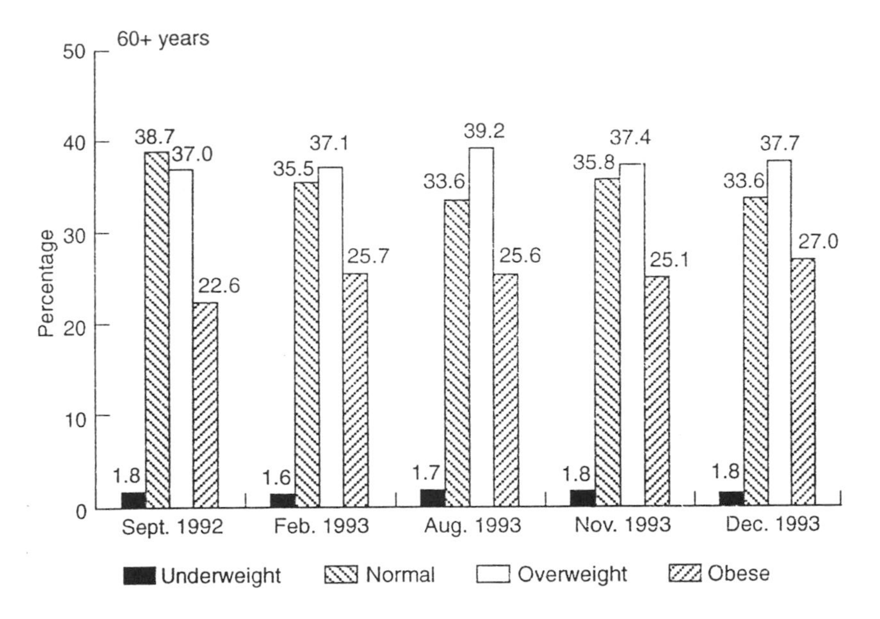

Figure 2.6 Continued

groups, there is a steady increase in the proportion of the population that are overweight and obese (according to WHO classifications). Among older adults and the elderly (those 30 years old and over), more than 55% of the population have weights above normal.

2.4.4 Elderly

It had been felt by many in Russia, as well as elsewhere in the West, that the elderly of Russia were most vulnerable to nutrition problems. These issues are reviewed in more detail elsewhere (Popkin, Zohoori and Baturin, 1996). One of the most visible sources of information on the nutritional status of the elderly in Russia was a report based on a survey conducted in two Russian cities – Moscow and Ekaterinburg – and in Yerevan, Armenia (Centers for Disease Control, 1992; McNabb *et al.*, 1994; Rubin, Posner and Peterson, 1994). Initial reports from this survey pointed to the high proportions (37–50%) of the elderly in these samples who reportedly lost more than 5 kg during the 6 months prior to the survey. However, there are a number of important potential sources of bias in this study. First, relatively small samples of only 200–300 elderly people above age 70 (mean age of those older than 70 in each city was 78, 75 and 78 years, respectively) were interviewed in each city. Secondly, this information was based on weight loss reported by the interviewees, as part of a rapid assessment survey used to target humanitarian relief efforts of CARE. Thirdly, the study also noted that the pension levels of the sampled elderly were below their government's poverty levels, another indication that these elderly persons were at risk of malnutrition. Also, the survey used a poverty line that was actually about 120 rubles, or about 25%, below the official poverty line at the time of their survey. Although publications based on later and more careful analysis of these data have toned down some of these earlier conclusions, the impression still exists that the elderly, particularly those living alone, have suffered considerably.

This concern was expanded by many news reports of long queues of the elderly waiting to purchase food and related reports about their economic difficulties.

In general, these reports have not been correct. As we show, over the first 2 years, pensioners (as the Russian elderly are often termed) have been less adversely affected than have other age–gender groups. Their pensions have been indexed to the inflation rate and they have handled the changes during this period quite well (Mroz and Popkin, 1995; Popkin, 1995; Popkin, Zohoori and Baturin, 1996).

Economic conditions of the elderly. In Table 2.4 one sees that the elderly living in households with adults and children under the age of 60 are five or more times more likely to be very poor and have an income less than half of

Table 2.4 The distribution of poverty among the Russian elderly, 1992–4 (proportions of each age group with incomes below the Russian poverty line) (Reprinted with permission from *Mortality Patterns and Adult Health Interventions in the Newly Independent States*. Copyright 1995 by the National Academy of Sciences, Courtesy of the National Academy Press, Washington DC.)

	September 1992		August 1993		December 1994	
	<50%	50–100%	<50%	50–100%	<50%	50–100%
Elderly living in extended households						
60–69	7.9	29.1	9.5	27.1	16.6	34.0
70+	7.8	26.8	8.0	25.6	17.3	35.5
Total 60+	7.8	28.3	8.9	26.5	16.8	34.5
Elderly living by themselves						
60–69	1.2	15.7	1.3	7.4	2.6	8.1
70+	2.1	15.8	1.1	7.7	1.1	12.8
Total 60+	1.5	15.7	1.3	7.5	2.1	9.6
Total sample of elderly people						
60–69	2.9	19.1	3.3	12.0	8.2	18.5
70+	3.7	18.9	3.0	12.8	7.4	21.9
Total 60+	3.2	19.1	3.2	12.3	7.9	19.7

Statistics for the September 1992 and August 1993 surveys have been weighted to the Russian census. The December 1994 survey is self-weighting.

the poverty line. By contrast, the elderly living alone are much less likely to be poor. Table 2.4 shows the pattern of poverty in 1992, 1993, and 1994. Clearly there was a marked shift in the fortunes of older Russians. A much larger proportion, 27.6% were poor in December 1994 than in either September 1992 (22.3%) or August 1993 (15.5%) (the total proportion of poor is the summation of the proportion of the elderly with incomes below 50% of the poverty line and those between 50 and 100% of the poverty line). In another study, we show a marked shift in the distribution of poverty away from the elderly to children, the working poor and the unemployed in Russia during this transition. There we showed that over 40% of children in 1992 and over 46% of children in 1993 were poor – double the rates for the elderly. This same ratio existed at the time of the December 1994 survey, namely 60.7% of preschool children were poor and only 27.6% of the elderly.

Table 2.5 presents economic information on income distribution by source. We present this separately for elderly persons living in extended families and for families in which only the elderly live. Among persons aged 60 and older, about two-thirds live by themselves outside extended family situations involving other adults and children. Elderly persons who live alone receive over three-quarters of their income from state transfer programmes. In contrast, the elderly residing in extended family situations receive less than half of their income from this source. It is important to note that a considerable proportion of income of the Russian elderly comes from individual private plots of land (termed non-cash income from the private sector in Table 2.5), which has been an important source of in-kind income for this population. This represents about 10% of the income of the elderly in all households and did not vary greatly according to household structure. As is also seen in Table 2.5, transfers from relatives living outside the home and from private charities (both cash and in-kind) have declined since 1992. The large size of the state transfers component of income means that older Russians are as a consequence very vulnerable to the political process and to a bureaucracy which is highly concerned about their welfare but also faces extreme financial constraints. For this reason, it is easy to see that the diet and nutritional status of the Russian elderly could change rapidly if the real value of pensions is eroded by inflation.

It is important to note that the major reason why the Russian elderly have not suffered more from the economic turmoil facing their country is that the current laws governing the transfer system are quite good. Transfer payments are based on the poverty line for older persons and are indexed on a quarterly basis to changes in the cost of living.

These retired people appear to be particularly vulnerable to rising food prices (data not presented). In the poorest 20% of families where the household head is a pensioner, over 80% of expenditure went for food in 1992–94. The results are identical for families with a pensioner present in the house-

Table 2.5 Distribution of sources of income (proportion of income by source) (Reprinted with permission from *Mortality Patterns and Adult Health Interventions in the Newly Independent States*. Copyright 1995 by the National Academy of Sciences, Courtesy of the National Academy Press, Washington DC.)

	Households with person aged 60 and older living by themselves			Households with persons aged 60 and older living with other individuals		
Sources of income	September 1992	August 1993	December 1994	September 1992	August 1993	December 1994
Income from work for state-owned organizations	5.6	4.8	4.2	41.2	36.2	23.9
Income from work for non-state owned organizations	0.3	0.1	0.9	3.8	2.8	8.9
Transfers from the state (pensions, unemployment benefits, stipends, state allowances	75.0	78.3	79.1	38.8	44.9	46.7
Cash income from private sector	0.9	1.2	1.6	1.6	2.0	4.6
Non-cash income from private sector	12.1	11.9	9.6	7.7	9.4	10.5
Sale of personal belongings	0.4	0.1	0.4	0.7	0.9	1.1
Sale of personal property/dividends	0.0	0.2	0.5	0.0	0.5	1.0
Family and charity transfers	5.8	3.5	3.6	6.2	3.3	3.0
Total monthly income	100%	100%	100%	100%	100%	100%

Statistics for September 1992 and August 1993 have been weighted to the 1989 Russian census. The December 1994 survey is self-weighting.

hold unit. In 1993, these families spent 12% of their total income on bread and pasta products, 17% on meat, 12% on dairy products and 14% on cakes, pies, and other sugar-rich confections. Expenditure on potatoes comprises only 3% of their income because this is the major crop grown on home plots. About 10% of total expenditure represents food from home production.

Weight changes. Figures 2.7 and 2.8 show the changes in the distribution of weight for the Russian elderly between 1992 and 1993. This is the period referred to in the Centers for Disease Control publications noted above as the one with potentially important difficulties. Figure 2.7 shows weight changes classified by initial BMI. Only 54 adults fell into the chronic energy-deficient group (BMI below 18.6) in 1992. Most of them had an increase in weight, with 27.8% experiencing an increase in weight over 3 kg. Adults who had higher BMIs in 1992 experienced a much greater likelihood of losing weight than did underweight individuals. However, even among the normal and overweight individuals, a greater proportion gained weight than lost it. Only among the overweight and obese individuals do we find a larger percentage losing weight. These data provide no indication of a significant trend toward weight loss among the adult population during this period.

To assess the situation of the very old (the population comparable to the one studied in the CARE report), this pattern of weight loss among those 70 years old and over is examined in a comparable way in Fig. 2.8. Again the pattern is similar. In fact, there is no weight loss among the underweight between 1992 and 1993, and among those who were of normal weight in 1992, only 4.2% lost more than 3 kg during the next year.

In summary, our thorough analysis of the elderly, presented partially here and in more detail elsewhere, revealed that there were no acute problems. The circumstances of the elderly in December 1994 had worsened, however, and required careful attention.

2.5 Summary

The RLMS is a rapid assessment survey of a large representative cohort of the Russian population. The rapidity of the resampling (initially twice yearly) of the same households and subjects makes this one of the most information-dense dietary monitoring systems in the world. The panel design underlying this survey will allow sensitive analyses of intraindividual change over time. This chapter only highlights a few key results and gives an overview of dietary and anthropometric status changes in the pre- and post-reform periods. It does not include all the range of economic and health analyses that have been conducted.

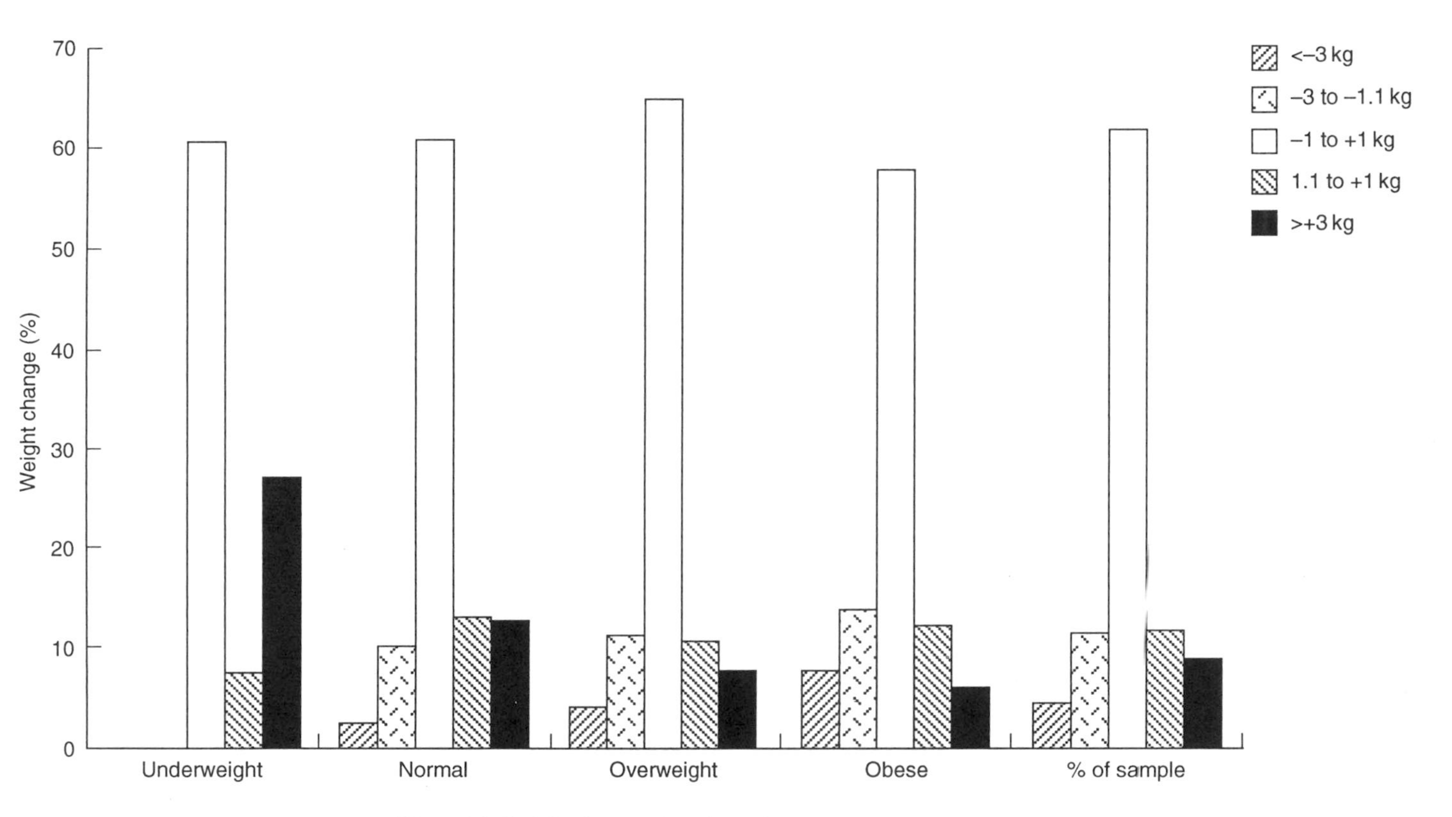

Figure 2.7 Weight change – Russian elderly, 1992–93.

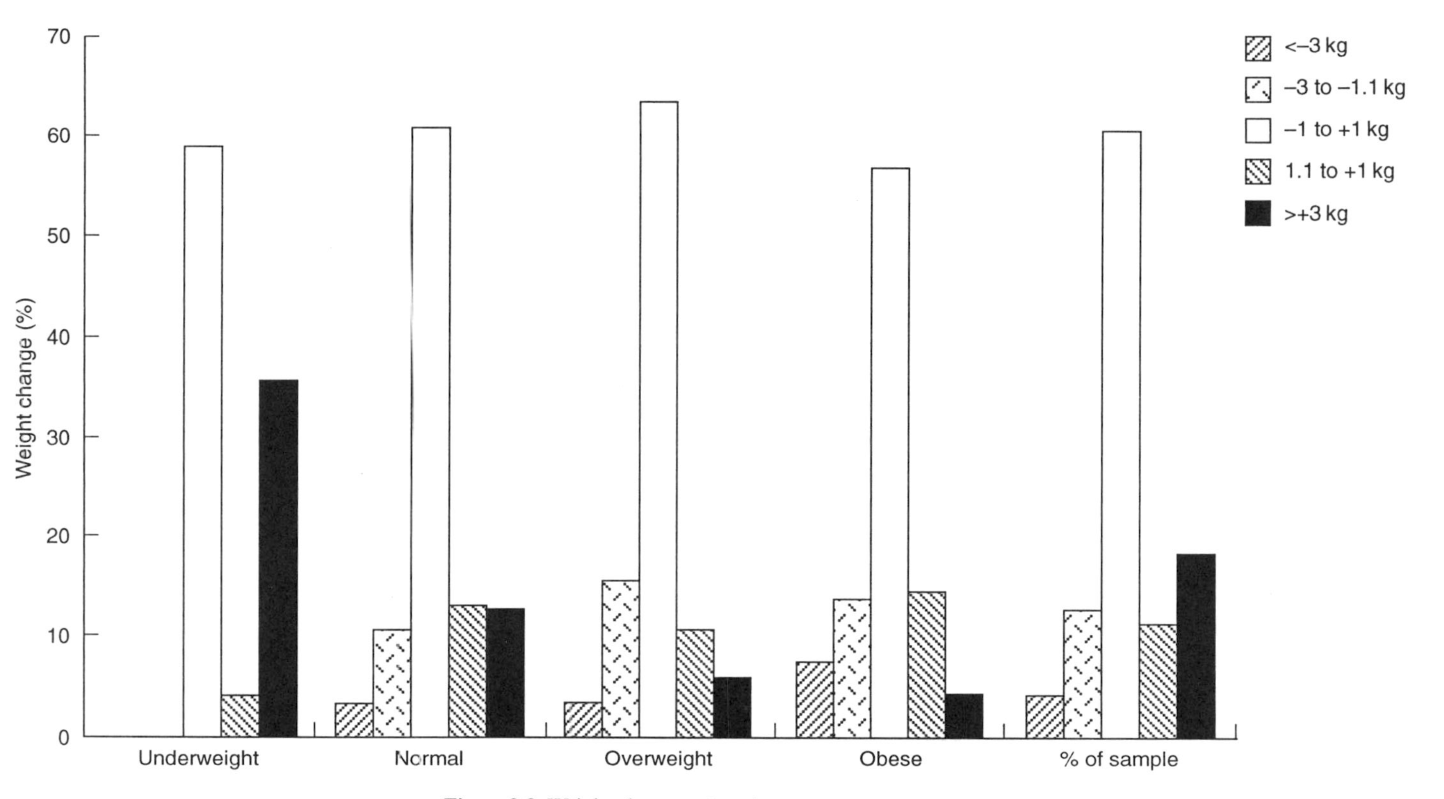

Figure 2.8 Weight change – Russians aged 70+, 1992–93.

This survey has provided timely information on the economic status of the Russian population and indicators of population changes in important health behaviours, including changes in smoking, alcohol and fat consumption, and their acute consequences, in terms of anthropometric indices, during the turbulence following the break up of the former USSR. Nutritional surveillance in this study is limited to dietary assessment by trained interviewers of what was consumed during the previous 24 hours. This tool provides a robust estimate of population mean intakes per day and provides a solid basis for evaluation of changes at the group level in consumption of foods and nutrients over time. Biochemical assessment of body fluids was not logistically or financially possible. The utilization of 24-hour dietary recalls, and storage of the information per meal, has allowed in-depth assessment of the dietary adequacy of micronutrients as well, and assessment of primary food sources and bioavailability. These analyses can point out emerging problems and save resources by directing more expensive conformational measures to the most vulnerable populations. Direct anthropometric measures in this panel design will continue to serve as a sensitive indicator of unfavourable changes in energy balance in adults and growth in children.

Select results of the first four rounds of the survey indicate that alcohol consumption and smoking habits have been radically altered during this transition, and require further monitoring, as well as public health policies to prevent long-term detrimental health effects. Dramatic reductions in the percentage of energy from fat are being noted in the population at large. Short-term changes in the weight status of the adult and elderly population are not obvious. However, infants and children appear to be suffering from the political turbulence, with increases in stunting.

The survey, in turning over analyses of a nationally representative sample within a year of data collection, is among the fastest worldwide. We hope that the placement of the original survey data on the worldwide web will set a precedent in data sharing and will promote its use by all interested scientists and policy makers.

Acknowledgements

Data collection funding for the 1992 round of the Russian Longitudinal Monitoring Survey (RLMS) was provided by the World Bank and for the 1993 and 1994 rounds by the US Agency for International Development. Additional funding for file creation has come from the National Institutes of Health (NIH) (1 RO1HD30880), for collaborative travel and research design work from the National Science Foundation (NSF) (SBR-9223326), and considerable support has come from the Carolina Population Center. This was a collaborative project of the University of North Carolina at

Chapel Hill (UNC-CH), the Goskomstat, the Russian Center of Preventive Medicine (RCPM), the Russian Institute of Nutrition (RIN) and the Russian Institute of Sociology (ISRosAN). Key collaborators of the authors in this survey are: Barbara Entwisle, Lenore Kohlmeier, Thomas Mroz and Michael Swafford, US; Alexander Nikolaevitch Ivanov and Igor Ivanovitch Dmitrichev, Goskomstat; Polina Kozyreva and Michael S. Kosolapov, ISRosAN; Svetlana Shalnova and Alexander Deev, RCPM; and Arseni Martinchik, Russian Institute of Nutrition. Leslie Kish and Steve Heeringa of the University of Michigan were the senior US sampling researchers for Phase 2 and William Kalsbeek, UNC-CH, was the leading sampling scholar for Phase 1. In both phases, Michael Kasalopov, Institute of Sociology, Russian Academy of Sociology, and Michael Swafford, a US sociologist, played central roles in implementing the sampling. A number of persons have provided important assistance in this work on nutrition. Most important have been Karin Gleiter, Laura Kline, David Robinson, Elena Glinskaya, Michael Lokshin, and Andrey Lukoshov, all at UNC-CH, for analysis of the Russian data. Frances Dancy assisted with support in administrative matters, Amanda Lyerly provided graphics support and Lynn Igoe, editorial support. All are thanked.

References

Brezhnev, L.I. (1967) The report of the General Secretary of the Central Committee of the Communist Party of the Soviet Union, in *The Proceedings of the XXIV Congress of the CPSU*, Gospolitizdat, Moscow, p. 48.

Centers for Disease Control and Prevention (1992) Nutritional needs surveys among the elderly – Russia and Armenia, 1992. *MMWR. Morbidity and Mortality Weekly Report*, **41**, 809–911. Reprinted in *Journal of the American Medical Association*, **268**, 3298.

Gabovich, R.D. (1960) *Uchebnik Gigieni*, Medgiz, Moscow (in Russian).

James,W.P., Ferro-Luzzi, A. and Waterlow, J.C. (1988) Definition of chronic energy deficiency in adults. Report of a working party of the International Dietary Energy Consultative Group. *European Journal of Clinical Nutrition*, **42**, 969–81.

Joint FAO/WHO/UNU (Food and Agricultural Organization of the United Nations/World Health Organization/United Nations University) Expert Consultation on Energy and Protein Requirements (1985). Energy and Protein Requirements: Report of a Joint FAO/WHO/UNU Expert Consultation. *WHO Technical Report no. 724*.

Kruschev, N.S. (1961) The report of the First Secretary of the Central Committee of the CPSU, in *The Proceedings of the XXII Congress of the CPSU*, Gospolitizdat, Moscow, pp. 171–2.

McNabb, S.J., Welch, K., Laumark, S. *et al.* (1994) Population-based nutritional risk survey of pensioners in Yerevan, Armenia. *American Journal of Preventive Medicine*, **10**, 65–70.

Ministry of Health, USSR (1968) *Recomenduemie velichini phisiologicheckich potrebnostey v pischevich veschestvach I energii*, Minzdraw, Mockow (in Russian).

Ministry of Health, USSR (1982) *Phisiologicheskich potrebnostey v pischevich veschestvach I energii razlichnich grup naselenia*, Minzdraw, Mockow (in Russian).

Ministry of Health, USSR (1991) *Normi phisiologicheskich potrebnostey v pischevich veschestvach I energii razlichnich grup naselenia SSSR*, Minzdraw, Mockow (in Russian).

Mroz, T. and Popkin, B.M. (1995) Poverty and the economic transition in the Russian Federation. *Economic Development and Cultural Change*, **44**, 1–31.

Popkin, B.M. (1994) The nutrition transition in low-income countries: an emerging crisis. *Nutrition Review*, **52** (9), 285–98.

Popkin, B.M., Zohoori, N. and Baturin, A. (1996) Elderly nutrition in Russia: is there a public health problem? *American Journal of Public Health*, **86**, 355–60.

Rubin, C.H., Posner, B.M. and Peterson, D.E. (1994) Nutritional survey of an elderly Russian population. CARE International Working Group. *American Journal of Preventive Medicine*, **10**, 71–6.

3 Nutritional surveillance programme of Bulgaria

STEFKA PETROVA

3.1 Introduction

In Bulgaria today there is a high and increasing morbidity and mortality rate of the chronic non-communicable diet-related diseases as well as the high risk for micronutrient deficiencies which has grown significantly in recent years. The transition to a market economy provides a reasonable opportunity to implement effective interventions to improve the nutritional situation in this country. During the past decades a few programmes directed at reducing the dietary risk factors have been developed but their partial implementation did not bring any positive changes. An important factor contributing to the programme's failure was the lack of information on the efficiency of the interventions, the evaluation and the feedback needed to develop an adequate nutritional strategy. The establishment of a continuous nutritional surveillance as the backbone of the national nutritional policies is strongly recommended from the IUNS Committee (Kohlmeier, Helsing and Kelly, 1990). The assessing, analysing and monitoring of nutritional situations was identified by the International Conference on Nutrition (ICN) in Rome, 1992 as one of the priority areas for action that can have a major impact on nutrition (ICN, 1992).

3.2 Past surveillance of nutrition in Bulgaria

Nutritional status surveys, designed to obtain information on food and nutrient intake, dietary habits, nutritional anthropometry, biochemical and clinical indices of the nutritional status of different population groups and diet related non-communicable diseases morbidity have been conducted in Bulgaria since the 1960s and include the following.

Implementing Dietary Guidelines for Healthy Eating. Edited by Verner Wheelock. Published in 1997 by Blackie A&P, an imprint of Chapman & Hall, London. ISBN 0 7514 0304 0

3.2.1 Nutritional survey of the Bulgarian population (1961–70)

This is the only representative nutritional survey of the Bulgarian population conducted so far (Tashev, 1972). The survey has been household based and included 1458 randomly selected households and 5357 individuals aged 3 months and older. Biochemical investigations have been performed on a subsample of 1000–1450 persons. Weighed records of all foods and drinks consumed over 10 consecutive days have been administered for collection of dietary data in the spring and autumn. Habitual physical activity has been investigated. Anthropometric status has been assessed by measuring height and weight, skin folds and circumferences. Blood pressures have been measured and electrocardiograms have been taken. Urine ascorbic acid has been used as a biomarker of the vitamin C intake. Total protein, protein fractions and amino acids in serum have been determined. The lipid status has been assessed on the basis of total cholesterol, lecithin, β-cholesterol, β-lipoproteins, total lipids and esterified fatty acids levels in serum. Haemoglobin, serum iron and transferin saturation have been determined for assessment of iron-deficient anaemia. Vitamin A status has been assessed using the indicator 'night blindness', serum levels of vitamin A and β-carotene. The status of thiamin, riboflavin, niacin, ascorbic acid and vitamin B12 have been investigated. The prevalence of specifically defined chronic diseases relation to nutrition has been estimated.

3.2.2 Survey of the population in two regions of the country (1988–89)

The survey was directed mainly at the assessment of the prevalence of chronic non-communicable diseases and their relation to nutritional habits. The study was household based and included 6854 individuals aged 3 years and older (Balabanski, 1991). The anthropometric status was determined by measuring height, weight, skin folds and circumferences. The lipid status of 1370 individuals was assessed on the basis of total cholesterol, high density lipoprotein (HDL) and low density lipoprotein (LDL) cholesterol and triglyceride serum levels. Iron-deficient anaemia was investigated in only 109 adults clinically suspected for anaemia, by determination of haemoglobin, serum iron and total iron-binding capacity. Vitamin status was not studied.

3.2.3 Small-scale nutritional studies of risk groups

The studies were conducted on at-risk population groups (children of different ages, adolescents, elderly people, pregnant women), urban and rural populations, different professional groups (Ivanova, 1985; Hadjiiski *et al.*, 1986; Ivanova and Polonov, 1987; Angelova-Gateva, 1988; Petrova,

Doicheva and Valova, 1990; Dejanov, Kerekovska and Doncheva, 1993; Pentieva *et al.*, 1996). The studies were carried out in different settlements and their design has been quite different. Most studies included dietary intake and anthropometric measures only. Biomarkers of the nutrient intakes as well as indices of the biochemical nutritional status were seldom determined and on a very limited number of individuals, mainly because of financial reasons.

3.2.4 Monitoring haemoglobin of pregnant women and infants

Haemoglobin levels of women during pregnancy and of infants once every 3 months in the first year of life have been monitored for 30 years by local outpatient clinics in the country. The data obtained are used for individual treatment only and are not collected nor analysed for assessment of the prevalence of anaemia.

3.2.5 Iodine deficiency disorders surveys

Since 1956 iodine deficiency disorders (IDD) have been monitored in Bulgaria. A large survey of goitre on 1 044 359 school-age children from 4085 sites in the country was the basis for identification of endemic areas. Since then four goitre prevalence surveys have been carried out in different settlements of the endemic regions only (Lozanov, 1995). Goitre grade, examined by palpation, has been mainly used as an indicator for IDD. Biochemical indicators (urinary iodine in schoolchildren and adults, and thyroid stimulating hormone in newborns) for assessment of IDD prevalence were used for the first time in a UNICEF survey conducted in 1991 on limited groups of individuals from endemic areas (DeLange and Gutekunst, 1992).

3.2.6 Strengths and weaknesses of the nutritional surveys

The large representative nutritional survey, conducted in 1961–70, described the nutritional status of the Bulgarian population and provided reliable and broad information as a basis of the national nutritional policy for the following years. The IDD problem was identified on the basis of data obtained from the national representative survey of goitre grade in 1956, which provoked the development and implementation of a national intervention programme.

However, since then nutritional and IDD data have not been collected on a systematic basis and have not been based on a representative sample of the Bulgarian population. Many surveys did not collect information on important indicators. Methods for the assessment of dietary and nutritional status were often not standardized and reliable enough. These factors influence the conclusions drawn from the data. The need for improvement of dietary methods in nutritional epidemiological studies in all eastern European countries was pointed out by Szostak (1994). Quality control in dietary surveys is necessary to minimize the errors in field work (Haralsdóttir, 1993) but has not been performed in most of the Bulgarian surveys. The collection, processing and analysis of the data were time consuming. In general most of the gaps in the dietary survey methodology in Bulgaria are very similar to those identified in other countries in eastern Europe (Charzewska, 1994) and in some countries in western Europe (Pietinen and Ovaskainen, 1994).

The nutritional surveys conducted on different risk and professional groups of the population in the 1980s were the basis for the development of specific requirements and regulations for nutrition of these populations but, in general, the data obtained do not provide information for setting adequate nutritional goals and decision making on a national level. There is not enough current information concerning protein–energy malnutrition and the risk groups are not identified. While iron deficiency is known to be a problem in some populations, there are no nationally representative data on the extent, magnitude and high-risk groups for anaemia. The limited data on other micronutrient deficiencies do enable identification of the problem at present. While the prevalence of goitre in the endemic regions is monitored and well established, the present distribution of goitre in the country is largely unknown. The iodine intake was not monitored until 1994.

3.3 Current nutritional surveillance programme

The national nutritional surveillance programme was developed in 1992–95 (Petrova and Ivanova, 1992, 1993; Petrova and Angelova, 1995). The purpose, objectives, strategies, organizational structure and management of a nationwide nutritional surveillance system were defined, the nutritional surveillance activities were determined and initiated. The nutritional surveillance programme was accepted by the Ministry of Health in 1995 and was included in the new National Health Strategy.

3.3.1 Purpose

The overall purpose is to reduce the risk of malnutrition as well as the risk of morbidity and premature mortality from chronic non-communicable diseases related to nutrition. Risk reduction will be attained by improvement in nutritional status through public health interventions based on regular, reliable and timely information on nutritional status and diet-related health problems.

3.3.2 Objectives

To assess the nutritional status and diet-related health of the Bulgarian population and to monitor their changes over time for decision making, a nationwide nutritional surveillance system will be established. The objectives of its activities, along the lines of those formulated by the United Nations Expert Committee Report (Mason *et al.*, 1984) and the International Conference on Nutrition in 1992 (ICNB, 1992) are:

- to describe the nutritional status of the Bulgarian population and to identify nutritional problems and groups at risk;
- to assess the prevalence, magnitude and distribution of diet-related health problems;
- to provide information that could contribute to the determination of causes and nutrition-related risk factors;
- to monitor the nutritional intervention programmes and evaluate their effectiveness;
- to update the strategies of the national nutritional policy, if necessary; and
- to measure the progress towards long-term nutritional goals.

3.3.3 Strategies

The main strategies for achieving the objectives of the national nutritional surveillance programme most effectively include:

- establishment of a nutritional surveillance system with an effective framework of defined efficient lines of responsibilities, supervision and communications;
- human resource development and integrated training of the personnel involved at all levels in the surveillance system so that they can perform their determined role;
- use of the available information concerning food consumption, nutritional status and health status related to nutrition;
- collection of data that could be used for making decisions; to avoid spending large amounts of time, effort and resources on collecting data that do not help toward achieving the objectives of the nutritional surveillance programme;
- use suitable criteria and indicators as well as current and standardized methods for assessing dietary and nutritional status;
- establishment of a system of quality control to ensure that data collected are accurate and valid;
- introduction of an analytical quality assurance;
- the information, interpretation of information and recommendations for

intervention are to be communicated back to decision makers in a timely, comprehensible, meaningful and compelling format;
- data dissemination, providing timely and regular information to public health personnel and the community.

3.4 Nutritional surveillance system management

3.4.1 Policy and decision making

The nutritional surveillance system is under the general direction of the Deputy Minister at the Ministry of Health who established policies concerning the operation and staffing of the surveillance system. The Deputy Minister liaises with other ministries and national institutions concerning the objectives and activities of the surveillance system. The Chief of the Department of State Sanitary Control at the Ministry of Health (MOH) and two experts in nutrition from the staff of the Nutrition Unit at this department assist the Deputy Minister to pursue the policy of the Ministry.

3.4.2 Co-ordination and advisory functions

An Advisory Board for Nutrition will be established within the Ministry of Health to ensure general co-ordination and strategy of the nutritional surveillance system activities and to advise on policy issues. The Advisory Board will include representatives of all the institutions included in the survey and *ad hoc* members depending on the issue discussed.

3.4.3 Planning, management and evaluation

The head of the Department of Nutrition at the National Center of Hygiene at the Ministry of Health has the primary responsibility for planning, implementation and evaluation of the nutritional surveillance system. The responsibilities of the staff of the Department of Nutrition, which includes 35 co-workers, are defined according to the following functions:

- survey design and management;
- questionnaire development;
- methodological assistance;
- training/manual development;
- conducting the feasibility/pilot studies;
- field supervision and quality control;
- biochemical analyses;

- data assessment and reporting;
- data dissemination;
- proposals for intervention.

3.4.4 *Implementation*

A network of nutrition monitoring units is established at the 28 existing regional Hygiene and Epidemiology Inspectors (HEI), comprised of staff of the Department of Food Hygiene and Nutrition and the Department of Child and Adolescent Hygiene. The field workers from HEI will have close collaboration with the physicians, nurses and dentists from the local outpatient clinics and schools. The functions of the Regional Nutrition Monitoring Units will be:

- organization and management of the nutritional surveys at a regional level;
- collection of the socio-demographic, nutrition and health information on questionnaires;
- physical measurements (anthropometry, blood pressure);
- collection and processing of blood specimens;
- data entry;
- information dissemination.

3.4.5 *Supporting services*

Higher Medical Institute in Sofia. A team of specialists (statisticians, program engineers) from the Department of Social Medicine at the Higher Medical Institute in Sofia is defined according to the following activities:

- development of entry software programs;
- training the field staff to enter the data.

Center for Health Information. The head of the Department of Statistics is responsible for the design of the surveys and representative sample size determination. The data obtained from the surveys will be processed and analysed by the defined team of experts and technical assistants.

National Clinical Center of Endocrinology. A team of specialists from the Department of Thyroidology, National Clinical Center of Endocrinology under the management of the department head will provide:

- goitre size assessment (palpation and ultrasound);
- training of IDD survey teams;

- IDD assessment and reporting;
- proposals for IDD intervention activities.

Primary health providers. Physicians, nurses and laboratory assistants from the local outpatient clinics and the schools at the settlements included in the different surveys will be engaged in the physical examinations and the collection of blood specimens.

3.5 Data management

Data are collected on questionnaire forms and will be checked, validated, cleaned and analysed using the Bulgarian program for diet analysis, Epi Info, SPSS. The data obtained will be presented to decision makers (Ministries of Health, Education, Economics, Council of Ministers, Parliament, President); primary health providers and nutritionists; non-governmental organizations in the country; and international organizations.

The results of the surveys will be distributed by:

- scientific and technical reports (to be submitted to the decision makers);
- national workshops;
- mass media;
- presentations at national and international scientific meetings; and
- publication of the data in books and articles.

3.6 Surveillance activities and main characteristics of the surveys

3.6.1 Nutritional surveillance of the age groups of the Bulgarian population

This will be along the lines of the Diet and Nutrition Survey Programme of the United Kingdom (Gregory *et al.*, 1995) which includes four separate surveys, conducted on different age groups of the population. The US nutrition monitoring approach (Interagency Board for Nutrition Monitoring and Related Research, 1992; Kuczmarski, Moshfegh and Briefel, 1994), where surveys (NHANES I–III) are carried out on the whole population, is not so suitable in Bulgaria because dealing with the great amount of data obtained will take a lot of time. The Bulgarian nutritional surveillance programme includes four separate surveys, each examining a nationally representative sample drawn from different age population groups. The surveys will be conducted for approximately 2½ years each and the cycle will take about 10 years to complete. The surveillance programme will start with the nutrition survey of schoolchildren in 1996, as a national Program for Improvement of Nutritional Status of Schoolchildren was initiated in 1995 and the data obtained in the survey will form a basis for assessing the efficiency of the interventions.

The main characteristics of the nutrition surveys are:

Target population. Individuals of the age groups of both sexes as follows:

- children aged 1–6 years;
- schoolchildren aged 6–18 years;
- adults aged 18–60 years;
- adults aged 60 years and older.

Sample size. The total effective samples must be nationally representative with respect to age, sex, urban/rural and ethnic (Bulgarian, Turkish) distribution as well as to the classification of social class. Subsamples to assess the biochemical nutritional status will be studied.

Design and methods. The surveys will be designed as cross-sectional with a multistage stratified cluster sample of households and random sampling of individuals (only the nutrition survey of schoolchildren will be school based). To allow for assessment of the seasonal changes in eating behaviour, field work will be distributed over two waves, in autumn and in spring each of three months' duration. Nutrition data will be obtained by 3-day record (in the case of young children, from their mothers). A face-to-face interview will be used to collect information on socio-demographic circumstances, the subject's eating patterns, micronutrient supplements, health and habitual physical activity. A record of smoking and drinking habits, and contraceptive use among the older age groups will be taken. Physical examination will be performed: anthropometric measurements (height, weight, mid-upper arm circumference and, for children over the age of 10 years and adults, waist and hip circumferences) and measurement of blood pressure. Biochemical analyses of whole blood and serum to assess some indicators of the nutritional status or dietary biomarkers will be performed. Dental examination will be conducted.

Descriptive variables. Gender; age; ethnicity; religion; urban/rural setting; family income; family structure; education; employment and marital status.

Outcome variables of interest. Food intake; nutrient and energy intake; sources of nutrients; nutrition knowledge, attitudes and behaviour; vitamin supplementation; smoking, alcohol and contraceptive use; physical activity level; overweight; iron-deficiency anaemia; vitamin status (vitamins A, D, C, thiamin, riboflavin, folate, vitamin B_{12}); zinc status; lipid status; chronic non-communicable diet-related diseases. The variables will be specified according to the age of the studied group.

3.6.2 Nutritional surveillance of socially deprived groups of the Bulgarian population

The nutritional surveillance programme also includes nationally representative surveys directed at socially deprived institutionalized children and adolescents in Bulgaria. The first survey of school-aged children (7–14 years old) began in 1995. Food and nutrient intakes in different seasons, physical activity, anthropometric measures and total morbidity rate have been studied. In 1997 a nutrition survey of institutionalized infants and children aged 1–3 years will start. Each survey will be carried out for about 2 years. The periodicity of these surveys will be about 10 years.

3.6.3 Surveillance of anaemia prevalence in risk population groups

Special attention is paid to anaemia in high-risk groups such as pregnant women. A national representative survey on anaemia prevalence in pregnant women will be conducted at the beginning of 1997. In this survey the existing system for monitoring pregnant women in outpatient clinics will be used and the available data of haemoglobin levels of women in the third trimester of pregnancy will be analysed. Additional information about the nutrition, demographic and socio-economic characteristics of the pregnant women will be collected. The periodicity of the surveys will be approximately 5 years.

3.6.4 Surveillance of iodine deficiency disorders

A national representative survey for assessment of iodine deficiency disorder (IDD) prevalence and distribution in the Bulgarian population was conducted in September–October 1996. This survey is to estimate the efficiency of the IDD prevention and control programme, which started in 1994, and to measure the progress towards the long-term goal – IDD elimination by the year 2000. A National Laboratory for Urinary Iodine Analysis was established and equipped at the Department of Nutrition, National Center of Hygiene and a pilot study was conducted in the endemic region of Smolian in 1995.The target population of the survey is schoolchildren aged 7–10 years. Goitre grade by palpation and urinary iodine were determined. The survey is designed as cross-section, school based with two-stage cluster sampling. The IDD prevalence will be monitored in the endemic regions every 5 years.

Since 1993 screening of thyroid stimulating hormone (TSH) of newborns in Bulgaria has been carried out. The data of neonatal TSH distribution will be used to assess the iodine status of the population, for primary screening for IDD severity and distribution and as an indicator for effectiveness of the programme for IDD control (Peneva *et al.*, 1995).

Monitoring of the iodine level in iodized salt was introduced in 1994. The samples are collected by sanitary inspectors from the Departments of Food Hygiene and Nutrition at the Sanitary and Epidemiology Inspectorates in the country. The iodine level is determined in the laboratories at the inspectorates.

3.7 Conclusion

The establishment of a nutritional surveillance programme in Bulgaria is the prerequisite for provision of reliable data for the development, implementation, evaluation and updating of an efficient and successful national nutrition policy.

References

Angelova-Gateva, P. (1988) Incidence of iron deficiency in children of early and preschool age, brought up at home. *Hygiena I Zdraveopazvane*, **XXXI**, (6), 65–71.

Balabanski, L. (ed.) (1991) *New Data for Nutrition and Epidemiology of Social Important Metabolic Diseases*, MA, NIGN, Sofia (Bulg.)

Charzewska, J. (1994) Gaps in dietary-survey methodology in Eastern Europe. *American Journal of Clinical Nutrition*, **59S**, 157S-160S.

Dejanov, Chr., Kerekovska, M. and Doncheva, N. (1993) Nutritional habits, lipid metabolism and prevalence of arterial hypertension and coronary heart disease among industrial workers. *Hygiene and Public Health*, **XXXVI**, (6),24–6.

DeLange, F.R. and Gutekunst, R. (1992) Iodine deficiency in Eastern Europe. *Report of ICCIDD, UNICEF and WHO.*

Gregory, J., Collins, D., Davies, P. *et al.* (1995) *National Diet and Nutrition Survey: Children Aged 1½ to 4½ years. Vol.1: Report of the Diet and Nutrition Survey*, HMSO, London, pp. 1–4.

Hadgiiski, R., Miteva, U., Doseva, T. *et al.* (1986) *Nutrition and Physical Activity of Medical Students.* Abstracts of the IV Congress on Nutrition, Plovdiv, p. 375.

Haraldsdóttir, J.(1993) Minimizing error in the field: quality control in dietary surveys. *European Journal of Clinical Nutrition*, **47**, (Suppl. S2), S19–S24.

ICN (International Conference on Nutrition) (1992) *Nutrition and Development – A Global Assessment*, FAO and WHO, pp. 96–101.

Interagency Board for Nutrition Monitoring and Related Research (ed. J. Wright) (1992) *Nutrition Monitoring in the United States: The Directory of Federal and State Nutrition Monitoring Activities*, Public Health Service, Hyattsville, Maryland.

Ivanova, L. (1985) Study on nutrition of the workers producing antibiotics and some of the basic requirements. *Hygiena i Zdraveopazvane*, **XXVIII**, (6), 79–82.

Ivanova, L. and Polonov, K. (1987) Problems of organized nutrition of elderly people. *Hygiena I Zdraveopazvene*, **XXX**, (2), 71–7.

Kohlmeier, L., Helsing, E., Kelly, A. *et al.* (1990) Nutritional Surveillance as the backbone of national nutrition policy: Recommendations of the IUNS Committee on nutritional surveillance and programme evaluation in developed countries. *European Journal of Clinical Nutrition*, **44**, 771–81.

Kuczmarski, M.F., Moshfegh, A. and Briefel, R. (1994) Update on nutrition monitoring activities in the United States. *Journal of the American Dietetic Association*, **94**,(7), 753–60.

Lozanov, B. (1995) *The Prevalence and Control of Endemic Goiter in Bulgaria*. Abstracts of the 5th National Congress of Endocrinology, Varna, p. 2.

Mason, G.B., Habicht, J., Tabatabai, H. and Velverde,V. (1984) *Nutritional Surveillance*, WHO, Geneva.

Peneva, L., Jadkova, L. Grigorova, R. *et al.* (1995) *Organization and Prospect of Neonatal Thyroid Screening in Bulgaria*. Abstracts of the 5th National Congress of Endocrinology, Varna, p. 3.

Pentieva, K., Petrova, S., Ivanova, L. *et al.* (1995) Food and nutrient intake of healthy pregnant women during the transitional period. *Hygiene and Public Health*, **38** (6), 40–43.

Petrova, S. and Angelova, K. (1995) Dietary and nutritional status monitoring system – scientific basis for nutrition policy. *Hygiene and Public Health*, **XXXVIII**, (1) 23–6.

Petrova, S. and Ivanova, L. (1992) *Program for Surveillance of Dietary and Nutritional Status of Bulgarian Population.* Abstracts of the National Conference on Hygiene and Health Prophylactics, Lovetch, p. 18.

Petrova, S. and Ivanova, L. (1993) *Draft Proposal for Micronutrient Deficiencies Surveillance System in Bulgaria*, Program Against Micronutrient Malnutrition – USA Publication, Atlanta, GA.

Petrova, S., Doicheva, P. and Valova, A. (1990) Study on the physiological needs and nutrition of the workers from three petro-chemical productions. *Hygiena I Zdraveopazvane*, **XXXIII**, (5), 82–7.

Pietinen, P. and Ovaskainen, M. (1994) Gaps in dietary-survey methodology in Western Europe. *American Journal of Clinical Nutrition*, **59S**, 161S–163S.

Szostak, W.B. (1994) The need for improved methods of diet assessment of developing and monitoring food policy in Eastern Europe. *American Journal of Clinical Nutrition*, **59S**, 273S–274S.

Tasher, T. (ed.) (1972) *Nutrition, Physical Development and Health Status of Bulgarian Population,* BAN, Sofia (Bulg.)

Part Two

National Policies

4 Nutritional policy: Bulgaria

STEFKA PETROVA

4.1 Geographical and demographical characteristics

Bulgaria is situated on the Balkan Peninsula in eastern Europe. The country covers 110 993.6 km^2 but more than half of it is covered by mountains. Bulgaria has a population of 8.427 million. After the Second World War a consistent increase in the urban population was observed – in 1946 its proportion was 24.7% of the total population but by 1994 it was 67.6% (National Institute of Statistics, 1995a). In the past decades there has been a significant tendency for birth rate reduction as well as death rate increase and the population growth has shown negative values since 1990; in 1994 it was –3.8 (Fig. 4.1). As a result, the proportion of the elderly people is increasing – the number of pensioners was 2.035 million in 1994. Bulgaria is one of the few European countries where life expectancy – one of the most fundamental indicators of health status – has virtually stagnated since 1970 (Table 4.1). For men, life expectancy has actually been declining since the late 1960s.

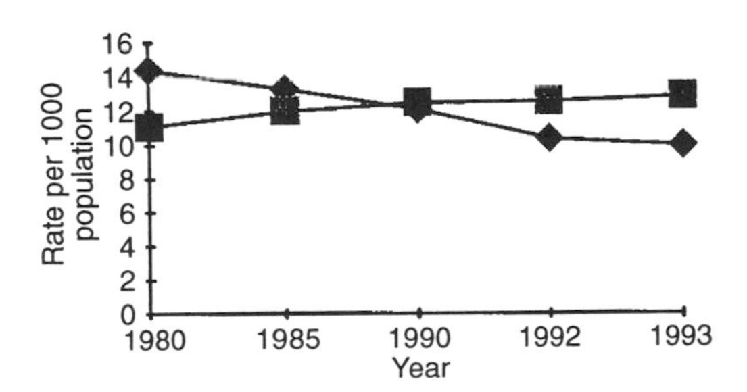

Figure 4.1 Birth rate (◆) and mortality rate (■) (source: National Institute of Statistics, 1995a).

Implementing Dietary Guidelines for Healthy Eating. Edited by Verner Wheelock. Published in 1997 by Blackie A&P, an imprint of Chapman & Hall, London. ISBN 0 7514 0304 0

Table 4.1 Life expectancy of the Bulgarian population by gender in selected time periods (years of life) (source: National Institute of Statistics, 1994)

Time period	1927–34	1935–39	1956–57	1960–62	1965–67	1969–71	1974–76	1978–80	1984–86	1988–90	1991–93
Total	48.40	51.75	65.89	65.59	70.66	71.11	71.31	71.14	71.19	71.33	71.00
Male	47.81	50.98	64.17	67.82	68.81	68.58	68.68	68.35	68.17	68.12	67.50
Female	49.09	52.56	67.65	71.35	72.67	73.86	73.91	73.55	74.44	74.77	74.77

Table 4.2 Agriculture production in 1990–94 (source: National Institute of Statistics, 1995a)

Year	Wheat (thousand tonnes)	Corn (thousand tonnes)	Tomatoes (thousand tonnes)	Potatoes (thousand tonnes)	Grapes (thousand tonnes)	Meat (thousand tonnes)	Milk (million litres)	Eggs (million)
1990	5292	1221	846	433	731	901	2385	2460
1994	3786	1362	443	476	498	516	1322	1532

4.2 Food production and manufacturing

Agronomy and food production have always been important components of the Bulgarian economy. In the 1980s agricultural production began to fall off but since 1990, during the period of transition to an open market, it has slumped sharply – the wheat output by 28.4%, output of vegetables by 50%, the output of milk by 44.5% and meat production by 42.7% (Table 4.2). The following basic reasons have been pointed out: a reduction in the use of fertilizers and pesticides because of lack of finances; irregular watering due to high taxes on water and electrical energy; perishing and slaughtering of the domestic animals because of inadequate forage; unused bank credits because of high interest rates, etc. (Institute of Economics, 1994). This has led to a deterioration in both quality and quantity of food. Furthermore because of the high prices, there has been a tendency for consumers to switch to cheaper and/or poorer quality foods (see section 4.3).

The significant growth of food production and manufacturing by private farms is an outstanding feature of this period – from 20–50% of the total foodstuffs in 1990 to 60–92% in 1994.

4.3 Food supply

4.3.1 Information source

The national household budget survey system was established in 1951 and the surveys have been conducted annually by the National Institute of Statistics since 1953. The surveys cover the whole country, the urban and rural population and the major socio-economic strata. At present, 2508 households are selected randomly through a two-stage sampling procedure from 271 urban and 147 rural settlements. The quantities of purchased, home-produced or bartered foods, as well as food consumed away of the chosen households, are recorded all the year (National Institute of Statistics, 1995b).

4.3.2 Trends of food consumption

The consumption of meat and meat products tended to increase until 1990, when meat consumption was 100 g daily per capita and that of meat products was 49.3 g/capita/day (Fig. 4.2). In the next few years of the economic transition a significant reduction of total meat consumption occurred – in 1994 it had reached 70.7 g/day/capita of the population. An unfavourable balance of different meats consumed has developed in recent decades. The proportion of pork, which has a high fat content, increased – from 28% in 1975 to 43.6% in 1990, while there was a decrease in the consumption of more lean beef and veal (19% of total meats in 1975; 7.7% in 1990). In the past few years, the consumption of beef and veal has continued to fall but the proportion of pork has also declined due to the growth in demand for lamb, mutton and other meats.

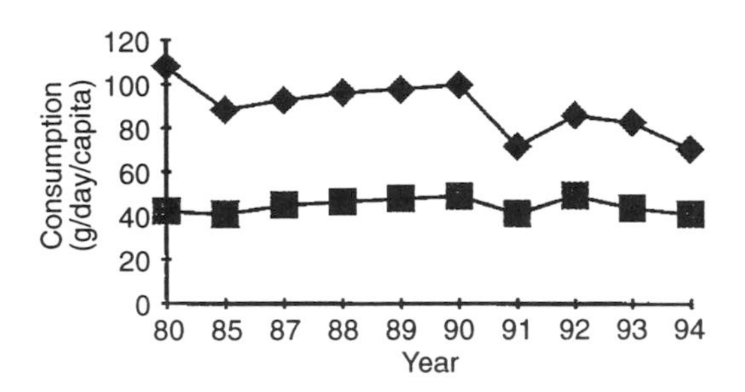

Figure 4.2 Consumption of meat (◆) and meat products (■) (source: National Institute of Statistics, 1995b).

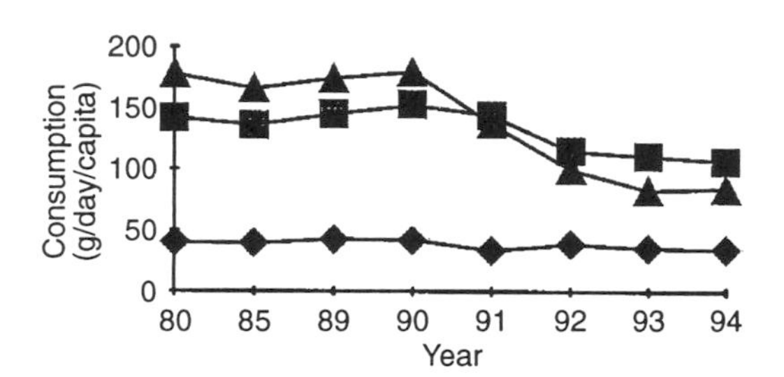

Figure 4.3 Consumption of milk (■), yogurt (▲) and dairy products (◆) (source: National Institute of Statistics, 1995b).

The fish consumption is traditionally low. The average daily intake per capita has been around 7–10 g since 1965.

The reduced availability and high prices of milk and yogurt are the main reasons why consumption has fallen during the transition period (Fig. 4.3). This applies particularly to the traditional and favourite Bulgarian yogurt, consumption of which has decreased by 52.3% by 1994 in comparison with 1990.

Total fat consumption has grown significantly during the past decades. While it was 47 g daily per capita in 1975, it had reached 54 g in 1989. The use of sunflower oil in cooking is traditionally high – 37–40 g daily per capita during the past 20 years. Lard has been widely used in the past but by 1990, consumption had decreased to 2.5 g daily per capita. In the transition period the price of butter has been increased significantly, resulting in a reduction in consumption of 48%. As a consequence, lard consumption has recovered somewhat, with an increase of 100% by 1994 as compared with the value for 1990.

There has been a trend for reduced consumption of fresh fruits and vegetables since the 1970s (Fig. 4.4). The great seasonal changes in their presence in the diet of the Bulgarian population have an adverse effect on nutritional quality (Fig. 4.5). The seasonal differences in consumption of fresh fruits and vegetables are more pronounced in rural populations and can alter by as much as a factor of ten.

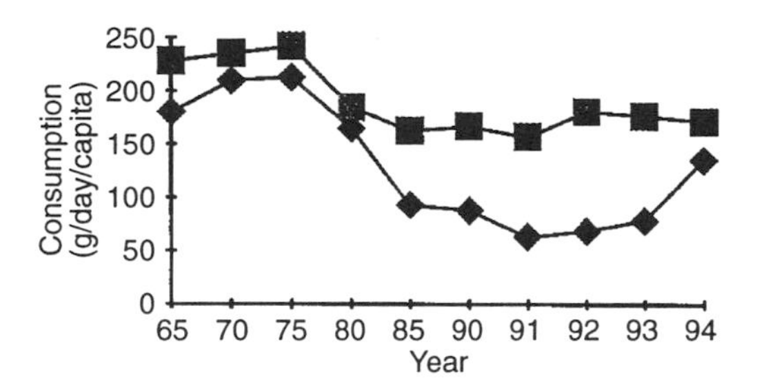

Figure 4.4 Consumption of fresh fruits (◆) and vegetables (■) (source: National Institute of Statistics, 1995b).

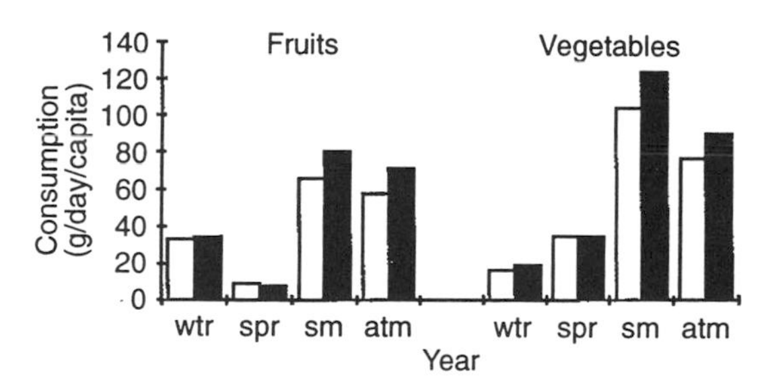

Figure 4.5 Seasonal changes in consumption of fresh fruits and vegetables in 1992. □, Towns; ■, villages; wnt, winter (December–February); spr, spring (March–May); sm, summer (June–August); atm, autumn (September–November) (source: National Institute of Statistics, 1995b).

Bread and bakery products are traditionally consumed in large quantities (over 400 g daily per capita) but especially high (496 g/day/capita) in the critical year, 1991. Then the prices of all foods were sharply increased but those of bread were comparatively constant. An unfavourable trend of falling wholemeal bread consumption has been developing during the period after the Second World War; in the 1980s wholemeal bread consumption as a proportion of total bread used was 0.4–0.8%. One of the few positive changes in the transition period has been the substantially increased intake of dark breads to about 2% in 1994.

There has been a tendency to lower the consumption of sugar, sweets and pastry with the onset of economic difficulties associated with the transition period. While the proportion of energy derived from sugar was 12% in 1989, in 1994 it had fallen to under 10%.

The alcohol consumption by the Bulgarian population was high during the 1960s–80s; in 1985–89 the apparent annual intake of alcoholic beverages was in the range of 4.9–5.5 litres/capita (expressed as ethanol). The consumption of all alcoholic beverages has shown a tendency to decrease in the past 5 years – the apparent total alcohol consumption was 3.7 litres (as ethanol) per capita in 1994. The reduction in wine and beer intake has been significantly greater than that of spirit drinks – in 1994 the intake was about 50% of that in 1985 (Fig. 4.6) As a result the proportion of the ethanol intake by spirits had increased up to 44% in 1994.

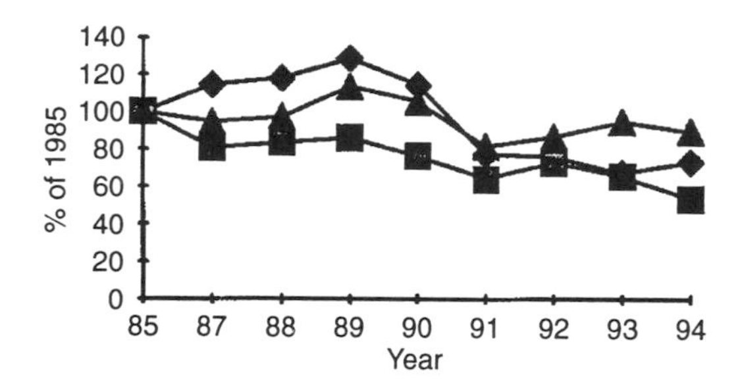

Figure 4.6 Percentage change in apparent per capita consumption of alcohol beverages: ◆, beer; ■, wine; ▲, spirits. (source: National Institute of Statistics, 1995b).

4.3.3 Expenditure on food

The data show that in general the relative amounts spent on food are higher than in most European countries (Table 4.3). The dynamic changes in national economics and market have influenced the structure of household expenses. The percentage of the total budget spent on food was reduced from 40.9% in 1985 to 36.3% in 1990 but it grew significantly in the next few years of the transition period – by 1993 it had grown to 42.9% from the total expenses. The expenditure on alcoholic drinks and cigarettes does not

Table 4.3 Consumer expenditure (annually per capita) (source: National Institute of Statistics, 1995b)

Expenditure	1985		1987		1988		1989		1990		1991		1992		1993	
	Leva	%	Leva	%	Leva	%	Leva	%	Leva	%	Leva	%	Leva	%	Leva	%
Total expenditure	1836	100	2011	100	2141	100	2332	100	2920	100	7772	100	13234	100	200890	100
Expenditure on food	752	40.9	808	40.4	847	39.5	888	38.1	1057	36.3	3681	47.4	5753	43.4	8622	43
Expenditure on alcoholic beverages	73	4.0	69	3.4	73	3.4	80	3.4	96	3.3	246	3.2	298	2.3	430	2.1
Expenditure on cigarettes	47	2.6	50	2.5	49	2.3	53	2.3	65	2.2	229	2.9	252	1.9	437	2.2

reflect their widespread use by the Bulgarian population but is due to the greater increase in food prices compared with those of cigarettes and alcoholic beverages.

Despite the marked growth in expenditure on food recently there has been a fall in consumption of most foodstuffs (Figs 4.2–4.4). Apparently the data show the existence of a financial crisis in Bulgarian households. The reduced food production causes a price increase of the basic foods, which explains the reduction in food consumption.

4.4 Dietary and nutritional status

4.4.1 Energy and nutrient intake

The available data show that for decades the diet of Bulgarians has not been a healthy one. The studies conducted on food consumption and nutrient intake of different population groups show common features within the age and social groups. One of the main characteristics of the Bulgarian diet is the limited variety of the foods consumed.

The energy intake was adequate for the whole population in the period 1975–89 (Marinova and Doichinova, 1986; Petrova, Ivanova and Vatralova, 1991). Since 1990 the tendency for overnutrition has been decreased significantly in some age and social groups, especially elderly people (Ivanova *et al.*, 1996c), and the unemployed.

The protein intake has been greater than the reference values and has usually provided 10–13%of the energy of the diet of the Bulgarian population during recent decades, including the past 5 years (Mladenova, 1986; Petrova *et al.*, 1993b). The proportion of the animal protein averaged 50% of the total protein consumed by adults and elderly people and about 50–65% of the total protein intake of the children and adolescents until 1990 (Tashev, 1972; Petrova *et al.*, 1989; Vatralova *et al.*, 1994). The reduced consumption of meat, milk and dairy products during the transition period resulted in a decrease in the proportion of animal protein in the diet by an average 10% (Pentieva *et al.*, 1996).

The intake of total fats is high (35–50%) for all the age and social groups (Petrova *et al.*, 1992). Not only have the saturated fats been higher than the limit of 10E% but the intake of polyunsaturated fatty acids has been much higher than 7% due to the traditional high usage of sunflower oil in cooking meals (Panchev and Andreeva, 1986; Dimitrova, 1993).

The carbohydrate intake has usually been lower than 50E%. The energy derived from refined sugar has been over 10% in the diet of children and adolescents (12–13E%) (Baikova *et al.*, 1993; Doichinova and Dimova, 1995). The data obtained from studies conducted in recent years show a decrease by 2–3E% of the sugar intake, corresponding to the irregular availability and the raised price of sugar as well as the higher prices of sweets and pastry (Ivanova *et al.*, 1996c; Pentieva *et al.*, 1996).

One of the most negative characteristics of the Bulgarian diet is the very high intake of sodium. During recent decades people over 1 year old have consumed very high amounts of sodium. In different age and social groups in some regions the sodium intake has been up to 3–4 times higher than the dietary reference values (Tashev, 1972; Panchev and Andreeva, 1986; Petrova, Ivanova, Bogdanov *et al.*, 1993).

Intakes of some vitamins (thiamin and riboflavin, as well as vitamin C and folate in the winter and spring) and minerals (iron, zinc, magnesium and calcium) have been 30–40% lower than the corresponding reference values in some population groups. At highest risk of inadequate micronutrient intake are young children, school-aged children, pregnant women, women of fertile age and the elderly (Duleva *et al.*, 1994; Petrova *et al.*, 1994; Ivanova, Petrova, Pentieva *et al.*, in press).

4.4.2 Protein–energy malnutrition

Protein–energy malnutrition of the type causing marasmus or kwashiorkor has not been recognized in the epidemiological studies in Bulgaria during the past decades.

Breast-feeding. The proportion of babies whose mothers do not breast-feed them at all or partially breast-feed until the third month of life has been increasing. It was 18.2% in 1985; 19.2% in 1990 and by 1993 it had increased to 22.4% (National Center of Health Information, 1993). An unfavourable characteristic of the nutrition of babies who are not breast-fed is that the breast milk often has been substituted by diluted yogurt or cow's milk. This applies especially to mothers in the villages as well as from those with low income who cannot afford the high prices of imported humanized milks.

Infant mortality. Infant mortality rate is strongly influenced by nutritional factors. A tendency for increasing infant mortality rate has been observed since 1988 (Fig. 4.7). This could be due to the nutritional status (anaemia) of the pregnant women, the permanent increase in numbers of babies who are not breast-fed and/or are fed with inadequate milks, as well as the environmental and socio-economic factors in the country during recent years.

Low birth weight. Low birth weight (less than 2500 g) is associated with both neonatal and post-neonatal mortality. The proportion of newborns with low birth weight was comparable to that of developed countries in the

1980s (6.21% of total newborn babies in 1989). During the past few years, there has been tendency for the proportion of underweight newborns to increase – in 1993 it had reached 8.25%, mainly because of babies born to young mothers (Fig. 4.8).

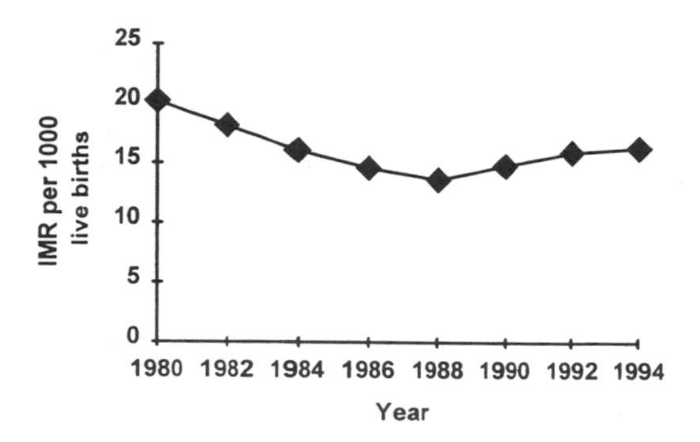

Figure 4.7 Infant mortality rate (IMR) (source: National Institute of Statistics, 1994).

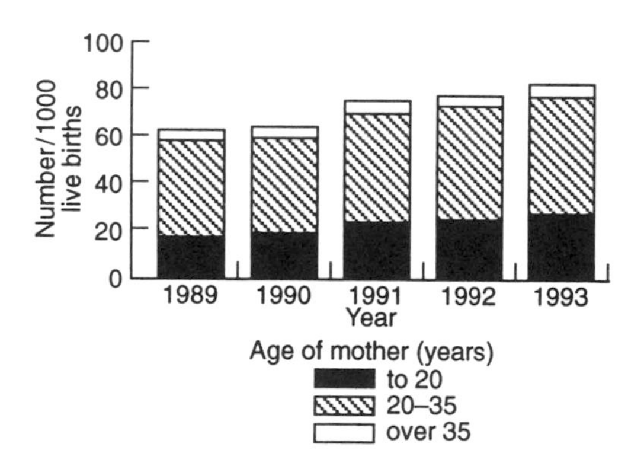

Figure 4.8 Low birth weight rate by age of mother (source: National Institute of Statistics, 1994).

4.4.3 Lipid status

Investigations into the biochemical nutritional status show widespread lipid disturbances among the population. The levels of serum cholesterol of 54% of 1370 individuals in the large epidemiological survey (1988–89) have been moderate or high elevated. Serum triglycerides were raised in 31% of the population group; high-density lipoprotein (HDL) cholesterol has been low in 8.8% of studied persons (Naumova, Belokova and Kerekovska, 1991). According to these data the risk for coronary heart disease is high in about one-third of the investigated population.

4.4.4 Micronutrient deficiencies

The studies on micronutrient status of Bulgarian population are limited mainly because of financial reasons. In a survey conducted in two provinces in 1989, the iron status of 109 adults clinically suspected for anaemia has been studied. Iron deficiency anaema has been found in 33% of those investigated (Balabanski *et al.*, 1991a). Iron deficiency anaemia has been found in 18.6% of 44 women in the third trimester of pregnancy from Sofia, investigated in 1992. Serum magnesium levels below the cut-off value have been found in 30.7% of pregnant women; serum calcium has been below the reference level in 25.6% of pregnant women, but zinc has been low in the serum of 42.8% of the investigated women (Ivanova *et al.*, 1996a,b). Ascorbic acid deficiency has been revealed in 29% of the pregnant women, and riboflavin deficiency in 60% (Petrova *et al.*, 1994). A study on the prevalence of anaemia, cited by WHO, was conducted on 203 young women aged 18–24 years from Sofia in 1995 (Baikova, 1996). Anaemia assessed on the basis of haemoglobin level has been determined in three women only. A study on the food intake of a representative group of pensioners from Sofia was carried out in 1994 but the biochemical nutritional status of only 38 elderly people has been determined. The data obtained did not recognize iron deficiency to be a problem in the study group (Ivanova *et al.*, 1996c). Studies conducted during the period 1983–92 on workers exposed to different occupational pollutants (lead, cadmium, carbon disulphide, styrene) revealed a high prevalence (20–80%) of vitamin deficiencies (vitamin C, vitamin E, thiamin, riboflavin and niacin) and mineral deficiencies (iron, zinc, copper and magnesium) (Petrova *et al.*, 1992). While the studies have been conducted on a small number of population subgroups, no data were available on a national level to identify the problems of micronutrient deficiencies, their extent, magnitude and high-risk groups. Only the iodine deficiency problem is defined.

At present the population on part of the territory of Bulgaria (about one-third) is affected by moderate to severe iodine deficiency resulting in a potential risk of brain damage and impairment of the intellectual capacities of the future generation. Despite iodized salt prophylactics given to the population in endemic regions, studies undertaken in 1987–88 on representative groups of these populations have shown a goitre prevalence of 23.3% (13–40% in the different settlements), which represents a twofold increase when compared with data collected in 1974 (Lozanov, 1995). The most affected groups were children, adolescent females and women of fertile age.

A small-scale study on 300 schoolchildren aged 8–16 years from the town of Smolian was conducted in 1995 and revealed almost the same goitre prevalence – 21% of the studied group.

4.5 Non-communicable diet-related diseases

The morbidity and mortality rates of non-communicable diet-related diseases of the Bulgarian population are high and show negative tendencies.

4.5.1 Cardiovascular and cerebrovascular diseases

The diseases of the circulatory system are the leading causes of death in Bulgaria. In 1992 the mortality rates per 100 000 population were 812.7 for males and 724 for females – the highest rates in Europe for males, and second-highest (after Hungary) for females (Table 4.4). The mortality due

Table 4.4 Main causes of death by gender in European countries, per 1000000 population (source WHO, 1994; National Institute of statistics, 1995).

Countries	Year	Gender	Causes of death			
			Diseases of the circulatory system	Neoplasms	Diseases of respiratory system	Infectious and parasitic diseases
Austria	1992	Males	475.8	255.8	55.2	4.3
		Females	629.1	237.0	44.6	2.3
Bulgaria	1992	Males	812.7	218.0	88.3	9.4
		Females	724.9	146.0	53.5	4.7
Czech Republic	1992	Males	634.1	311.8	58.2	3.9
		Females	664.8	230.7	41.0	3.4
Denmark	1992	Males	501.9	307.8	94.1	12.3
		Females	508.4	290.6	84.5	6.3
France	1991	Males	288.0	306.1	69.0	12.2
		Females	326.8	185.4	57.5	12.0
Germany	1991	Males	492.5	272.0	76.8	6.9
		Females	642.2	254.9	58.3	7.0
Great Britain	1992	Males	491.7	300.0	119.8	5.4
		Females	510.0	262.4	121.0	4.8
Hungary	1992	Males	739.4	369.5	85.5	12.7
		Females	738.0	260.9	50.0	5.9
Italy	1990	Males	387.5	304.2	77.4	4.1
		Females	425.7	201.7	47.0	2.9
Poland	1992	Males	541.4	227.3	45.6	10.6
		Females	533.5	159.5	24.2	4.6
Romania	1992	Males	694.2	180.9	116.0	19.5
		Females	720.8	122.1	72.1	5.5
Russia	1991	Males	519.6	233.3	72.5	19.6
		Females	711.6	163.0	41.3	5.4

to diseases of the circulatory system accounted for over 62% of all deaths in the Bulgarian population in 1993. The main causes of this high mortality rate are cerebrovascular diseases and ischaemic heart diseases.

In contrast to the decreasing trend in western European countries, the mortality rates for cardiovascular and cerebrovascular diseases are increasing. The mortality rate for ischaemic heart disease has increased since 1980 by more than 43% (Fig. 4.9).

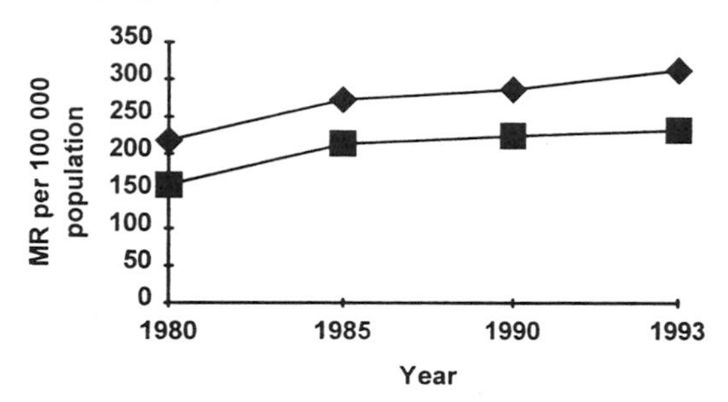

Figure 4.9 Mortality rate for ischaemic heart disease: ◆, men; ■, women (source: National Institute of Statistics, 1994).

The mortality rate for myocardial infarction, especially in males, has been steadily increasing since 1980 (Fig. 4.10) and represents the main reason for the high mortality due to ischaemic heart diseases.

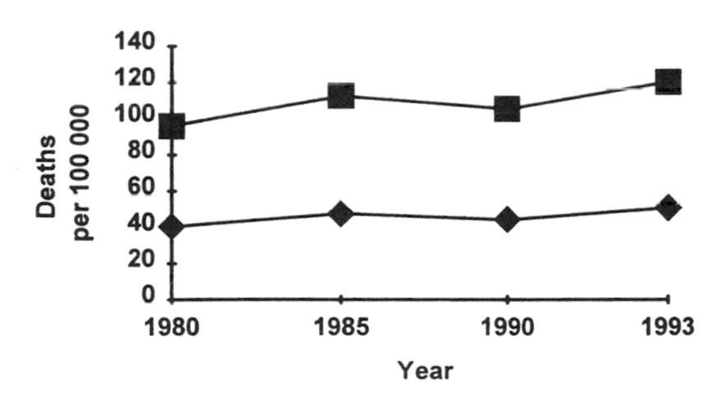

Figure 4.10 Mortality rate for acute myocardial infarction: ◆, women; ■, men (source: National Institute of Statistics, 1994).

The mortality rate for hypertension, a risk factor for ischaemic heart disease and cerebrovascular disease, increased in the 1980s but a decrease has been recorded in recent years (Fig. 4.11).

The mortality rate for cerebrovascular diseases in Bulgaria has been the highest in the world for the past decade but since 1990 there has been a sharp increase in the mortality rate, by 1993 it was up to 294.9 for males and 273.1 for females per 100 000 population (Fig. 4.12).

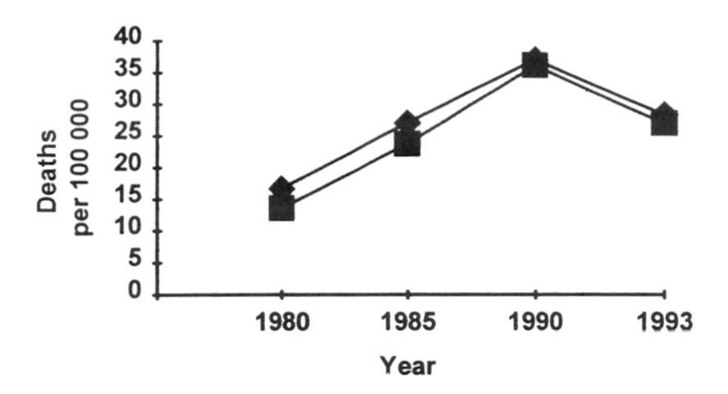

Figure 4.11 Mortality rate for hypertensive disease: ◆, men; ■, women (source: National Institute of Statistics, 1994).

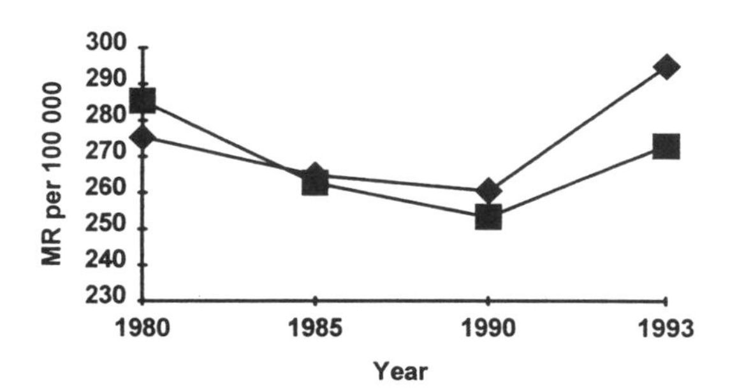

Figure 4.12 Mortality rate of cerebrovascular disease: ◆, men; ■, women (source: National Institute of Statistics, 1994).

4.5.2 Cancer

Malignancies are the second most frequent cause of death in Bulgaria and in 1993 accounted for 17% of all deaths. The cancer mortality rate has not changed in the past decade but the changes in morbidity have been considerable in this period (Fig. 4.13). The morbidity rate for stomach cancer

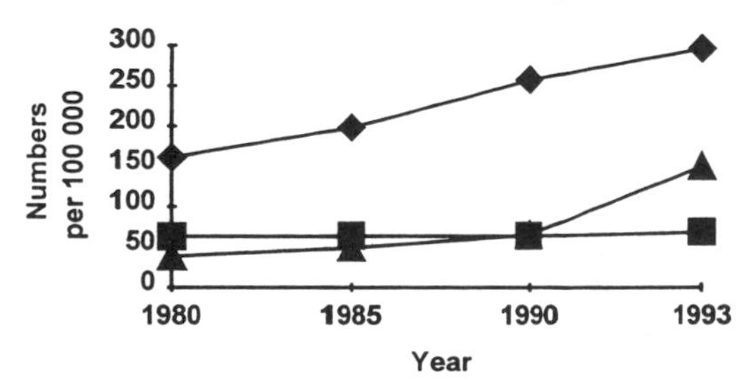

Figure 4.13 Incidence of registered cases of breast (◆), stomach (■) and colorectal (▲) cancer (source: National Institute of Statistics, 1994).

remains high. In the past few years, however, the number of registered cases of colon cancer (related to fat and dietary fibre intake, and excess body weight) has grown sharply – in 1993 it was 130% higher than in 1991. There is a permanent and significant increase in breast cancer morbidity, which has grown by 84% in the period 1980–93.

4.5.3 Obesity

Obesity, a risk factor for hypertension, non-insulin-dependent diabetes mellitus and hypercholesterolaemia is common in Bulgaria. Surveys in two regions of the country conducted in 1988–89 using international standards have found that 35–40% of the sample population suffered from obesity, while another 20–30% was overweight (Balabanski *et al.*, 1991b). The obesity has also increased in children and adolescents – its prevalence was under 1% in the 1970s but since 1985 it has increased to 4–20% in the studies carried out in different settlements and regions of the country (Boiadgieva, 1993). The frequency of obesity is much higher in females (Vatralova, Ivanova and Petrova, 1994).

4.5.4 Diabetes mellitus

The frequency of diabetes mellitus among the Bulgarian population is increasing steadily – during the period 1980–93 it has increased by 57% (Fig. 4.14). In 1991 there were 101 029 cases of diabetes representing 11.25 per 1000 of the whole population. The mortality index related to diabetes was 20.8 in 1993.

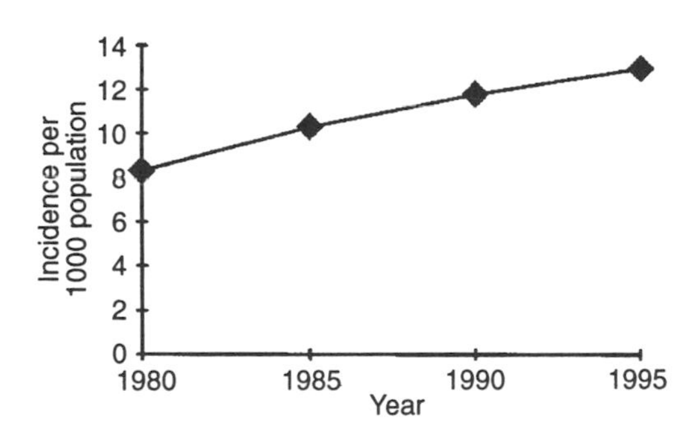

Figure 4.14 Incidence of registered cases of diabetes mellitus (source: National Institute of Statistics, 1994).

4.5.5 Dental caries

The frequency of dental caries is very high among the Bulgarian population of all groups. The epidemiological studies conducted through the entire country show that 90–100% of the population is affected by dental caries (Skopakova-Lukanova, 1986). The outstanding characteristic is that this disease is very frequent in early childhood – about 70% of young children are affected. The low fluorine content of the drinking water in many country regions contributes to this situation.

4.5.6 Osteoporosis

The study on osteoporosis prevalence was started in 1990 by the Clinical Center of Endocrinology and Gerontology. The data obtained show that 35–40% of women between the ages of 45 and 55 years suffer from osteoporosis, resulting in vertebrae deformations in 49% of the investigated women and pathological fractures in 39% (Todorova, unpublished).

4.6 Food safety and quality

The supply of good-quality, safe food has been inadequate for most of the 1980s because of inappropriate agricultural, industrial and environmental policies. This situation has further deteriorated since 1989 as a result of dramatic changes in the political, social and economic situation. Thus, food-borne pathogens and contaminants present a widespread public health problem, and are an important cause of reduced economic productivity. Besides the considerable direct health and social costs, unsafe food can adversely affect the national food industry and food exports, as well as important sectors such as tourism, thereby resulting in significant economic losses.

4.6.1 System for control

A nationwide network of 28 Hygiene and Epidemiology Inspectorates has been established for 40 years. This includes Departments of Hygiene which control food quality and safety of both home-produced and imported foods in Bulgaria. The responsibilities for food control are shared with the Ministry of Agriculture and a few other institutions. These have their own control networks which are not efficient, and are poorly coordinated, with outdated equipment and methodology.

4.6.2 Microbiological safety

The reported incidences of food-borne diseases in 1992–93 were low in Bulgaria (Table 4.5) but they were within the same range as in previous years. The determined incidences and outbreaks of food-borne disease are significantly lower than those in the western European countries. This seems unusual and the reliability of the data must be questioned. Food-borne diseases in Bulgaria generally cause mild illness and people usually do not seek treatment through the primary health services. Also, the likelihood of the outbreaks coming to the attention of health authorities depends on the physicians' awareness, their interest, surveillance activity of the local agencies and their motivation to report the incident.

Table 4.5 Food-borne disease outbreaks by causative agents, 1992–93 (source: Ministry of Health)

Causative agent	1992		1993	
	Number of outbreaks	Cases	Number of outbreaks	Cases
Salmonella, total	17	582	12	189
S. enteritidis	14	455	9	150
S. typhimurium	3	127	2	17
S. branderburg, gr. B	–	–	1	22
Staphylococcus aureus	3	100	2	30
Clostridium botulinum	16	16	17	17
Trichinella	10	69	9	116
Others	–	–	6	114
Unknown	1	10	3	65
Total	47	777	49	531

Viral hepatitis A, which is most frequently transmitted by food, is a serious health problem in Bulgaria. In 1992, the number of cases with expressed clinical symptoms was 9823 (110.7 per 100 000 population). This is mainly a disease of young children, school-aged children and young adults. The disease is usually mild.

As a result of the liberalization of the country's economy during the transition period it became clear that there is:

- no economically effective system able to guarantee the microbiological, parasitic and mycotoxicological safety of some animal and vegetable raw materials (milk and dairy products, meat, cereals, etc.);
- a low level of hygiene in food manufacturing, catering establishments and food trade activities.

4.6.3 Chemical contaminants

The nitrate levels in foods have been monitored by the Hygiene and Epidemiology Inspectorates regularly throughout the whole country for 5 years. Monitoring of heavy metals in foods was initiated 15 years ago but since 1989 it has been limited and irregular, mainly because of the lack of financial support. In the 1960s and 1970s the pesticide levels in foods were controlled, but since then they have not been monitored as they were not considered to be a problem.

Failure to control the use of pesticides and fertilizers in agriculture during recent years led to the presence of pesticide residues in foodstuffs and seasonal increase in the content of nitrates in some vegetables (Vachkova-Petrova *et al.*, 1993). There are several well-defined regions in Bulgaria with environmental problems, particularly soil pollution with heavy metals. As a consequence some staple foods are seriously contaminated.

4.6.4 Food quality

In recent years there has been a tendency for the quality of manufactured foods to deteriorate, so there is a growing proportion of foods that do not correspond to the Bulgarian State Standards. This results in foods which have high contents of fat and sodium. Another problem is that sausages can contain high levels of nitrates.

4.7 Main reasons for the negative characteristics of the nutritional situation

The poor standards in food supply and nutrition may be related to:

- a deterioration in the economic, technical and social basis of agriculture;
- inadequate attention to the needs of the home market with reference to agriculture production, import and export of foods;
- unreasonable price policy, resulting in a lack of economic motivation for production of safe, good-quality and healthy foods;
- inadequate storage facilities for the preservation of fresh fruits and vegetables, so that high quality cannot be maintained throughout the year;
- insufficient refrigerator basis and lack of refrigerator chains in the country;
- insufficient modern technologies in the food industry which could ensure better preservation of the biological value of processed foods;
- high cost of food which causes consumption of cheaper foods which are often of bad quality;
- lack of priority amongst consumers with respect to their own health maintenance because of the low living standard;
- lack of information and awareness about foods and healthy nutrition;
- some unhealthy traditions in the national dietary pattern, e.g. consumption of salt and savoury foods, pork meat, alcohol, etc.

A national food and nutrition policy has not been established up to now but many measures have been initiated which represent elements of such a policy.

4.8 Past nutrition policy until 1990

The main measures related to food and nutrition policy in the period 1960–90 were:

- A National Programme for the Prevention of Iodine Deficiency Disorders (IDD) was devised in the 1960s. Iodized salt was produced and introduced into the determined endemic regions and supplementary potassium iodine tablets were given to schoolchildren. However, the protection provided by iodized salt and tablets has not been regular. The iodine level in the table salt has not been monitored and the awareness of the population in the endemic regions concerning IDD has not been a subject of attention.
- In the 1970s 130 000 plots were distributed to workers and employees for personal use in order to improve the food supply. Subsidiary farms were established to factories to improve the food supply to factory canteens. The food supply for canteens in crèches, kindergartens and schools has not been supported in any way; here the food supply was much worse and more irregular compared with that for workers.
- The production of babies' and children's foods and drinks has taken place (1968). However, the production of dietary foods has not been regular and in sufficient quantities.
- Above 100 documents connected with the manufacturing, preservation, transport, selling, quality and safety of goods have been developed and introduced, but have not been incorporated with national food law.
- Recommended dietary allowances for the population in Bulgaria have been developed (1972, 1980).
- The first national food composition tables have been elaborated (1975).
- Programmes and practical recommendations for improvement of children's and adolescents' nutrition were developed in the 1970s. Because of problems with the supply of fresh fruits and vegetables, lean meats and the variety of foods in canteens of schools, it has not always been possible to follow the requirements for a healthy diet. Refreshment bars were opened in schools but they offered mainly pastry and sugar products. Nutrition education for teachers and schoolchildren has not been introduced.
- Practical recommendations for the nutrition of pregnant and breast-

feeding women, institutionalized elderly people and people exposed to occupational pollutants were elaborated in the 1980s.

- Medical control of mass-catering has been initiated but very often it has been inefficient.
- Two national programmes were accepted by the Ministry of Health for implementation: a system for the healthy nutrition of the Bulgarian population (1984) and a national programme for the prevention of socially important diseases (1987). These were launched but have not been very successful because of lack of commitment from the governments.

4.9 Current nutritional policy

4.9.1 Current problems in food and nutritional policy

The transition of the country from a centrally planned to a market economy since 1990 has led to many economical problems arising from the abolition of subsidies for agricultural production. These include a decrease in production of agricultural products; a drastic increase in food prices and a greater proportion of consumer expenditure accounted for by food expenses; significant increases in numbers unemployed; a decrease of the real income of the population and especially of those on pensions or social benefits. These increased the risk of nutrient deficiencies and extended the problems of the unbalanced and unhealthy diet of the Bulgarian population, especially of socially deprived groups.

At the beginning of this period the IDD prevention measures were stopped because of problems in the production of iodized salt and lack of finances for providing potassium iodine tablets, as well as frustration of the organization.

The great reduction of the subsidies provided by the state budget for the provision of canteen food for schoolchildren and the continuous increase of the prices of main foodstuffs and electricity led to an increase in the cost of meals. Hence there was a significant decrease in the number of schoolchildren taking their lunch in canteens (49% in 1991, 30% in 1993 and 28% in 1994). In Sofia only 10% of schoolchildren eat in school canteens. In an attempt to keep prices reasonable many school canteens offer cheap foods and meals which do not adhere to the dietary guidelines. The lack of united governmental policy in 1990–94 concerning mass catering for schoolchildren enabled some local authorities to use the state subsidies for other purposes and to close down the canteens in the schools to save money. There has been a real risk of elimination of canteen meals for schoolchildren in this country.

The privatization of the agriculture and food industry, and the establishment of many new private shops and restaurants with inexperienced staff has created major problems with respect to the control of food quality and safety.

4.9.2 Current measures and action areas of food and nutritional policy

The first draft of a Food and Nutritional Policy of Bulgaria was developed in 1991. A national seminar with the participation of representatives of all the ministries related to the food and nutrition problems, private and governmental food producers and informal organizations was conducted in 1992 and the issues of the national food and nutrition policy were discussed. In November 1992 the final draft was developed and since then it has been waiting to be considered by the government, which has changed several times during this period. The present Ministry of Health is going to establish an Inter-sector Committee on Food and Nutrition Policy to review the project, update it and present it to the government and parliament. In the meantime, many elements of the food and nutritional policy are being developed.

Nutritional policy measures.

- The Reference Values of Energy and Nutrient Intake for the Bulgarian population were updated in 1994 (Petrova *et al.*, 1993a; Dietary Reference Values for Food Energy and Nutrients for Bulgarian Population, 1994).
- Dietary guidelines for Bulgarians were developed (Petrova, 1996). They are directed at the whole population as well as at the specific groups of pregnant and lactating women.
- Dietary guidelines for the prevention of chronic non-communicable diseases, directed at primary health providers, have been developed (Pctrova, 1995).
- Bulgarian Food Composition Tables were updated in 1996.
- A governmental decree and programme for IDD control were adopted in May 1994 (Decree No. 96 on measures for prevention and elimination of Iodine Deficiency Disorders and Diseases, 1994). They include iodine fortification of table salt for humans, the salt for animal consumption and for food production as well as iodine supplementation by tablets for young children, schoolchildren, pregnant and lactating women. Non-iodized salt is not permitted for sale in the country. The Ministry of Industry is considering measures to complete the salt-producing plant, including iodination. Monitoring of the iodine content of iodized salt was started in 1994. A specialized laboratory for measurement of iodine in urine samples was established, equipped and

started work in 1995. Neonatal thyroid screening by determination of the thyroid stimulating hormone (TSH) in all newborn children in the country (about 80 000/yr) was introduced in 1993 for a period of 3 years. By June 1995 141 625 newborns had been investigated (Peneva *et al.*, 1995). Neonatal thyroid screening is a very important measure for early diagnosis and treatment of congenital hypothyroidism and for prevention of mental retardation. Awareness of the iodine deficiency problem is gaining pace, reflected both in the media and in the official establishment of a National Expert Committee on the Iodine Deficiency Disorders.

- A programme for improving the nutrition of schoolchildren was developed in 1995 and is in the process of being adopted by the government. This includes legal and economic measures for nutritional improvement in school canteens and refreshment bars, and provision for an increase in the state aid for school meals. Measures for improvement of nutritional knowledge, attitudes and behaviour of schoolchildren and teachers represent an important part of this programme. A proposal for the integration of food and nutritional issues into the curriculum of primary and secondary schools, as well as modules for teachers' training, have been developed and discussed with the Ministry of Education.
- A national network of Health Promotion Schools has been set up, and by 1995 included 97 primary and secondary schools, as well as 35 kindergartens, which have priority for training on healthy nutrition.
- Bulgaria was included in the WHO Country Integrated Non-communicable Disease Intervention (CINDI) programme in 1994. A national committee at the Ministry of Health was established. It includes representatives of different professions related to the non-communicable diseases, governmental and informal organizations and institutions. Strategies and programmes for intervention directed at positive changes in the dietary habits of the Bulgarian population were developed and discussed. The programme started in two regions in the country where local committees of representatives of the main authorities and the community were established. The programme was given much publicity, with policy advocacy as well as financial support from private and governmental institutions.
- A Nutritional Surveillance Programme was developed with the object of identifying the nutritional problems at a national level, population groups at risk, and assessing the prevalence and distribution of diet-related health problems. Such information will be used to understand the trends in nutritional status in the Bulgarian context, define dietary guidelines for the population, and develop, implement and evaluate interventions for promoting healthy diets.
- A Programme for Fluorine Fortification of Milk has started, directed towards the prevention of dental caries in children. The technologies for

production of milk enriched with fluorine are to be introduced. The food standards and regulations for implementation of fluorine-enriched milks are to be ratified by the government.

Food quality and safety policy measures.

- A basic Food Law has been drafted. This has been reviewed by the Ministry of Health and at present is being moved through inter-ministerial review and put to the vote in parliament.
- An extensive updating of existing food regulations and standards has been started. These will be harmonized in line with the WHO, FAO and European Union directives.
- A National Register of the foods produced in and imported into Bulgaria is being developed. Up-to-date telecommunication technologies will be established for prompt expansion of information between the Ministry of Health, National Center of Hygiene, and Hygiene and Epidemiology Inspectorates on the problems related to food quality and safety.
- A project for strengthening the regulatory control over foods through co-ordinated administrative, inspection and laboratory capabilities has been developed. The restructuring of food control functions is expected to result in a significant increase in both efficiency and effectiveness.
- The new economic conditions created by the private initiative and the market mechanisms require the development of both voluntary and mandatory compliance systems. A project funded by the United Nations has been prepared by the Ministry of Agriculture. The project will consider extension services and an efficient food export certification system.
- Adapting and applying the internationally recognized system of food safety – Hazard Analysis Critical Control Point – has been initiated. It will shift the emphasis from end-point product testing to preventive control of critical aspects of food production.

4.10 Conclusion

The enormous complexity and the gravity of the problems in food supply, quality and safety, and the unfavourable trends of food consumption and nutritional status, as well as the great morbidity and mortality rates of non-communicable diet-related diseases, reinforce the necessity of a national food and nutritional policy. It requires very serious political commitment on behalf of the Bulgarian authorities as well as the participation and support of governmental and private institutions, in fact the entire community. Much effort is required to ensure that food and nutritional problems and their health consequences get much more publicity and that the Bulgarian population recognizes the need to change its own nutritional behaviour.

References

Baikova, D. (in press) Anemia prevalence in young women from Sofia. *Hygiene and Public Health.*

Baikova, D., Lipova, M., Duleva, V. and Spasov, B. (1993) *Nutrition of Schoolchildren from Sofia During the Economic Crisis.* Abstracts of the V National Congress of Nutrition, Plovdiv, p. 117. (in Bulgarian).

Balabanski, L., Timev, I. *et al.* (1991a) Nutrition and anemias, in *New Data for Nutrition and the Epidemiology of Socially Important Metabolic Diseases*, (ed. L. Balabanski), MA, NIGN, Sofia, pp. 68–71 (in Bulgarian).

Balabanski, L., Stankusheva, T., Naumova, R. *et al.* (1991b) Overnutrition and obesity – morbidity rate, clinical characteristics and relation to nutrition, in *New Data for Nutrition and the Epidemiology of Socially Important Metabolic Diseases*, (ed. L. Balabanski), MA, NIGN, Sofia, pp. 29–36 (in Bulgarian).

Boiadgieva, P. (1993) Epidemiological data for the obesity of the adolescents in Bulgaria. *Hygiene and Public Health,* **XXXVI**, (2), 35–7.

Decree No. 96 on measures for prevention and elimination of iodine deficiency disorders and diseases (1994) *Darjaven Vestnik*, No. 43 (in Bulgarian).

DeLange, F. and Gutekunst, R., (1992) Iodine deficiency disorders in Eastern Europe. *Report of ICCIDD, UNICEF and WHO.*

Dietary Reference Values for Food Energy and Nutrients for Bulgarian Population (1994) *Darjaven Vestnik*, No. 64 (in Bulgarian).

Dimitrova, M. (1993) *Problems of Nutrition of the Schoolchildren in Town of Lovetch.* Abstracts of V National Congress on Nutrition, Plovdiv, p. 114 (in Bulgarian).

Doichinova, A. and Dimova, E. (1995) *Assessment of Nutrition of Young Children*, NCH, Sofia (in Bulgarian).

Duleva, V., Baikova, D. *et al.* (1994) *Vitamin Intake of Schoolchildren from Sofia.* Abstracts of VI National Congress on Hygiene and Health Prophylactics, Sofia, p. 136.

Institute of Economics, Bulgarian Academy of Sciences (1994) *Agrarian Market and Regulation of the Agrarian Production*, Goreks Press, Sofia (in Bulgarian).

Ivanova, L., Pentieva, K., Petrova, S. *et al.* (1995a) Dietary intakes, iron status and anemia prevalence in pregnant women. *Obstetrics and Gynecology*, **XXXIV**, (1), 6–8.

Ivanova, L., Pentieva, K., Petrova, S. *et al.* (1995b) Serum levels of calcium and magnesium in pregnant women and their relation to the diet. *Hygiene and Public Health*, **XXXVIII**, (4–5), 50–52.

Ivanova, L., Pentieva, K., Petrova, S. *et al.* (1995c) Serum zinc level and its relation to the diet in the last trimester of the pregnancy. *Obstetrics and Gynecology*, **XXXIV**, (3), 17–19.

Ivanova, L., Pentieva, K., Petrova, S. *et al.* (1996a) Food and nutrient intake of elderly people from Sofia. *Hygiene and Public Health*, in press.

Lozanov, B. (1995) *The Prevalence and Control of Endemic Goiter in Bulgaria.* Abstracts of the 5th National Congress of Endocrinology, Varna, p. 2.

Marinova, M. and Doichinova, A. (1986) Nutrition of young children from Sofia. *Pediatrics*, **XXI**, (2), 78–84.

Ministry of Health (1992) *Food and Nutrition Policy of Bulgaria – Draft Project*, Ministry of Health, Sofia (in Bulgarian).

Mladenova, S. (1986) *Nutrition of the Non-institutionalized Elderly People in Haskovo region.* Abstracts of IV National Congress of Nutrition, Bulgaria, Plovdiv, p. 384 (in Bulgarian).

National Center of Health Information (1993) *Information Bulletin*, **XX**, (1) (in Bulgarian).

National Institute of Statistics (1994) *Population*, Sofia (in Bulgarian).

National Institute of Statistics (1995a) *Reference Book of Statistics*, Sofia (in Bulgarian).

National Institute of Statistics (1995b) *Budgets of the Households in Republic of Bulgaria*, Sofia (in Bulgarian).

Naumova, P., Belokova, R. and Kerekovska, M. (1991) Study on lipid status disorders and their relation to the nutrition of the population in Bourgass and Dobrich regions, in *New Data for Nutrition and the Epidemiology of Socially Important Metabolic Diseases*, (ed. L. Balabanski). MA, NIGN, Sofia, pp. 36–44 (in Bulgarian).

Panchev, P. and Andreeva, M. (1986) *Nutrition in Different Age and Professional Groups in Russe Region*. Abstracts of IV National Congress of Nutrition, Bulgaria, Plovdiv, p. 267 (in Bulgarian).

Peneva, L., Jadkova, L., Grigorova, R. *et al.* (1995) *Organization and Prospect of Neonatal Thyroid Screening in Bulgaria*. Abstracts of the 5th National Congress of Endocrinology, Varna, p. 3.

Pentieva, K., Petrova, S., Ivanova, L. *et al.* (1996) Food and nutrient intake of healthy pregnant women during the transitional period. *Hygiene and Public Health*, in press.

Petrova, S. (1995) Dietary guidelines for prevention of chronic non-communicable diseases, in *Guidelines for Prevention of Chronic Non-Communicable Diseases of Bulgarian Population*, MH, Sofia, pp. 58–67 (in Bulgarian).

Petrova, S. (ed.) (1996) *Dietary Guidelines for Bulgarians*, MH, Sofia (in Bulgarian).

Petrova, S., Ivanova, L., Atzeva, E. *et al.* (1989) Recommended dietary allowances for elderly people in Bulgaria – approaches and criteria for their updating. *Hygiena i Zdraveopazvane*, **XXXII**, (6) 23–9.

Petrova, S., Ivanova, L. and Vatralova, K. (1991) *Food and Nutrient Intake of Different Social and Professional Groups*. Reports of XII Session des Journées Médicales Balkaniques, Constanta – Mamaia, Romanie, pp. 46–51.

Petrova, S., Haralanova, M. *et al.* (1992) Case study: Bulgaria, Report. *Preparatory meeting on ICN for Central and eastern European countries*, Nitra, Czechoslovakia.

Petrova, S., Angelova, K., Pentieva, K. *et al.* (1993a) Recommended dietary allowances and daily food guide for Bulgarians, Abstracts of GEN 3th Annual Symposium. Ernährung, **17**, (6), 335.

Petrova, S., Ivanova, L., Bogdanov, B. *et al.* (1993b) Food and nutrient intake of Bulgarian population, Abstracts of GEN 3th Annual Symposium. Ernährung, **17** (6), 332.

Petrova, S., Pentieva, K., Ivanova, L. *et al.* (1994) *Vitamin Intake and Status of Pregnant Women*. Abstracts of VI National Congress on Hygiene and Health Prophylactics, Sofia, p. 131 (in Bulgarian).

Skopakova-Lukanova, K. (1986) *Nutrition and Dental Caries in Schoolchildren*. Abstracts of IV National Congress on Nutrition, Plovdiv, p. 46 (in Bulgarian).

Tashev, T. (ed.) (1972) *Nutrition, Physical Development and Health Status of Bulgarian Population*, BAN, Sofia (in Bulgarian).

Todorova, M. (unpublished) Osteoporosis in postmenopausal women in Bulgaria (in Bulgarian).

Vachkova-Petrova, R., Vassileva, L., Stavreva, M. *et al.* (1993) Evaluation of risk for health of high nitrate intake in rural population. *Hygiene and Public Health*, **XXXVI**, (4–5), 46–8.

Vatralova, K., Ivanova, L. and Petrova, S. (1994) *Anthropometric Measures of Elderly People*. Abstracts of VI National Congress on Hygiene and Health Prophylactics, Sofia, p. 131 (in Bulgarian).

Vatralova, K., Kadiska, A., Angelova, K. and Ovcharova, D. (1994) Dietary intake of professional groups with light occupational activity. Abstracts of Symposium on Current research into eating practice, Potsdam, Germany. *Appetite*, **23**, (2), 201.

WHO (1994) *World Health Statistics*, WHO, Geneva.

5 The development of national nutritional policy in Canada

PETER W.F. FISCHER

The development of a national nutritional policy in Canada has progressed from the mid 1930s to the present time. The development of this policy has relied on a number of different strategies designed to improve the nutritional status of Canadians. These were initially concerned with the prevention of nutritional deficiencies, but in more recent years, with the minimization of nutritionally related risk factors for the development of chronic diseases. The strategies include a set of recommended nutrient intakes (originally referred to as the Dietary Standard), a food guide, a set of nutritional recommendations, a mandatory food fortification programme, food consumption surveys and a policy on nutritional labelling. It is the objective of this chapter to provide a description of the evolution of these approaches and how they contribute to the present policy aimed at enabling Canadians to select a healthful diet.

5.1 Early measures – concern about nutritional deficiencies

5.1.1 The dietary standard

During the Great Depression which began in 1929, there was no scarcity of food, but there was an inability of a large percentage of the population to buy food. During this time, a large number of people became dependent upon government authorities for their meals. Consumption surveys carried out at this time in a number of Canadian communities indicated that there was malnutrition in some areas and, as a result of these findings, the Department of Pensions and National Health appointed a nutritional advisory committee. The idea of establishing such an advisory committee originated from the Final Report of the Mixed Committee of the League of Nations, who suggested that national committees be established to deal with the situation of 'starvation in the midst of plenty'. This committee, named The Canadian Council on Nutrition, was first appointed in 1937.

Implementing Dietary Guidelines for Healthy Eating. Edited by Verner Wheelock. Published in 1997 by Blackie A&P, an imprint of Chapman & Hall, London. ISBN 0 7514 0304 0

The Council consisted of 25 members, headed by the Deputy Minister of the Department of Pensions and National Health. Its membership consisted of a collection of scientists, medical experts and welfare workers from universities, welfare and health organizations and government. The Council's mandate was to discover, study and discuss nutritional problems of regional and national significance and to make recommendations as to their solutions (Morrell, 1963).

During the first year of its existence, the Council adopted a Canadian Dietary Standard. In the previous year, the Health Organization of the League of Nations had published the first food standard, which was based on a study of the physiological requirements for nutrients and was intended for international use. This standard recommended average values of calories and protein on the basis of age, gender, body weight and activity. No requirement for fat, minerals or vitamins was given. After considering this standard, the Council decided that its recommendations were inappropriate for Canadians, and thus devised the first Dietary Standard for Canada (Canadian Council on Nutrition, 1940). This standard contained recommendations for total calories, protein (50% should be from animal sources), fat (not less than 30% of total calories), calcium, iron, iodine (the general use of iodized salt was recommended), ascorbic acid and vitamin D. Specific recommendations were made for milk consumption, as milk was considered an ideal source of several nutrients, including protein, fat, vitamin D and calcium. Energy recommendations for men and women were based on physical expenditure. Women were classified as doing 'no manual work' or doing 'housework or similar'. In addition, there were recommendations for pregnant and lactating women. For men, there were five levels ranging from 'no manual work' to 'very hard manual work'. It was a standard that recommended minimum requirements which could be used to determine whether intakes reported during surveys were adequate (Canadian Council on Nutrition, 1940).

In 1942, for the sake of uniformity, the Canadian Council on Nutrition adopted the Recommended Allowances of the US National Research Council, with some modifications. There was concern that Canadians needed more calories because of the cold and more vitamin A for the mucous membranes because they lived in 'overheated houses'. At this time, recommendations were added for thiamin, riboflavin and niacin (Anonymous, 1945). This dietary standard was used in a number of ways, including planning food supplies for various groups; educational purposes in regard to the use of food; construction of regulations under the Food and Drugs Act; and evaluating the adequacy of observed intakes.

The use of the allowances to evaluate intakes had demonstrated widespread deficiency which was not borne out by the evidence. The allowances were based, for the most part, on a maximum designed for individuals, thus covering most members of the population. It was concluded that because the accuracy of the US allowances were falsely conveyed and because of the seriousness of their misuse, it was advisable to discontinue their use in Canada. It was suggested by the Council on Nutrition that, although the construction of a dietary standard is made difficult by lack of information regarding individual requirements, the meagre available data could be used to set a standard which would allow for the planning of food supplies for a population with the provision that it would not be good enough to assess adequacy of intakes of individuals. A new Canadian Standard, based on the above approach was adopted in 1945 (Anonymous, 1945).

This standard tended to assign a range, rather than a specific amount, on the basis that normal physiological requirements vary, even within a group category. It was stated that the distribution of requirement for any one nutrient would take the form of a Gaussian curve, assuming the knowledge of individual requirements was sufficient and extensive. Consequently, individual intakes should not be evaluated in terms of mean alone but of the complete curve, together with other associated evidence (Young, 1949).

In 1948, for the first time, the concept of body size was incorporated into the Dietary Standard. This concept was developed to avoid the use of figures representing the highest requirement that any individual might have, since the chief cause for the reason why individuals' dietary needs differ is the variation in metabolic body size. The intent of this standard was to indicate a 'nutritional floor' beneath which the maintenance of health could not be assumed. It was defined as the maintenance requirement for 'purely sedentary living without unnecessary exercise'. The statement was made that the ingestion of more of a nutrient than serves a clear physiological need is undesirable, especially in the face of a world scarcity of food, and may even be harmful to the individual in certain circumstances. 'More' should not be regarded as 'better' and excess ingestion of nutrients should not be confused with an adequately nourished state sometimes referred to as 'optimal nutrition'. The standard was expressed in terms of body size and, for adults, activity level. It included recommendations for calories, protein, calcium, iron, vitamin A, thiamin, riboflavin, niacin, ascorbic acid and vitamin D. No provision for a margin of safety was included since 'these are based more on opinion than on physiological observations' (Canadian Council on Nutrition, 1949).

The 1948 standard was revised by the Canadian Council on Nutrition and approved in 1963. In this standard, the term 'nutritional floor' was dropped since it was misinterpreted as meaning that the entire standard was an absolute minimum. In this standard, the maintenance requirements were given, with definitions of the degree of activity. The different activity levels were clearly defined in relation to occupation and recreation. Minimum and recommended intakes were given for those nutrients for which adequate knowledge existed. The recommended intakes were set above the minima to allow for biological variation and also to compensate for incomplete information concerning optimum levels for health. The recommended intakes were considered adequate for maintenance of health among the majority of Canadians. It was stated that all the nutrients except for vitamin D can be obtained at recommended amounts from the diet. Vitamin D must be obtained from pharmaceutical preparations or from foods to which it has been added. This standard, as the previous ones, was used for planning diets and food supplies for groups of healthy individuals and as a basis for establishing the need for a public health nutritional programme or for evaluating the success of such a programme. The objective of such a programme was to achieve a level of intake that supplies approximately the amount of nutrients recommended in the standard. It was again reiterated that the standard should not be used for the appraisal of the nutritional status of individuals or groups. The recommendation for calories represented average requirements because the harm of excessive intakes of energy was recognized. The statement was made that there is no evidence that any benefit is derived from intakes of fat constituting above 25% of calories. However, to ensure adequate intakes of essential fatty acids the recommendation was made that at least 25% of calories should be provided by fat. Fat consumption in Canada, in fact, was rising from 34% of calories in 1936 to about 40% at the time of these recommendations (Anonymous, 1964).

The 1975 revision of the standard would adopt the FAO/WHO Expert Group recommendations whenever possible and would present a clear rationale for the daily nutrient intakes recommended. The standard recommended daily intakes for energy and 27 nutrients, an increase of 12 over the 1964 standard. The age, weight and gender groups were changed and the recommendations no longer were tied to activity levels. Body weights for the different age groups were those observed during the Nutrition Canada Survey. The recommended amounts were considered adequate to meet the physiological needs of practically all healthy people in the population, and because of this, exceeded the minimum requirements of most individuals. Only energy estimates were based on the requirements of the average person, where characteristic activity patterns for each age group were assumed. It was pointed out that the recommended intakes should be achieved by eating a variety of foods because unknown nutrients may be present which are essential for the maintenance of health. This standard was used in a similar fashion as the previous one, but also provided basic information regarding the production, distribution and consumption of food. It was used by government and industry in the formulation of fabricated foods, for policies on nutritional fortification and as a basis for advertising (Bureau of Nutritional Sciences, Department of National Health and Welfare, 1975).

In 1983, the Dietary Standard was again revised and its name was changed to Recommended Nutrient Intakes for Canadians, since the old term led to confusion with various other dietary guides describing patterns of food use rather than nutrient requirements. This revision contained a lengthy discussion on the meaning of terms and concepts, since previously there had been considerable confusion about the interpretation and use of the recommended intakes. Requirement was defined as that level of intake that meets an individual's needs for the establishment and maintenance of a reasonable level in tissues or body stores. In the case of energy, this was a level needed to maintain appropriate body size and meet the energy requirements for expected work and leisure activities. It was stated that there is an individual variability of requirement so that a group of similar individuals will show a range of requirements and an average requirement can be calculated. The recommended nutrient intake was defined as the level of dietary intake thought to be sufficiently high to meet the requirements of almost all individuals in a group with specified characteristics. It therefore takes into account individual variability and, of necessity, exceeds the requirement of almost all individuals. While an individual whose intake is below the recommended nutrient intake is not necessarily below his or her requirement, the lower the intake in relation to the recommended nutrient intake, the greater the risk of not meeting the requirement. The 1983 revision of Recommended Nutrient Intakes for Canadians added chapters on carbohydrate and fibre, manganese, selenium and chromium (Bureau of Nutritional Sciences, Department of National Health and Welfare, 1983). This was the last of the revisions that was concerned solely with the prevention of nutritional deficiency.

5.1.2 Fortification programme

In 1942, the Canadian Council on Nutrition first considered the addition of nutrients to white flour. This was stimulated by proposals from other countries to add synthetic B vitamin to ordinary white flour to improve its nutritional value in relation to wholewheat flour. The Council was opposed to the addition of synthetic nutrients and instead promoted the production and sale of higher extraction flour. Vitamin B white flour (Canada Approved) was introduced in 1942. This flour was not an outstanding success since it did not perform as well as other white flour in baking (Morrell, 1963). The Council issued statements in 1941, 1944 and 1949 that did not support fortification. The statements indicated that when staple foodstuffs for any reason are inadequate, encouragement should be given to improving their nutritional quality by whatever means are most sound from the standpoint of nutrition and economy. The Council claimed that there was evidence that the proper use of natural foods is more beneficial for general health than placing reliance on an assembly of chemicals, whether as ingredients of a food or of a pharmaceutical. It therefore reaffirmed its views that higher extraction of wheat, such as used to make Canada Approved white flour, was a proper step toward assisting the public in the selection and use of foods for adequate nutrition rather than the addition of nutrients (Canadian Council on Nutrition, 1949).

It was not until Newfoundland joined Canada in 1949 that fortification of staple foods gained acceptance. In the isolated fishing villages of Newfoundland, there was evidence of deficiency diseases such as night blindness, beriberi, rickets and scurvy (Aykroyd, 1930). By the 1940s, although some of these conditions had improved, there were cases of low blood ascorbic acid levels and inadequate intakes of thiamin, riboflavin and niacin. To deal with these deficiencies, the Newfoundland Medical Association set up a nutrition council in 1942, which advised that all pregnant women and children should receive concentrated orange juice as a source of vitamin C. By 1944, there was a programme for the fortification of flour with riboflavin, thiamin, niacin, calcium and iron, and of margarine with vitamin A (Adamson *et al.*, 1945). When Newfoundland joined Canada, it had the assurance of the Canadian government that it would be able to continue its fortification programme (Anonymous, 1949).

In 1952, a national standard for enriched bread was introduced which required the addition of thiamin, riboflavin, niacin and iron to white flour. The introduction of this standard contributed to the final demise of vitamin B white bread (Canada Approved) (Morrell, 1963). In 1950 the addition of vitamin D to condensed, evaporated, dried, whole and skimmed milk was permitted (Anonymous, 1950).

In Canada, one of the most significant programmes that affected public health was the mandatory addition of potassium iodide to table salt, started in 1949. This virtually eliminated iodine deficiency goitre which was common in some areas of Canada. Another fortification programme, the addition of ascorbic acid to evaporated milk, was responsible for the elimination of infantile scurvy in some eastern parts of the country. The fortification of fluid milk with vitamin D resulted in the virtual disappearance of rickets in Canada by the late 1960s.

Nutrients may be added to foods for a number of reasons. The first is for the replacement of nutrients lost during processing. Examples are the mandatory addition of thiamin, riboflavin, niacin and iron, as well as the optional addition of other nutrients, so that their level in white flour is equivalent to that found in wholewheat flour. Other examples are the restoration of B vitamins and iron in breakfast cereal to replace those lost during processing and the addition of vitamin A to all skimmed and partially skimmed milk to replace that lost with the butter fat during the skimming process. The second reason for nutrient addition is to ensure that the nutritional quality of substitute foods is equivalent to that of the foods being replaced. Thus, the Food and Drug Regulations specify specific nutritional requirements for a number of products, such as simulated meat and meat products, infant formulas, fruit drinks, margarine and meal replacements. The third reason is to correct nutritional deficiencies in segments of the population. Examples are the mandatory addition of vitamin D to all milk to combat rickets and the addition of iodine to salt to overcome goitre (Bureau of Nutritional Sciences and Long Range Planning Directorate, 1979; Verdier, 1994).

5.1.3 Canada's Food Guide

Canada's Food Guide has become one of the most useful tools for the nutritional education of the public and dissemination of the recommendations contained in the dietary standards and recommended nutrient intakes.

The advent of the Second World War and the results of dietary surveys in 1941 paved the way for the establishment of a nutritional service, funded by a war appropriation, in the Department of Pensions and National Health. This nutritional service later received full government funding and became the Division of Nutrition in the Department of Health and Welfare. It was the mandate of this original nutritional service 'to assist the public generally to maintain and improve nutrition in Canadian homes by advising as to suitable purchases and methods of preparation' (Verdier, 1994). Several mimeographed pamphlets for home economists and pay envelope inserts were initially produced.

In 1942 a 36-page pamphlet entitled *Healthful Eating* was published. This was Canada's first food guide, at that time called Canada's Official Food Rules. These Food Rules were produced by the Nutrition Service and were based on food lists previously published by the Canadian Medical Association. The Food Rules were to become the focal point of the Canadian Nutrition Program, a wartime programme to inform Canadians about the relationship of food to health (Verdier, 1994).

The Food Rules are shown in Table 5.1. The first Food Rules were replaced in 1944. The recommendation for milk was increased and this resulted in objections from the Department of Agriculture, since there was a scarcity of milk during the Second World War. However, the Canadian Council on Nutrition concluded that a food list of this type should not be based on existing supply. The Food Rules should serve as a guide to the selection of foods which would provide the necessary nutrients from day to day (Anonymous, 1944). The Food Rules still consisted of five food groups and the 'official' was deleted from the title. In 1949, it was slightly revised to meet the new dietary standard. The recommendations for the milk group was targeted at three different age groups and the statement that 'at least' plus quantity was added to provide more latitude in the interpretation of quantity (Canadian Council on Nutrition, 1949).

Table 5.1 Canada's official Food Rules (Verdier, 1994)

Eat these foods every day:	
Milk	Adults – ½ pint, children – more than 1 pint Some cheese as available
Fruits	One serving of tomatoes daily, or of citrus fruit, or of tomato or citrus-fruit juices, and one serving of other fruits, fresh, canned or diced
Vegetables	(In addition to potatoes, of which you need one serving daily). Two servings daily of vegetables, preferable leafy green, or yellow, and frequently raw
Cereals and bread	One serving of a whole-grain cereal and four to six slices of Canada-approved bread, brown or white
Meat, fish etc.	One serving a day of meat, fish or meat substitutes. Liver, heart or kidney once a week.
Eggs	At least 3 or 4 weekly
Fish-liver oils	These oils are essential for children and should be given as recommended by a physician. They may also be required by adults

The amounts specified are minimum daily food requirements. It is important to remember that these are wartime Food Rules and may be further conditioned by problems of supply

In 1961, taking into account advances in nutritional knowledge and availability of food supplies, as well as flexibility in the variety of life styles, the Food Rules were changed to Canada's Food Guide (Anonymous, 1961). The five food groups were retained to provide the most effective basis for teaching and to prevent confusion with the four groups used in the United States (Verdier, 1994). The 'at least' term was deleted and guidance for pregnant and lactating women was added. The guide was produced as a coloured leaflet, a poster and an explanatory pamphlet (Verdier, 1994).

In 1982 the revision of the Food Guide (Health Promotion Directorate, 1982) underwent a major shift. In the mid 1970s, a set of nutritional recommendations, aimed at decreasing the nutrition-related risk factors associated with cardiovascular and other chronic diseases, was accepted by the Department of National Health and Welfare. The Food Guide incorporated these recommendations. It was also based on the publication *Recommended Nutrient Intakes for Canadians* (Bureau of Nutritional Sciences, Department of National Health and Welfare, 1983) in order to aid in achieving a nutritionally adequate diet. In integrating Nutrition Recommendations (discussed below) with Canada's Food Guide, three major principles emerged:

1. variety in food choices and eating patterns;
2. moderation in use of fat, sugar, salt and alcohol;
3. balance between energy intake and expenditure.

The overall objective of this guide was to provide a framework to assist in choosing foods which satisfy the Recommended Nutrient Intakes and incorporate Nutrition Recommendations. The Food Guide depicted four food groups: fruits and vegetables; breads and cereals; milk and milk products; and meat, fish, poultry and alternatives. The Guide indicated variety in food selection by providing examples of food choices within food groups and a range of numbers and sizes of servings. This Food Guide was widely used to provide uniform advice in national, regional, provincial and local programmes for education, community/public health, agriculture and mass media (Health Promotion Directorate, 1982).

The Food Guide was again revised in 1992. This revision was designed to be much more of an implementation tool for the revised Nutrition Recommendations. It will be discussed in greater detail in section 5.2.3.

5.1.4 Nutrition Canada Survey

Although numerous food consumption surveys had been carried out in Canada, most were small and were restricted to specific regions. The Nutrition Canada Survey was the first national nutritional survey and the most comprehensive ever conducted. During the survey, medical, dental and anthropometric data were collected. A 24-hour recall of food intake was collected, and urinary and blood analysis were performed to assess the nutritional health of the population.

The Nutrition Canada Survey was initiated because there was a need to have knowledge about the nutritional status of Canadians, since nutritional health is fundamental to normal general health and prevention or reduction in the severity of disease. There had been tremendous changes in the food supply and eating habits and it was important to know how this affected nutritional status. The information could also be used as a starting point and scientific base to encourage people to improve their nutrition where needed and to monitor changes continually in the future. The data would also serve as a basis for planning future informational, educational, public health and welfare programmes; for the evolution of food and drug regulations affecting the nutritional quality of the national food supply; and for the identification of problems where existing knowledge was inadequate and warranted further research.

The Nutrition Canada Survey was designed to determine the prevalence of nutritional diseases in the Canadian population on the basis of geographical location, type of community, season, age, gender, pregnancy and income level. It was also designed to identify and determine the quantity of food items consumed by Canadians. This, in turn, would allow calculation of nutrients consumed, would provide information on food consumption patterns and the degree of variation in these patterns, would allow for a re-evaluation of food enrichment and fortification policies and programmes, as well as an estimation of consumption of substances such as food additives and pesticide residues.

The evolution of the Survey began in 1964, when the Canadian Council on Nutrition recommended that a comprehensive nutritional survey be undertaken. The Dominion Council on Health supported this recommendation, and the Food and Drugs Directorate (now the Health Protection Branch) examined the feasibility. The concept received wide support of health officials at the federal and provincial levels and within the nutrition and related scientific communities. The programme content and the funding was approved in August of 1969.

Staff were organized at Headquarters and national and regional directors were appointed. A series of committees defined the scope, the overall survey design and population sampling, specific methods for data collection, standards for data interpretation and the actual interpretation itself. Provincial health departments were the major organizers of the field operations. The field work commenced in September 1970 and was completed in December 1972. Over 18 million individual pieces of information were collected from over 19 000 individuals of all ages (Bureau of Nutritional Sciences, Department of National Health and Welfare, 1973). One report per province, plus Indian, Inuit, dental, food consumption patterns and anthropometric reports were published.

The chief findings were that there was a lack of clinical evidence of widespread nutritional deficiency diseases. In the majority of cases, intakes were more than adequate. Those with the least satisfactory nutritional status were native people, the elderly and those with the lowest incomes. One-half of the adults studied were considered overweight, due to a sedentary life style and/or small caloric excesses over a long period of time. Ten per cent of the males and 30% of the females were obese. The intake of protein generally exceeded recommended levels, except for the elderly, who had intakes that were marginal. Frank iron deficiency anaemia was low, but a substantial number of Canadians, particularly women of child-bearing age, had poor iron intakes and low iron stores. Thiamin, riboflavin and niacin intakes of most groups surveyed were adequate, although biochemical tests revealed some evidence of poor thiamin status in middle-aged and elderly individuals. Calcium intakes were generally satisfactory, but low intakes by some teenage girls and pregnant women were of some concern. Serum ascorbic acid levels were low in a significant proportion of the elderly, particularly men and those with low incomes (Bureau of Nutritional Sciences and Long Range Planning Directorate, 1979).

The results of the Nutrition Canada Survey tended to change the direction of nutritional policy, away from the prevention of nutritional deficiencies to the alleviation of diet-related risk factors for chronic disease.

5.2 Concern about diet and chronic diseases

5.2.1 Dietary guidelines

In an attempt to provide guidelines for improved health, a document was released by the Minister of Health and Welfare in 1974 entitled *A New Perspective on the Health of Canadians* (Lalonde, 1974). This document argued that there were health problems in the Canadian population that were sufficiently pressing that risk factors should be reduced. Subsequently, the government was urged to develop guidelines that could assist the population in making judicious food choices which might be beneficial in decreasing the onset of chronic disease. A committee was set up whose mandate it was to provide advice to the public about how certain dietary patterns might decrease risk factors associated with cardiovascular disease, the major cause of mortality in Canada. The Report of the Committee on Diet and Cardiovascular Disease (Mustard Report, since the committee chairman was Dr Fraser Mustard) was submitted in 1976 (Committee on Diet and Cardiovascular Disease, 1976). Before adoption of the recommendations, interdepartmental negotiations were necessary which resulted in a number of changes, specifically deletion of the mention of cholesterol. Neither public health officials nor Agriculture Canada considered that the evidence was strong enough to warrant recommending decreased intakes of dietary cholesterol, and therefore, eggs. The Department of National Health and Welfare agreed, although their position was from a different perspective. The Health Department felt that it was not wise to deprive people of an important source of nutrients, while the Agriculture Department did not want to damage an established egg industry. After being widely discussed, the following list of relatively moderate recommendations was adopted in 1977 (Murray and Rae, 1979):

1. The consumption of a nutritionally adequate diet, as outlined in Canada's Food Guide.
2. The reduction in calories from fat to 35% of total calories. Include a source of polyunsaturated fatty acid (linoleic acid) in the diet.
3. The consumption of a diet which emphasizes whole-grain products and fruits and vegetables and minimizes alcohol, salt and refined sugars.
4. The prevention and control of obesity through reducing excess consumption of calories and increasing physical activity. Precautions should be taken that no deficiency of vitamins and minerals occurs when total calories are reduced.

There were also a number of recommendations that were directed at government and the food industry. These were:

1. Active and continuous promotion of the recommendations for dietary changes.
2. The development and production of food products consistent with the above dietary recommendations and clearly labelled for adequate consumer information.
3. Encouragement and support for
   (a) research on the relationship of nutritional, environmental and lifestyle factors to cardiovascular disease;
   (b) research directed at the most effective methods for dispersing essential knowledge to all citizens;
   (c) increased research on, and production of, primary agricultural products for development of food items consistent with dietary recommendations.

These recommendations were accepted as national policy and became the basis of nutritional programmes. It became recognized that the applicability of these recommendations was much broader than cardiovascular disease. They were endorsed by all the provincial and territorial departments of health, by more than 50 national professional associations, organizations and agencies concerned with health, education, fitness, and the food service industry, food product development and agriculture.

The recommendations were conservative, nutritionally sound, with positive influences on all segments of the population and were compatible with current trends in nutritional education. They were flexible enough to allow for regional and local differences in food habits and practices. They stressed moderation, that is, cutting down rather than cutting out, thus making them easier to comply with and more acceptable to the Canadian public.

The guidelines that were conveyed to the public to assist them in following the Nutrition Recommendations were stated in a simpler, more comprehensible fashion. They advised individuals to consume a nutritionally adequate diet, as outlined in Canada's Food Guide; avoid overweight through appropriate food selection and increased physical activity; limit the total amount of fat, sugar, salt and alcohol in the diet; and increase the intake of vegetables, fruits, and whole-grain cereals, and include sources of polyunsaturated fatty acid (linoleic acid) (Murray and Rae, 1979).

These recommendations remained the basis of Canadian nutritional policy until 1990, when a revision was released.

5.2.2 Setting dietary standards, taking into account the prevention of chronic disease

For more than 40 years, dietary guidelines had provided advice to Canadians on how to consume a nutritionally adequate diet. It was not until the late 1970s, when Nutrition Recommendations were integrated into Canada's Food Guide, that the influence of diet on chronic disease became a part of the advice to the public. In the 1980s, there was a change in the emphasis of programmes of nutritional education. The primary focus became the reduction of risk factors for chronic diseases, supplanting the prevention of nutrient deficiencies. This approach was understandable, given the lesser threat from nutrient deficiency compared to cardiovascular disease and cancer. However, the prevention of nutrient deficiency could not totally be dismissed, since this is the primary reason for eating. Consequently, it became clear that a balanced approach was necessary; the recommended diet should meet the need for nutrients while, at the same time, provide maximum protection against chronic diseases (Scientific Review Committee, Health and Welfare Canada, 1990).

In October 1987, the Minister of National Health and Welfare announced the appointment of two committees which were jointly charged with 'the review and revision of nutrition recommendations for a healthy Canadian population to ensure up-to-date recommendations for professionals and the public which will promote and maintain health and reduce the risk of nutrition-related diseases' (Scientific Review Committee, Health and Welfare Canada, 1990). The first committee was the Scientific Review Committee, which was responsible for the review of scientific evidence from the public health perspective in order to revise the Nutrition Recommendations. The second committee was the Communications and Implementation Committee, which was responsible for the expression of the updated nutritional recommendations as dietary advice for the consumer and for the recommendation of implementation strategies. This sharing of responsibilities was unique. Previously, the process had been completed by several committees, operating independently, and at different times. It was anticipated that the integrated review would better meet the needs of those who make use of the advice (Scientific Review Committee, Health and Welfare Canada, 1990).

In order to achieve the balance between meeting the needs for nutrients and protection against chronic diseases, the Scientific Review Committee conducted a combined review of nutritional requirements and nutrient/disease relationships. The process thus provided not only a revision of the 1977 Nutrition Recommendations, but also an updated set of Recommended Nutrient Intakes for Canadians. The Recommended Nutrient Intakes provided recommended levels of intake of essential nutrients for different age and gender groups, while the Nutrition Recommendations suggested dietary patterns that would provide nutrients at the recommended amounts, while minimizing the risk of chronic diseases.

The membership of the Scientific Review Committee consisted of experts in nutritional sciences, cardiology, pediatrics and epidemiology. The committee enlisted other experts to draft chapters. These chapters were subjected to peer review by at least two external reviewers before final revision and acceptance by the Scientific Review Committee. This process of using a single review to develop both the Nutrition Recommendations and the Recommended Nutrient Intakes required an increased emphasis on nutrient/disease relationships in the development of the latter. Nutrient/disease relationships were considered only within the context of the diet; the pharmacological use of nutrients was not considered. An overriding consideration in the review was that the whole diet, not just individual nutrients, is involved in the diet/health equation. Consequently, a number of non-nutrient dietary components, such as alcohol, artificial sweeteners and caffeine were also included in the review (Scientific Review Committee, Health and Welfare Canada, 1990).

The Report of the Scientific Review Committee was published in 1990 (Scientific Review Committee, Health and Welfare Canada, 1990). The first part of the report dealt with nutritional recommendations, including a discussion on nutrition and disease. The second part of the report contained chapters on each nutrient which described the rationale for the establishment of the recommendations and the recommended nutrient intakes. The recommended intake of nutrients was believed to be sufficiently high to meet the requirements, including reducing the risk of chronic diseases, if appropriate, for almost all individuals in a group with specified characteristics (age, gender, physiological state). Since these Recommended Nutrient Intakes were designed to meet the needs of almost all normal individuals, they exceeded the actual needs of most. Where the information was sufficient, the average requirement was increased by two standard deviations to take into account individual variability assuming a normal distribution. Restrictions on the intake of dietary components because of toxicity or association with an increased risk of chronic diseases were also taken into account (Scientific Review Committee, Health and Welfare Canada, 1990).

The set of Nutrition Recommendations produced as a result of this Review are as follows (Scientific Review Committee, Health and Welfare Canada, 1990):

1. *The Canadian diet should provide energy consistent with the maintenance of body weight within the recommended range.* This recommendation was based on evidence indicating that there is increased risk of a number of chronic diseases if body weight is either above or below the recommended range. However, controlling weight should not be done by energy restriction alone, since there is danger of ingesting suboptimal amounts of nutrients. Thus, physical activity should play a role in the control of body weight. It was concluded that a desirable level of activity would be one that permits the intake of at least 1800 kcal/day, while keeping weight within the recommended range.
2. *The Canadian diet should include essential nutrients in amounts recommended.* This recommendation was made not only to provide assurance that sufficient amounts are ingested, but also that excessive amounts should not be eaten. The review indicated that there was no evidence to indicate that intakes in excess of the Recommended Nutrient Intakes confer any health benefits. It was noted, however, that in the case of protein and vitamin C, whose habitual intakes greatly exceeded the Recommended Nutrient Intakes, there is no reason to suggest that these be reduced.
3. *The Canadian diet should include no more than 30% of energy as fat and no more than 10% as saturated fat.* This recommendation was made because diets high in fat have been associated with a high incidence of heart disease and certain cancers, and that a reduction in total fat would also significantly reduce saturated fat. It was also stated that dietary cholesterol, though not as important as saturated fat in increasing blood cholesterol levels, is not without importance. A reduction in cholesterol intake would normally accompany a reduction in total fat.
4. *The Canadian diet should provide 55% of energy as carbohydrate from a variety of sources.* It was concluded that carbohydrate would be the preferred replacement for dietary fat, since protein intakes already exceeded requirements. Also, there was some evidence indicating that the consumption of complex carbohydrates has been associated with a lower incidence of heart disease and cancer.

5. *The sodium content of the diet should be reduced.* The committee concluded that, although there was insufficient evidence to set a quantitative recommendation for sodium, the present food supply contains amounts greatly in excess of requirements.
6. *The Canadian diet should include no more than 5% of total energy as alcohol, or two drinks daily, whichever is less.* The reasons cited by the Committee for this recommendation were that alcohol dilutes the nutrient density of the diet, it has a deleterious influence on blood pressure, and it is associated with detrimental effects during pregnancy.
7. *The Canadian diet should contain no more than the equivalent of four regular cups of coffee per day.* There was some evidence which linked caffeine consumption to an increased risk of cardiovascular disease.
8. *Community water supplies containing less than 1 mg/litre should be fluoridated to that level.* This recommendation was made because fluoridation of community water supplies has proved to be a safe, effective and economical method for improving dental health.

5.2.3 Implementation strategies for Nutrition Recommendations

It was the mandate of the second committee, the Communications and Implementation Committee, to take the updated scientific evidence that defined a healthful diet, which was provided by the Scientific Review Committee, and make it accessible to, and comprehensible by, the public. The Communications and Implementation Committee did this in a number of ways, including translation of the Nutrition Recommendations into an easy to understand set of Guidelines for Healthy Eating and the initiation of a complete revision of Canada's Food Guide, which incorporated these Guidelines. The Committee also recommended strategies to be used by governments, health organizations, food industry, the food services sector and the general public for the implementation of the Guidelines (Communications and Implementation Committee, Health and Welfare Canada, 1990a).

The translation of the Nutrition Recommendations resulted in Canada's Guidelines for Healthy Eating. These Guidelines are as follows (Communications and Implementation Committee, Health and Welfare Canada, 1990a):

- enjoy a variety of foods;
- emphasize cereals, breads, other grain products, vegetables and fruits;
- choose low-fat dairy products, lean meats and foods prepared with little or no fat;

- achieve and maintain a healthy body weight by enjoying regular physical activity and healthy eating;
- limit salt, alcohol and caffeine.

These Guidelines were aimed at healthy Canadians over the age of 2 years.

It was considered important that there be collaboration and co-ordination among the many stake-holders to promote a single set of Canada's Guidelines for Healthy Eating. Prior to release of these Guidelines, there were as many as 11 different nutritional recommendations and dietary guidelines from such sources as the Heart and Stroke Foundation, the Canadian Consensus Conference on Cholesterol, the Osteoporosis Society of Canada, the Canadian Cancer Society, the Canadian Dental Association and the Canadian Dietetic Association, as well as government. In addition, there were various guidelines used at the provincial and local levels in many parts of the country, and the Canadian public was exposed to recommendations concerning diet and nutrition coming from the US through the media. As part of the implementation strategy, all interested parties, including those who already had guidelines, were consulted and it was recommended that they all adopt and promote the single set of Canada's Guidelines for Healthy Eating (Communications and Implementation Committee, Health and Welfare Canada, 1990a). Compliance with this recommendation was excellent.

Three subcommittees of the Communications and Implementation Committee were set up to aid in data gathering and implementation. The subcommittees were the Task Group on Canada's Food Guide, the Task Group on Food Consumption and the Technical Group on Canada's Food Guide (Communications and Implementation Committee, Health and Welfare Canada, 1990b).

The mandate of the Task Group on Canada's Food Guide was to review the literature addressing a historical overview of Canada's Food Guide; consumer research findings regarding issues such as awareness, use, acceptability and compliance; and experiences with food guides in other organizations and countries. The Group was also to obtain expert input from other organizations, federal/provincial/territorial nutritionists, etc. They were also to identify issues concerning a new revised guide and analyse issues in the context of the scientific statements coming from the Scientific Review Committee. Finally, they were to prepare reports including recommendations on a new revised guide (format, style, approach, name, etc.) (Communications and Implementation Committee, Health and Welfare Canada, 1990b). The group reported that previously the Food Guide provided advice only on choosing a basic diet, which was directed only at the prevention of nutritional deficiencies. The Guide did not consider the need for certain people to limit certain nutrients or foods, nor did it take into account the availability of a wide variety of manufactured, processed or combined food dishes that characterize the diet. The Task Group suggested that the Nutrition Recommendations be incorporated into the Guide, and that foods that did not traditionally fit in the Guide also be included. The task group also examined the types and numbers of food groups that should be incorporated into a new Food Guide. They also modelled diets and analysed them for their nutrient content to ensure that it would be possible from a practical aspect to follow the Nutrition Recommendations and the Recommended Nutrient Intakes (Communications and Implementation Committee, Health and Welfare Canada, 1990b).

The Task Group on Food Consumption was to provide information on food consumption patterns and the distribution of nutrients in the Canadian food supply. It was to relate this information to the Nutrition Recommendations and to predict the impact of the revised recommendations on the food supply and the development of new products. The work of this group was hampered by the lack of current data, since no national food consumption surveys had been carried out since the Nutrition Canada Survey in 1972. There were the Apparent Per Capita Food Consumption data, collected by Statistics Canada from supply and disposition balance sheets. There were also data from the Family Food Expenditure surveys carried out by Statistics Canada every 2 years. These, however, only provided gross estimates of consumption. The former only reported national data on food disappearance while the latter provided information on household food purchases. Neither source reflected actual consumption. The recommendation was consequently made that financial resources be provided by the Department of National Health and Welfare, and that it collaborate with partners, to generate baseline and ongoing national data. Food and nutrient consumption surveys have now been initiated in partnership between the Federal and provincial health departments. As of April 1995, six provinces have either completed or are conducting surveys. It is anticipated that all provinces will participate to enable the establishment of a current national database.

The Task Group on Food Consumption also reviewed the results of nutrition awareness surveys. These indicated that consumers did change their food habits in response to the 1977 Nutrition Recommendations. For example, the consumption of fish and poultry increased, as did that of fruits and vegetables, while the ingestion of red meat, fat, fried foods and salt decreased. Fifty-six per cent of those interviewed indicated that they watched their diet for health reasons, although not everyone was clear about how to lower the risk factors for chronic disease. In the Nova Scotia Heart Health Survey (Nova Scotia Department of Health and Fitness and Department of National Health and Welfare, 1987), nearly all respondents knew that blood cholesterol levels affected health, but less than one-half knew that this could be decreased by reducing the consumption of fatty foods. The Task Group found that Canadians were receptive to nutritional and health messages, although they would not understand 'reduce your fat intake to 30% of calories'. It was recommended that local efforts, which capitalize on current consumer interest, should be stressed. These efforts were thought to be necessary to implement the Guidelines. It was suggested that they be incorporated into programmes, policies, legislation, media campaign and be used by the formal education system (Communications and Implementation Committee, Health and Welfare Canada, 1990a).

The recommendation was also made that provincial, territorial and municipal governments examine social assistance allowances, and adjust them, if necessary, to ensure that recipients can achieve Canada's Guidelines for Healthy Eating. The Nova Scotia Nutrition Council had conducted a study to determine whether social assistance allowance was adequate in terms of being able to afford a nutritious diet. The study revealed that the food allowance fell significantly short of the cost of purchasing foods required for a healthful diet. As a result, the food allowance was increased. For a period of time, Agriculture Canada had published a Nutritious Food Basket, which was an ongoing study of the cost of purchasing nutritious foods to meet the Recommendations, carried out in 18 cities across Canada. The Department added a Thrifty Nutritious Food Basket based on food consumption patterns of low-income Canadians and selected to meet Recommended Nutrient Intakes. This was designed to assist local planners (Communications and Implementation Committee, Health and Welfare Canada, 1990a).

In order to meet the drastic reduction in the quantities of total and saturated fat consumed, concerted efforts on the part of the food and food services industries, as well as consumers, was required. The types of efforts that were targeted were government support, through legislation and regulations, that promote the development of foods with reduced levels of fat or with unsaturated fats substituting for saturated fat. Nutritional labelling regulations supported this. Manufacturers were allowed to make label claims, such as low fat, fat free, light, etc. These claims required mandatory nutritional labelling using standard guidelines. Also, to enable claims to be made, certain compositional requirements had to be met. The low-fat claim, for instance, required that the product contain no more than 3 g of fat per serving, or no more than 15 g of fat/100 g of dry matter (Department of National Health and Welfare, 1981).

It was also recommended that provincial, territorial and municipal governments integrate the teaching of nutrition into the curriculum at all levels of the formal education system, including teacher education (Communications and Implementation Committee, Health and Welfare Canada, 1990a).

A wide variety of other recommendations were made to assist in implementation of the Guidelines. These recommendations for actions were the results of consultations with many partners. Because of these consultations, these partners share ownership of the recommendations and therefore a responsibility for their implementation.

The major implementation strategy that the Communications and Implementation Committee initiated was the revision of the Food Guide, which would incorporate Canada's Guidelines for Healthy Eating. The Technical Group on Canada's Food Guide was given the task of assessing the practical implications of shifting from a Guide that recommended only a foundation diet to one that advised in accordance with the revised Nutrition Recommendations and meets the Recommended Nutrient Intakes. The Technical Group developed a food guide, referred to as the Base Food Guide. This Base Food Guide was then subjected to numerous revisions, following focus group testing and consultations with a large number of interested parties. The entire process took about 2 years and resulted in the development of a Food Guide Tear Sheet, consumer booklet and fact sheet for communicators (Health and Welfare Canada, 1992).

During the development of the Food Guide, it was tested with groups of consumers in four different cities to provide input about the design and content. These consumers were all responsible for meal preparation, the majority had not finished high school, and all had children aged 4 to 10 years. Consultations were also held with readability experts. The Food Industry was also consulted during the development since they would be involved in the implementation.

The Food Guide was based on a total diet approach which assists in the selection of all foods to meet both nutrient and energy needs. Previous guides provided guidance only on the amounts of nutrients and kinds of foods, but did not take into account energy needs. The new category of other foods was introduced. The actual Guide consists of a rainbow design chosen to communicate a positive message about how food groups work together to help establish healthy eating patterns. This design continues to reinforce the importance of each of the four food groups and visually demonstrates that the amount needed from each group varies. The key message that it conveys is that one should eat a variety of foods and choose lower-fat foods more often (Department of National Health and Welfare, 1981).

5.3 Summary

The National Nutrition Policy, which relies on nutritional education based on sound scientific evidence, has largely proved to be effective. Consumers are selecting lower-fat foods, for instance, and industry is producing these. An example is the shift from whole milk to partially skimmed milk which has taken place in the past 15 years. The incidence and mortality from cardiovascular disease is declining; however, it is still unclear how much dietary changes have contributed to this, since many other factors, such as decreased smoking and improved medical care, also have had an effect.

One of the most successful strategies was the establishment of a communication and implementation mechanism for nutritional policy which involved government, non-government health groups and industry. Since all sectors had a stake in seeing a successful implementation of guidelines, all worked together towards a common goal.

References

Adamson, J.D., Jolliffe, N., Kruse, H.D. *et al.* (1945). Medical survey of nutrition in Newfoundland. *Canadian Medical Association Journal*, **52**, 227–50.

Anonymous (1944) *Healthful Eating*, National Health Series No. 109, Pensions and National Health, Ottawa.

Anonymous (1945) The construction and use of dietary standards. *Canadian Journal of Public Health*, **36,** 272–5.

Anonymous (1949) The story of nutrition in Newfoundland. *Canadian Nutrition Notes*, **5**, 25–6.

Anonymous (1950) Canadian Council on Nutrition. *Canadian Nutrition Notes*, **6**, 39–40.

Anonymous (1961) Rules out – guide in. *Canadian Nutrition Notes*, **17**, 49–50.

Anonymous (1964) Dietary Standard for Canada.*Canadian Bulletin on Nutrition*, **6**, 1–76.

Aykroyd, W.R. (1930) Beriberi and other food deficiency diseases in Newfoundland and Labrador. *Journal of Hygiene*, **30**, 357–86.

Bureau of Nutritional Sciences and Long Range Planning Directorate (1979) *Occasional Paper No. 5, Nutrition and Health in Canada*, Health and Welfare Canada, Ottawa.

Bureau of Nutritional Sciences, Department of National Health and Welfare (1973) *Nutrition Canada, National Survey*, Information Canada, Ottawa.

Bureau of Nutritional Sciences, Department of National Health and Welfare (1975) *Dietary Standard for Canada*, Information Canada, Ottawa.

Bureau of Nutritional Sciences, Department of National Health and Welfare (1983) *Recommended Nutrient Intakes for Canadians*, Supply and Services Canada, Ottawa.

Canadian Council on Nutrition (1940) The Canadian Dietary Standard. *National Health Review*, January 1940.

Canadian Council on Nutrition (1949) A new dietary standard for Canada, 1949. *Canadian Journal of Public Health*, **40**, 420–6.

Committee on Diet and Cardiovascular Disease (1976) *Report of the Committee on Diet and Cardiovascular Disease*, Health and Welfare Canada, Ottawa.

Communications and Implementation Committee, Health and Welfare Canada (1990a) *Action Towards Healthy Eating ... Canada's Guidelines for Healthy Eating and Recommended Strategies for Implementation, The Report of the Communications/Implementation Committee*, Supply and Services Canada, Ottawa.

Communications and Implementation Committee, Health and Welfare Canada (1990b) *Action Towards Healthy Eating ... Technical Report, The Report of the Task and Technical Groups on Canada's Food Guide and the Task Group on Food Consumption*, Supply and Services Canada, Ottawa.

Department of National Health and Welfare (1981) *Departmental Consolidation of the Food and Drugs Act and of the Food and Drug Regulations, amendments to 1993*, Supply and Services Canada, Ottawa.

Health and Welfare Canada (1992) *Canada's Food Guide to Healthy Eating*, Supply and Services Canada, Ottawa.

Health Promotion Directorate (1982) *Canada's Food Guide Handbook (Revised)*, Health and Welfare Canada, Ottawa.

Lalonde, M. (1974) *A New Perspective on the Health of Canadians*, Health and Welfare Canada, Ottawa.

Morrell, C.A. (1963) Looking back over twenty-five years at the Canadian Council on Nutrition. *Canadian Nutrition Notes*, **19**, 49–55.

Murray, T.K. and Rae, J. (1979) Nutrition recommendations for Canadians. *Canadian Medical Association Journal*, **120**,1241–2.

Nova Scotia Department of Health and Fitness and Department of National Health and Welfare (1987) *The Nova Scotia Heart Health Survey*, Halifax.

Scientific Review Committee, Health and Welfare Canada (1990) *Nutrition Recommendations, The Report of the Scientific Review Committee*, Supply and Services Canada, Ottawa.

Verdier, P. (1994) Canada's Food Guide revisited, Part 1: Canada's five food group rules and guide. Unpublished Report.

Young, E.G. (1949) The use and abuse of dietary standards. *Canadian Journal of Public Health*, **40**, 327–31.

6 National policy: Denmark

LARS OVESEN

6.1 Introduction

The national policy on nutrition and health is described in the Health Promotion Programme of the Government of Denmark (Ministry of Health, 1992) presented to the Danish parliament in 1989. The overall specific goals of this programme are:

- to reduce the number of premature deaths;
- to reduce the number of people who are disabled and suffering; and
- to enable more people to maintain their quality of life when they grow old.

The government selected certain priority areas where health promotion efforts were considered to be particularly valuable for possible gain in population well-being. The prevention of cancer and cardiovascular diseases was among such areas given preferential attention.

The relevance of a national policy on the prevention of diseases associated with life-style factors is emphasized by adverse developments in mortality rates and diet composition in this country during the past 20 years.

6.1.1 Dietary recommendations and guidelines

The national policy on nutrition derives its rationale from the dietary recommendations, prepared jointly by experts from the Nordic countries. The latest edition of the Nordic recommendations was sanctioned by the Danish authorities in 1989 (National Food Agency of Denmark, 1989).

The Nordic dietary recommendations originate from the present nutritional situation in the Nordic countries, and aim at forming the basis for planning a diet with a composition that:

- covers the physiological need for nutrients for growth and everyday function; and

Implementing Dietary Guidelines for Healthy Eating. Edited by Verner Wheelock. Published in 1997 by Blackie A&P, an imprint of Chapman & Hall, London. ISBN 0 7514 0304 0

- gives the conditions needed for good health and reduces the risk of diet-related diseases.

The recommendations for adults and children older than 3 years concerning dietary macronutrient composition are:

- protein: 10–15% of total energy intake;
- fat: maximum 30% of total energy intake;
- carbohydrate: 55–60% of total energy intake, and not more than 10% should come from sugar;
- dietary fibre: at least 3 g/MJ/day, corresponding to 25–30 g/day for an adult.

For children less than 3 years old a higher fat intake is recommended (6–12 months, 35–45 E% fat; 1–3 years, 30–35 E%). During the first 6 months of life nutritional needs should be covered by breast feeding.

The dietary recommendations also contain recommendations for the intake of vitamins and minerals, salt and alcohol, and reference values for energy intake.

The Nordic recommendations are regularly updated. The next edition will be published in 1996.

The dietary guidelines are in accordance with the Nordic recommendations. New guidelines have recently (1995) been published by the National Consumer Agency in Denmark. The dietary guidelines for the Danes are:

- eat plenty of grains;
- eat fruit and plenty of vegetables daily;
- eat potatoes, rice or pasta daily;
- eat fish often – and choose different kinds of fish;
- choose milk products and cheese with a low content of fat;
- choose meat with a low content of fat;
- use butter, margarine and oils sparingly; and
- cut down on sugar and salt.

Compared to the prior dietary guidelines the present ones are more action-oriented and emphasize the increased intake of foods rich in carbohydrate rather than the more 'negative' guidelines of a reduction in fat intake.

6.2 Mortality rates

During the past 20 years Denmark has only experienced a very modest improvement of life expectancy compared to most other countries in Europe (Danish Institute for Clinical Epidemiology, 1993). In 1990–91 life expectancy at birth in Denmark was 72.2 years for men and 77.7 years for women. In 1970 Denmark was number 4 for men and number 8 for women on the list of 23 OECD countries. By 1990 Denmark had dropped to number 18 and number 21 on this list for men and for women, respectively.

The problematic development is caused by higher mortality rates for both sexes, but especially for middle-aged (35–64 years) women in Denmark, who demonstrate a higher mortality rate than women in other European countries. On average, there is an excess mortality of 10% in Denmark compared to other European countries.

The country has, like most countries in Western Europe, experienced a decrease in mortality from ischaemic heart disease since the mid 1960s. However, mortality from cancer has shown a slight increase during the past 60 years. Mortality from these two diseases alone constitutes about half of all deaths in Denmark.

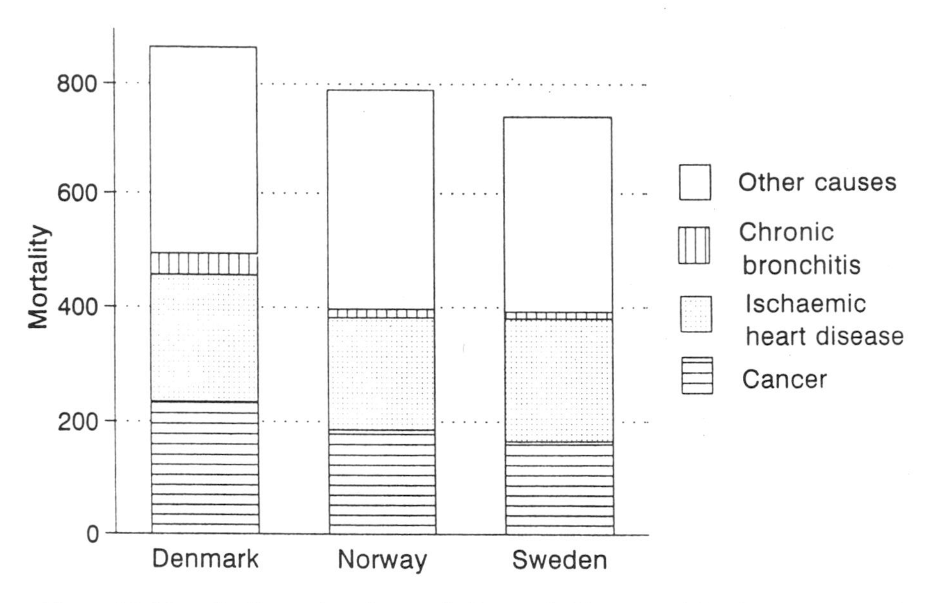

Figure 6.1 Mortality from selected causes in Denmark, Norway and Sweden. Age-standardized rates per 100 000; men and women combined, 1988.

Analysis of specific disease causes shows that Denmark has excess mortality from cancer, especially cancers of the lung, large intestine and breast, and ischaemic heart disease and chronic bronchitis compared to many other countries in Europe. Mortality rates in the Nordic countries are given in Fig. 6.1. If mortality from these diseases is reduced to the level found in other European countries excess mortality largely disappears.

Lung cancer, intestinal cancer, breast cancer, heart disease and chronic bronchitis have scientifically established connections to environmental factors, most notably to smoking habits and diet. Thus, a clear and coherent national policy for food and nutrition is considered to be a *sine qua non* to improving the disturbing high mortality rates in Denmark.

6.3 Food and nutrient intake

A nationwide survey of the dietary habits of adults in Denmark was carried out by the National Food Agency in 1985 (National Food Agency of Denmark, 1986). The study was performed on adults only (15–80 years of age). It showed a high average fat intake of 44% of energy intake (E%). More than 95% of the population derived more than 30% of their dietary energy from fat, and more than 20% had more than 50 E% fat. Saturated fat in butter, margarine, meat, milk and cheese constituted almost the entire fat intake. Carbohydrate intake was correspondingly low with an average intake of 42 E%, of which slightly less than 10 E% came from simple sugars, and an intake of dietary fibre of around 22 g/10 MJ.

The second national dietary intake study, completed in 1995, included 1261 children (1–14 years) and 1837 adults (15–80 years). This study demonstrated rather substantial changes in macronutrient intakes during the 10-year period (data not published). In adults the fat intake had decreased to 37.5 E% and the carbohydrate intake had increased to 47.3 E% (Fig. 6.2). More than 90% of the Danish population derive more than 30 E% from fat, so the fat intake for most of the population is still more than the recommended intake. Sugar and dietary fibre intakes were stable at about 10 E% and 20 g/10 MJ, respectively. The energy percentage from fat was somewhat lower in the children's diet. However, the lower fat E% for the children was explained by a higher content of simple sugars (Fig. 6.2).

For some nutrients (vitamins A, B_2, B_{12}, niacin and the minerals calcium and phosphorus) the daily intake was more than recommended. For other nutrients (vitamins B_1, B_6, folacin, C, E, and the minerals magnesium and zinc) the intakes were somewhat lower, but still within reasonable levels. For a third group of nutrients the intakes were low compared to the recommendations. These nutrients were iron (for menstruating women), iodine, selenium and vitamin D (especially for children).

Data from food balance sheets indicate an increase in fat intake from 36 E% in 1955 to around 40–42 E% in the mid-1960s, and seemingly unchanged until 1990 (National Food Agency of Denmark, 1992). In the same period, the percentage of energy derived from carbohydrates in the diet has gone from 53 to 42%. The daily dietary fibre consumption has decreased from 38 g in 1955 to 27 g in 1990. Average annual alcohol consumption in persons 14 years or older has increased from 4.3 litres (calculated as pure alcohol) in 1955 to 11.6 litres in 1990, decreasing slightly during recent years. However, intake data from food balance sheets are not as reliable as intake data derived from dietary history or registration techniques.

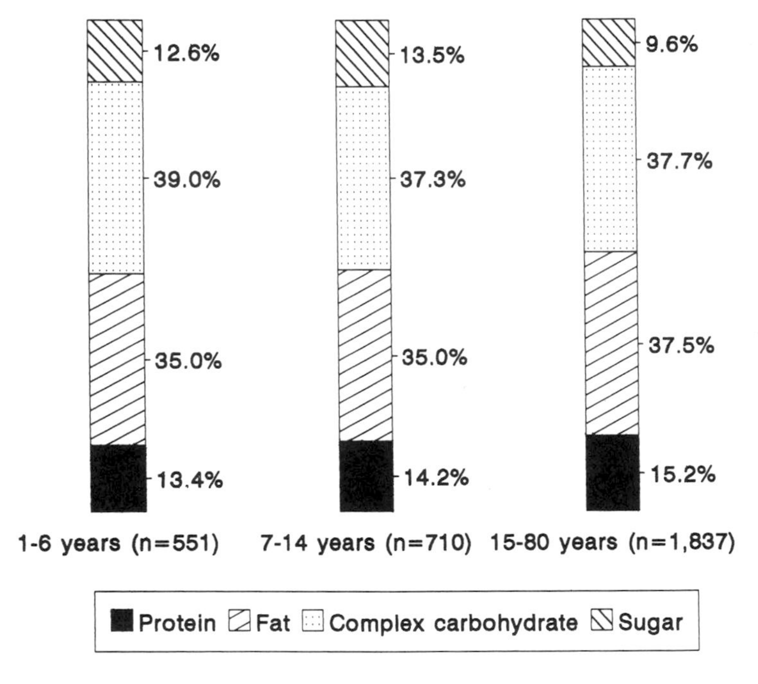

Figure 6.2 Energy distribution in the Danish diet (excluding alcohol).

The most important contributors to fat consumption are butter, margarine, meat and dairy products (Fig. 6.3). Cereals and sugar contribute most to the carbohydrate consumption (Fig. 6.4).

Thus, although the intake data seem to indicate a shift in dietary macronutrient intake in recent years, i.e. decreased fat intake and increased carbohydrate intake, the average Danish diet still contains too much fat, sugar and alcohol and too little complex carbohydrate and dietary fibre.

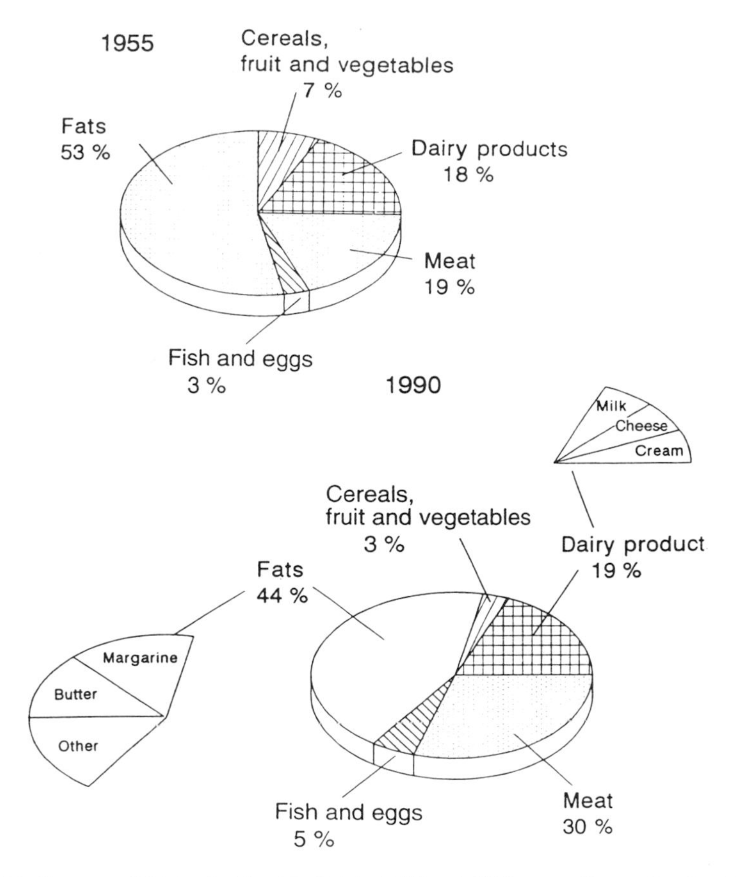

Figure 6.3 Sources of fat in the Danish diet in 1955 and 1990, according to the Danish food balance sheets. Calculated on edible portion.

6.4 The policy on nutrition and food

The overall goal with the nutritional and food policy of the Danish government is to 'contribute to helping to motivate the population to choose a diet that provides the nutrients required to promote health and prevent disease, and assuring consumers wholesome food'. The nutritional policy deals with the supply of foods and, with that, the intake of nutrients, i.e. the energy-supplying fat, carbohydrate, protein and alcohol, and the non-energy-supplying nutrients, vitamins, minerals and dietary fibre. The food policy deals with food quality and problems regarding the misleading of consumers. The Danish food policy will not be dealt with in this chapter.

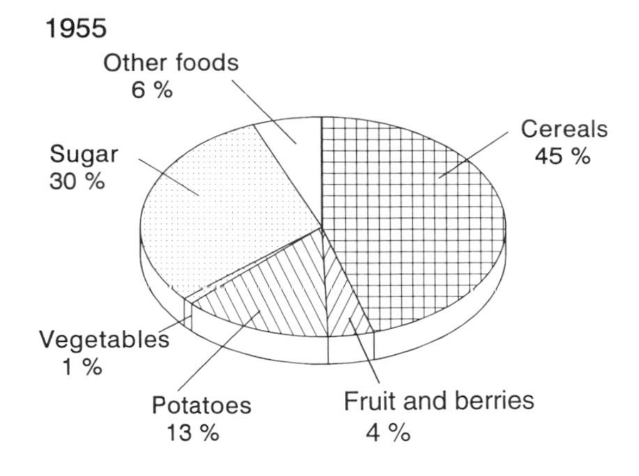

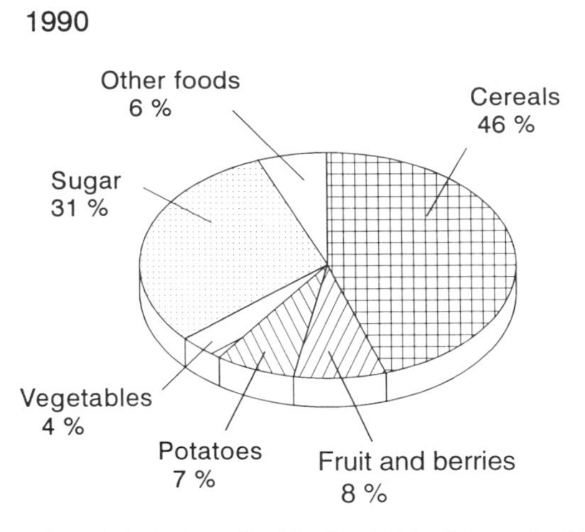

Figure 6.4 Sources of carbohydrate in the Danish diet in 1955 and 1990, according to the Danish food balance sheets. Calculated on edible portion.

The nutritional policy includes the entire complex of political initiatives in the area of food and health, which is expected to influence nutritional status in the population. Nutritional policy considerations should therefore enter into decision making when policies on, for example, agriculture, fishing, industry and taxation are being implemented.

6.4.1 Aims of the Danish nutritional policy

The superior aim of the Danish nutritional policy is to promote healthy dietary habits to foster good health and prevent disease.

Nutritional factors associated with cardiovascular disease and cancer are the high fat intake, the low fibre intake, the high salt intake and the high alcohol intake in Denmark. It is characteristic that the diseases are difficult to cure. A prophylactic initiative is consequently a necessity to reduce the occurrence in the population.

Other diseases of nutritional relevance are hypertension, diabetes mellitus, osteoporosis, constipation and dental caries. Obesity is a risk factor for many diseases – cardiovascular disease, hypertension, diabetes mellitus and some cancer diseases, and muscular and skeletal diseases – and therefore of obvious nutritional relevance. The occurrence of obesity has increased during recent years in Denmark.

The following nutritional policy goals are given the highest priority:

- to reduce the intake of fat to less than 35 E%, eventually reaching a level of about 30E%;
- to increase the intake of dietary fibre to about 30 g/day;
- to secure children and young people a diet that provides a solid foundation for growth and development;
- to secure elderly people a diet which enables them the opportunity to enjoy retirement, e.g. by reducing the risk of functional disorders and preserving the quality of life; and;
- to develop increased knowledge on dietary habits and health as well as the factors that determine dietary habits.

Thus, dominant elements in the Danish nutritional policy are a reduction in foods rich in fat, that is mainly margarine, butter and fat-rich meat and dairy products, and an increase in foods rich in complex carbohydrates and fibre, such as bread, vegetables and fruits, in concordance with the Nordic guidelines for nutrition.

The instruments to achieve the goals of the nutritional policy are:

- information about nutrition; education and labelling of food;
- influencing the supply and demand for food;
- public mass catering; and
- research and surveys.

6.4.2 *Nutritional information, education and food labelling*

Information and education are important instruments in the nutritional policy. Two governmental departments take care of preparing nutritional information for the public: the National Food Agency of Denmark (the Ministry of Health) and the National Consumer Agency (the Ministry of Industry).

The National Food Agency prepares the authoritative basis for nutritional education and educates the public on food, while the National

Consumer Agency is responsible for providing information on nutrition and issues related to nutrition, such as hygiene, shopping, preparing food and home economics.

The main target for the information on healthy nutrition is the population as a whole (mass strategy). The purpose is to influence attitudes and behaviour in the entire population. The reason for choosing a mass strategic approach is that unhealthy eating habits are not limited to any particular risk group in Denmark, but rather involves the major part of the population.

However, information activities are often targeted towards specific population groups. The groups given prime attention are:

- population groups of particular nutritional importance, e.g. schoolchildren, children in day-care centres and the elderly;
- key persons directly or indirectly professionally engaged with communicating nutritional knowledge, e.g. teachers, health-care professionals, food producers and food retailers; and
- persons who are approaching important changes in their lives motivating them to alter their diet, e.g. parents-to-be and elderly persons planning retirement.

The two agencies responsible for nutritional information have, during recent years, implemented several general media campaigns, as well as campaigns directed towards specific target groups. Four media campaigns have until now focused on reducing fat intake.The campaigns have focused on the visible fat, butter and margarine in the diet, which contribute to more than 40% of the Danes' total fat intake, and on the traditional Danish gravy. Basically, the campaigns have concentrated on easy and practical ways to reduce the use of fat without loss of meal quality.

It is a common belief that healthy food is more expensive, takes more time to prepare and is less tasty than unhealthy food. The campaigns have sought to refute these misunderstandings.

Several awareness studies – some including simple questions about fat use – have been performed as a sequel to the campaigns.

Future campaigns will, according to the dietary guidelines given above, be concentrated on foods rich in complex carbohydrates and fibre (National Food Agency of Denmark, 1994).

During the past couple of years co-operation on nutritional information between the public authorities and the retail trade and food manufacturers has increased. As an example, a recent campaign included five large food chains, which advertised wholesome (low-fat) foods. Also, the dairy industry is engaged in nutritional information, specifically towards children in child-care institutions and schools, according to the nutritional guidelines laid out by the public authorities.

Nutritional education and information at the local level will in the future gain increased significance. One advantage of local activities is the widened possibility of personal engagement and the direct dialogue with people whose dietary behaviour one wants to change. This dialogue is probably of principal importance to change the behaviour of many people.

In Denmark several organizations are communicating information on food and nutrition. In addition to the public contribution, there are non-governmental organizations for disease prevention (e.g. the Danish Heart Association, the Danish Cancer Society) and the privately established Danish Nutrition Council (funded by the Danish Medical Association in conjunction with food manufacturing organizations, primarily the Danish Dairy Council, which has its own nutritional information programme), as well as food manufacturers and retailers. Furthermore, the consumers have their own organization: the Danish Consumer Council.

Concerning food labelling, Denmark is subjected to EU legislation. According to this legislation health claims of foods are prohibited.

A Nordic working group has just finished its task concerning the nutritional relevance of nutrient claims. The conclusion is that food content of fat, sugar, dietary fibre and salt are the only nutrients suitable to claim. The report will discuss which categories of claims are appropriate. The report will be published soon.

Symbol labelling is allowed under certain conditions, but is not widely used in Denmark. The Danish government has been hesitant to promote symbol labelling because this kind of labelling may counteract the essential nutritional message that a food is not healthy in itself; rather one should aim at a healthy composition of the diet over a longer period.

Specific risk groups. There are some indications that children below 3 years of age run an increased risk of getting too little energy if a low-fat diet is given by well-meaning and health-conscious parents. Therefore, information campaigns directed towards parents with small children have been carried out to call attention to the fact that the recommendations to decrease the intake of fat do not apply to children under 3 years of age.

Several studies have demonstrated a protective effect of periconceptional folic acid supplementation on the occurrence of neural tube defects (myelomeningocele, encephalocele and anencephali), which are rare congenital malformations (Rasmussen, Andersen and Ovesen, 1994). There is reason to believe that a diet in accordance with the dietary guidelines, i.e. with high intakes of cereals, vegetables and fruit, will secure an intake of folacin of around 400 μg daily (with a sufficient supply of other micronutrients), which is most likely sufficient to decrease the occurrence of neural tube defects. Future nutrition campaigns will be directed specifically towards women of child-bearing age, particularly if they are contemplating pregnancy. The National Board of Health will advise general practitioners of folic acid supplementation to women at risk of folic acid deficiency, e.g. with a deficient dietary intake or with certain gastrointestinal disorders, or to women who have had a pregnancy complicated by neural tube defect.

The national authorities (the National Food Agency and the National Board of Health) have recently established expert groups to evaluate the scientific basis for guidelines to prevent and treat anorexia nervosa and osteoporosis.

6.4.3 Influencing the supply and demand for food

The co-operation between the authorities and food producers to develop nutritious foods of high quality, including the development of new food products, has gained increased momentum during recent years through several large-scale research programmes funded by both the authorities and the food industry. To strengthen the demand for healthy and nutritious food products it is important to follow up on product development with nutritional information and proper marketing, giving consumers a necessary basic knowledge of health and nutrition.

As mentioned above, the health promotion programme also pledges to work towards including nutritional policy considerations as part of the basis for making decisions related to policies concerning agriculture, fishery, industry, taxation and to municipal and regional planning, so that the policies adopted in these areas do not contradict the nutritional policy targets. However, concrete initiatives have been difficult to implement.

6.4.4 Public mass catering

Present figures indicate that about 800 000 meals are served by public mass catering. In Denmark there are increasing numbers of old people living at home who become dependent on public catering arrangements. Thus, a large and increasing proportion of the population is, for shorter or longer periods, dependent on some kind of public – or private – collective provision of meals.

Meals from the public mass catering system should set an example of food of good nutritional and culinary quality. The meals offered by the system should take their basis from the needs and wants of the users of the system. The public mass catering system is regarded as an area where the effect of a preventive effort concerning nutrition may bear fruit.

Recommendations for nutrient and food composition of the diet provided by the public to institutionalized people have just been completed. Recently, the Ministry of Health has established a committee to gain insight into the extent and distribution between customer groups of public meals, and the nutritional quality of the meals, to propose activities and give lines of directives within the field of public mass catering. The committee's work was planned to be completed by summer 1996.

Other fields of interest and current work are:

- to offer instruction, information, management instruments and information on new technology to public kitchens;
- to propound guidelines for labelling of food from public and private mass catering; and
- to execute research projects with respect to the nutritional quality of food produced by different production systems.

6.4.5 Research and surveys

Increased knowledge of the dietary intake of all population groups, on the relationship between diet and disease, and on factors that determine people's choice of diet is considered to be the foundation for up-to-date nutritional guidelines and for sound, adequate and timely nutritional information.

Many projects and programmes, of which some have been mentioned above, are presently in progress to fulfil this goal of the national nutritional policy. Among these projects are repeated dietary surveys, such as the ones in 1985 and 1995, to follow the dietary intakes (of food, nutrients and contaminants) in representative samples of the Danish population, including children and the young. Large-scale dietary intake studies are planned to be repeated every 10 years.

It is important to monitor the nutritional situation continuously to evaluate whether the objectives of the policy are fulfilled, and to what extent and where special initiatives are needed. This means that data on the occurrence of nutrition-related diseases and nutrient intake for various sectors of the population must be available. Such data are presently not accessible in Denmark. However, a working group under the Ministry of Health is being established to evaluate the possibility of making a database, which would make it possible to follow developments in the nutritional situation of various groups within the Danish population.

6.5 Recent changes in food consumption patterns

During the past 10 years the Danish population has shown increased interest in changing dietary habits towards more healthy food choices, i.e. less fat-rich products, such as whole milk (replaced by low-fat milk), margarines and eggs, and more carbohydrate-rich products, primarily fruit, vegetables, rice and pasta (The National Food Agency of Denmark, unpublished data).

Studies carried out in 1985–87 and repeated in 1994 have demonstrated an increased awareness in the adult population of the need to include for health reasons especially fruit and vegetables (from 65% of the population in 1986–87 to 77% in 1994), and high-fibre bread (from 60% to 71%) in the diet (Danish Institute for Clinical Epidemiology, 1995).

Has this increased awareness of healthy eating been transformed into healthy food choices? Many facts indicate that this is occurring.

Fats used as spreads and for frying (margarine and butter) constitute a large part of the total fat intake in Denmark. Calculations indicate that scraping the fat off the bread and throwing away the frying fat – instead of using it for making gravy – will cut the total fat intake by one-third. Consequently, many campaigns for healthy nutrition have focused on these two areas using simple and action-oriented messages.

Studies indicate that this strategy is having an impact. From 1991 to 1994 the Danes have reduced the amount of spreadable margarine and butter on bread by 25% without a simultaneous reduction in the intake of bread or an increase in the use of high-fat meat, cheese or other products spread on bread (National Food Agency of Denmark, 1996). These results are in accordance with the results from the recent national dietary intake study, which have shown that a major explanation for the reduced fat E% from 1985 to 1995 is a reduction in the intake of fats (from margarine, butter and oils) from about 70 g/day to about 45 g/day.

Another indication of changing consumer habits is that many retailers in Denmark now have information initiatives – often in co-operation with the National Food Agency – on sound nutrition included in their sales strategies. Increased attention to nutrition has happened at the same time as the average consumer increasingly is demanding food of good quality, produced under well-regulated environmental and ethical conditions. The changed consumer behaviour has resulted in a new consumer strategy, which will soon be implemented by the largest supermarket chain in Denmark, with more attention directed to such issues as nutrition, animal ethics, ecology and production methods.

6.6 Food fortification

Nutritional surveys indicate that the population's intake of most micronutrients is sufficient. A common basic principle in Denmark is that the addition of micronutrients to food is only permissible if it is nutritionally justifiable. Further, if the justification for fortification is a nutritional deficiency in the population, this deficiency has to be documented (Nordic Council of Ministers, 1989). Consequently, nutrients are added to a very limited selection of foods, and nutrients are solely added for restoration (vitamin C to juices and mashed potato powder; vitamin B_1 and B_2, niacin and iron to breakfast cereals; vitamins B_1 and B_2, iron and calcium to flour; and calcium and iron to oatflakes) or substitution purposes (vitamin A to margarine and minarine).

Food fortification is presently not undertaken in Denmark. However, studies during recent years have shown that the intake of iodine in large parts of the Danish population is low compared to recommended intakes, and that the occurrence of non-toxic goitre is endemic among the elderly in certain areas of the country. A working group established by the National Food Agency has just finished its work, and concludes that iodine fortification (to all salt) is necessary to bring the intake up to recommended daily intakes (National Food Agency of Denmark, 1995).

As indicated above, there might be a problem reaching a sufficient folacin intake for women of child-bearing age. However, concerning this vitamin, it has been decided that supplementation of target groups is more suitable than fortification.

6.7 Breast-feeding

Most infants (95%) are breast-fed from birth. At the age of 4 months slightly fewer than 50% are nourished exclusively by breast milk, and another 15% are nourished partly by breast milk. At the age of 6 months 25% are fully breast-fed and 25% partly breast-fed. Very few mothers continue to breast-feed their babies without supplement after the age of 6 months. Denmark has experienced an increase in breast-feeding frequency and length from the middle of the 1970s. During the past 10 years frequencies have stabilized.

Several studies have shown that if the intake of newborns is supplemented by formula milk in the maternity ward they will consume less breast milk, and these babies will breast-feed for a significantly shorter period than babies who are not fed infant formula. Supplementary feeding in the maternity ward influences the mother's flow of milk negatively, in some studies until as late as 4 months after birth.

The authorities are continuously promoting and encouraging breast-feeding of babies during their first year of life through information to health personnel and directly to pregnant women and new parents. Furthermore, there are activities in progress to get as many hospitals as possible to comply with the requirements of the Baby-Friendly Hospital Initiative launched by UNICEF and WHO in 1991. The object of this initiative is to promote breast-feeding, primarily by ensuring a very early commencement of breast-feeding after birth at the maternity ward. Presently, 25–50% of Danish newborns will receive an infant formula supplement during their stay in the maternity ward. The figure was about 75% in 1988.

References

Danish Institute for Clinical Epidemiology (1993) *Middellevetid og dødelighed* [*Life expectancy and mortality*].

Danish Institute for Clinical Epidemiology (1995) *Sundhed og sygelighed i Danmark 1994* [*Health and disease in Denmark 1994*].

Ministry of Health (1992) *The health promotion programme of the Government of Denmark.*

National Food Agency of Denmark (1986) *Danskernes kostvaner 1985* [*Dietary habits in Denmark 1985*], Publication No. 136.

National Food Agency of Denmark (1989) *Næringsstofanbefalinger 1989* [*Recommended daily intakes 1989*], Publication No. 182.

National Food Agency of Denmark (1992) *Udviklingen i danskernes fødevareforbrug* [*Development of food consumption in Denmark 1955–1990*], Publication No. 214.

National Food Agency of Denmark (1994) *Kulhydrater – sundhed og sygdom* [*Carbohydrates – health and disease*], Publication No. 224.

National Food Agency of Denmark (1995) *Jod – er der behov for berigelse af kosten* [*Iodine – is there a need for fortification of the diet*], Publication No. 230.

National Food Agency of Denmark (1996) *Levnedsmiddelstyrelsens ernæringsoplysning 1991–1995* [*Nutrition education by the National Food Agency*].

Nordic Council of Ministers (1989) *Tilsætning af vitaminer og mineraler til levnedsmidler* [*The addition of vitamins and minerals to foods in the Nordic countries*].

Rasmussen, L.B., Andersen, N.L. and Ovesen, L. (1994) Folacin and neural tube defects. Should pregnant women take supplements. *Scandinavian Journal of Nutrition*, **38**, 15–17.

7 Nutritional policy in Greece

ANTONIA TRICHOPOULOU and ARETI LAGIOU

7.1 Introduction

Nutritional policy has emerged as an important issue, probably as a result of the growing realization of the potential of healthy nutrition to prevent disease; a scientifically based nutritional policy can advance a wide range of health objectives and at the same time accommodate economic considerations and reflect environmental priorities.

Three elements appear to be essential to any comprehensive policy for food and nutrition; namely, fundamental prerequisites (food and nutrition situation analysis, as well as setting clear and explicit goals and objectives), a series of activities (or means of obtaining the objectives) and well-defined organizational responsibility for implementation of the policy (Helsing, 1990a).

In this chapter, the development of the efforts towards a nutritional policy in Greece during the past 15 years is described. The emphasis has been on developing a valid information system about the contemporary dietary patterns of the Greek population and on setting nutritional guidelines and general objectives of a comprehensive policy that has potential for promoting public health.

7.2 The policy environment

There is no official nutritional policy in Greece, but there has been a series of rather uncoordinated activities, undertaken by several, frequently unrelated, governmental agencies and *ad hoc* committees. The governmental bodies most frequently involved in nutritional policy-related activities are:

- 'Nutrition and Food Committee', National Board of Health, Ministry of Health

Implementing Dietary Guidelines for Healthy Eating. Edited by Verner Wheelock. Published in 1997 by Blackie A&P, an imprint of Chapman & Hall, London. ISBN 0 7514 0304 0

- 'Committee on Foods' (licensing), National Drug Administration, Ministry of Health
- 'Supreme Chemical Council', Ministry of Economics
- 'Consumers Officer', Ministry of Trade
- 'Office of Home Economics', Ministry of Agriculture

It is strange, and a little ironic, that nutritional policy was actually practised in Greece in the aftermath of the Second World War, when food shortages made it necessary to make rational, health-based choices for food production, importation and distribution. However, when the food procurement gradually returned to normal in the late 1950s, a combination of factors led to changes of priorities in setting agricultural policy objectives and to devaluation of health considerations. Several factors have contributed to these unfortunate developments, including the fragmentation of related administrative responsibilities, the domination of unrelated market forces and the lack of nutrition-oriented academic centres.

In the late 1970s the issue of nutritional policy was raised again, but it failed to capture the attention of health policy makers, who were preoccupied with other pressing problems in the health care field. Furthermore, the agriculture section remained largely indifferent, if not hostile; many influential people in that sector have assumed that their interests would not be served by an increasing emphasis on health considerations in the context of an integrated nutritional policy (Helsing, 1990b).

The first political action towards the establishment of a co-ordinated nutritional policy in Greece took place in May 1981, when a committee was set up in the Ministry of Health with the mandate to explore the feasibility of, and prepare the ground for, the development of a national nutritional policy. Recommendations were issued but they were never implemented or, indeed, accounted for in subsequent actions. The term 'nutritional policy' resurfaced in 1984, in a round table discussion organized by the Greek Society of Nutrition and Foods together with the Department of Nutrition and Biochemistry of the Athens School of Public Health.

A sound nutritional policy should be based on reliable data concerning the current nutritional status of the population and the formulation of nutritional guidelines. The sequential steps towards the development of such an information system and the objectives of a health-promoting nutritional policy are presented.

7.3 Food and nutrition situation analysis

In the early 1980s, in Greece, reliable information concerning food consumption on a national basis did not exist. Only a few studies concerning dietary habits in small population groups, done at different times, using different methodologies were available. Efforts to secure funds for the development of a nutritional survey were undertaken but with no success.The Department of Nutrition of the Athens School of Public Health urgently needed information. The only source of information at national level was food balance sheets data of the Food and Agriculture Organization of the United Nations. An analysis, based on the FAO data, revealed a disquieting situation. In Greece, as well as in several other countries which have joined the group of so-called developed countries in the past 20 years or so, there has been a remarkable change in the consumption of proteins and fats of animal origin, whereas the consumption of vegetables, fruits and cereals has remained relatively stable. These changes have been correlated in time and place with changes in the incidence (as reflected in mortality) of several major and common diseases, including coronary heart disease, colon cancer, breast cancer, diabetes mellitus, etc. (Trichopoulou and Efstathiades, 1989; Trichopoulou *et al.*, 1993).

These data were supplemented with the food availability data from the Greek household budget surveys. It was noticed that although there were obvious differences in average per capita amounts, the trends shown in these two data sources were virtually parallel (Figs 7.1 and 7.2). These findings

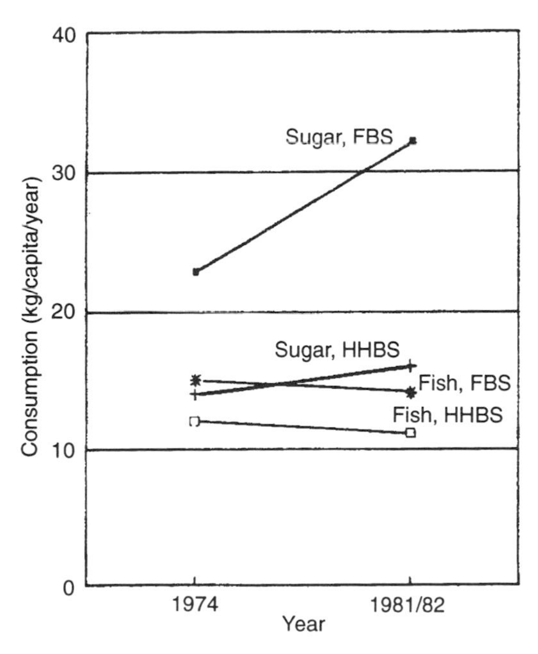

Figure 7.1 Differences between data for sugar and fish consumption from the FAO food balance sheets (FBS) and the Greek household budget survey (HHBS) (source: Trichopoulou, 1989).

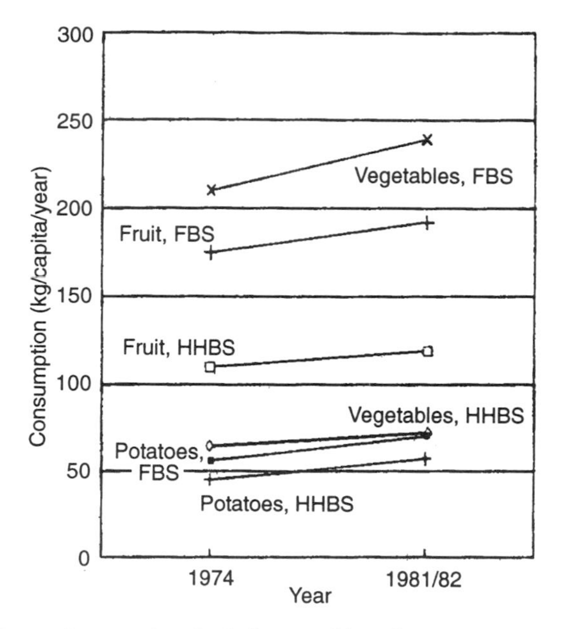

Figure 7.2 Difference between data for fruit, vegetable and potato consumption from the FAO food balance sheets (FBS) and the Greek household budget survey (HHBS) (source: Trichopoulou, 1989).

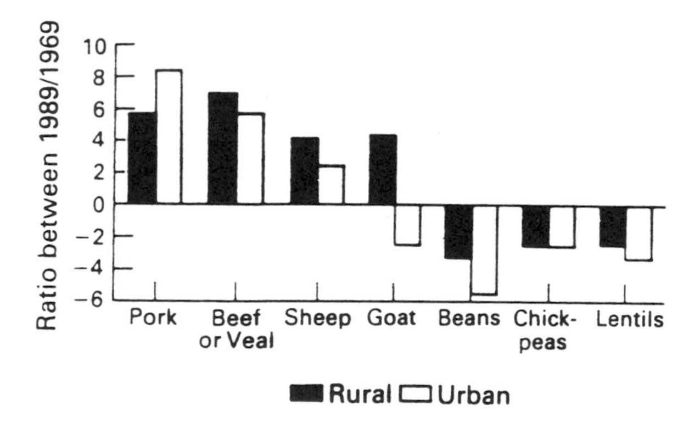

Figure 7.3 Comparison of frequency of consumption of selected food items between 1989 and 1969 (source: Trichopoulou, 1993).

were published in order to sensitize the health authorities and to warn the public (Trichopoulou, 1989).

In 1989 the dietary habits of the present time and of 20 years ago of 404 adults (men and women) were studied in urban and rural areas of Greece. The methodology used was a food frequency questionnaire coupled with a 24-hour diet recall. The comparison of frequency of consumption of selected food items between 1989 and 20 years previously in rural and urban population groups is presented in Fig. 7.3 (Trichopoulou, Katsouyianni and Gnardellis, 1993). As previously indicated, the most profound changes in dietary intakes concern the increased consumption of pulses (beans, lentils and chickpeas) (Katsouyianni *et al.*, 1991). The changing patterns of food habits in Greece are also evident in Crete, and they are compatible with an increase in plasma cholesterol. Mean plasma cholesterol concentration has risen by 36% over 26 years, as reported by Kafatos *et al.* (1991).

7.3.1 HBS data and the potential of their contribution, the DAFNE project

The need for surveillance and for a reliable, easily accessible and continuously updated nutrition information system for formulating the objectives and monitoring the effects of the policy was emphasized. The next step was to have a more careful look at the dietary data in the national household budget surveys (HBSs). Although HBSs are designed not for nutritional purposes but in order to analyse economic implications of trends in food consumption and to obtain the necessary information for the estimation of price indices, they represent a unique source of data on dietary patterns. A large amount of information concerning nutrition is collected in almost all European countries through HBS at variable time intervals. This information could be of great help for assessing nutritional patterns of different population groups, differentiating between regions, education level, income and age group, for the identification of high-risk groups for nutrition-related diseases and for nutritional strategy planning; utilizing household budget survey data might provide a new insight on how variable and changing economic and social conditions have affected the food patterns of the Greek population (Trichopoulou, 1992).

The National Nutrition Center of Greece and the Greek Society of Nutrition and Foods have undertaken, since 1987, a series of studies and other activities aiming at the development of the most appropriate way of using food and related data from the household budget surveys. The culmination of these activities was the development of the DAFNE (DAta Food NEtworking) project which involves 10 European countries (Belgium, Denmark, Germany, Greece, Hungary, Ireland, Poland, Portugal, Spain, United Kingdom). The tasks of the Scientific Network for Pan-European Food Data Bank based on household budget surveys (DAFNE) include the study of current methods of HBS data collection and processing, as well as the resolution of all scientific and technical issues for the consolidation of the national databases. The end product of this effort, which is supported by the European Union, is the creation of an operational European HBS Food Data Bank (European Parliament, 1995).

Some preliminary representative results of the DAFNE project are summarized in Tables 7.1 and 7.2, in which availability of selected food groups for years 1982 and 1987 is presented (Trichopoulou and Vassilakou, 1995). Over this period cereal consumption decreased. Meat consumption, which increased in previous years, was stable at around 140 g/capita/day, while the consumption of milk and dairy was still increasing. The disquieting issue concerns the reduction in olive oil consumption and the increase of seed oil and margarine consumption.

Table 7.1 Availability (in g/capita/day) of main foods in Greece for 1981–82 and 1987–88 (source: Trichopoulou and Vassilakou, 1995)

Food items	1981–82	1987–88
Bread	177	218
Cereals and products	107	85
Meat	143	145
Fish	35	39
Oils and fat	79	83
Milk and dairy	161	201
Pulses	18	16
Potatoes	158	155
Vegetables	202	241
Fruits	332	343
Sugar and confectionery	57	44

Table 7.2 Availability (in g/capita/day) of oils and fat in Greece for 1981–82 and 1987–88 (source: Trichopoulou and Vassilakou, 1995)

Food items	1981–82	1987–88
Olive oil	69	64
Seed oils	2	11
Butter	1	1
Margarine	3	5
Cooking fat	4	2

7.3.2 *The European Prospective Investigation into Cancer and Nutrition (EPIC) study*

Sources of data concerning food availability of intake range from the nationally collected and FAO assembled food balance sheets to specifically designed food consumption surveys and nutritional epidemiological investigations. One of the main advantages of prospective studies is that data on current diet can be collected at the time of the subject's enrolment in the study; repeat measurements of diet can be made at any time during the follow-up period in order to investigate whether dietary changes have occurred.

A large modern prospective study, the EPIC study of diet and chronic diseases, is under progress in nine European countries and valuable data are being collected on food intake, other life-style and environmental factors and anthropometry, as well as biological samples in a cohort of about 400 000 healthy European adults. The subjects will be followed up to investigate the incidence of, and mortality from, cancer in relation to epidemiological data and biochemical markers (Riboli, 1992). In the Greek component of the EPIC study it is planned to recruit about 40 000 subjects, with about equal numbers of men and women. Men will mainly be recruited in the age range of 40 to 63 while for women the age range will be 35 up to 69. Geographical distributions and target populations from which subjects are drawn will provide a broad and representative picture of the contemporary dietary habits as well as evidence of the determinants of consumer food choices in the Greek population.

7.4 Nutritional guidelines

In 1985, based on the information about the contemporary Greek dietary pattern that we obtained from the FAO data, the Greek Society for Nutrition and the Department of Nutrition of the Athens School of Public Health developed the following nutrition guidelines, which have been adopted and used by the Ministries of Health and Commerce:

- eat more fruits, vegetables, cereals and pulses;
- eat less red meat and more poultry and fish;
- eat fewer lipids and prefer those of vegetable origin;
- eat less butter, eggs and sausages;
- eat less refined sugar;
- reduce consumption of sugar-containing beverages;
- reduce salt intake;
- eat in a pleasant environment;
- walk and exercise more.

Until more reliable data concerning (1) the nutritional status of the Greek population, appropriately stratified, (2) the occurrence patterns and trends of diet-related diseases and conditions, and (3) the complex interaction between social, economic, nutritional and epidemiological parameters, become available these interim guidelines have been extensively utilized in nutritional education courses and for the production of educational material for the general public.

In 1994, the Greek Ministry of Health adopted the 'Mediterranean diet pyramid' (Fig. 7.4) which was first introduced in the International Conference on Mediterranean Diet, Boston, 1993. The National Center of Nutrition contributed to the development of the graphic illustration of the pyramid and the formulation of the accompanying guidelines (Willett *et al.*, 1995).

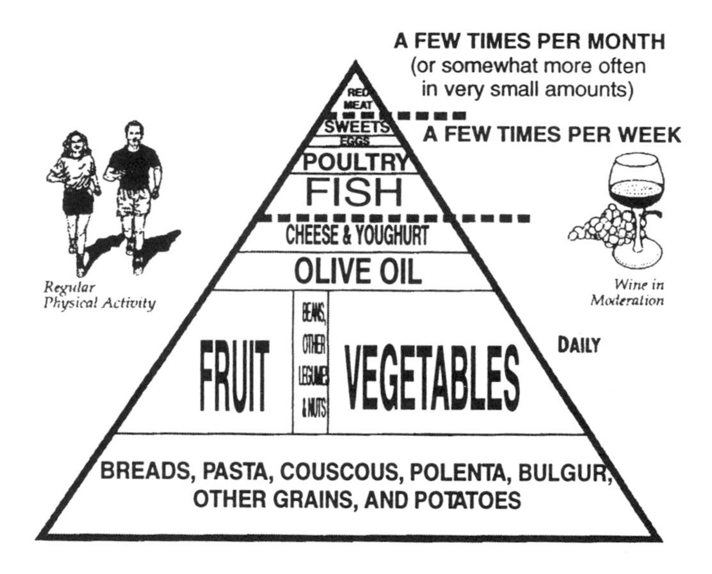

Figure 7.4 The Mediterranean diet pyramid: a cultural model for healthy eating (source: Willett *et al.*, 1995).

The objective was to translate current nutritional knowledge to a recommended eating pattern in terms of food groups and a general sense of frequency of servings, as well as an indication of foods to favour in a healthy Mediterranean-style diet.

In generic terms, the Mediterranean diet may be described as a diet low in saturated fat, with added fat mostly in the form of olive oil; high in complex carbohydrates from grains and legumes; and high in fibre, mostly from vegetables and fruits. Total fat may be high (around 40% of total energy intake as in Greece) or moderately high (around 28% of total energy intake, as in Italy), but in all instances, the monounsaturated-to-saturated fats ratio is elevated (usually 2 or more). The high content of fresh plants and cereals in the diet, and the abundant olive oil, guarantee a high intake of β-carotene, vitamin C, tocopherols (vitamin E), various important minerals and several possibly beneficial non-nutrient substances, such as polyphenols and antocyanines.

In terms of foods and frequency of consumption the historical pattern of the Mediterranean diet includes the following components (European Parliament, 1995):

1. An abundance of food from plant sources, including fruits and vegetables, potatoes, breads and grains, beans, nuts and seeds.
2. Emphasis on a variety of minimally processed and, wherever possible, seasonally fresh and locally grown foods. Freshness maximizes the health-promoting micronutrient and antioxidant content of these foods.
3. Olive oil as the principal fat, in place of other fats and oils.
4. Total fat ranging from less than 25% to over 35% of energy, with saturated fat no more than 7–8% of energy (calories).
5. Daily consumption of low to moderate amounts of cheese and yoghurt.
6. Weekly consumption of low to moderate amounts of fish and poultry and a few eggs per week.
7. Fresh fruit as the typical daily dessert. Sweet with significant amounts of sugar and saturated fats consumed not more than a few times per week.
8. Red meat a few times per month.
9. Regular physical activity at a level compatible with fitness, healthy weight and well-being.
10. Moderate consumption of wine, normally with meals and mostly by adult men.

7.5 Nutritional education

In Greece, nutritional education courses have been been organized for health professionals, teachers and the general public. A systematic effort was undertaken by the Department of Nutrition and Biochemistry of the Athens School of Public Health. The target was to provide knowledge but also methodology of attitude and behaviour change. A great deal of this effort has been concentrated in programmes for school teachers. School teachers consist of a 'critical mass' of people deserving high priority because of their influential role on the formulation of the young generation's nutritional habits.

7.6 The challenge for further policy development in Greece

Nowadays, overall evidence is sufficiently strong for the authorities who are seeking to reduce cardiovascular and malignant disease to issue dietary guidelines which have much in common with the characteristics of the traditional Mediterranean diet.

In Greece several important developments are changing the background in which nutritional policy activities are and will be taking place in the future. Mortality rates from diet-related cardiovascular diseases and several forms of cancer (including those of the breast and large bowel) appear to be increasing (Trichopoulou, Lagiou and Trichopoulos, 1994). Furthermore, studies have shown that the progressive abandonment of the traditional diet by the low- and middle-class segments of the population have striking effects on the serum lipid profiles of adolescents and young adults in the respective populations (Petridou *et al.*, 1995). In this context, there is an urgent need to reverse the trends that tend to take contemporary Greeks away from their health-promoting nutritional traditions, to preserve and revitalize the traditional Mediterranean diet within a modern life-style. The Mediterranean diet constitutes a centuries-old tradition that contributes to excellent health, provides a sense of pleasure and well-being, and forms an integral and important component of a healthy-promoting life style.

7.7 Conclusions

In Greece, as in other European countries, the development of nutritional policy has had a snowball effect. The National Nutrition Center has taken a leading role in the initiation and propagation of activities, as well as in the scientific substantiation and overall promotion of the various aspects of an integrated national nutritional policy. Since nutritional policy was brought into the discussion in the early 1980s, considerable work has been done; it is even more important that slowly but steadily more dedicated people have joined in this effort, allowing all of us to look to the future with confidence.

Acknowledgement

We would like to thank Mr Pericles Karathanasis for his technical support.

References

European Parliament (1995) *STOA Report on Nutrition in Europe: Nutrition policy and public health in the European Community and models for European eating habits on the threshold of the 21st century*, (in press).

Helsing, E. (1990a) *A Comprehensive Nutrition Policy*. First European Conference on Food and Nutrition Policy. Report of a conference, World Health Organization, Regional Office for Europe, pp. 43–8.

Helsing, E. (1990b) The case of Greece, in Initiation of national nutrition policies. University of Athens. Doctoral thesis, pp. 1–35.

Kafatos, A., Kouroumalis, E., Vlachonikolis, I. *et al.* (1991) Coronary heart disease risk-factor status of the Cretan urban population in the 1980s. *American Journal of Clinical Nutrition*, **54**, 591–8.

Katsouyianni, K., Trichopoulou, A., Trichopoulos, D. and Willett, W. (1991) *Dietary Variability in Greece*. A report to the Secretariat of Research and Technology, Ministry of Industry, Research and Technology, Athens.

Petridou, E., Malamou, H., Doxiades, S. *et al.* (1995) Blood Lipids in Greek Adolescents and their Relation to Diet, Obesity, and Socioeconomic factors. *Ann. Epidemiol.* **5**, 286–291. Elsevier Science, New. York.

Riboli, E. (1992) Nutrition and cancer: background and rationale of the European Prospective Investigation into Cancer and Nutrition (EPIC). *Annals of Oncology*, **3**, 783–91.

Trichopoulou, A. (1989) Nutrition Policy in Greece. *European Journal of Clinical Nutrition*, **43**, (Suppl. 2), 79–82.

Trichopoulou, A. (1992) Monitoring food intake in Europe: A food data bank based on household budget surveys. *European Journal of Clinical Nutrition*, **46**, (Suppl. 5), 3–8.

Trichopoulou, A. and Efstathiades, P. (1989) Changes of nutrition patterns and health indicators at the population levels in Greece. *American Journal of Clinical Nutrition*, **49**, 1042–7.

Trichopoulou, A. and Vassilakou, T. (1995) *Food availability in Greece per capita 1981–82 and 1987–88*, National Nutrition Center and Greek Society of Nutrition and Foods.

Trichopoulou, A., Katsouyianni, K. and Gnardellis, Ch. (1993) The traditional Greek diet. *European Journal of Clinical Nutrition*, **47**, (Suppl. 1), 76–81.

Trichopoulou, A., Toupadaki, N., Tzonou, A. *et al.* (1993) The macronutrient composition of the Greek diet: estimates derived from six case-control studies. *European Journal of Clinical Nutrition*, **47**, 549–58.

Trichopoulou, A., Lagiou, P. and Trichopoulos, D. (1994) Traditional Greek diet and coronary heart disease. *Journal of Cardiovascular Risk*, **1**, 9–15.

Willett, W., Sacks, F., Trichopoulou, A. *et al.* (1995) Mediterranean Diet Pyramid: a cultural model for healthy eating. *American Journal of Clinical Nutrition*, **61**, (Suppl.), 1402–6.

8 Promoting good nutrition and health for all in Ireland

URSULA O'DWYER

8.1 Overview

In Ireland in the 1990s, there has been increasing recognition of the vital role played by improved nutrition in achieving optimum health gain. This has led to the development of many new initiatives on healthy eating. These vary from government-based to those from voluntary organizations, community actions and food industry programmes.

An overview of some of these programmes will be presented here. Particular emphasis will be given to government initiatives for the 1990s and beyond, which have been developed to help Irish people achieve their maximum health potential.

8.2 Introduction

Healthy nutrition can make a major contribution to the prevention of coronary heart disease, some cancers and other diet-related diseases. In Ireland, levels of avoidable illness and premature death are higher than in many other parts of Europe. Up to half of our adult population is overweight or obese, 25% of adults die prematurely (before the age of 65) from coronary heart disease and 33% of adults die prematurely from cancers (Department of Health, 1995).

National and other nutritional surveys have shown that the Irish diet does not conform to current nutritional guidelines. The Irish diet is high in fat, particularly in saturated fat, and low in fibre. Consumption of fruit and vegetables is among the lowest in Europe.

The challenge to improve the health of people in Ireland is a long-term process requiring careful planning for maximum impact. To meet this challenge a five-year action plan, *Nutrition Health Promotion – Framework for Action* was drawn up in 1991 (Department of Health, 1991). This action plan has been endorsed and built on by subsequent Department of Health

Implementing Dietary Guidelines for Healthy Eating. Edited by Verner Wheelock. Published in 1997 by Blackie A&P, an imprint of Chapman & Hall, London. ISBN 0 7514 0304 0

strategies: *Shaping a healthier future. A strategy for effective healthcare in the 1990s* (Department of Health, 1994) (Fig. 8.1) and *A Health Promotion Strategy* (Department of Health, 1995).

Figure 8.1 *Shaping a healthier future* cover.

More recently the Nutrition Advisory Group to the Minister for Health has, at the request of the Minister, drawn up *Recommendations for a Food and Nutrition Policy for Ireland* (Nutrition Advisory Group, 1995). These recommendations are expected to form the working basis for an Irish policy on food and nutrition.

8.3 What are Irish people eating?

The Irish diet is based around four main food staples: bread, meat, potatoes and milk, which combined provide 55% of energy, 75% of protein, 40% of fibre and a large proportion of essential minerals and vitamins. The traditional image of the Irish diet as being heavily reliant on potatoes still holds true; for example, potatoes provide 30–40% of vitamin C intakes. In recent years, there has been an increase in the consumption of processed potatoes (such as chips) and a rise in rice and pasta intake (Lee and Cunningham, 1990).

Figure 8.2 Potatoes in basket.

Data from the Kilkenny Health Project and national food balance sheets indicate that the Irish diet is undergoing changes. Although milk consumption is higher than in other EU countries, there has been a sharp drop in butterfat consumption, mediated through a drop in butter usage and an increase in low-fat milk consumption (Foley, 1995).

While fruit and vegetable consumption is one of the lowest in Europe, the population average is about 3 servings/day (Health Promotion Unit, 1996) and fruit consumption is rising steadily. A similar picture is seen for fish consumption, intakes are rising slowly although overall consumption remains low.

In general the Irish diet is well balanced. However, like most Western countries, the balance of energy-providing nutrients is skewed towards a diet high in fat. National and subgroup surveys have indicated that average intake of dietary fat ranges from 36 to 41% of total food energy (Foley, 1995). Data from the Irish National Nutrition Survey 1990 showed that meat, dairy products and spreadable fats were the main sources of fat, indicating that a high percentage of dietary fat is likely to be saturated. Fibre intakes are low when compared to the recommended dietary allowance (RDA) of 25–35 g/day. Calcium intakes were adequate for the majority of the population, but only reached approximately 75% of the RDA of 1200 mg for 12–18-year-olds. Folic acid intakes were below the RDA for 90% of Irish women and iron intakes were below the RDA in 75% of women aged 12–50 years (Lee and Cunningham, 1990).

It is obvious from the above picture that the Irish diet does not conform to current nutritional guidelines. These guidelines are set out below and emphasize gradual changes required for healthy eating.

8.4 Healthy eating guidelines

The healthy eating guidelines are recognized as the cornerstone for nutrition health promotion. These were recently updated by the Nutrition Advisory Group to the Minister for Health (Nutrition Advisory Group, 1995). Consideration was given to setting qualitative and quantitative targets for the Irish population. However, there was inadequate information on nutrient intakes and on the rate of dietary change to set quantitative targets. Furthermore, many people have difficulty in interpreting numerical targets and in estimating the extent of proposed dietary change. Therefore the Nutrition Advisory Group prepared two sets of qualitative guidelines. The first set of guidelines applies to the general population.These are called the Healthy Eating Guidelines and are presented below. In addition, guidelines for special groups were also drawn up.

8.4.1 Healthy Eating Guidelines

1. *Eat a wide variety of foods.* By incorporating a wide variety of foods in the diet most dietary requirements will be met. The diet should be based on fresh foods as far as possible. It is important to taste food before seasonings are added. Herbs and spices including pepper can enhance the flavour of food. Reliance on salt to flavour food is not recommended.
2. *Balance energy intake with physical activity levels.* Food provides energy or fuel for the body. It is recommended that a high energy intake, to ensure an adequate intake of nutrients, be balanced with sufficient physical activity to maintain a healthy weight.

   Exercise should be incorporated into the daily routine on at least 5 days a week. This will not only improve physical fitness and well-being but can also protect against a number of diseases, including coronary heart disease and osteoporosis.
3. *Eat plenty of fruit and vegetables. Aim to eat at least four servings every day.* Irish people have very low intakes of fruit and vegetables in

comparison to those living in southern European countries. Fruit and vegetables are rich sources of micronutrients such as folic acid and the antioxidant vitamins, beta-carotene (vitamin A), vitamin E and vitamin C. There is evidence that these antioxidant vitamins play a role in the prevention of coronary heart disease and certain cancers. Adequate intake of folic acid in early pregnancy reduces the incidence of neural tube defects. Fruit and vegetables are also rich sources of dietary fibre. Four or more servings of fruit and vegetables per day are likely to ensure adequate intakes of these nutrients. (1 serving = ½ glass fruit juice, 2 tablespoons cooked vegetables or salad, small bowl of homemade soup, 1 medium-sized fresh fruit, 2 tablespoons of cooked or tinned fruit (preferably in natural juice).)

4. *Starchy foods such as bread (preferably wholemeal), cereals, pasta and rice, as well as fruit and vegetables, should be eaten daily. The frequent consumption throughout the day of foods containing sugar should be avoided, especially by children.* Starchy foods include bread, potatoes, rice, cereals, cereal-based foods, fruit and vegetables. Qualitative research shows that many Irish people restrict their intake of the starchy foods because they are perceived as being 'fattening' (Kearney, 1994). However, there is substantial evidence that diets rich in carbohydrates are less likely to lead to excess weight compared with diets which are high in fat. People, especially those who are physically active, are advised to eat more starchy foods to ensure an adequate intake of energy, vitamins and dietary fibre.

   It is recommended that frequent consumption throughout the day of foods containing sugar be avoided to reduce the risk of dental caries, particularly among children.

5. *Total fat intake should be reduced, with emphasis on reducing saturated fats. Some saturated fat may be replaced by unsaturated fats. Oily fish is a good source of unsaturated fats as well as some essential fatty acids. Current evidence suggests that there should be no increase in* trans *fatty acid intake.*

   There is a need to reduce the total fat intake of the Irish population and to attain an appropriate balance of fats in the diet. This should be achieved primarily by reducing the intake of saturated fats.

   The fat content of food can be decreased by using different cooking methods. Boiling, braising, baking, steaming and poaching may be used to reduce fat intake. Microwave ovens can also reduce the amount of fat used in cooking.

   If fat is added to foods, using an unsaturated oil or spread, either monounsaturated or polyunsaturated, improves the balance of fat in the diet. Oily fish is a good source of unsaturated fats and of some essential fatty acids. Salad dressings based on unsaturated oils may be substituted for traditional mayonnaise or salad cream which are high in saturates.

Much of the fat (especially saturated fat) eaten in Ireland is consumed in confectionery, biscuits and cakes. These too are also likely to provide a substantial proportion of the *trans* fatty acids in the Irish diet.

Starchy foods such as bread, potatoes, cereals, fruit and vegetables are all low-fat foods. Other low-fat choices include lean meat, fish and chicken. Foods with a fat content lower than the original product are becoming increasingly available.

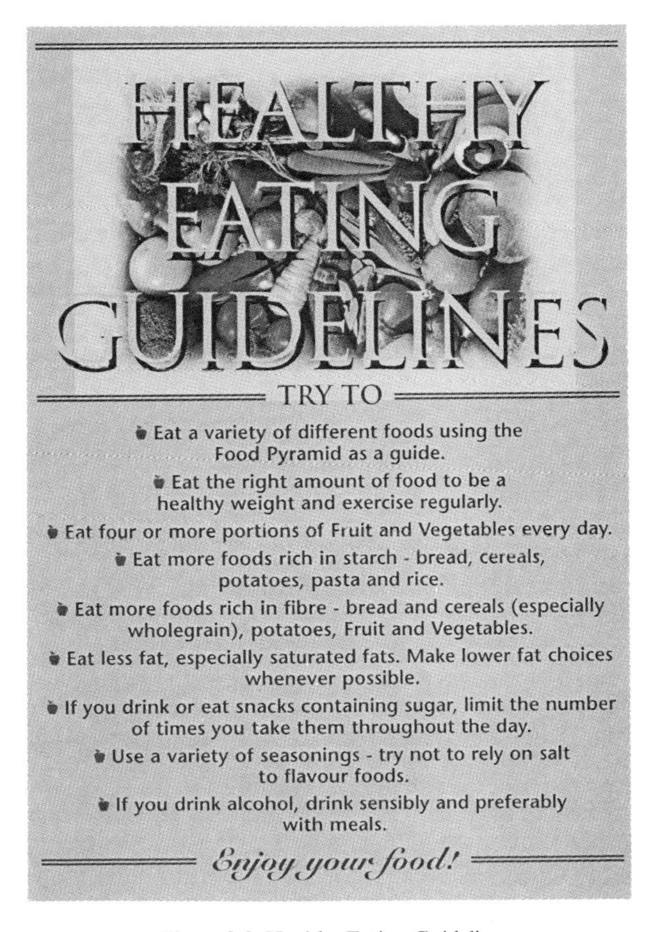

Figure 8.3 Healthy Eating Guidelines.

6. *Alcohol recommendations*. The Department of Health has published a policy document on alcohol. The main policy objective is to promote moderation in alcohol consumption, for those who wish to drink, and reduce the prevalence of alcohol-related problems in Ireland, thereby promoting the health of the community.

8.4.2 Consumer Healthy Eating Guidelines

Figure 8.3 shows the Healthy Eating Guidelines as presented in more consumer-friendly wording in nutritional health promotion materials intended for the general public.

8.5 Recommendations for a policy on food and nutrition

The Nutrition Advisory Group to the Department of Health was responsible for the development of Recommendations for a Food and Nutrition Policy for Ireland. This group was established in 1991 and its first term of reference was to assist in the formulation of a national policy on food and nutrition to improve nutrition and health in Ireland. The recommendations were presented to the Department of Health in November 1995 and a consultation process with major players in the area of food and nutrition is taking place. Once this has been completed, it is envisaged that the recommendations from the report will be endorsed by the Department of Health and a policy on food and nutrition will be adopted and implemented in Ireland.

The report aims to:

- outline the food and nutrient intake which would maintain and promote health and prevent disease;
- update dietary guidelines for the population in the context of what is known about nutrition and health in Ireland;
- consider the barriers to the attainment of optimum nutrition by consumers;
- consider the implications of dietary recommendations for the national food supply and particularly for the Irish food industry;
- make recommendations for the further development and implementation of the policy on food and nutrition in Ireland.

In compiling the report, the Nutrition Advisory Group considered that the concept of a food and nutrition policy should be elaborated, the elements of a healthy diet should be discussed and the particular nutritional and health circumstances pertaining to Ireland should be described.

Figure 8.4 Recommendations for a Food and Nutrition Policy for Ireland.

The Group considered that a revised statement on dietary guidelines was necessary and was also aware of the many non-nutritional issues that influence food consumption. Finally, the Nutrition Advisory Group in its recommendations sought to chart the way forward for the formulation and implementation of an appropriate policy on food and nutrition for Ireland.

The key recommendations in the report for health gain through improved nutrition are:

1. Food and nutritional policy development and implementation will require long-term, sustained commitment by government.
2. Organizational structures relevant to food and nutrition policy should include a mechanism for consultation with food producers and consumers.
3. The activities of state and semi-state agencies should be compatible with the national policy on food and nutrition.
4. National food consumption surveys of sufficient detail to meet the needs of both nutritional assessment and the monitoring of food safety should be carried out every 5 years.

5. A proactive approach should be taken to the dissemination of nutritional information to the public.
6. A community nutritional and dietetic service should be provided throughout the country.
7. Monitoring of changes in food consumption and in nutrition-related diseases is essential to the evaluation and ongoing development of policy on food and nutrition in Ireland.

8.6 Additional components of policy on food and nutrition

The National Nutrition Surveillance Centre, established by the Department of Health in 1992 in the Department of Health Promotion, University College Galway, will have a key role in providing data on food and health. It is a centralized source of information with three functions:

- to provide relevant information on nutrition in an accessible form at short notice;
- to monitor trends in health status, correlated with food supply and consumption and advise health planners on these findings;
- to provide a source of information and research expertise, particularly in epidemiological or surveillance methodology, to those wishing to mount specific projects such as micro-dietary surveys (National Nutrition Surveillance Centre, 1993).

The annual reports from the National Nutrition Surveillance Centre (National Nutrition Surveillance Centre, 1993, 1994) provide a review of available data on nutrition-related diseases in Ireland, as well as on food production, supply and consumption.

The Food Safety Advisory Board was established by the Minister for Health in 1995. The functions of the Board include advising 'the Minister on matters relating to food with particular reference to nutrition'.

The Nutrition Committee of the Food Safety Advisory Board has now taken over the work of the Nutrition Advisory Group.

8.7 Action on healthy eating

While preparations for a national policy on food and nutrition were being considered in 1991, it was agreed that, in tandem with such preparations, action on healthy eating initiatives should also be progressed, hence the publication of the *Nutrition Health Promotion – Framework for Action* (Department of Health, 1991).

Table 8.1 Summary of Nutrition Health Promotion – Framework for Action

Target audience	Areas for action
Community	Nutritional awareness and eating behaviour programmes Primary health care nutrition conferences Establishment of community dietitian posts National Healthy Eating Week
Schools	Schools' nutrition programme Schools' nutrition information campaign Schools' information on healthy meal choices
Industry/workplace	Workplace healthy eating materials Workplace nutrition education programmes
Population subgroups	Low-income groups' nutrition programme Local authority school lunches programme Nutritional information campaign for the elderly Infants and young children nutrition education materials
Food industry	Food producers' and processors' nutrition briefings Retail outlets' healthy food choices award scheme Restaurant and hotel healthy eating campaign Food labelling education programme
Networking with other organizations	Joint nutrition education programmes with organizations such as the Irish Heart Foundation, Irish Cancer Society and Irish Hyperlipidaemia Association Dissemination of nutritional education materials via professional groups Networking with groups such as the Irish Countrywomen's Association Partnerships with the food industry Media nutrition briefings and conferences

A summary of the Framework for Action is outlined in Table 8.1. Table 8.2 includes additional nutritional goals, targets and actions as published in the national Health Promotion Strategy (1995). Examples or case studies for some of these actions are presented below.

8.8 Case studies – nutritional initiatives

8.8.1 Successes and lessons learned

The food pyramid (Fig. 8.5) and the Healthy Eating Guidelines (Fig. 8.3) are the basic nutritional education tools used by the Health Promotion Unit of the Department of Health (Health Promotion Unit, 1996). Depending on the target audience, these healthy eating 'messages' are packaged in appropriate 'wrappers'.

Table 8.2 Nutrition goals, targets and actions

The ongoing implementation, within the next 5 years, of the Department of Health's Healthy Eating Guidelines including:

- educating and motivating Irish people to eat a wide variety of foods in line with current recommendations as illustrated in the food pyramid
- the encouragement of the achievement and maintenance of a healthy weight through healthy eating and regular exercise
- the encouragement of a reduction in total fat intake (to no more than 35% of energy) by the year 2005 and to attain an appropriate balance of fats
- the achievement of a moderate reduction of 10% in the percentage of people who are overweight and a reduction of 10% in the percentage of people who are obese by the year 2005 (this target has been set understanding the difficulties associated with reducing overweight and maintaining a healthy weight)

Actions planned in these areas include:

- implementing the Five Year Framework for Action on Nutrition
- establishing a community nutrition service in each health board
- continuing to promote healthy eating through initiatives like National Healthy Eating Week
- continuing nutrition education for health professionals
- expanding community-based healthy eating initiatives for lower socio-economic groups

Packaging the Healthy Eating Guidelines and communicating an achievable realistic goal to the general population can often be difficult, as shown by the following example.

Research in Ireland into the general public's knowledge and attitudes towards healthy eating is similar to that in many other developed countries. Some people have a good level of nutritional knowledge but many, including health professionals, are confused. Some people feel that changes need to be made by other people but that their own diet is adequate (Conroy, 1994).

Some research carried out specifically into consumer interpretation of healthy eating guidelines has found that simple healthy eating guidelines can often be misinterpreted by the general public; for example the guidelines on eating less fat often translates to eating less red meat and less dairy products, instead of choosing low-fat varieties of these nutritious foods (Flynn *et al.*, 1993).

Therefore the single most important goal in promoting the healthy eating guidelines is to ensure accuracy and consistency in nutritional information. Often this is difficult, for a number of reasons:

- As nutritionists we need to put across a simple and clear message.
- As nutritionists we know what we mean, but the consumer may interpret the message differently.
- The media are more interested in sensational food information and this is often reported instead of sound healthy eating advice. Healthy eating

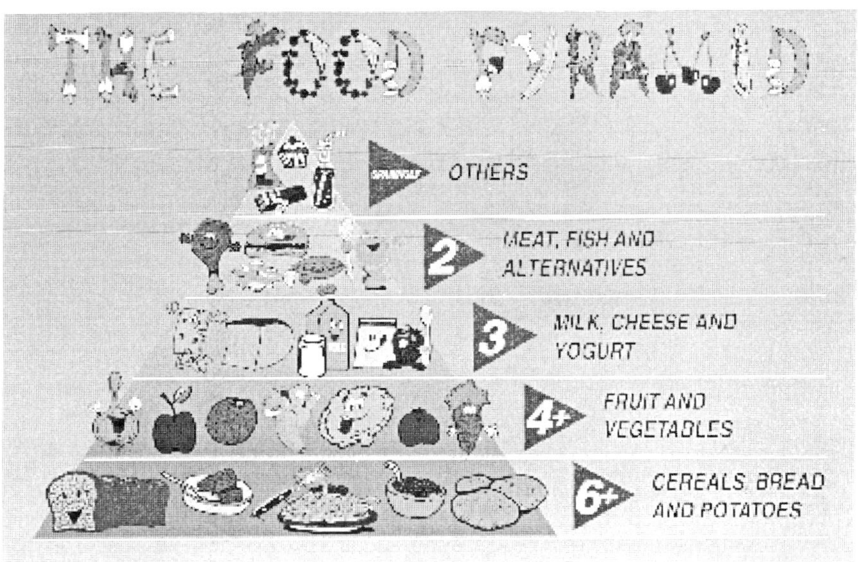

Figure 8.5 (a) Food pyramid; (b) schoolchildren's food pyramid.

messages are perceived as 'boring', although this picture seems to be changing. Perhaps the most important thing we have learned in recent years is the need to talk to our target audience, whether they are the general public, health professionals, caterers or retailers. Then, based on informed discussion regarding attitudes and perceived barriers to healthy eating, this research can be used to produce tailored nutritional education programmes.

Eat More Fruit and Vegetables Campaign. A perfect example of the problems associated with promoting simple, clear healthy eating messages is the message to increase fruit and vegetable consumption.

In 1993, when the food pyramid was being launched, the Health Promotion Unit decided to include fruit and vegetables together on one shelf and to recommend four or more servings a day. Four or more servings were chosen because this seemed a realistic achievable target:

- The national average daily intake was then two servings, so increasing this to four meant doubling current consumption. Recent research has indicated that intake is rising and average intake is about three servings a day, although men generally and those on lower incomes have lower intakes of fruit and vegetables (Health Promotion Unit, 1996).
- For lower socio-economic groups where access to shops may be difficult, coupled with other potential problems such as lack of transport, higher cost in local shops, lack of finances and larger families, four seemed a realistic target.
- Saying four or more means four minimum and more if you can.

Figure 8.6 '4 or more a day' logo.

However, some Irish nutritionists felt that four was too ambitious and perhaps three would have been a better figure to aim for. On the other hand, the fruit and vegetable industry wanted to know why we hadn't chosen five like national promotions in the UK and the USA. The goal chosen for the 1996 Health Eating Campaign was to increase fruit and vegetable intake. So what message should be used – 4 or more a day, 5 a day or simply 'Eat more fruit and vegetables'?

'Eat more fruit and vegetables' was agreed on as the main healthy eating message. However, recent consumer research has shown that many people eating only about two portions of fruit and vegetables a day thought this was enough, so the idea of a target number, which is a realistic target, has also been built into the campaign. So the message is 'Eat more fruit and vegetables' with a by-line '4 or more a day'.

Figure 8.7 'Eat more fruit and vegetables' poster.

So what action was necessary?

- Survey consumers to find out about fruit and vegetable consumption, attitudes to fruit and vegetables and barriers against consuming more.
- Develop nutritional health promotion materials based on survey findings and test these with focus groups before printing.
- Evaluate campaign at the end of the year and also individual key components such as National Healthy Eating Week.

8.8.2 National Healthy Eating Week

Following the launch of the *Nutrition Health Promotion – Framework for Action*, the first National Healthy Eating Week (1992) took place in the Dail Eireann restaurant, Irish Government Buildings. The focus was on healthy options being made available to Ministers, Deputies and Senators, and on informal discussions with the Department of Health dietitian at lunchtimes. This, together with the media focus, led to considerable press coverage and general interest in healthy eating messages.

In 1993, this action was expanded into a National Healthy Eating Week. In order to facilitate national coverage, liaison officers were appointed in each of the eight Irish Health Boards. The liaison officers are central to active regional participation in National Healthy Eating Week as they plan and implement local 'on the ground activities'. The overall theme, media participation and support materials are organized centrally by the Department of Health.

Themes for National Healthy Eating Weeks were:

- 1993 – 'Eat a wide variety of food in the correct amounts' and the food pyramid was introduced to the Irish public (Health Promotion Unit, 1993).
- 1994 – 'Be a healthy weight' – building on the food pyramid concept (Health Promotion Unit, 1994).
- 1995 – 'Eat more breads, cereals and potatoes' – again the emphasis was on the bottom shelf of the food pyramid and highlighted the importance of starchy carbohydrates and high-fibre foods as the basis for a healthy diet (Health Promotion Unit, 1995).
- 1996 – 'Eat more fruit and vegetables' is the theme – focusing on creating awareness of aiming to eat four or more servings of fruit and vegetables a day for better health (Health Promotion Unit, 1996).

Year-Long Healthy Eating Campaign. In 1996 a new approach has been taken – it has been decided to expand the Week into a year-long campaign, launching the theme with a very strong media and community focus during National Healthy Eating Week, but making it a year-long promotion. A year-long focus on fruit and vegetables provides the following benefits:

- more flexibility
- better use of resources
- more opportunity to promote the theme
- reinforcement of a nutritional message
- longer lasting resource materials.

As with all national campaigns on healthy eating, the food pyramid will remain the cornerstone of the promotion, with the fruit and vegetable shelf of the food pyramid being strongly promoted. This approach provides for ongoing continuity with past and future campaigns.

Six main features of the campaign

- Year-long theme
- Key focus National Healthy Eating Week
- Retail industry focus
- Regional resources
- Opportunistic activity
- Evaluation.

The main media and community focus will still be during National Healthy Eating Week for the following reasons:

1. It is possible to enlist the support of liaison officers in each of the Health Boards to plan and implement a week-long intensive activity campaign.
2. It is possible to enlist the help of a wide range of health professionals for one week's activity. These include dietitians (62 participated in National Healthy Eating Week 1996), public health nurses, home economic teachers, physical education teachers and a wide range of media personnel.

The Healthy Food Magazine. The *Healthy Food Magazine*, a 44-page free magazine with healthy eating recipes, was a key ingredient in the success of National Healthy Eating Week in 1995 and 1996.

In 1996 over 300 000 copies were distributed together with more than 500 000 leaflets. The magazine is user friendly and has been used, not only in consumers' own homes, but also in schools, in doctors' and dentists' waiting rooms and with a wide range of audiences.

Other support materials include wooden mobile food pyramids, National Healthy Eating Week street banners, balloons, posters, stickers and logos for media campaigns.

Figure 8.8 Cover of *Healthy Food Magazine.*

Key target audiences for National Healthy Eating Week campaign. The consumer, or food purchaser, and therefore all Irish adults (and many teenagers and schoolchildren), are the key targets for the National Healthy Eating Week campaign. To gain access to as wide a consumer group as possible the following bodies or organizations play a key role:

- Health Boards and health professionals media
- retail trade – supermarkets and shops
- national food agencies
- media, ministers, deputies and senators; personalities
- teachers and other educators
- voluntary health agencies, e.g. Irish Heart Foundation
- workplaces, industrial catering contractors

Figure 8.9 Cover of *Eat more Fruit and Vegetables Magazine*, 1996.

- restaurants and their associations
- Food Writers' Guild
- Irish Countrywomen's Association.

Food Writers' Guild. The Irish Food Writers' Guild is a major component in the success of National Healthy Eating Week. A series of recipes from the Irish Food Writers' Guild is commissioned each year by the Health Promotion Unit and these appear in the healthy eating materials. These recipes are then used by the food writers themselves and other journalists to publicize National Healthy Eating Week and to publicize the healthy eating message throughout the year. Most of the food writers have access to newspapers and magazines via their own columns. Food photography accompanies all recipes.

In 1996, syndicated recipe tapes including healthy eating tips on fruit and vegetables were sent to local and national radio stations to tie in with seasonal bursts of media activity.

8.8.3 Retailers' initiative

One of the criticisms of earlier National Healthy Eating Week campaigns, when the focus was specifically on one week, was that major resources, energy and personnel were being invested in a short-term campaign. The Department of Health needed to consider a campaign that provided on-going information and motivation to the general public to choose healthy food. To satisfy this requirement, a retailer award scheme was devised which included the following key ingredients:

- door stickers for participating supermarkets;
- blank posters for monthly healthy eating special offers;
- monthly action return forms;
- mail out of backup support materials monthly.

In principle the campaign seemed like an excellent idea and met with enthusiasm from many supermarket chains. However, on the ground the support for the campaign varied, depending on priorities of individual supermarkets. A number of problems arose:

- too many supermarket chains were invited to participate in the pilot campaign;
- commitment by the Chief Executive/General Manager of a supermarket chain didn't necessarily translate into commitment on the ground at local level;
- central distribution of materials did not work;
- returning monthly report forms was too time consuming;
- maintaining year-long healthy eating activity proved to be too difficult; many retailers indicated an interest in promoting healthy eating at a few different times throughout the year;
- at individual level, supermarkets requested some one-to-one support to initiate and motivate the campaign.

Evaluation on the ground showed little visibility in the supermarkets for the campaign. Given the level of funding involved it was decided to terminate the campaign and look at how it could be revamped and implemented more successfully, perhaps with a small core group of supermarkets where the one-to-one support could be provided by a community nutritionist or a health promotion officer. Ideas for this revamp are now being discussed with a small number of supermarkets. The key emphasis will be that only three or four bursts of activity per annum on the supermarket floor will be necessary for participation, and that the retailer initiative ties into the year-long healthy eating campaign theme. Another key feature in 1996 was the merchandising carried out by the Health Promotion Unit (with permission from supermarket chains. This was found to be necessary if visibility of healthy eating messages is to be achieved.

8.8.4 Health professionals – public health nurses' initiatives

Having decided to use the food pyramid as a key nutritional education tool together with the Healthy Eating Guidelines, public health nurses were surveyed with regard to the most effective nutritional education approach for them. The following nutritional education programme was decided on:

- An information package including an 8-minute audio-visual cassette on healthy eating using the food pyramid, performed by two actors in one of Ireland's most popular TV soap operas.
- Posters, leaflets and an A4, 20-page, full-colour book with healthy eating information and recipes.
- A list of most often asked questions and answers.
- A briefing by a dietitian at monthly group meetings.

The programme was initiated with a briefing session for superintendent public health nurses from all community care areas in Ireland. This meeting took place in the Department of Health and facilitated direct liaison with dietitians in setting up regional briefing sessions. This programme worked very well, with approximately 90% take-up. Evaluation showed that those who participated, particularly those who had a healthy eating briefing by a dietitian, found the programme to be very useful.

An initiative for general practitioners, which involves a case study approach together with a healthy eating guidelines briefing, is currently being investigated.

8.8.5 National Ploughing Championships

The major rural exhibition event in Ireland each year is the National Ploughing Championships, which is attended by more than 150 000 farmers, their wives and children. In 1995, the Health Promotion Unit in association with the Cereals Association of Ireland exhibited at the championships. The exhibition stand included a free tea/coffee facility for the public which attracted large gatherings throughout the three-day event and offered lots of opportunities to talk about healthy eating with the dietitians. An interactive quiz 'Is your child's diet healthy?' was used to initiate discussion with mothers, and copies of materials, in particular the *Healthy Food Magazine* (available free), were extremely popular.

Participation in this event is to become an annual feature of the nutritional health promotion programme as it allows direct access to Irish farmers and their families – a very important target group who may be difficult to access otherwise.

8.8.6 Low-income groups

A peer-led nutritional initiative has been shown to be a successful method to impact health messages among low-income groups. 'Food and Health' is a nutritional education project, currently under way in a lower socio-economic area of Dublin. Initiated by the Health Promotion Unit of the Department of Health and the Eastern Health Board, it is a peer-led project. A community development approach that views the health professional as a resource to the community is used and the experiences of the community are recognized as contributing to the education process. The project is targeted towards low-income women, as research has shown that women are still pivotal in determining the diets of their families.

During the initial 2-year pilot phase, 13 local women were trained as 'Food and Health' leaders, receiving training in nutritional education and facilitation skills. The nutritional education component centred around a 10-week course covering all aspects of healthy eating and included a practical cooking session to help develop cooking skills. This training course provided the template for courses that the leaders would run themselves. A working resource pack for use by the leaders was written by the project dietitian and reviewed by the leaders, so that the final project was tailored to meet the needs of target groups. The trainers are presently involved in running their own courses within their communities.

At all stages of the project, formal and informal feedback has been actively provided by leaders, participants and project facilitators, with adjustment of the design and format of the 'Food and Health' course and the overall project being made accordingly.

Evaluation of this project is ongoing and a final report from the pilot phase is expected shortly. Early indications from the evaluation show that among the leaders, the percentage of energy from fat dropped significantly with a corresponding improvement in the balance of fats eaten. Daily fibre, folate and vitamin C intakes rose significantly. Nutritional knowledge and attitudes also improved among both leaders and participants on courses, indicating that a peer-led project is an acceptable and effective method to impart nutritional messages among low-income groups. (McDonnell and Foley, 1995)

8.8.7 Other nutrition programmes

A wide range of other nutrition programmes is also under way throughout the country, organized by voluntary organizations, such as the Irish Heart Foundation and the Irish Cancer Society, and generic food agencies.

The Happy Heart Programme described below is a community action programme, which has been developed by the Irish Heart Foundation and has been ongoing since 1990.

The generic food agencies also have a range of consumer nutrition projects, many promoting their products in the context of the food pyramid and using the Healthy Eating Guidelines of the Department of Health. These include the National Dairy Council, An Bord Bia (The Irish Food Board), An Bord Glas (the Irish Fruit and Vegetable Board), An Bord Iascaigh Mhara (The Irish Sea Fisheries Board) and the Cereals Association of Ireland.

Happy Heart Programme. This programme is a heart disease prevention programme run at local community level by volunteers and is developing gradually in counties throughout Ireland. It is supported by the Irish Heart Foundation and the Health Promotion Unit, Department of Health and provides opportunities for health promotion activities, including attention to healthy eating. Counties involved at present include Donegal, Cork, Carlow, Wexford, Mayo, Waterford, Sligo, Galway and the town of Malahide, which initiated and piloted the Happy Heart Programme.

At local level in the Happy Heart areas, nurses, general practitioners, dietitians and other health professionals are working in a voluntary capacity along with lay people to 'spread the word' about healthy life style, including healthy eating.

Two nutrition-related Happy Heart programmes have been under way since 1993.

Happy Heart Eat Out. This is an initiative to provide healthy food choices on menus in selected restaurants, hotels and pubs in the Dublin area and in the Happy Heart areas. The initiative was introduced, supervised and evaluated by dietitians to assess acceptability to caterers and customers. It is hoped that the principles of healthy eating will continue to be included in the menus of the establishments which participated during this one-week programme. Plans for a Happy Heart Eat Out Award for restaurants are currently under way.

Happy Heart at Work. This is being developed by the Irish Heart Foundation to provide a heart-health promotion structure for the workplace. This initiative includes a programme on healthy eating. To date, over 50 companies have been awarded the Happy Heart Healthy Eating Symbol following a catering audit and monitoring visit by a dietitian.

The Irish Heart Foundation published its Nutrition Policy in 1991 (Graham *et al.*, 1991) and this is outlined below.

Irish Heart Foundation Nutrition Policy. The Irish Heart Foundation Nutrition Policy was developed as part of the Foundation's response to the high incidence of heart disease in Ireland. The policy deals primarily with nutritional recommendations for the general population. There is also reference to nutritional recommendations for high-risk individuals and some general recommendations and suggestions regarding the implementation of the policy (Graham *et al.*, 1991).

The nutritional recommendations for the general public are:

- Irish people should be advised to adopt a diet which reduces total fat intake from the current level of 35–40% of food energy to less than 35%. As a longer-term objective, a fat intake of less than 30% of food energy is recommended.
- These recommendations do not apply to children below 5 years of age.
- Not more than one-third of dietary fat should come from saturated fat.
- Saturated fat should be partially replaced by polyunsaturated and monounsaturated fats. Fats from polyunsaturated sources should not comprise more than 10% of total energy.
- Changes in specific foodstuffs to reduce saturated fat intake include the use of low-fat dairy products, lean meat, poultry, fish and vegetable proteins, and reducing consumption of biscuits, cakes and processed meats. Fish consumption should be increased. Low-fat unsaturated spreads are recommended.
- Intake of food energy should be reduced, if necessary, to correct overweight and adjusted to maintain ideal body weight.
- Increased consumption of fruits, vegetables and cereals is recommended. Such foodstuffs provide fibre and help to reduce fat intake.
- Salt intake should be reduced by avoiding table salt, minimizing salt in cooking and by reducing consumption of high-salt processed foods.
- Alcohol consumption should not exceed 21 units/week for men and 14 units/week for women. One unit of alcohol means half a pint of beer, one glass of wine or one small measure of spirits.

The policy expands on these recommendations, translating them into appropriate food choices. A section outlining the scientific background to the document is included, as well as reference to the need for attention to other risk factors for coronary heart disease, along with dietary change.

8.9 The future challenge for the Department of Health

At the end of 1996, the *Nutrition Health Promotion – Framework for Action* 5-year plan has been implemented (Department of Health, 1991). Many of the activities are ongoing; however, a review of the framework and a new plan for the next 3 years, focusing on implementing the recommendations for a Food and Nutrition Policy for Ireland, are currently being developed.

The key recommendations for the further development and implementation of policy on food and nutrition are:

- Policy development and implementation will require the long-term, ongoing and sustained commitment of government. All government departments should be required to take health considerations into account when deciding on policies that influence food production and consumption.
- One organization should be responsible for the implementation and coordination policy measures for food and nutrition.
- Mechanisms for consultation should be established where account can be taken of the views of consumers, scientists, the agri-food industry and regulatory authorities.
- National food consumption surveys of sufficient detail to meet the needs of both nutrition and food safety should be carried out every 5 years.
- Methods to promote healthy eating among at-risk groups should be further investigated.
- A database should be established on national, European Union and international regulations concerning food standards.
- Food producers, processors, retailers and restaurateurs should be encouraged and supported to increase the range of healthy food choices available to consumers.
- A proactive approach should be taken to the dissemination of nutritional information to the public.
- All educational establishments should formulate and implement a nutritional policy and review it regularly.
- Community nutrition and dietetic services should be provided throughout the country. In addition, clinical nutrition services should be developed, in association with general practitioners, in hospitals, nursing homes, ante-natal clinics and day centres for the elderly.
- Monitoring of changes in food consumption and in nutrition-related diseases is essential to the evaluation and ongoing development of policy on food and nutrition in Ireland.

Priority areas for action, based on these recommendations, will be identified for the next 3 years and an action plan developed to meet the challenge of promoting good nutrition and health for all in Ireland into the twenty-first century.

References

Conroy, R.M. (1994) Culture, health beliefs and attitudes in a rural Irish community. *Anthropology Ireland*, **4**, (1), 22–32.

Department of Health (1991) *Nutrition Health Promotion – Framework for Action*, Department of Health, Dublin.

Department of Health (1994) *Shaping a Healthier Future. A Strategy for Effective Healthcare in the 1990s*, Department of Health, Dublin.

Department of Health (1995) *A Health Promotion Strategy*, Department of Health, Dublin.

Flynn, M.A., Codd, M.B., Gibney, M.J. and Sugrue, D.D. (1993) How effective is healthy eating advice for women from different socio-economic groups? *The Proceedings of the Nutrition Society*, **52**, 28A (abstract).

Foley, R.S. (1995) Dietary Changes in the Kilkenny Health Project, 1985 to 1990. MSc Thesis, Trinity College, Dublin.

Graham, I.M., Kilcoyne, D., O'Dwyer, U. and Reid, V. (1991) Irish Heart Foundation Nutrition Policy. *Irish Medical Journal*, **84**, 135–43.

Health Promotion Unit (1993) *Healthy Eating*, Department of Health, Dublin.

Health Promotion Unit (1994) *Be a Healthy Weight*, Department of Health, Dublin.

Health Promotion Unit (1995) *Healthy Food*, Department of Health, Dublin.

Health Promotion Unit (1996) *Eat more Fruit and Vegetables*, Department of Health, Dublin.

Kearney, M. (1994) Studies on attitudes and beliefs for healthy eating promotion: PhD Thesis, Trinity College, Dublin.

Lee, P. and Cunningham, K. (1990) *Irish National Nutrition Survey 1990*, Irish Nutrition and Dietetic Institute.

McDonnell, R.J. and Foley, R.S. (1995) A Community Intervention Project – Nutrition, submitted for publication.

National Nutrition Surveillance Centre (1993) *Nutrition Surveillance in Ireland 1993: Series Report I*, Centre for Health Promotion Studies, University College Galway, Ireland.

National Nutrition Surveillance Centre (1994) *Health Status of the Irish Population 1994: Series Report II*, Centre for Health Promotion Studies, University College Galway, Ireland.

Nutrition Advisory Group (1995) *Recommendations for a Food and Nutrition Policy for Ireland*, Department of Health, Dublin.

9 Nutritional policy in Italy: state of the art

ANNA FERRO-LUZZI and CATHERINE LECLERCQ

9.1 Introduction

The ultimate aim of nutritional policy is to reduce the prevalence of nutrition-related diseases and the social costs and human suffering resulting from them. Nutritional policy is developed according to the specific national circumstances in terms of food supply, food culture, economic conditions and disease patterns. In many aspects, the Italian context is similar to that of other Western affluent societies, with problems of over-consumption and wrong dietary choices rather than of insufficient availability of food. However, Italy presents some specific characteristics which have influenced the elements of nutritional policies developed in the past and that will be crucial for the future of nutritional policy in this country.

Before analysing the Italian situation, it might be useful to recall what is meant by food and nutritional policy and which are the landmarks of its success. According to the definition of the WHO Regional Office for Europe, the food and nutritional policy consists of 'a concerted set of actions based on scientific principles and intended to ensure the safety and the nutritional quality of the food supply and the accessibility of good, affordable and properly labelled food to all population groups, as well as to encourage and facilitate the healthy use of food' (WHO, 1991). In this chapter we shall deal only with the nutritional quality of foods and the associated risks and shall not touch on aspects related to food safety.

It is common wisdom that policies, in order to succeed, require that a consensus exists between all parties concerned, that the interest of the population be the main objective, and that the government is actively involved and supportive. Nutritional policy is no exception. For it to succeed it is necessary that the production, manufacturing and distribution sectors be involved and that this involvement rests on the conviction that it is in their own long-term economic interest to achieve overall healthy nutrition by responding to the documented needs of the population.

Implementing Dietary Guidelines for Healthy Eating. Edited by Verner Wheelock. Published in 1997 by Blackie A&P, an imprint of Chapman & Hall, London. ISBN 0 7514 0304 0

Suggestions of how to develop comprehensive food and nutritional policies in the European context have been offered by Helsing (1991) and are summarized here. First of all it is deemed important that all nutritional policy activities be co-ordinated by a body whose tasks would be to allocate duties to all actors. Two steps are then considered necessary prerequisites: one is the setting up of an information system that will provide useful indicators relative to the status of food and health; the other is the definition of clearly defined and feasible targets (quantitative goals for food and health indicators). The actual implementation of a nutritional policy requires a number of initiatives that can be classified in two broad categories:

1. Actions directed towards the consumers, intending to help them to maintain or modify their life styles. The training of professionals of the health and education sectors, the education of the public, nutritional labelling, food fortification and the legislation intended for ensuring the safety of food all belong to this category.
2. Actions that create an appropriate context for people to make the correct food choices. These actions consist of policy deliberations that are inspired by health and nutritional concerns: agriculture policy, food processing regulations, policy of prices, mass catering regulation, food trade regulation.

There are no set rules about how to develop and implement a food and nutritional policy, because these need to be adapted to the needs and means of each particular country. Analysis of the Italian dietary and public health circumstances allows the specific needs of Italy to be revealed.

9.2 The Italian food consumption patterns

9.2.1 Traditional Italian Mediterranean diet

The geographical position of Mediterranean countries has bestowed them special characteristics as regards climate and soil, leading to an agriculture unique for the variety of its products (Pilo, 1991). Moreover, thanks to its history of land and maritime commercial activity, and to the large place occupied in the culture by delight in good food, a very rich culinary tradition has developed. As the result of these and other factors, the Mediterranean diet is considered a most varied and complete way of eating (Keys, 1995).

The diet consumed by the rural population of Southern Italy in the early 1960s attracted considerable scientific interest, and is often referred to as the typical Mediterranean diet. This diet was based primarily on cereals, fresh vegetables and olive oil. It was low in fat, in animal protein and in cholesterol, and high in fibre (Ferro-Luzzi and Sette, 1989). Dietary styles in Italy were then characterized by a large regional variability. Although differences existed even between neighbouring regions, the largest contrast in dietary patterns was that between northern and southern Italy. At that time, the northern areas consumed a diet three times richer (in g/day) in animal foods (milk, meat, cheese), higher in sugar and with less plant foods, except for potatoes. It also contained far less olive oil, which was substituted by animal fats (Ferro-Luzzi and Branca, 1995). The most contrasting food patterns were found in rural areas due to traditional local habits and recipes for food preparation.This north/south trend has survived to a great extent even today, but was sharper in the 1960s.

9.2.2 Recent trends of the Italian dietary profiles

The largest quantitative and qualitative changes in the Italian diet have occurred since the Second World War (Ferro-Luzzi and Sette, 1989), with a gradual shift towards a higher nutrient density and a progressively altered structure of the diet (Ferro-Luzzi and Sette, 1989; Cialfa, 1991). A recent review points out the early 1950s as the time when the consumption of animal foods (meat, milk and dairy products) and of edible fats began to increase (Ferro-Luzzi and Branca, 1995). Also the consumption of sugar, fruit and vegetables increased, whereas that of cereals decreased slightly. The extent of these changes has been more marked in the south, with the WHO population goals for disease prevention of 'no more than 30% energy from fat' (WHO, 1990) being gradually approached and then even exceeded: the percentage of energy from fat increased from 28% in the 1960s to 36% in the 1980s (ICN, 1992). As a consequence, the north/south differences have been greatly attenuated. However, a clear-cut north/south trend persists within Italy for olive oil intake (80% of total fats and oils in the south versus 20% in the north) and for tomatoes and other fruiting vegetables (almost three times as much in the south with respect to the north). The same north/south trend found within Italy persists between other northern and southern European countries for the same items: these are still key foods characterizing the Mediterranean diet (Ferro-Luzzi *et al.*, 1994a).

Among countries situated around the Mediterranean Basin, the current Italian diet is, with the Greek and the Spanish, that with more 'Mediterranean characteristics'. This emerges quite sharply from the analysis of food balance sheets (Fig. 9.1). In 1988–90, the estimated percentage of energy derived from olive oil was 9% in Italy, far higher than that reported in Portugal (3%) and in France and Yugoslavia (less than 1%). Estimated intake of fruit was 380 g/day in Italy, higher than in Portugal, France and Yugoslavia (mean 200 g/day). Intake of vegetables was 470 g/day in Italy versus 330 g/day in France and 210 g/day in Yugoslavia.

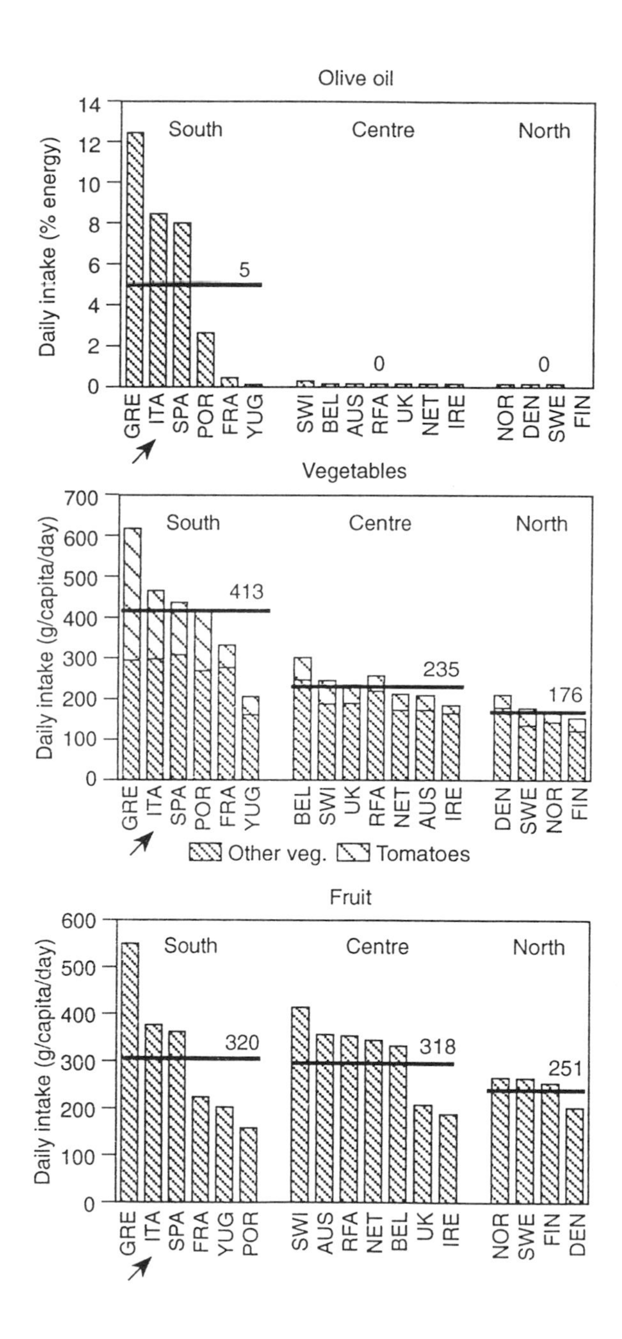

Figure 9.1 Estimated daily intake of some 'key' Mediterranean food items, Europe, 1988–90 (modified from Ferro-Luzzi *et al.*, 1994a).

9.3 Nutrition-related diseases in Italy: scope for prevention?

As in other Western countries, the two first causes of mortality in Italy are cardiovascular diseases and tumours. A clear north/south trend is observed within Italy for standardized mortality rates for coronary heart diseases in men, with higher rates in the north than in the centre and south (Fig. 9.2). In terms of time trends, mortality rates for coronary heart diseases have increased in Italy until the 1970s. A declining trend has been observed in both sexes from the early 1980s, more than 10 years later than in the US and in other Western countries but gathering pace. During the same period, a biologically compatible decreasing trend has been observed in the level of the major coronary risk factors (Menotti and Scanga, 1992). In the south the decrease in coronary heart diseases has been far less important than in the north (Barchielli and Cecchi, 1990).

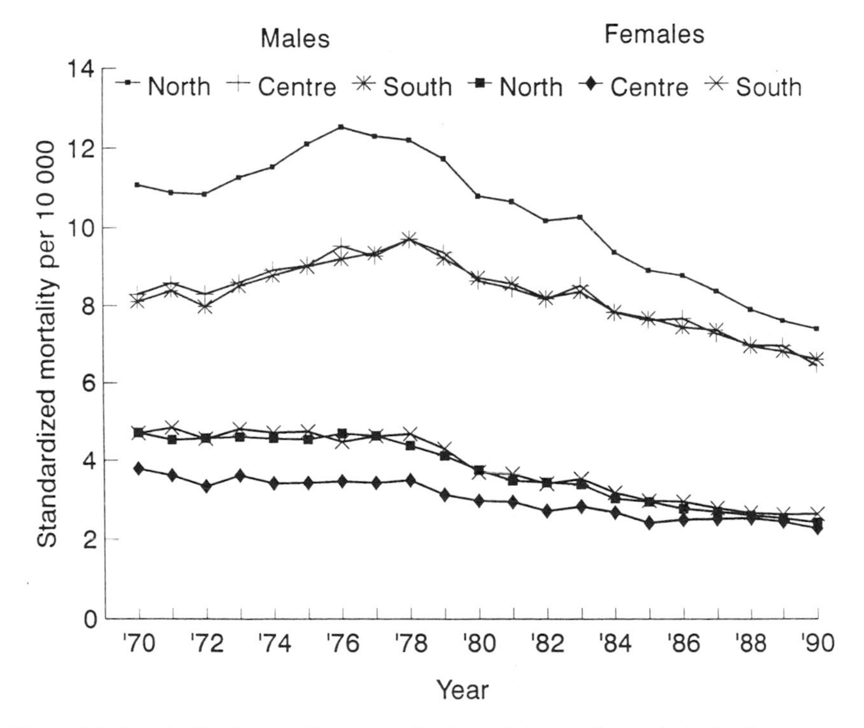

Figure 9.2 Standardized mortality rates of ischaemic heart disease in Italy (the rates were standardized for the 1971 Italian population census). Time trends by gender and by broad geographical areas (1970–90) (source: Capocaccia *et al.*, 1993).

As for nutrition-related tumours, mortality in both sexes is still lower in southern European countries than in the northern ones, even if a systematic tendency towards levelling of various rates is observed, with increasing rates in

Mediterranean countries (La Vecchia *et al.*, 1991). Among these countries, the lowest rates are found in Greece, Italy, Portugal and Spain. A character shared by all European countries is the large within-country geographical variability in tumour rates. Italy is no exception: for all tumours with a recognized dietary risk factor, the ratio between the highest and the lowest regional standardized mortality rate is 2 or more (Capocaccia *et al.*, 1993). On the whole, rates are higher in northern Italy than in southern Italy (Merlo *et al.*, 1991). In terms of time trends, the only nutrition-related tumour with decreasing death rate during the past 10 years was stomach cancer. For the others, death rates were either stable or on the increase. The same unfavourable trends have been observed in other Mediterranean countries (La Vecchia *et al.*, 1991).

How much these trends can be attributed to dietary habits is difficult to say. However, the very existence of trends over time and across regions in the death rates due to the two main groups of nutrition-related diseases suggests that there is scope for prevention. In fact these trends are presumably determined by environmental factors – diet among them. Based on this consideration, IARC (The International Agency for Research on Cancer) suggests using the lowest rates observed as the target level to be achieved through preventive measures (Smars, Muir and Boyle, 1992).

Other nutrition-related conditions with high social costs are obesity (the Italian prevalence is one of the highest in Europe), non-insulin-dependent diabetes, osteoporosis, liver cirrhosis, goitre, iron deficiency anaemia and tooth decay (Ferro-Luzzi *et al.*, 1994b). For most of these diseases the prevention measures through dietary intervention are well defined and their efficacy is proven.

9.4 Nutritional policy in Italy: relevant mandate of public institutions and their activities

The Italian institutional bodies that are somehow involved in activities of relevance for a nutritional policy and their current activities are illustrated in Fig. 9.3. The two main authorities involved in nutritional policy activities at national level are the Ministry of Health and the Ministry of Agriculture. The regional districts have their own authorities involved in such activities, both at regional level, through the Regional Health Authority and the Regional Agriculture Authority, and at subregional level, through the Local Health Centres. As yet, there is no central intersectorial structure with the overall authority to plan and co-ordinate the parallel activities undertaken by the whole set of bodies involved. A detailed analysis of the functions and competence of these bodies, of their links and of their activities in the past 20 years is given below. Since the agriculture sector and the public health sector have moved in a somewhat independent way, their mandate and activities will be illustrated separately.

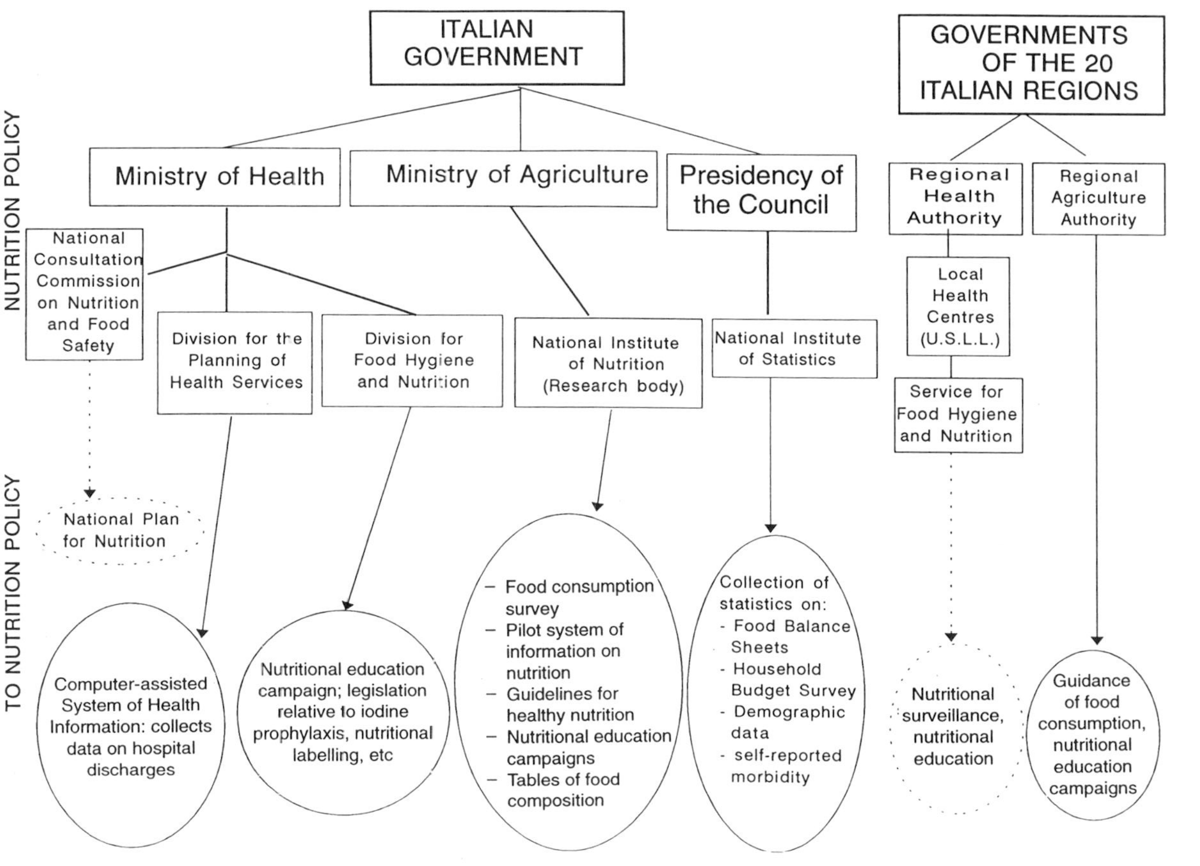

Figure 9.3 Nutritional policy in Italy in the 1990s: the main bodies and their areas of intervention.

9.4.1 The agriculture sector

The Italian Ministry of Agriculture is in charge of the national food policy, which is developed mainly in three divisions: Agricultural production, Economics of mountainous areas and forests, Economic monitoring of agricultural products. Ensuring the supply of sufficient food at national level is no longer a problem for Italy: food policy is now directed at ensuring the quality and reliability of agricultural products, either processed or not. The main tool is legislation which governs the methods and procedures of agricultural production and of the preservation, processing and distribution of food (Saccomandi, 1991). Another important instrument of food policy is the Common Agriculture Policy which disciplines most of the agricultural production in all EU countries.

Although unintentionally, the national food policy inevitably affects the dietary pattern of the population and therefore its nutrition status. Thus, for example, the stabilization of the price of olive oil through subsidies of the European Union for its production and sales has enabled its consumption to be maintained by compensating its higher production costs and has avoided its substitution with fats with less favourable fatty acid profiles or antioxidative properties. There are many other examples of interference between food policy and nutritional status; they will not be dealt with here. It is worth mentioning that the rationale for decisions such as subsidies has been the support of agricultural and economic sectors and not the improvement of the nutritional status of the population. Thus, Italian food policy may not at present be considered part of a nutritional policy since decisions are taken without an explicit nutritional concern.

However, since the 1960s the Ministry of Agriculture has also promoted other important initiatives aimed at assessing and improving the nutritional status of the population. These initiatives have been realized in collaboration with the National Institute of Nutrition which depends on the Ministry of Agriculture and conducts research in food science and in human nutrition. It also hosts a WHO collaborating centre for nutrition policy. This institute has received specific funding from the Ministry of Agriculture to perform activities of nutritional surveillance and of nutritional education and has co-ordinated the process of setting tools and targets for nutrition.

Activities of nutritional surveillance. In 1980 the Ministry of Agriculture funded the first nationwide survey on food consumption in Italy, specifically aimed at nutritional surveillance. It was conducted by the National Institute of Nutrition and covered 10 000 households (Cialfa, Turrini and Lintas, 1991). A second survey is under way and is also nationwide. Despite the reasonable interval between the two surveys, this was a chance happening rather than a planned outcome. In fact, no permanent provision exists for the periodic repetition of the survey, thus it may not be considered an element of a continuous surveillance system.

Tools and target-setting process. National tables of food composition are an important tool for assessing the nutrient intake of the population. The first Italian tables were developed by the National Institute of Nutrition in 1946. The last revised edition of these tables was published in 1994.

A second important tool is the list of recommended daily allowances (RDAs) for the Italian population. They were first formulated in 1973 by an *ad hoc* expert group as an initiative of the Italian Society for Nutrition (SINU). They are adapted to the specific Italian circumstances and are revised periodically (Italian Society for Human Nutrition, 1996).

The Dietary Guidelines for a Healthy Nutrition have been elaborated in 1986 by an *ad hoc* expert advisory commission co-ordinated by the National Institute of Nutrition. They are qualitative rather than quantitative and largely reflect the traditional Italian dietary pattern. They consist of a folded colourful leaflet with a voluminous scientific dossier (National Institute of Nutrition, 1986). They are now being updated.

Educational campaigns. In the past 20 years several national campaigns have been performed by the Ministry of Agriculture in collaboration with the National Institute of Nutrition. In 1986 the regular conduct of educational campaigns was formalized through the Agriculture Act n. 752. In this act, the Interministerial Economic Planning Committee designated the National Institute of Nutrition as the appropriate body to organize national information campaigns directed at the consumer to guide food consumption patterns for nutritional education purposes.

Various campaigns have been realized for the promotion of individual foods considered healthy, e.g. olive oil, 'blue fish'. We shall illustrate only those campaigns that addressed the entire diet. Both their information content and the strategy of its transfer to the population have evolved over time in the attempt to respond to the true information need of the Italian population and to become increasingly more effective.

The first national campaign was conducted in 1975. In those years, problems of undernutrition still persisted, especially in the less developed areas of southern Italy. The main objective of the campaign was thus to promote the consumption of a sufficient and nutritious diet. Therefore the issues addressed by this campaign were the nutrient content of foods, how to avoid losses of nutrients during the cooking process, which foods should be present in the diet, etc. A national conference on nutritional education was organized in Rome, involving the scientific community and the information and education sectors. It was followed by a series of courses held in eight cities throughout the country aimed at updating secondary school science teachers in nutritional matters. Science teachers were expected then to transfer the information to schoolchildren. The campaign included the publication and distribution of the proceedings to the education sector and of two books to the general population: *Nutrition of Mother and Child* (Pedicino, 1979) and *Foods as They are Consumed* (Spina, 1980).

A second campaign was conducted in 1981. The aim in this case was the promotion of the nutritional and health benefits of the Mediterranean diet for the prevention of chronic degenerative diseases. The population was advised to combine seven food groups in their diet:

1. meat, fish and egg products;
2. milk and milk products;
3. cereals and tubers;
4. legumes;
5. fats;
6. fruit and vegetables, main sources of carotenoids;
7. fruit and vegetables, main sources of vitamin C.

The third campaign was conducted between 1986 and 1988. The prevention of chronic degenerative diseases was the main objective. The seven messages (National Institute of Nutrition, 1986) contained in Dietary Guidelines for a Healthy Nutrition were:

1. mind your body weight;
2. more vegetable starch and more fibre;
3. salt: little is better;
4. why and how to vary your diet;
5. alcohol: if you drink do so in moderation;
6. sweets: how and how much;
7. less fats and cholesterol.

These are advisory guidelines of a non-quantitative nature that emphasize the importance of an overall healthy eating pattern rather than promoting the consumption of single food items. The leaflets were printed in a simple and attractive way. Four million guidelines were dispatched to 23 000 family physicians and 3 million to 9000 chemists throughout Italy (Ticca, 1991). The choice of using health professions as a channel to the general population was guided by the thought that these professionals could act as guarantors of reliability of the campaign and single out the families at higher risk and thus needing nutritional advice with higher priority. In addition to the leaflets, the physicians were sent a complete set of documentation, including the scientific dossier of the guidelines, a commented version of the Italian RDAs and a commented version of the Italian tables of food composition (see above) so that they would be updated on the matter and provide correct nutritional advice to their patients.

Different media were used: the dietary guidelines, with the same striking multicoloured logo, were transmitted through television, magazines and newspapers so as to reach as many Italians as possible, and more than once. A series of seven instructional films, each relative to one of the seven dietary guidelines, was diffused during a very popular television programme (audience 4 million to 8 million Italians). This material was integrated with specifically developed cartoons and a set of seven videotapes was produced for free distribution to any organization requiring it. A set of two simpler videotapes was produced for schoolchildren. Collaborations were also established with food processing and food catering firms which reprinted and distributed the dietary guidelines.

The real novelty of this wide and well-designed campaign was that it included an evaluation of impact. The efficacy was assessed by a representative sample of housewives extracted in 81 municipalities (Crisci, 1988). Out of 800 women, 62% remembered the main slogan of the campaign 'eat better to live better' whereas individual guidelines were remembered by 12–19%. The women that had been exposed more than once to the message (for example, because they read at least two magazines participating in the campaign) were better at recalling the messages. All this indicated, in advertising terms, that the campaign had had a real communicative efficacy. The women were asked to report any modification in their frequency of consumption of various food items during the period of the campaign. A decrease in frequency of consumption of red meat and an increase in white meats, fruit juice, milk and eggs were noted.

Altogether, more than 7 million leaflets containing the dietary guidelines were distributed in that campaign. The proportion of the population reached was therefore relatively higher than in the USA where 8 million copies of dietary guidelines were distributed for a population four times that of Italy.

The production sector was simultaneously involved in a campaign for the promotion of 10 native products of Italian agriculture. They were were fruit products (fruit juice, citrus fruit, grapes and peaches) and animal products (rabbit, ovine meat/goat meat, trout, poultry, bovine meat, eggs). These foods are characterized by either overproduction or by the availability of potential new markets within Italy. The mandate was economic (to support weak sectors of Italian agriculture and to support the payment balance of the country) whereas the promotional messages were based on both the nutritional value and the gastronomic attributes of the products (Istituto di Tecnica e Propaganda Agraria, 1987). This campaign was funded by the Ministry of Agriculture but was not in full agreement with the campaign for Healthy Nutrition: out of the 10 products promoted, six were of animal origin (including one red meat), contrary to the recommendations of the dietary guidelines. However, on the whole, the combination of the two campaigns was positive. Perhaps it was due to their involvement in the promotional campaign that the Italian supply sector did not react negatively to the dietary guidelines. A strong reaction, such as that of US food producers, could have counteracted the suggestion to moderate the consumption of some food products (salt, alcohol, animal fats and sugar) and this might have reduced the impact of the overall campaign.

Independent of the activities of the Ministry of Agriculture, several regional districts – especially in the north of Italy – have taken initiatives of nutritional education, mainly through primary and secondary schools. In fact, since 1977, the regional agriculture authorities have been delegated the task of promotion and guidance in food consumption matters and of planning interventions according to the specific needs of the population. Such a mandate has been given to them by a Presidential Decree (n. 616/77, art. 77) of the central government which granted the 20 Italian regional governments with great autonomy of decision and action in various sectors. The central government is theoretically in charge of co-ordinating and directing all activities undertaken by the regional authorities but no structure has been given the specific mandate to co-ordinate activities in the sector of nutritional education. The ensuing autonomy of decision and of action led to an undesirable fragmentation of all the operations undertaken throughout Italy in this sector (Ticca, 1988).

9.4.2 The public health sector

The Italian Ministry of Health is involved in nutritional policy activities mainly through two Divisions: the Division for Food Hygiene and Nutrition and the Division for the Planning of Health Services. It also acts upon food safety and hygiene matters through one of its bodies, the National Institute of Health. This body is omitted in Fig. 9.3 as we do not deal in this chapter with these aspects of nutritional policy.

Nutritional education by the Ministry of Health. Preventing nutrition-related diseases through diet modification represents a highly challenging option for the health sector of most countries. Italy is no exception and the Ministry of Health has formally adopted nutritional education as its main *modus operandi*.

One of the largest educational campaigns ever launched by the Ministry of Health has been the 'National Campaign for Nutrition Education and

Information' conducted in 1990. Although not co-ordinated with the campaigns of the Ministry of Agriculture, its messages were checked by the National Institute of Nutrition and brought into line with the national dietary guidelines (see above). The first aim of the campaign was to give technical and scientific support to the local health centres of the National Health Service in their task of educating people in food matters (Ticca, 1991). Public health staff were the main target of the campaign. They received sets of six small volumes related to the 'Theory and practice of healthy eating' (Ministry of Health, 1990):

1. Principles of Human Nutrition
2. Varied and Balanced Eating Patterns for the Adult
3. Food Consumption in Specific Physiological Conditions
4. Eating Pattern for the Prevention of Some Prevalent Pathologies
5. Safety of Food and Beverages from Production to Consumption
6. Methodological and Operational Aspects of Nutrition Education

A set of eight booklets was also prepared for distribution to the general population, in collaboration with consumer associations:

1. Balanced Eating Pattern for Women during Pregnancy and Lactation
2. Balanced Eating Pattern from Birth to Adolescence
3. Balanced Eating Pattern for the Adult
4. Balanced Eating Pattern for the Elderly
5. Safety Aspects of Foods and Beverages from Production to Consumption
6. Alcoholic Drinks: Invitation to Moderation
7. Diet, Cholesterol and Prevention of Cardiovascular Diseases
8. Prevention of Food Intolerance

Another means of educating the population in nutrition matters is to label foods for their nutritional content. The aim of nutritional labelling is quite ambitious: the general population should read the labels (at present very few do so in Italy), understand the information and modify their consumption accordingly. To fulfil the EU Directive (90/496/CEE), an Italian Presidential Decree (16 February 1993, n. 77) authorizes the labelling of any food with its content in macronutrients according to a precisely defined format; it also makes such labelling compulsory for food items that bear a nutritional claim. The nutritional label may also include the content of those vitamins and minerals present or added in a 'significant quantity', i.e. at least 15% of the RDAs in 100 g of products and/or in a standard portion. In this case, the exact proportion of the RDA covered must be mentioned on the label in order to increase the capacity of the consumer to interpret the information given (Scarpa, 1995).

Regional activities of the public health sector. The operational units of the Italian public health sector are the local health centres (USSL) which are co-ordinated by the Regional Health Authorities (Assessorati Regionali alla Sanità). Health services are provided and managed through the various departments in which the USSL are organized. In 1993, a Decree (n. 517/93) created within their Department of Prevention a new service, the Service for Food Hygiene and Nutrition, whose mandate is to control the hygiene of food and beverages and to conduct nutritional surveillance and nutritional education activities. With this aim in mind, the USSL are requested to collect their own data on food consumption so as to monitor the dietary risk and the nutritional status of the local population. However, neither the funding nor the technical staff are as yet in place, thus these services are operational only in a few pilot USSL.

First steps towards an integrated nutrition policy: the National Consultation Commission for Nutrition and Food Safety and the National Plan of Action for Nutrition. Since 1990, the Directorate for Food Hygiene and Nutrition of the Italian Ministry of Health has been very active in trying to design an integrated nutritional policy within the health sector. An important step was the creation of the National Consultation Commission for Nutrition and Food Safety (Consulta Nazionale per la Nutrizione e la Sicurezza degli Alimenti), a central organ of decision aimed at co-ordinating the activities undertaken within a national nutritional policy and at monitoring their effects. It was established in 1990 with the mandate of co-ordinating:

1. the updating of dietary recommendations for the population;
2. prevention initiatives such as education in nutrition and healthy food choices;
3. the development of a system of information on nutrition (Ministry of Health, 1990).

The members are senior staff of the Ministries of Agriculture, Industry, Health, and of regional authorities, together with representatives of consumer associations. The Consultation Commission remains nevertheless an organ of the Ministry of Health. It has its own Scientific Committee, which includes scientists of the National Institute of Nutrition, technical personnel of the health system and university lecturers and has a consultative mandate. Since the creation of the National Advisory Commission, the Scientific Committee has been consulted twice, once in relation to the implementation of a Nutrition Information System at national level and once to comment on the mandates that should be given to the Services of Food Hygiene and Nutrition of the local health centres (see above).

As a further step, the Division of Food Hygiene and Nutrition has drafted a National Plan of Action to be developed in application of the commitments made by the Italian Ministry of Health at the FAO/WHO International Conference of Nutrition (Scarpa, 1995). This draft proposal is now under examination by the Italian parliament. It is quite ambitious and would revolve around a Centre of Information on Nutrition which would elaborate the data collected by a System of Information on Nutrition, to be established within the already existing Health Information Network (SIS). A pilot national nutritional surveillance system has recently been developed by the National Institute of Nutrition by request of the Ministry of Health (Ferro-Luzzi *et al.*, 1994b) and will probably be useful to this aim. The system is meant to warn the Ministry in relation to undesirable changes in the eating habits of the population and in the prevalence of nutrition-related diseases. The main feature of the system is that it makes exclusive recourse to secondary data. It is described in detail in Chapter 1 of this volume.

9.5 An overall analysis of nutritional information from public and private sources in Italy

The cardinal element of nutritional policy in Italy has always been nutritional education through public campaigns. The past 20 years have been characterized by evolution of the messages and strategies of such campaigns. However, there is scope for further improvement. A close look at Fig. 9.3 shows that five bodies are in charge of nutritional education: the first and second – the Division for Food Hygiene and Nutrition of the Ministry of Health and the National Institute of Nutrition (depending on the Ministry of Agriculture) – both operate at the national level; the third and fourth – the Regional Health Authorities and the Regional Agriculture Authorities – have jurisdiction in each of the 20 regional districts; and the fifth – the Local Health Centres – have a catchment area limited to the subprovincial level. The educational campaigns launched by these public structures have suffered so far by lack of follow-up, by lack of standardization of the messages to the public and by lack of co-ordination between the diverse campaigns. In fact, the budgetary decisions taken in this sector have not allowed, until now, the planning of nutritional education activities and their monitoring in the long term. Moreover, regional and local initiatives have not been adequately controlled at central level. Duplication of efforts (elaboration of messages, editing and printing of booklets, identification of suitable channels for distribution, etc.) and heterogeneity of messages have probably led to high costs/benefit ratios compared to the ratio that might be obtained with centrally co-ordinated campaigns (Ticca, 1991).

Of course, messages related to nutrition coming from private sources are not standardized. As we shall see, these messages often openly contradict each other and, what is worse, those generated by public institutions.The two main private sources of nutritional information are the food industry and the mass media.

The promotion of products is essential to food industries: their investment in advertisements is understandably large and, compared to the budget of the public sector for nutritional information, it appears disproportionally greater. Thus, in 1994, 4146 billion Italian lire were spent on advertisements for food and beverages, whereas overall 255 billion lire were spent on public information relative to health (Nielsen and NASA, unpublished data). Since nutritional information represents less than 25% of health information (Ercoli, 1988), it can be stated that in 1994 the budget of the public sector for nutritional education amounts to less than 2% of that spent by the food industry for food and beverage promotion. Among all sources of information on food and nutrition, advertisements are likely to have had the largest impact on food choices. The quality of the information generated by the food industry is varied. In a few cases, the promotional messages place a specific food product in the context of an overall healthy eating pattern, for example pasta has been promoted as part of a desirable diet by a major Italian food company. However, most food industries either promote their individual line of products without any reference to nutritional aspects or with incorrect nutritional information.

Those industries that produce foods that are to be maintained at lower levels of consumption in the context of a healthy diet often enter the scientific debate with unsound information directed to stir up any existing scientific controversy. Thus, for example, the consumption of milk and milk products and red meat should be moderated due to their cholesterol and saturated fatty acid content. The producers' associations of both these sectors have reacted to such advice. A poster is now hanging in most Italian butcher shops extolling the health-promoting qualities of meat. On the other hand, the Italian dairy sector is the sponsor of many scientific conferences on the topic of milk and health, in which the problems related to high intakes of dairy products are not mentioned.

In other cases, food products have been promoted with scientifically unsupported nutritional claims that may lead a health-conscious consumer to assign wrong priorities in his food choices or to choose the wrong product.

This source of misinformation is now being brought under more effective control. Since 1992 private citizens or associations who believe that an advertisement is misleading can appeal to an *ad hoc* Guarantor (Decree 25.2.92, n.74). The Guarantor can avail itself of technical expertise on the matter. In the case of food products, the National Institute of Nutrition is one of the expert structures called upon to provide this expertise. A later Decree (16.2.93 n. 77) particularly refers to nutritional claims as used for the promotion of food products; it specifies that nutritional claims may not mention any effect on health but must be limited to description of the specific nutrient content of the product. The draft of the National Plan of Action (see above) goes one step further when it specifies that the above-mentioned Guarantor will in future systematically check all advertisements for products aimed at weight reduction. The government is obviously attempting, through expanding legislation, to make it increasingly difficult for the food industry to disseminate misleading nutritional information through advertisement.

The other private source of nutritional information is the mass media. The press may magnify scientific controversies on the health impact of foods and nutrients, or present the information out of an overall context or even distort new evidence, so that the reader might end up in some cases being confused or led to incorrect conclusions. For example undue stress may be put on the risk of a specific food or nutrient, contrary to the dietary guidelines which advise moderation in consumption of some foods without excluding any of them. This manipulation of the information might be decreasing as an increasing number of national newspapers and magazines are now submitting their articles to the National Institute of Nutrition for guidance on scientific accuracy and consistency with the dietary guidelines.

9.6 Conclusions

Italy lacks, as yet, a multisectorial integrated nutritional policy. None the less, if one looks more closely at the current picture, a certain number of prerequisites are already present in terms of legislation, institutional bodies and actions undertaken. Integration of the initiatives and expertise already existing would easily lead to a relatively advanced nutritional policy.

The high degree of decentralization in Italy undoubtedly creates a substantial challenge. Policies need to be modulated at regional level, given the regional variability of the dietary risks and of the disease patterns. However, there is an obvious need for central co-ordination of all activities to be undertaken, involving both the Ministry of Health and the Ministry of Agriculture in an integrated food and nutritional policy.

Preserving and rediscovering the Mediterranean diet is recognized as the most appropriate measure for the prevention of nutrition-related diseases in Italy. The promotion of the traditional dietary pattern is an easily accepted message as this diet is still part of the local culture. It is also likely to be effective since a large body of evidence shows that this dietary profile is consistent with lower rates of ischaemic heart diseases and of various cancers. Typical Italian food products tend to feature among the foods classified as being health-protective, including olive oil, fruit, pasta, garlic, onions, tomatoes and other vegetables. The implication of this measure is that the promotion, for purely economic purposes, of these lines of products would have a positive spin-off for the health of the consumer. At the same time, it should be relatively easy to recruit the interest and the support of the majority of the Italian food production and manufacturing sectors to a nutritional policy. However, the objectives of the supply side and of the health sector diverge on some aspects, and the consumption of some local food products needs to be kept under control for health promotion reasons. Politicians need to be convinced that such losses are small with respect to the long-term benefits to be derived by the whole nation from a decrease of nutrition-related diseases.

Acknowledgements

The authors are most grateful to Dr F. Branca, Dr L. Martino, Dr B. Scarpa and Professor M. Ticca for their helpful comments.

References

Barchielli, A. and Cecchi, F. (1990) Le malattie cardiovascolari, in *La Salute Degli Italiani.* Rapporto 1990 (ed. M. Geddes), La Nuova Italia Scientifica, Rome, pp. 63–80.

Capocaccia, R., Farchi, G., Prati, S. *et al.* (1993) *La Mortalità in Italia Nell'anno 1990.* ISTISAN report, National Institute of Health, Rome.

Cialfa, E. (1991) Food consumption in Italy: present situation and trends, in *Food and Nutrition Policy in Mediterranean Europe.* Proceedings of a WHO Symposium. WHO C.C. Nutr. Ser. n. 1 (eds A. Ferro-Luzzi, E. Cialfa and C. Leclercq), National Institute of Nutrition, Rome, pp. 63–82.

Cialfa, E., Turrini, A. and Lintas, C. (1991) A National Food Survey. Food balance sheets and other methodologies. A critical overview, in *Monitoring Dietary Intakes* (ed. I. Macdonald), Springer-Verlag, Berlin, pp. 23–44.

Crisci, M.T. (1988) *Verifica dell'efficacia di una campagna di informazione alimentare attraverso la stampa.* Atti del convegno 'L'informazione alimentare e le istituzioni', Parma, 6 May 1988. National Institute of Nutrition and Ministry of Agriculture and Forestry, Rome, pp. 24–8.

Ercoli, E. (1988) *Informazione ed educazione alimentare nei programmi del Servizio Sanitario Nazionale.* Atti del convegno 'L'informazione alimentare e le istituzioni', Parma, 6 May 1988. National Institute of Nutrition and Ministry of Agriculture and Forestry, Rome, pp. 19–24.

Ferro-Luzzi, A. and Branca, F. (1995) Mediterranean diet, Italian-style: prototype of a healthy diet. *American Journal of Clinical Nutrition*, **61**, (S), 1338–45.

Ferro-Luzzi, A. and Sette, S. (1989) The Mediterranean diet: an attempt to define its present and past composition. *European Journal of Clinical Nutrition*, **43**, (S2), 13–29.

Ferro-Luzzi, A., Cialfa E., Leclercq, C. and Toti, E. (1994a) The Mediterranean diet revisited. Focus on fruit and vegetables. *International Journal of Food Sciences and Nutrition*, **45**, 291–300.

Ferro-Luzzi, A., Leclercq, C., Martino, L. and Berardi, D. (1994b) *SIN – Sistema Informativo Nutrizionale*. Monografie dei Quaderni della Nutrizione, National Institute of Nutrition, Rome.

Helsing, E. (1991) Development of a food and nutrition policy, in *Food and Nutrition Policy in Mediterranean Europe*, Proceedings of a WHO Symposium. WHO C.C. Nutr. Ser. n. 1 (eds A. Ferro-Luzzi, E. Cialfa and C. Leclercq), National Institute of Nutrition, Rome, pp. 83–94.

ICN (International Conference on Nutrition) (1992) *Italian Country Paper for the International Conference on Nutrition*, National Institute of Nutrition, Rome.

Istituto di Tecnica e Propaganda Agraria (1987) *Per una Sana Alimentazione Italiana.Le Basi Scientifiche. La Campagna di Valorizzazione MAF. L'informazione*, Istituto di Tecnica e Propaganda Agraria, Rome.

Italian Society for Human Nutrition (1986) *Livelli di Assunzione Giornalieri Raccomandati di Energia e Nutrienti per la Popolazione Italiana*, 2nd edn, National Institute of Nutrition, Rome.

Keys, A. (1995) Mediterranean diet and public health: personal reflections. *American Journal of Clinical Nutrition*, 61, 1321S-1323S.

La Vecchia, C., Lucchini, F., Negri, E. and Levi, F. (1991) Patterns and trends in mortality from selected cancers in Mediterranean countries, in *The Mediterranean Diet and Cancer Prevention* (eds A. Giacosa and M.J. Hill), National Institute for Cancer Research, Genova.

Menotti, A. and Scanga, M. (1992) Trends in coronary risk factors in Italy. *International Journal of Epidemiology*, **21**, 883–91.

Merlo, F., Filiberti, R., Reggiardo, G., Giacosa, A. and Visconti, P. (1991) Regional and temporal differences in the Italian diet and their relationship with cancer risk, in *The Mediterranean Diet and Cancer Prevention* (eds A. Giacosa and M.J. Hill), National Institute for Cancer Research, Genova.

Ministry of Health (1990) *Teoria e Pratica Della Sana Alimentazione*, Campagna Straordinaria di educazione alimentare e di informazione dei consumatori, Ministry of Health, Rome.

National Institute of Nutrition (1986) *Linee Guida per una Sana Alimentazione Italiana*, Dossier scientifico di base, National Institute of Nutrition, Rome.

Pedicino, V. (1979) *L'alimentazione della Madre e del Bambino*, Ministry of Agriculture and Forestry and National Institute of Nutrition, Rome.

Pilo, V. (1991) Gearing the Mediterranean agro-alimentary sector to a health-promoting dietary model, in *Food and Nutrition Policy in Mediterranean Europe*. Proceedings of a WHO Symposium. WHO C.C. Nutr. Ser. n. 1 (eds A. Ferro-Luzzi, E. Cialfa and C. Leclercq), National Institute of Nutrition, Rome, pp. 205–10.

Saccomandi, V. (1991) Linking agricultural policy with policy for food and nutrition, in *Food and Nutrition Policy in Mediterranean Europe*. Proceedings of a WHO Symposium. WHO C.C. Nutr. Ser. n. 1 (eds A. Ferro-Luzzi, E. Cialfa and C. Leclercq), National Institute of Nutrition, Rome, pp. 201–4.

Scarpa, B. (1995) Necessità di una migliore informazione alimentare, in *Alimentarsi bene da piccoli, per crescere sani e restare in salute da adulti*. Proceedings of a workshop of the European Food Information Council, Milan, 7 November 1995.

Smans, M., Muir, C.S. and Boyle, P. (1992) *Atlas of Cancer Mortality in the European Community*, IARC Scientific Publications n. 107, IARC, Lyons.

Spina, A.A. (1980) *Gli Alimenti Così Come li Consumiamo*, Ministry of Agriculture and Forestry and National Institute of Nutrition, Rome.

Ticca, M. (1988) *L'informazione Alimentare Pubblica in Italia*. in Atti del convegno 'L'informazione alimentare e le istituzioni', Parma, 6 May 1988. National Institute of Nutrition and Ministry of Agriculture and Forestry, Rome, pp. 15–17.

Ticca, M. (1991) Food and nutrition policy: the Italian experience, in *Food and Nutrition Policy in Mediterranean Europe*. Proceedings of a WHO Symposium. WHO C.C. Nutr. Ser. n. 1 (eds A. Ferro-Luzzi, E. Cialfa and C. Leclercq), National Institute of Nutrition, Rome, pp. 153–60.

WHO (1990) *Diet, nutrition, and the prevention of chronic diseases.* Report of a WHO Study Group. *WHO Technical Report Series 797.*

WHO (1991) *Food and Nutrition Policy in Europe*, Report of a WHO Conference, WHO Regional Office for Europe, Copenhagen.

10 The national nutritional policy in New Zealand

JANET WEBER and JULIET WISEMAN

10.1 Introduction

New Zealand is an agricultural country with a high national consumption of beef, sheep meat, dairy products and bread. The diet is British based but with some influence from traditional Maori eating, for example the use of kumara (sweet potatoes), and from a wide range of immigrant populations including Chinese and European. Information about the New Zealand diet is scarce, only three national surveys have been carried out – one in 1926 (Gregory *et al.*, 1934) one in 1977 (Birkbeck, 1980) and the Hillary Commission Survey in 1990 (Horwath *et al.*, 1991). Some trends in food consumption can be seen from food balance sheets, published by the Department of Statistics since 1982. Recent changes include consumption of more processed foods (i.e. less flour but more biscuits, less potatoes but more chips and crisps) and an increasing number of meals eaten away from home (Bailey and Earle, 1993).

Diet-linked health issues have changed from concern about under-nutrition earlier this century, particularly iodine deficiency. Today cardio-vascular diseases and diet-associated cancers are the main causes for concern. Food is the most important industry in New Zealand and food industries have clearly influenced food policy. For example, prior to 1972 margarine could not be obtained except on prescription; the sale of margarine in New Zealand was strongly opposed by the dairy industry. A recent example of food industry influence is on the fortification of foods. New Zealand has traditionally been anti-fortification with few foods fortified (salt, margarine and baby foods). However, in 1995 the government was persuaded to take a more liberal view of fortification by adopting the Australian standard on fortification, which will facilitate import of foods from Australia, such as fortified breakfast cereals.

Past food policy was implemented mainly through legislation and included the mandatory fortification of salt with iodine and the provision of free school milk. Recent attempts to promote dietary change have mainly been through consumer education. In addition to government-funded activities,

Implementing Dietary Guidelines for Healthy Eating. Edited by Verner Wheelock. Published in 1997 by Blackie A&P, an imprint of Chapman & Hall, London. ISBN 0 7514 0304 0

non-government organizations, e.g. The National Heart Foundation, The Cancer Society and The Nutrition Foundation, and primary producer boards are active in nutritional education.

The establishment of a policy on nutrition for New Zealand, resulting in production of universal guidelines on food and nutrition, has encouraged the many voluntary players in nutritional education to have consistent messages. Implementation of nutritional policy has been hampered by the lack of nutritional research and through lack of a continuing voice on nutrition within the ministries. Advisory committees on nutrition have existed intermittently. Recent restructuring of the health service, the disbanding of the Public Health Commission, the introduction of a user-pays system and contracting out of many services has opened new opportunities for nutrition as well as highlighting a lack of co-ordination.

10.2 Development of nutritional policy

The New Zealand government has influenced nutrition throughout the twentieth century by means of both legislation and allocation of funds to consumer education. Earlier in the century actions were in response to specific problems. In 1981 the first Dietary Goals were published and since 1991 a nutritional policy document has been available to guide actions. For most of the twentieth century there was no dietary standard (recommended nutrient intake figures) for New Zealand. Dietitians used the Australian, British, American and FAO/WHO standards, mainly for clinical and menu planning purposes.

Early initiatives were chiefly via legislation or were recommendations aimed at preventing specific nutrient deficiencies, for example the 1908 Margarine Act (changed in 1972), which banned purchase of margarine in this country, except on prescription. In 1943 iodine was first added to table salt at the recommendation of the Department of Health Goitre Committee – to combat the problem of endemic goitre resulting from low iodine levels in the soil. In 1946 the flour extraction rate was raised to 80% (higher than many other westernized countries) in an attempt to maintain nutritional value without fortification. Also in 1945 legislation was brought in to ensure that milk trucks should be covered to protect the riboflavin content of milk. In 1954 water was fluoridated on the recommendation of nutritionists and dentists.

In 1977 a Nutrition Advisory Committee (NAC) was set up to advise the Minister of Health and develop a dietary standard and nutritional goals for New Zealand. This was the first in a series of multidisciplinary committees set up to advise the government on nutritional issues. This committee consisted of physicians, a nutritionist, two food technologists, a dietitian, health educator and a representative of federated farmers. It was the first time that a nutritionist and others with a broad range of interests had a direct means of influencing nutritional policy.

In 1981 the first Dietary Goals for New Zealanders were produced by the NAC. They were nutrient goals, not expressed in food terms, and were a mixture of recommended individual actions and recommendations to educators (Nutrition Advisory Committee, 1981):

1. Education of the public in the importance of consuming a wide variety of foods in their daily diet.
2. Limit total energy intake to balance energy expenditure. Since moderate exercise is beneficial to health, there should be an increase in expenditure through exercise as well as a reduction in intake to achieve this goal.
3. Reduce intake of simple sugars, principally cane sugar, and increase intake of complex carbohydrates, principally starch.
4. Reduce total fat intake, especially saturated fat.
5. Reduce intake of animal protein, and consume relatively more protein from vegetable sources. Animal protein foods, however, are an important source of nutrients such as iron, zinc and vitamin B_{12} and should still be consumed in moderation.
6. Reduce the amount of salt added to the diet.
7. Increase the intake of dietary fibre of all types by greater emphasis on cereals, fruits and vegetables.
8. Reduce considerably the intake of all alcoholic drinks.
9. Pay attention to the dietary habits of pregnant and nursing mothers.
10. Promote breast-feeding and better infant feeding practices, and provide sound nutritional advice to mothers who cannot breast-feed.
11. Actively discourage young people from starting smoking and urge all persons already smoking to stop the habit.
12. Maintain and extend fluoridation of water supplies.

These goals were used as the basis of nutritional education for the next 6 years. There was no mechanism for regular review of the goals, although members of the nutritional community advised that this should be done (Birkbeck, 1985).

The Nutrition Advisory Committee also produced the first, and only, set of recommended nutrient intake figures for New Zealand, published in 1983 (Nutrition Advisory Committee, 1983). This was a two-tier system giving minimum safe intake figures (MSI) and adequate daily intake figures (ADI). These were in use until 1991 when it was recommended that the Australian standard should be adopted for New Zealand use until the New Zealand figures could be updated (Nutrition Taskforce, 1991).

In 1984 the Nutrition Advisory Committee was disbanded, due to restructuring and cost cutting in the ministry. This was clearly regretted by the nutritional community as it was seen as the breakdown of the only means for direct communication with the government (Scott, 1984).

In 1986 the Department of Health devised the first dietary guidelines for New Zealanders (Department of Health, 1987). The guidelines were based on the 1985 USA Dietary Guidelines. They were as follows:

1. Eat a variety of foods.
2. Maintain weight within a reasonable range.
3. Don't eat too much sugar.
4. Eat adequate dietary fibre.
5. Don't eat too much salt.
6. Don't drink too much alcohol.
7. Don't eat too much fat.

The guidelines were presented as a four-page document with explanations of each guideline and notes relating how they could be interpreted for babies, teenagers, pregnant and breast-feeding women, and the elderly. Emphasis was given to the first guideline which was explained in terms of the four food groups, although no suggestion was given of the quantity of food to be eaten from each group.

Major differences from the earlier Dietary Goals are that all recommendations are made for individual action, the goal referring to intake of animal protein is dropped, and the wording is changed from 'reduce intake' to 'don't eat too much'.

There may have been disagreement from some parties about the guideline on fat, which, unlike in the earlier goals, is given a low priority (being placed last) and contains the qualifying statement: 'There is some controversy about the recommendations for the amount of fat in the diet of New Zealanders but it is certainly appropriate for adult men in particular to reduce fat. It is also desirable for people who are overweight or with a family history of premature heart disease, high blood pressure or diabetes' (Department of Health, 1987).

In 1988 a Nutrition Taskforce was set up by the Department of Health, once again providing means for nutritionists (and others) to influence nutritional policy decisions. The Taskforce was chaired by a physician/gastroenterologist and included three nutritionists (academics), a practising dietitian, a health economist, an epidemiologist, a representative of the Maori Women's Welfare League, a health educator, a food technologist and a representative of the dairy industry.

The Nutrition Taskforce stated its aim as: 'To recommend a food and nutrition policy which encourages nutritionally appropriate eating habits, promotes health and well-being, and which takes into account social, economic, ethnic and cultural factors' (Nutrition Taskforce, 1991).

The aim of the Taskforce was in line with one of the 1989 Health Goals and targets: 'To reduce the incidence of dietary related health disorders by improving nutrition' (Nutrition Taskforce, 1991).

The Taskforce pulled together all available evidence from research on nutrition in New Zealand, as well as applying overseas research to the New Zealand situation. One hundred and eighty-one submissions were received and interested parties, including representatives of the food industry and consumer groups, were invited to give oral evidence.

In shaping policy recommendations the Nutrition Taskforce reviewed existing policy in other countries as well as considering 'social, economic, cultural, spiritual and political issues'. So, for instance, the recommendation regarding alcohol takes into account its 'established place in the social activity of many New Zealanders' (Nutrition Taskforce, 1991). The report indicates that although the Nutrition Taskforce acknowledges the importance of wellness and 'sense of well-being' there is little research on these issues on which to base recommendations.

The Taskforce, consisting of a wide range of people representing different interests, had much discussion and disagreement about some parts of the report (Parnell, 1991). The final report represents a compromise. However, the make-up of the Taskforce (including food industry representatives) may have ensured that the final recommendations made were widely acceptable.

After 3 years the Nutrition Taskforce produced a comprehensive report, which was a milestone for nutrition in New Zealand. The report proposed a nutritional policy, including goals, targets, strategies to achieve the goals and a suggested means of administering the policy.

Goals are given for a wide range of individual nutrients, as well as for foods, traditional foods, education, food quality and safety, administration, surveillance and research. Nutrient goals are accompanied by measurable targets and each goal is followed by strategies to help reach the targets. A total of 423 strategies are given, including 126 for policy makers, 100 for industry, 63 for health professionals, 55 for researchers and 79 for individuals. Examples of goals, targets and strategies for energy and for food are as follows.

Energy:

- Goal: For all New Zealanders to maintain body weight within the healthy range by balancing energy intake with expenditure.
- Target: To reduce the frequency of obesity (body mass index (BMI) greater than 30) in adults to below 8% by the year 1995, and to below 5% by the year 2000.

Strategies (several strategies are suggested for each group, these are just one example from each):

- For individuals: Undertake regular and appropriate physical activity.
- For health professionals: Learn to interpret and use BMI charts and waist:hip ratios.

- For the food industry: Extend the range of energy-reduced products and label them clearly to indicate their energy content.
- For policy makers: Ensure that food labelling is implemented to enable consumers to choose energy-reduced foods.
- For researchers: Direct research towards establishing whether BMI is an appropriate measure of obesity for Maori and Pacific Island people, and to investigating alternative indices.

Food supply

- Goal: To achieve and secure a wide variety of safe, affordable, tasty, convenient and nutritious foods which allow all New Zealanders to maintain a healthy diet.

Strategies are given for each group for nine food groupings, as well as for distribution and storage, retail, pre-prepared foods and new technology. The following is an example of strategies relating to fish and seafood:

- For individuals and health professionals: Promote the consumption of fish on a regular basis.
- For food industry and producers: Develop and implement a code of practice for fish handling to maintain optimum quality.
- For policy makers and researchers: Ensure access is provided to the Maori for traditional sources of fish.

The strategies suggested were very detailed and far-reaching. The Taskforce recognized that co-ordination of the policy was essential, thus recommended two targets related to administration of the policy:

1. An independent advisory council to provide advice, to oversee the co-ordination of policy strategies, to assess progress.
2. A professional food and nutrition unit within the Department of Health to provide technical information and to develop and implement the policy.

The Nutrition Taskforce also advised on the production of the updated National Nutrition Guidelines in 1991. These are known as *Food Fantastic, Nga Kai Tino Pai Rawa – New Zealand Food and Nutrition Guidelines* (Department of Health, 1991). (The inclusion of the Maori name for the guidelines was the first recognition of New Zealand's bicultural nature in food and nutritional recommendations.)

The 1991 guidelines for adults are as follows:

1. Eat a variety of foods from each of the four major food groups every day.
   - vegetables and fruit (three and two servings)
   - bread and cereals (six-plus servings)

  - milk and milk products, especially low fat (two servings)
  - lean meat, chicken, seafood, eggs, nuts and pulses (one serving)
2. Prepare meals with minimal added fat (especially saturated fat) and salt.
3. Choose prepared foods, drinks and snacks that are low in fat (especially saturated fat) and salt.
4. Maintain a healthy body weight by regular physical activity and by healthy eating.
5. Drink plenty of liquids each day.
6. If drinking alcohol, do so in moderation.

Differences from the earlier guidelines include: a more definite recommendation on fat reduction without any qualifying statements, recommendations on food preparation and the number of servings from each food group, more emphasis on physical activity and a guideline on fluid intake. In addition, recognition is given to the consumption of prepared foods (even though guideline number three is difficult to put into practice in many parts of the country). The mention of 'low-fat products' is also new and does not appear in earlier guidelines, possibly because of lack of availability. For instance low-fat dairy products have only been readily available since deregulation of the milk industry in 1991.

The guidelines were produced as both a small leaflet, including the basic guidelines and some explanation, and as a larger booklet with more information for health professionals and educators. More recently guideline booklets for separate population groups have been published, including: infants, children, adolescents, older people, pregnant and breast-feeding women.

Following the release of *Food for Health*, the report of Nutrition Taskforce, the Nutrition Taskforce ceased to exist which meant that nutritionists had reduced means of influencing government nutritional policy.

In 1992 the Department of Health launched the first Government Food and Nutrition Policy, endorsing the recommendations made in the Taskforce report. The policy was launched by the Minister of Health at a conference attended by nutritionists and food industry representatives. The policy states: 'National Nutrition Policy aims to improve health and reduce disease through the food we eat.' This policy has three goals:

1. To increase longevity and reduce nutrition-related morbidity and mortality.
2. To modify, where necessary, the foods we eat to meet the specific health nutrient goals as contained in the New Zealand Food and Nutrition Guidelines.
3. To promote healthy food choices, through collaboration with industry, researchers, educators and nutrition experts.

Strategies for achieving these goals include:

- communication of nutritional information
- co-ordination amongst key partners
- food legislation
- nutritional research
- monitoring and evaluation (Department of Health, 1992a)

In 1993 the Department of Health was restructured to form the Ministry of Health and the Public Health Commission (PHC). The role of the Public Health Commission was to purchase services, provide advice to the minister, and carry out research needed for Public Health priorities, including nutrition. The nutrition unit in the PHC took on the role of implementing the Nutrition Policy and updating dietary guidelines. A Nutrition Advisory Committee was set up to advise the PHC on nutritional issues. The Advisory Committee consists of physicians, nutrition educators, dietitians and food industry representatives. (Thus the administration of the Policy was similar to that recommended by the Taskforce.)

Between 1993 and 1995 (when the PHC was disbanded) the PHC produced two reports on nutrition (*Advice to the Minister on Nutrition, 1993–94* (PHC, 1994a) and *National Plan of Action for Nutrition* (PHC, 1995a)), updated the dietary guidelines, purchased research and monitored progress towards nutritional goals. The PHC employed two full-time nutritionists and one was employed in the Ministry of Health.

10.3 Food policy in New Zealand – the present situation

The Nutrition Taskforce report (Nutrition Taskforce, 1991) was the major development in policy on food and nutrition, giving a series of quantified nutrient goals as well as suggesting strategies for meeting these goals. The strategies suggested for policy makers, the food industry, health professionals and individuals included much more than just educational measures.

The *National Plan of Action for Nutrition* (PHC, 1995a) builds on the Taskforce report and is now the strategic direction for food and nutrition in New Zealand.

The *National Plan of Action for Nutrition* (NPAN) is presented in three parts: food security, food quality and safety, and appropriate diets and healthy life styles. As a plan for public health it contains objectives, outcome targets and targets/recommendations for public policy, public health programmes, and research and information. There are no specific targets for individuals, health professionals or the food industry as in the

Taskforce report. Most of the strategies are stated as proposals for action by the PHC, for example, 'the PHC will investigate', 'the PHC will support', 'the PHC will purchase'.

The NPAN reflects participation by New Zealand in several international agreements. New Zealand's participation in the International Conference on Nutrition in Rome, 1992, appears to be a major influence in the format of the NPAN, especially the prominence given to food security. The strategies of the *Ottawa Charter for Health Promotion* (WHO, Health and Welfare Canada, Canadian Public Health Association, 1986) are in agreement with those recommended in the NPAN. Lastly, the NPAN concurs with the commitment to sustainable development on the part of the New Zealand government as indicated from the signing of Agenda 21 in the Rio Declaration (Ministry of External Relations and Trade and Ministry for the Environment, 1992).

New Zealand policy papers also influenced the NPAN. Consultation by the PHC in 1993 resulted in *A Strategic Direction to Improve and Protect the Public Health* (PHC, 1994b). Objectives from this report are referred to in each of the three sections of the NPAN. Two policy papers, *Food and Nutrition* (PHC, 1994a) and *Food Safety* (PHC, 1994c) provide much of the basis of the NPAN.

Other influences include the relevant scientific literature (reviewed by the PHC) and the Australian Food Policy. The Maori view of holistic health is cited by the PHC as contributing to the overall approach and the NPAN is said to be in agreement with the Treaty of Waitangi. At the time of writing the NPAN, hunger, as evidence by people using foodbanks, was more visible in New Zealand than it had been in the recent past, probably because of changes in social welfare policy and high unemployment.

A major difference between the 1991 Nutrition Taskforce report and the Nutrition Plan of Action is in consideration of food security. The objective from *A Strategic Direction to Improve and Protect the Public Health* (PHC, 1994b) which influences this aspect of nutrition is 'To improve and protect the public health by developing strategies to reduce the impacts of unemployment, inequalities in wealth and housing, transport, and literacy problems on health.'

An outcome target is not set because of lack of New Zealand information but it is suggested that the 1997 national dietary survey will provide some of the information needed.

Healthy Public Policy Recommendations include (in order of priority):

- that the PHC investigates national and international experiences and policy options for improving food security;
- that the PHC facilitates communication with appropriate services to establish a joint process to ensure sufficient and sustainable food supplies for all.

Public Health Programme Recommendations include (in order of priority):

- that the PHC evaluates current programmes available in economic cooking with the aim of providing nationally available resources to support programmes;
- that the PHC investigates the current work on the cost of a healthy diet to determine whether it is being used appropriately to help maintain people's purchasing power with respect to food.

Research and Information Recommendations include (in order of priority):

- that the PHC works with other agencies to establish baseline information on the dietary intakes, nutritional status, food purchasing power and level of food skills and knowledge of the population, including those on a low income and other at-risk groups, including Maori and Pacific Island people;
- that the PHC ensures that adequate samples of people on low income, beneficiaries and the unemployed are included in the national nutritional survey.

There are no quantified outcome targets for food quality and food safety. This section focuses almost exclusively on food safety in setting targets, although issues of food quality are discussed in the text. This is a change from the Taskforce report which included strategies such as certification of organic food and reduction of food additives.

The section of the report on 'Healthy diets and appropriate lifestyles' contains eleven quantified outcome objectives (fewer than the nutrients covered in the Taskforce report). Several of these are similar to those of the Taskforce report. However, the targets to be achieved are shifted to a later date or modified, for example:

- National Plan of Action for Nutrition (obesity) rates should not increase from the current rates of 11% for males and 13% for females by the year 2000.
- Taskforce report – reduce frequency of obesity to less than 8% in 1995 and less than 5% by the year 2000.
- National Plan of Action for Nutrition (fats) to decrease intake of total fats by approximately 20% from 37–38 g to 30–33 g by the year 2005.
- Taskforce report – to reduce total fat intake to 30–35% by 1995 and further to 30–33% by the year 2000.

It is obvious that the authors of the *National Plan of Action for Nutrition* do not feel that some of the goals of the Taskforce report are achievable at all or in the given time.

In writing the NPAN the PHC has the benefit of information from the Hillary Commission 'Life in New Zealand' Survey (Horwath *et al.*, 1991), which provided the first national information on food consumption for 14 years. This was a government-funded project carried out jointly by the Nutrition Department of the University of Otago and the Hillary Commission (a charity involved in promotion of sports and exercise).The survey provided a baseline of nutritional information from which to monitor progress towards nutrient goals. It indicated some changes from the survey carried out in 1977, including a reduction in the average fat intake for men and women from 41% of total energy in 1977 to 37–38% in 1989.

It is also clear that the authors of the NPAN do not feel that goals set out for 1995 have been attained. There are two possible reasons for these changes in targets. First the authors of the later report may feel that the earlier goals were unrealistic; secondly, strategies to achieve them may have been unsuccessful or may not have been carried out. The reasons for modifying the Taskforce targets are not discussed in the later report.

Some of the targets from the NPAN refer to foods, as opposed to nutrients, for example: 'To increase the consumption of vegetables and fruit so that 75% of New Zealanders eat at least five servings per day by the year 2000'. The strategies proposed to achieve these outcome targets are less specific than those proposed in the Taskforce report, for example:

- that the PHC develops a strategy to encourage governmental departments and the food and agricultural industries to further develop nutritional policies for their organizations and that progress towards this end is monitored;
- that the PHC supports the role of community dietitians to the regional public health providers;
- that the PHC purchases programmes for improving the nutrition of Maoris.

The NPAN, although it claims to have a holistic view of health, focuses predominantly on strategies within the health system, and related research, to implement nutritional policy. In this way the NPAN is more narrow than the Taskforce report, but it may also be more realistic in only proposing what may actually be achieved in the current political climate.

10.4 Implementing nutritional policy

Government, Crown Health Enterprises (which have replaced Area Health Boards) and non-government organizations, such as the National Heart Foundation, the Cancer Society and the Nutrition Foundation, have all been involved in nutrition-related activities which have assisted in implementing the nutritional policy. The food industry has also carried out education campaigns or taken other action (e.g. voluntary labelling and product development) which might allow the nutritional goals to be reached.

Early initiatives seem to have occurred without specific direction or co-ordination, for example earlier legislation. There was concern that the various voluntary organizations involved in nutritional education were not providing consistent messages (New Zealand Nutrition Foundation, 1986).

The development of dietary goals, followed by the Nutrition Taskforce report (and later the National Plan of Action for Nutrition) has provided some guidance for other groups involved in nutritional education and for organizations, such as schools and food manufacturers, wishing to develop their own nutritional policies. However, there has not been an official co-ordinating body for activities aimed at implementing the policy, except for the Public Health Commission (between 1993 and 1995).

One of the criticisms of policies on food and nutrition in any country, or organization, is that they might become simply paper exercises. Much time and expense goes into formulating recommendations which are then ignored. It is clear that some of the recommendations of the Nutrition Taskforce have been carried out, for example the expansion of the Food and Nutrition Guidelines. On the other hand, some objectives, particularly non-educational ones such as nutritional labelling (the importance of which is quite clearly stressed in the Taskforce report), have not occurred. Lack of co-ordination may be one reason for this lack of implementation.

The PHC fulfilled the co-ordinating role in part by allocation of funds to priority projects and in an advisory capacity to non-government groups. The co-ordinating role has now moved to the Ministry of Health. The purchasing function of the PHC is now carried out by Regional Health Authorities.

Actions needed to implement the dietary goals can be divided into the following areas:

1. *Research*. The lack of New Zealand research in many areas has hindered goal-setting. In addition, research is needed to monitor progress towards goals.
2. *Education*. Materials and personnel are needed for educating the public, health professionals and the food industry. In addition the content of other programmes, e.g. national curriculum and campaigns by NGOs (non-governmental organizations), needs to be consistent with dietary goals.
3. *Legislation*. Legislation is needed to control health claims about foods, to stop misinformation and ensure consistent nutritional labelling.
4. *Influencing the food supply*. Changes in the food supply can be brought about by nutritional organizations and nutritionists working with the food industry on product development and on developing food policy. Consumer demand and the potential for health marketing may also influence the industry.

5. *Influencing public policy*. Policy in many areas impacts on nutrition, as indicated by objectives in the NPAN. Nutrition needs to be considered not just in obvious areas of agricultural, health and technology, but also in transport, education, employment, housing and social welfare.

The NPAN is divided into the three areas under which the work should proceed: food security, food quality and safety, and appropriate diets and healthy life styles. The first two areas have traditionally been considered separately from nutrition in New Zealand. Recently some work is being done on food security by dietitians. This work involves primarily educational activities associated with budget cooking, food banks and school meals. There are no provisions for influencing the level of social welfare benefits, minimum wage, etc. But as evidence of lack of food security accumulates it is possible that the NPAN may influence people to work in more advocacy roles.

The placement of Nutrition in Health Protection units, along with food safety, facilitates implementation of food safety objectives. For instance, dietitians in the Public Health Service are currently working on food safety campaigns.

Most of the obvious work being carried out towards implementing the NPAN is in the area of appropriate diets and healthy life styles. Much activity has been in education, but other activities have also been carried out.

10.5 Education

Government involvement in food and nutritional education has been primarily through publication of materials and through provision of nutritional information by various health workers. Non-government organizations and the food industry have been active in carrying out national educational campaigns on issues of food and nutrition. Recently the PHC has purchased health education programmes, including programmes in which Maori community health workers work in specific areas.

The Dietary Guidelines for all age groups are freely available through the Public Health Units. The Public Health Commission has, over the past 2 years, produced seven sets of dietary guidelines for: babies and toddlers (PHC, 1995b), children 2–12 years (Department of Health, 1992b), adolescents (PHC, 1993), older people (PHC, 1994d), pregnant women (PHC, 1995c), breast-feeding women (PHC, 1995d) and a new version of the adult guidelines (PHC, 1995e). All these guidelines are consistent with dietary goals and are versions of the original guidelines with additions for specific groups. For example, the guidelines for adolescents pay particular attention to vegetarianism and other topics important to this group. The guidelines for pregnant and breast-feeding women emphasize the need to avoid alcohol. Iron is emphasized in the baby and toddler guidelines The food examples given show that more attention has been given to the needs of Maori people than in previous guidelines.

A number of people in New Zealand within the Public Health System provide nutritional information. These include: GPs, Plunket nurses, community health workers, public health nurses, dental nurses, community dietitians and a few community nutritionists.

Community dietitians are employed in two different roles: first, there is the traditional role which involves one-to-one help with clinical problems, this is often carried out by the dietitians employed by community services; secondly, there is a more promotional role which seems to be expanding in New Zealand (as evidenced by recent changes in dietetics training), this includes both education of health professionals and of the general public. Dietitians in health promotion roles tend to be employed in the Public Health Units of the Crown Health Enterprises. However, not all Public Health Units employ a dietitian.

There is no clear nationwide system for priority setting by health workers engaged in work on community nutrition. Dietitians working in a Public Health Unit work to a business plan which must be approved by their manager and the local funding agency. The business plans are influenced by perceived local needs, overall objectives (e.g. focus on vulnerable groups), overall strategies (for example, one Public Health unit has a policy not to actively participate in the national campaigns organized by NGOs), local expertise and the NPAN.

Community dietitians working in other roles appear to respond to requests as they arise, depending on the time they have available. They may give a talk to a school or local group in co-operation with a public health nurse or dental nurse or they might participate in promoting national campaigns, such as the Cancer Society 'Fit Food' campaign or the 'Iron' education programme run by the Beef and Lamb Marketing Board. Restructuring of the health services has meant that the amount of one-to-one counselling by the community dietitians has increased so that the amount of time available for community education has decreased. In some areas dietitians are instructed to charge for their time, either for all groups, or just for commercial groups, e.g. industry. This effectively reduces the amount of community education work.

Other health workers include nutritional education in their work as the need and opportunity arise. They use a variety of educational resources, including the Food and Nutrition Guidelines as well as resources from the National Heart Foundation and Cancer Society and from the food industry. This has been the main avenue for nutritional education, but once again restructuring is having effects, for example increasing the number of schools to be covered by a school dental nurse decreases opportunities for her/him to carry out nutritional education.

There are relatively few dietitians/nutritionists with health promotion roles, so one of their priorities is to provide support to other health workers.

The physical placement of dietitians/nutritionists can aid or hinder this co-operation. For example, nutrition in the Public Health Service is situated in health protection, along with food safety and communicable diseases. In some areas they are housed in the same building with health promotion which, in the view of staff, increases their ability to include nutrition in a variety of health promotion activities which are taking place. Personal networks between health workers also facilitate wider inclusion of issues on food and nutrition.

It seems that activities within the health system are fairly fragmented and there there is no nationwide system in place for implementing the guidelines at a local level. However, personal communication with nutrition workers in various parts of the country indicates that activities consistent with the nutritional goals were being carried out.

The non-government organizations are very important in nutritional education. Recent successful campaigns include the 'Fit Food' campaign from the Cancer Society (1994) and campaigns from both the National Heart Foundation and the Nutrition Foundation. Although no evidence is available on dietary change as a result of these campaigns, research has shown increased awareness (Cancer Society of New Zealand, 1992; Casswell, Peach and Dehar, 1992a, b).

All these food education initiatives are in line with dietary goals. However, in the past, the different organizations may have appeared to be giving conflicting messages. For this reason, and for reasons of efficiency, the agencies joined in 1993 to form Agencies for Nutrition Action (including the Nutrition Foundation, Cancer Society, Heart Foundation, Dietetic Association, Te Hotu Manawa Maori (Maori Heartbeat) and the Hillary Commission). The first joint project for the group is planned for 1996 and is an obesity prevention programme for 18–23-year-olds.

Food industry and food industry groups have always been involved in nutritional education and there are examples of campaigns which do support the dietary goals and those which in the past have not done so. A recent campaign from the Dairy Advisory Bureau, run jointly with the Arthritis Foundation, promotes consumption of dairy products by young people, in line with the dietary goals. However, a campaign run in 1991 which questioned the need for dietary fat reduction would not have helped to achieve dietary goals and was criticized by nutritionists. Possibly, recent industry consultation via the PHC in setting dietary goals may have ensured better co-operation from the food industry.

10.6 Research

Nutrition research in New Zealand has in the past been hampered by lack of funding. The Health Research Council and other organizations such as the National Heart Foundation and Cancer Society annually support a number of projects. Funding groups may well use the National Plan of Action for Nutrition to assist them in decision making. The PHC also contracted out research projects and may have helped to identify priority projects for other funding bodies. The major government funding needed for a National Dietary Survey has not been available until now.

The National Nutrition Survey is currently being contracted out by the Ministry of Health and will take place in 1997. It is expected to provide baseline data on which to assess the success of nutrition initiatives and to fill some gaps in information, such as the groups not represented in the Hillary Commission Survey (Horwath *et al.*, 1991) – low-income groups, Maori and Pacific Islanders. Much of the needed information cited in the NPAN will come out of this survey.

Over the past 2 years the PHC has also monitored changes in the New Zealand diet using available evidence – the food disappearance figures from the food balance sheets from the Department of Statistics. For example, in 1995 the PHC produced a fact sheet giving estimated average fat intakes much lower than in the past (32% energy).

A continuing programme of research into the composition of New Zealand foods is being undertaken by Crop and Food Research Institute. Over the past few years considerable progress has been made with the production of New Zealand food tables and a food analysis program for computers, which has been sold to universities and some CHEs (Crown Health Enterprises). In total, 1782 foods have been analysed for a range of up to 423 food components. The funding for this programme comes partly from the Ministry of Health and mostly from the Public Good Science Fund (PGSF). The interest of the PGSF is mainly in agricultural and food industry applications of the information.

10.7 Food legislation

Recent changes in food legislation have provided more comprehensive nutritional labelling and closer controls over nutritional claims. Food labelling and food composition are governed by the 1984 Food Regulations. There is no mandatory nutritional labelling in New Zealand unless a claim is made. An amendment to the Food Regulations brought in 1991 (in force by 1995) means that a nutrient claim must be accompanied by a nutritional label, which must be of a certain format. Claims must only be made given levels of nutrients. Definitions of 'high', 'low' and 'reduced' are given for certain nutrients and foods. Many nutritionists would welcome tighter control over claims made and would also like to see universal nutritional labelling. However, the 1991 amendment was seen as great progress and brought in some recommendations for which the Food Standards Committee had been pressing for some years.

The Food Standards Committee has been, since 1973, the means of reviewing food legislation. It has included a nutritionist and this has meant that nutritionists have had a role in changing the legislation. The Food Standards Committee has now been disbanded while a means of joint standard setting with Australia is developed. Currently the system for review which will replace the Food Standards Committee is not in place.

The Nutrition Taskforce stressed the importance of food industry co-operation in achieving dietary goals and especially the importance of providing simple nutritional labelling. Some progress has been made towards reaching this goal, but the need for harmonization with Australian food regulations is currently the priority.

A recent change in the food regulations allows the manufacture of a wider range of fortified foods in New Zealand, which has in the past preferred to restrict the number of nutrient-fortified foods. Nutritionists here have encouraged the addition of nutrients to foods to combat recognized deficiencies (e.g. iodine) but are reluctant to allow it on any other grounds (this point of view is endorsed in the Nutrition Taskforce report). However, the decision has been taken to allow more fortified foods really to facilitate trade with Australia.

Recent changes to legislation regulating alcohol advertising, which now allow advertisements on television, are not in line with the dietary guidelines.

10.8 Influencing the food industry

As indicated in the present dietary guidelines, the composition of prepared foods has a major influence on diet.

The New Zealand Nutrition Foundation has always maintained close links with the food industry and is partially industry funded. It offers a service to food manufacturers to help in developing nutritional policies which are consistent with national nutritional goals. In addition the Foundation is currently developing nutritional education for food technologists.

There is evidence of poor consultation between policy makers/nutritionists and the food industry in the past. For example, the PHC's *Advice to the Minister of Health* document (1993) was criticized by some members of the industry as being 'commercially unrealistic'. It is clearly important that food industry co-operates with nutritional strategies and this will involve good communication. Following the 1993 document release a Food Industry Forum was set up to consult with the PHC. The current Nutrition Advisory Group, which still advises the Ministry of Health, includes two food technologists.

One initiative which has directly influenced the food supply is the National Heart Foundation 'Pick the Tick' nutrition signposting scheme. This was started in 1992 and was not fully approved by the PHC. To enter the programme (which is sometimes described as a food endorsement programme) some manufacturers have modified their products by reducing the fat and salt content. The scheme is currently quite small and is restricted by lack of funding.

The NHF is currently working with a meat product manufacturer to develop a lower fat version of Povi Massima – corned beef popular with Pacific Island people.

The National Heart Foundation has also developed a means of influencing caterers through the Heartbeat Catering scheme and Schools Heartbeat, both of which have been successful programmes receiving some government funding.

The linkages between nutritional agencies and the food industry are likely to be important in implementing dietary goals and it is possible that the Agencies for Nutrition Action will be in a stronger position to influence and develop joint programmes with industry. The NPAN also indicates that much government-funded action will take place in this area.

10.9 Influencing public policy

The need to influence public policy in all areas impacting on nutrition is mentioned in the NPAN. This is perhaps the biggest challenge in implementing nutritional policy, particularly in a political environment of 'user pays' and in a country with a powerful food industry. Recently, legislation has been changed to allow liquor advertising on television, in allowing this to occur the government has shown less than total commitment to promoting the nutritional guidelines, moderation of alcohol intake being a feature of all the guidelines. Another recent decision made by government is that the 'follow-on' formulas should not have to conform to the WHO Code on Breastmilk Substitutes. This will allow them to be advertised, and again could be seen as encouraging people towards actions contrary to the nutritional goals. The guidelines promote breast-feeding of infants until 12 months, whereas the 'follow-on' formulas are said to be appropriate for babies from 6 months, so this could encourage early weaning of some breast-fed babies.

Concern about food security is leading some in the nutritional community to explore ways of influencing a wider range of public policies. For example, the Public Health Nutrition Unit in Christchurch recently made a submission on placement of large supermarkets for city planning. It is possible that the NPAN will help broaden nutritionists' view of their role and result in more attempts to influence public policy.

10.10 Summary

New Zealand food policy development has made considerable progress in the past 5 years. There is now in existence a fairly broad policy. Successful implementation of the policy is dependent on the Health Service and current re-structuring raises some uncertainty about the future of health promotion. Non-government agencies and the food industry will also be important in policy implementation. At this time, with the lack of current New Zealand nutritional research, it is too early to say if much progress is being made towards New Zealand's dietary and health goals.

References

Bailey, R. and Earle, M. (1993) *Home Cooking to Takeaways. A History of New Zealand Food Eating 1880–1990*, Massey University, Palmerston North.
Birkbeck, J.A. (1980) *New Zealanders and their Diet*, A Report to the National Heart Foundation of New Zealand.
Birkbeck, J.A. (1985) Nutrition goals for New Zealand: Are they still appropriate? *Journal of New Zealand Dietetic Association*, Oct., 67–72.
Cancer Society of New Zealand (1992) *Fit Food Report*, Cancer Society of New Zealand, Wellington.
Casswell, S., Peach, R. and Dehar, M. (1992a) *Report of Outcome Evaluation of Heartbeat Awards in Workplace Cafeterias Project*, Alcohol and Public Health Research Unit, Auckland.
Casswell, S., Peach, R. and Dehar, M. (1992b) *Report of Outcome Evaluation of Heartbeat Awards in Schools Project in Secondary and Intermediate Schools*, Alcohol and Public Health Research Unit, Auckland.
Department of Health (1987) *Nutrition Guidelines for New Zealanders*, Department of Health, Wellington.
Department of Health (1991) *Food Fantastic, Nga Kai Tino Pai Rawa New Zealand Food and Nutrition Guidelines*, Department of Health, Wellington.
Department of Health (1992a) *National Nutrition Policy*, Department of Health, Wellington.
Department of Health (1992b) *Eating for Healthy Children 2–12 years*, Department of Health, Wellington.
Gregory, E., Todhunter, E.N., Thompson, H.M.S. and Chambers, E.C. (1934) *The Adequacies of Some New Zealand Dietaries*, Home Science Department, Otago University, Dunedin.
Horwath, C., Parnell, W., Birkbeck, J. *et al.* (1991) *Life in New Zealand Commission Report Volume VI: Nutrition*, University of Otago, Dunedin.
Ministry of External Relations and Trade and Ministry for the Environment (1992) *United Nations Conference on the Environment and Development, 3–14 June 1992, Rio de Janeiro, Brazil, Outcomes of the Conference.*
New Zealand Nutrition Foundation (1986) *Nutrition News*, March, no. 7.
Nutrition Advisory Committee (1981) National Nutrition Goals for New Zealanders. *Journal of New Zealand Dietetic Association*, Oct., 6–7.
Nutrition Advisory Committee (1983) *Recommendations for Selected Nutrient Intakes of New Zealanders*, Department of Health, Wellington.
Nutrition Taskforce (1991) *Food for Health*, Department of Health, Wellington.
Parnell, W. (1991) A Food and Nutrition Policy for New Zealand. *Journal of the New Zealand Dietetic Association*, April, 5.
PHC (1993) *Eating for Adolescents*, Public Health Commission, Wellington.
PHC (1994a) *Food and Nutrition. The Public Health Commission's Advice to the Minister of Health 1993–94*, Public Health Commission, Wellington.
PHC (1994b) *A Strategic Direction to Improve and Protect the Public Health? The Public Health Commission's Advice to the Minister of Health 1993–94*, Public Health Commission, Wellington.
PHC (1994c) *Food Safety: the Public Health Commission's Advice to the Minister of Health 1993–94*, Public Health Commission, Wellington.
PHC (1994d) *Eating Well for Healthy Older People*, Public Health Commission, Wellington.

PHC (1995a) *National Plan of Action for Nutrition. The Public Health Commission's Advice to the Minister of Health 1994–95*, Public Health Commission, Wellington.

PHC (1995b) *Healthy Eating for Babies and Toddlers,* Public Health Commission, Wellington.

PHC (1995c) *Eating for Healthy Pregnant Women,* Public Health Commission, Wellington.

PHC (1995d) *Eating for Healthy Breastfeeding Women*, Public Health Commission, Wellington.

PHC (1995e) *Healthy Eating for Adult New Zealanders*, Public Health Commission, Wellington.

Scott, P.J. (1984) Nutrition, science and social responsibility. *Journal of the New Zealand Dietetic Association*, April, 31–5.

WHO, Health and Welfare Canada, Canadian Public Health Association (1986) *Ottawa Charter for Health Promotion*, World Health Organization, Ottawa.

11 Food and Nutrition Policy in Norway

LARS JOHANSSON, GRETE BOTTEN,
KAARE R. NORUM and
GUNN-ELIN Aa. BJØRNEBOE

11.1 The history of the policy

The Food and Nutrition Policy of Norway today is a consequence of work carried out nationally and internationally over a long period. It may be dated from 1930s when the League of Nations raised the issue that it should be a collective duty of a society to take on the responsibility for a policy on food and nutrition. In Norway, the General Director of Health, Karl Evang, strongly subscribed to that idea, arguing that the question of the diet of the people was a national responsibility, demanding solutions through appropriate measures in many sectors in the society. The idea of prevention and health promotion as intersectorial work has since then gradually gained support in our country and is now a platform in the newly formed health promotion policy. The establishment of a National Nutrition Council in Norway in 1937 was closely related to development in the League of Nations. A specific task of this Nutrition Council was to create a Food and Nutrition Policy that the government and parliament could adopt.

In 1939 a major initiative was undertaken in Norway to improve the nutritional status of the population, with the participation of the Ministries of Health, Agriculture, Fishery and Trade. This initiative was mainly taken as means to prepare the population for difficulties if Norway was involved in the war in Europe. However, the nutritional problems in Norway then were caused by poverty, and the measures were closely linked to stimulate economic growth and even distribution. In addition, nutritional information was considered very important.

During the Second World War, 1940–45, when the national food supplies were scarce, few negative nutritional effects were observed in the population. On the contrary, measured as mortality of coronary heart disease and tooth decay, the nutritional situation improved (Strøm, 1954).

Implementing Dietary Guidelines for Healthy Eating. Edited by Verner Wheelock. Published in 1997 by Blackie A&P, an imprint of Chapman & Hall, London. ISBN 0 7514 0304 0

The idea behind the establishment of the Food and Agricultural Organization of the United Nations (FAO) after the Second World War in 1945 was a 'marriage' between health promotion (through better nutrition) and food production. FAO requested each of its member nations to establish a national nutrition council which should have the responsibility to prepare and co-ordinate implementation of an intersectorial policy on food and nutrition. In Norway this led to a re-establishment and strengthening of the National Nutrition Council. The body was located within the Ministry of Health and Social Affairs. In most other FAO member countries similar councils were organized within the Ministries of Agriculture.

Until around 1950 the main challenges for the Norwegian policy on food and nutrition were to ensure enough healthy food for all people. After 1950, however, the dietary problems changed in character. Problems such as overnutrition and unbalanced diet became more evident and the responsibility for the society to address such nutritional problems steadily became more obvious. There was an enormous increase in mortality from coronary heart diseases, an increase which was due to life-style changes. In 1963 an official Norwegian report on the relationship between dietary fat and cardiovascular disease recommended a decrease in the fat content of the national diet to 30% of the dietary energy (Nicolaysen *et al.*, 1963). This document formed a basis for the subsequent work with the formulation of an official Norwegian Food and Nutrition Policy. However, it took quite some time before this new nutritional challenge became an important target in an official policy.

At the FAO/WHO World Food Conference in Rome in 1974 it was again stated that each nation should have a policy on food and nutrition. The Norwegian delegation at the conference was headed by the Minister of Agriculture, Torstein Treholt. He stated in his main talk to the conference that the industrialized countries should formulate a nutritional policy, and when he returned to Norway he immediately took the initiative to establish a Norwegian Nutrition and Food Policy. A white paper was presented to the parliament through Report No. 32 (1975–76) *On Norwegian nutrition and food policy* from the Ministry of Agriculture (Royal Norwegian Ministry of Agriculture, 1975–76). The objectives and considerations which this policy should co-ordinate may be summed up:

1. Healthy dietary habits should be encouraged.
2. The Nutrition and Food Policy should be drawn up in accordance with the recommendations of the World Food Conference.
3. By reason of the supply situation the aim should be to increase production and consumption of Norwegian food products and improve the degree of self-sufficiency in food products.
4. On grounds of regional policy, greater weight must be attached to exploiting food resources in areas with weak economy.

In 1982 the government presented a follow-up white paper: Report No. 11 (1981–82) *On the Follow-Up of Norwegian Nutrition Policy* (Royal Ministry of Health and Social Affairs, 1981–82). This time the Ministry of Health and Social Affairs was responsible for the report. In 1993 the Food and Nutrition Policy was integrated in Report No. 37 (1992–93) *Challenges in Health Promotion and Prevention Strategies* (Royal Ministry of Health and Social Affairs, 1992–93). These three white papers define the nutritional goals to be striven for in Norway, and the measures that the government intend to employ to improve the Norwegian diet. In all three reports it is underlined that dietary changes should be voluntary. The task of authorities is to facilitate the choice of healthy foods and to stimulate and encourage the desired development in nutritional behaviour. Emphasis is placed on the need to co-ordinate the Food and Nutrition Policy within the health sector as well as with other sectors of the society, such as agriculture, fishery, consumer affairs, education and others that have bearing on the food and nutrition situation of the people. Though it will remain entirely an individual decision what to eat, it is a public and community responsibility to ensure that the circumstances are as good as possible to enable the individual to choose a nutritionally favourable diet.

11.2 Dietary changes

During the twentieth century, Norway has developed from a poor country to a very rich country. Dietary habits have changed during this period (National Nutrition Council, 1994). Many of the major health problems encountered in Norway today are diet-related. The most important health problems are associated with the fact that the diet contains too much fat, especially saturated fat, too little starch and fibre, too much salt and sugar, and too little of certain nutrients such as vitamin D and iron. These dietary habits may contribute to the development of diseases and conditions such as cardiovascular diseases, some types of cancer, obesity, tooth decay, iron deficiency, and gastrointestinal complaints. Vitamin D deficiency exists among small children in immigrant groups. Other deficiencies are rare. Osteoporosis is common in Norway; however, the dietary component as a risk factor is still not understood well.

Changes in diet in the first half of the present century can be described briefly as a substantial decrease in the consumption of food grain and potatoes (Table 11.1). The consumption of cereal products has increased during the past 10 years, and the share of wholemeal flour has risen in recent years, and now comprises about 21% of total sales, compared to 17% in 1975. After an initiative from the National Nutrition Council the Norwegian Dairies introduced partially skimmed milk (low-fat milk) with a fat content of 1.5% into the Norwegian market. This milk has now a considerably higher share of the market compared to skimmed milk and standard milk. Meat consumption has increased considerably in the past 20 years, whereas the consumption of fish has been less than desirable for a long time.

Table 11.1 Food consumption at wholesale level (kg/person/year)

	1890	1934–38	1953–55	1970	1980	1993[a]
Cereal including rice	230	119	98	71	80	82
Potatoes[b]	144	120	93	79	60	50
Potato products[c]	–	–	–	7	12	23
Vegetables	10	19	35	40	51	57
Fruit, berries	9	33	41	67	75	81
Meat and offal	44	38	36	43	55	59
Eggs	2	7	7	10	11	11
Fish[d]						
Whole milk (3.8%)	81	188	195	172	164	50
Low-fat milk (1.5%)	–	–	–	–	–	85
Skimmed milk (0.1%)	77	6	10	14	28	29
Cheese	8	6	8	9	12	14
Cream	–	–	5.0	6.7	7.1	6.7
Butter	6.2	7.6	3.8	5.4	5.6	3.1
Margarine, total	3.9	23	24	19	16	13
Oil and other fats[e]	–	–	3.8	4.4	4.7	4.0
Sugar, syrup, honey, etc.	9	37	40	42	43	43

[a]Provisional figures
[b]Potato excluding those for industrial uses.
[c]Potatoes used to produce potato products.
[d]Figures for fish consumption are unreliable and not published.
[e]Includes cooking oils, cooking fats, and fat used in food manufacturing for mayonnaise, salads, chocolate, biscuits, etc.

Consumption of fruit and vegetables has shown a rise over a prolonged period. Vegetables produced in Norway make up 70% of total consumption, while imports comprise about 70% of the total amount of fruit consumed. The consumption of potatoes has decreased while the consumption of processed potato products is increasing. Potatoes as raw materials for further processing now comprise about 30% of all potato sales, compared to 10% in 1975. In particular, the sale of potato chips has increased.

The consumption of edible fat has dropped steadily over several years due to reduced consumption of margarine and butter. The proportion of soft margarine (i.e. with a relatively large content of vegetable oils) has increased and now makes up 56% of total margarine consumption. The consumption of low-fat margarine has increased. Wholesale figures for sugar have been higher than desirable for a long time. Of the total consumption of sugar on a wholesale basis, sweetened soft drinks contribute on average 6 kg/person/yr. The sale of such drinks has risen from 45 litres/person/yr in 1974 to 100 litres in 1993. The consumption of artificially sweetened soft drinks is now increasing at the expense of sugar-containing soft drinks.

Table 11.2 Dietary energy and energy-providing nutrients at wholesale level (per person per day)

	1890	1934–38	1953–55	1970	1980	1993
Energy (kcal)	3275	3200	3070	2860	3170	2980
Protein (g)	98	96	89	85	94	96
Fat (g)	67	120	128	126	135	112
Carbohydrate total (g)	570	433	392	352	390	391
Starch (g)			238	185	185	185
Sugar (g)			109	115	120	122
Dietary fibre (g)					23	23
Percentage distribution of energy						
Protein (%)	12	12	12	12	12	13
Fat (%)	18	34	38	39	38	34
Carbohydrate (%)	70	54	50	49	50	53
Sugar (%)			14	16	15	17

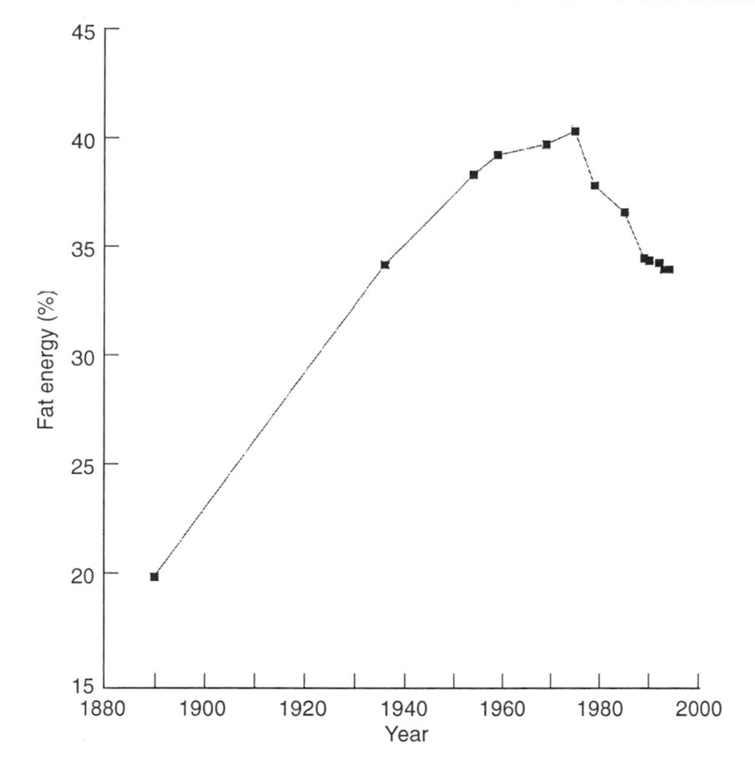

Figure 11.1 Dietary fat, percentage of total energy. Food supply, Norway.

Calculations on the energy content of the food supply show that the population as a whole has had sufficient food throughout the entire period from the turn of the century (Table 11.2). The energy content has steadily been approximately 3000 kcal/person/day. Calculations based on wholesale figures and on household consumption studies show that the energy% from fat in the diet increased from 20% in 1900 to 40% in the 1970s and since then decreased to 34%. It is difficult to point out when the peak in dietary fat content occurred (Fig. 11.1). According to food supply data the peak was in the middle of the 1970s, but household consumption surveys and dietary surveys show a fat content above 40 energy% (E%) in the 1960s or even earlier.

The three most important sources of dietary fat are (1) margarine, butter and other edible fats; (2) milk and milk products; and (3) meat and meat products (Table 11.3). The relationship between dietary sources of fat has changed since the mid 1970s. The proportion of fat derived from margarine has shown a marked decrease. In spite of a reduced contribution of fat from milk, the proportion of fat from dairy products has nevertheless not changed much, due to higher consumption of other dairy products. 'Other fats' and 'other foods' have increased in significance as sources of dietary fat. The proportion of fat derived from meat has remained fairly constant. The dietary fatty acid pattern has changed considerably. Around 1900, polyunsaturated fatty acids accounted for 15% of the dietary fat content; the level decreased to below 10% in 1950. Since the beginning of the 1960s it has increased to 17%. The dietary content of *trans* fatty acids was very low around 1900, and reached its peak level of 5 E% in the 1950s. It is now about 3 E%.

Table 11.3 Dietary sources of fat at wholesale level (g/person/day)

	1975	1993
Margarine	39	27
soft	16	9
low-fat	–	3
other	23	15
Oils, other fats	12	11
Dairy products	42	32
milk	18	10
cream	6	8
cheese	8	9
butter	10	5
Meat	21	22
Other foods	15	20
Total fat %	129	112
Fat energy %	40	34

Measurements of serum cholesterol in large samples of men and women aged between 40 and 42 years show approximately a 10% decrease in serum cholesterol level during the past 15 years. Figure 11.2 shows the death rate from coronary heart diseases in Norway. During the Second World War,

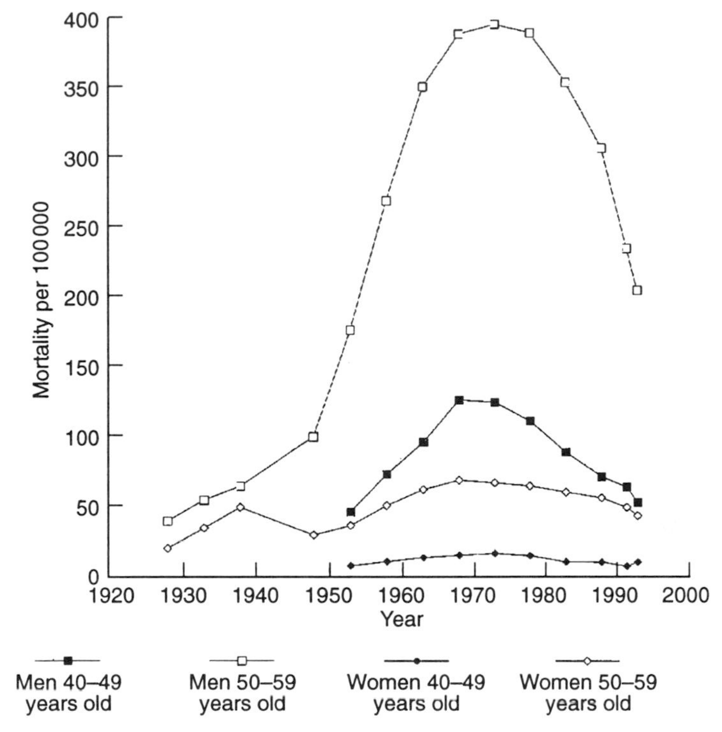

Figure 11.2 Coronary heart disease in Norway, mortality per 100 000.

1940–45, the rate decreased, and in the 1950s there was a rapid increase. During the past 20 years there has been a rapid decline, since 1976, of about 41% in men and 26% in women aged between 50 and 50 years.

11.3 The Food and Nutrition Policy in Norway of today

In Report No. 37 to the Storting (1992–93) *Challenges in Health Promotion and Prevention Strategies* the Food and Nutrition Policy is integrated into the health policy. The policy is based on the experiences gathered during the follow-up of the preceding parliamentary white papers and the modern Norwegian Food and Nutrition Policy has the following four main objectives.

1. *To reduce the prevalence of dietary-related diseases and damage to health in the population.* To ensure such a reduction, the government intends to implement a policy that will support the following issues:

- A national diet in line with the recommendations of the National Nutrition Council;
- Breast-feeding of babies should continue to be encouraged;
- The nutrition-related differences in health status in the population should be reduced;
- Dietary treatment should be integrated into primary and secondary prevention of diet-related diseases within the health services.

The objectives deal with both the national diet, including that of infants, the present inequality in health, especially cardiovascular diseases, and objectives to change approaches within the health services. Special emphasis should be made to change food consumption so that it fulfils the nutritional goals presented below:

- Reducing the proportion of energy in the diet from fat to 30E% by lowering the proportion of saturated fat.
- The fibre content of the diet should be increased to 25 g/person/day by increasing the consumption of cereals, potatoes, vegetables and fruit.
- Sugar should contribute no more than 10% of energy.
- Salt intake should be reduced to 5 g/person/day..
- Increased consumption of fish.
- A change in dairy products, meat and meat products in favour of those with lower fat content.
- The consumption of butter, hard margarine, high fat potato products and snacks should be reduced.
- A frequent intake of grilled, fried, smoked or salted foods should be avoided.

These are in line with the present recommendations given by the National Nutrition Council.

2. *To ensure that food products are safe in terms of health.* The policy shall facilitate the following aims:

   (a) Foods free of infectious agents and approved food additives in quantities which are a risk to health.
   (b) Consumer demands for food quality, safety and security.

   Special emphasis should be placed on improving the mapping, monitoring and warning systems for food-borne diseases. Included in this part of the policy is ensuring a water-supply satisfying the quality requirements laid down by the Norwegian authorities.
3. *To strengthen consumers' influence on the Food and Nutrition Policy* the government will ensure that it is really possible for consumers to provide themselves with a health-promoting diet. In order to maintain this a consumer policy that stimulates a health-promoting diet through differential prices, food availability, food labelling/claims and information and marketing will be implemented.

4. *To contribute to safe production, distribution and marketing of food products and to safe consumption patterns in terms of health, the environment and appropriate use of resources.* This includes that food production shall satisfy society's requirements for safe and ethical acceptable norms and allow for the protection of animals and plants, genetic and environmental resources. This aspect of the Food and Nutrition Policy is an adjustment to sustainable development, meaning that production is ecologically sustainable for the next generations. This links the modern Food and Nutrition Policy to international work for environmental protection and human rights for food and health. In this respect, it is appropriate to quote the following recommendations regarding food production from The Brundtland Commission: 'The industrialized countries must reduce overproduction of agricultural products, so that world market prices will reflect the real production costs. In the short term this implies higher costs for food-importing from developing countries. But it will mean a real stimulus to increase production in developing countries.'

Traditionally the Norwegian Food and Nutrition Policy has been linked to the world food situation. This is also the case today. At the International Nutrition Conference held in Rome, December 1992, a declaration and a plan of action were approved. The primary objectives are to eliminate famine, and to reduce, as much as possible, the prevalence of disease and suffering caused by hunger and malnutrition. At the national level, it was expected that each country should prepare a plan of action by the end of 1994. Based on the objectives in the plan of action, the Ministry of Health and Social Affairs emphasizes the need to strengthen co-operation between ministries and subordinate bodies as well as between local and central levels, the private sector and other relevant agencies.

11.4 Governmental implementation bodies

At the ministerial level two official bodies are given the responsibilities of co-ordinating the implementation of the Food and Nutrition Policy: the National Food Control Authority and the National Nutrition Council. There are clear distinctions between the responsibility of these two bodies.

11.4.1 The National Food Control Authority

This was established in 1988 in order to administer legislation related to food products, and it is responsible for co-ordinating and guiding the executive control system. Before 1988 this work was done by the Directorate of Health. A Local Food Control Authority is responsible for inspecting production, presentation, import, storage and transport of foodstuffs. Running costs of the local authority are met through the municipal budgets and the work is part of the local health services. The Local Food Control Authority consists of 82 units covering all municipalities. During the past few years the work of some Local Food Control Authorities has been strengthened and involved in broader nutritional work in collaboration with the local health services.

11.4.2 The National Nutrition Council

This was established in 1946. The Council is today an expert body consisting of 23 members and an administration of 10 employees. Knowledge within nutritional biology, clinical nutrition, epidemiology, agricultural economy, community nutrition and nutrition policy is represented in the expert body. The mandate for the Nutrition Council is to:

- be an advisory body to Ministries and others in matters concerning food supply and nutrition;
- describe and evaluate the nutritional situation in Norway;
- propose new strategies and measures in order to reach nutritional goals;
- give assistance and proposals to research councils and research institutions;
- contribute in promoting and co-ordinating professional work on diet and nutrition, nationally and internationally;
- be actively engaged in nutritional education and ensure that public information on nutrition is according to recommendations.

One important task for the Council is the formulation of the Norwegian dietary guidelines. Such guidelines were first published in 1954, and have been the theoretical basis for nutrition-related health promotion, and incorporated as the scientific basis in the Food and Nutrition Policy. The latest revised guidelines have been prepared in co-operation with the other Nordic countries.

During the past few years the administration of the Council has been strengthened from being a small secretariat to an efficient administrative body with broad nutritional knowledge, operating in close contact both with the Ministry and with the Council and its members. This has been very important because it has to be able to implement and co-ordinate activities in many different sectors of the society. An intersectorial approach is one of the most important elements in the Norwegian Food and Nutrition Policy. The Nutrition Council has an extensive co-operation with relevant participants at national as well as on local level.

11.5 Important characteristics of the food and nutrition policy and its implementation

A basis for the policy is an agreement on the idea that many factors affect the diet and the prevalence of diet-related health problems (Fig. 11.3). Of

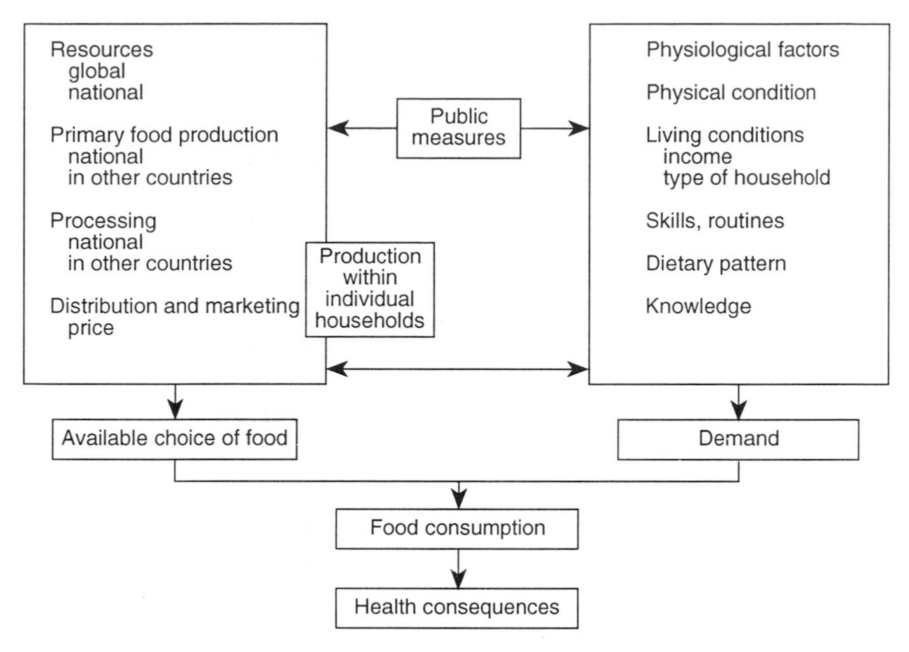

Figure 11.3 Factors influencing food consumption.

major importance for the implementation of the Norwegian Food and Nutrition Policy is the consensus achieved about the goals and the strategies of the policy. This has been achieved by founding the goals of the policy on sound scientific basis and by stimulating scientists to participate in the implementation of the policy. As a consequence, the message given to the public has been consistent, whether the message has been transmitted by voluntary organizations or public agencies. Our experience has shown that the content of a strategy intended to influence the diet in a desired direction should define:

1. *The goal.* The strategic effort must be expressed generally and in terms of principle. Thematically, the objective can be linked to reduced risk of disease, better growth and development, more optimal supply of nutrients or a healthier diet in general.
2. *The target groups.* These should be identified. They may be narrowly or broadly defined.
3. *The measures.* These may be implemented in a number of arenas. Often, several arenas will be used synergistically in a total effort to achieve the goal.

The fundamental background for choosing where to invest the effort will be the knowledge of nutritional problems existing in the population, or risk factors and the wish to reduce these problems. If the priorities in the nutritional work are to be decided on the basis of the occurrence of nutritional problems, epidemiological surveys are required to provide information on relevant conditions, such as growth and development among children and adolescents, the occurrence of diet-related problems and biological risks. It is particularly important to identify any specific social or biological groups who may be more susceptible to the problem than the population in general, in order to design a strategy that will include measures to reach these groups. In response to the epidemiological basis in the strategy, the work on monitoring the situation of Norwegian food and nutrition has been strengthened considerably in the past years.

Politicians and bureaucrats at different levels are important target groups for the nutritional work. The members of this group influence both food supply and the consumers' options and preferences, by deciding the overall framework of different sectors. The professions employed in the public services, such as medical and nursing services, the social welfare sector, the educational sector and the cultural sector have a large number of personnel and resources at their disposal that may be used to reduce the risk of dietary problems.

It is important to make it more attractive to sell healthy food. The National Nutrition Council has worked to influence consumers' choices by information and advice through various communication channels. The goal of our work has been to influence what consumers purchase by, for example, adequate labelling, marketing and by changing the relative prices and the availability of different foods. Co-operation with manufacturers and merchants has been important during this process.

The strategies used within the field of disease prevention and health promotion are often grouped into mass strategies, target group strategies and high-risk group strategies. In the case of a mass strategy, the target group is the general population. Several long-lasting nationwide campaigns, general education and training have been important elements of the mass strategy initiated by the National Nutrition Council. In target group strategies the focus has been directed at various specific groups of the population, e.g. schoolchildren, infants and immigrants. In the high-risk strategy persons, who have been identified to be at high risk of developing diet-related disease, are given advice or preventive treatments. The national high-risk strategies have been based on screening of large groups of the adult population to identify persons at high risk, and then introducing measures directed specifically towards the identified individuals.

A wide range of measures has been used to improve the diet since 1975. In Report No. 37 (1922–93) the different types of measures are classified in the following areas: monitoring and surveys, information, legislation and control, and the efforts in the different sectors.

Legal measures define the framework for the food supply, including nutritional composition and conditions of sale. In addition, the legislation determines the frameworks for the design and content of the public services that can appropriately be used in nutritional work, such as health services and education. *Economic measures* refer to both the relative prices of products and the level of income of the population. Government taxes and subsidies can be changed to favour purchase of healthy foods. In addition, the demand can be turned towards healthier products through the income and distributional policy. **Organizational measures** include how the supplies of food and the associated services are designed and implemented. Examples include the food offered in public enterprises, e.g. at schools and at public institutions such as hospitals and military barracks. The purpose of *educational measures* is to try, by means of various forms of information and communication, to direct preferences. During recent years nutritional education has been carried out in co-operation with non-governmental organizations and consumer organizations, school and health workers, food industry, policy makers and media.

The choice of strategy also includes identifying the arena for intervention. Relevant arenas include public services, especially the health and social welfare services, including the curative and preventive health services. Organizations, including government organizations, employers and employees' organizations, and the various non-governmental organizations, have been major contributors in the work to promote health via better nutrition. The food industry has also been of major importance, and the retailers are relevant areas for strategic nutritional work.

11.6 Concluding remarks

In our opinion the official Food and Nutrition Policy papers have been very useful strategic documents in the efforts to improve public health in Norway the past 20 years. The National Nutrition Council has played an important role in implementation by formulating a consistent and scientifically sound basis for the policy. The Council has often been consulted in connection with widespread efforts in various sectors, in addition to the health sector.

The basic idea that Food and Nutrition Policy must be carried out across different sectors of the society was already underlined when the policy was designed in the mid 1970s, and since then this principle has been further emphasized and applied. Increased attention has been drawn to health promotion and prevention of disease.The most important nutritional goal will now be to reduce dietary intake of fat from 34 to 30 E%,. To achieve this, it is important to remember that the formulation of a policy and the work of implementing it requires knowledge of diet-related problems as well as strategic knowledge of the changing society.

References

National Nutrition Council (1994) *The Norwegian Diet and Nutrition and Food Policy*, National Nutrition Council, Oslo.

Nicolaysen, R. *et al.* (1963) *Betenkning om forholdet mellom fett og hjerte-kar-sykdommer. Skrevet av en sakkyndig komité oppnevnt ved kgl. resolusjon av 22. desember 1960*, Nasjonalforeningen for folkehelsen, Oslo.

Royal Ministry of Health and Social Affairs (1981–82) *Report No. 11 to the Storting. On the Follow-Up of Norwegian Nutrition Policy*, Royal Ministry of Health and Social Affairs.

Royal Ministry of Health and Social Affairs (1992–93) *Report No. 37 to the Storting. Challenges in Health Promotion and Prevention strategies*, Royal Ministry of Health and Social Affairs.

Royal Norwegian Ministry of Agriculture (1975–76) *Report No. 32 to the Storting. On Norwegian nutrition and food policy*, Royal Norwegian Ministry of Agriculture.

Strøm, A. (1954) *The influence of wartime on health conditions in Norway*, Report from Institute of Social Medicine, University of Oslo, Akademisk Trykningssentral, Blindern, Oslo.

12 Implementing dietary guidelines: the Scottish perspective

ANNIE S. ANDERSON and MICHAEL E.J. LEAN

12.1 Nutrition and health in Scotland

Until the nineteenth century the 'traditional' Scottish fare of oats, barley, kail, milk and locally grown produce was the stuff of legends, nurturing a nation of giants wielding claymores and tossing cabers. It has become a long-forgotten menu, superseded, in the course of the past century as shipping and trade boomed, by an abundance of imported wheat for white bread, syrup, treacle and jam from the colonies, and a surfeit of meat from more recent alterations in farming practices (Carnegie UK Trust, 1955). After the depression of the 1920s and '30s, which saw Glasgow plunge from the 'second city of the Empire' to become one of the most deprived, came wartime rationing followed by reckless opportunism resulting in a pie, chips and Irn Bru take over, the Big Mac and deep-fried Mars bars. The foolhardy protest that the Scots will survive it all – they have always been a hardy race, still produce the best heavyweight athletes and get into the World Cup finals! The medical establishment begs to differ.

Since the middle of the nineteenth century, when rickets and malnutrition became common amongst urban Scots, the physical health of the Scottish highlander (and lowlander) has been a cause of concern. Recruits for the Boer War (1889–1902) in 1889 were described as having a poor physique, anaemia and were mostly rejected for active service on health grounds. Concern, however, did not lead to action. In the 1930s Boyd Orr published his classic analysis of the relationship between poverty, poor diet and ill health and a series of government initiatives followed which helped feed and nourish the population (Boyd Orr, 1936). During the Second World War a comprehensive UK food policy incorporating food rationing, mass nutritional education and widespread dietary supplements illustrated that an adequate and nutritious food supply could be provided and consumed by an entire nation. Health improved rapidly and these measures helped to eliminate the killer diseases of previous centuries, such as tuberculosis. The cause of disease in the mid-twentieth century combined

Implementing Dietary Guidelines for Healthy Eating. Edited by Verner Wheelock. Published in 1997 by Blackie A&P, an imprint of Chapman & Hall, London. ISBN 0 7514 0304 0

classical undernutrition with overnutrition. The health of Scots in the last decades of the twentieth century now focuses strongly on the results of overnutrition with increasing rates of obesity, cardiovascular disease, diabetes and cancers, but undernutrition is still frighteningly common in some population groups – and overprovision with calories – revealing gross imbalance in nutrient intakes. The socially deprived form a larger part of the Scottish population than in other parts of Britain, and it is in the socially deprived that both undernutrition and obesity are most common.

The current diet of excess stems partly from post-war government encouragement for Scottish agriculture and food manufacturing to provide an abundance of meat, milk and dairy products at a cost so low that they could be afforded by all. In addition, sugar, in its many forms in beverages, confectionery and manufactured foods, and fat, in a range of meat products, baked goods and pastries, provide excess intake of saturated fat and calories at low cost. Such foods, promoted by highly effective advertising and marketing, set the scene for current health promotion attempts at changing the diet of a nation.

Scottish agriculture has seen steady changes over the past 40 years, from the small mixed farm growing a variety of crops for consumption by the local community to a subsidy-driven industry producing a limited number of crops sold to wholesalers outside Scotland which in turn process and package products and send them back for Scottish consumers. Remarkably, however, Scotland remains a major producer of soft fruit, a commodity not generally considered a major component of the diet, probably because the bulk of this produce is exported for jam manufacturers! The jam- and marmalade-making industry centred around Dundee, which combined imported sugar with local soft fruits, now imports its fruit from eastern Europe.

Processed foods have become a major feature of the Scottish diet, with a decreased consumption of fresh produce such as fish, fruits and vegetables. Popular stereotypes of a diet high in meat pies, chips and alcohol and low in fruit and vegetables (Horowitz, 1992) have been confirmed by national and local studies (Whichelow, 1987; Tunstall-Pedoe, Smith and Crombie, 1989; Gregory *et al.*, 1990; Bolton-Smith, 1991; Anderson and Hunt, 1992; Wreiden *et al.*, 1993; Anderson *et al.*, 1994; Forsyth, Macintyre and Anderson, 1994). These studies show that, in all age groups, the Scottish diet is 'high in sweet and salty snacks, baked goods of inappropriate composition accompanied by excessive amounts of sugary drinks and alcohol. As a result the Scottish diet is characteristically low in antioxidant vitamins and fibre and contains an excess of fat, saturated fat, *trans* fatty acids, refined sugars and salts' (Scottish Office, 1993). Furthermore, the Scottish diet report (Scottish Office, 1993) describes Scotland as having 'a more unhealthy diet than any other country in the Western world'.

12.2 Scottish Office policy for change

Activities in the area of healthy eating were generally stimulated following the publication of the NACNE (Health Education Council 1983) report and the COMA publication *Diet and Cardiovascular Disease* in 1984 (DHSS, 1984). These reports were further boosted by the Scottish Home and Health Department (1990) publication on the prevention of coronary heart disease in Scotland. More recently, the government publication *Scotland's Health – A Challenge to Us All* (Scottish Office, 1992) which set out health targets for the country was followed by the establishment of a working party on the Scottish diet under the chairmanship of Professor Philip James of the Rowett Research Institute, Aberdeen. The remit of this group was 'to survey the current diet of the Scottish people; to assess the relevance of diet to health; to make proposals, if appropriate, for improvements in the Scottish diet; and to assess their likely impact'.

The ensuing report from the working party *The Scottish Diet* (Scottish Office, 1993) detailed a sad picture of Scottish health and disease. Scottish men and women have the highest premature mortality from coronary artery disease in the world, and Scotland has one of the highest rates of stroke in the Western world, reflecting diet components and inactivity; 75% of adult Scots have total cholesterol levels above the acceptable range of 5.2 mmol/l, and overweight affects over half of all middle-aged adults. Smokers in the West of Scotland have double the usual risk of lung cancer, with low antioxidant vitamin intakes from fruit and vegetables aggravating the effect of high smoking rates. Furthermore, rates of breast-feeding are reduced to less than 50% and as low as 10% in some urban areas, reducing the health-protective effects for the nation's babies. This report comes in an era where initiatives aimed at healthy eating are abundant and suggests a widespread failure to produce fundamental changes in Scottish eating habits, at least in the short term.

A series of nutritional targets (Table 12.1) aimed principally at decreasing intake of the energy% derived from fat, saturated fats and sugar and increasing the energy% derived from starchy carbohydrates, fibre, fruit and vegetables were proposed in this report. To focus on the needs for implementation of these targets a novel analysis of the changes required in consumption of key foods was also undertaken. This showed that it would be possible to modify the current Scottish diet and achieve international targets (Tables 12.2 and 12.3). These changes focus mainly on increasing intake of fruit, vegetables, fish, bread and cereals, and decreasing intake of cakes and pastries, meat products, all fats, confectionery, savoury snacks and soft drinks. It was felt critically important to provide quantitative guidelines for these changes. Following consultation over this report, the Scottish Office announced in 1994 a set of targets to be achieved by the year 2005, and established a Scottish Diet Action Group with representation from food production, processing, manufacturing, retailing, catering, consumer organizations, education, health promotion, health services and government to agree 'an action plan for delivering the Scottish dietary targets which set out what is required, by whom and on what timescale; and to commission action accordingly'.

Table 12.1 Scottish diet report – nutrient targets for 2005

	Current average intake	Direction of change	Proposed average for the Scottish diet
Vegetables and fruit (g) (excluding potatoes)	181.0	⇑	>400
Carbohydrates			
Starch E%	25.3	⇑	>40
Fibre (g) (as non-starch polysaccharide)	10.5	⇑	>16
Sugars E%	16.3	↓	<10
Total fat E%	40.7	↓	<35
Saturated	16.6	⇓	<11
Salt consumption as sodium (mmol)	163.0	⇓	100
Potassium consumption (mmol)	62.0	⇑	80

Table 12.2 Scottish diet report – proposed increases in foodstuffs by 2005 needed to achieve targets

	Problem	Solution
Vegetables	Consumption inadequate	(1) Fresh and frozen vegetable intake to double (2) Potato intake to increase by 25%
Fruit	Consumption inadequate	Fresh fruit intake to double
Fish	Maintain white fish Oily fish consumption inadequate	Maintain white fish Oily fish intake to double
Bread	Maintain white bread consumption Wholemeal and brown bread consumption inadequate	Increase total bread intake by 45% mainly using wholemeal and brown bread Manufacturers to reduce salt content
Cereals	Consumption inadequate	Breakfast cereal intake to double Manufacturers to reduce salt and sugar content

Table 12.3 Scottish diet report – proposed decreases in foodstuffs by 2005

	Problem	Solution
Cakes and pastries	Consumption too high	Cakes, biscuits and pastry intake to reduce by half
Meat	No further increase in lean meat consumption Processed meat products consumption too high	Processed meat and sausage intake to reduce by half Bacon and ham intake to reduce by 20%
Fats	Consumption of total fat and saturated fats too high	(1) Butter intake to reduce by two-thirds (2) Replacement of saturated fat margarines and spread with low saturated fat equivalents
Milk	No change in total milk consumption	Whole milk replaced by semi-skimmed milk except for infants aged 1–2 years
Sugar	Consumption too high	Average intake of NME sugars in adults not to increase Average intake of NME sugars in children to reduce by half
Confectionery, soft drinks, savoury snacks	Consumption too high, especially by children and adolescents	Cut adult intake by 33%, 50% for children and adolescents

12.3 National action plan and the food network in Scotland

Clearly, changes in food consumption do not involve the consumer alone. Change is also needed at all sections of the food network (producers, manufacturers, processors, retailers, caterers, education, health promotion, media, government and consumer). While the bulk of this chapter is concerned with describing health promotion initiatives stemming from efforts to increase consumer demand for a healthier diet, the supply side must not be forgotten.

12.3.1 Primary producers

Primary producers (namely the farming, fish and horticulture industries) are important links in the food chain. Although a relatively small proportion of all foods consumed in Scotland is produced here, developments such as quality assurance schemes in the livestock sector to assist in the provision of lower-fat cuts of meat and leaner breeds of cattle are important steps in the right direction. Fish farming has also increased the supply of salmon and trout for the Scottish consumer. Likewise, fruit and vegetable growers have made wider attempts to reach consumers by the provision of farm sales and 'pick your own' fruit supplies.

12.3.2 Food manufacturers and processors and bakers

These have already contributed to healthier eating by the provision of low-fat, low-sugar and low-salt products, although progress has been slow. The provision of a wide range of basic products which are lower in sugar/fat/salt needs to be addressed. For example, bakers could substantially reduce the salt content of bread; soft drinks manufacturers could reduce the sugar content of drinks.

12.3.3 Retailers and caterers

They also have a strategic role to play in the delivery of the nation's diet. What is clear is that these supply-side factors need to be reassured that moves to provide appropriate foodstuffs will be matched by consumer demand.

It is recognized that the action plan must involve both changes in demand and supply, and should incorporate models of good practice from existing initiatives and foster new programmes. Essentially, the action plan will help to devise a more co-ordinated and committed national approach to changing behaviour, a fundamental design omitted from previous attempts at change. Clearly, long-lasting health improvements can only be achieved if everyone, from central and local government, employers, voluntary organizations and the media to individuals, agree objectives and work together, with necessary resources made available to ensure stability and profitability through a period of major change.

12.4 Healthy eating initiatives – a general view

Since the publication of the NACNE report in 1983 a wide range of agencies have been involved in helping to design, facilitate and encourage the implementation of dietary recommendations. These include the Scottish Office, local authorities (regional councils), Health Boards (health promotion and nutrition and dietetic departments), retailers, food manufacturers, employers, enterprise organizations, churches and charities and the media. The type of action in the community arena is particularly diverse and ranges from food co-ops, mobile shops, community cafés and tasting and cooking demonstration classes through provision of fruit for crèches and schools.

Initiatives with an impact on food supply and consumption can be categorized as having the following aims:

- principally concerned with the transfer of knowledge or skills relating to food and nutrition;
- principally concerned with improving availability of and access to a range of good-quality, affordable foods;
- a combination of both of these aims.

Work in the first category represents classical health education approaches, focusing on attempts to increase awareness of the importance of a healthy diet, awareness of healthy eating messages, knowledge of what is in food and how to put healthy eating advice into practice. A wide range of innovative approaches has been used to achieve this aim, across all ages and sections of society. Written healthy eating guidelines in colourful, artistic design have been produced by central and local health promotion agencies, food retailers, manufacturers, producers, television companies, professional associations, academic departments, education departments and restaurants. Verbal advice on the construction of a healthy diet is a popular component of radio and TV programmes, evening classes and health professional communication. Indeed, Scots are said to be bombarded with such information. However, there remains confusion over nutritional messages, limited quantitative information on how to achieve a healthy varied diet at each meal, how to assess personal intake, and a generalized distrust of information sources (especially those perceived as representing English paternalism). The setting up of a central nutritional information and advisory bureau which could be pro-active in guiding independent food activities towards a common goal would be a helpful move in co-ordinating activities to improve behaviour change.

The second category is generally concerned with addressing the barriers relating to insufficient means, costs of healthy eating, poor access and a lack of cooking facilities and equipment. All these are common problems and the issue of access to food is partially relevant with respect to food costs in Scotland. A wide range of good-quality foods at reasonable cost has not always been available throughout Scotland, but urban centres are now served by national food retailers who supply 70% of all food consumed in Scottish homes. Such retail provision means that a wide choice of food is available within cities, although Scottish cities are still characterized by a lack of fresh food markets (notably fruit and vegetables) which might promote competition and value for money. Compounding this problem, especially for the poor and elderly who do not have private transport, is the siting of the larger supermarkets at out-of-town sites. This has resulted in a general downgrading of local shops, further disadvantaging people in urban areas who are already physically and financially disadvantaged by having to pay more and choose from a smaller range of (often poor-quality) goods.

Research carried out in Glasgow by the Medical Research Council Medical Sociology Unit (Forsyth, Macintyre and Anderson, 1994) suggests that current food patterns are best explained 'by a dynamic model which takes into account household resources, local availability and cultural factors such as traditional beliefs about appropriate or healthy diets'. Thus, retail outlet and food provision play a key role in influencing food choice through a combination of equally important factors.

A comprehensive review of community initiatives in Scotland, commissioned by the Health Education Board for Scotland, is currently being undertaken by Anderson *et al.* in order to gain an insight to the wide range of activities in this area. The following pages describe some of the best known activities aimed at changing diet intake, many of which are aimed at long-term change.

12.5 Facilitating dietary change: agencies involved

12.5.1 Local authorities

Local authorities (Regional and District Councils up to May 1996) have enormous scope to facilitate and encourage Scots to attain current dietary targets. Most action has involved the regional education departments which are responsible for both the provision of school meals and teaching nutrition within the curriculum.

Strathclyde Region, which includes almost half of all Scots, was the first regional authority with a food and health policy including school meals. A school meals programme 'Keep your balance' was developed to implement the Food and Health Policy, and operated in primary schools, using educational materials and food coding and promoting healthier food choices at school lunches. Fundamental to the implementation of such a policy has been the incorporation of nutritional specifications in the contracting process, menu development, food production methods and recipe development, and addressing special needs including ethnic groups, the under- and overnourished. This example could act as a model for other local and regional catering services, including community centres, residential and day care centres and staff menus. However, it is increasingly clear that to be effective nutritional expertise is required by both contractor and commissioner, and that independent or bilateral evaluation of the service is needed to ensure that the nutritional conditions are met.

Local authority education departments are also responsible for ensuring that home economics is taught to all schoolchildren in Scottish state schools for 80 minutes/week during the first (S1) and second (S2) years of secondary education, of which about half involves nutrition, including practical skills. Home economics programmes allow pupils to apply their knowledge about healthy eating to food preparation and to appreciate that food has social as well as health dimensions. Pupils also have opportunities to evaluate their own eating patterns and to consider sustainable ways of improving their diet. After S2 pupils may continue with home economics standard and higher grade or, in some cases, a 40-hour Scottish Education Board short course in Health Studies including Health and Food Choices. Courses in higher-grade home economics include an in-depth study of nutrition and diet and an independent study of a particular topic (in 1995 topic options included 'Develop a means of encouraging young children to take an active interest in healthy eating'). The continuation of home economics in the curriculum is widely supported in Scotland, but is under threat from political influences and influences from the south: England and Wales have recently removed home economics as a core subject.

Additional ways in which schools have promoted healthy eating are described in Table 12.4. The concept of 'health-promoting schools' was pioneered in Scotland but has been more widely adopted in Europe. Considerable effort is needed to develop a school health education policy which would encourage development of health-promoting schools and allow some influence over food provision within the school. The lack of training in basic principles of nutrition and health amongst schoolteachers is of concern.

Table 12.4 School actions to promote healthier eating

Increasing availability of healthy eating choices
Provision of breakfast prior to commencement of classes
Offering healthy choices in fund-raising tuck shops and vending machines
Staff making appropriate food choices as role models
Organizing cooking competitions to promote healthy ingredients
Involving parents in such initiatives as healthy packed lunch schemes
Selling healthy food for fund-raising activities (e.g. freshly made bread)

Many local authorities are also involved in food initiatives originating as part of social strategies or anti-poverty initiatives. These include the City of Edinburgh District Council which runs a food co-operative development project to resource food co-operatives by bulk buying, offering storage space, including cold storage, and a van delivery service. Strathclyde Regional Council provides support for food enterprise, such as start-up grants for food co-operatives, e.g. Kirkwood Food Co-operative. Such food and poverty initiatives may not always focus on optimal nutritional quality, but are an important structure in a community food network.

Clearly, there is a role for local authorities in facilitating healthy eating, ranging from supporting business ventures, town and country planning, child and adult education to the provision of healthy meals through all catering outlets. Actions to date are admirable, especially where food policies have been drawn up and concentrated, and co-ordinated efforts are clearly needed before widespread implementation will happen.

The greatest need at local government level is for an individual or group with nutritional training to co-ordinate, initiate, inform and sustain activities in a range of sectors. Health alliances between health authorities and health boards have opened a potential channel to process this need, linking with health promotion agencies.

12.5.2 Health service activities

The NHS is an ideal setting for initiating dietary changes (Anderson and Lean, 1987). It already has a health agenda, it houses a health profession specializing in food (dietitians) and it has the potential to reach large numbers of the population through primary care and hospital referrals. Additionally the NHS, as one of the biggest employers in the UK, has one of the country's largest catering organizations with great potential to provide practical examples of healthy food choices.

Many of the post NACNE efforts to reduce the burden of chronic diet-related disease in Scotland have been initiated through the NHS health boards and health trusts. Following on from the implementation of local food and health policies in England, the Scottish Office required all health boards in Scotland to have food and health policies in place within NHS establishments by March 1994. For most health boards this has involved the production of information leaflets on healthy eating for staff and patients, changes to staff and patient menus to facilitate healthy choices (in some areas with preferential pricing), in-service nutritional education for many types and grades of staff, displays and demonstrations (or open days) to provide further information, practical ideas on how to replace high-fat/high-sugar foods with healthier alternatives and opportunities to discuss food issues and concerns with dietitians. In Greater Glasgow Health Board this had included the production of appropriate materials for ethnic minorities.

More recently (in 1991), *Framework for Action* (the companion document to the *Patient Charter*) charged the NHS with working together with organizations at a local level to tackle health issues and to establish health alliances. This initiative has helped to foster two main actions in the community. The first of these is the development of Healthy Eating Award Schemes (e.g. Ayrshire and Arran and Forth Valley). These schemes aim to encourage restaurants to provide a significant number of 'healthy choices', appropriately labelled and promoted. There have, however, been concerns about the need to ensure that 'healthy' meals reach nutritional targets. The meal is the smallest unit of diet to which nutritional recommendations can be usefully applied, and it is possible to include all foods, in appropriate amounts, in a healthy balanced meal. It is therefore to be hoped that awards for quality in catering should be based on the efforts of the caterer to provide a properly nutritionally balanced meal and not on use of individual courses or foods in isolation (although there is scope for considerable modification in individual dishes). Greater nutritional awareness is needed amongst caterers, and access to simple and cheap nutritional analysis services would be a great advantage.

Grampian Health Promotions (GHP) is an example of a health board working in partnership with other agencies and organizations, including local food producers and retailers. As Grampian is a major food manufacturer and exporter, GHP is currently designing a 'Health Food Product Award' to provide a further opportunity to raise awareness of the importance of 'healthier' convenience food products. Secondly, many health board dietitians have worked with local schools (section 12.5.1) (e.g. Forth Valley, Shetland), in the promotion of appropriate food choices in tuck shops, vending machines and school canteens. In some areas (e.g. Highland) this has involved a novel approach using 'Smart cards' which enable children to purchase school meals with the card and receive 'bonus points' each time they pick a choice in line with nutritional guidelines.

Other activities by health board staff (mostly community dietitians and health education staff) include activities in deprived areas (e.g. Inverclyde) which focus on increasing access to healthy foods by assisting in the development of bulk buying and co-operative schemes, development of a food saving scheme for the elderly (Dumfries and Galloway) and the development of healthy eating clinics where people are referred on a one-to-one basis to the health promoter by the primary care team (Glasgow). A food coupon scheme in Dalmarnock, Glasgow (giving discount to healthy foods) and healthy tuck shops in Drumchapel, Glasgow have also been initiated by health board staff in the past 5 years.

Traditionally, there has been a wide range of innovative approaches involving NHS dietitians and aimed at encouraging healthy eating. These include 'Get Cooking' classes, which is a national project (not NHS-led) that aims to teach young people basic cooking skills to help enable them to adopt a healthier diet. In some areas health board staff have also worked with local retailers to initiate sweet-free checkouts (Orkney). Community dietitians have been particularly active in Scotland at attempting to publicize effective dietary strategies aimed at achieving a nutrient change. However, there are few full-time posts and these are often combined with clinical practice in a community setting (e.g. one-to-one consultations in GP obesity clinics). Overall, there is an impression that health boards are committed to promoting healthier eating and it is clear that many staff are well motivated and enthusiastic to spread the word. However, scepticism remains in some quarters over the appropriateness of acute hospitals being the correct setting for promoting changes in diet. Sadly, the effect of such actions on nutrient intake will probably never be described as monitoring and evaluating are often low on the agenda of health activists, who may only carry out simple monitoring, such as the uptake of key foods (usually milk, breads and sugar in drinks), which is insufficient to evaluate dietary change.

The Health Education Board for Scotland (HEBS) gives leadership to the health education effort in Scotland. This new health board came into being in 1991 with new terms of reference and an emphasis on the evaluation of its activities. The main aims of HEBS initiatives on healthy eating are:

- to promote awareness of the benefits of healthy eating;
- to enhance awareness of what constitutes healthy patterns of eating with particular regard to healthful changes in the consumption of fats, salt, sugar, fish, fibre and fresh fruit and vegetables;
- to promote a positive image of healthy eating;
- to enhance skills in the choosing and preparation of healthy foods and meals;
- to encourage implementation of policies which promote healthy eating.

Action is directed through specific programmes (schools, workplace, community, health service, general public and special programmes). During 1993–94 HEBS mounted a poster campaign concentrating on encouraging the consumption of fruit (using the slogan 'Fruit, The Healthy Snack') and involved the use of adshell poster sites through Scotland, schools and local community outlets. Press campaigns during the same period have used consistent messages to encourage increased consumption of pasta, bread, fish and vegetables, which have been supported by practical recipe ideas. In particular, the Sea Fish Industry Authority has been jointly involved in promoting a press initiative to increase fish intake.

HEBS also produce a variety of materials to encourage dietary change, notably the 'hassle-free' cookery book directed towards people with limited budgets and cooking skills. These are available to health boards and pilot work is under way to examine the effectiveness of distributing these booklets through small retailers as well as community and health settings. Initiatives by HEBS in schools and the workplace and with ethnic minorities are in place or planned.

It is clear that health promotion, including dietary factors, is now a major feature for Scottish health boards. The way forward involves implementing food policies but also sharing NHS expertise with other agencies. While this seems straightforward in many ways, it may involve a complete attitude change, an understanding of how apparently healthy people perceive the value of dietary change, as well as some knowledge of how lifestyle factors are influenced by daily and societal pressures. For example, while selection of a healthy diet may be the ultimate objective, priority factors of taste and cost may be the only way to promote this goal, health issues being of less importance to large numbers of the population.

12.5.3 Scottish Office: urban partnership

The concept of health promotion now extends well beyond that of health education alone and includes prevention (or services available to the population), and health protection (policies and regulations aimed at the promotion of positive health and the prevention of ill health) (Tannahill, 1988). Another crucial strand for achieving health is the strengthening of community action and public participation. Central to this is the empowerment of communities, their ownership and control of their own endeavours and desires (WHO, 1986)

In Scotland the settings for such community food initiatives have been areas of urban deprivation where a strong commitment to community participation already exists. These projects are predominantly 'bottom up', where action is said to 'begin with those who will be responsible for implementation' (Crosswaite and McQueen, 1993) compared to 'top down' approaches which begin with a policy decision and involve a process of setting precise objectives. To have an effect on behaviour, both these approaches are necessary.

After the publication of *Scotland's Health* (Scottish Office, 1992) the government provided financial backing for pilot work in each of four urban 'partnership' areas to fund local initiatives, based on local needs, of how best to encourage dietary improvement. These areas are in the periphery of urban conurbations and housing estates which were poorly serviced, with food provision largely through unevenly scattered small shops. The availability of fruit and vegetables is low and the quality may be poor. Usually the range of foods is limited and prices high. The main areas of dietary action in these estates are listed in Table 12.5 and show that many of these are focused on mothers and children. Nutrition is not an overt theme. None of these projects has provided only nutritional education and all have made genuine efforts to create opportunities for residents to experience new food horizons in terms of a range of items, new recipes and practical suggestions. Such projects have developed from an understanding of the practical barriers to dietary change within these communities. Initial evaluation of these schemes suggests that local people have been actively involved in the projects. Media coverage has supported these activities and this has been valuable in encouraging residents to participate.

In the long term, such projects highlight fundamental issues of community health, such as the need for lay training, networking and structural issues, including the problems of food access in urban areas. The lessons learned from these demonstration projects provide support for the arguments for the developments of food co-ops and cheap subsidized transport to shops. These issues are not uniformly addressed by the large multiple retailers. It is clear that retailers with a strong sense of social conscience would find opportunities to develop outlets in these areas, and local planners could play a greater part in improving health.

Table 12.5 Urban partnership projects

Project	Target group	Project description	Project personnel	Development
Westerhailes, Edinburgh (spin-off project: target group – young tenants)	Primary school children Parents Teachers Retailers	Lunch vouchers, using an incentive system (points given for healthy food choices and prizes) during school holidays	Manager Assistant	
Castlemilk, Glasgow	Local residents (including children)	Baseline research to establish costs of food purchases in different areas and local perceptions about the availability and costs of food; production of local healthy recipe book; funding to community cafés, for equipment, and supports taster days to encourage participation; formation of 'Jeely Piece' club offering fresh fruit and milk at lunchtimes.	Representatives from Healthy Castlemilk, Health Promotion Dept The Castlemilk Partnership Project co-ordinator	Initial projects have been further developed
Ferguslie Park, Paisley	Local residents	Local food prices survey; distribution of information folder on diet; provision of mini-bus and crèche facilities to improve opportunities, especially for fresh food; food taster days	Health project staff The Ferguslie Park, Partnership The Women's Food Poverty Action Group Strathclyde Regional Council	
Whitefield, Dundee	Mother and toddlers; young unemployed	Provision of kitchen running healthy eating and budget cooking classes	Project worker; supported by a steering group representing the Health Promotion Dept Social Work Dept	Project extended by 3 months

It is reassuring that the Scottish Office has played a major role in reviewing the position of diet in relation to health in Scotland. Urban partnerships are a splendid example of community-led initiatives which could be usefully developed and expanded. In particular developments within rural areas would be welcome in many parts of Scotland, following on the model of many Scandinavian countries.

12.5.4 Catering

In line with other European countries, the expenditure on meals and snacks eaten outside the home has increased by 10% between 1992 and 1993 (UK figures) largely arising from an increase in takeaway fast food outlets and new, more formal restaurants. The proportion of food provided by the catering industry looks set to rise with a shift towards greater provision of ordinary meals, rather than special occasion catering. The quality of food provided by caterers in Scotland has improved in terms of variety and creativity but not obviously in terms of nutrition and quality. It remains cheap, by international standards, and tends to make use of materials available as industrial waste, such as fat skimmed from milk, and back fat from pigs imported from Denmark and The Netherlands, for inclusion in sausages and pies. Apart from some interest in healthy eating award programmes, little visible or measurable effort has been made on the part of catering to improve dietary intake.

Large, multiple catering chains such as McDonalds (Scottish only in name) are now widespread throughout the country and do provide nutritional information to help consumers select their meals, although constructing a healthy balanced meal from their provision may be challenging. It is hoped that other outlets will follow suit and provide guidelines for wise food choices, focusing on the meal as the unit of nutrition.

Caterers receive only rudimentary training in nutrition or none at all and respond largely to consumer demand. Unlike many North Americans, Scottish consumers are not yet demanding more nutritious options when eating out. This may be partly the result of failure to provide information in nutritional terms (i.e. relating to nutrition and health recommendations). Information tends to be in terms of food chemistry (e.g. g/100 g) which cannot readily be converted to nutritional information. This is an area where effective training will clearly be needed to complement better health promotion. A central service to provide nutritional analysis of foods, recipes and whole meals would assist caterers and provide an independent reference point for consumers.

12.5.5 Retail industry

Most of the large supermarket chains operating in Scotland have gone some way towards fostering healthy eating:

- providing nutritional labelling on all products;
- provision of healthy eating leaflets and information directed at meal design;
- increased availability and range of fruit and vegetables, low-fat and low-sugar products;

- removal of confectionery from check-out points;
- transport from deprived areas.

These activities have included individual actions, such as promoting basic healthy foods (e.g. baked beans, wholemeal bread) with money-saving offers widely advertised in the local press. National supermarket promotions have also been run in line with dietary guidelines, such as eating 'five a day' of fruit and vegetables.

However, it is true that 'added-value' foods, whose cheap contents are heavily marketed (e.g. soft drinks), represent ready profits for retailers; other foods such as fruit and vegetables could also offer high profit margins.

No retailers (or indeed brands) have their products endorsed by bodies such as The Health Education Board for Scotland or the Dietetic Association. This is a sensitive issue as it fails to address the issues surrounding 'healthy' diets as opposed to 'healthy' foods and many view such an approach suspiciously as it is seen to benefit the commercial interest with a loss of credibility to the health promoter.

There is interest in Scotland from bodies such as the Scottish Consumer Council in extending the role and responsibility of major retailers into the community, particularly with respect to deprived areas. Efforts to locate better, larger supermarkets nearer deprived areas need the support of sympathetic planning departments and practical access, such as the provision of buses.

12.5.6 Independent activities, worksites, churches and charities

Throughout the country, independent agencies (alone or in partnership) have initiated action aimed at improving dietary intake. For example the Barri Grub enterprise in Edinburgh has initiated a shop and mobile fruit and vegetable van, selling fruit to primary schools, sheltered housing occupants and community centres.

To date, there have been few worksite activities in Scotland aimed at healthy eating, apart from on NHS premises. The Polaroid factory in Fife has been a setting for worksite activity where fruit and vegetable offers at local stores have been highlighted and samples of healthy foods and nutritional information provided.

Charity work aimed at reducing undernutrition includes the action of churches, Salvation Army, Instant Neighbour Trust and St Vincent de Paul Society. The principal aim in these actions is provision to the needy rather than healthy eating and includes the provision of soup kitchens and food distribution. Recent initiatives by charities such as Crisis in London in their 'Fare Share Scheme' which transports fresh produce (fruit and vegetables) left at the end of the day from retailers to day centres for the homeless has yet to happen in Scotland.

12.6 Dietary impacts

Cumulatively, the impact of all the efforts to improve the diet of Scots over recent years has not been radical, but there is some evidence to indicate that slow changes in the trends in disease rates, nutrient intakes and food habits are starting. For example, National Food Survey (NFS) data which record food entering households for domestic consumption show that between 1985 and 1994 the percentage energy derived from fat decreased from 41.5 to 41% and that from saturated fats from 18.1 to 16.0%. The NFS also shows that folic acid intake has risen from 198 μg/day in 1984 to 208 μg/day in 1994 (MAFF, 1996) and vitamin E intakes have shown a steady increase, rising by 50% in the 10-year period from 1980 to 1990 (6.43 mg/day to 9.43 mg/day) (Scottish Office, 1993).

These results, although encouraging, must be considered in the light of evidence that the intake of sodium and the proportion of energy from fat and saturated fat remain greater in Scotland than in England and Wales (MAFF, 1996). Similarly, intakes of vitamin C and beta-carotene in Scotland have not increased, although trends in food consumption are encouraging. National Food Survey data (Table 12.6) also show considerable decreases in milk, cream, meat and meat products and sugar intakes between 1985 and 1994, although fruits and vegetables, potatoes and cereals have been more variable. It must be remembered that NFS data have only recorded foods coming into the home, so trends may not totally reflect changing patterns of eating. It is likely that an increasing proportion of total food is now eaten outside the home and there may well be increases in fats in snacks and fast foods.

Table 12.6 Changes in household food (per person per week) in Scotland 1985–90 (source: MAFF, cited in *The Scottish Diet* (Scottish Office, 1993) and MAFF (1996))

Food groups	1985	1990	1994
Milk and cream (pints)	4.19	3.80	3.69
Sugar and preserves (oz)	10.06	8.57	5.88
Meat and meat products (oz)	35.99	34.48	33.20

Data from the Scottish Milk Marketing Board (1990) show that reduced fat milk consumption increased dramatically from 0.3 pints/head/week in 1983 to 1.56 pints/head/week in 1989, and it appears to be continuing to increase with up to 68% of milk consumers now regularly using semi-skimmed and skimmed milk (Grampian Health Board, 1995).

Data from the Computer Assisted Telephone Interviewing (CATI) survey at the Research Unit in Health and Behavioural Change in Edinburgh report that in the years between 1988 and 1993 there has been a significant decrease in the frequency of adding salt to food at the table 'most of the time' – from 42.2 to 38.7% of consumers – and the use of butter – from 32 to 14.9% amongst Scottish consumers (Robertson and Uitenbroek, 1993; Robertson, Uitenbroek and Hay, 1993).

Although nutritional and dietary changes may be rather small to date they can be interpreted as showing that people are making appropriate changes for food purchases and that some eating habits in the home are heading in the right direction. Encouraging changes in disease profiles are in agreement, but still quite small and provide further evidence of the need for continuous progress. Rates of death for acute myocardial infarction before the age of 65 continue to fall (2118 in 1993, compared to 1799 in 1994). Cancer deaths below the age of 65 have also fallen from 2203 in 1993 to 2104 in 1994 in men, although rates rose slightly in women (Scottish Office, 1995). The decrease in smoking in men has had a major impact on these figures but it is likely that other aspects of life-style change, including diet, have played an important role.

These small changes in disease patterns are encouraging for health promotion and dietary educationalists but the slow rate of change emphasizes the need for greater action, partnership between agencies and co-ordinated activities from all members of 'the food network' not just individual actions by the consumer. The present awareness of the role of diet in long-term health and disease prevention has been well promoted by NHS staff through dietetic and health promotion departments and assisted by some changes in food supply, notably the range of low-fat and low-sugar products available. However, it is clear from surveys of attitudes that there is considerable complacency about changing dietary habits (Anderson *et al.*, 1994) and it is unlikely that major changes needed to reach government targets for diet can come about from the present focus on individual activities. Ultimately, reaching these targets, which would certainly lead to a great improvement in health, can only be met if there is a change in total food provision in the country. Policy guidelines on food composition for the producer, processor and caterer are likely to be considerably more effective than further emphasis on actions carried out at an individual level. The work of the Scottish Diet Action Group emphasizes the need for a co-ordinated programme of change in all divisions of the food supply system.

12.7 The future

Scotland's ill health is clearly still a cause for concern. The biggest worry is the high level of preventable ill health, and diet composition is a critical part. Chronic diet-related diseases are a major burden on the workforce, health service and national economy. However, actions to facilitate dietary change have been seen in almost every area and it is hoped that initial (often innovative) work will be developed and expanded.

Amongst health activists there is tremendous energy and enthusiasm to continue the current trends to promote change in food selection. Dietitians and health promoters have much to offer the food industry and food network in general. The NHS has set an example for change which might be followed by others, although there is still great potential for further action. For example, many large hospitals now have retail outlets attached – these should provide healthy eating opportunities in line with food policy guidelines but this is not necessarily the case (as witnessed by the attempts to locate a McDonalds at the Southern General Hospital in Glasgow). There is a need for health boards and trusts to identify a senior person with understanding and training in nutrition to inform policy and strategies in all areas.

Clearly, food is of interest and concern to many agencies – not just because of its health properties but also because of its social value, its role in aiding communication and its central role in family life. Any and all attempts to change dietary intake need to take a wide view of how such actions will be received. Social and cultural 'traditions' of the past two decades are strong and the values attached to familiar, everyday foods cannot be dismissed. Change needs to evolve from within communities as well as from external forces and it cannot be imposed by a 'nanny state'.

Change also needs to be monitored and evaluated. Nutrient intakes in Scotland are monitored by the UK National Food Survey and within the National Diet and Nutrition Survey, and changes in food selection will also be monitored by the Scottish Health Survey, which commenced in 1995. Accurate profiles of health, disease, nutrition and food intakes are required to retain credibility, monitor disease trends and to sustain enthusiasm for healthy food choices and changes where necessary in the twenty-first century.

In conclusion, achieving dietary change will mean alterations in the supply of healthier foodstuffs from producers as well as increased consumer demand. Although there have been, to date, a wide range of food-related actions, the time is ripe for a co-ordinating body to unify action and fully realize the potential of all aspects of Scotland's food network for promoting healthy eating. National dietary targets and guidelines now need to be translated into dietary action.

References

Anderson, A.S. and Hunt, K. (1992) Who are the 'healthy eaters'. Eating patterns and health promotion in the West of Scotland. *Health Education Journal*, **51**, 3–10.

Anderson, A.S. and Lean, M.E.J. (1987) Setting an example: food and health policy with the National Health Service. *Health Education Research*, **2**(3), 275–85.

Anderson, A.S., Hunt, K., Ford, G. and Finnigan, F. (1994) One apple a day? Fruit and vegetable intake in the West of Scotland. *Health Education Research*, **9**(3), 297–305.

Anderson, A.S., Foster, A., Lean, M.E.J. and Marshall, D. (1994) Ripe for change – fruit and vegetable consumption in Scotland. *Health Bulletin*, **52**, 51–64.

Bolton-Smith, G. (1991) The diets of Scottish men and women in relation to nutritional recommendations for health. *Health Bulletin*, **49**, 264–72.

Boyd Orr, J. (1936) *Food, health and income*, Macmillan, London.

Carnegie UK Trust (1955) *Family Diet and Health in Pre-war Britain*, Report of the Carnegie Trust for the Rowett Research Institute.

Crosswaite, C. and McQueen, D.V. (1993) *The Implementation of Smoking and Nutrition Policies in Scotland and Finland: A Report*, Research Unit in Health Behavioural Change, Edinburgh.

DHSS (1984) *Diet and Cardiovascular Disease*, Report on health and social subjects 28, HMSO, London.

Forsyth, A., Macintyre, S. and Anderson, A.S. (1994) Diets for disease? Intraurban variation in reported food consumption in Glasgow. *Appetite*, **22**, 259–74.

Grampian Health Board (1995) *Adult Lifestyle Report*, GHB, Aberdeen.

Gregory, J., Foster, K., Tyler, H. and Wiseman, M. (1990) *Dietary and Nutritional Survey of British Adults*, HMSO, London.

Health Education Council (1983) *A discussion paper on proposals for nutritional guidelines for health education in Britain (NACNE)*, HEC, London.

Horowitz, T. (1992) To die for: lethal cuisine takes high toll in Glasgow, West's sickest city. *Wall Street Journal*, 23rd September, p. 1, col. 1.

MAFF (Ministry of Agriculture Fisheries and Food) (1966) *National Food Survey, 1994: Annual Report on Household Food Consumption and Expenditure*, HMSO, London.

Robertson, B. and Uitenbroek, D. (1993) *Health Behaviours among the Scottish General Public, 1993 Report*, Research Unit in Health and Behavioural Change, University of Edinburgh.

Robertson, B., Uitenbroek, D. and Hay, S. (1993) *Health Behaviours among the Scottish General Public 1994 Report*, Research Unit in Health and Behavioural Change, University of Edinburgh.

Scottish Home and Health Department (1990) *Prevention of Coronary Heart Disease in Scotland*, SHHD, Edinburgh.

Scottish Milk Marketing Board (1990) *The Household Market for Milk in Scotland*, Scottish Milk Marketing Board, Paisley.

Scottish Office (1992) *Scotland's Health – a challenge to us all*, HMSO, Edinburgh.

Scottish Office (1993) *The Scottish Diet*. Report of a working party to the Chief Medical Officer for Scotland, HMSO, Edinburgh.

Scottish Office: Information Directorate (1995) *Chief Medical Officer Reports Scotland's Health Improving Steadily*, HMSO, Edinburgh.

Tannahill, A. (1988) Health promotion and public health: a model in action. *Community Medicine*, **10**(1), 43–51.

Tunstall-Pedoe, H., Smith, W.C.S. and Crombie, I.K. (1989) Coronary risk factor and lifestyle variation across Scotland: results for the Scottish Heart Health Survey. *Scottish Medical Journal*, **34**, 355–60.

Whichelow, M. (1987) Dietary habits, in *Health and Lifestyle Survey* (eds B. Cox *et al.*), London Research Trust.

WHO (1986) *Ottawa Charter for Health Promotion*, World Health Organization, Ottawa.

Wreiden, W., Bolton-Smith, C., Brown, C. and Tunstall-Pedoe, H. (1993) Fruit and vegetable consumption in Glasgow; some results from the MONICA study of 1986 and 1989. *Proceedings of the Nutrition Society*, **52**, 12A.

13 Nutrition and dietary guidelines for the Spanish population. Tool for a nutrition policy in Spain

LLUÍS SERRA-MAJEM, JAVIER ARANCETA and GROUP OF NUTRITION GUIDELINES OF THE SPANISH SOCIETY OF COMMUNITY NUTRITION*

Spain can be considered a typical Mediterranean country that enjoys the so-called 'Mediterranean diet'. The term 'Mediterranean diet' has become popular in recent years, and has entered the language not only of the general public but also of scientific publications, with consistently positive, albeit rather vague, connotations. However, the term is used loosely and for varying purposes, and uncertainties remain about the dietary pattern it applies to, where in the Mediterranean region such a diet is to be found and precisely what it is expected to do for health (Ferro-Luzzi and Sette, 1989; Keys, 1995; Nestle, 1995a).

The particular composition of the Mediterranean diet and its beneficial effects on health were first pointed out by Keys *et al.* (Keys and Keys, 1975; Keys, 1980) and confirmed in his 'seven countries' study. More recently, the major characteristics of this dietary pattern have been defined (Helsing and Trichopoulou, 1989; Serra-Majem and Helsing, 1993) as have its time trends and potential use as a dietary guide for non-Mediterranean countries (James *et al.*, 1989; Nestle, 1995b; Willett *et al.*, 1995).

Since the 'seven countries' study, further studies in Mediterranean countries have linked dietary patterns to the occurrence of chronic diseases. A comparative analysis of these data with those from Western and Nordic countries includes estimates of risk and attributable proportions, that should

*Group of Nutrition Guidelines of the Spanish Society of Community Nutrition: Chairman: J. Mataix, University of Granada; Secretary: J. Aranceta, Basque Government; Members: V. Arija, University of Rovira i Virgili; M. De Oya, Spanish Society of Arteriosclerosis; P. Espí, Autonomous Government of Valencia; C. López-Nomdedeu, Spanish Ministry of Health; G. Lloveras, Autonomous Government of Catalonia; A. Mariné Font, University of Barcelona; O. Moreiras, University Complutense of Madrid; J. Peña, Spanish Society of Paediatrics; C. Pérez, Municipality of Bilbao; L. Ribas, University of Barcelona; E. Ros, Spanish Society of Arteriosclerosis; L. Serra-Majem, University of Las Palmas; A. Sierra, University of La Laguna; G. Varela, Spanish Society of Nutrition; F. Villar, Spanish Ministry of Health; J. Vioque, Spanish Society of Epidemiology.

Implementing Dietary Guidelines for Healthy Eating. Edited by Verner Wheelock. Published in 1997 by Blackie A&P, an imprint of Chapman & Hall, London. ISBN 0 7514 0304 0

be especially useful for understanding the magnitude of diet as a risk factor for chronic diseases in the Mediterranean as compared to other countries (La Vecchia, Harris and Wynder, 1988; Doll, 1994; Tavani and La Vecchia, 1995).

Does the Mediterranean diet still exist? Recently, several authors have reviewed changes in patterns of fat intake in Mediterranean countries (Serra-Majem and Helsing, 1993). Significant changes have occurred in the consumption of some – but not all – foods, in both positive and negative directions with respect to dietary recommendations. The negative changes have included an increase in consumption of animal products, particularly pork, beef and poultry, and a decrease in cereals, potatoes and pulses. Positive changes have included an increase in fruit consumption and a decrease in lard consumption, and some improvements in food quality. Therefore, the Mediterranean diet still exists, but it is now quite different from dietary patterns of the 1960s (Ferro-Luzzi *et al.*, 1984; Helsing, 1993). As for the future, the continued existence of traditional Mediterranean dietary patterns seems possible only if comprehensive nutritional policies are developed to ensure its survival (Serra-Majem *et al.*, 1996).

13.1 Dietary and nutritional patterns in Spain

To illustrate the reasons for this conclusion, we review recent changes in the dietary patterns of Spain. Because agricultural policy in this country is largely determined by the European Union (EU), the EU also determines nutritional policy through its decisions related to cattle-raising, trade relations and food labelling. Thus, the European geopolitical system is characterized by an upward devolution of responsibility to the EU government in Brussels, and a downward devolution towards regional governments, with profound effects on nutritional policies.

Within this policy context, nutritional planning requires an understanding of local food consumption patterns. Two types of dietary data are collected regularly in most European countries, including Spain: agricultural supply and utilization data in the form of food balance sheets as prepared by the Food and Agriculture Organization of the United Nations (FAO), the Organization for Economic Co-operation and Development (OECD), Eurostat or national administrations, and household budget survey data. In addition, some countries sporadically conduct special dietary surveys based on nationally representative population samples.

Special surveys, conducted at regular intervals, could be used to describe the usual food consumption and nutrient intake patterns of the population (Sekula, 1993). However, the high cost of these surveys has prohibited their establishment in Spain on a national level; instead, they only have been conducted at the regional or local level, and the methods used were not always the same.

Table 13.1 shows trends in consumption of key food groups in Spain from 1964 to 1991, as derived from household budget surveys. Such surveys tend to overestimate consumption of foods such as bread, potatoes, pulses, vegetables, fruit, milk and vegetable oils as compared to individual dietary records, and to underestimate data on food balance sheets by at least 20%. Data in Table 13.1 demonstrate an increase in consumption of fruit, meats, fish and seafood and dairy products, and a decrease in edible fats, cereals, potatoes, pulses and sugar.

Table 13.1 Trends in food consumption in Spain (g/person/day; 1964–91) (source: Moreiras, Carbajal and Campo, 1995)

	1964	1981	1991
Milk and dairy products	228	381	375
Cereals	476	272	239
Potatoes	300	196	145
Fish	63	72	76
Red meat	47	87	90
Meat products (sausages)	16	33	39
Poultry meat	14	59	58
Edible fat	68	65	55
Eggs	32	45	35
Pulses	41	24	20
Fruits	162	282	300
Vegetables	151	202	173
Sugar	39	37	29

In Spain, dietary surveys have been conducted only at the regional level, using 24-hour recalls (from 1 to 3 days) combined with a food frequency questionnaire. A comparison of macronutrient intake from four regions is given in Table 13.2. Surveys have been conducted in Catalonia (Serra-Majem *et al.*, 1996), the Basque Country (Aranceta *et al.*, 1990), Madrid (Aranceta *et al.*, 1994), Valencia (Vioque and Quiles, 1995), Murcia (Violan, Stevens and Molina, 1991), and the Canary Islands (Doreste, 1987). In these surveys, fat intake ranged from 100–108 g/day among men, and from 71–91 g/day among women; saturated fat intake ranged from 32–38 g/day among men, and from 21–32 g/day among women. Regional differences were much greater among women than men.

13.2 Nutritional policy in Spain

With the exception of Malta, no European Mediterranean country has a policy on nutrition at the national level. Most countries have developed nutritional objectives and dietary guidelines as well as some system for monitoring nutritional information, but no structured nutritional policies. Several reasons explain this gap. Nutrition receives scant attention from the public health sector, perhaps because it is less relevant as a risk factor in the Mediterranean than in northern Europe. The role of the EU in agricultural policies also affects development of nutritional policies. Another reason is the less interventionist attitude toward health policy in the Mediterranean. Finally, there is great emphasis placed on consumer demand in formulating nutritional policy in Mediterranean countries. Such issues have affected policy development in Malta, Italy and Spain, as well as in the other countries in the region.

The modern history of Spain begins with the failure of two attempts to construct a parliamentary Republican system that led to civil war in 1936 and a totalitarian regime that was to last until 1975. The post-civil war period was one of deep economic and social crisis, aggravated by the Second World War. The period from 1961 to 1975 was one of expansion and development that included not only an invasion of tourists, but also large-scale internal migration leading to unprecedented urbanization. Since 1975, the country has been governed by a democratic system. From 1985 to 1991, Spain experienced decisive social, economic and political changes leading to its present situation. Today, the Spanish state is composed of 17 autonomous communities, each with a parliament and executive government that have assumed considerable responsibility from the central administration. Three of these communities retain historic names going back to earlier periods of self-determination: Catalonia, the Basque Country and Galicia. Spain joined the EU in 1985 (MAE, 1986). Today, its population is 39.1 million.

Like the other southern European countries, Spain has no formal nutritional policy, but the Ministries of Agriculture and Health conduct many related activities (MAPA, 1991a, 1991b). The major sources of information about food availability and dietary intake in Spain are:

- food balance sheets – FAO, OCDE, Ministry of Agriculture, Industry, Trade;
- household budget surveys – National Institute of Statistics (every 10 years and continuously);
- household consumption surveys – Ministry of Agriculture (every year);
- individual dietary surveys (at regional level only)
  Canary Isles (1983–85)
  Catalonia (1986)
  Basque Country (1989)
  Murcia (1990)
  Madrid (1992–93)
  Catalonia (1992–93)
  Valencia (1993–94)

Despite these many sources of information, there is no co-ordinated food consumption monitoring system at the national level. Furthermore, the periodic evaluations of Spain's health objectives do not probe nutritional indicators, except for obesity which is estimated using self-reported weight and height (Regidor, Gutiérrez and Rodriguez, 1993; Serra-Majem *et al.*, 1993).

In Spain, the 17 autonomous regions are responsible for development of health plans consistent with the World Health Organization Regional Office for Europe (WHO–Europe) 'Health for All for the Year 2000' initiative and with the Spanish health law. To date, 10 regions have reinforced their health plans with a law or decree, and only four have not yet approved one.

All the regions have received the authority in health promotion and health protection, except those concerning international health, but only six have received the authority in health care planning and administration (Catalonia received them earlier, in 1982, five years before the Basque Country, Valencia and Andalusia) (MSC, 1994).

Nearly all of the regional health plans have included an analysis of the situation, health objectives and describe specific programmes and activities to develop. Some regional health plans do not include nutritional objectives, even though nutritional information from household budget surveys can be desegregated at the regional level. In addition, recent nutritional surveys have been conducted or are ongoing in several regions, and surveys were also conducted in the Canary Islands and in Catalonia 10 years ago (see above: Doreste, 1987; Aranceta *et al.*, 1990, 1994; Violan, Stevens and Molina, 1991; Vioque and Quiles, 1995, Serra-Majem *et al.*, 1996). Additional information also could be derived from the results of school feeding programmes in Bilbao (Aranceta and Perez, 1986), school catering interventions in Barcelona (Maldonado and Villalbí, 1995), supermarket interventions in Valencia (Vaandrager *et al.*, 1993) and others. However, since 1995, no nutritional and dietary guidelines had been defined for the Spanish state.

13.3 Nutritional objectives for Spain

Present-day scientific and epidemiological knowledge points to a clearly marked relationship between consumption of fats and various high-profile chronic diseases, and this has led a group of FAO/WHO experts to recommend that fat intake not above 30% of daily energy be set as the aim for the population. Very low-fat diets can cause problems in satisfying energy and nutrient needs. This group, therefore, suggested that the lower limit for fat intake should be set at 15% of daily energy, a sufficient level for covering needs for essential fatty acids and fat-soluble vitamins. The group, like many other bodies, recommended distributing the energy intake evenly between saturated fats (10%), monounsaturates (10%) and polyunsaturates (10%), though no excessively scientific criterion existed, except with saturated fats (<10%).

In Spain, as in the rest of the Mediterranean countries, these general WHO recommendations are difficult to implement. In our diet the contribution of olive oil represents between 13 and 20% of consumed energy (according to regions) which makes it difficult to carry out the plan to reduce the contribution of energy from fats to 30%.

In the context of the Mediterranean diet it would be possible to maintain the present level of olive oil consumption and aim at reducing by 3–4% the energy provided by fats derived from polyunsaturated fatty acids (PUFA).

Data from the latest food surveys carried out in Spain, generally, put the energy intake from fats at between 37 and 42% (Table 13.3). Though it involved modifying the WHO recommendations somewhat, the Spanish Association for Community Nutrition is carrying out a set of nutritional recommendations with the assent of the Nutrition Unit of the WHO Regional Office for Europe, which is compared in Table 13.3 with the rest of the aims or nutritional guidelines analysed. This proposal of nutritional aims for the Spanish population was analysed and debated at the meeting on 24 October 1994 during a consensus meeting held in Barcelona. The main point is to recommend a relative intake of fat below 35% of energy if olive oil is the most important fat consumed (as happens in most of the Spanish regions).

Table 13.2 Results of various nutritional surveys in Spanish autonomous regions (source: Aranceta *et al.*, 1990, 1994; Violan, Stevens and Molina, 1991; Serra Majem *et al.*, 1996)

		Catalonia 1992–93	Madrid 1992–93	Murcia 1990	Basque Country 1989
Energy	M	2334	2697	2610	2944
(kcal)	W	1809	2116	1760	2049
Protein	M	100	106	97	109
(g/day)	W	81	86	70	78
Total fat	M	97	105	105	105
(g/day)	W	77	89	71	86
Saturated fat	M	33	35	32	36
(g/day)	W	26	28	21	29
Cholesterol	M	474	430	441	608
(mg/day)	W	388	334	317	429

M, men; W, women

Table 13.3 Nutritional objectives for Europe (WHO–Europe) and Spain (Spanish Society of Community Nutrition)

	Estimated present situation in Spain	Nutritional objectives (WHO)[a]	Nutritional objectives (SENC)[b]
Body weight	BMI = 25–26	BMI 20–25	BMI 20–25
Total fat (% energy)	40[c]	20–30	≤35[d] ≤30[e]
Saturated fat (% energy)	13	10	≤10
PUFA (% energy)	7	10 PUFA/SFA=1	≤7 UF/SF≥2.0
Cholesterol (mg/1000 kcal)	150	<100	≤100
Sugar (% energy)	10	10	≤10
Complex CH (% energy)	33	45–55	>50
Fibre (g/day)	≤20	30	>25
Nutrient density	Acceptable	↑	↑
Salt (g/day)	9	5	<6
Proteins (% energy)	>15	12–13	13
Alcohol (% energy)	6	Limit	Reduce ≤1–2 glasses of wine/day
Fluorides in water (mg/l)	<0.3	0.7–1.2	–
Iodine prophylaxis	Variable	+	Fluoridated-iodinated salt

Data adapted from different studies.
[a]From WHO–Europe, 1987 (James, Duthie and Whale, 1989).
[b]SENC, Spanish Association of Community Nutrition. Guidelines adopted in a consensus meeting held in Barcelona (Serra-Majem, Aranceta and Mataix, 1995).
[c]Alcohol-free energy.
[d]In case of frequent use of olive oil.
[e]In case of not using olive oil frequently.
SFA, saturated fatty acids; PUFA, polyunsaturated fatty acids; UF/SF, unsaturated fats/saturated fats.

13.4 Dietary guidelines

In order to achieve the nutritional aims set, health promotion programmes envisaging different types of community intervention strategies need to be developed and implemented. A big part in these actions is played by the planning of food and nutritional policies from a global viewpoint, involving all sectors in the final aim of guaranteeing the health of the population.

With this in mind, dietary guidelines are published, translating the nutritional aims – scientifically formulated and expressed in numerical terms as quantities of nutrients and percentages of energy – into more everyday terms. In these guidelines, the recommendations are expressed qualitatively as the most positive foods, portions and trends for health. The dietary guidelines are directed to the individual and, therefore, put in a friendly, persuasive or suggestive mode (Guthrie, 1987; Bengoa *et al.*, 1988). The dietary guidelines are necessary as a reference point for nutritional education among different groups of the population and as suggestions and a reference framework for the food industry. Most of the changes recommended are directed toward the whole population, though some guidelines have in mind specific advice to vulnerable groups.

At present there are nutritional aims and dietary guidelines in many countries. Some of these documents have been drawn up by official bodies and others by scientific bodies or associations (RMHSA, 1982; NACNE, 1983; DHHS, 1985; MHW, 1985; CDH, 1987; TGFW, 1991).

The main recommendations included in the dietary guidelines refer to maintaining a proper weight, moderation in the consumption of saturated fats, an increase in the consumption of complex carbohydrates, moderate consumption of alcohol and salt and promotion of moderate physical exercise. As a complement, some countries include in their recommendations promotion of breast-feeding (Australia and Canada), care of culinary techniques (Germany and Quebec), increasing the consumption of fish (Norway), maintaining the consumption of animal proteins (France and New Zealand) or happy eating for the happy family (Japan). A list of key points is used, groups of foods are depicted in a food wheel, as they were in Canada, France and Spain. In order to translate the nutritional aims into a more accessible language for the United States population, the US Department of Agriculture in 1991 designed a dietary guide chromatically and conceptually included within a pyramid (USDA, 1992). At the base of the pyramid were included those foods that it was thought necessary to promote (bread, cereals, rice and pasta). The section immediately above was primarily made up of the group of greens and vegetables, followed by the groups of dairy and essentially protein foods, clearly putting over the idea of moderating the consumption of oils, fats and sugar.

Recently, this concept of a guidelines with a pyramid structure has been adapted to the situation of the Mediterranean diet (ICDM, 1993), modified in some aspects in the 1994 Oldways–Harvard University, and WHO version (Oldways Preservation, Exchange Trust and Harvard School of Public Health, WHO–Europe, 1994).The format of the USDA pyramid has also been adapted to the Hispano-Mexican diet (PSNC, 1993). The latest qualitative adaptation of the pyramid to the Mediterranean diet has been that carried out by means of a chromatic design by the group of the Public Health School of the University of Athens (Trichopoulou, 1994). The proposal to design a dietary guide for the Spanish population in a pyramidal chromatic structure has also been discussed and was debated at the consensus meeting (Fig. 13.1). We can cite as an antecedent of this present initiative, the guidelines designed for the general population of the Basque people (1991) (Departamento de Sanidad, 1991), once their usual feeding profile was epidemiologically known. In the Basque Country, they had as complementary support material a food wheel drawn with an aerograph (Aranceta, 1991). In Catalonia, a table has been adopted in place of the wheel, the term in Catalan ('taula') meaning both figurative table and real table (Serra-Majem and Salvador, 1988) and in the state as a whole, the Ministry of Public Health also published a wheel of foodstuffs in the context of the EDALNU Food Education Programme.

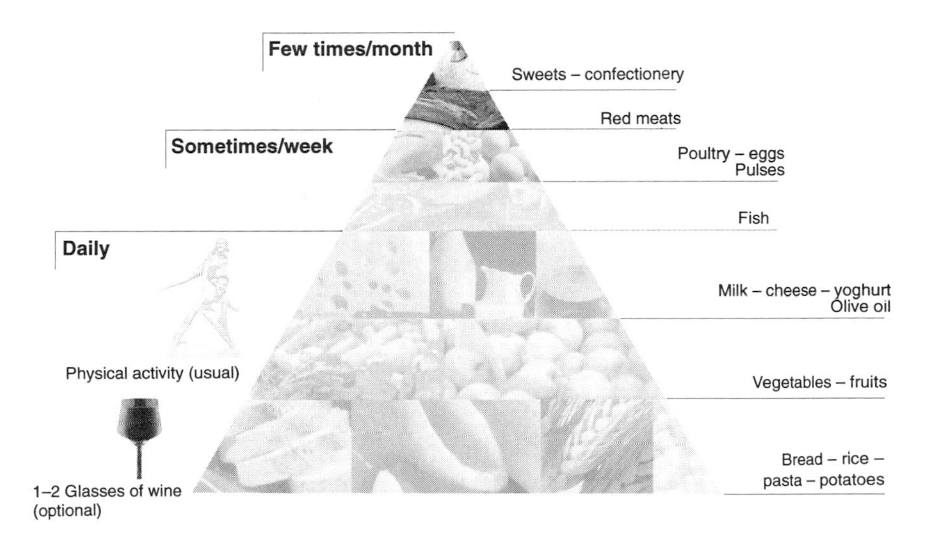

Figure 13.1 Pyramid of the healthy diet. Dietary Guidelines for the Spanish population (source: J. Aranceta, L. Serra-Majem, C. Perez and J. Mataix; Spanish Association of Community Nutrition, 1995).

In general, the drawing of dietary guidelines should be a dynamic process brought up to date and adapted to new technologies. In this context, it is very important to keep in mind that these need to be addressed to the general population, to industry and also to those politically responsible. It is desirable that the drawing up of nutritional aims and dietary guidelines be carried out by interdisciplinary work groups, working harmoniously together. In this way the scientific bases of the recommendations may be more correctly drawn up and, at the same time, a better way may be found for transmitting the message in a friendly and attractive form to the population (dietary guidelines). In the future, the Spanish Association of Community Nutrition intends to advance this line of work, which will culminate in the publication of the first food guidelines for the Spanish population and perhaps with consensus on nutritional policy at state level throughout Spain.

Acknowledgements

The authors thank Mr Anthony Currant for his valuable editorial support, and Mrs Vicky Serra for typing the manuscript.

References

Aranceta, J. (ed.) (1991) *Programa de educación nutricional para la Comunidad Autónoma del País Vasco*, Dirección de Salud Pública, Departamento de Sanidad, GobiernoVasco.

Aranceta, J. and Pérez, C. (1986) Evaluación y hábitos alimentarios de los escolares de los colegios públicos de la villa de Bilbao. *Arch. Pediatr.* **37**, 523–34.

Aranceta, J., Pérez, C., Eguileor, I. *et al.* (1990) *Encuesta Nutricional del País Vasco*, Gobierno Vasco, Vitoria.

Aranceta, J., Pérez, C., Amela, C. and García Herrera, R. (1994) *Encuesta de Nutrición de la Comunidad de Madrid.* Consejería de Salud de la Comunidad de Madrid, Madrid.

Bengoa, J.M., Torún, B., Béhard, M. and Scrimshaw, N.S. (1988) *Guías de Alimentación: Bases para su Desarrollo en América Latina*, Universidad de las Naciones Unidas y Fundación Cavendes, Caracas, Venezuela.

COH (Commonwealth Department of Health) (1987) *Towards better nutrition for Australians. Report of the Nutrition Task Force of the Better Health Commission*, Commonwealth Printing Office, Canberra.

Departamento de Sanidad (1991) *Rueda de los alimentos,* Servicio de publicaciones. Gobierno Vasco, Vitoria.

DHHS (1985) Nutrition and your health. Dietary guidelines for Americans, 2nd edn. *Home and Garden Bulletin*, no. 232, US Government Printing Office, Washington, DC.

Doll, R. (1994) The use of meta-analysis in epidemiology: diets and cancers of the breast and colon. *Nutr. Review*, **52**, 233–7.

Doreste, J.L. (1987) Encuesta de alimentación y valoración nutricional de la comunidad canaria. Doctoral thesis, Universidad de la Laguna, La Laguna.

Ferro-Luzzi, A. and Sette, S. (1989) The Mediterranean diet: an attempt to define its present and past composition. *Eur. J. Clin. Nutr.* **43**, (Suppl. 2), 13–30.

Ferro-Luzzi, A., Strazzulo, P., Scaccini, C. *et al.* (1984) Changing the Mediterranean diet: effects on blood lipids. *Am. J. Clin. Nutr.* **40**, 1027–37.

Guthrie, H. (1987) Principles and issues in translating dietary recommendations to food election: a nutrition educator's point of view. *Am. J. Clin. Nutr.* **45**, 1394–8.

Helsing, E. (1993) Trends in fat consumption in Europe and their influence on the Mediterranean diet. *Eur. J. Clin. Nutr.* 47, (Suppl. 1), 4–12.

Helsing, E. and Trichopoulou, A. (eds) (1989) The Mediterranean Diet and Food Culture – a Symposium. *Eur. J. Clin. Nutr.* **43**, (Suppl. 2), 1–92.

ICDM (International Conference on the Diets of the Mediterranean) (1993) *Optimal Traditional Mediterranean Diet.* Preliminary Concept. ICDM.

James, W.P.T., Duthie, G.G.. and Wahle, K.W.J. (1989) The Mediterranean diet: protective or simply non-toxic? *Eur. J. Clin. Nutr.* **43**, (Suppl. 2), 31–42.

Keys, A. (ed.) (1980) *Seven Countries. A Multivariate Analysis of Death and Coronary Heart Diseases*, Harvard University Press, Cambridge, MA.

Keys, A. (1995) Mediterranean diet and public health? personal reflections. *Am. J. Clin. Nutr.* **61**, (suppl.), 1321S–1323S.

Keys, A. and Keys, M. (1975) *How to Eat Well and Stay Well, the Mediterranean Way*, Doubleday, New York.

La Vecchia, C., Harris, R.E. and Wynder, E.L. (1988) Comparative epidemiology of cancer between the United States and Italy. *Cancer Res.*, **48**, 7285–93.

Maldonado, R. and Villalbí, J.R. (1995) Educación nutricional y comedor escolar. Concordancia o discrepancia? *An. Esp. Pediatr.*, **42**, 100–14.

MAPA (Ministerio de Agricultura Pesca y Alimentación (1991a) *Consumo Alimentario en España 1990*, Tomos I y II, Dirección General de Política Alimentaria, Madrid.

MAPA (Ministerio de Agricultura Pesca y Alimentación) (1991b) *Dieta Alimentaria Española 1990,* Dirección General de Política Alimentaria, Madrid.
MHW (Ministry of Health and Welfare) (1985) Dietary guidelines for health promotion. Vol 29. Health Promotion and Nutrition Division. Health Services Bureau. Ministry of Health and Welfare, Tokyo. *The Nutrition of Japan*, **20**, (4), 29/172–177.
MAE (Ministerio de Asuntos Exteriores) (1986) *Comunidades Europeas: adhesión de España: trat. hecho en Lisboa y Madrid el día 12 junio 1985; ratificado por Instr. 20 sept. 1985*, BOE (núm. 1) de 1 de Enero, Madrid.
Moreiras, O., Carbajal, A. and Campo, M. (1995) Tendencias de los hábitos alimentarios y estado nutricional en España. Resultados de las encuestas de presupuestos familiares, in *Documento de consenso: guías alimentarias para la población española* (eds L. Serra-Majem, J. Aranceta, J. Mataix *et al.*), Sociedad Española de Nutrición Comunitaria – SG Editores, Barcelona.
MSC (Ministerio de Sanidad y Consumo) (1994) *Dirección General de Alta Inspección y Relaciones Institucionales 'Estudio descriptivo de los Planes de Salud en España'*, Mimeo.
NACNE (National Advisor Committee for Nutrition Education) (1983) *National Research Council. A discussion paper on proposals for nutrition guidelines for health education in Britain*, Health Education Council, London.
Nestle, M. (1995a) Mediterranean diets: historical and research overview. *Am. J. Clin. Nutr.*, **61**, (Suppl.), 1313S–1320S.
Nestle, M. (ed.) (1995b) Mediterranean diets. *Am. J. Clin. Nutr.* **61**, (suppl.), 1313S–1427S.
Oldways Preservation, Exchange Trust and Harvard School of Public Health,WHO-Europe (1994) *The Traditional Healthy Mediterranean Diet Pyramid*, Oldways Preservation and Exchange Trust, Boston.
PSNC (Penn State Nutrition Center) (1993) *Pyramid Packet*, Penn State University, University Park.
Regidor, E., Gutiérrez, J.L. and Rodríguez, C. (1993) *Indicadores de salud. Segunda evaluación en España del programa regional europeo salud para todos*, Ministerio de Sanidad y Consumo, Madrid, pp. 143–4.
RMHSA (Royal Ministry of Health and Social Affairs) (1982) *Report No. 11 to the Storting. On the Follow-Up of Norwegian Nutrition Policy*, RMHSA, Oslo.
Sekula, W. (1993) Nutrition information systems in Europe, in *Food and Nutrition Policy in Europe* (eds D.G. Van der Heij, M.R.H. Löwik and Th. Ockhuizen), Pudoc Scientific Publishers, Wageningen, pp. 101–12.
Serra-Majem, L. and Helsing, E. (eds) (1993) Changing patterns of fat intake in Mediterranean Countries. *Eur. J. Clin. Nutr.* **47**, (Suppl. 1), 1–100.
Serra-Majem, L. and Salvador, G. (eds) (1988) Recomanacions alimentàries, in *Llibre Blanc: Hàbits alimentaris i consum d'energia i nutrients a Catalunya*, Departament de Sanitat i Seguretat Social, Barcelona.
Serra-Majem, L., Ribas, L., Lloveras, G. and Salleras, L. (1993) Changing patterns of fat consumption in Spain. *Eur. J. Clin. Nutr.* **47**, (Suppl.), S13–S20.
Serra-Majem, L., Aranceta, J. and Mataix, J. (eds) (1995) *Documento de Consenso. Guías Alimentarias para le Población Española*, SG-Editores, Barcelona, pp. 1–317.
Serra-Majem, L., Ribas, L.,García-Closas, R. *et al.* (1996) *Llibre Blanc: Avaluació de l'estat nutricional de la població catalana* (1992–1993), Departament de Sanitat i Seguretat Social, Barcelona.
Tavani, A. and La Vecchia, C. (1995) Fruit and vegetables consumption and cancer risk in a Mediterranean population. *Am. J. Clin. Nutr.*, **61**, (Suppl.), 1374S-1377S.
TGFW (The Guild of Food Writers) (1991) *The Coronary Prevention Group. Eat well – live well*, The Coronary Prevention Group, London.
Trichopoulou, A. (1994) *Mediterranean Diet*, Department of Nutrition and Biochemistry. Athens School of Public Health, Athens.
USDA (1992) The food guide pyramid. Human Nutrition Information Service, *Home and Garden Bulletin*, no. 252, USDA, Washington DC.
Vaandrager, H.W., Koelen, M.A., Ashton, J.R. and Colomer Revuelta, C. (1993) A four-step health promotion approach for changing dietary patterns in Europe. *Eur. J. Public Health*, **3**, 193–8.
Violan, C., Stevens, L. and Molina, F. (1991) *Encuesta de Alimentación en la Población Adulta*

de Murcia 1990, Serie informes n°7, Consejería de Sanidad, Dirección General de Salud, Región de Murcia.

Vioque, J. and Quiles, J. (1995) Resultados preliminaries de la encuesta de Nutrición de la Comunidad valenciana, in *Documento de consenso: guías alimentarias para la población española* (eds L. Serra-Majem, J. Aranceta, J. Mataix *et al.*), Sociedad Española de Nutrición Comunitaria-SG Editores, Barcelona, pp. 121–4.

Willett, W.C., Sacks, F., Trichopoulou, A. *et al.* (1995) Mediterranean diet pyramid: a cultural model for healthy eating. *Am. J. Clin. Nutr.*, **61**, (Suppl.), 1402S–1406S.

14 Implementing dietary guidelines: Sweden

ÅKE BRUCE

14.1 Background

14.1.1 Public health

The following text is a summary from Sweden's contribution to the FAO/WHO International Conference on Nutrition 1992 (Swedish Ministry of Health and Social Affairs, Swedish Ministry of Agriculture, 1993).

In an international context Sweden's nutritional status is very good. As the socio-economic situation has improved, so has the health and nutrition situation. Life expectancy is among the highest in the world. Access to food is not a problem; there is no shortage of energy or individual nutrients. However, the high standard of living enjoyed by Swedes in recent decades has also created new problems. The most serious diseases in the Swedish middle-aged population today are cancer and cardiovascular diseases, both of which are clearly linked to life styles.

Public health has continued to improve in recent years. However, despite this general improvement, there are great differences as regards ill-health and mortality not only between different age groups, but also between the sexes, between different socio-economic groups and between different parts of the country, as well as between native Swedes and immigrants.

Almost all kinds of ill health are more common among the elderly than among the young. Class differences as reflected in health status are twice as great in the 61–71 age group as in the 15–30 age group. As regards mortality, class differences are most pronounced in the 34–45 age group and diminish in higher age groups. After retirement class differences between men disappear altogether, but can still be observed among women.

There are unmistakable social patterns for various categories of disease. Strokes are more common among blue-collar workers than among salaried employees. Different sectors of the population contract different types of cancers: for example, lung cancer and stomach cancer are more common among blue-collar workers than among salaried employees, while the

Implementing Dietary Guidelines for Healthy Eating. Edited by Verner Wheelock. Published in 1997 by Blackie A&P, an imprint of Chapman & Hall, London. ISBN 0 7514 0304 0

reverse is true of cancer of the colon, breast cancer and probably cancer of the prostate. Generally speaking, farmers run less risk than other groups of contracting cancer, and urban populations are more at risk than rural populations as regards most types of cancer. However, in an international perspective the differences between socio-economic groups in Sweden are less noticeable than in many other countries.

The aim of Sweden's health policies is to improve the health status of the population as a whole and to diminish the social differences in this respect. In the implementation of this policy, food and nutrition is only one of the areas where measures are taken, but an important one.

The regional differences that do exist are probably mainly due to differences in social structure, i.e. the ratio of blue-collar to white-collar workers. There are, however, some differences in the general health status of the population in the north of Sweden compared with the south, particularly in relation to cardiovascular disease and certain cancers (such as stomach cancer). There is also some evidence of differences between coastal and inland populations. These differences may to some extent be attributable to variations in eating habits and, as regards cardiac infarcts, to climatic factors (cold) and perhaps differences in the quality of drinking water. As regards bone mineral status and fractures, women in rural areas are in a better position than those who live in cities.

About 10% of the population has an immigrant or refugee background. Studies indicate higher morbidity among this group as compared with the rest of the population. Many immigrants and refugees come from countries with very different socio-cultural and natural environments. Their eating habits often change for the worse, since they tend to adopt some of the less desirable dietary practices of the industrialized world, such as increased consumption of sugar and fat, with resultant adverse effects on their health. Due to language and cultural barriers it is difficult to get nutritional messages through to immigrants. The nutritional consequences of immigration constitute an area that probably requires greater attention than it has received so far.

14.1.2 Political attitudes to diet and health

In January 1983, the Swedish government appointed a committee to formulate proposals for a new national food policy for the coming 10–15 years. The Food Committee of 1983 appointed several different groups of experts for the purpose of investigating and laying the basis for the Committee's report. One of these subcommittees was an Expert Group for Diet and Health, which presented its report in 1984 (Bruce, 1987).

In the government's directive to the Food Committee and its Expert Groups, it was stated that consumers should have access to foods, which from a nutritional and health point of view are satisfactory. Prices should be reasonable. The consumers should, however, be free to choose these foods according to taste and liking. The Expert Group was requested to report whether changes in consumption are desirable with respect to public health and, if so, suggest how these could be achieved and consider the implications for food production.

The report by the Expert Group gave a brief description of how health and nutritional matters had been approached in earlier reports on Swedish agricultural policy, where the primary consideration had been quantity, i.e. the volume of food produced. Nutritional aspects had been given little attention. The Expert Group devised guidelines concerning the changes in diet that are desirable to improve health. The Group defined a number of goals for reasonable changes up to the year 1990 and then a final goal for the year 2000.

For various reasons, the suggestions by this Expert Group had little impact on the immediate policy, but several of the proposals such as that on symbol labelling of foods, became effective during the beginning of the 1990s.

During recent years, the preparatory work for the International Conference on Nutrition (ICN) in Rome 1992 and subsequent activity has been of great importance in formulating a comprehensive national Swedish food and nutrition policy (Swedish Ministry of Health and Social Affairs, Swedish Ministry of Agriculture, 1992).

14.1.3 Administration

Public health is the responsibility of many different authorities and organizations. Preventive health care is largely provided at the local and regional levels. The government agencies and ministries that are immediately concerned with dietary matters are the National Food Administration and the Ministry of Agriculture, the National Board of Health and Welfare and the National Public Health Institute under the Ministry of Health and Social Affairs, and the National Board for Consumers Policies and the Ministry of Public Administration. The relationships between the ministries and the administrations are presented in Fig. 14.1. Other authorities with responsibility for

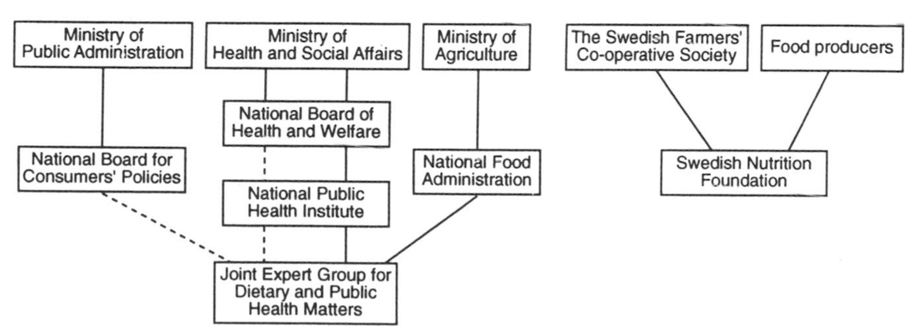

Figure 14.1 Relations between Swedish ministries and administrations, etc. responsible for national food and nutritional activities.

education, consumer policy, agricultural policy and environmental and chemical matters may also be concerned with public health in the broadest sense of the term.

A joint Expert Group for Dietary and Public Health Matters has been set up with representatives from the National Food Administration and the Public Health Institute. Most of the members of this group represent various medical disciplines. Its task is to monitor developments in research on the connection between dietary habits and health. Where necessary, the group is to draw the attention of the relevant authorities to the need to take measures. It is also to take account of matters relating to the production, processing and handling of food products that are likely to be associated with the effects of these products on health.

14.1.4 The food industry and distribution sector

In Sweden this sector is characterized by a very high degree of centralization, which is mainly due to its domination by three large national food store chains. As a result, local factors have very little impact on the nutritional content of food produced in Sweden. Likewise, traditional regional differences in dietary habits have tended to disappear, so that only marginal differences remain, such as higher consumption of crispbread and dairy products in the north of Sweden. In forested areas hunting (for elk meat) is still of importance.

The food distribution sector in Sweden is characterized by concentration into increasingly large and fewer units. Another feature of the industry is the domination of domestic production. Only about 10% (by value) of all food sales are from imports, which mainly consist of processed foods. The food sector is dominated by Swedish companies. The concentration in this sector exists, moreover, both in terms of geography and ownership. The Swedish Farmers' Co-operative Society has a strong position in certain processing industries (e.g. dairy and meat-packing) with market shares of between 70 and 100%. Food distribution is also concentrated in a small number of companies and the distribution stage is characterized by substantial vertical integration. The number of employees in the Swedish food industry in 1988 was about 67 000.

14.1.5 Institutional households and restaurants

There are about 35 000 institutional households in Sweden, two-thirds of which are in the public sector. The rest are staff restaurants, which are provided by practically all large workplaces. About two-thirds of the meals served by private restaurants are lunches, and the restaurants concerned thus fulfil the same function as staff restaurants in this respect.

Practically all schoolchildren and many adults are dependent on institutional food services of one kind or another for one of their main meals outside the home. Approximately 4.8 million meals a day are served by institutions or workplaces and therefore these services play an important part in eating and dietary habits.

Fast-food restaurants are also classed as institutional food services. Previously, people used to go to these for a snack, but nowadays fast-food meals increasingly seem to replace main meals. Today, fast-food outlets serve about 10% of all meals provided by institutional food services.

A number of studies of the food and nutritional quality provided by staff and private restaurants have been carried out in various parts of the country. The findings of these studies indicate that there are wide variations in nutritional content and that the majority of lunches served by such restaurants contain too much fat and salt. If the institutional food services followed the nutritional recommendations that have been issued, this would probably have a substantial impact on public health. This will only take place when the staff are sufficiently well trained and when there are sufficient nutrition-based recipes.

14.1.6 The Swedish dietary habits

Traditionally, Swedes have a large breakfast, lunch at midday and supper at 5 or 6 p.m., the latter two consisting of cooked food. The staple foods of the traditional Swedish diet were potatoes, bread, milk and other dairy products. The main course at lunch and supper used to consist of meat or fish, while vegetables, especially green vegetables, were not considered to be a very important item. Around the beginning of the twentieth century there was an increase in the consumption of fatty foods, such as edible fat and high-fat dairy products and sugar, both in cooking and because of increased consumption of pastries and confectionery. During the years before, during and after the Second World War a typical lunch consisted of meat and potatoes, a glass of milk and a piece of crispbread with plenty of butter.

Since the 1950s, however, a change has taken place in this diet, involving increased consumption of rice and pasta at the expense of potatoes, where pizzas and hamburgers have tended to replace traditional Swedish food. Milk consumption has decreased, but this has been offset by increased cheese consumption. Moreover, there has been an increase in the consumption of fresh fruit, fruit juice and vegetables (Fig. 14.2). In the past two or three decades eating habits have changed even more due to the impact of foreign travel and immigration. The traditional mealtimes are also undergoing changes.

The question of food quality has been the subject of much discussion in Sweden in recent years. To many people quality means food products that look and are fresh, as well as being free of colouring agents and preservatives. Quality can be perceived as freedom of choice between food that differs in taste, origin, method of production and degree of processing. In the

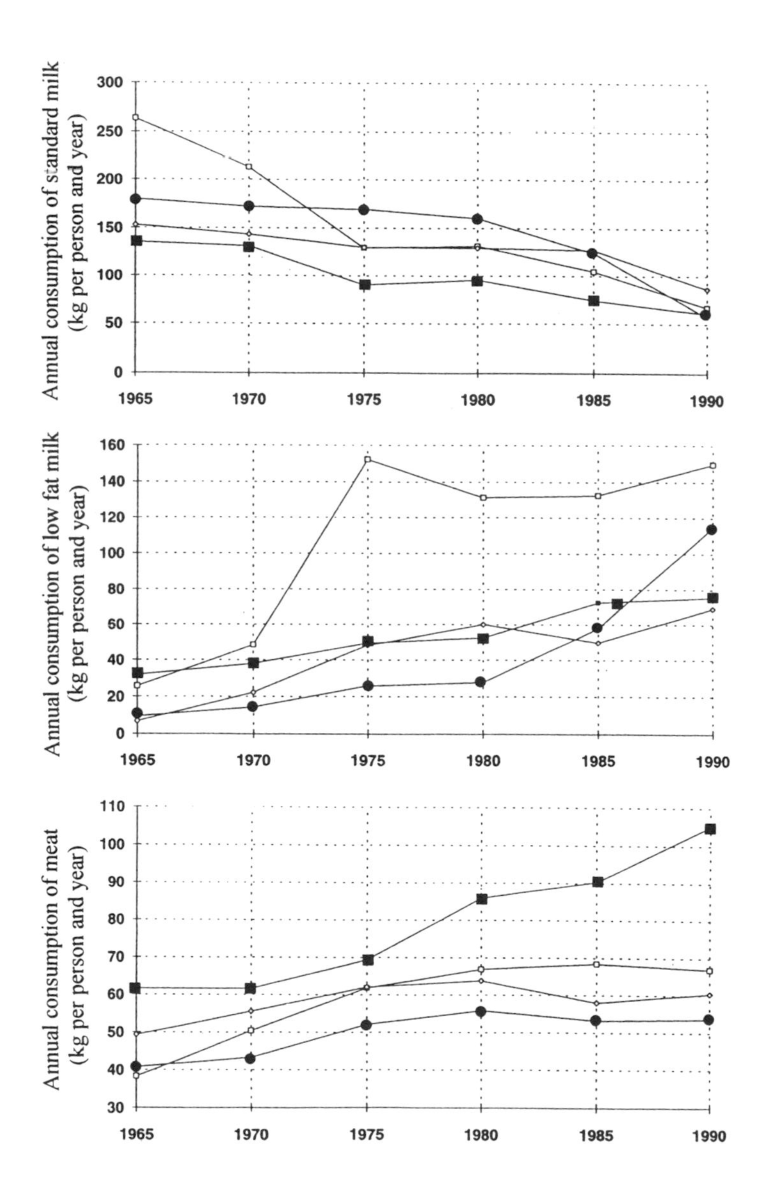

Figure 14.2 Annual consumption of some groups of food in the Nordic countries, 1965–90 and fat intake (g/day and energy percent). ■, Denmark; □, Finland; ●, Norway; ◊. Sweden. Data from national food balance sheets (Nordic Council of Ministers, 1992)

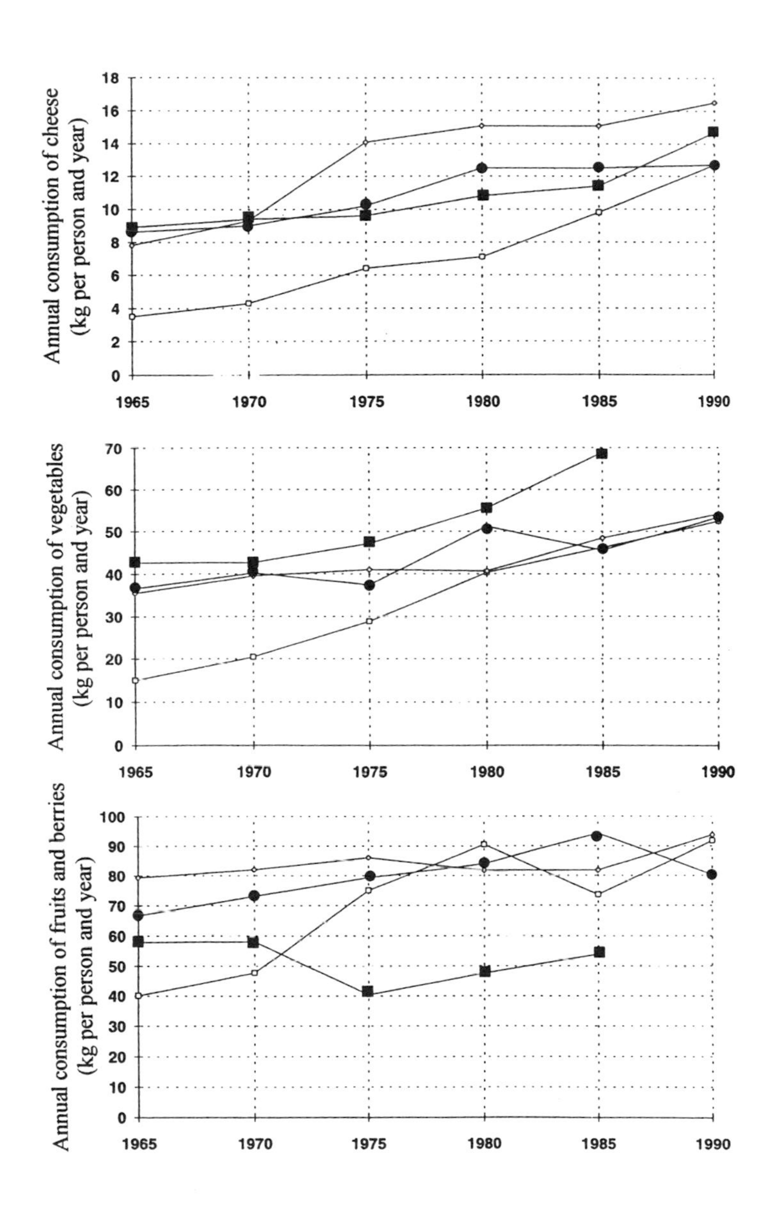

Figure 14.2 *Continued*

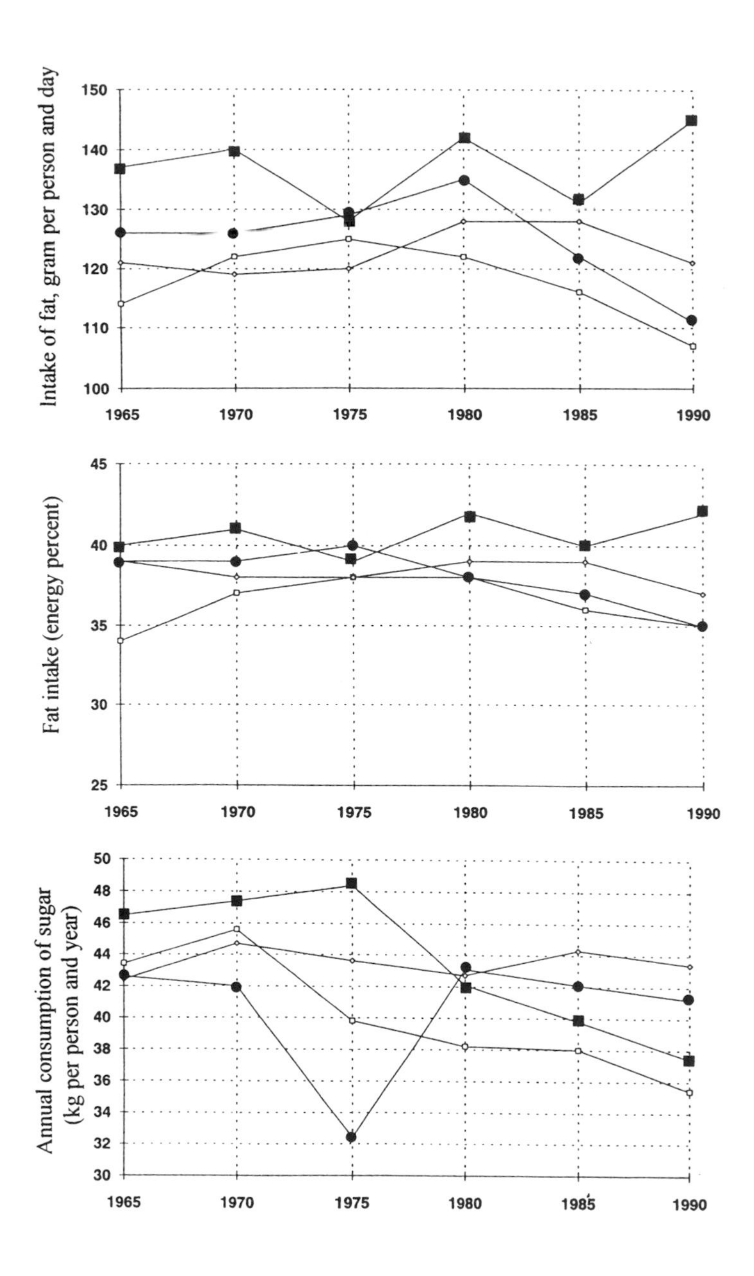

Figure 14.2 *Continued*

past few years there has been increasing interest in 'green' or local produce. Informative labelling and freedom of choice are essential to allow consumers to meet their individual requirements, the legislation on labelling is especially important in this context. Consumers generally possess relatively good theoretical knowledge about health diets, especially on fibre and fat, but lack of practical knowledge in this area makes it difficult to put this knowledge into practice.

14.2 The Swedish nutritional recommendations

At the first Nordic Nutrition Conference in Stockholm in 1977 it was decided that common nutritional standards for the Nordic countries should be elaborated (Bruce, 1990). The recommendations were presented 3 years later and were more or less accepted in the Nordic countries during the subsequent years. New editions of these recommendations were further elaborated and the next Swedish version was published in 1989 (Kost, Motion and Hälsa, 1988–92). A new edition is expected in 1996.

The recommendations are based on the present nutritional situation and aim at defining the basis for planning a diet that:

1. satisfies the primary nutritional requirements, i.e. meets the physiological requirements of each individual for growth and function (= nutrient recommendations); and
2. provides the prerequisites for general good health and reduces the risk of diseases caused by faulty diets (= dietary guidelines).

A major part of the recommendations is for the planning of diets for adults and children above 3 years of age. In these diets, protein should provide 10–15% of the total energy intake and fat ≤30%. Essential fatty acids should contribute at least 3% and not more than 10% of energy. Carbohydrates should provide 50–60% of the energy intake, of which ≤10% of the energy should be provided by refined or industrially produced sugars (sucrose and other sugars).

The need for nutrients is most easily met if the diet is varied and each day contains leafy vegetables, fruit, potatoes and root vegetables, dairy products, meat, fish or eggs, cereals and edible fats (= the Swedish food circle, Fig. 14.3).

Recommendations for a suitable meal pattern also are given. Diets, which comply with these recommendations and are varied and consumed in such a quantity that the individual's requirement for energy is met, should as a rule provide a person with sufficient amounts of the individual nutrients.

14.3 The Swedish dietary guidelines

The joint Expert Group for Dietary and Public Health Matters, mentioned earlier, was formed around 1970. The primary task of this group was to draw up a scientific basis for information on diet and exercise. The first report of this group was published in 1971 and the last edition in 1992 (Bruce, 1987; Kost, Motion and Hälsa, 1988–92). The reports describe the present dietary situation, its importance for public health, the principles for desirable changes in dietary habits and physical exercise, and how these principles could be carried out in practice.

Today the Swedish dietary guidelines include the following recommendations:

- gentle physical activity ought to be undertaken regularly, even daily;
- avoid overweight by adopting energy intake to the expenditure of energy; for most people this means increased daily physical activity;
- the intake of fat should not exceed 30% of energy intake; for most people, this means a decrease in fat consumption, which ought to occur primarily through a decreased consumption of saturated fatty acids to not more than 10% of energy;
- the intake of dietary fibre should increase to 3 g/MJ/day, which corresponds to 25–30 g/day;
- the intake of refined sugars should be 10% of the energy intake or less, especially for low-energy users;
- the intake of salt should gradually decrease to 5–6 g/day;
- alcohol consumption ought to be moderate or entirely avoided;
- the consumption of foods rich in starch should increase – most Swedes should eat more bread and other grain products, pasta, rice, potatoes and root vegetables;
- food from all seven food groups (Fig. 14.3) ought to be consumed every day;
- avoid prolonged frying of meat and fish;
- the daily intake of energy ought to be divided into three main meals and two or more snacks;
- each meal should include several vegetables, root vegetables, fruit and/or berries.

14.4 Implementing dietary guidelines

14.4.1 The seven-food group system, the Swedish 'food circle'

Over the years there have been several different ways of teaching nutrition. The method of dividing foods into food-group systems has been used since the beginning of this century, and the present Swedish version was elaborated during the 1950s. As can be seen in Fig. 14.3, it comprises seven food groups: vegetables; fruit and berries; potatoes and root vegetables; bread, flour and grains; edible fats; milk and cheese; meat, fish and eggs. The recommendation is that foods from each group in the food circle should be consumed every day. Moreover, the products in the lower half of the 'circle; used to be referred to as the 'base', which provides the foundation for a nutritious and inexpensive diet and can remain approximately the same from day to day. Base food should be supplemented with foods from the upper half, which could vary from day to day and between seasons.

Figure 14.3 The 'food circle' (source: The National Board for Consumer Administration, The National Board of Health and Welfare, the National Food Administration, Sweden).

14.4.2 The 'plate model'

Among health professionals who provide dietary advice, there has long been a need for a simple education tool for use when advising individuals what to eat. A fat-balanced, fibre-enriched diet is to be recommended, not only for healthy people, but also for patients with diabetes, hyperlipidaemia, hypertension and obesity (Nydahl *et al.*, 1993).The need for a more simple method to teach proper daily nutrition has led to the development of a plate model (Fig. 14.4).

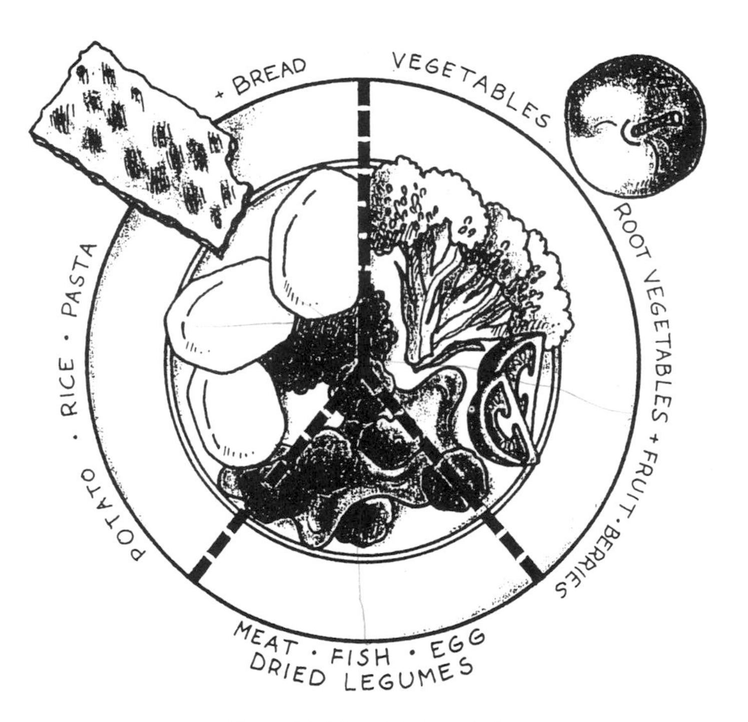

Figure 14.4 The 'plate model'.

The plate is divided into three sections, by an inverted 'Y'. The smallest part, a maximum of one-quarter of the surface, represents the dietary contribution from meat, cheese, fish and eggs. The other two sections are of equal size and represent the dietary contribution from vegetables and fruit or rice, pasta, potatoes and bread, respectively. It should be noted that the plate model describes the promotions of different foods in a meal and not only what is actually on the plate. This means that in a lunch or dinner bread and fruit should be included to fulfil the dietary recommendations. In the case of a meal such as soup, stew or pizza, for example, it is obviously difficult to divide the plate into the three sections, but the whole meal should still be considered from the plate model aspect.

During recent years the plate model has become widely accepted and applied in dietary education. The message appears to be easy to understand, memorize and use in daily life. Furthermore, it is also useful as an educational tool for patients with diabetes, hyperlipidaemia, hypertension and obesity, which is important, as these risk factors are often interrelated and frequently exist concurrently in the same patient.

14.4.3 Symbol labelling

In 1989 the Swedish National Food Administration decided that a number of foodstuffs which had either a low-fat content or were rich in dietary fibre could be labelled with a special symbol (a keyhole in a green or black circle, Fig. 14.5). The purpose of this decision was to make it easier for the consumer when shopping to choose foodstuffs that are desirable from a nutritional point of view and to encourage the food producers to broaden the supply of low-fat or fibre-rich products.

Figure 14.5 The 'keyhole' symbol.

The 'keyhole' symbol can be printed on the package of the accepted products, attached on the shelves in the shops or used in advertising or marketing of the products. The symbol is free to use and no previous acceptance or licensing is necessary. Its application is supervised by the local public health administration. However, the products must meet with the standards set up by the National Food Administration and the symbol must be printed in green or black.

The symbol labelling only applies to groups of foodstuffs which vary in the fat and fibre contents. The symbol is restricted to those products considered to be desirable, i.e. those with relatively low fat or relatively high fibre. Groups of foodstuffs that only include products that are low in fat or rich in dietary fibre (for instance, vegetables and fish) are not labelled.

Today the keyhole symbol has become a simple aid for choosing healthy food when making food-purchase decisions. An increasing percentage of the consumers knows what the keyhole means and they are guided by the symbol when buying food. It is now found on almost all products, which comply with the relevant one of the following standards:

- Milk – the fat content should be 0.5 g or less per 100 g.
- 'Natural' fermented milk – the fat content should be 1.5 g or less per 100 g, and sugar should not have been added.
- Fermented milk with added sugar and/or jam, etc. – the fat content should be 0.5 g or less per 100 g.
- Skimmed milk-powder – the fat content of the product for sale should be 1.5 g or less per 100 g.
- Cottage cheese – the fat content should be 4 g or less per100 g.
- Processed cheese and whey products – the fat content should be 10 g or less per 100 g.
- Other types of cheese – the fat content should be 17 g or less per 100 g.
- Margarine and similar cooking fats – the fat content should be 41 g or less per 100 g.
- Edible ices – the fat content should be 6 g or less per 100 g.
- Unmixed (whole) meat products and minced meat – the fat content of the product for sale should be 10 g or less per 100 g.
- Mixed meat products, including sausages – the fat content of the product for sale should be 15 g or less per 100 g.
- Bread, biscuits, rusks, pasta products and breakfast cereals – at least half of the cereal components should be wholemeal flour or the product should contain at least 7% dietary fibre (dry weight).
- Flour, cereals and grains – the product should be based on wholemeal grain or contain at least 11% dietary fibre (dry weight).
- Breakfast cereals – the product should contain at least two-thirds wholemeal grain or at least 9% dietary fibre (dry weight) and contain less than 13% sugar.
- 'Ready-to-eat' foods: entire meals; restaurant dishes, based on meat, fish or vegetables and with potato, rice or pasta – the fat content of the product (as a dish) should be 30% of energy or less.

14.4.4 Health claims

There is a great public interest in matters relating to health and food and, as a result, it has become increasingly common to use health arguments in the labelling and marketing of food products. In recognition of the need to avoid misleading or false information when using health claims for the purpose of marketing food products, the food industry has prepared a programme of action in consultation and agreement with the National

Food Administration and the National Board for Consumer Policies. The programme includes a number of generally accepted principles with respect to the use of health claims in the labelling and marketing of food products. It is stated that the health claims used must be limited to generally recognized and well-documented causal connections between food and health. Marketing and information material containing health claims should promote consumer awareness of the connection between food and health. The claims should be presented in such a way as to enhance public confidence in food products and the food industry. These rules are applicable to all use of health claims in the marketing of food products, for example package labelling, advertising, product leaflets, recipes, information brochures and video, film and TV commercials.

Since it is not possible to outline in detail and in advance all the issues that may arise in connection with the use of health claims in the labelling and marketing of food products, and since the relevant research is constantly making new advances, the agreement will be revised when required. An expert on nutritional matters at the Swedish Nutrition Foundation is available to give advice and comments on the factual content of health claims to food manufacturers.

Claims and arguments about effects on physiological conditions and specific diseases must conform to official recommendations. Such claims must fulfil the requirement that normal use of the product contributes to a substantially improved diet from a nutritional point of view. In order to avoid the use of misleading or incorrect health claims, the food industry has prepared a number of rules. These rules, which are based on up-to-date research findings in this field, must be observed. In addition, various special legal requirements relating to certain food products must also be observed. The labelling of food products must also comply with the international and Swedish marketing rules, which contain provisions requiring that marketing information must be correct and objective and that the arguments used must not be misleading.

Health claims and arguments are allowed for a number of conditions. For each of these there are special requirements regarding acceptable statements:

- Obesity – a diet with a low or reduced energy content is a significant factor in the prevention and treatment of obesity. No other properties of individual food products or components have any specific effect on obesity.
- Cholesterol level in the blood – a reduction of the intake of saturated fats, either by reducing the total fat content or replacing them with mono- or polyunsaturated fats can help to lower blood cholesterol levels. Some soluble, gel-forming kinds of fibres can also help to reduce cholesterol levels.

- Blood pressure – a reduced intake of salt (NaCl) can counteract high blood pressure. The use of mineral salts containing potassium can help to reduce the intake of salt, but otherwise has no proven effect on blood pressure.
- Atherosclerosis – a high blood cholesterol level and high blood pressure are diet-related risk factors for atherosclerosis. Measures to reduce these factors reduce the risk of atherosclerosis and related cardiovascular diseases.
- Constipation – dietary fibre speeds up the passage of food through the intestinal tract and counteracts constipation caused by low intake of dietary fibre or lack of exercise.
- Osteoporosis – a calcium intake corresponding to official recommendations, together with physical activity and abstention from smoking, provides the best protection against osteoporosis. There is no reliable evidence that a higher calcium intake has any additional beneficial effects on health.
- Dental caries – the absence of sucrose and other easily fermentable carbohydrates in products that are frequently eaten between meals reduces the risk of caries.
- Iron deficiency – foods that are rich in iron provide protection against iron deficiency. Another significant factor is whether food constituents stimulate or inhibit absorption.

Health claims can make a worthwhile contribution in spreading information about the connection between food and health and the composition of a healthy diet. Moreover, they provide an incentive for the development of healthier food products for which health claims can be made.

14.4.5 Changes in food consumption

The national changes in the consumption of some important food groups and intake of macronutrients between 1965 and 1990, based on food balance sheets, have recently been compared by a Nordic expert group (Nordic Council of Ministers, 1992). Figure 14.2 shows these findings for fat, fat as percentage of energy, sugar, low-fat and standard milk, cheese, meat, vegetables and fruit and berries. In most respects there are similar consumption trends among the countries. Regarding Sweden, it is difficult to attribute the positive trends in the consumption of low-fat versus standard milk, vegetables, etc. and the concomitant decrease in fat intake to any specific activities. Most of the effects of the symbol label scheme became effective after this period.

In 1989 a combined nationwide dietary and household budget survey was taken to obtain for the first time data on the food and nutrient intake among a representative sample of the Swedish population. This study will be repeated in 1996 and, if possible, more frequently in future. These surveys will provide the authorities with detailed data regarding consumption of various foodstuffs, intake of all nutrients, etc., in various age and socio-economic groups.

14.5 Final comments

During the past 5 years, most of the governmental activities within the 'diet and health' sector have been accomplished by the Food Administration and the Public Health Institute, together with the scientific support of the Expert Group. One frame for these activities has been the WHO/FAO ICN initiative (International Conference on Nutrition). Both before and after the ICN in Rome, 1992, Sweden elaborated and amended a national nutritional policy. The final version of the document was released by the government in 1995 and it will now form the basis for future activities.

Another, and perhaps the most important, initiative is the 'keyhole' symbol on various foods. The introduction of this simple symbol encouraged the relevant food producers to develop lean varieties of the traditional Swedish cheeses, mixed meat products, etc., as well as new varieties of wholemeal bread. Today almost all relevant products are labelled, even when packed abroad! Several studies have shown that most Swedes are aware of the meaning of the symbol. In some food groups the symbol definitely has increased the consumption of lean varieties, and particularly the mixed meat and ready-to-eat products. It has been less easy to evaluate the effect of the symbol regarding different types of milk and margarines, since the low-fat varieties often are identified in other ways. The present introduction of the symbol in the catering sector is a challenge and the future will show to what extent it will affect the fat content of the dishes.

References

Bruce, Å. (1987) The implementation of dietary guidelines. *Am. J. Clin. Nutr.*, **45**, 1378–82.

Bruce, Å. (1990) Recommended dietary allowances: the Nordic experience. *Europ. J. Clin. Nutr.*, **44**, (Suppl. 2), 27–9.

Bruce, Å. and Becker, W. (1989) Svenska näringsrekommendationer. *Vår Föda*, **41**, (5–6), 271–80.

Nordic Council of Ministers (1992) Comparison of the per capita statistics for foods in the Nordic countries (working paper), 586.

Kost, Motion, and Hälsa, (1988–92) *Socialstyrelsen och Statens Livsmedelsverk*, Allmänna förlaget, Stockholm.

Nydahl, M., Gustafsson, I.-B., Eliasson, M. and Karlström, B. (1993) A study of attitudes and use of the plate model among various health professionals giving dietary advice to diabetic patients. *J. Hum. Nutr. Diet*, **6**, 163–70.

Swedish Ministry of Health and Social Affairs, Swedish Ministry of Agriculture (1993) *Sweden's Country Paper to the FAO/WHO International Conference on Nutrition 1992*, National Food Administration, Uppsala.

15 Developments in healthy eating in Great Britain since the Second World War

VERNER WHEELOCK

15.1 Introduction

In Great Britain, there has been an enormous change in attitudes towards food since the Second World War. During the war itself, the overriding concern was to ensure that enough food was available for the whole population. Hence various measures were introduced to achieve this objective. These included rationing and initiatives to increase supplies of home-produced food.

When hostilities ceased, these measures were gradually relaxed so that prices and incomes became the main factors influencing consumer choice of food. There was relatively little concern about nutrition – it was generally assumed that provided a person consumed a varied diet all the requirements for essential nutrients would be fulfilled.

However, since then it has become clear that the composition of the diet is a key factor in the development of chronic diseases such as cardiovascular disease and various cancers. In this chapter, my objective is to describe and discuss some of the crucial developments over the past 20–30 years in relation to diet and health that have occurred in Great Britain. These will be considered from the perspective of government, industry and consumers.

15.2 The role of government

The government has a major impact on both the availability of food and public attitudes towards food. On the one hand, there is a responsibility to ensure that there is an adequate supply of safe food available. Invariably, a shortage of food can lead to serious criticism of the authorities and sometimes even riots on the streets. On the other hand, there is also a responsibility for health. In the light of our current knowledge on the relationship between diet and health, governments can come under pressure to provide advice on what should be eaten and even to control the

Implementing Dietary Guidelines for Healthy Eating. Edited by Verner Wheelock. Published in 1997 by Blackie A&P, an imprint of Chapman & Hall, London. ISBN 0 7514 0304 0

composition and availability of certain foods. Inevitably, conflicts can arise. For example, recommendations to reduce the consumption of certain nutrients may pose a threat to the markets of some foods. Not surprising, those directly involved usually take steps to defend their own interests.

15.2.1 Committee on Medical Aspects of Food Policy

One of the critical issues is the interpretation of scientific knowledge. A topic such as the relationship between diet and chronic disease is extremely difficult to research because:

- these diseases are normally multifactoral – diet is not the only factor involved;
- several different nutrients in the diet may have a role;
- it is practically and ethically impossible to conduct definitive experiments using humans;
- research that contributes to our knowledge of this topic is spread over many different disciplines;
- the time scale is very long; as a general rule, the chronic diseases can take 20, 30 or even more years to develop before obvious symptoms manifest themselves.

In the UK administration, the Committee on Medical Aspects of Food Policy (COMA) is the official government body with responsibility for evaluating existing scientific knowledge. Panels are established as required and consist of a number of independent experts in the topic under investigation with a secretariat drawn from the Department of Health. Observers from various other government departments, such as the Ministry of Agriculture, Fisheries and Food (MAFF), Welsh Office, Northern Ireland Office and Scottish Office of Home and Health, may be invited to attend. The Panel reviews the existing relevant literature, issues an open invitation for submissions and produces a report for publication, which is available for purchase. Reports include a narrative explaining the current state of knowledge and recommendations to government and others, such as the food industry, health professionals and consumers. The recommendations to government are not necessarily incorporated into official policy. Invariably many other influences come into play when policy is being formulated.

As far as dietary guidelines are concerned, the first significant COMA report was published in 1974, entitled Diet and Coronary Heart Disease (Committee on Medical Aspects of Food Policy, 1974). Its recommendations included:

- 'obesity should be avoided both in the child and the adult ... those individuals who are already obese should so reduce their food intake in relation to their physical activity that they are no longer obese'.

- '... the amount of fat in the UK diet, especially saturated fat from both plant and animal sources, should be reduced' (majority recommendation).
- '... the consumption of sucrose, as such or in foods and drinks, should be reduced, if only to diminish the risk of obesity ...'.

This report had absolutely no impact on the public and it is highly unlikely that it had any influence on the various government policies dealing with food and its supply.

A few years later, the Centre for Agricultural Strategy (1979) at the University of Reading published a report outlining the case for a National Food Policy in the UK. This report reviewed the various UK government and European Community Common Agricultural Policy measures which had a direct influence on food supplies. In particular, it challenged the belief that consumers determine the nature and range of foods actually supplied. It is clear that government support for agricultural commodities has a direct influence on the price and availability of food. Therefore, it would be reasonable to expect the government to take account of the human health dimension in determining the nature of support for agriculture.

The attitude of the government of the day is clearly illustrated in this extract from an official press release (Ministry of Agriculture, Fisheries and Food, 1979) issued in response to the Reading report:

> The Report calls for a national food policy. If by this the authors mean, as their press release indicates, that the Government should ensure that an adequate range of wholesome foods is available and that the consumer has the means and knowledge to choose his foods wisely, then this is already Government policy. But if, as the Report itself seems to indicate, the writers are arguing for more active interference with food supplies and consumption there must be doubts about whether this would be practicable or desirable. The relationship of food to health is not sufficiently understood to provide the kind of precise nutritional blueprint that this approach would require. Nor, short of introducing rationing, would it be practicable for the Government by direct action to prevent people from overeating, which is probably the most serious health problem. Furthermore, action on agricultural policies and support is not possible independently of the EEC. And more generally it would not be desirable for the Government to exercise such a degree of regimentation over consumers and the public.

This reaction clearly reflects the fact that at the time MAFF was dominated by agricultural interests with virtually no input from consumers. In reality, there was little awareness generally that diet could be an important factor in the development of heart disease or other chronic conditions. The press release also conveniently ignored various reports which had been published during the 1970s in many different countries, including the USA, which focused on the relationship between heart disease and the habitual diet.

15.2.2 Background to the NACNE report

Meanwhile, in the Department of Health and Social Security (DHSS) it was recognized that if nutritional education was to be brought up to date, there was an urgent need for a point of reference which would provide simple and accurate information on nutrition (Department of Health and Social Security, 1978). As a consequence, the National Advisory Committee on Nutrition Education (NACNE) was established under the aegis of the British Nutrition Foundation and the Health Education Council (HEC). Very early on, it was realized that it would not be possible to make progress until there were some guidelines on what actually constituted a healthy diet. As a result, the Committee asked Dr (now Professor) Philip James to assemble a group with the object of preparing guidelines. The James group decided to rely on eight reports prepared by official or professional bodies as a basis for its recommendations (National Advisory Committee on Nutrition Education, 1983a):

- Department of Health and Social Security (1978);
- Committee on Medical Aspects of Food Policy (1974);
- Royal College of Physicians of London and British Cardiac Society (1976);
- Royal College of Physicians of London (1981);
- National Academy of Sciences (1980);
- Department of Health and Social Security (1981);
- WHO Expert Committee (1982);
- Royal College of Physicians of London (1983).

The significant aspect of the report is that the recommendations (Table 15.1) quantified the changes considered to be desirable.

There is no question that the NACNE report and the machinations surrounding its publication represent a turning point in public policy and in consumer awareness towards dietary guidelines in the UK.

In July 1983, Geoffrey Cannon (1983) a journalist and campaigner wrote an exclusive article for *The Sunday Times* in which he claimed that the initial conclusions were presented to the DHSS in 1981. The government had continually refused to accept the recommendations. The article included several quotations from senior executives in major food companies opposed to the concept of dietary guidelines, with the clear implication that pressure was being applied to the government.

A few months later extracts from the report were published in the authoritative medical journal, the *Lancet* (National Advisory Committee

Table 15.1 Summary of NACNE recommendations (source: National Advisory Committee on Nutrition Education, 1983a)

Dietary constituent	Baseline	Short term	Long term
Energy	No change		
Protein	No recommendation		
Cholesterol	No recommendation		
Total fat (% total daily energy intake)	38	34	30
Saturated fat (% total daily energy intake)	18	15	10
Polyunsaturated fat (% total daily energy intake)	4	5	?
Polyunsaturated/saturated (P/S) fat ratio	0.24	0.32	?
Sugar (% total daily energy intake)	14	12	7
Alcohol (% total daily energy intake)	6	5	4
Dietary fibre (g/head/day)	20	25	30
Salt (g/head/day)	12	11	9

on Nutrition Education, 1983b). Shortly afterwards, the document itself was published but the detailed title made clear that it was a discussion document prepared by an *ad hoc* working party. This meant that it did not have any official status.

The Cannon article stimulated enormous media interest and alerted many people, including professionals such as dietitians, doctors, home economists, nutritionists, food scientists, technologists and marketeers, to the existence of NACNE and the James report. Not surprisingly, when it was published the HEC was overwhelmed by the demand. The first printing was soon exhausted and in total about 4000 copies were distributed.

In the longer term, the contents were to be quite profound. Many courses in colleges and universities were amended to incorporate the recommendations. Health authorities developed healthy eating policies using the NACNE report as a key input. In food companies, opportunities for new product development and marketing were being identified. On the other hand, there were many food companies and agricultural interests, especially those with products high in saturated fat and/or sugar, which clearly regarded the recommendations as a very serious threat to their business. Many of these took steps to criticize and challenge the James report.

15.2.3 Back to COMA again

At the same time, a COMA panel, which included Philip James, was studying the latest research on diet and cardiovascular disease and the report (Committee on Medical Aspects of Food Policy, 1984) was published in July 1984 – 9 months after the NACNE report was released. Basically, the recommendations were very similar to those of the NACNE report and quantitative values were given (Table 15.2).

Table 15.2 Summary of 1984 COMA recommendations (source: Committee on Medical Aspects of Food Policy, 1984)

Dietary constituent	Baseline	Recommendations
Total fat (% total daily energy intake)	42	31–35[a]
Saturated fat (% total daily energy intake)	20	15
Polyunsaturated fat (% total daily energy intake)	4.7	3.5–6.8[a]
P/S fat ratio	0.23	0.23–0.45
Simple sugars		No increase
Dietary fibre		Advantages in compensating for a reduced fat intake with increased fibre-rich carbohydrates
Salt		No increase – consideration should be given to ways and means of decreasing it
Energy		A combination of regular exercise and appropriate food intake
Cholesterol		No specific recommendation
Protein		No specific recommendation
Alcohol		Avoid excess – defined as 100 ml/day (80 g/day) for men and 65 ml/day (52 g/day) for women

[a]Depends upon the P/S ratio; the upper limit corresponds to the recommended ratio of approximately 0.45.

A reduction of 25% in saturated fat was recommended and officially Britain finally fell into line with many other countries by recognizing the desirability of increasing the amount of polyunsaturated fatty acids (PUFA) in the national diet. To crown it all, the report was accepted by the government.

It is widely believed that the key person who insisted that the COMA report should not be pigeon-holed was John Patten, who was Parliamentary

Secretary for Health (i.e. a junior Minister) at the time. In a newspaper interview he stated that '... I have learned since taking this job how much you can do to prevent health problems by your daily lifestyle. I am interested in preventive medicine!'.

Announcing the report in the House of Commons, Secretary of State for Health and Social Security, Norman Fowler (Patten's boss) said:

> I welcome this report. Heart attacks kill more men under 65 than any other disease – 30 000 each year in England and Wales alone. This is an important scientific report based on a very careful study of all the available evidence on the relationship between diet and health. (Hansard, 1985)

The 1984 COMA report did not restrict itself to the diet, but actually went on to make recommendations on how the changes in food consumption could be facilitated. These included:

> Those responsible for health education should inform the general public of the recommendations and how to implement them. In particular, advice should be given on how to construct diets and regulate physical activity in order to minimise the risk of cardiovascular disease and avoid obesity.
>
> The percentage by weight of fat and of saturated fat, polyunsaturated and *trans* fatty acids in butter, margarine, cooking fats and edible oils should be printed on the container or wrapping in which they are sold. Consideration should also be given to providing in addition (i.e. not in place of) uniform and more simple labelling codes to enable the general public to distinguish easily between fats and oils with low or high fat contents of saturated acids.

The report also recommended that detailed information on fat consumption be provided for all other foods with a fat content of more than 10% by weight, or which are major contributors to fat intake. This information should be included on the label of pre-packed food. Those which are not pre-packed should have the information prominently displayed at the point of sale. Similar information should be provided by caterers.

The government was recommended to take appropriate steps to improve the quality of nutritional education for the general population as well as in schools. Action should be taken to ensure that public knowledge on the composition of food is improved, for example by the introduction of legislation on labelling. Farmers should be encouraged to reduce the amount of fat in sheep, cattle and pigs.

The official response was very positive because, in his statement, Norman Fowler went on to say that:

> The Government are committed to increasing the amount of scientific knowledge on nutrition, diet and health and making this information widely available in an easily understood form so that people can decide for themselves what is the best food for them. I am now giving the report to the British Nutrition Foundation and the Health Education Council and requesting these two bodies to ask their joint advisory committee on nutrition education to turn the advice from the report into practical guidance on a sensible healthy diet for families throughout the United Kingdom: the Scottish Health Education Group would also be involved. The Government want to discuss with the relevant medical bodies how best to take forward the report's recommendations about special dietary advice for people most at risk. The Government have already begun talks with the food industry about fat content labelling and are considering the longer term recommendations to produce less fatty and less salty foods. (Hansard, 1985).

It was clear that there had been a fundamental shift in the approach by the government as far as the Department of Health was concerned. The momentum generated by the publication of the NACNE report was being reinforced by the COMA report coupled with the very positive statement from the Minister responsible for health.

15.3 Action by food manufacturers and retailers

The fact that the recommendations now had official backing acted as a stimulus to the food industry. The retail multiple Tesco decided to launch a Healthy Eating Programme in January 1985.

Food manufacturers began to recognize that 'healthy eating' was becoming an important issue with consumers. As a result, the nutrition/health dimension was increasingly used as a factor in product development and food marketing. Various foods such as low-fat spreads, low-fat yoghurts, semi-skimmed milk and high-fibre breakfast cereals were actively promoted as 'healthy' and sales increased steadily. A study by Juliet Slattery (1986) surveyed the various products which were marketed as healthy. Some of them are shown in Table 15.3.

Unfortunately, marketeers responsible for products which were high in fat and/or sugar were unable to take advantage of the NACNE and COMA recommendations to promote their products. So they decided to use alternative strategies. For example, butter was promoted as 'natural' even though it was a major contributor to the saturated fat in the British diet. At about the same time, public interest in and concern about food additives was generated by popular books and media coverage. This proved to be

Table 15.3 Some food products launched recently which are being marketed as 'healthy' (Slattery, 1986)

Product	Example of manufacturer[a]
Wholemeal rusks	Farleys
Low-fat rice pudding	Ambrosia
Low-fat ice-cream	Loseley
Low-fat crisps	KP; Smiths; Bensons
Reduced sugar jams[b]	Robertsons
Sugar-free fruit spreads	Harmony Foods
High-fibre cake mix	Greens
High-fibre cakes and biscuits	Allinsons; Vitbe
Low-salt biscuits	Fox's
Low-fat sausages	Walls; Bowyers
Low-fat spreads	St Ivel; Van den Berghs
Canned vegetables without added salt	Sainsbury
Canned fruit without added sugar	Del Monte
Milk with natural fat replaced by vegetable fat	Pritchett Foods
Hard cheese made with vegetable oil	Kallo (Soderasens)
Vacuum-packed meat cuts and mince with reduced fat	Sainsbury
Calorie-counted ready meals	Findus (Lean Cuisine); St Michael; McCains
Wholewheat canned pasta	Buitoni
Branburgers	Dunkerley's Frozen Foods
Baked beans without added sugar	Harmony Foods
Wholemeal fish fingers	Findus

[a]For most of the products shown above there are several more manufacturers than those indicated.
[b]For the term 'jam' to be used, there is a legal requirement for a minimum quantity of sugar to be incorporated in the product.

opportune for some marketeers who were able to present products as healthy by promoting them as 'free of additives' or 'no artificial preservatives' even though they contained high concentrations of sugar and fat. This kind of activity undoubtedly confused the messages to consumers about 'healthy eating' and made it even more difficult to communicate the dietary guidelines to the public.

15.3.1 Generating further momentum

In 1991, a conference entitled 'The food network: achieving a healthy diet by the year 2000' was organized by the British Dietetic Association and the Health Education Authority (Hurren and Black, 1991). This meeting brought together key representatives from many different sectors of the food network. In particular, there were delegates from retailers, caterers, manufacturers, farmers, consumers, government, educators and health professionals. The opening addresses were given by David Maclean, Minister responsible for food in MAFF and Lady Hooper, his opposite number in the Department of Health. David Maclean explained that government support for food research was being focused so that there would be greater emphasis on food safety and nutrition. New initiatives for research on dietary fat, calcium and fibre had been taken. A new research programme had been established which was designed to understand the factors affecting consumer choice of food. Steps were also being taken to provide dietary advice for the public with the publication of a booklet *Eight Guidelines for a Healthy Diet* and to require consistency in the way nutritional information was presented on food packaging.

Lady Hooper emphasized that messages for consumers must be clear and consistent. She mentioned that formal liaison arrangements between the Department of Health and MAFF meant that the two departments were now working closely together, without making reference to difficulties which had arisen in the past.

It is difficult to identify specific achievements that occurred as a result of this conference. Nevertheless, it was noteworthy because it provided a forum for people from all parts of the food chain, who between them covered a range of interests. This demonstrated that interest in the subject was obviously growing. From the perspective of the food companies, some of them would obviously benefit from growing public awareness of the dietary guidelines. By contrast, others may have felt threatened and were there to defend their interests, if necessary. Nevertheless, their presence in itself was an indication that 'healthy eating' was having an impact on food markets.

15.4 The health of the nation

During the 1980s, the government recognized that there was a need to conduct a critical examination of health policy in order to respond to changes in society, the economy and patterns of disease. Government thinking was outlined in a green paper (Department of Health, 1991) which was published in June 1991. In his introduction, the Secretary of State for Health, William Waldegrave, emphasized that:

- A major theme in the green paper is the prevention of ill health and promotion of good health.
- There is a need for people to change their behaviour because many of the main causes of premature death and unnecessary disease are related to how we live our lives. He considered that for too long the health debate has been bedevilled by the two extreme claims: on the one hand, 'It's all up to individuals', and on the other 'It's all up to the government'.

  While there is a need to have a proper balance between individual responsibility and government action, it was important for the government to ensure that individuals have the necessary information with which to exercise informed free choice.

- Setting objectives and targets for improvements in health is an essential discipline.

The strategy was to focus on key areas, judged against the following criteria:

- The area should be a major cause of premature death or avoidable ill health (sickness and/or disability) either in the population as a whole or amongst specific groups of people.
- The area should be one where effective interventions are possible, offering significant improvement in health.
- It should be possible to set objectives and targets in the chosen area and monitor progress towards achievement through indicators.

The green paper identified the following causes of substantial mortality:

- coronary heart disease
- stroke
- cancers
- accidents.

It also identified factors that contributed towards both mortality and morbidity and to healthy living, including diet and alcohol consumption.

After extensive discussions and debates, the white paper (the formal policy document) was issued in July 1992 (Department of Health, 1992). Cardiovascular disease was designated as one of five key priority areas. It was pointed out that coronary heart disease (CHD) accounted for about 26% of all deaths in England in 1991. It is both the largest single cause of death, and the single main cause of premature death. It accounts for 2.5% of the total spending in the National Health Service (NHS) and results in 35 million lost working days per year. Stroke caused about 12% of all deaths in England in 1991. It is also a major cause of disability especially amongst older people. Stroke accounts for 6% of total NHS expenditure and results in the loss of about 7.7 million working days per year.

The following targets were specified:

- To reduce death rates for both CHD and stroke in people under 65 by at least 40% by the year 2000 (from 58 per 100 000 population in 1990 to no more than 35 per 100 000 for CHD and from 12.5 per 100 000 population in 1990 to no more than 7.5 per 100 000 for stroke).
- To reduce the death rate for CHD in people aged 65–74 by at least 30% by the year 2000 (from 899 per 100 000 population in 1990 to no more than 629 per 100 000).
- To reduce the death rate for stroke in people aged 65–74 by at least 40% by the year 2000 (from 265 per 100 000 population in 1990 to no more than 159 per 100 000).

As part of the strategy to achieve the targets for CHD and stroke, the following targets were set for diet and nutrition:

- To reduce the average percentage of food energy derived by the population from saturated fatty acids by at least 35% by 2005 (from 17% in 1990 to no more than 11%).
- To reduce the average percentage of food energy derived by the population from total fat by at least 12% by 2005 (from about 40% in 1990 to no more than 35%).

Opportunities for promoting 'healthy eating' by different sectors of the food chain were listed:

1. Health education authority, food producers, manufacturers and retailers
   - continuing to develop nutrition education resources for health professionals and for the public;
   - increasing further the variety and availability of manufactured foods with lower saturates, fat and sodium content than in current versions;
   - reformulating more standard foods as far as practicable to reduce saturates, fat and sodium;
   - offering throughout the country plentiful and easily accessible supplies of starchy staples, vegetables and fruit;
   - moving at an early date to full nutritional labelling;
   - developing marketing practices more conducive to healthy food choices.
2. Caterers
   - offering menus which enable and encourage people to choose healthy diets;
   - using government nutritional guidelines;
   - identifying models of healthy catering practice and disseminating them throughout the catering network;
   - ensuring adequate nutrition education and training of professional and other catering staff.
3. Health and local authority services
   - ensuring adequate nutrition education and training of all appropriate professional and other staff;
   - ensuring adequate dietetic expertise in the health and education sectors;
   - maximizing opportunities for educating people about healthy eating;
   - encouraging the use of government nutritional guidelines in catering facilities.
4. Media/advertisers
   - giving the public information about diet, nutrition and health which encourages healthy eating.

5. Voluntary sector
   - taking initiatives nationally and locally which support the aim of encouraging healthy eating;
   - co-ordinating activities within the voluntary sector and with government and others.

Lastly, targets were set to overcome obesity. These were: to reduce the percentages of men and women aged 16–64 who are obese by at least 25% for men and at least 33% for women by 2005 (from 8% of men and 12% of women in 1986–87 to no more than 6% and 8%, respectively)

15.5 Action to achieve the targets – the Nutrition Task Force

The Nutrition Task Force was established to develop and co-ordinate a programme of action to implement the nutritional aspects of *The Health of the Nation*. It consisted of representatives from retailing, catering, food manufacturing, health professionals, consumer organizations, the media, research and government agencies chaired by Professor Dame Barbara Clayton. Working groups on information and education, catering, food chain and NHS and health care professionals were set up to consider individual sectors.

A report *Eat Well* (Department of Health, 1994) was published in March 1994. This identified 17 different tasks which were to be undertaken by 16 project teams:

1.1 Guidelines for educational materials to assist people writing materials for use in schools, in the training of health professionals, in health settings and by the public.

1.2 Accreditation scheme for food and nutrition education materials.

2. Graphical nutrition labelling. To consider the contribution that can be made to the development of a scheme for graphical nutritional labelling, jointly with the Food Advisory Committee.
3. Meal signposting scheme. To draw up criteria, establish potential users and feasibility, checking procedures and promotion.
4. Advertising codes of practice. To identify need/scope for amendments to advertising codes of practice to reflect nutritional aspects of *The Health of the Nation*.
5. Promotion of positive advertising. To initiate discussions with marketing and advertising media, television producers, public relations firms, BBC and the food industry.
6. Nutritional guidance for hospital caterers. To review advice and guidance currently available and draw up practical nutritional guidance for use by hospital caterers and appropriate health professionals, including special hospitals.

7. Nutritional guidance for school meal providers. To review systematically the advice and guidance available to school meals providers and draw up nutritional guidance.
8. Nutritional guidance for fast food outlets and restaurants. To draw up statements of healthy catering practice and consult on a basis of guidance.
9. Nutritional guidance for workplace catering. To draw up guidance for workplace catering and agree on dissemination and monitoring.
10. Training for caterers. To consider and identify appropriate nutritional components to NVQs (National Vocational Qualifications). Review GNVQs (General National Vocational Qualifications). Consider nutritional component of undergraduate courses, management training and in-house training.
11. Product development. To develop the proposal for a fat audit and modest reductions in fat content of products.
12. Product promotion. To promote the consumption of food products such as fruit and vegetables, cereal products, pasta and fish.
13. NHS contracts handbook. To draw up a handbook to contain advice to managers on appropriate nutritional aspects of the contracting process.
14. Training for NHS and health professionals. To look at the nutrition content of basic and in-service training of health professionals.
15. Primary health-care team. To consider effectiveness of training for primary health-care teams.
16. Low income. To collate and disseminate examples of good practice and of local initiatives to help encourage those on low incomes to eat a healthy diet.

At the time of writing a number of the working groups had completed their remit and a report was published. However, the Nutrition Task Force was disbanded in the middle of 1995 and it is doubtful if all the project teams will actually report.

15.6 Nutrition Task Force reports

To give an indication of the work of the Nutrition Task Force, here are brief details of three reports:

15.6.1 Nutrition – core curriculum for nutrition in the education of health professionals

The general public places considerable faith in the advice provided by health professionals. They expect them to provide clear information and to offer support with dietary changes. However, the professional experience and education of some health professionals have not been designed to equip them well for this task.

The classical curricula for courses in nutrition often contain a wealth of information relevant to diet and nutrition within the context of physiology and biochemistry. By contrast, it is rare to find an approach which addresses the subject from the perspective of the whole body in order to help students understand how function is maintained in health and disturbed by diseases.

This report (Nutrition Task Force Project Team on Nutrition Education and Training for Health Professionals, 1994) concluded that health professionals with expertise in nutrition should be able to:

- appreciate the importance and relevance of nutrition to the promotion of good health, the prevention and treatment of disease;
- describe the basic scientific principles of human nutrition;
- give consistent and sound dietary advice to people in an appropriate manner and know when and how to refer to a State Registered Dietitian for more specific advice;
- know and be able to promote the explain current dietary recommendations and the advantages of breast-feeding;
- provide appropriate and safe clinical nutritional support, and know when and how to refer to a State Registered Dietitian or another specialist in clinical nutrition;
- understand the relative costs and benefits of nutrition compared with other approaches to preventive and therapeutic care;
- assess the validity of nutritional literature and nutritional reports in the media.

In order to achieve this, proposals are presented which would act as a core for nutritional curricula. This would consist of three broad categories, dealing with:

- the principles of nutritional science
- nutrition in public health
- clinical nutrition including nutritional support.

The details are shown below.

A. Principles of nutrition science
   1. Diets, foods and nutrients (substrates and cofactors).
   2. Metabolic demand, digestion and absorption, balance and turnover, physical activity, metabolic effects of excess, obesity.
   3. Requirements, essentiality, bioavailability, limiting nutrients, effect of nutrient status on biochemical and organ function.
   4. Adaptation to low-nutrient intakes, body composition (form and function).

5. Assessment of diet and nutritional status.
6. Physiological mechanisms that determine appetite, sociological, psychological, economic and behavioural aspects of food choice.

B. Public health nutrition
1. The average British diet, including subgroup differences (e.g. region, gender, ethnic origin), life-style, risk factors and epidemiology (socio-economic factors, smoking and activity).
2. Pre-conception, pregnancy, breast-feeding, infant nutrition, growth and development, ageing.
3. Dietary Reference Values (DRVs), dietary recommendations and guidelines, diet and coronary heart disease and stroke, *The Health of the Nation* targets.
4. Nutritional surveillance and identification of markers and nutritional status.
5. Achieving change, education and motivation (education resources, theory and skills).
6. Food supply, monitoring, cost/benefit of nutritional interventions, legislation, food labelling and policy which affects food consumption.

C. Clinical nutrition and nutritional support
1. Assessment of clinical and functional metabolic state, effect of functional state on nutritional intake and status, effect of status on clinical outcomes.
2. Anorexia and starvation, response to injury, infection and stress.
3. Altered nutritional requirements in relevant disease states, unusual requirements.
4. General principles of nutritional support, routes of support.
5. Basis of nutrition-related diseases, therapeutic diets (diabetic, renal), weight reduction.
6. Drug–nutrient interactions.

It is suggested that the level of complexity can be varied depending on the needs of the different professional groups.

Ideally, for comprehensive coverage a course of 18 hours with supporting practical experience would be required.

15.6.2 Nutrition and health: a management handbook for the NHS

The National Health Service (NHS) is particularly well placed to have a big impact on the nation's diet. Therefore, managers have many opportunities to have an influence on people's eating habits. This report (Nutrition Task Force Project Team on the National Health Service, 1994) suggests various ways in which these can be implemented and gives a number of case studies illustrating what can actually be achieved. Examples of issues that might be considered:

1. Provisions of services
   - Has provision been made for assessment of the nutritional status of hospital patients?
   - Do catering/hotel services for staff and clients include agreed nutritional standards for menus?
   - Is a range of healthy food choices offered to patients and staff, with appropriate menu labelling?
   - Are healthy options offered in hospital shops and out-patient shops?
   - Are healthy choices promoted at point of sales to encourage people to try them?
2. Primary health care
   - Have members of the team identified their training and education needs on the subject of nutrition?
   - Does the team know enough to be able to identify the factors influencing the diets of their populations?
   - How are people with special dietary or nutritional needs identified?
   - Does the team work with other agencies to promote the nutritional aspects of health in their community?
3. Continuing specialist training and education
   - Has a co-ordinator been appointed to oversee the implementation of *Health of the Nation* plans?
   - Are all teaching staff aware of *Health of the Nation* targets?
   - Is the extent to which *Health of the Nation* nutritional targets have been addressed a factor in course content?

Because this report presents a range of specific ideas and suggestions, it is likely to be very helpful to managers in the NHS who wish to take a positive approach to *The Health of the Nation* strategy.

15.6.3 Obesity: reversing the increasing problem of obesity in England

One of the targets in *The Health of the Nation* is to reduce the incidence of obesity in both men and women to the 1980 levels. Unfortunately, the latest available information shows that the incidence has increased substantially – from 8% in 1986–87 to 13% in 1993 for men and from 12% to 16% for women over the same period.

This report (The Nutrition and Physical Activity Task Force, 1995) considers the background research in detail and, as part of its work, the project team organized a special conference, for which a number of experts were requested to prepare background papers.

The Task Force recommended that a preventive population-based approach be adopted because of the large and increasing proportion of the population which is already overweight or obese. A targeted approach is also needed for those at high risk. The preventive approach needs to be combined with new therapeutic strategies for those who are already obese.

The two principal ways of limiting excess weight gain – in preventive terms – are increasing all forms of physical activity and reducing the energy density, essentially the fat content of the diet.

Various strategies for achieving the objectives are set out in the report. In order to ensure that progress is maintained, the project team recommended that the Department of Health should establish an Obesity Focus Group.

15.7 The practicalities of implementing dietary guidelines

Developments within government are obviously important because of the signals that are sent out to industry, public sector, consumers and the media. There is no doubt that a majority of consumers in Great Britain now accept that diet is an important factor influencing health. However, it is quite a different matter when it comes to making an assessment of their diet and deciding if changes are desirable. Nowadays, consumers are bombarded with information on all aspects of food through the media, health professionals and books, as well as advertising and promotion by the food industry. Enormous sums of money are spent to promote individual products. For example in 1983, Heinz spent £4.6 million on baked beans while Kellogg's spent £5.8 million on one product – All Bran. It is inevitable that marketeers will present their products in the best possible light by emphasizing what are considered to be the most desirable characteristics and making little or no reference to those considered undesirable. Hence products which are promoted because of a high fibre content may also be relatively high in sugar and/or salt.

Similarly, the media do not always portray a balanced objective view of nutritional knowledge. Sometimes they are more interested in controversy and confrontation.

Academics and researchers regularly disagree. The arguments often spill out into the public domain and this undoubtedly leads to a confused picture. For example, despite the fact that, in 1994, the latest COMA report (Committee on Medical Aspects of Food Policy, 1994) dealing with cardiovascular disease recommended a reduction of 30% in the sodium content of the average British diet, some academics have persistently rejected the scientific rationale behind the recommendation. As a consequence, the Chief Medical Officer is unwilling to advise the government to endorse this particular COMA recommendation.

One of the most important developments has been initiatives by retailers. In Great Britain, a small number of supermarket chains dominate food retailing. Furthermore, 'own label' products can account for up to 60% of the food items available.

The two leading chains have both developed healthy eating programmes. As mentioned earlier, Tesco launched its programme in 1985 and this was the subject of a major revision at the start of 1995, when the Tenth Birthday was celebrated. The Sainsbury programme was launched in 1994 (Chapter 20).

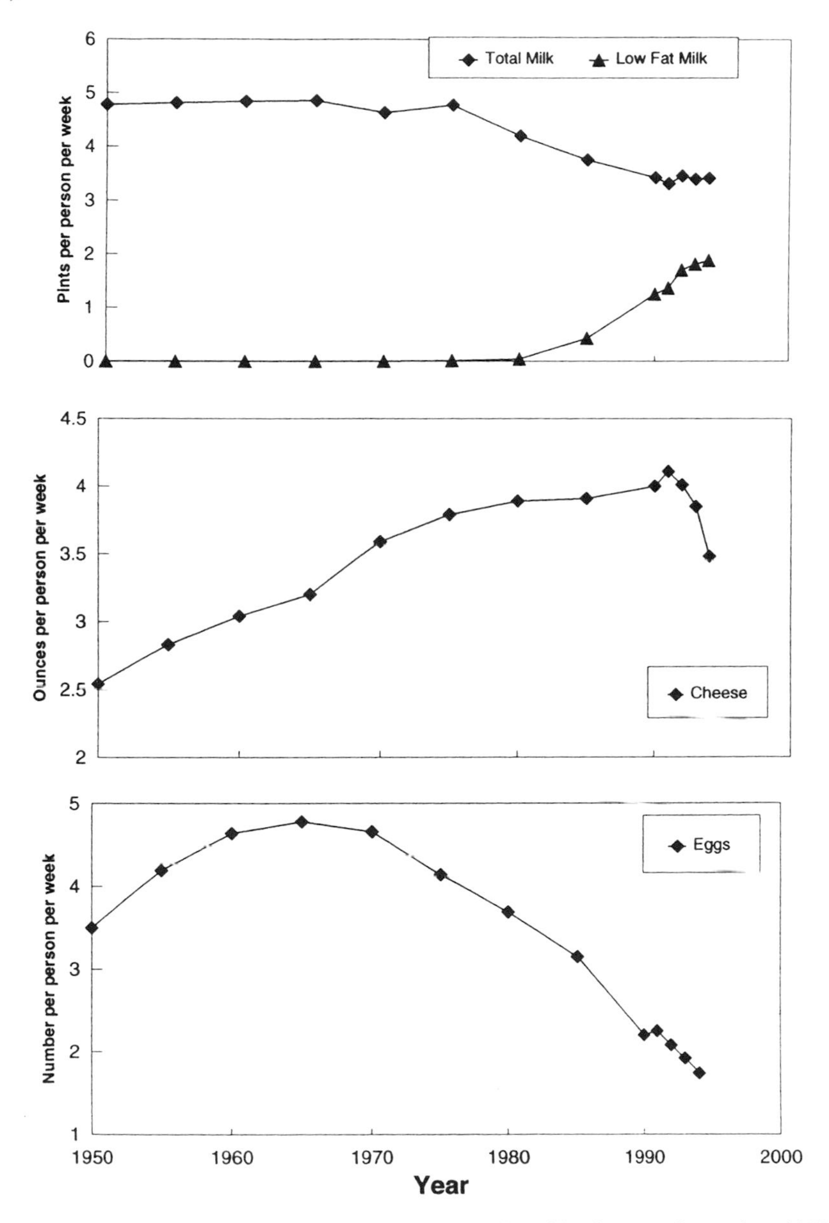

Figure 15.1 Changes in demand for total milk, low-fat milk, cheese and eggs since 1950.

15.8 Changes in food consumption patterns

The National Food Survey (NFS) (various years) provides data on food purchased for use in the home. Although it does not include food bought and consumed outside the home, it, nevertheless, measures a high proportion of the food that is eaten and gives a relative picture of trends. Therefore, it is worth examining this information in order to obtain some insight into the effect of nutritional factors on choice of food.

Demand for milk remained steady until 1975 (Fig. 15.1). Since then it has fallen by about 30% but the most significant feature has been the growth in demand for low-fat milks over the past 15 years. On the other hand, there has been a steady growth in the demand for cheese, although a small reduction has occurred in the past few years. Demand for eggs has slumped since the peak observed in 1965.

There has been a fall in demand for bacon and ham while demand for pork has remained fairly constant except for a surge in the early 1980s (Fig. 15.2). Demands for both beef/veal and mutton/lamb have fallen steadily in recent years. By contrast, demand for poultry has expanded rapidly.

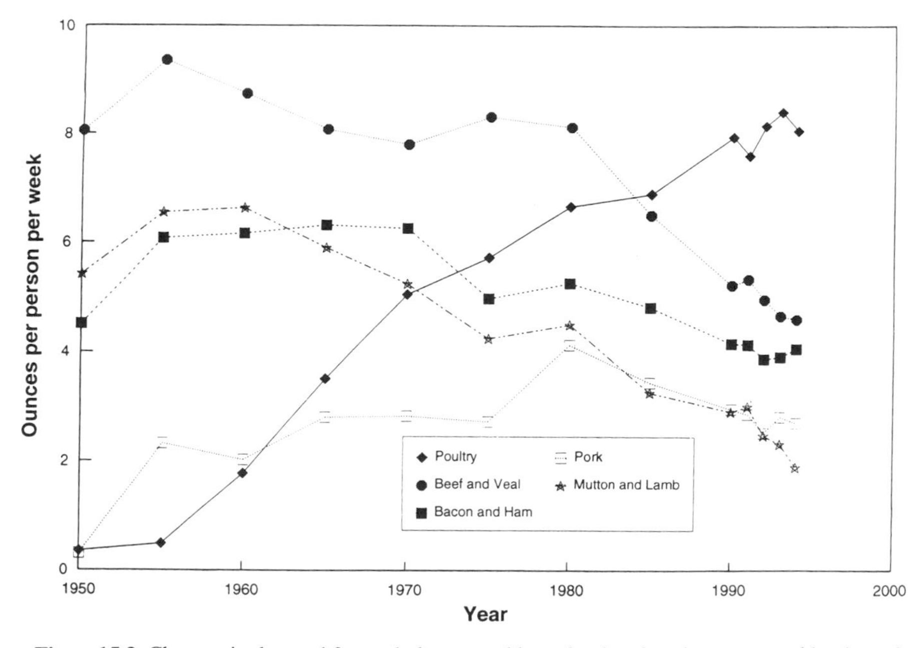

Figure 15.2 Changes in demand for pork, bacon and ham, beef and veal, mutton and lamb, and poultry since 1950.

Demand for total fats has fallen steadily over the past 15 years (Fig. 15.3). In the early 1980s, margarine became more popular than butter although in the past few years, demand for margarine has also fallen, while that for other fats has been growing. In the 1950s and '60s, the 'other fats' consisted mainly of lard. However, since then demand for lard has almost disappeared and most of the 'other fats' are cooking oils and low-fat spreads.

Demand for sugar expanded markedly in the 1950s and remained virtually constant until 1970. Since then it has fallen by well over 50%. Demand for preserves has fallen steadily since 1950.

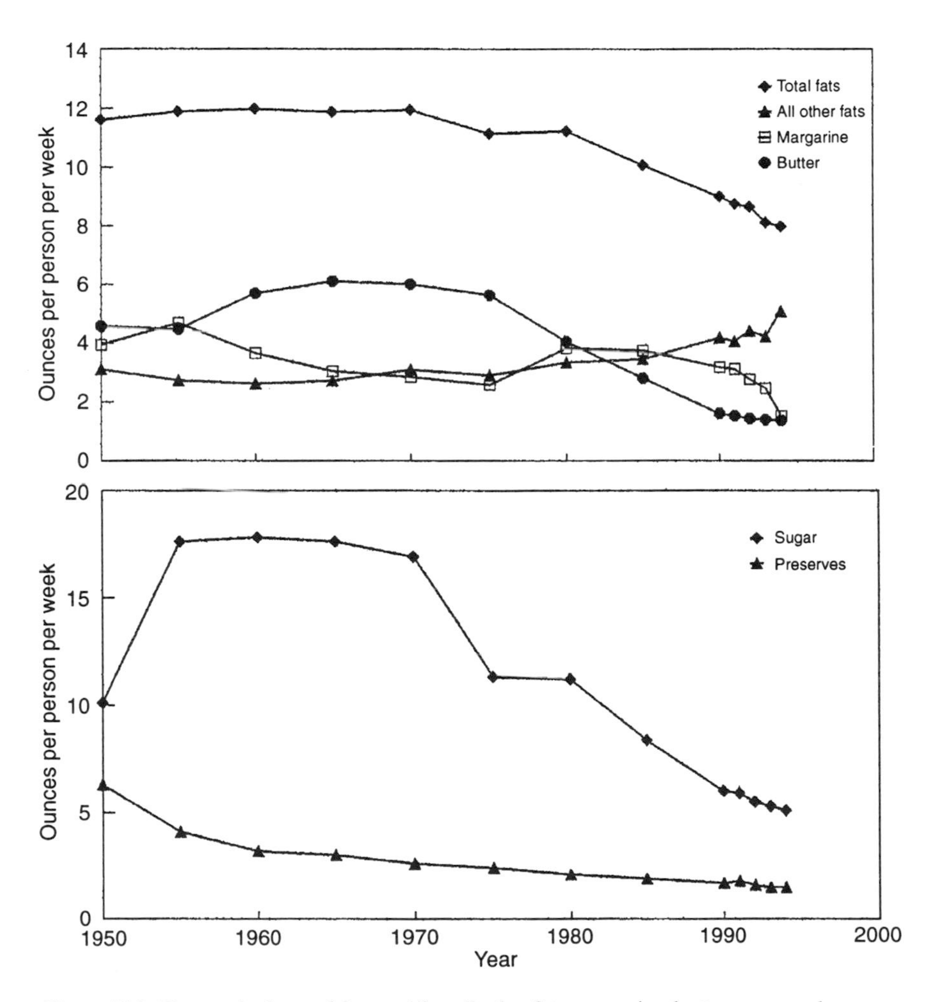

Figure 15.3 Changes in demand for total fat, all other fats, margarine, butter, sugar and preserves since 1950.

Consumption of fresh fruit is now much higher than it was in the 1950s (Fig. 15.4). There has also been a steady growth in the consumption of fruit juices. With vegetables, the outstanding feature has been the collapse in the demand for fresh potatoes. There has also been a small decrease in demand for fresh vegetables (excluding potatoes). On the other hand, the demand for vegetable products has expanded substantially.

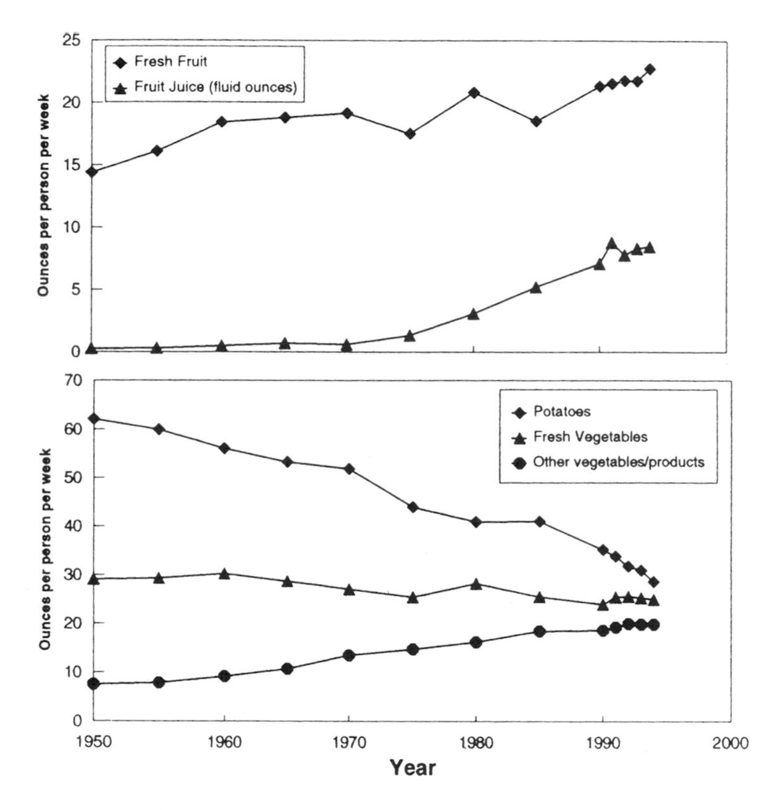

Figure 15.4 Changes in demand for fresh fruit, fruit juice, potatoes, fresh vegetables and other vegetables/products since 1950.

Demand for breakfast cereals has grown steadily since 1950 (Fig. 15.5) but consumption of bread has declined by over 50%. There was also a steady decline in demand for cakes and pastries between 1965 and 1985 but there has been some recovery in the past 10 years. Demand for biscuits has also fallen since 1965.

It is clear from these data that many of the staples such as bread, sugar, potatoes, beef, mutton and eggs have experienced big decreases in the

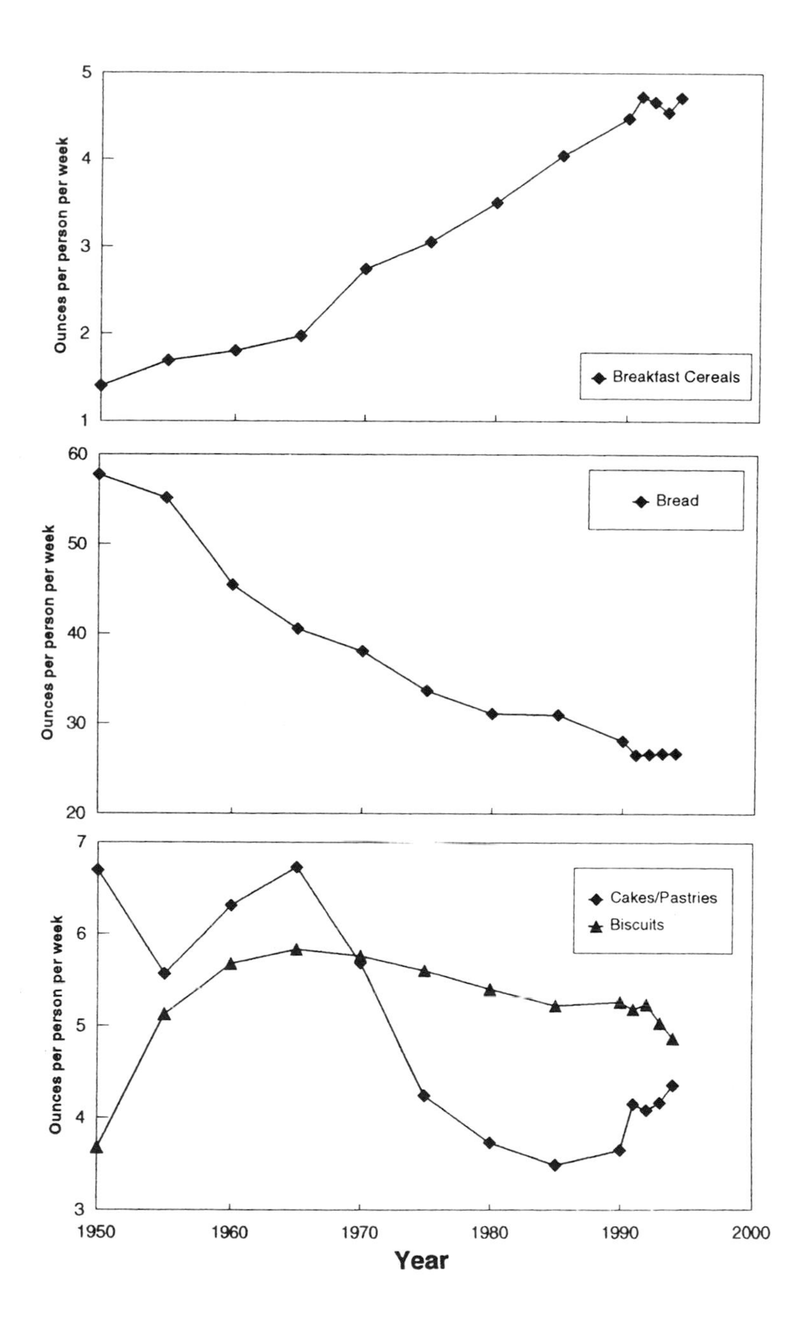

Figure 15.5 Changes in demand for breakfast cereals, bread, cakes/pastries and biscuits since 1950.

amounts consumed. To some extent, these have been balanced by growth in the markets for cheese, poultry, breakfast cereals and fruit.

However, it is important to appreciate that total energy consumption, as measured by the NFS, has fallen (Fig. 15.6). Average energy consumption has fallen from over 2600 kcal/head/day in the 1950s to under 1900 kcal/head/day in the 1990s. Intake of total fat and of saturated fat has also fallen substantially in the past 25 years. To some extent, the decrease may be an overestimate because the NFS does not include food prepared and eaten away from home. Eating out in cafés and restaurants certainly has increased but the growth in this activity is partially offset by the decline in 'industrial catering', i.e. the provision of meals at the place of employment. It follows, therefore, that the reductions in consumption which have occurred are largely because people are eating less food.

It is self-evident that changes in life style do have a major impact on how the food consumption patterns have been evolving. Clearly, convenience has played an important part. A key force has obviously been the growth in proportion of married women at work. Women who spend a substantial

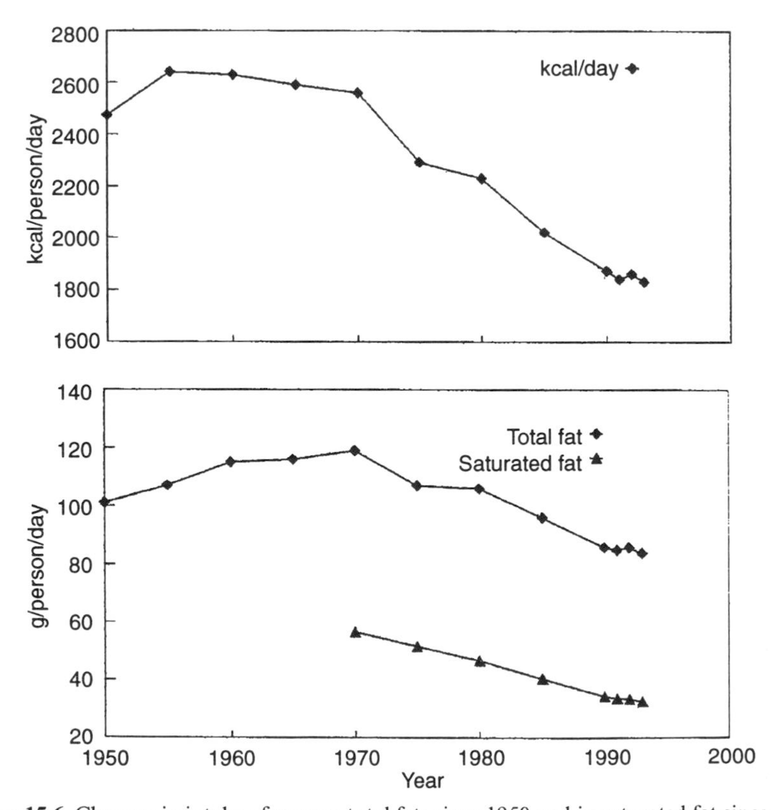

Figure 15.6 Changes in intake of energy, total fats since 1950 and in saturated fat since 1970.

proportion of their day away from home expect to purchase food which can be served quickly and easily. Much less home baking is done now, which, to some extent, is the reason why demand for sugar, fat and eggs has fallen.

From a nutritional perspective, the most interesting changes are the growth in demand for low-fat milks, fruit juices, fruit and vegetables, cooking oils, breakfast cereals and poultry. It would be simplistic in the extreme to conclude that concern about diet and health is the only reason for these changes. Ease of preparation undoubtedly contributes to the growth in demand for breakfast cereals, while the fall in the price of poultry relative to that of red meats has been critical to the large growth in demand that has occurred.

Perhaps the most striking development has been the increase in the proportion of semi-skimmed milk, which has grown from virtually zero in 1986 to over 50% of the total liquid milk market today. Switching from whole milk to semi-skimmed milk is an effective way to reduce fat intake because the change is easy to make. Furthermore, semi-skimmed milk is purchased and used in exactly the same way as whole milk. The price is the same and the difference in taste is relatively small. In fact, after a period of adjustment, whole milk can taste rather fatty. The spreading fats also exhibit some interesting changes with a big drop in consumption of butter, which is high in saturates. Over the past few years, demand for margarine has fallen sharply while there has been an increase in 'all other fats', which are mainly spreads containing less than 80% fat characteristics of margarine. It is also worth noting the steady decline in consumption of total fat.

In conclusion, it is clear that some of the dietary recommendations are getting through to some of the people and that the effect is growing. Nutritional concerns are certainly not the only factors involved in choice of food. In this context, the most significant progress is likely to be made when the changes are easy to make and when they are reinforced by other factors which generate pressure for alterations in the habitual diet. It follows, therefore, that if substantial progress is to be made, food manufacturers and retailers have a crucial role to play in developing and promoting products which facilitate consumers wishing to purchase a healthy diet.

References

Cannon, G. (1983) Battle for the British diet. *The Sunday Times,* 3 July.

Centre for Agricultural Strategy (1979) *National Food Policy in the UK*, Centre for Agricultural Strategy, University of Reading, Reading.

Committee on Medical Aspects of Food Policy (1974) *Diet and Coronary Health Disease*, Report on Health and Social Subjects, No. 7, HMSO, London.

Committee on Medical Aspects of Food Policy (1984) *Diet and Cardiovascular Disease*, Report on Health and Social Subjects No. 28, HMSO, London.

Committee on Medical Aspects of Food Policy (1994) *Nutritional Aspects of Cardiovascular Disease*, Report on Health and Social Subjects No. 46, HMSO, London.

Department of Health (1991) *The Health of the Nation – A Consultative Document for Health in England*, Cm 1523, HMSO, London.

Department of Health (1992) *The Health of the Nation – A Strategy for Health in England*, Cm 1986, HMSO, London.

Department of Health (1994) *Eat Well! An Action Plan from the Nutrition Task Force to achieve the Health of the Nation Targets on Diet and Nutrition.* Available from Department of Health, PO Box 410, Wetherby, Yorkshire LS23 7LN, UK.

Department of Health and Social Security (1978) *Report of the Working Party on Nutrition Education*, HMSO, London.

Department of Health and Social Security (1978) *Prevention and Health – Eating for Health*, HMSO, London.

Department of Health and Social Security (1981) *Report on Avoiding Heart Attacks*, HMSO, London.

Hansard (1985) House of Commons, 12 July, Column 665.

Hurren, C. and Black, A. (eds) (1991) *The Food Network: Achieving a Healthy Diet by the Year 2000*, Smith-Gordon, London.

Ministry of Agriculture, Fisheries and Food (1979) Press Notice No. 390, 19 November.

National Academy of Sciences (1980) *Towards Healthful Diets*, National Academy of Sciences, Washington DC.

National Advisory Committee on Nutrition Education (1983a) *A Discussion Paper on Proposals for Nutritional Guidelines for Health Education in Britain*, Health Education Council, London.

National Advisory Committee on Nutrition Education (1983b) Proposals of nutritional guidelines for health education in Britain. *Lancet*, **2**, 719.

National Food Survey Committee (various years) *Household Food Consumption and Expenditure*, HMSO, London.

Nutrition and Physical Activity Task Force (1995) *Obesity: Reversing the Increasing Problem of Obesity in England.* Available from Department of Health, PO Box 410, Wetherby, Yorkshire LS23 7LN, UK.

Nutrition Task Force Project Team on the National Health Service (1994) *Nutrition and Health: A Management Handbook for the NHS.* Available from Department of Health, PO Box 410, Wetherby, Yorkshire LS23 7LN, UK.

Nutrition Task Force Project Team on Nutrition Education and Training for Health Professionals (1994) *Nutrition – Core Curriculum for Nutrition in the Education of Health Professionals.* Available from The Nutrition Unit, Department of Health, Room 501A, Skipton House, 80 London Road, London, SE1 6LW, UK.

Royal College of Physicians of London (1981) *Report on the Medical Aspects of Dietary Fibre*, Royal College of Physicians, London.

Royal College of Physicians of London (1983) Obesity. *Journal of the Royal College of Physicians*, **17**, 3–58.

Royal College of Physicians of London and British Cardiac Society (1976) Prevention of Coronary Heart Disease. *Journal of the Royal College of Physicians*, **10**, 213–75.

Slattery, J. (1986) *Diet/Health: Food Industry Initiatives*, Food Policy Research, University of Bradford, Bradford.

WHO Expert Committee (1982) Prevention of Coronary Heart Disease, *WHO Tech. Rep. Ser. 678*.

Part Three

Public Sector Policy Initiatives

16 A nutritional policy at regional level: the Catalonia case study

LLUÍS SERRA-MAJEM, LOURDES RIBAS, GONÇAL LLOVERAS and LLUÍS SALLERAS

16.1 Introduction: a health policy for Catalonia

Catalonia is a region of Europe, situated in the north-east of the Iberian Peninsula. It has a population of 6 million inhabitants and a history, a culture and an idiosyncrasy which, compared with its surrounding regions, bestow a very different character upon it. In 1979, when the Autonomous Community Statute was approved, Catalonia gained its own government and the ability to organize itself within the framework of the Spanish State and the EC. The commitment to the idea that Europe should operationally organize itself on the basis of regional policy leads us to support all State and EC initiatives that tend towards encouraging regional policies in all areas including, obviously, health (Salleras *et al.*, 1994b).

Throughout most of the twentieth century, the Spanish State's health policy – similar to those of other European countries – has been dominated by the aim to reduce the number of premature deaths and increase the population's total life expectancy. It was simply a matter of 'adding years to life'. In 1985, the Spanish government passed the General Health Act which, under the protection of the Spanish constitution, clearly encouraged decentralization and development of a pluralistic system in which each autonomous community would establish its own body to administer all public health centres, health services and health establishments (Ministry of Health, 1986).

In Catalonia, parliament passed the Reorganization of Health Services in Catalonia Act, creating the Catalan Health Service (CHS) (Generalitat Catalunya, 1990). This Act also mandated a Health Plan for Catalonia as the guiding instrument and reference framework for all public actions in the health sector in the region. Under this Act, the Plan was to establish targets, guidelines and actions needed to guarantee constitutional rights to health protection. In doing so, the Plan was to respond to the population's health

Implementing Dietary Guidelines for Healthy Eating. Edited by Verner Wheelock. Published in 1997 by Blackie A&P, an imprint of Chapman & Hall, London. ISBN 0 7514 0304 0

needs and be implemented on the basis of specific health targets – not on demands for care or service (Terris, 1990; CHS, 1992). As developed, the Health Plan for Catalonia incorporates many of the innovative strategies embodied in the WHO–Europe 'Health for All' initiative (WHO, 1981, 1985).

The government of the Generalitat of Catalonia, following the recommendations of WHO–Europe, has included the two modern dimensions of health policy aimed at 'adding years to life' and 'adding health to life' within the current health policy in Catalonia (WHO, 1981). With the introduction of the two modern dimensions, the emphasis on health policy in Catalonia is placed more on quality than quantity. The change is really quite rational. The first strategy, 'adding years to life', was justifiable in Spain at the beginning of the twentieth century when life expectancy at birth was about half what it is now (about 37 years in Catalonia in the year 1900). The strategy is still justifiable in developing countries where life expectancy at birth is not very different from that of European countries at the beginning of the twentieth century. However, in the Catalonia of the last decade of the twentieth century, where the life expectancy at birth is now 77 years, it is clear that the emphasis should be placed on quality of life by increasing expectation of life in good health of the population and the positive health of the population. The priority given in the framework document to health promotion and disease prevention as activities to be implemented by the Catalan Health Service is clearly established (Via and Salleras, 1991). In fact, positive health, adding health to life, mostly depends on the health promotion actions aimed at modifying health-damaging life styles and promoting health-enhancing ones. On the other hand, it has been clearly proven that preventive measures are always more effective and efficient than curative ones. They also have greater potential for increasing the expectation of life in good health than curative measures. In fact, the improvement in the expectation of life in good health of the population mostly depends on preventive measures, and on primary prevention in particular. Assessing the potential increase in the expectation of life in good health was the main criterion used in the selection of priority actions for the health policy in Catalonia, from now until the year 2000 (Dillard, 1983; Via and Salleras, 1991). In particular, WHO–Europe has recommended a reorientation of health-care services in order to guarantee equity and community involvement, to place emphasis on primary health care, and to give priority to health promotion and disease prevention. It has also recommended acknowledging the important role of intersectorial and international co-operation when it comes to the health policies developed in the member states. Catalonia's policies also followed directives of the EU, particularly in the health protection area and some aspects of health promotion and disease prevention (cancer, cardiovascular diseases, eating habits, smoking and alcohol) (Richards and Smith, 1994).

In developing its Health Plan, Catalonia took into consideration the experience of other countries that have implemented modern health policies (e.g. Canada, the USA and the UK: (Gouvernement du Québec, 1989; SSH, 1991; USPHS, 1991). These countries have recognized that health personnel who are implementing new policies must be actively involved, through their scientific and professional associations, in the formulation of Health Plans (Dixon and Gilbert, 1991). Developing consensus about preventive activities has also proved to be an essential element. Thus, health professionals require education about policy targets, motivation to become involved in the new policy and training to carry out new policies within the framework of their day-to-day activities (Lawrence and Mickalide, 1987; Dixon and Gilbert, 1991).

16.2 Nutritional policy planning

Health Department experts followed several steps in setting priorities for health problems and actions to address them. They first analysed the extent of the key health problems in terms of mortality, morbidity, years of life lost due to premature death, temporary or permanent disability, number of days lost from the workplace, days of hospitalization and health and social costs. They also estimated the prevalence and potential consequences of chronic disease risk factors: imbalanced diet, cigarette smoking, hypertension, lack of physical exercise, excessive alcohol consumption, hepatitis B and C virus infections and others. They then estimated the extent of improvement in health indicators that might occur as a consequence of reducing or eliminating risk factors and health problems. Then they examined the organizational, political and financial feasibility of potential actions that might be taken to solve the problems or control the risk factors. Finally, they assessed the potential of such actions to improve the health of the population (adding health to years) (Pineault and Daveluy, 1986).

On the basis of these criteria, the Department identified priorities for the year 2000; these included 13 health problems and 18 interventions or actions. Of the top ten priority health problems, six were directly related to food or alcohol habits. Dietary intervention was ranked as the third priority need for implementation. Overall, the framework document of the Health Plan for Catalonia contained 263 health, risk reduction and operational targets, 53 of which related to nutrition, food quality, overweight or hypercholesterolaemia. Along with these targets, the Department identified implementation activities, the human, material and financial resources that would be required to carry out the activities, and a plan for evaluation of the structure, process and results of the interventions (Champagne, Constandriopoulos and Pineault, 1985; Salleras, Lloveras and Serra-Majem, 1993).

16.3 Dietary goals

For targets related to eating habits and physical exercise, WHO–Europe did not set quantitative attainment goals (WHO, 1985). Furthermore, WHO nutritional guidelines for Europe (James *et al.*, 1988) did not consider issues related to the Mediterranean diet, especially where fat intake is concerned, because its goals referred to a pattern typical of northern countries: less than 30% of energy from fat (10% saturated, 10% monounsaturated and 10% polyunsaturated fatty acids). For this reason, Catalonia adapted its goals to its Mediterranean situation (DSSS, 1988; Helsing and Trichopoulou, 1989) (Table 16.1).

Some of its goals derived from a survey of a random sample of the Catalan population carried out in 1986. This survey identified several nutritional problems: excessive intake of energy, total lipids (41.7% of energy intake), saturated fatty acids (13% of energy), cholesterol and protein; and insufficient intake of carbohydrates, especially complex carbohydrates, and fibre. Individuals aged 64 and over were most likely to suffer from nutritional deficiencies, and women aged 19 and over were most likely to exhibit folic acid and iron deficiencies.

In order to promote nutritional health some dietary guidelines (Table 16.2) were drawn up for the Catalan population (DSSS, 1988; Salleras, Lloveras and Serra-Majem, 1993):

1. meat and animal fat consumption should be moderated;
2. consumption of foods rich in complex carbohydrates such as bread, pulses, pasta, rice, etc. should be increased;
3. olive oil intake should be maintained and promoted;
4. the consumption of full-fat dairy products should be moderated, preferably by choosing their skimmed or semi-skimmed versions instead; and
5. the intake of fruit and vegetables should be increased.

The issue of fat intake was of particular concern. A 1992 workshop in Barcelona examined the changing patterns of fat intake in the Mediterranean countries in order to draw conclusions about their public health nutritional significance. Much more attention has been given to the relationship of dietary fat and health in northern Europe than in the south, and the Barcelona meeting attempted to redress this imbalance (Serra-Majem and Helsing, 1993). On this basis, Catalonia established nutritional objectives relating to fat intake that focused much more on limiting saturated fatty acid intake to less than 10% of energy, than on total or unsaturated fat.

Six years after formulating the Catalan dietary guidelines, 250 professionals from different parts of Spain met in Barcelona, on 24 and 25 October 1994, to discuss the present knowledge of the nutritional status of the Spanish population and its relationship with the health indicators, and to draw nutritional and policy objectives for the nation. A review of the most recent dietary surveys and a discussion on the food consumption patterns in different parts of Spain and the trends over the past decades occupied the first part of the conference. After a diagnosis of the nutritional status of the Spanish population, the nutritional objectives were discussed and analysed; some dietary guidelines were therefore studied and consensus was reached (Serra-Majem, Aranceta and Mataix, 1995; Serra-Majem *et al.*, 1996).

16.4 Dietary counselling in primary care

By consensus, representatives of the Department of Health, the Catalan Society of Family and Community Medicine, the General Medicine Society and the Catalan Society of Nursing developed a preventive interventions package for asymptomatic adults. Only interventions approved by Canadian and American experts during the past 15 years were included (CTFPHE, 1979; Oboler and Laforce, 1989; USPSTF, 1989; Hayward *et al.*, 1991). Among these interventions, dietary counselling is one of the most relevant. Materials and protocols have been developed to help health professionals perform appropriate nutritional interventions (Salvador *et al.*, 1992; DSSS, 1995). Indeed, more than half of the Catalan health centres have developed structured dietary advice for visiting patients.

One major change stemming from the new organization of the Catalan health system is the separation of financing of services from their provision, in a manner similar to that of England and New Zealand (Killoran, 1992; Bhopal, 1993; Harris and Shapiro, 1994). The system distinguishes between the service contractor – the Catalan Health Service – and the providers of health care through a service provision contract. The Health Plan establishes the basis of the relationship between payers and providers, and the contract process modulates implementation of the Health Plan by defining the types of services, principles of service delivery – criteria of equity, access to services, quality of activities, priorities – and mechanisms for co-ordination and evaluation. The contracts also establish criteria for clinical documentation, drug selection and continuing education for professionals. Most important, the Health Plan mandates contracts for preventive – as opposed to health care – activities related to priority health problems (Chisholm, 1990).

During the 1994 contract negotiations, Primary Health Care Team (PHCT) professionals sat alongside health service and primary care providers, ensuring incorporation of feasibility criteria and participation by all parties involved in health service delivery. Thus, the contract is not only the primary instrument for implementation of the Health Plan, but it is also a primary means for orienting the work of health professionals toward priority targets and the need to evaluate success in attaining them.

The Health Plan recognizes the importance of continuing education on preventive activities for primary care personnel as a crucial factor for attaining health targets, as seen in several countries with new health policies (ACP, 1994; ATPM, 1994; Egger and Parkinson, 1994). It also recognizes that protection from environmental risks, and reduction of behavioural risk factors, depends largely on decisions and actions taken in sectors other than health, such as environment, agriculture, industry, government, employment, social security, transport and the economy. As compared to the health sector, the agriculture and commerce sectors play only minor roles in Catalan nutritional policy, but their participation is important.

16.5 What are the chances of developing a nutritional policy at regional level?

The chances are the same as those at national level, with slight variations depending on the powers devolved from the central government. Figure 16.1 shows the areas of action that can be carried out by governments to develop a Food and Nutrition Policy. The areas for action include food supply, food quality and food demand; some of these actions could be developed at regional level, it is advisable for regional governments to implement some of them and some others can only be developed at national or supranational (European Union) level. Food supply regulation is the responsibility of the European Union and the possibility of modifying agricultural policies at regional or national level within the EU is remote.

The role of the regions in a nutritional policy is often limited to actions concerning food demand – nutritional education, information, etc. – missing real opportunities for developing an intersectorial policy involving all links in the food chain. In Catalonia, intersectorial co-operation in the development of a nutritional policy for the region has been of extreme importance, particularly in the development of new food technology. There are several examples in the field of olive trees and fruit production.

In Catalonia, nutritional policy has two strands, one developed as a part of the health policy already mentioned, and a second developed as a part of an agricultural policy. The agricultural policy is mainly focused on promoting indigenous products, such as olive oil, fruits, vegetables, rice, pulses, nuts, cheese, cured sausage, meats, fish and wine, and has developed a comprehensive Food Quality Control, also establishing several Food Quality Standards (Tarrago Colominas, 1994). This policy is co-ordinated with the first at a technical and political level.

The development of the nutritional policy within the health policy followed the analysis of a nutritional survey conducted in 1986 and also of a household budget survey conducted in 1981. Other monitoring systems, such as food balance sheets, have a national application and their use at regional level is not feasible.

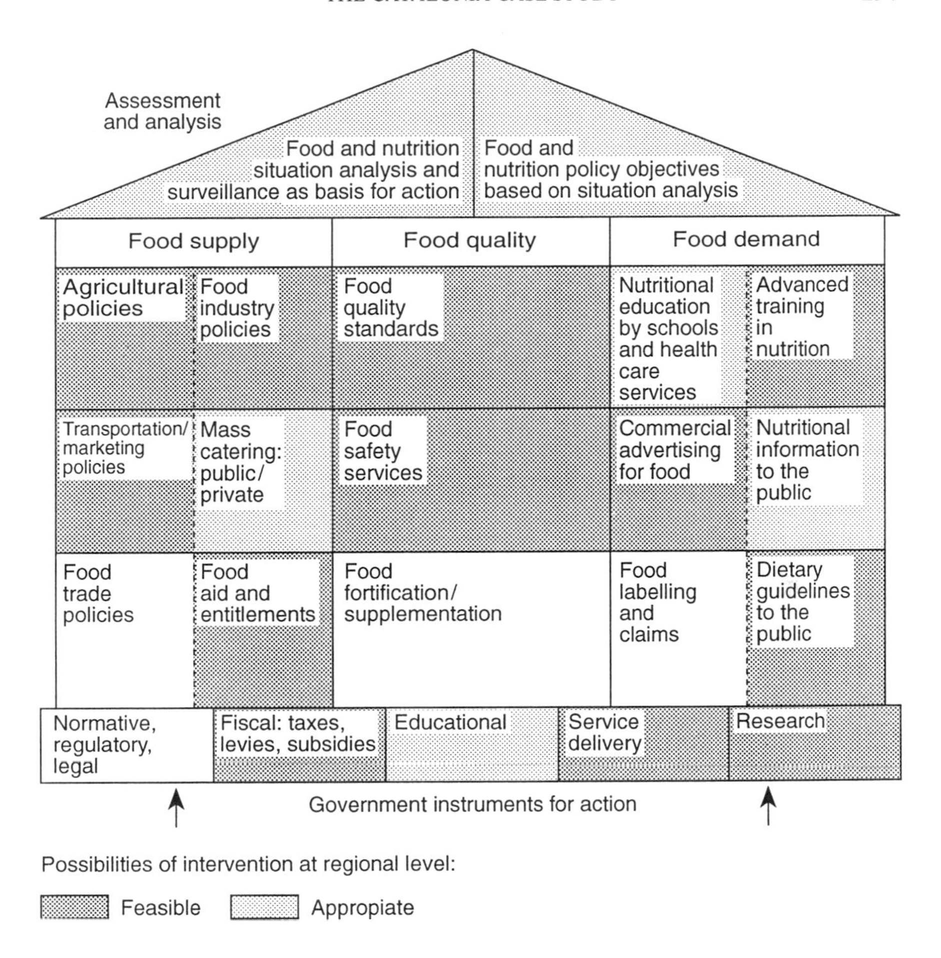

Figure 16.1 Outline of the elements of a food and nutrition policy. Possibilities of intervention at regional level (modified from Helsing, 1995, reproduced with permission of the Spanish Association of Community Nutrition).

The Health Plan for Catalonia 1993–95 formulates intervention proposals dealing with priority health problems and efficient services to solve them. Decentralized elaboration of the health plan, based on preliminary health plan projects for eight health regions of the Catalan Health Service, is a new working methodology that also involves different institutions and professionals. The results of a recently analysed nutritional survey, conducted in 1992 and 1993 over a random sample of 2757 people of the Catalan population, has shown important regional differences that will be taken into account when developing each Regional Health Plan between 1996 and 1999. In fact, the priorities for intervention within the health sector will be analysed at this eight-region level, and nutrition could be chosen as a first priority in one region but as a second or third priority in others; differences are remarkable for certain nutrients, for example saturated fat and carotenoid intake, explained by differences in meat, fish and fruit consumption.

16.6 Evaluation and surveillance

Evaluation of the structure of health-care implementation (e.g. the existence of suitable suppliers) and its process is accomplished mainly through the contracting out of services to providers. Evaluation of the results of implementation – achieving health and risk-reduction targets – is accomplished by analysing epidemiological data obtained from a variety of sources (Salleras *et al.*, 1994a).

Table 16.1 presents the results of several surveys designed to monitor nutritional objectives in the Catalan Health Plan. These data were obtained through two cross-sectional surveys conducted in the region in 1986 and 1992–93. This second survey included a comprehensive evaluation of nutritional status obtained by measuring several anthropometric, dietary and biochemical indicators. These data indicate that the Catalan population generally met dietary objectives.

Table 16.1 Nutritional trends and objectives in Catalonia

	1986	1992–93	Objectives 2000
Energy supplied by			
Fat (%)	41.7	38.3	≤35
SFA (%)	13.7	12.9	≤10
Protein (%)	15	18.3	≤15
Carbohydrates (%)	41.5	42.1	≥50
Fibre (g)	15	16.8	25–30
Iron deficiency anaemia (%)		2.2	<2
Urinary iodine excretion (μg/l)[a]	79	176	>160
Cholesterolaemia (mg/dl)	211	204	<200
Hypercholesterolaemia (≥250 mg/dl) (%)	19	12.7	<15
BMI[a]			
≥25 and <30 kg/m^2 (%)	28.9	31.7	
≥30kg/m^2(%)	11.9	11.1	<10

[a]Data for 1983–85.
BMI, body mass index; SFA, saturated fatty acids.

Table 16.2 presents operational targets for nutrition in the health policy of Catalonia and compares them to the baseline situation of 1992. These data suggest that a large proportion of the Catalan population is largely

Table 16.2 Operational targets for nutrition in the health policy of Catalonia (1991)

Awareness of:	
The meaning of following a balanced diet	70%
Food rich in animal fat, salt and sugars	85%
Food containing iron among fertile women and health consequences of iron deficiency	80%
Consumption of:	
Iodinated salt in endemic areas (current situation: 60%)	90%
Milk and dairy products (preferably low-fat), twice a day (current situation: 71%; only 23% low-fat)	80%
Food rich in complex carbohydrates, five times a day (current situation: 42%)	80%
Bread, daily (current situation: 90%)	100%
Fruit and vegetables, four times a day (current situation 60%)	90%
Olive oil related to other vegetable oils (%) (current situation: 81%)	90%
Instruments for action	
Proportion of health professionals able to give dietary advice (current situation: estimated <40–50%)	80%
Use of standardized dietary protocols in health services (current situation: 40%)	100%
Proportion of schools including nutritional education programmes (current situation 29%)	90%
Proportion of collective dining rooms having nutritional control and advice (current situation: unknown)	100%

aware of nutritional advice and follows dietary recommendations. However, only 40–50% of surveyed health professionals are able to give dietary advice, the same percentage of health services are using dietary protocols routinely and only 29% of schools are offering nutritional education.

The integration of a nutritional policy into a health policy has, from our experience, several advantages at regional level:

1. It deals with other behavioural risk factors for chronic diseases that are clearly related to diet and nutrition, integrating the efforts to combat them.
2. It can easily use existing resources within the health administration, such as primary health-care teams, school education programmes, continuous education programmes for health professionals, etc.
3. It increases participation from the community through the health-care system.
4. It may be more efficient as costs are reduced because they are shared.

Among disadvantages, an excessive medicalization may occur, leaving aside the agricultural implications of such policies while focusing exclusively on the food demand.

A detailed analysis and study should be made of the competence of the various entities involved in policy making – the EU and national, regional and local governments – and especially in the planning and development of nutritional policies. Further study is also needed of the advantages and disadvantages of integrating nutritional policies into health plans or policies, an option currently favoured by all the countries of the southern European region, and already supported by hopeful results from regions such as Catalonia.

Acknowledgements

The authors thank Mr Anthony Currant for his valuable editorial support, and Mrs Vicky Serra for typing the manuscript.

References

ACP (American College of Physicians) (1994) Positive Paper: The role of the future general internist defined. *Ann. Intern. Med.*, **121**, 616–22.

ATPM (Association of Teachers of Preventive Medicine) (1994) *An Inventory of Knowledge and Skills Relating to Disease Prevention and Health Promotion*, ATPM, Washington DC.

Bhopal, R.S. (1993) Public health medicine and purchasing health care. *Br. Med. J.*, **306**, 381–2.

CTFPHE (Canadian Task Force on the Periodic Health Examination) (1979) The periodic health examination. *Can. Med. Assoc. J.*, **121**, 1193–254.

Champagne, F., Constandriopoulos, A.P. and Pineault, R. (1985) Cadre conceptuel à l'évaluation des programmes de santé. *Rev. Epid. et Santé Pub.*, **33**, 173–81.

Chisholm, J.W. (1990) The 1990 contract: its history and its content. *Br. Med. J.*, **300**, 853–6.

CHS (Catalan Health Service) (1992) *Health Plan for Catalonia 1993–1995*, Departament de Sanitat i Seguretat Social, Barcelona.

Dillard, S. (1983) *Durée ou Qualité de la Vie?* Gouvernement du Québec, La Santé des quebecois, No. 4, Bibliotèque National de Québec, Quebec.

Dixon, J. and Gilbert, H. (1991) Priority setting. Lesson from Oregon. *Lancet*, **337**, 891–4.

DSSS (Departament de Sanitat i Seguretat Social) (1988) *Llibre Blanc: Hàbits Alimentaris i Consum d'Aliments i Nutrients a Catalunya*, Departament de Sanitat i Seguretat Social de la Generalitat de Catalunya, Barcelona.

DSSS (Departament de Sanitat i Seguretat Social) (1995) *Basis for the Integration of Prevention into Health Care Practice*, Departament de Sanitat i Seguretat Social, Generalitat de Catalunya, Barcelona, Doyma.

Egger, R.W. and Parkinson, M.D. (1994) Preventive medicine and health system reform: improving physician education, training and practice. *JAMA*, **272**, 688–93.

Generalitat Catalunya (1990) *Llei 15/1990 de 9 juliol, d'ordenació sanitària de Catalunya*, DOGC No. 1324, 30 July 1990.

Gouvernement du Québec (1989) *Ministere de la Santé et des Services Sociaux. Pour améliorée la santé et le bien-être au Quebec*, Orientations, Quebec.

Harris, A. and Shapiro, J. (1994) Purchasers, professionals and public health, A need for more radical appraisal of roles. *Br. Med. J.*, **308**, 426–7.

Hayward, R.S.A., Steinberg, E.P., Ford, D.E. *et al.* (1991) Preventive care guidelines 1991. *Ann. Intern. Med.*, **114**, 758–83.

Helsing, E. (1995) The scientific basis for the formulation of a nutrition policy. *Rev. Esp. Nutr. Comunitaria*, **1**, 23–7.

Helsing, E. and Trichopoulou, A. (1989) The Mediterranean diet and food culture – a symposium. *Eur. J. Clin. Nutr.*, **43**, (Suppl. 2), 1–92.

James, W.P.T., Ferro Luzzi, A., Isaksson, B. and Szostak, W.B. (eds) (1988) *Healthy Nutrition: Preventing Nutrition Related Diseases in Europe*. Copenhagen:WHO Regional Office for Europe,

Killoran, A. (1992) *Putting Health into Contracts. The Role of Purchasing Authorities in Commissioning Health Promotion and Disease Prevention Services*, Health Education Authority, London.

Lawrence, R.S. and Mickalide, A. (1987) Preventive Services in Clinical Practices. Designing the Periodic Health Examination. *JAMA*, **257**, 2205–7.

Ministry of Health (1986) *Ley 14/1986 de 25 de Abril*, General de sanidad, BOE Nos. 101 and 102 of 28 and 29 April 1986.

Oboler, S.K. and Laforce, F.G.M. (1989) The periodic physical examination in asymptomatic adults. *Ann. Intern. Med.*, **110**, 214–26.

Pineault, R. and Daveluy, C. (1986) *La Planificatión de la Santé. Conceps, Méthodes, Strategies*. Agence d'ARG, (les éditions), Montreal.

Richards, T. and Smith, R. (1994) How should European health policy develop? A discussion. *Br. Med. J.*,**309**, 116–21.

Salleras, L., Lloveras, G. and Serra-Majem, L. (1993) Foreword. Nutrition in the health policy context of Catalonia. *Eur. J. Clin. Nutr.*, **47** (Suppl. 1), 1–3.

Salleras, L., Rius, E., Tresserras, R. and Vicente, R. (1994a) *Working together for health gain at regional level. The Experience of Catalonia. Implementing for Health.* European Health Policy Conference 'Opportunities for the future', Copenhagen, 5–9 December 1994. Departament de Sanitat i Seguretat Social, Barcelona.

Salleras, L., Serra-Majem, L., Warner, M. and Ritsatakis, A. (1994b) *Prospects for Health Promotion in European Regions*, Generalitat of Catalonia and WHO Regions for Health Network in Europe, Barcelona.

Salvador, G., Lloveras, G., Serra-Majem, L. *et al.* (1992) *Protocols Dietètics per a l'Atenció Primària: Manual pel Sanitari*, Departament de Sanitat i Seguretat Social, Barcelona.

Serra-Majem, L. and Helsing, E. (eds) (1993) Changing patterns of fat intake in Mediterranean Countries. *Eur. J. Clin. Nutr.*, **47** (Suppl. 1), 1–100.

Serra-Majem, L., Aranceta, J. and Mataix, J. (eds) (1995) *Documento de consenso: Guías Alimentarias para la Población Española*, SG-Editores, Barcelona, pp. 1 317.

Serra-Majem, L., Ribas, L., García-Closas, R. *et al.* (1996) *Llibre Blanc: Avaluació de l'estat Nutricional de la Població Catalana (1992–1993)*, Departament de Sanitat i Seguretat Social, Barcelona.

Serra-Majem, L., Aranceta, J., Group of Nutrition Guidelines of the Spanish Society of Community Nutrition (1997) Nutrition and dietary guidelines for the Spanish population. Tool for a nutrition policy in Spain in *Implementing Dietary Guidelines for Healthy Eating* (ed. V. Wheelock) Blackie A&P, Chapman & Hall, London, pp. 233–44.

SSH (Secretary of State for Health) (1991) The Health of the Nation, HMSO, London.

Tarrago Colominas, J. (1994) *Una Politica Agrària i Alimentària per a la Cuina Catalana*, Congrés Català de cuina, Girona, December 1994.

Terris, M. (1990) Public health policy for the 1990s. *Ann. Rev. Public Health*, **11**, 39–51.

USPHS (US Public Health Service) (1991) *Healthy People: National Health Promotion and Disease Prevention Objectives*, US Department of Health and Human Services, Washington DC.

USPSTF (The US Preventive Services Task Force) (1989) *Guide to Clinical Preventive Services. An Assessment of the Effectiveness of 169 Interventions*, William and Wilkins, Baltimore.

Via, J.M. and Salleras, L. (eds) (1991) *Framework Document for the Formulation of the Health Plan for Catalonia*, Departament de Sanitat i Seguretat Social de la Generalitat de Catalunya, Barcelona, pp. 1–229.

WHO (1981) *European Regional Strategy for Attaining Health for All*. World Health Organization, Copenhagen.

WHO (1985) *Targets for Health for All*, WHO Regional Office for Europe, Copenhagen.

17 High fat intake: policy implications for The Netherlands

MICHIEL R.H. LÖWIK, KARIN F.A.M. HULSHOF, MARIJKE RIEDSTRA, HENNY A.M. BRANTS and SIGRID N. VAN WECHEM

17.1 Introduction

Both the quantity and the type of fat in the diet have an important influence on the serum lipoprotein pattern, which in turn influences the risk for coronary heart disease (WHO, 1994). The strongest dietary determinants of blood cholesterol levels are saturated fatty acids (National Research Council, 1989). Fat intake, especially the intake of saturated fatty acids, is given the strongest emphasis in several policy statements regarding nutritional education because the scientific evidence of its relationship to health is strongest and the likely impact of a change in fat intake on public health is greatest (National Research Council, 1989; Seidell and Löwik, 1993). In The Netherlands, the mean contribution of fat to daily energy intake was about 40% in 1987–88 which was much higher than the Dutch guideline of 30–35 energy%.

Based on this observation, the Dutch Steering Group for a Healthy Diet (installed in 1987), in which several organizations in industry, government and nutritional education participate, chose to take measures aimed at a reduction of fat intake by the Dutch population of 10% within 4 years. Besides the expected effect on public health of a lower fat intake, sole attention to fat allows an effective (simpler message than a prudent diet) preventive strategy that could be supported by food industry and retailers. As to the implementation, a national intervention programme called 'Fat Watch' was launched in 1991. This campaign, concentrating its activities in March, was repeated over 4 consecutive years (Riedstra *et al.*, 1993). This implies that as far as fat intake is concerned the policy processes are in the phase of implementation, and research should be oriented more towards an assessment of the effects and processes of the campaign. An assessment of the effects of these campaigns on buying and consumption behaviour is

Implementing Dietary Guidelines for Healthy Eating. Edited by Verner Wheelock. Published in 1997 by Blackie A&P, an imprint of Chapman & Hall, London. ISBN 0 7514 0304 0

given in this chapter. Throughout this campaign there was special interest in its effect on changing fat consumption of the Dutch population. For this a comparison between the results of the first and second Dutch National Food Consumption Surveys (DNFCSs) was carried out.

17.2 Results of the first DNFCS

In 1987–88, the mean contribution of fat to daily energy intake was about 40%. At that time major sources of fat were oils and fats (accounting on average for 32% of total fat intake), meat (products)/poultry (20%), milk (products) (10%), cheese (8%), biscuits and pastry (7%), and nuts, seeds and snacks (7%) (Löwik *et al.*, 1994). A simulation study showed that a massive preference of consumers for lower-fat variants of the first four food groups would result in a substantial reduction in fat intake (Löwik and Kistemaker, 1994). It was calculated that if 43% of the products with the highest fat content were replaced by lower-fat variants, the average contribution of fat to energy intake would be 35%. A complete substitution would result in an average contribution of fat of 28%. From the results it was concluded that the present supply of food does not need a dramatic change in order to realize the goal of lower fat consumption. By choosing leaner and lower-fat variants within basic food groups, instead of those with a higher fat content, it is possible to lower the fat consumption (as a percentage of total energy intake) substantially. Therefore, it was concluded that it was worth starting a campaign, since a successful campaign might have a substantial effect on fat consumption.

17.3 Risk groups

The variation in food consumption data shows that there is no such thing as a uniform diet in The Netherlands. Various subgroups, based on socio-demographic variables, such as household size, socio-economic status, region and degree of urbanization, revealed only relatively small differences in mean intake values (Brants *et al.*, 1989; Westenbrink *et al.*, 1989; Löwik *et al.*, 1992), which also holds for indicators of the fat intake (Brants *et al.*, 1989). This implies that the relevance of segmentation in terms of expected biological effect of the existing difference, and therefore targeted public health measures, is limited. For instance, those with a higher level of education obtained less energy from fat, whereas the average total fat intake of this group was still substantially higher than the guideline of 30–35 energy%.

In spite of statistically significant differences in mean values, the intake distributions in the various population groups overlap to a great extent.

Therefore, the dietary risks are dispersed throughout Dutch population groups. Combining such factors as education level and household size came up with greater differences, as shown in Fig. 17.1, but at the same time the size of the groups becomes smaller and this may be prohibitive for the implementation of nutritional policies, which have then to be tailor-made for a lot of separate groups. Costs will be increased substantially by such a strategy.

These and other analyses have been used by the Steering Group for a Healthy Diet in the development and implementation of the 'Fat Watch' campaign.

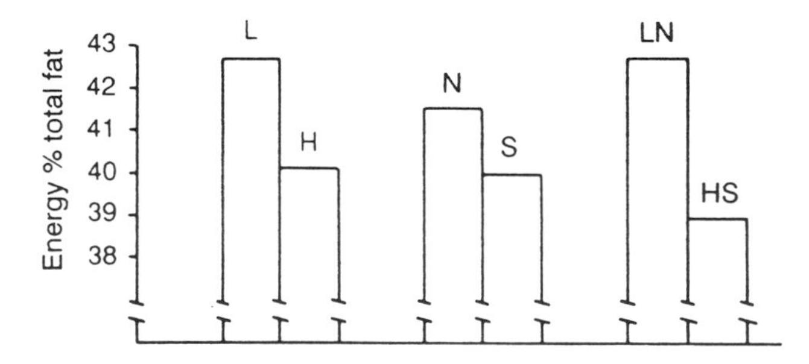

Figure 17.1 Percentage of energy derived from fat among 22–49-year-old women according to education (L, lower; H, higher education) and household size (S, solitary; N, non-solitary).

17.4 Fat Watch Campaign

In 1991, a nationwide intervention programme, named 'Fat Watch', was organized by the Steering Group for a Healthy Diet. The primary target group of the Fat Watch Campaign was consumers who are mainly responsible for household food purchases. In The Netherlands, this is mainly females. Mass media (television, radio, newspapers and magazines, and intermediate channels, especially supermarkets (brochures and posters)) were used to convey the message. Retailers and food producers were stimulated to initiate additional activities. Supermarkets were considered as a good channel for information dissemination. Each year the content of the printed material and TV and radio commercials were devised according to the goal set for that year. A logo marked all campaign materials. The 1991 TV spot was broadcast 92 times and the spots of 1992 and 1993 65 and 42 times, respectively. Radio commercials were broadcast 25 times in 1992 and 1993, but not in 1991. In the third year, 2317 billboards were placed in 19 large towns for 1–2 weeks. In 1991, supermarkets and pharmacies served as intermediaries. In 1992 and 1993 post offices, libraries, fish shops, dietitians, home nursing services and local health units participated as well; in 1993 hotel and catering services were also among the participating intermediaries (Riedstra *et al.*, 1993).

17.5 Evaluation studies

The nationwide Fat Watch Campaigns of 1991, 1992 and 1993 were evaluated by TNO Nutrition and Food Research Institute in collaboration with ResCon and A.C. Nielsen, whereas the campaign of 1994 was evaluated by the State University, Groningen. These studies consisted of a process evaluation and an effect evaluation. For more detailed information on the activities during the campaign and campaign awareness among the primary target group see Riedstra *et al.* (1993). In this chapter the sales figures of the effect evaluation are presented only, whereby actual (buying) behaviour is the topic of interest.

For the sales of food products A.C. Nielsen Marketing Research collected data among national samples (326 stores in 1991 and 345 stores in 1992) of all supermarkets. A sample of comparable size in 1990 was used as the reference year and starting point for the evaluation of the Fat Watch Campaigns regarding the sales of food products. In the sampled supermarkets the sales over 2-month periods were estimated by:

$$[\text{sales}] = [\text{stock at start}] + [\text{purchases}] - [\text{stock at this moment}],$$

whereby sales are expressed in Dutch guilders (market value).

Weighting factors for the individual supermarkets of the sample were used in the calculations to obtain a representative sample. These factors were based on the differences between the sample and the total number of supermarkets regarding characteristics such as type and size of store and region.

17.6 Results of the Fat Watch Campaign

17.6.1 Methodological aspects

For studies on sales figures it is essential to classify products of a large number of food groups as precisely as possible according to quantity and type of fat. The food groups that were used are:

- biscuits
- chocolate products/candy bars
- cocktail snacks
- dry sauces/saté sauces/soya sauces

- frozen chips
- frozen pastry
- coffee creamer
- cake/gingerbread
- margarine/low-fat margarine/household shortenings
- Dutch cheese
- nuts/peanuts/rice crackers
- salad dressing/mayonnaise/oil
- meat products
- table sauces/ketchup
- sweet milk drinks/chocolate drinks

A product can be qualified as 'favourable' or 'less favourable' on the basis of the quantity and type of fat (primarily the content of polyunsaturated fatty acids) it contains. This qualification is used within food groups and hence refers to the fat content of the product relative to other products in the same group. The product groups were selected on the basis of data from the 1987–88 Dutch National Food Consumption Survey and coverage by A.C. Nielsen in their food index.

The information on fat content (total and polyunsaturated fatty acids) was based at first on the fat content mentioned in the 1989 Netherlands Nutrient Databank (NEVO). A further source of information was the product labels.

The classification into 'favourable' and 'less favourable' products according to type of fat could not be applied to products in all food groups because the composition of some products was not sufficiently known. The food groups 'biscuits' and 'cake/gingerbread' were incompletely classified according to type of fat in some years (12% and 14% of the products, respectively, could not be classified in December 1991/January 1992). These food groups, as well as the group 'frozen chips' (80% of the products could not be classified in December 1991/January 1992), were therefore excluded from analyses according to fat type.

The statistical analysis was based on the sales figures in three 2-month periods in three successive years (1990–92), as shown schematically in Fig. 17.2. By taking into account only the proportion of 'favourable' products

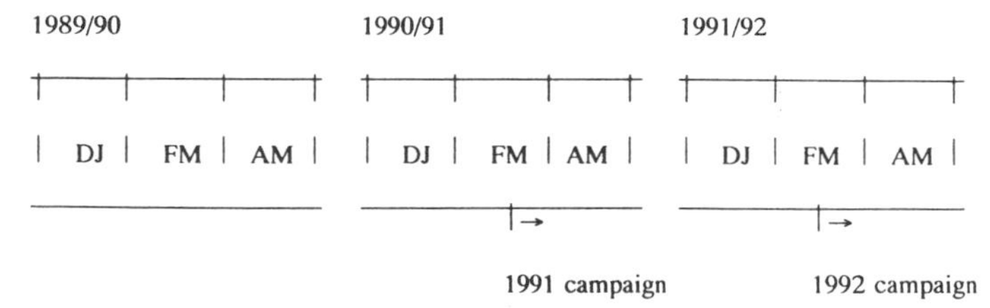

Figure 17.2 Survey periods for sales figures. DJ, December/January; FM, February/March; AM, April/May.

rather than their quantities the results are corrected for changes in the market size. This approach also makes allowance for the most recent product introductions to the market.

The analysis was used to explore to what extent the ratio between 'favourable' and 'less favourable' products, expressed as market value (money), varied during the periods under survey. Price-cutting actions may have affected sales. These effects were corrected so as to arrive at an assessment of effects of the Fat Watch Campaign with maximum accuracy. To achieve this, a price elasticity of –1 was assumed, meaning that if the price is cut by 10%, the quantities sold increase by 10%, so that the sales in money value remain unchanged. To examine developments over time (1989–90, 1990–91, 1991–92), the market share of products qualified as 'favourable' in each food group was expressed as an index, taking the situation in 1989–90 or 1990–91 as starting point (100%).

17.6.2 Results: sales figures

The development in indices of the market share of 'favourable' products with regard to their quantity of fat are presented in Table 17.1. First, the effect of the second Fat Watch Campaign was standardized relative to 1990, i.e. the situation prior to the start of the first campaign, thus revealing the possible effect of both campaigns. In the indices, the three periods in 1989–90 (December/January, February/March and April/May) are set to 100, so that seasonal effects are corrected for. Next, the effect of the second campaign is expressed relative to the first one, thus revealing any additional effects of the second Fat Watch Campaign.

Table 17.1 Development of the indexed proportion of relatively 'favourable' products (according to quantity of fat) in 1990–91 and 1991–92[a]

	December/January	February/March			April/May		
	index	index	%[b]	SE[c]	index	%	SE
1989–90	100.0	100.0			100.0		
1990–91	101.4	104.8	3.4*	0.5	106.8	5.4*	0.5
1991–92	104.6	104.6	0.0	0.5	102.3	–2.3*	0.6

[a]Compared with December/January of the same year, standardized relative to the same period in 1989–90.
[b]Difference (%) in index relative to December/January of the same year.
[c]Standard error of the difference.
*Significantly different (two-sided; $P<0.10$).

Table 17.1 shows the developments in the indices of all available food groups taken together. The indices for the three periods in 1990–91 and 1991–92 were calculated relative to those in 1989–90.

To estimate the direct effect of the campaign months the results for the different periods in 1990–91 and 1991–92 must be indexed before examining the changes within a year. In 1990–91, 1.4 of the 4.8 shift noted in February/March 1991 had been affected by market developments. The remaining 3.4 can be attributed to the first Fat Watch Campaign. In April/May 1991, the cumulative effect of the campaign was 5.4 (6.8–1.4). When the period of data collection was more synchronized with the campaign activities of 1991 it was found that there was a larger effect during than after the campaign. Furthermore a separate analysis for participating and non-participating supermarkets showed a larger effect in participating supermarkets. These results suggest some degree of a dose–response relationship, making a direct effect of the campaign on shifts in sales figures in the favourable direction more plausible.

For 1991–92, this approach was more difficult because of two factors, namely the first Fat Watch Campaign and independent market developments, are indistinguishable. In the period February/March 1992, the cumulative increase of the index relative to 1989–90 was 4.6. However, this increase had already been achieved in December 1991/January 1992. In April/May 1992 the index was 2.3 lower than before the campaign of that year.

The general 'trend' over the years has been a development in a 'favourable direction' with regard to both the quantity and the type of fat. The results show that the second Fat Watch Campaign in March did not lead to an additional (measurable) increase in market share (in market value) of low-fat products. In contrast, in 1991, an increase in index regarding fat quantity was found during and immediately after the campaign.

The index was 104.6 in December 1991/January 1992 which was in fair accordance with the indices in February/March and April/May 1991. Thus, the changes that took place after the first campaign had remained for a whole year. Trend-like developments may have contributed to this picture. A clue for a general trend is the fact that the index was somewhat higher in December 1990/January 1991 than in December 1989/January 1990 (i.e. before the first Fat Watch Campaign).

However, in supermarkets with a fair degree of participation this development was less strong than in supermarkets that participated hardly or not at all. It may be expected that the supermarkets participating in 1992 participated in the 1991 Fat Watch Campaign as well (Riedstra, Hardeman and Schneijder, 1992). Therefore, differences in indices between participating and non-participating supermarkets would probably be larger if the indices were standardized relative to 1990. As already noted, the shifts in 1991 were larger for the participants. In 1992 a trend in a 'less favourable' direction was observed which was attenuated by the Fat Watch Campaign, as the differences found on the basis of degree of participation in the campaign of 1992 suggest. Splitting up supermarkets according to degree of participation in the second Fat Watch Campaign revealed that a direct effect is indeed conceivable, albeit in compensating for an undesired development. In Table 17.2 the overall results regarding type of fat are presented.

Table 17.2 Development of the indexed proportion of relatively 'favourable' products (according to type of fatty acids) in 1990–91 and 1991–92[a]

	December/January	February/March			April/May		
	index	index	%[b]	SE[c]	index	%	SE
1989–90	100.0	100.0			100.0		
1990–91	100.8	98.8	–2.0*	0.4	89.6	–11.2*	0.4
1991–92	103.2	103.3	–2.9*	0.4	92.9	–10.3*	0.5

[a]Compared with December/January of the same year, standardized relative to the same period in 1989–90.
[b]Difference (%) in index relative to December/January of the same year.
[c]Standard error of the difference.
*Significantly different (two-sided; $P<0.10$).

In 1991 as well as in 1992 a change in the unfavourable direction was observed in February/May when compared with the preceding months. The results of December/January suggest a trend over the years in the favourable direction. A limitation of these data is that not all food products available are covered by the Nielsen Food Index. Thus, the food groups were incomplete with regard to major sources of fat in the Dutch diet. For example, data on dairy products and fresh meat were lacking. However, it is unlikely that the consumer's purchasing behaviour has differed appreciably between food products and food groups included and those not included in the analyses.

The analysis on which the interpretation is primarily based was corrected for market developments that could have taken place independently of the Fat Watch Campaign. This enables us to estimate the effects of the activities in March as accurately as possible. However, the existence of a campaign extending over more than 1 year can result in a continuous influence and/or delayed effects. In this respect, a particular aspect is food supply. Shifts towards a desired level of fat consumption may be effected both through behavioural changes and through changes in food supply. The introduction of new products may have had its effect only after some time. Comparison of the market share of 'favourable' products in December/January over the 3-years under survey revealed a shift in the desired direction with regard to both quantity and type of fat.

17.7 Dutch Nutrition Surveillance System

The Netherlands Food and Nutrition Council (1987) recommended that the Dutch Nutrition Surveillance System should consist of two components, namely monitoring of the Dutch population with regard to food availability and consumption, and more detailed investigations into the nutritional status (and, if necessary, food consumption) of specific vulnerable groups. Insight into dietary patterns is the core target of nutritional surveillance, since this provides a comprehensive basis for nutritional risk assessment. In 1987–88, the first Dutch National Food Consumption Survey was carried out within the framework of the Dutch Nutrition Surveillance System (Löwik and Hermus, 1988; Hulshof and Van Staveren, 1991; Löwik *et al.*, 1994). A similar survey was carried out in 1992 (Anonymous, 1993a), whereby differences in time could be studied.

In 1992, the average fat consumption was much lower than in 1987–88 (Table 17.3). This change was mainly due to a lower intake of saturated and monounsaturated fatty acids. The intake of polyunsaturated fatty acids is similar in both surveys. These differences between the surveys are a significant and relevant change in the perspective of public health. Whether the Fat Watch Campaign has contributed to this change is an important question. However, there are several possible explanations for the observed differences, the effects of the Fat Watch Campaign being one of them, whereby this campaign could have had an effect on both the supply and demand of food products.

Table 17.3 Mean fat intake (± standard deviation)[a] by the Dutch population in 1987–88 and 1992, as observed in the first and second National Food Consumption Surveys

Intake	1987–88 (*n*=5898)	1992 (*n*=6218)
Total fat (g/day)	105 ± 41	92 ± 37
Saturated fat (g/day)	43 ± 17	35 ± 15
Monounsaturated fat (g/day)	41 ± 17	34 ± 15
Polyunsaturated fat (g/day)	18 ± 10	17 ± 9
Total fat (energy%)	40.0 ± 7.2	36.9 ± 6.9
Saturated fat (energy%)	16.5 ± 3.4	14.1 ± 3.3
Monounsaturated fat (energy%)	15.4 ± 3.4	13.6 ± 3.3
Polyunsaturated fat (energy%)	6.9 ± 2.7	6.8 ± 2.5

[a]Weighted calculations (for age and gender).

As to the causes of the differences between the first and second National Food Consumption Surveys four categories are distinguished, namely:

- methodology;
- changes in the socio-demographic characteristics of the Dutch population;
- changes in the composition of the food products;
- changes in the food choices of the Dutch population or groups (Löwik, Hulshof and Kistemaker, 1993).

These four potential causes will be discussed below.

17.7.1 Methodology

In comparing the data of the first Dutch National Food Consumption Survey (DNFCS) with those of the second DNFCS differences may be found that do not result from real changes in consumption patterns but from methodological differences between the surveys. Possible differences may be related to non-response, distribution among days of the week and distribution over the quarters of the year. The results of the first DNFCS have shown that energy and fat intake is higher at the weekend (Saturday/Sunday) than on weekdays (Löwik *et al.*, 1994). Further, the average intake of (saturated) fat (as a percentage of total energy intake) is subject to seasonal variation: the lowest average percentage was found in July–September (39.3%), and the highest in October–December (40.4%) (Hulshof, 1993). Although the magnitude of the effects of such methodological differences is not known yet, it is expected to be small relative to, for example, changes in product composition, and relevant only for specific questions and/or analyses based on small samples of the DNFCS.

17.7.2 Characteristics of the population

The development of the Dutch population is characterized, among other things, by ageing, a declining family size and an increase of average education level. The results of the first DNFCS have shown that the proportion of energy derived from fat is lower among young children (e.g. 33.6% for boys aged 1–4) than among older children or adults (Löwik *et al.*, 1994). If young children are relatively less represented in the second DNFCS, fat intake as a percentage of total energy intake averaged over the total population will be higher. Increase of education and declining family size might have a favourable effect on average fat intake because fat consumption is higher in larger family households and among those with lower education (Brants *et al.*, 1989). Because of the opposite effects of shifts in demographic and socio-economic characteristics, and because of the minor significance of these shifts to be expected in the course of 4 or 5 years, the effects on fat intake are likely to be small.

17.7.3 Composition of food products

The food industry is continuously marketing new and modified products. Changes in the composition of food products are covered by the Dutch Nutrient Database (NEVO). The 1986–87 version of the NEVO database was used for the first DNFCS, and calculations for the second DNFCS were based on the 1993 NEVO version. Because the NEVO database follows upon developments in supply, there is inevitably some degree of backlog relative to the actual situation.This backlog should be taken into account when interpreting the results.

This situation may be exemplified with meat products for which the meat sector noted that the fat content values used for calculations in the first DNFCS were too high. This was confirmed by a later comprehensive national study (Van Wijk, 1991; Van Wijk, Erp-Baart and Roomans, 1991) in which the meat products surveyed were purchased in 1990 (i.e. prior to the Fat Watch Campaigns). However, this does not imply that the results of the first or the second DNFCS, or both, were incorrect. Given the time and the technical and financial means available, it is still the most feasible approximation of reality. The example does show, however, that the period covered by the first DNFCS should not be confined to the period April 1987–March 1988 in which the diaries were filled in. To answer the question 'Has a change in fat consumption taken place under the influence of the Fat Watch Campaign?' a period restriction is necessary. For that purpose, information on fat consumption in the period immediately preceding the campaign (i.e. before March 1991) should be available because behavioural changes with regard to both food choice and food preparation, as well as the fat content of (new) products before the start of the campaign, are not a direct effect of the Fat Watch Campaigns if we assume that consumers have not anticipated future campaigns.

If the second DNFCS is calculated on the basis of the 1986–87 NEVO version, it appears that the difference in calculated fat intake can partly be ascribed to a changed composition of food products consumed (Anonymous, 1993a).

17.7.4 Shift from visible to invisible fat

In the second DNFCS, too, a delay in registration inherent in a nutrient database should be taken into account. For example, the Commodity Board for Margarine, Fats and Oils noted that the market share of reduced-fat products had increased from 8% in 1991 to 15% in 1992. The sales of shortenings and frying fats had increased by 2.3% and the supply to the food industry by more than 3% (Anonymous, 1993b).

These changes suggest a shift from visible to invisible fat. If this shift is real, the lowered consumption of visible must be read from the diaries. An increase in fat content of such products as biscuits and ready-to-eat meals, if any, should be recorded in the NEVO database. However, the period was too brief to enter such changes taking place in 1992 in the database version of early 1993. In this context, the lower calculated energy intake in the second DNFCS could be indicative of estimates for intake of macronutrients that were too high in the first DNFCS and/or too low in the second, if it is assumed that the average energy intake and energy requirement of the Dutch population has not changed between 1987–88 and 1992.

17.7.5 Choice behaviour

Shifts in choice behaviour in food consumption surveys pertain primarily to more or less conscious changes in the purchase, preparation and consumption of food. The topic of interest is now behavioural changes in population groups for which repeated assessments are the research method of choice. Most respondents to the second DNFCS have probably not participated in the first one. Even for those who have participated in both surveys, a comparison on an individual level is hampered by seasonal differences and differences in days of the week covered.

If the sample is of sufficient magnitude and representative of the Dutch population, there is a reasonable case for certain differences between both surveys being attributable to changed behaviour. The 'residual changes' after correction for differences in population sample, composition of products and methodology may be seen as resulting from changes in choice behaviour.

17.8 Conclusions

The above considerations led to the conclusion that the question 'Has fat consumption changed as a result of the Fat Watch Campaigns?' cannot be answered by just comparing the results of the DNFCS surveys. The possible explanations are so numerous that it is unlikely that any difference can be attributed unequivocally to the Fat Watch Campaigns. On the other hand, of course, the assertion that the campaigns have not contributed at all to possible changes in fat consumption is also untenable.

The national campaigns are at a disadvantage in 'proving' effects. A problem inherent in the evaluation of national campaigns is the absence of a control sample. Therefore, no information is available on developments in the absence of the Fat Watch Campaigns. This also holds, of course, for the sales figures included in the Nielsen Food Index, which were analysed in 1991 and 1992 especially for the purpose of the campaigns in these years (Riedstra, Hardeman and Schneijder, 1992).

However, there were indications (larger effect during than after the campaign, larger effect in participating supermarkets) that the shifts in a favourable direction could be attributed to the campaign (especially in the first Fat Watch Campaign). Further, sales figures suggested that the general trend between 1990 and 1992 with regard to both quantity and type of fat was favourable. By standardizing relative to a year in which there was no campaign (e.g. 1990), there is a reasonable explanation for possible changes being an (indirect) result of the Fat Watch Campaigns. The process evaluation of Fat Watch Campaigns showed that, especially in the first year, food manufactures and retailers had been very active. These activities (including the introduction of new low-fat products and temporary price reductions) can be seen as part of the campaign since the Steering Group for a Healthy Diet stimulated involvement of those responsible for the supply of food products. To our knowledge no other major independent public health initiatives oriented at food consumption were conducted during the period of the first years of the Fat Watch Campaign. Therefore, it is most likely that the Fat Watch Campaigns acted at least as a catalyst of (the already existing trend of) a reduction in the fat consumption. However, caution is needed when drawing conclusions regarding the direct and independent effect of the Fat Watch Campaigns on the fat consumption since these campaigns had the character of a mass-mediated intervention. For instance, from the Minnesota Heart Health Program with an intensive intervention programme it was found by Luepker *et al.* (1994) that, against a background of strong secular trends of increasing health promotion and declining risk factors, the overall programme effects were modest in size and duration and generally within chance levels.

References

Anonymous (1993a) *Zo eet Nederland, 1992*, Voorlichtingsbureau voor de Voeding, 's-Gravenhage.

Anonymous (1993b) Nederlands vetgebruik daalt. *MVO-magazine*, **23**, 1.

Brants, H.A.M., Aarnink, E.J.M., Hulshof, K.F.A.M. *et al.* (1989) *Vetconsumptie in Nederland. Vol. 1. Doelgroepsegmentatie (Voedselconsumptiepeiling 1987/1988)*, TNO-rapport V89. 436. TNO-Voeding, Zeist.

Hulshof, K.F.A.M. (1993) *De inneming van energie en voedingsstoffen naar seizoen-Voedselconsumptiepeiling 1987–1988*, TNO report V93.217, TNO Nutrition and Food Research, Zeist.

Hulshof, K.F.A.M. and Van Staveren, W.A. (1991) The Dutch national food consumption survey: Design, methods and first results. *Food Policy*, **16**, 257–60.

Löwik, M.R.H. and Hermus, R.J.J. (1988) The Dutch nutrition surveillance system. *Food Policy*, **13**, 359–65.

Löwik, M.R.H. and Kistemaker, C. (1994) Assessment of nutritional status in the Netherlands (Dutch Nutrition Surveillance System), in New aspects of nutritional status. (eds J.C. Somogyi, I. Elmadfa and P. Walter) *Bibl. Nutr. Diet.* **51**, 68–73.

Löwik, M.R.H., Hulshof, K.F.A.M. and Kistemaker, C. (1993) Lagere vetconsumptie in de tweede voedselconsumptiepeiling. Hebben de Let op Vet campagnes effect? *Voeding* **54**, (9), 27–9.

Löwik, M.R.H., Van den Berg, H., Westenbrink, S. *et al.* (1992) Risk groups among elderly people in the Netherlands: A review (Dutch Nutrition Surveillance System). *Age Nutrition*, **3**, 72–7.

Löwik, M.R.H., Brussaard, J.H., Hulshof, K.F.A.M. *et al.* (1994) Adequacy of the diet in the Netherlands in 1987–1988 (Dutch Nutrition Surveillance System). *International Journal Food Science Nutrition*, **45**, (Suppl. 1), S1–S62.

Luepker, R.V., Murray, D.M., Jacobs, D.R. Jr *et al.* (1994) Community education for cardiovascular disease prevention: Risk factor changes in the Minnesota Heart Health Program. *American Journal of Public Health*, **84**, 1383–93.

National Research Council (1989) *Diet and Health – Implications for Reducing Chronic Disease Risk*, National Academy Press, Washington.

Netherlands Food and Nutrition Council (1987) Mogelijkheden tot het opzetten van een voedingspeilingssyteem in Nederland. *Voeding*, **48**, 35–43.

Riedstra, M., Hardeman,W. and Schneijder, P. (1992) *De effecten van de tweede landelijke Let op Vet Campange, gehouden in 1992 – Verkoop van voedingsmiddelen naar hoeveelheid en soort vet*, TNO rapport V92. 455, TNO-Voeding, Zeist.

Reidstra, M., Brug, J., Hardeman, W. *et al.* (1993) Drie jaar landelijke Let op Vet Campagne: Wat is er gebeurd? *Voeding*, **54**, (9), 4–7.

Seidell, J.C. and Löwik, M.R.H. (1993) Voeding, in *Volksgezondheid toekomst verkenningen – De gezondheidstoestand van de Nederlandse bevolking in de periode 1950–2010* (eds D. Ruwaard and P.G.N. Kramers), SDU Uitgeverij, Den Haag, pp. 559–66.

Van Wijk, Th.A. (1991) *Bepaling van het vetgehalte van vleesprodukten*, TNO-rapport T91.038, TNO-Voeding, Zeist.

Van Wijk, Th.A., Van Erp-Baart, A.M.J. and Roomans, H.H.S. (1991) *Bepaling van het vet – en eiwitgehalte van bereid vlees*, TNO-rapport V91.324, TNO-Voeding, Zeist.

Westenbrink, S., Hulshof, K.F.A.M., Aarnink, E. *et al.* (1989) *De inneming van enkele microvoedingsstoffen door de Nederlandse bevolking. Voedselconsumptiepeiling 1987–1988, Zeist*, TNO Nutrition and Food Research report no. V89.213, Zeist.

WHO (1994) *Cardiovascular Disease Risk Factors: New Areas for Research*, Report of a WHO Scientific Group, Geneva.

18 Food for health: a nutritional initiative of the Nova Scotia Heart Health Program

DAVID R. MacLEAN, ANNE COGDON,
JANE FARQUHARSON, ROB HOOD,
KIM TRAVERS and ANDRES PETRASOVITS

18.1 Introduction

Cardiovascular disease (CVD) is the leading cause of death and disability in Canada (Heart and Stroke Foundation of Canada, 1995). Nova Scotia has the highest age-specific death rates attributable to CVD in the country, mainly because of higher rates of ischaemic heart disease (Nair *et al.*, 1989). The Nova Scotia Heart Health Survey (1986) revealed a high prevalence of the known modifiable risk factors for CVD and a high prevalence of multiple risks for CVD, throughout the province, with two-thirds of the adult population having one or more of the major risk factors (Nova Scotia Department of Health and Fitness, 1989).

The survey also disclosed that a substantial proportion of the population had little understanding of the causes of heart disease and the ways it could be prevented. The report concluded that the high rates of CVD in Nova Scotia result from unhealthy characteristics of average live style. The survey showed that 70% of adult Nova Scotians had one or more risk factors for CVD and 25% had two or more risk factors. Furthermore, the survey showed that higher levels of socio-economic status were associated with lower levels of risk (Kephart, Langille and MacLean, 1993).

As a consequence of these findings the province initiated, in 1989, the Nova Scotia Heart Health Program (NSHHP). The NSHHP was designed to be a public health approach to the CVD problem, utilizing health promotion and disease prevention strategies targeted to the whole population as well as to individuals at high risk. In this context it was to be a community-based intervention for the promotion of heart health and the prevention of heart disease. The programme was jointly funded by a grant from the Nova Scotia Department of Health (NSDOH) and a matching research grant from the National Health Research and Development Program (NHRDP), Health Canada.

Implementing Dietary Guidelines for Healthy Eating. Edited by Verner Wheelock. Published in 1997 by Blackie A&P, an imprint of Chapman & Hall, London. ISBN 0 7514 0304 0

The NSHHP draws upon the experience of community programmes for cardiovascular disease prevention in the United States and Europe, which have demonstrated that it is feasible to reduce cardiovascular disease risk in entire populations (Puska *et al.*, 1985; Farquhar *et al.*, 1990). The programme was designed to be developed and evaluated over a 5-year period, employing a demonstration model concept for its implementation.

The theoretical framework for the programme has applied aspects of social change theory to community health. The health promotion and disease prevention activities have been focused on the community, in addition to the individual. This emphasis results from the recognition that individual behaviour is greatly influenced by the environment in which people live and, in fact, without a conducive environment, individual change is extremely difficult (World Health Organization, 1992). Inherent in this approach is the recognition that local values, norms and behaviour patterns found at the community level have a significant effect on shaping an individual's attitudes and behaviours.

The link between diet and risk factors for cardiovascular disease, particularly obesity, hypertension and hypercholesterolaemia, is a recognized public health issue (Federal Provincial Working Group on the Prevention and Control of Cardiovascular Disease in Canada, 1991). Increased concern for CVD as a major public health problem is reflected in Canadian nutritional recommendations (Health and Welfare Canada, 1990). These recommendations have moved from a foundation dict approach (prevention of deficiencies) to a total diet approach (prevention of chronic disease) while concentrating on increased carbohydrate consumption and lower total dietary fat and saturated fat intake.

In 1991, the NSHHP carried out a province-wide nutritional survey in a representative sample of 2200 individuals. A key result was the finding that 80% of adult Nova Scotians have an estimated usual fat intake of over 30% calories from fat (after adjustment for intra-day variability) (NSHHP, 1993). Of particular concern, however, are persons living in low-income households, who were found to consume more fat than persons living in middle- and high-income households. The results of these studies suggest that low income may be a barrier to implementing nutritional recommendations. The findings from the nutritional survey contributed to raising the priority and visibility of this issue in the province and served to plan and launch the Food for Health Initiative in the context of the NSHHP.

18.2 Organizational structure of the Nova Scotia Heart Health Program

The Nova Scotia Heart Health Program has been designed to be situated at the interface between the formal public health sector, as represented by government, and the informal sector, as represented by the community and the organizations and agencies that operate there. In this manner the programme served as a linking agent between these sectors.

A co-ordinating committee of partners in development was the key mechanism by which the community/public health partnership was achieved. This committee which was appointed by the Minister of Health for the Province of Nova Scotia was the mechanism by which community resources and intersectoral support from the public, academic and private sectors was brought together to participate along with the Department of Health in the planning, development, implementation and the evaluation of the Heart Health Program.

The committee was chaired by the Principal Investigator and operated under terms of reference that had been approved by the Minister of Health. The development, implementation and evaluation of the programme activities, which were carried out over the first 5 years, were accomplished through a series of subcommittees of the parent group. These subcommittees developed the programme modules and work plans which were then presented to and approved by the co-ordinating committee.

The Nova Scotia Heart Health Program was designed to be a public health approach to cardiovascular disease prevention, using a partnership model. The essence of this approach was to test the feasibility of bringing about a community–public health partnership to plan, develop, implement and evaluate health promotion and disease prevention activities for heart health, directed at the population as a whole in Nova Scotia. The term 'public health' in this context includes both the formal and informal public health systems of the province. The formal system includes primarily the Department of Health, particularly its Public Health Division which includes the four Regional Health Units located throughout the province. This formal sector also includes other government departments, such as the Departments of Agriculture and Fisheries, particularly those components of these departments which impact directly upon, or have an interest in, health.

The informal public health system is much broader and less discretely defined, being made up of what is referred to in the context of this programme as the 'community'. It consists of a variety of community-based voluntary health and non-health organizations, the academic community, health professional groups, the private sector and a variety of specialized health care organizations such as the Maritime Heart Centre and Federation of Community Health Centres.

18.3 Evaluation design

The *Evaluation Guidelines for Heart Health* (Health Canada, 1993) developed by the Canadian Heart Health Initiative (Stachenko, 1993), served as the guide for evaluating the programme. The guidelines state 'program evaluation is taken to mean the ascertainment of:

- the extent to which a program meets its goals and objectives, and
- the key factors which explain program failure or success'.

Hence goals and objectives were stated for the provincial heart health programme and each of its component programmes, and programmes were evaluated based on measures of goal attainment.

Demonstration programme components were implemented and evaluated in settings such as workplace and grocery stores, and larger settings such as local communities and the province of Nova Scotia. Therefore, evaluation strategies of specific programme components differed, depending on the programme setting. To some degree, the site-specific programme evaluations were short-term evaluation designs, and the provincial programme valuations were long-term evaluation designs, as they will be used for long-term monitoring and evaluation of population heart health.

Other evaluation strategies have implications for current programme development and research that extends over 10–15 years (long-term evaluation). For example, the Nova Scotia Nutrition Survey was used to aid programme development for nutrition-related interventions, but also serves as a baseline of nutritional habits across Nova Scotia that can be compared to future surveys.

Many of the evaluation strategies and methods used were borrowed from other community-based heart health initiatives outside of Canada, primarily in the United States. However, most strategies were modified to fit the capabilities of the Nova Scotia programme. Evaluations from community-based heart health programme models (Stanford Five City Project, Pawtucket Heart Health Program, Minnesota Heart Health Program, and the Community Health Improvement Program) were comprehensive and costly. They incorporated quasi-experimental research designs which were not feasible for the Nova Scotia programme principally because of the costs involved and due to the fact that the Nova Scotia programme was not testing the efficacy of community intervention.

While the Nova Scotia programme relied less on experimental research approaches, more emphasis was put on community analysis, formative evaluation and process evaluation. This approach was consistent with the recommendations for lesser-funded programme made by researchers who have reviewed the findings of the programme in the United States referred to above (Mittelmark *et al.*, 1993). Primary data-gathering techniques included interviews, survey questionnaires and large cross-sectional surveys.

In summary, the evaluation design utilized a case-study approach which was employed to provide an analytical framework for, and the documentation of, the processes of partnership development, programme planning, development and implementation, community mobilization and activation, using primarily formative evaluation techniques. In addition, both process and outcome evaluations were conducted to assess the impact of the intervention modules, with respect to their specific objectives, which were planned, developed and implemented during the life of the whole programme.

18.4 Goals

The overall mission of the NSHHP, as articulated by the co-ordinating committee, was 'to promote the optimal health of Nova Scotians through community and individual empowerment and environmental change'.

To accomplish this mission a number of programme goals were developed by the NSHHP through a strategic planning process. A nutritional goal was one of these and was stated as: 'to enable all Nova Scotians to choose a heart healthy diet, including price and availability of food'. Specific objectives were defined as:

- To increase the awareness and knowledge levels of Nova Scotians on the relationship between diet and health.
- To influence the food industry (e.g. marketing boards, agriculture, fisheries, suppliers, grocery chains) to play a leading role in the development and availability of healthier food products.
- To create a consumer demand for healthier food products.
- To lobby for affordable healthier food products that are available to all Nova Scotians.
- To collaborate with professional organizations and governing bodies in the development of a nutritional policy for Nova Scotia.
- To encourage the avoidance of alcohol abuse.
- To ensure that the public are aware that alcohol abuse increased the risk of coronary heart disease and accidents.
- To encourage avoidance of overweight and obesity.
- To promote a diet which is: lower in fat, saturated fat, sugar, salt, alcohol and higher in fibre and carbohydrates.

18.5 Food for Health initiative

The nutritional strategy, referred to as 'Food for Health' was developed as the vehicle to implement the nutritional objectives and was one of the main components of the NSHHP. Its aim was to provide the public with positive information on healthy food choices and to secure co-operation from government departments (fisheries, agriculture) and the private sector to make it possible for people to make healthy choices about what they eat. Food for Health was viewed as the fundamental programme component to address the issue of excess fat consumption which likely lies at the heart of problems associated with elevated lipids in the population of Nova Scotia.

The Food for Health project had the following components:

- Shopping for Health;
- Take Breakfast to Heart;
- heart health training opportunities for chefs and food service personnel;
- accessibility to heart healthy foods;
- position paper on product labelling.

Translating nutrition messages into practical use is a continuing challenge for health professionals. There continues to be confusion over many diet and health relationships (National Institute of Nutrition, 1992; Reid and Hendricks, 1993). Strategies need to be developed to reach the less aware population and attention must be given to regional, demographic and cultural differences when developing nutritional health promotion programmes.

An intersectoral Food for Health Committee was established by the NSHHP to address these challenges. The committee included representatives from the Canadian Cancer Society, Canadian Council of Grocery Distributors, Heart and Stroke Foundation, Beef Information Centre, Pork Nova Scotia, Chicken Marketing Bord, Milk Maritime, National Sea Products, Chefs' Association, Restaurant and Food Services Association, Dietetic Association, Department of Health, Department of Fisheries, Department of Agriculture and Marketing and Nutrition Council.

The Food for Health Committee, in partnership with the Nova Scotia Department of Health and Health Canada, launched the nutritional programme with the public release of the results of the Nova Scotia Nutrition Survey on 3 March 1993. The Minister of Health chaired the launch which was held at Province House (provincial legislature). Immediately prior to the launch a briefing session was held in the morning by programme staff for 90 invited business and community leaders. The purpose of the session was to inform these leaders of the key findings, to discuss the potential nutritional interventions suggested by the Food for Health Committee, and to ask for broad support and assistance across all sectors toward the goal of 'reducing the total fat intake of adult Nova Scotians'.

Media coverage of the launch included articles in provincial newspapers, and news reports on television and radio the day of and the day following the launch.

The focus of Food for Health was to lower the total fat intake of adult Nova Scotians. The objectives were:

- To increase knowledge levels of Nova Scotians regarding the fat content of food choices.
- To work with the media in the dissemination of reliable nutritional information.

- To increase opportunities for Nova Scotians to acquire skills in the preparation of lower-fat meals.
- Within grocery stores, to identify and promote lower-fat foods.
- To advocate for 'consumer friendly' mandatory nutritional labelling.
- To increase the proportion of hospitality and food service industries that offer identifiable lower-fat food choices.

The decision to focus on fat intake resulted from the findings of the Nova Scotia Heart Health Survey (1986) and the Nova Scotia Nutrition Survey (NSHHP, 1993).

18.5.1 Shopping for Health

The aim of the Shopping for Health programme was to inform women about lower-fat food choices and lower-fat cooking methods to enable them to adopt a 'heart healthy' diet for themselves and their families. To achieve this aim, a multifaceted programme was implemented in grocery stores in the autumn of 1994.

This was a retail point-of-purchase pilot programme implemented in three grocery stores over a 10-week period. The target audience was women between the ages of 25 and 39. Focus groups were held with women in the target age groups to determine barriers and resistance points to lower-fat food selection and appropriate programme components, materials and message delivery. The programme consisted of employee training, an information book, a grocery store focus, a 1-800 number (free to callers) for information and advice, and taste testing demonstrations.

The interventions were designed and implemented by means of three Working Groups. The groups focused on a simple, lower-fat eating message, emphasizing appropriate cooking methods, correct portion sizes and food selection.

Educational brochures developed with input from the focus groups were made available in three stores. Food demonstrations were carried out by nutrition students from a local university, trained for the purpose. The stores supplied all the food necessary for the demonstrations. The Heart and Stroke Foundation of Nova Scotia made available its 1-800 Line/ Question Box to provide answers to consumers' questions about nutrition. The line was also used by volunteers needing technical support.

Evaluation consisted of pre- and post-programme surveys of the target population, focus groups with store employees, interviews with store managers and feedback from store tour participants.

To evaluate the effectiveness of the programme, knowledge and behaviour were measured for a sample of women before and after the in-store programme. The results showed positive changes in knowledge and behaviour for the women as a group. An indication of the impact of the project is given by Table 18.1.

Table 18.1 Number and percentage of correct responses for knowledge of low-fat foods, pre-test and post-test; and proportion of knowledge gained for each item

	Number of correct responses		
	Pre-test	Post-test	Net gain
Cheddar cheese is a good low fat snack	158 (75.6%)	171 (81.8%)	13 (6.2%)
Regular margarine contains less fat than butter	109 (52.2%)	147 (70.3%)	38 (18.2%)
If food is labelled 'cholesterol free' then it is good for the heart	174 (83.3%)	1809 (86.1%)	6 (2.8%)
All foods labelled 'lite' are low in fat	184 (88.0%)	189 (90.4%)	5 (2.3%)

As can be seen from the pre- and post-test results, modest gains were made in the knowledge of fatty foods. The evaluation design does not permit attribution of the changes solely to the project. Clearly a major change was not expected given the limited duration of the intervention.

The evaluation showed the feasibility of making positive changes in knowledge of consumers concerning lower-fat choices. These results support the position that there may be value in the further development and dissemination of the Shopping for Health programme in Nova Scotia to educate consumers about healthy eating.

18.5.2 Take Breakfast to Heart

This project was a nutritional education programme, co-developed by Nova Scotia Heart Health and Kellogg's Canada Limited. This educational campaign was implemented in the autumn of 1993 and again in 1994. The objectives of the programme were to encourage Nova Scotians to eat breakfast on a daily basis, to eat a breakfast that is balanced, low in fat and high in fibre and to continue this healthy eating pattern throughout the day.

The project objectives were to:

- promote the benefits of grains and cereals in a healthy diet;
- educate consumers about the benefits of eating a balanced, lower-fat breakfast on a regular basis;
- promote the consumption of a lower-fat, fibre-rich diet in support of Canada's Guidelines to Healthy Eating.

Major components of the programme remained the same for both of the years it was offered but fewer communities were targeted for the breakfast in 1994 due to budget limitations. The 1993 campaign had the following components;

- two television advertisements, one targeted to adults, the other targeted to children;
- delivery of free-standing inserts to 230 000 homes in Nova Scotia, either through newspaper delivery or a home flyer delivery service;
- community breakfasts at eight sites (the breakfasts included a free meal of cereal, a variety of breads, apples, juice, coffee and tea). Following the breakfast, adults participated in a seminar on nutrition led by a registered dietitian, while children were entertained with a variety of activities and games. Many sites provided local entertainment, prior to and during the breakfast meal.
- in-store promotions at 37 grocery stores across the province. An education display was staffed by professional demonstrators for 20 hours at each store. In addition, registered dietitians were available for 5 hours per store to answer consumer questions related to nutrition, lower-fat eating and the campaign objectives. Grocery store tours were also organized and conducted by the dietitian as necessary.
- Distribution of an educational brochure at all breakfast events and in-store displays.

Evaluation was carried out through a telephone survey of 400 Nova Scotians to assess awareness of the programme and to ascertain the impact of the programme in terms of consumers' attitudes towards this type of programme; to determine if consumers are supportive of a partnership between a private company and a government agency; and to determine if this programme is a method by which consumers want to receive nutritional information. In addition, the planning and implementation process was documented at each targeted site with qualitative data collected from community coordinators and planning committees.

The programme impact results of the 1994 survey were lower than those in 1993, although approximately half of the sample (45% and 56% respectively) strongly and somewhat agree that they were eating less fat at breakfast and less fat throughout the day, since the campaign (Table 18.2)

On the basis of the survey results, it was concluded that the Nova Scotian population found informational campaigns about the health benefits of breakfast and the health benefits of lower-fat choices useful. The 'Take Breakfast to Heart Program' has the potential to be offered to communities as a one of the nutritional 'products' during the dissemination phase of Heart Health Nova Scotia.

18.5.3 Trimming the fat

A programme consisting of a 10-week, continuing education course entitled, 'Trimming the fat: a heart healthy approach to cooking' was

Table 18.2 Percentage of individuals interviewed who agree with various statements pertaining to the 'Take Breakfast to Heart' campaign

	Strongly agree		Somewhat agree	
	1993	1994	1993	1994
Promotion made me conscious of the importance of a low-fat breakfast	40	36	324	30
Since this campaign, I am eating breakfast more regularly	10	20	18	14
Campaign made me more conscious of eating less fat at breakfast	31	36	38	29
Cereals like Kellogg's are an element of a low-fat breakfast	38	36	54	47
Since this campaign, I am eating less fat at breakfast	20	20	37	25
Since this campaign, I am eating less fat throughout the day	25	18	36	38

created to address the identified gap in the nutritional education of chefs and cooks. This pilot programme was offered at a private cooking school in a metropolitan area and was subsidized by the Regional Industrial Training Committcc (RITC) – Tourism, Government of Nova Scotia.

Once the course was approved by the RITC Tourism Board, two dietitians were hired on contract to develop the curriculum. Curricular materials were reviewed by several culinary institutes and information was collected from centres that had experience in this area or were in the process of developing training courses targeted to chefs (National Restaurant Association, Canadian Heart and Stroke Foundation, Canadian Restaurant and Food Association). The goal and objectives were developed and draft versions of the course outline were created and reviewed by working group members.

Nutritional and educational topics covered in the curriculum included:

- the relationship between nutrition and CVD, summary of results from Nova Scotia Heart Health Survey, 1986 and Nova Scotia Nutrition Survey (NSHHP), 1993;
- consumer food trends;
- recommended nutrient intakes;
- Canada's Guidelines for Healthy Eating and Canada's Food Guide;
- overview of fat, cholesterol, protein, simple and complex carbohydrates and fibre;
- healthy weight and healthy weight loss;
- vegetarian diets;

- label reading;
- consumer issues of processed meats, food additives and organic foods.

Students participated in interactive games, viewed videos, calculated their BMI and waist/hip ratio, completed a 24-hour dietary record and received a personal computer analysis of their nutrient intake, and modified recipes to make them more 'heart healthy'. The final session was devoted to an explanation of the Heart and Stroke Foundation's Heart Smart Restaurant Program and a discussion regarding the changes the students would make when they returned to their eating establishments.

Evaluation information was collected before and after the pilot courses. The evaluation served three purposes: to assist with curriculum development, to evaluate course content and procedures, and to assess changes in attitude, knowledge and behaviour specific to lower-fat food preparation.

A self-administered questionnaire was distributed to the chefs before the course. The questionnaire requested information on the name of the sponsoring restaurant, the type of clientele generally served, menu offerings (specialities, popular dishes), food preparation (use of ready-made versus made-from-scratch foods), availability of heart healthy menu choices, their views about the importance of providing heart healthy menu items, their intention to change their menu to include heart healthy items, the barriers they may face if they tried to introduce heart-healthy menu items and what they hoped to learn from participating in the course.

Out of a total of 15 chefs, 13 stated that they intended to change their menu to include items that were heart healthy. When questioned about what they hoped to learn from the course, most chefs wanted to learn how to make their menu selections 'healthy' and lower in fat. Many chefs in the second pilot also mentioned that they wanted to increase their knowledge and skills for personal reasons as well as for the benefit of their customers.

Information about the course content and procedures was collected by a post-programme questionnaire. The questionnaire requested information on: the relevance of the course to their work, what they enjoyed, suggested changes to the course, the nutrition topics they would like information about in the future, their rating of various aspects of the course and if they would recommend the course to other chefs. Thirteen chefs stated they would recommend the 'Trimming the fat' course to other chefs.

18.5.4 Accessibility to heart healthy foods

The Food for Health strategy included an investigation of the cost and availability of heart healthy foods. The project included the revision, development and validation of food baskets to represent current dietary recommendations with common foods; and a survey of 86 grocery stores to assess and compare the availability and price of these food baskets across the province.

In Canada, two standardized food baskets are used to examine food availability: Agriculture Canada's nutritious food basket (NFB) and the thrifty nutritious food basket (TNFB). However, the latest Canadian nutritional recommendations have not yet been incorporated into these baskets. The purpose of this study was to validate revised food baskets which incorporated the recent nutritional recommendations while considering the food preferences of Nova Scotians. The validated instruments were then used as tools to examine the availability, accessibility and cost of heart healthy dietary changes in Nova Scotia. Data were collected in 85 stores from the eight counties surveyed within the Nova Scotia Nutrition Survey. Results will be used to highlight food security issues to be addressed in the province.

The objectives of the study were:

- to develop and validate a food basket based primarily upon consumption patterns of Nova Scotians which meets Canadian nutritional recommendations (consumption food basket, CFB);
- to validate a food basket based upon substitutions of alternative/fat-modified foods (alternative food basket, AFB);
- to assess the availability of food items found within revised food baskets (CFB and AFB) across Nova Scotia;
- to compare the price of the revised food baskets (CFB and AFB) with the price of the current food baskets from Agriculture Canada (nutritious food basket, NFB; thrifty nutritious food basket, TNFB) across Nova Scotia.

For purposes of the study, accessibility was defined to include: sufficient personal income to purchase foods, ready access to quality grocery stores and food service operations, ready availability of a variety of foods at a reasonable cost, the freedom to choose personally acceptable foods, legitimate confidence in the quality of the foods available and easy access to understandable, accurate information about food and nutrition.

Existing food baskets from Agriculture Canada, the NFB and TNFB, were analysed for nutrient content as illustrated in Table 18.3. Results of nutrient analysis showed that the NFB and the TNFB do not meet the current recommendations, and consumption of a diet based upon foods from within these two baskets would provide a diet high in fat and lower in carbohydrate than that which is currently recommended. The amount of fat in the NFB for both males and females of 25–49 years of age was 38% of total calories. The fat content of the TNFB was 33% for males and 41% of total calories for females.

Table 18.4 summarizes the mean costs of each food basket across the province. The alternative food basket (AFB), a heart healthy basket based upon substitution of low-fat or 'lite' formulations of their regular counterparts in the standard Agriculture Canada's nutritious food basket (NFB), was the most expensive, costing almost $140 to feed a woman aged between 25–49 for 1 month. The consumption food basket (CFB), a second heart healthy basket based upon food consumption patterns from the Nova Scotia Nutrition Survey, was the second most costly, averaging almost $8.00 less per month than the AFB, but $13.00 more per month than the standard NFB. As expected, Agriculture Canada's Thrifty Nutritious Food Basket (TFB), a basket designed to include less expensive sources of nutrients, but also the basket with the highest fat content, was the least expensive. All differences in cost were statistically significant at $P<0.05$.

Table 18.3 Macronutrient values of various of food baskets

	NFB	TNFB	AFB	CFB	RNI (F 25–49 years)
Energy (kcal)	2200	2443	2257	2200	1900
Carbohydrate (% energy)	54.3	47.5	63	56.9	>55
Protein (% energy)	15.2	16.5	16	15.6	15
Fat (% energy)	31.7	37	25	30.2	<30

NFB, nutritious food basket; TNFB, thrifty nutritious food basket; AFB, alternative food basket; CFB, consumption food basket; RNI, recommended net intake; F, females.

Table 18.4 Mean cost ($) of various provincial food baskets

Basket	*n*	Price		% NFB cost ($/$NFB)
		Mean[a]	SD	
Alternative	75	$139.70	8.41	118
Consumption	80	$131.84	9.35	112
Nutritious	82	$118.13	9.40	100
Thrifty	82	$105.25	9.06	89

[a]All means are significantly different.

Based on the research completed by the working group and the results of the accessibility/pricing survey, the following conclusions were arrived at:

- the Nutritious Food Basket and Thrifty Food Basket are no longer applicable, as they do not adhere to the current nutritional recommendations or consider regional difference in food preferences; therefore:

- it might be appropriate to consider development of new national and regional baskets; and that these baskets be developed to incorporate the current nutritional recommendations and regional differences in food preferences;
- nutritional and food consumption surveys are necessary instruments to collect the necessary data to incorporate regional differences in food choices, into the new baskets;
- since the cost of the baskets is related to the size of the grocery store and the population of the community, the location of 'superstore' grocery stores in each region would allow rural residents an opportunity to access cheaper food;
- nutritional educators may be advised that their clients need not purchase 'designer' lower-fat food products in order to meet the current nutritional recommendations.

18.5.5 Let's Make It Clear

Let's Make It Clear was a position paper on the future of nutritional labelling in Canada and in support of nutritional labelling reform. The paper recommended the use of labels which are consistent across products and simple and easy to understand; a format that makes the fat content of the product easy to find and one in which information is accessible to all socio-economic groups and educational levels. The document was distributed to departments within Industry Canada and Health Canada, professional groups, interested businesses within the retail sector, provincial and federal representatives and provincial government departments.

In 1992, the National Institute of Nutrition surveyed over 800 primary shoppers in large urban centres across Canada (National Institute of Nutrition, 1992). The results showed that the majority of Canadians considered the availability of nutritional information to be important, but they rarely obtained this information from the nutrition panels on products. Consumers did not use the nutrition panel because it was too complex. Instead, they relied on accessing information from the product ingredient list and health claims. However, the same study indicated that consumer understanding of health claims was at best sketchy and frequently led to poor food choices. These findings were supported by Reid and Hendricks (1993) who concluded that complexity of nutritional information and format is a major barrier to the usefulness of product information for consumers.

Results of the 1993 Nova Scotia Nutrition Survey showed that the majority of Nova Scotians held positive attitudes toward nutrition and heart health and that the average person also had adequate knowledge about basic nutritional concepts. The survey also found that two-thirds of the population were trying to choose foods because of the nutrient, polyunsaturated fat or fibre content. In addition, 68% of Nova Scotians were choosing or avoiding foods because they were concerned about heart disease, cancer, osteoporosis, high blood pressure or their weight.

However, the survey also showed that when these Nova Scotians attempted to make lower-fat choices, they were not successful. Seventy-seven per cent of the respondents who believed they were avoiding foods because of the fat content were still consuming over 30% of their calories from fat in their diet. These results were similar for saturated fat intakes. In fact, there was little difference in the eating patterns between the Nova Scotians who were trying to choose lower-fat foods and those who were not.

The results of the Nova Scotian Nutrition Survey reinforced the suggestion that consumers require more skills and assistance in selecting healthy, lower-fat foods. Because consumers are using some of the information on product labels to guide their food choices, the nutritional information presented on the package should be easy to understand and instructive about the fat content.

The objective of the 'Let's Make It Clear' paper was 'to develop and distribute a documented statement that advocates for a clear, instructional food label that would enhance our efforts to reduce the total fat consumption of adult Nova Scotians'.

Background and research information was gathered from several sources including Med Line Search, Consumer and Corporate Affairs, the Canadian Dietetic Association, the Nova Scotia Food and Drug Administration, the Heart and Stroke Foundation, Health Canada and the Food Marketing Institute.

The paper made the following recommendations:

- use labels that are consistent across all products;
- present information that is simple and easy to understand;
- use a format that makes the fat content easy to find;
- present information that is understandable for people from all socio-economic groups and education levels.

An article was written about the paper in two newsletters – the Precis (from the Canadian Council of Grocery Distributors) and the Canadian Retailer (a bimonthly newsletter, serving the retail sector). Following distribution of these newsletters, requests for the position paper were received from several organizations in the private sector. The paper was distributed to all member organizations of the Food for Health Committee as well as to a number of government departments, community groups and organizations for their review.

18.6 Conclusions

The development and operation of the Food for Health Committee broke new ground in Nova Scotia. The Food for Health Committee membership consisted of a large number of groups and organizations representing the food industry and health sector. For the first time business, professional groups, health organizations and government worked together to plan and implement nutritional programmes which were targeted to specific populations and age groups.

The diverse membership also meant that the committee possessed a great deal of knowledge and expertise. Therefore, the group was able to draw upon the advice and experience of group members and seldom had to go outside the committee for assistance.

Relevant survey findings guided the planning and mobilized members around the issue. The committee relied heavily on the findings of the 1986 Nova Scotia Heart Health Survey and 1993 Nutrition Survey to provide direction for the project. The data from these surveys were invaluable in targeting the issue of fat reduction and the audiences for specific programme activities. Having this information enabled the committee to come to a consensus on the goal within a short time frame. Without this information, the committee members may have wasted time advancing their own organization's agenda instead of developing a common agenda.

An effort was made to support or advance the work of members' organizations. Resources and programmes developed by members' organizations were incorporated into Food for Health initiatives. Gaps identified by members became challenges for the entire committee to solve. Members also benefited by extending their networks, which increased the potential for future collaborative projects.

Historically, the dietetic community has taken responsibility for public education in the area of food and nutrition. Unfortunately, access to dietitians by the general public is limited in Nova Scotia and therefore access to nutritional education is also limited. Due to the great need and demand for nutritional education, opportunities need to be increased and readily available. The Food for Health Committee's process can be used as a model for effective public education. Dietitians were involved in the planning of all nutritional resources and programmes but a variety of groups, organizations and venues were used to deliver this education to the public. In this way, accurate and current information was disseminated through a variety of channels to a wider audience.

It may be concluded that the Food for Health Committee was successful in meeting its objectives through the implementation of five separate project areas. Therefore, the formation of a coalition to address nutritional concerns was shown to be feasible. The preceding points should be considered in the future if a similar coalition is formed to address nutrition in the province.

References

Farquhar, J.W., Fortmann, S.P., Flora, J.A. *et al.* (1990) Effects of community wide education on cardiovascular disease risk factors: The Stanford 5 City Project. *JAMA*, **264**, 359–65.

Federal Provincial Working Group on the Prevention and Control of Cardiovascular Disease in Canada (1991) *Promoting Heart Health in Canada: A Focus on Cholesterol*, Health and Welfare Canada, Ottawa.

Heart and Stroke Foundation of Canada (1995) *Heart Disease and Stroke in Canada, 1995*, Heart and Stroke Foundation of Canada, Ottawa.

Health and Welfare Canada (1990) *Nutrition Recommendations: The Report of the Scientific Review Committee*, Ministry of Supply and Services, Ottawa, Ontario.

Health Canada (1993) *Evaluation Guidelines for Heart Health*, The Canadian Heart Health Initiative, Health Canada, Ottawa, Ontario.

Kephart, G., Langille, D. and MacLean, D. (1993) Socioeconomic differentials in risk factors for cardiovascular disease in Nova Scotia. Unpublished manuscript, Dalhousie University, Halifax, Nova Scotia.

Mittelmark, M.B., Hunt, M.K., Heath, G.W. and Schmid, T.L. (1993) Realistic outcomes: lessons from community-based research and demonstration programs for the prevention of cardiovascular diseases. *Journal of Public Health Policy*, Winter 1993.

Nair, C., Colburn, H., MacLean, D.R. and Petrasovits, A. (1989) *Cardiovascular Disease in Canada*, Health Reports, Vol. 1, No. 1, Canadian Centre for Health Information, Statistics Canada, Ottawa.

National Institute of Nutrition (1992) *Consumer Use and Understanding of Nutrition Information on Food Package Labels*, TR #12375, Ottawa, Ontario.

Nova Scotia Department of Health and Fitness (1989) *The Report of the Nova Scotia Heart Health Survey*, The Nova Scotia Department of Health and Fitness, Halifax.

NSHHP (Nova Scotia Heart Health Program) (1993) *Report of the Nova Scotia Nutrition Survey, Halifax, Nova Scotia*, Nova Scotia Department of Health and Health Welfare, Halifax, Nova Scotia.

Puska, P., Nissinen, A., Tuomilehto, J. *et al.* (1985) Communication based strategy to prevent coronary heart disease: Conclusions from 10 years of North Karelia. *Annual Review of Public Health* **6**, 147–93.

Reid, J.D. and Hendricks, S. (1993) Consumer awareness of nutritional information on food package labels. *Journal of the Canadian Dietetic Association*, **54** (3), 127–31.

Stachenko, S.J. (1993) Towards a comprehensive public health policy: The Canadian Heart Health Initiative. *Canadian Journal of Cardiology*, **9**, (Suppl. D), 139D.

World Health Organization (1992) *Health Promotion and Chronic Illness* (ed. A. Kaplun), WHO Regional Publications, European Series, No. 44, Copenhagen.

19 Implementing dietary guidelines for elderly people

SALLY HERNE

19.1 Introduction

19.1.1 Demography and disease

In the second half of the twentieth century demographers have noted a worldwide gradual ageing of the population. According to the World Health Organization (WHO), by the year 2025 elderly people (defined as

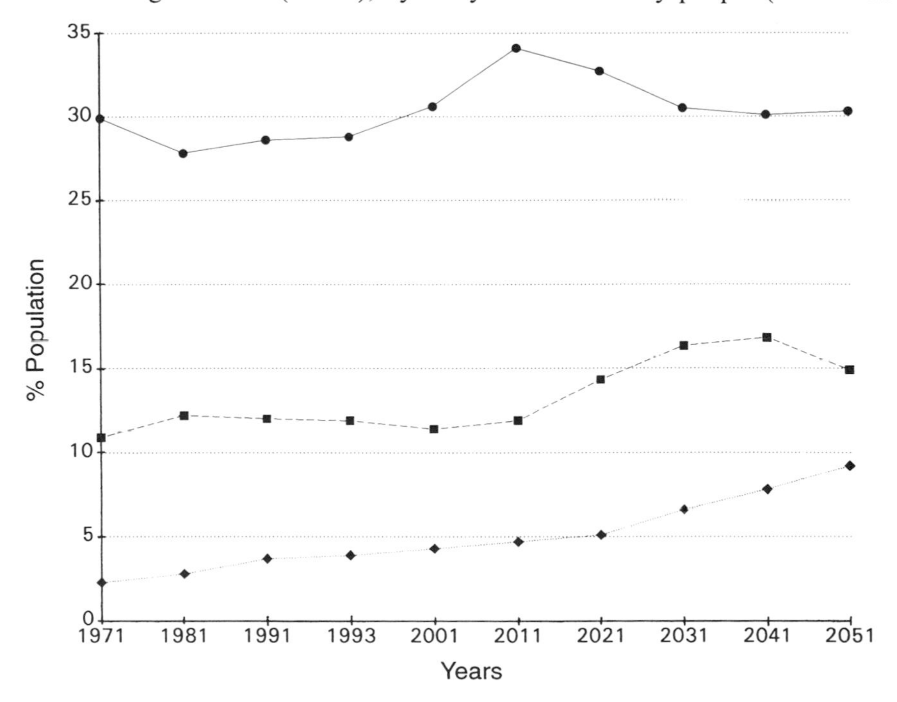

Figure 19.1 United Kingdom population by age; ●, 40–64; ■, 65–79; ◆, 80+ (source: *Social Trends 1995*. Central Statistical Office. Crown Copyright. 1995. Reproduced by the permission of the Controller of HMSO and the Central Statistical Office).

Implementing Dietary Guidelines for Healthy Eating. Edited by Verner Wheelock. Published in 1997 by Blackie A&P, an imprint of Chapman & Hall, London. ISBN 0 7514 0304 0

those aged 60 years and over) will number 806 million or 11.9% of the world's population (WHO, 1991). In the UK, projections based on census data suggest that the greatest demographic change will be amongst the 'old' old – those aged 75 years and over; whereas the group aged 40–64 was predicted to increase by 1.3% between 1971 and 2051, those aged 65–79 and 80+ are expected to increase by 27% and 75%, respectively (Fig. 19.1)

Although old age does not automatically equate with ill health, a number of chronic conditions exhibit a marked correlation with chronological age – ischaemic heart disease, stroke, cancer and diabetes mellitus, for example (Fig. 19.2).

As a result of the morbidity associated with these disease states, elderly people tend to be disproportionate users of health and community care services. In the UK alone, the elderly use approximately half of all hospital services, over one-third of all primary care resources and account for one-quarter of all prescribed drugs (Hall, MacLennan and Lye, 1993). The current scenario is that the demands on services are increasing at a time when the relative size of the workforce funding health care is shrinking. The Organization for Economic Cooperation and Development (OECD)

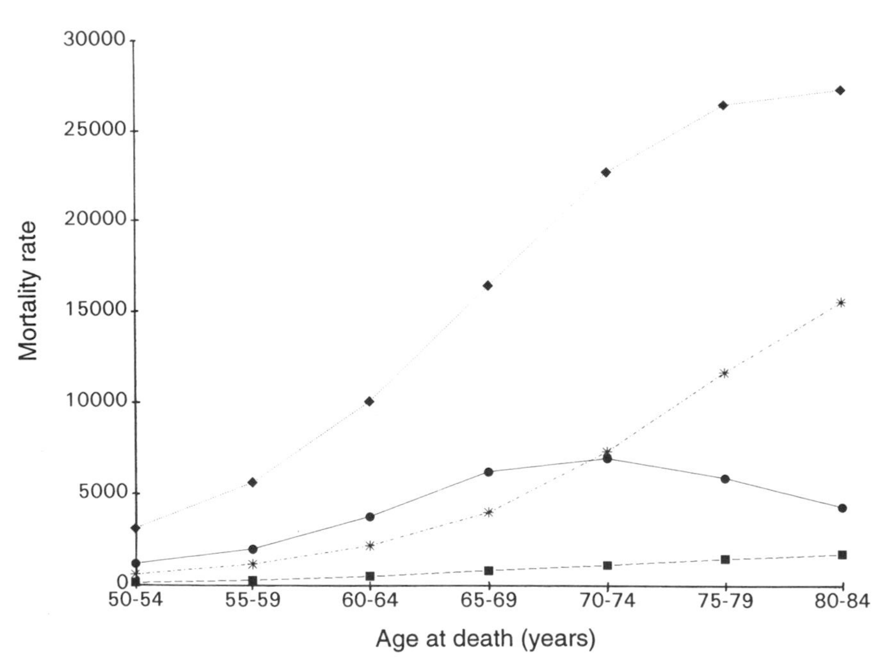

Figure 19.2 Mortality statistics by cause and age, England and Wales 1992. ●, Lung cancer – neoplasm of the lung, bronchus and trachea; ■, diabetes mellitus; ◆, ischaemic heart disease *; cerebrovascular disease. (Reproduced with permission from OPCS (1993) *Mortality Statistics by Cause England and Wales*, 1992).

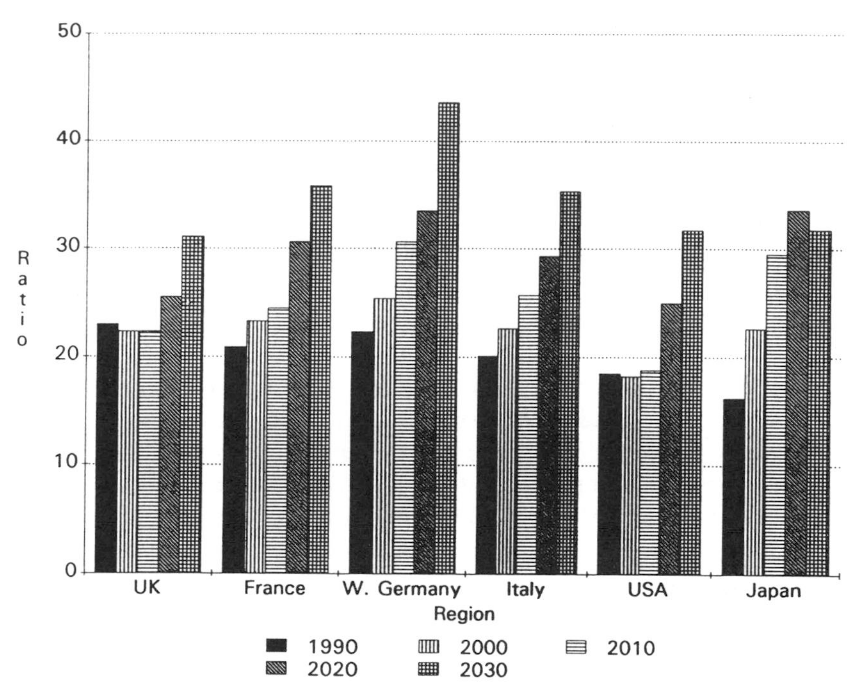

Figure 19.3 Projected aged dependency ratio of selected countries, 1990–2030. Aged dependency ratio = population aged 65+ as a percentage of the population aged 15–64 (Copyright OECD, 1988, *Ageing Populations: The Social Policy Implications*. Reproduced by permission of the OECD).

estimates that throughout Europe, the US and Japan, those aged 65+ will represent at least 30% of the size of the population aged 15–64 by the year 2030 (Fig. 19.3).

In Britain the effects of degenerative disease on both individual well being and the national economy are vast. Coronary heart disease (CHD) accounted for 26% of all deaths in England in 1991 – the largest cause of death and the single main cause of premature death. It accounts for 2.5% of National Health Service (NHS) expenditure and results in 35 million lost working days/year. In addition, approximately 12% of all deaths in the same period were as a result of stroke, which is also a major cause of disability in older people. Stroke accounts for 6% of NHS expenditure and results in the loss of about 7.7 million working days/year (Department of Health, 1992a).

19.1.2 Health promotion in old age

Despite the scale of such disease in later life, traditionally only a small proportion of health care budgets has been allocated to preventive health promotion measures; in the US recent estimates put it at a mere 3% (Anonymous, 1993). However, governments are becoming more aware of the need to implement co-ordinated health policies to tackle diet-related diseases. In the UK this has taken the form of 'The Health of the Nation' (Department of Health, 1992a), a strategy which identifies the major causes of morbidity and mortality, sets targets for their reduction and recommends means of achieving them. The policy has two major objectives directly relevant to the health of older people:

1. to reduce the death rate for CHD in people aged 65–74 by at least 30% by the year 2000; and
2. to reduce the death rate for stroke in people aged 65–74 by at least 40% by the year 2000.

In order to achieve these particular targets, and a more general one to maintain body mass index of between 20 and 22, the Department of Health (DoH) has highlighted dietary change as being of paramount importance. This represents a significant change in the thinking on nutrition and its role in the health of the elderly. In previous nutritional guidelines (NACNE,1983) it had been thought that, apart from increasing dietary fibre, the recommendations on reducing fat, saturates, salt, sugar and alcohol were inappropriate for the majority of elderly people. In effect, the assumption was that healthy eating post-retirement was too little too late. However, as research results accumulated disputing this idea (e.g. Weber, Barnard and Roy, 1983), the DoH commissioned a working party to examine the evidence. The conclusions of the report were striking, suggesting that the assumption behind NACNE was not a safe one to make because of a general lack of research into nutritional needs later in life. Thus, the overall recommendation of the committee (Department of Health,1992b, p. 1) was that:

> ... the majority of people aged 65 years or more should adopt, where possible, similar patterns of eating and lifestyle to those advised for maintaining health in younger adults ... elderly people should reduce dietary intakes of fat and simple sugars and increase intakes of starchy foods, non-starch polysaccharides and vitamin D.

This change in approach is now embodied in the Health of the Nation programme. In particular, the reduction of total fat and saturates has been emphasized as a key element in improving health in later life. The dietary targets set are:

1. to reduce the average percentage food energy derived from saturated fatty acids by at least 35% by the year 2005, from 17% to no more than 11%;
2. to reduce the average food energy derived by the population from total fat by at least 12%, from approximately 40% to no more than 35%.

Nutritional problems in old age are complicated by a further phenomenon; not only are elderly people the main sufferers of the so-called 'diseases of affluence', they have also been identified as a group susceptible to nutritional deficiency, often due to insufficient quantity as well as quality of food intake. The last large-scale study in the UK, conducted in the 1960s, found that 8% of men and 6% of women living in their own homes were malnourished. However, malnutrition was twice as common in the over-80s as it was in the younger elderly (DHSS, 1979). Rates for those living in institutions have consistently been quoted as running at several times this level, with particularly low intakes of energy, vitamin D, folate and zinc (Abbasi and Rudman, 1994).

Clearly, healthy eating and nutritional guidance have major roles to play in improving the health of elderly people on a general scale, but what makes elderly people prone to poor dietary habits and diet-related disease? How can health promotion target both policy and information correctly at an older audience? In order to address these questions, the rest of this chapter will focus on:

1. the barriers to healthy eating brought about by biological ageing and the social, economic and psychological changes which accompany it; and
2. how progress might be made in these areas.

19.2 Types of malnutrition occurring in old age

According to Davies (1990) four types of malnutrition may affect elderly people:

1. Specific malnutrition: this is frequently associated with the presence of clinical disease such as osteomalacia. The appearance of other diseases such as respiratory infection may also be indicative of an underlying deficiency.
2. Sudden malnutrition: generally caused by marked changes in the elderly person's food intake following either a physical trauma (e.g. major surgery) or a mental trauma, bereavement for example.
3. Recurrent malnutrition: severe malnutrition following a gradually worsening cycle of illness and poor nutrition.
4. Long-standing malnutrition; there can be a long latent period between the adoption of poor eating habits and signs of clinical diet-related disease. This is particularly true of the chronic degenerative disease mentioned in the introduction.

This categorization of nutritional problems in old age sheds some light on the kinds of factors involved in diet-related illness. A more comprehensive list was compiled by Exton-Smith (1979), dividing the causes of poor eating habits and nutritional deficiency into primary and secondary factors (Table 19.1).

Table 19.1 Causes of nutritional deficiency (reproduced from *Nutrition and Lifestyles* (ed. M. Turner), Applied Science Ltd. 1979, with permission)

Primary	Secondary
Ignorance	Impaired appetite
Specific isolation	Masticatory inefficiency
Physical disability	Malabsorption
Mental	Alcoholism
Iatrogenic	Drugs
Poverty	Increased requirements

The classification suggested here will be used as a framework to describe:

- the numbers affected by these factors;
- research on the links between these factors and dietary problems;
- implications for healthy eating.

19.3 Primary causes of nutritional problems in old age

19.3.1 Ignorance about nutrition

Elderly people are disadvantaged in being able to make informed decisions about the food they eat in several ways:

1. They are more likely to have left school at a young age. Figures from the General Household Survey (GHS) show that people aged 60+ are 14 times more likely to have left school at age 15 years or less than 40–49-year-olds, and more than twice as likely to have left education at age 16 or less than 30–39-year-olds (Table 19.2). In addition, nearly four times as many 60–69-year-olds had no qualifications when they left school compared to 20–29-year-olds (OPCS, 1990).

Table 19.2 Age on leaving full-time education (reproduced with permission from OPCS (1990) General Household Survey 1988)

Current age	Under 15	Under 16 (cumulative percentage)	Under 17	Under 18
20–24	1	8	57	70
25–29	1	8	61	71
30–39	3	35	60	69
40–49	5	56	73	80
50–59	32	67	82	86
60–69	69	77	88	91

2. The majority of elderly people received little or no nutritional education as part of their schooling (Davies, Anderson and Holdsworth, 1985).

3. Messages on what constitutes a 'healthy' diet have only been widely disseminated from the 1980s onwards, when elderly people have already accumulated several decades of eating habits. Dietary changes can therefore necessitate overcoming ingrained ideas about meal composition.

The cumulative effect of these factors has been that a number of older consumers have relatively short educational lifespans and low levels of educational attainment. Various studies have linked the number of years in education with poor nutritional knowledge (e.g. Clancy, 1975). As a result, elderly people are generally not proficient in identifying sources of nutrients, do not read labels which use terms they cannot understand and, hence, find it difficult to discriminate healthy foods from the vast range of products on offer. Ignorance of the basic facts of nutrition has been shown to be prevalent in elderly women but appears to be an even greater problem for men. Fusillo and Beloian (1977) suggested that this may be because those with the responsibility for shopping and preparing (traditionally women) have higher levels of food knowledge and also circulate information amongst themselves. As far as the implications for healthy eating are concerned, although knowledge about healthy eating does not automatically lead to positive action, it is unlikely that consumers will be motivated to change their eating habits without some information on the benefits. To illustrate this Charny and Lewis (1987) noted a consistent association between the level of nutritional knowledge, dietary quality and an intention to make positive dietary changes. Those subjects changing their diet for health reasons had particularly high levels of nutritional knowledge, whereas those changing more for reasons of appearance had their knowledge concentrated in specific areas – cholesterol, margarines and high-fibre diets.

Furthermore, Probart *et al.* (1989) suggested that those people with comparatively high levels of knowledge are more orientated towards seeking out further information from both traditional sources (medics, dietitians, published literature) and other sources. They then showed a tendency to use this information to purchase more 'healthy' foods. At the other end of the scale there was also a relationship between low knowledge, a tendency to seek information from non-traditional sources (chiropractors, naturopaths and health food shop personnel) and a higher acceptance of misinformation. The cycle of disadvantage therefore appears to be quite potent – those who start off with little knowledge approach less well-used sources of information, are more likely to believe incorrect information and, as a result, are less well equipped to adopt healthy eating habits.

Although healthy eating is now a subject more in the public domain, there is a change in attitude necessary on the part of older people. There is a tendency for them to view healthy eating as having little impact and that degenerative disease and disability are natural consequences of the ageing process (Backett and Davidson, 1992). Work carried out in the US has emphasized the ability of elderly people to make changes, but blames inaction on the trend for nutritional education to focus on what individuals cannot eat, rather than advising them of what they can choose (Popkin, Haines and Patterson, 1992).

With regard to the future, it has been possible to improve both the retention and positive action of elderly subjects by more accurately targeting information. Older people were found to be more receptive to nutritional education that focused on issues that affected them directly (Davies, Anderson and Holdsworth, 1985), such as the relationship between calcium, vitamin D and bone strength. In a similar vein, those already suffering from diseases which could be moderated by diet demonstrated high levels of nutritional knowledge and evidenced positive behavioural change, presumably because of their motivation to get well (Charny and Lewis, 1987). This does suggest that advice at points of treatment – GP surgeries, clinics and hospital departments – would be of value. However, despite their perceived 'expertise' British medics are ill-equipped to identify symptoms of malnutrition, treat undernutrition and pass on dietary advice (Lennard-Jones, 1992). Developing training in nutrition at undergraduate and postgraduate level for medics and other health professionals involved in the care of elderly people is recommended to maximize opportunities in health promotion.

19.3.2 Social isolation

In 1993 it was estimated that 16% of those of pensionable age in the UK lived alone. This is more than double the level recorded in 1961 (OPCS, 1993). Of this number, a large proportion are elderly women, due to the differing life expectancies between the sexes.

Living alone was associated with being older, having a lower income and experiencing less flexible food budgets (Bransby and Osborne, 1953). It is therefore unsurprising that this group needed more help with shopping and housework than married people, spent less on food and were more reliant on gifts of food from friends and relatives. As a result, both men and women living alone ate less foods which required some preparation than married couples – potatoes, puddings, sauces, fish, cakes, biscuits and fruit, for example. Men living in a married couple had an average intake of 2109 kcal compared with 2048 kcal for men living alone; whereas for women the figures were 1791 kcal and 1675 kcal, respectively. Men living in a couple had more vitamin C but less vitamin A than those living alone, whereas married women had higher intakes of protein and fats than those living alone. Similar findings of the relative poverty of people in single-person households have been reported by a large number of studies, with the result being lower dietary variety, fewer hot meals per week and lower body weights (e.g. Schwartz,

Henley and Zeitz, 1964). Brockington and Lempert's study in Stockport, Manchester (1966) clarified the impact of household composition further – by finding that the general benefits of living together tended to transcend marital status – 41.3% of households with two single people living together and 48.8% of those consisting of two widowed people had a hot meal daily, compared with 27% of single people living alone and 24.5% of widowed people living alone. Elderly widows have also reported fewer material resources, lack of support networks and adequate transport, all of which may act to limit their choice (Fengler, Danigelis and Little, 1983).

As the number of elderly people continues to grow, so it is likely that there will be even greater numbers of single-pensioner households. Community services, such as meals on wheels and luncheon clubs, have an important part to play in ensuring at least a basic main meal every day for the most vulnerable. Currently only 4% of pensioners in the UK receive meals on wheels and 3% attend luncheon clubs. This low take-up is likely to be due to a number of factors, not least the timing of meals (often too early), their unappealing appearance and poor nutritional quality as well as lack of transport to attend luncheon clubs (Davies, 1991). Suggestions on how to improve the health of older people through large-scale catering have already been made by Davies (1991). The ideas contained in this report are supported – particularly with regard to innovations in meal distribution. The current tendency for local authorities to use frozen meals with table-top steamers is certainly a step forward in achieving higher nutritional quality, better presentation of meals and improved microbiological safety.

19.3.3 Physical disability

Particularly amongst the 'old' old, physical disability and dependency are widespread – 27% of men and 33% of women aged 85 and over questioned in 1990 rated their health as 'not good' in the preceding year (Department of Health, 1992c). It has been estimated that 22% of elderly people in the UK have severe disabilities and 8% are housebound (DHSS, 1979). Commonly cited causes of long-term disability are stroke, arthritis, rheumatism, respiratory disorders and heart disease. As well as the direct problems caused by the disease state itself, e.g. breathlessness and poor hand grip, disability has numerous possible repercussions on the motivation to eat healthily, the ability to shop and prepare food and the amount of food the elderly person feels able to consume:

- Fatigue, inertia, lack of vigour. In Horwath's study of elderly people in Adelaide (1987), a lack of energy was associated with poor diets. When elderly respondents experienced fatigue, preparing meals, getting to the shops and carrying food home were more frequently regarded as arduous chores. As a result less effort was made to prepare and eat regular meals.

- Difficulty in swallowing is usually associated with a major or minor stroke. In the study carried out by the DHSS (1979) elderly people with a damaged swallowing reflex found it difficult to consume sufficiently nutrient-dense diets. Those people who rely on puréed or soft food are faced with the additional difficulty of unappealing presentation.
- Immobility. Exton-Smith, Stanton and Windsor (1972) conducted one of the foremost studies of housebound elderly people in the UK. Although restricted movement could be detrimental to the ability to self-care, it was found that dietary quality could remain adequate as long as the elderly person received the support they needed for cooking and shopping. Ensuring that these services are available and accessible is therefore a priority. The main nutritional difference in intakes between housebound and more active people was a deficiency of vitamins C and D in the immobile group. Here it is possible that supplementation has a role in preventing increased risk of femur fracture, osteoporosis, etc.
- Lower physical activity. A cohort of 68-year-old men was studied by Hanson, Mattisson and Steen (1987) in Malmö, Sweden. Low physical activity was found to be an independent risk indicator of inadequate dietary habits. Krondl *et al.* (1982) proposed that this may be due to the more varied diet consumed by physically and socially active people. It is possible that the difference could be due to the appetite stimulus of physical activity or because it symbolizes continuing engagement in society and better morale. Certainly, elderly people in residential care have been found to take a greater interest in food and not require appetite stimulants when programmes of activities have been introduced into their daily routine (Anonymous, 1989). Giving residents the freedom to make their own decisions, prepare snacks and drinks for themselves and to engage in activities outside residential homes is also central to the philosophy of 'Home Life', the code of practice on residential care (CPA, 1984).

19.3.4 Mental health problems

As well as physical deterioration in later life, certain degenerative mental conditions are also prevalent. Five per cent of those aged 65+, and 20% of those aged 80+ suffer from dementia in the UK. The disease has a devastating effect on the ability to self-care and also affects nutritional status through a mechanism as yet unknown. The increase in energy requirements in Alzheimer's disease can be as much as 1600 kcal/day, making it difficult to meet this calorific need through normal eating habits. As a result both weight loss and protein–energy malnutrition can occur. According to Gray (1989), food preferences may change with the onset of dementia because of difficulties recognizing and detecting food odours, and degenerative changes in the brain detrimentally affecting appetite. Some subjects develop unusual food habits, refuse to eat, or compulsively put anything, including non-foodstuffs, into their mouths. Various problems are also associated with sufferers not chewing food properly and choking. While research on the causes of dementia grows, the only feasible means of protecting nutritional status in dementia patients is through intensive supplementation.

The second major mental health problem in old age is depression. Symptoms of depression have been reported in between 30 and 50% of elderly people in one cross-cultural study (Andrews *et al.*, 1986). With such a high prevalence rate, concern has rightly focused on the role of depressive states (particularly the impact of bereavement) in influencing food choice and dietary quality in older populations. Numerous studies worldwide have correlated depression, apathy, bereavement and accompanying social isolation with general undernutrition and avitaminosis (e.g. Exton-smith, Stanton and Windsor, 1972; DHSS, 1979; Davies 1981; Horwath, 1987). The cause of the depression largely determines the approach necessary. In the case of bereavement social support is vital, particularly for those pensioners taking on previously unfamiliar roles. Men with little or no experience of cooking for themselves will require the most support and advice.

19.3.5 Iatrogenic problems

Iatrogenesis is the term coined for health problems caused by medical intervention. In the case of nutrition, iatrogenesis is related to the dietary regimes prescribed by physicians and other health professionals. Those elderly people with a history of gastric surgery or peptic ulcers are particularly at risk as the traditional gastric diet is low in vitamin C. Greater emphasis on pharmacological iatrogenesis and suggestions for improvements in drug treatments will be covered later.

19.3.6 Poverty in old age

Census data in the US reveals that at the beginning of the 1990s 42% of women and 17% of men aged 65 and over had incomes of less than $6000 per year (US Bureau of the Census, 1990). Similarly in the UK, retired people are three times more likely to experience poverty than younger, working people (Walker, 1987).

Numerous studies in the US and Europe have made the general link between low income and less nutritionally adequate diets, but how does this happen? In examining previous research on this area, a number of factors appear to be involved:

1. Those people in higher income brackets spent 38% more per person on food than poorer people in 1983. However, as a proportion of their income, poorer people spent 30% as opposed to 12% on food (Cole-Hamilton and Laing, 1986). The poorest in society are therefore disproportionately affected by rises in inflation, other price rises and proposals for VAT on food.
2. Monotony of diet. The Health Education Authority's study of healthy eating in low-income groups (1989) discovered that consumers with very little money to spend adopted a 'tunnel vision' approach to shopping for food, choosing the same familiar foods each time. This was not because of any desire to consume a repetitive diet but out of concern to avoid waste. Shoppers bought large amounts of convenience foods because of their speed and ease of preparation and their acceptability to family members. Those who lacked confidence in their cooking skills particularly worried about waste when cooking from scratch. This was a finding supported by research by Wilson (1989) which described consumers being denied the opportunity to experiment with new foods and recipes in case these were not acceptable to their families and their money wasted as a result. Instead the emphasis was on pleasing taste preferences and filling people up, with health coming a poor second. The result tends to be a diet which lacks any great variety – Bransby and Osborne (1953), Davidson *et al.* (1962) and Davis *et al.* (1985) have all noted that people in lower-income groups have lower dietary diversity scores; for example 14% of elderly people in the study by Davis *et al.* ate five or fewer foods a day.
2. Flexible food budgets. In a study of low-income groups by Manchester Polytechnic, retired people mentioned food, fuel and rent/mortgage as the most important items in their budget (Laing *et al.*, 1984). However, because fuel and housing costs were not regarded as flexible, it was food that suffered when money was tight (also see Lennon and Fieldhouse, 1982). Twenty-three per cent of the elderly reported cutting down their food budgets in times of financial hardship, despite the belief by nearly two-thirds of them that 'food is important to health'.
4. Missed meals. As a direct result of this tendency to sacrifice money intended for food to pay other bills, elderly people have also commonly reported missing meals. In the same study around Manchester, 5% of retired people had missed at least one meal in the past year because of a lack of money. Forty-six per cent disagreed with the statement 'Do you usually have enough money for food all week?' and 25.2% had missed at least one meal in a 24-hour recall period. Furthermore, the effect of income was found to operate independently of household composition – the proportion of those living alone having seven hot meals a week fell from 32.5% in the highest-income group to 15.2% in the lowest. The reduction was equally striking when two people were

living together – 66.7% down to 29.3% respectively (Brockington and Lempert, 1966).

5. Income and health. Income has been found to have a complex relationship with health – arguments have been put forward that low income predisposes someone to poor health and conversely that poor health condemns an individual to low income. Realistically it seems likely that both situations can interact. In terms of eating habits a number of studies have correlated financial problems (particularly amongst the very elderly) with poor appetites and in turn poor nutrient intakes (McIntosh, Shiflett and Picou, 1989), poor dental health and chewing difficulties (Davidson *et al.*, 1962). In the largest recent cross-cultural study of diet and the elderly (SENECA), researchers in Switzerland concluded that food budgeting problems were associated with poorer self-rated health, low intakes of various nutrients and food shopping difficulties. It appeared that ill health and living alone were obstacles which were overcome by the majority of respondents but that low income, especially for those in advanced old age, remained a perennial problem (Schlettwein-Gsell and Barclay, 1995).
6. Knowledge about food. In a study of 'average' Americans, Fusillo and Beloian (1977) associated increasing age, lower educational attainment, low social class and low income with low nutritional knowledge. Age in particular was a major determinant of nutritional scores. However, other evidence seems to condemn this approach as simplistic. Respondents in other studies (Cole-Hamilton and Laing, 1986; Health Education Authority, 1989) had absorbed healthy eating messages and made changes where possible, but they consistently quoted lack of money as a serious impediment to altering their diet more radically.
7. Different foods eaten. The results of surveys on income and food choices are strikingly similar to those mentioned earlier under social class. Poorer people are less likely to consume 'healthy' foods – milk and milk products, meats, fresh fruit and vegetables, bread and cereals – and are more likely to use white bread, whole milk, sugar, potatoes, tea, juice, eggs, butter and bacon (Probart *et al.*, 1989; Ryan and Bower, 1989). Elderly men living alone on lower incomes fared particularly badly – half consumed less than one serving of milk products, meat, fruit and vegetables daily (Davis *et al.* 1985). This lack of fresh produce ties in with the observations mentioned earlier that low-income groups make extensive use of convenience foods when compared to their wealthier counterparts (Cole-Hamilton and Laing, 1986; Health Education Authority, 1989).
8. Fewer material resources. Other than money itself, the importance of the assets it can buy should not be underestimated. Cooking and storage facilities and transport (particularly car ownership) all have important implications for the frequency with which a consumer shops, which

> outlets they can choose, the price they pay for food and the variety of foods available to them. Elderly people have reported lower rates of ownership of freezers, microwave ovens and fridges than many other population groups (OPCS, 1986), limiting options for cooking, storage and shopping. In a similar vein, car ownership amongst pensioners remains low, especially amongst females (e.g. Beuret, 1991) and consequently transport is often cited as a barrier to being able to shop more frequently (Midwinter, 1991). This obviously has implications for the amount of foods with a relatively short shelf-life that can be bought – particularly fresh fruit and vegetables.

Those elderly people restricted by lack of money, disability and no car are dependent on local shops and discount food stores. Although these shops offer low prices, they only tend to stock a limited range of goods (usually around 750 items) and may not sell fresh fruit and vegetables at all (London Food Commission, 1985). Lack of transport and shopping difficulties have been correlated with poor dietary intakes by researchers such as Davies (1981) and Horwath (1987). In the UK, as the trends for out-of-town shopping developments and cuts in rural transport services continue these aspects of access to food can only take on greater significance.

Although the take-up of private pension schemes and insurance are increasing, these can only have a minor impact on the elderly of today. Instead it is important that the poorest in society receive state support at a level which enables them to be more discriminating in their eating habits. Investment in welfare benefits should be seen as part of the health promotion strategy to reduce diet-related disease.

19.4 Secondary causes of malnutrition

19.4.1 Impaired appetite

Initial studies on older people have noted that intakes of most nutrients fall with increasing age. Studies by Exton-Smith, Stanton and Windsor (1972) have determined that most changes occur between the ages of 70 and 80 years. In this 10-year period calorific intakes were found to fall by 19%, fat by 30%, protein 28%, carbohydrate 6%, calcium 12%, iron 21% and vitamin C 27%. Risk of poor intakes seems to be concentrated in the area of micronutrients so that respondents were least likely to be deficient in protein but reported low levels of vitamin B_1, niacin, vitamins C and D (Le Clerc and Thornbury 1983). Claims have been made for this to be due to a decrease in the amount of total food eaten (Slesinger, McDivitt and O'Donnell, 1980) and also for a decrease in the variety of the diet in old age (Fanelli and Stevenhagen, 1985).

Undoubtedly the tendency for elderly people to be less physically active (section 19.3.3) will affect their perceived need for food. However, physiological mechanisms controlling the sensations of hunger and thirst and the sensory appreciation of food do undergo change in later life. Particularly important are the senses of smell and taste:

- Sense of smell. Doty *et al.* (1984) tested smell identification ability in subjects ranging from 5 to 99 years of age and found that 60% of subjects aged 60–80 had major deficits in their sense of smell. Above the age of 80 this increased to 80%. This does translate itself into a decreased ability to detect food aromas and the stimulation these aromas provide – salivation, gastric acid flow and secretions from various endocrine organs. Apart from this sensory loss being associated with age, it can also be induced by many of the drug treatments commonly given to elderly people – antihypertensives, antidepressants and some strong painkillers, for example (Schiffman, 1994).
- Sense of taste. Similar losses in sense of taste in older people have also been reported. For example, elderly people were impaired in their ability to detect salt in samples of soup, requiring twice as much to be present in order to notice it (Stevens *et al.*, 1991). Loss of taste tends to occur gradually over long periods of time and may begin as early as the mid-thirties, diminishing its impact on the elderly person. However, noticeable losses can decrease the acceptability of foods because of the strength of taste as a determinant in choice. Schiffman and Warwick (1989) reported that flavour enhancement and amplification could increase the intake of nutrient-dense foods. Since the most agreeable flavours to Western palates are salt and sweet, this does present some problems. In order to increase the palatability of food and hence increase nutrient intake it seems likely that concentrations of sugar and salt in food have to be increased. Both these substances have been implicated in obesity, hypertension, dental caries and other diseases. Evidently it is important that less harmful means of flavour enhancement are found. In the meantime, the use of low-sodium salt and artificial sweeteners is recommended. Some development to improve the quality of the latter would be beneficial. Again, like smell, taste can also be affected by common pharmacological treatments for hypertension, Parkinson's disease, infection, hypoglycaemia, rheumatism and arthritis, for example (Schiffman, 1994).
- Visual stimulus. More controversial is the idea that colour and its perception are linked to the ability to distinguish particular flavours and the acceptability of food. This may be related to the idea that certain colours make a food familiar and therefore more acceptable. In Clydesdale (1994) elderly subjects relied heavily on visual cues to determine the characteristics of foods. An increase in colour resulted in

higher quality and acceptability ratings being given to the foods. Obviously this reliance on the appearance of food as a guide to its suitability has important ramifications for those elderly people with failing eyesight.

- Hunger and thirst. Changes in homeostatic mechanisms make elderly people less sensitive to both external and internal changes. This includes a decreased sensitivity to the sensations of hunger and thirst and consequent lower intakes of both food and fluid (Rolls and Philips, 1990). More research has been carried out on fluid intake where a vicious circle has been found to exist – those elderly patients who had already been dehydrated later developed a reduced thirst sensation and were therefore not able to maintain a suitably high fluid intake to restore fluid balance (Philips, Johnston and Gray, 1991).

19.4.2 Masticatory inefficiency

Andrews *et al.* (1986) have found that dental problems were one of the most common difficulties reported, and that the percentage of those with dental impairment increased with age. Research in the UK and the US suggests that dentition affects eating habits in several ways – edentulous states, problems with dentures or oral disease.

Amongst others, Smith (1979) reported a positive correlation between poor diet and difficulties with natural or false teeth. In interviews with 274 elderly people in the Nottingham area (mean age 73 years), 74% of the sample had no natural teeth left; 98% of these had full upper and lower dentures but only 10% of these were found to be satisfactory in a clinical examination. Many of the dentures were old and did not fit properly – 25% had been wearing the same set of dentures for at least 10 years. The poor fit, coupled with poor cleaning in many cases led to a high incidence of lesions of the mouth.

Of the 26% who had at least some of their natural teeth remaining, 40% had some decayed teeth and 20% had teeth which were so badly decayed they needed to be extracted. The ramifications of such poor dental health were varied – 40% experienced pain on eating (due to decay or the high rates of gingivitis found), 30% had difficulty chewing and 20% had been embarrassed by their dentures 'dropping' in public. To compensate, 12% had changed their diet accordingly. Horwath (1987) disputes that dentition has any great effect on the types of food eaten – despite finding similar problems to those mentioned here, subjects did not eat significantly differently from their less restricted counterparts. Only women who perceived that they had some chewing difficulties had a higher milk and milk product consumption. Even foods which would be expected to cause problems – crisp fruits, steak, chops and nuts – and those which might be seen as good alternatives – stewed fruit, bananas and casseroles – were not eaten in significantly different quantities. Respondents in the study did not change the type of food eaten but managed to maintain their dietary patterns by changing the form the food was served in (e.g. finely chopping fruit) or by swallowing food less well chewed.

Dental problems of the kinds mentioned here are, of course, both preventable and treatable. Elderly people with dentures do not experience difficulties eating foods such as fresh fruit and vegetables because they wear dentures but because the dentures do not fit, are old or damaged. Primary care services in the UK have promoted medical check-ups for the over-75s. In view of the prevalence of dental problems it seems logical that this idea should be extended to dental care, with check-ups being free of charge. Other health professionals such as community nurses, health promotion departments and general practitioners should aim to encourage elderly people to take their dental health as seriously as their general physical health.

19.4.3 Malabsorption

Many physiological changes occur during the ageing process. Those which affect the gastrointestinal systems of older people have the potential to affect the digestion and absorption of a wide range of macro- and micro-nutrients. Those that have been noted are:

- A loss of gastric parietal cells decreases the secretion of hydrochloric acid, causing hypochlorhydria which decreases absorption of calcium and iron (particularly non-haem iron), folic acid and vitamin B_{12}. According to Chen (1986) 15–25% of individuals over 60 suffer from hypochlorhydria.
- Protein digestion may be impaired (Holmes, 1990).
- Decreased acidity permits bacterial overgrowth which may bind vitamin B_{12}, and cause reduced bile salt function as well as fat and fat-soluble vitamin malabsorption (Holmes, 1990).

In order to minimize the effects of malabsorption, those elderly people with small bowel ischaemia, gluten sensitivity and hypochlorhydria should be identified at the earliest possible stage. Dietary advice should emphasize the importance of consuming nutrient-dense sources of the nutrients involved – red meat, eggs, fortified cereals, milk and milk products, for example. Vitamin B_{12} injection and appropriate supplementation may also be used in cases of severe deficiency. Following the current trend in multi-disciplinary health care teams, a hospital or community dietitian should be involved in the care of such patients.

19.4.4 Alcoholism

In general, evidence shows that alcohol consumption is lower in elderly people than in other population groups (Gomberg, 1982). However, it is not clear whether this represents a fall in alcohol consumption through the ageing process or is the result of changes in attitudes towards drinking during this century; those people currently aged 60+ have been more exposed to ideas of temperance and moderation as well as practical restrictions on drinking, such as prohibition.

For those who do drink alcohol in later life, indications are that the damage caused increases with age. This may be due to the lower ratio of water: fat in the body associated with ageing or because alcohol metabolism declines. Jacques *et al.* (1989) found that, even in apparently well-nourished elderly people as alcohol intake increased blood levels of folate, riboflavin, copper, zinc, urea nitrogen and creatinine declined.

Studies in Europe and the UK have estimated that between 3.6 and 10.1% of the elderly are 'heavy drinkers' (Iliffe *et al.*, 1991; Posner *et al.*, 1994). These means conceal a distinct variation between the sexes – whereas 4.7% of women in Posners' study drank 5 fluid oz or more of alcohol per week, the rate amongst men of a comparable age was 17.1%.

Approximately one-third of these heavy drinkers have identifiably poor dietary habits which may ultimately lead to disease (Steen, Isaksson and Svanborg, 1977). Usually, deficiency disease occurs as a result of alcohol replacing more nutrient-dense food as the main source of calorific intake. However, high alcohol intake has also been more directly associated with a number of chronic diseases known to be major sources of mortality and morbidity:

- raised blood pressure (Potter, Bannan and Beevers, 1984);
- higher incidence of cerebrovascular disease (BMA, 1986);
- oral and oesophageal cancers (MacSween, 1982).

Although the problem of alcoholism in old age does not appear to be widespread, it is compounded by the fact that those people affected are often disadvantaged in other ways – male heavy drinkers are also more likely to be tobacco users and to be socially isolated (isolation as a risk factor for poor dietary quality has already been mentioned). Programmes of health promotion in these groups therefore need to focus not just on the drinking but also on the social circumstances of the sufferer. A combination of medical advice and social support in the form of lunch clubs, meals on wheels and home helps is recommended for those at risk. Outside the core of problem drinkers elderly people are more likely to be non-drinkers or light drinkers compared to younger groups (Falconer and Rose, 1991). Problems are more likely to occur when younger generations reach retirement age and beyond and carry their comparatively heavier drinking habits with them. In the intervening time continuing education about safe levels of alcohol consumption for the population in general is a priority. Current targets set in *The Health of the Nation* (Department of Health, 1992a) are to reduce the proportion of men and women drinking more than the recommended intake of alcohol to 18% and 7%, respectively, by 2005, with initiatives in both the statutory and voluntary sectors reinforcing health promotion messages.

19.4.5 Drugs

In the UK three-quarters of elderly people take prescribed drugs. The majority of these take between one and three drugs, with the rest taking between four and six simultaneously (Williamson, 1978). Older people visiting their GP are more likely to be given a prescription, including a repeat prescription (Bliss, 1985). Drugs can have a potent effect on nutritional status in two main ways: either they have side-effects which affect the elderly person's motivation or ability to eat, or they react with foods, altering their nutritional value. These mechanisms are outlined in Table 19.3.

Table 19.3 Effects of drugs on food and nutrient intakes

Mechanism	
Ability and motivation	Chemical changes
Appetite suppressant	Absorption
Alters sense of smell	Special reactions
Alters sense of taste	
Bulking	
Induces nausea/vomiting	

Table 19.4 Drug effects on appetite and nutritional value of food

Drug	Use	Effect
Phenolphthalein	Laxative	Calcium, vitamin D and potassium lost
Methotrexate	Leukaemia	Folic acid antagonist
Azulfidine	Anti-inflammatory	Folic acid lost
Glutethimide	Sedative	Impairs calcium transport
Methyldopa	Antihypertensive	Vitamin B_{12}, folic acid and iron lost
Phenindione	Anticoagulant	Affects sense of taste
Glipizide	Hypoglycaemic	Affects sense of taste
Streptomycin	Antibiotic	Affects sense of smell
Codeine	Analgesic	Affects sense of smell

- Appetite. A number of drugs have the effect of suppressing the appetite centres of the brain, including commonly prescribed drugs such as insulin. This produces weakness and also an aversion to foods. Obviously without supplementation this leads to a fall in dietary quality.

- Taste and smell changes. A loss of taste (dysgeusia) may be attributed to various anti-cancer agents, treatments for Parkinson's disease and some diuretics. Others, such as antibiotics and drugs for hypertension, cause losses of both smell and taste. Examples are included in Table 19.4. The role of smell and taste in appetite and enjoyment of food has been discussed in section 19.4.1.
- Bulking of food. Constipation is a common complaint among the elderly for which dietary fibre agents tend to be prescribed. Elderly people are also prone to self-medicate using raw, unprocessed bran or laxatives in large quantities. Both methods of treatment can have repercussions by creating a feeling of fullness without actually contributing any nutrients, or preventing absorption by binding with nutrients or causing food to pass through the gut more rapidly.
- Nausea. Treatments such as chemotherapy can reduce appetite and hence food intake because of the persistent nausea they cause for the elderly patient.
- Absorption Several drugs cause primary malabsorption of micronutrients. Colchicine is commonly prescribed for gout and yet it may cause severe vitamin B_{12} deficiency and megoblastic anaemia. Further examples are included in Table 19.4.
- Special adverse reactions. The need for special, often restrictive, diets may be precipitated by certain drug treatments such as monoamine oxidase inhibitors. These anti-depressants react with dietary amines causing an array of symptoms ranging from nausea and headache to stroke and heart problems. A diet low in tyramines is essential, which means cutting out beans, yeast extracts, red wine, herrings, bananas and many other 'healthy' foods.

Evidently the detrimental effects of drugs on food intake have to be balanced against their therapeutic effects on disease states. However, evidence is gathering that pharmacological treatment of disease is not always appropriately administered:

1. prescription of drugs is not always related to the dependency of the patient, in fact, sometimes the most active and independent people are prescribed the most drugs (Wade, Sawyer and Bell, 1983);
2. only a minority of elderly people are given warnings about the side-effects their drugs may have (Busson and Dunn, 1986);
3. drugs are prescribed repeatedly over long periods of time without review, often leading to duplication of medication and diuretics in particular (Herne, 1994);
4. alternative therapies, such as dietary change and exercise programmes, are underused both in the community and institutional settings (Lan and Justice, 1991).

Certainly, for many of the more common conditions of obesity, hypertension and constipation dietary change have a valuable role to play in health promotion. No doubt the medical profession has shied away from these means because they are not 'traditional' and they require the patient to make long-term changes in their life styles. However, dietary therapy has the advantages of being cheaper than pharmacological methods, with few side-effects and often spin-off benefits such as weight loss, increased continence and better-quality sleep (Anonymous, 1989). Details of how dietary therapy might be promoted (particularly in institutions) have been given by Herne (1993); these will be summarized later in the discussion.

19.4.6 Increased requirements

It is generally supposed that old age brings with it a decreased requirement for most nutrients. More recently, however, arguments have been put forward that because of the poor absorption of some micronutrients elderly people actually require greater intakes than some other groups, particularly of vitamins D, B_6 and B_{12} (Russell, 1992). Although this theory remains contentious, there is no doubt that various illnesses, particularly infectious disease, can increase nutritional requirements dramatically, often by 50% (Scrimshaw, 1977). Infections of the respiratory tract, urinary tract, skin and eyes are prevalent in elderly populations, occurring in 15–20% of those in care (Garibaldi, Brodine and Matsumiya, 1981). The need for extra nutrients at a time of illness can create complex cyclical problems leading to the recurrent malnutrition described by Davies (1990) (section 19.2). Despite the need for extra nutrients, the symptoms of fatigue, nausea, fever, vomiting, etc. associated with infectious disease reduce the appetite of the elderly person and his or her ability to self-care. Food intake declines and this, in turn, affects immunity to further infection. Further infection can cause further disease and continuing low nutrient intakes. In the case of those under the care of homes and hospitals, supplementation has already been suggested by the Kings Fund Centre (Lennard-Jones, 1992). In its report the centre estimates that supplementation along with enteral and parenteral nutritional support could save the health service £266 million per year, decrease re-admission to care and shorten the length of stay by 5 days for an estimated 10% of the hospital population.

19.5 Discussion and recommendations

In the context of old age the concept of 'healthy eating' goes far beyond ideas of reducing fat, sugar and salt and increasing complex carbohydrates. It must also encompass the more general aim to promote quantity and quality of intake for elderly people in order to avoid deficiency states. From the data presented in this chapter it is clear that there are many apparent barriers to achieving this aim, particularly in terms of social problems such as poverty. The implementation of broad-based public health measures is a step forward in tackling the disease and disability of diet-related disease, but it must also be linked to initiatives in the food industry, retailers, fiscal policy, education and social services.

Examples of possible strategies to achieve better health in later life are:

1. Comprehensive nutritional education pre- and post-retirement, concentrating on the health issues of greatest relevance to older people. Guidance should include written materials detailing food sources of various nutrients, the importance of exercise, advice on the appropriate use of supplements and cooking suggestions. Some guidelines which are specifically aimed at this age group are already available. For younger adults continuing education on the benefits of healthy eating needs to emphasize that diet can still have an impact on health in later life. Efforts should be concentrated on the areas where elderly people are most likely to be vulnerable – vitamin D deficiency, the need for daily intakes of vitamin C, and so on.
2. Dissemination of written and oral advice on healthy eating and special diets at points of treatment, whether these be hospital or community based.
3. More comprehensive nutritional education for medics, community nursing services and other health professions in close contact with the elderly. Elderly people tend to listen and heed the advice of general practitioners and therefore education of this group is especially important. Improved liaison with community and hospital dietitians should aid the flow of information to its appropriate target groups.
4. In order to boost the take-up of community meals services, they need to be both more affordable and better quality. Current initiatives based on frozen foods, reheated in the home using table-top units seem to be the best way forward in this area, provided elderly people are supplied with the necessary equipment. However, it is important to give elderly people advice on the correct procedure for re-heating meals and storing/re-heating any leftovers to prevent food safety problems.
5. Careful monitoring of the severely incapacitated, both in hospital and in the community through social and medical services. Supplementation should be used where it is not possible for the elderly person to eat a sufficiently nutrient-dense diet by normal means. Particularly for those in institutions, emphasis needs to be placed on creating more physical and mental stimulation for patients and residents, both as an aid to appetite and a means of maintaining engagement.
6. Further research into the mechanisms by which dementias affect nutritional status and possible ways of minimizing nutritional risk in these patients.

7. Extended voluntary and statutory aid for those suffering from depression, particularly related to bereavement. This may involve formal supply of frozen meals as described in point 4, or take the form of the American 'buddy' system where 'at-risk' individuals are supported by a single case worker, equipped to help both on a practical level and in giving advice.
8. Targeting of welfare payments to the poorest and most vulnerable elderly people. This needs to include:
   - education on what elderly people are entitled to;
   - encouragement to use social services such as home helps, meals on wheels, lunch clubs, saving schemes for other bills such as fuel;
   - more one-off payments for items such as cookers, freezers and fridges to aid food storage and shopping.
9. Improvements in transport systems directly to major supermarkets and in rural areas, where deregulation of services has had a profound effect on accessibility of food outlets.
10. Development of more acceptable flavour enhancement for foods such as meal replacements, ready meals, fortified products, drinks and so on. Further research on the role of colour in increasing acceptability may yield useful information for institutional caterers, trying to improve the quality of their products.
11. More emphasis on the need for adequate fluid intakes in older people, particularly those suffering from confused states who may forget to drink sufficient quantities. Providers of community, hospital and residential home meals should ensure that all residents/patients have drinks supplied with their meals and snacks. More independent people should have the facilities to make drinks as and when they wish.
12. Initiatives to promote dental health; in particular, check-ups for the over-70s should be promoted.
13. Identification of those with conditions linked to malabsorption states and suitable treatment using supplements and educational strategies. Patients need to be made aware of the food sources of the nutrients likely to be lacking in their diet, preferably in the form of written information from a dietitian.
14. A comprehensive re-shaping of the current prescribing practices for older people. Systems of regular review need to be incorporated, particularly in general practice, in order to avoid unnecessary repeat prescriptions and duplications of drug treatments. At present communication between primary- and secondary-level health care services is poor – hospital consultants and general practitioners have a slow exchange of information which may not be in an intelligible form to the other party. Such deficiencies allow the current problems in the pharmacological treatment of older patients to be perpetuated. Initiatives in some areas of the UK have encouraged meetings between

the two parties, as well as more telephone discussion of cases. Projects of this nature appear to be successful in combating many of the problems in the health service and should be fostered on a more wide-scale basis.

15. Education of patients about their drug treatments and any likely side-effects they may encounter. If possible this should come from the practitioner or pharmacist, rather than relying on patients to read the small print of manufacturers' leaflets.
16. Guidance from trained professionals for patients and caterers affected by special diets, particularly those which require a radical change in habits, such as those with diabetes. Diet sheets should be tailored to suit each individual, particularly with regard to cultural, religious, ethnic or taste preferences. For those institutions with little expertise in this area, special diet products or whole meals can be supplied by various distributors. These often have quantities (g) of fat, carbohydrate and calories already calculated.
17. Increased use of meal replacements and supplements for those with diseases that raise the metabolic rate. This is particularly important for those people being treated with drugs known to deplete certain nutrients.
18. Greater use of enteral and parenteral feeding for elderly people in hospital (especially those recovering from surgery) and for those convalescing in the community.

Evidently there are infinite ways in which the health of elderly people can be improved through changes in policy. In general, governments have recognized that the need to adapt health and community care to ageing societies is there; more questionable is the extent to which resources are backing this commitment.

To avoid the burden of ill health and its consequent expense, programmes that tackle the root causes of diet-related disease must be instigated before the numbers of elderly are due to take off in the early part of the twenty-first century. Several of the recommendations made here are currently being implemented, but if real success is to be achieved nutritional policy has to be more proactive in its approach. Lessons can be learned from the Australian government, which drew up a formal national nutritional policy in consultation with manufacturers, retailers, consumers and the media. The food and nutrition policy encompasses three main ideas – promoting the availability of 'healthy' foods, the affordability of such foods and understanding of the links between nutrition and health. Implementation of such a policy is seen as part of a strategy to enhance 'social justice' – a concept particularly apt for elderly people as one of the more disadvantaged groups in most societies.

References

Abbasi, A.A. and Rudman, D. (1994) Undernutrition in the nursing home: prevalence, consequences, causes, prevention. *Nutrition Reviews*, **52**, (4), 113–22.
Andrews, G.P., Esterman, A.J., Braunack-Mayer, A.J. and Rungie, C.M. (1986) *Ageing in the Western Pacific*, World Health Organization Regional Office for the Western Pacific, Manila.
Anonymous (1989) Cutting out drug induced apathy. *Social Work Today*, **20**, (18), 8–10.
Anonymous (1993) Health care reform legislative platform: economic benefits of nutrition services. *J. Am. Diet. Assoc.*, **93**, (6), 686–90.
Backett, K. and Davidson, C. (1992) Rational or reasonable? Perceptions of health at different stages of life. *Health Education Journal*, **51**, (2), 55–9.
Beuret, K. (1991) Women and transport, in *Women's Issues in Social Policy* (eds M. McLean and D. Groves), Routledge, London, pp. 61–75.
Bliss, M.R. (1985) Prescribing for the elderly. *Br. Med. J.*, **283**, 203–6.
BMA (British Medical Association((1986) *Diet, Nutrition and Health*, BMA, London.
Bransby, E.R. and Osborne, B. (1953) A social and food survey of the elderly living alone or as married couples. *Br. J. Nutr.*, **7**, 160–80.
Brockington, C.F. and Lempert, S.M. (1966) *The Social Needs of the Over 80s. The Stockport Survey*, Manchester University Press.
Busson, M. and Dunn, A. (1986) Patients' knowledge about prescribed medicines. *Pharmaceutical Journal*, **236**, 624–6.
Central Statistical Office (1995) *Social Trends*, Vol. 25, HMSO, London.
Charny, M. and Lewis, P.A. (1987) Does health knowledge affect eating habits? *Health Education Journal*, **46**, (4), 172–6.
Chen, L.H. (1986) Biomedical Influences on the Nutrition of the Elderly, in *Nutritional Aspects of Ageing* (ed. L.H. Chen), CRC Press, Boca Raton, FL., pp. 53–73.
Clancy, K.L. (1975) Preliminary observations on media use and food habits of the elderly. *Gerontologist*, **15**, (6), 529–32.
Clydesdale, F.J. (1994) Changes in color and flavor and their effect on sensory perception in the elderly. *Nut. Rev.*, **52**, (8), S19–S20.
Cole-Hamilton, I. and Laing, T. (1986) *Tightening Belts: A Report of the Impact of Poverty on Food*, London Food Commission Report 13, LFC.
CPA (Centre for Policy on Ageing and the Department of Health and Social Security) (1984) *Home Life: a Code of Practice for Residential Care*, CPA, London.
Davidson, C.S., Livermore, J., Anderson, P. and Kaufman, S. (1962) The nutrition of apparently healthy ageing persons. *Am. J. Clin. Nutr.*, **10**, 181–909.
Davies, L. (1981) *Three Score Years and Then? ... A Study of the Nutrition and Well-being of the Elderly at Home*, Heinemann, London.
Davies, L. (1990) Socio-economic, psychological and educational aspects of nutrition in old age. *Age and Ageing*, **19**, (4), (Suppl. 1), S37–42.
Davies, L. (1991) *Opportunities for Better Health in the Elderly Through Mass Catering*, WHO, Copenhagen.
Davies, L., Anderson, J.P. and Holdsworth, M.D. (1985) Nutrition education at the age of retirement from work. *Health Education Journal*, **44**, (4), 187–92.
Davis, M.A., Randall, E., Forthofer, R.N. *et al.* (1985) Living arrangements and dietary patterns of older adults in the United States. *J. Gerontol.*, **40**, (4), 434–42.
Department of Health (1992a) *The Health of the Nation: A Strategy for Health in England*, HMSO, London.
Department of Health (1992b) *The Nutrition of Elderly People: Report of the Working Group on the Nutrition of Elderly People of the Committee on Medical Aspects of Food Policy*, HMSO, London.
Department of Health (1992c) *The Health of Elderly People – An Epidemiological Overview*, HMSO, London.
DHSS (Department of Health and Social Security) (1979) *Nutrition and Health in Old Age*, Reports on Health and Social Subjects No. 16, HMSO, London.
Doty, R.L., Shaman, P., Appelbaum, S.L. *et al.* (1984) Smell identification ability: changes with age. *Science*, **226**, 1441–3.

Exton-Smith, A.N. (1979) Eating habits of the elderly, in *Nutrition and Lifestyles* (ed. M. Turner), Applied Science, London, pp. 179–94.
Exton-Smith, A.N., Stanton, B.R. and Windsor, A.C.M. (1972) *The Nutrition of Housebound Old People*, King Edwards Hospital Fund for London.
Falconer, P. and Rose, R. (1991) *Older Britons: A Survey*, Centre for the Study of Public Policy, Glasgow.
Fanelli, M.T. and Stevenhagen, K.J. (1985) Characterising food consumption patterns by food frequency methods: core foods and variety foods in diets of older Americans. *J. Am. Diet. Assoc.*, **85**, 1570–76.
Fengler, A.P., Danigelis, N. and Little, V.C. (1983) Later life satisfaction and household structure: living with others and living alone. *Ageing and Society*, **1**, 357–77.
Fusillo, A.E. and Beloian, A.M. (1977) Consumer nutrition knowledge and self-reported food shopping behaviour. *Am. J. Public Health*, **67**, (9), 846–50.
Garibaldi, R.A., Brodine, S. and Matsumiya, S. (1981) Infections among patients in nursing homes: policies, prevalence, problems. *N. Engl. J. Med.*, **305**, 731-5.
Gomberg, E. (1982) Alcohol use and alcohol problems among the elderly, in *National Institute on Alcohol Abuse and Alcoholism and Health Monograph 4*, US Department of Health and Human Services, Rockville, MD, pp. 263–90.
Gray, G.E. (1989) Nutrition and dementia. *J. Am. Diet. Assoc.*, **89**, 1795–1802.
Hall, M.R.P., MacLennan, W.J. and Lye, M.D.W. (1993) *Medical Care of the Elderly*, John Wiley and Sons, Chichester.
Hanson, B.S., Mattisson, I. and Steen, B. (1987) Dietary intake and psychosocial factors in 68 year old men. *Compr. Gerontol.*, **1**, 62–7.
Health Education Authority (1989) *Diet, Nutrition and Healthy Eating in Low Income Groups*, HEA, London.
Herne, S. (1993) Healthy eating in old age. *Br. Food. J.*, **95**, (5), 36–9.
Herne, S. (1994) Private residential care for elderly people. PhD Thesis, Department of Biomedical Science, University of Bradford.
Holmes, S. (1990) Nutrition and older people: a matter of concern. *Nursing Times*, **90**, (42), 31–3.
Horwath, C.C. (1987) A random population study of dietary habits in elderly people. PhD Thesis, Department of Community Medicine, University of Adelaide.
Iliffe, S., Haines, A., Booroff, A. *et al.* (1991) Alcohol consumption by elderly people: a general practice survey. *Age and Ageing*, **20**, 120–3.
Jacques, P.F., Sulsky, S., Hartz, S.C. and Russell, R.M. (1989) Moderate alcohol intake and nutritional status in non-alcoholic elderly subjects. *Am. J. Clin. Nutr.*, **50**, 875–83.
Krondl, M., Lau, D., Yurkiw, M.A. and Coleman, P. (1982) Food use and perceived food meanings of the elderly. *J. Am. Diet. Assoc.*, **80**, 523–9.
Laing, T. *et al.* (1984) *Jam Tomorrow: A Report of the First Findings of a Pilot Study of the Food Circumstances, Attitudes and Consumption of 1000 People on Low Incomes in the North of England*, Manchester Polytechnic.
Lan, S.J. and Justice, C.L. (1991) Use of modified diets in nursing homes. *J. Am. Diet. Assoc.*, **91**, (1), 46–51.
LeClerc, H.L. and Thornbury, M.E. (1983) Dietary intakes of Title III Program recipients and non-recipients. *J. Am. Diet. Assoc.*, **83**, (5), 573–7.
Lennard-Jones, J.E. (1992) *A Positive Approach to Nutrition as Treatment*, Kings Fund Centre, London.
Lennon, D. and Fieldhouse, P. (1982) *Social Nutrition*, Forbes Publishing, London.
London Food Commission (1985) *Food Retailing in London*, LFC.
McIntosh, W.A., Shifleet, P.A. and Picou, J.S. (1989) Social support, stressful events, strain, dietary intake and the elderly. *Medical Care*, **27**, (2), 140–53.
MacSween, R.N.M. (1982) Alcohol and cancer. *Br. Med. Bull.*, **38**, 31–3.
Midwinter, E. (1991) *The British Gas Report on Attitudes to Ageing 1991*, British Gas, London.
NACNE (National Advisory Council on Nutrition Education) (1983) *Proposals for Nutritional Guidelines for Health Education in Britain*, Health Education Council, London.
OPCS (Office of Population Censuses and Surveys Social Survey Division) (1986) *General Household Survey 1985*, HMSO, London.

OPCS (Office of Population Censuses and Surveys) (1990) *General Household Survey 1988*, HMSO, London.

OPCS (Office of Population Censuses and Surveys) (1993) *Mortality Statistics by Cause England and Wales, 1992*, HMSO, London.

Organisation for Economic Cooperation and Development (1988) *Ageing Populations: The Social Policy Implications*, OECD, Paris.

Philips, P.A., Johnston, C.I. and Gray, L. (19910 Thirst and fluid intake in the elderly, in *Thirst: Physiological and Psychological Aspects* (eds D.J. Ramsay and D. Booth), Springer-Verlag, New York, pp. 403–11.

Popkin, B.M., Haines, P.S. and Patterson, R.E. (1992) Dietary changes in older Americans 1977–1987. *Am. J. Clin. Nutr.*, **55**, 830–2.

Posner, B.M., Jette, A., Smigelski, C. *et al.* (1994) Nutritional risk in New England elders. *J. Gerontol.*, **49**, (3), M123–133.

Potter, J.F., Bannan, L.T. and Beevers, D.G. (1984) Alcohol and hypertension. *Br. J. Addiction*, **79**, 365–72.

Probart, C.K., Davis, L.G., Hibbard, J.H. and Kime, R.E. (1989) Factors that influence the elderly to use traditional or non-traditional nutrition information sources. *J. Am. Diet. Assoc.*, **89**, 1758–62.

Rolls, B.J. and Philips, P.A. (1990) Ageing and disturbances of thirst and fluid balance. *Nutr. Rev.*, **48,** 137–44.

Russell, R.M. (1992) Micronutrient requirements of the elderly. *Nutr. Rev.*, **50**, (12), 463–6.

Ryan, V.C. and Bower, M.E. (1989) Relationship of socio-economic status and living arrangements to the nutritional intake of the older person. *J. Am. Diet. Assoc.*, **89**, 1805–7.

Schiffman, S. (1994) Changes in taste and smell: drug interactions and food preferences. *Nutr. Rev.*, **52**, (8), S11–S14.

Schiffman, S. and Warwick, Z.S. (1989) Use of flavour amplified foods to improve nutritional status in elderly persons, in *Nutrition and the Chemical Senses in Ageing: Recent Advances and Current Research Needs* (eds C. Murphy, W.S. Cain and D.M. Hegsted), New York Academy of Science, 267–76.

Schlettwein-Gsell, D. and Barclay, D. (1995) Dietary habits and attitudes in healthy ageing, in *Adaptations in Ageing* (eds J.LC. Dall *et al.*), Academic Press, NY.

Schwartz, D., Henley, B. and Zeitz, L. (1964) *The Elderly Ambulatory Patient: Nursing and Psychological Needs*, Macmillan, New York.

Scrimshaw, N. (1977) Effect of infection on nutrient requirements. *Am. J. Clin. Nutr.*, **30**, 1536-44.

Slesinger, D.P., McDivitt, M. and O'Donnell, F.M. (1980) Food patterns in an urban population: age and socioeconomic correlates. *J. Geront.*, **35**, (3), 432–41.

Smith, J.M. (1979) Oral and dental discomfort a necessary feature of old age? *Age and Ageing*, **8**, 25–32.

Steen, B., Isaksson, B. and Svanborg, A. (1977) Intake of energy and nutrients and meal habits in 70 year old males and females in Gothenburg, Sweden. A population study. *Acta. Med. Scand., Suppl.*, **611**, 39.

Stevens, J.C., Cain, W.S., Demarque, A. and Ruthruff, A.M. (1991) On the discrimination of missing ingredients: Ageing and salt flavor. *Appetite*, **16**, 129-40.

US Bureau of the Census (1990) *Statistical Abstract of the United States 1990*, US Government Printing Office, Washington DC.

Wade, B.E., Sawyer, L. and Bell, J. (1983) *Dependency with Dignity*, Bedford Square Press, London.

Walker, A. (1987) The poor relation: poverty among older women, in *Women and Poverty in Britain* (eds C. Glendinning and J. Millar), Wheatsheaf Books, London.

Weber, F., Barnard, R.J. and Roy, D. (1983) Effects of a high complex carbohydrate low fat and daily exercise regime on individuals 70 years of age and older. *J. Gerontol.*, **38**, (2), 155–61.

Williamson, J. (1978) Prescribing problems in the elderly. *Practitioner*, **220**, 749–55.

Wilson, G. (1989) Family food systems, preventive health and dietary change: a policy to increase the health divide. *J. Soc. Pol.*, **18**, (2), 167–85.

World Health Organisation Regional Committee for Europe (1991) *Healthy Ageing*, WHO, Copenhagen.

Part Four

Industry Initiatives

20 The Sainsbury's Healthy Eating Initiative

G.D. SPRIEGEL

In 1991 the Committee on Medical Aspects of Food Policy (COMA) produced their report: *Dietary Reference Values for Food Energy and Nutrients for the UK*. This report received wide press coverage and was generally regarded by the nutrition community in the UK as the most comprehensive report ever produced on the current nutrient needs for different groups of the UK population and reviewed the function of the nutrients and identified their role in health and disease. The report assessed dietary consumption patterns in this country in relation to incidence of key degenerative diseases and set population guidelines for intakes of selected nutrients and fibre. Guidance was provided in the report of the key changes in nutrient intake which needed to be undertaken by the UK population in order to help improve the health status of the country.

The key changes to the British diet recommended by the COMA Report were:

- A reduction in the percentage of calories derived from total fat in the diet from over 40% to approximately 35% (33% with moderate alcohol intake).
- A reduction in the percentage of calories derived from saturated fat from around 18% to approximately 11%.
- A reduction in sugar intake – especially non-milk extrinsic sugars.
- An increase in dietary fibre from an average of 12 g/day to an average of 18 g/day.
- A reduction in sodium intakes. The panel set a figure of 1.6 g/day, but noted that current average intakes were needlessly high, i.e. in excess of 3.2 g/day. They recommended that these should not increase. A subsequent COMA Report recommended that average intakes should be reduced by about one-third.

In addition there was a growing body of research evidence to support the need for increased consumption of fruits and vegetables, not only as a

Implementing Dietary Guidelines for Healthy Eating. Edited by Verner Wheelock. Published in 1997 by Blackie A&P, an imprint of Chapman & Hall, London. ISBN 0 7514 0304 0

contributor of dietary fibre, but also to increase intake of anti-oxidant vitamins and phytoprotective compounds.

This evidence was certainly supported by the World Health Organization, which had proposed an increase in daily fruit and vegetable consumption that had been converted to the more consumer-friendly '5-a-Day' campaign by nutritional organizations in the United States.

The COMA Report was followed, in 1992, by the publication of the *Health of the Nation* white paper, a strategy for health in the UK which, although covering a broad spectrum of health concerns, identified the contribution that improved diet could make to a reduction in the incidence of degenerative diseases such as coronary heart disease, stroke, cancer and obesity-related conditions. The report in effect recognized the increasing medical costs of a greying population and proposed the philosophy of disease prevention through a healthier life style as a more cost-effective health management strategy.

In order to ensure that the momentum established by the COMA Report and the *Health of the Nation* white paper was not lost, the government set up a Nutrition Task Force under the chairmanship of Professor Dame Barbara Clayton of Southampton General Hospital to identify means by which the targets laid down within the *Health of the Nation* document could be achieved.

Sectors of the food industry – manufacturers, caterers and retailers – were requested to identify strategies by which companies could make a significant positive contribution to improving the health status of the population through product development and reformulation, and improved customer awareness and information.

From a commercial standpoint it was clear that, as the links between diet and disease became more clearly established, customers would expect responsible food companies to develop products or marketing strategies consistent with the change in dietary trends that were to be encouraged if the *Health of the Nation* targets were to be achieved in the proposed timescale.

In the autumn of 1992 a Board decision was taken within Sainsbury's that a food and nutrition strategy should be developed that would help our customers make an informed choice in food purchasing decisions to benefit their health and that of their families. In many ways, Sainsbury's, as the leading food retailer, was in an ideal position to motivate change because:

- The company had direct contact with 9 million customers per week – an excellent interface for communication.
- As a retailer with a major own-brand programme product formulation was under its own control.

- As the company marketed the entire range of food products it was not tied to a particular product sector and could take a holistic view – there was no vested interest in promoting or defending a particular product sector.

To achieve this Board objective a cross-functional Working Group was set up, under technical leadership, to determine how the company could rise to the challenge laid down by the *Health of the Nation* document and help meet the objectives of the Nutrition Task Force.

The first meetings of the multifunctional Working Group were unable to agree a clear way forward. The relative backgrounds and, in certain cases, entrenched views, of marketing, legal, technical, purchasing and home economics departments were not conducive to prompt agreement on strategy.

It was, therefore, decided to conduct market research to assist our understanding of our customers' thoughts and perceptions of healthy eating so that we could develop a strategy to meet their needs. The market research consisted of in-depth group discussions with women who claimed to be interested in healthy eating to a varying extent. While excluding extremists at either end of the spectrum, we attempted to consult respondents who represented a broad spectrum of interests, level of information and commitment. The following key points emerged from the research:

1. *Most customers want to eat more healthily.* This was not surprising as, confronted with the choice of eating more healthily it could be anticipated that most customers would respond positively.
2. *Nutritional information is comprehensive.* During discussion it emerged that customers were amazed by the amount of nutritional information which is available to them generally on pack. It had always been our policy to provide comprehensive nutritional information in full compliance with legislation. The problem was not the availability of the information but the comprehension of the information. In short, nutritional information is comprehensive but not comprehensible.
3. *Customers are confused.* Most customers were very confused about the content of a balanced diet. They were highly critical of the mixed messages that they received from nutritionists through various channels and a number quoted the advice offered during the 1970s to reduce consumption of starch, compared with the current advice, which is to eat more starch, but less fat. The common question asked was 'When will you change the advice again?'
4. *Misunderstanding of fat and fat contents.* The nature of fats, fatty foods and the level of fat in a food were poorly understood. Customers generally regarded any food which was considered fattening or high calorie to be so because of a high fat content. For example, 'lager is

fattening, therefore, lager contains fat'. Knowledge of fat contents of food was extremely low.

5. *The need for benchmarks.* Calories and alcohol were better understood than other food components due to well-publicised benchmarks. The alcohol benchmark system of 14 units for a woman per week, and 21 units per man per week, were well publicized and understood. There was agreement that similar advice on fat would be useful. Customers were concerned that although the general advice was to eat less fat the concern was 'How much less – and when will I know when I get there?'
6. *Healthy eating is boring.* There was an overriding perception that foods that were 'healthy' tended to be tasteless, uninteresting and generally inconvenient. Foods that were 'unhealthy' tended to be exciting and tasty.

The discussion groups were then asked to help in the development of a strategy which could be implemented by the company in order to help customers select a more balanced diet.

From the discussions a number of key points arose. These were:

1. *Clearer indication of the type of foods constituting a balanced diet.* There was a strong desire for bold descriptors on foods – especially those foods low in fat. Customers were keen on symbols to identify food that would be more beneficial to them in terms of their overall diet without the need to study detailed nutritional information.
2. *Nutritional information.* Most customers were enthusiastic about key nutritional information being presented in the format of serving size rather than the content per 100 g as required by legislation. Even customers who were interested in eating more healthily were not prepared to conduct mathematical gymnastics to convert information as presented into something more practical. The food components of greatest interest were calories and fat.
3. *Benchmarks to be developed for calories and fat* – along the lines of the alcohol benchmarks with which they were already familiar. This would enable guidance of the amount of calories and/or fat which could be consumed in a day within the healthy eating guidelines of the COMA Report.
4. *Respondents were also keen that every effort was made to convey healthy eating as enjoyable, convenient and affordable.*
5. *Information to enable an informed choice.* Overall, customers were very positive about receiving information that would enable them to make an informed choice to provide a more balanced diet for themselves and their families. However, they were strictly of the view that any attempt to coerce or persuade would be resisted. There was a strong feeling that positive simple messages on nutrition needed to be absorbed as snippets

of information to enable them to build up their own databank. Any technique that would improve their knowledge and understanding of a balanced diet through leaflets, recipe suggestions and simple messages was well received. They wanted a strategy for foods based on foods, rather than food components. Customers understand food – not food chemistry.

The major benefit of the market research was to give the Working Party a clear focus based upon the company's commitment to meet the needs of our customers. After some deliberation a strategy was devised that would move our customer offer from providing choice – to providing informed choice. The three key components of the strategy were as follows:

1. improved on-pack presentation and labelling;
2. a customer communication programme;
3. a strategy to assist special dietary groups.

20.1 Improved product presentation and labelling

20.1.1 Healthy eating symbol

A Sainsbury's healthy eating symbol was developed by our design studio to act as a co-ordinating link between the various components of the strategy. After market research the symbol (Fig. 20.1) was selected.

Figure 20.1 Sainsbury's Healthy Eating Symbol.

The symbol is designed to portray fitness and vitality but, at the same time, was of appeal to both men and women. The symbol would appear on packs, on recipe cards and in any advertising conducted to support the strategy.

20.1.2 On-pack presentation

The next problem was to determine which products should carry the new symbol. At about this time much attention was being given to the healthy eating pyramid which had been developed by the Flour Advisory Bureau and the Dunn Nutrition Centre (Fig. 20.2). The food pyramid was a

THE BRITISH HEALTHY EATING PYRAMID

A GUIDE TO CHOOSING A HEALTHY DIET

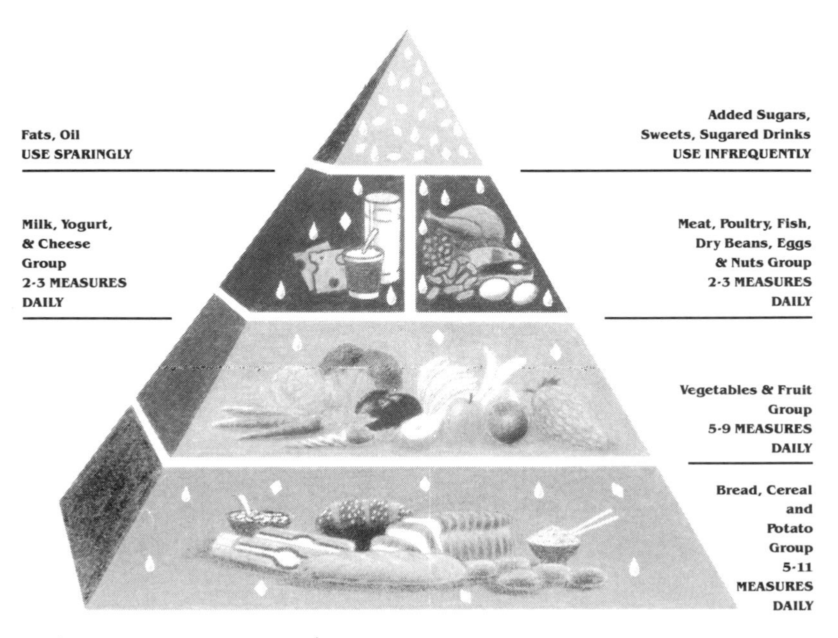

KEY Fat (naturally occurring and added) Sugars (added) These symbols show fats, oils and added sugars in foods.

Each day choose foods from all five groups.

Eat most of the large bread/cereal group at the bottom.

Eat least of the small fat and sugar group at the top.

A measure is a small portion, or a unit of food (eg slice of bread, piece of fruit).

Young, active, not overweight: Eat the larger numbers of measures shown.

Older, inactive, overweight: Eat the smaller numbers of measures shown.

Produced by the Flour Advisory Bureau and the Dunn Nutrition Centre

Figure 20.2 Food pyramid.

pictorial representation of the proportions in which food should be consumed in order to achieve a properly balanced diet. As part of the activities of the Nutrition Task Force the Department of Health decided to research the food pyramid with a range of alternative pictorial or graphical representations of the balanced diet.

After a range of options had been discussed, the final options were the food pyramid, and the tilted food plate (Fig. 20.3). After much debate and market research, the tilted plate was finally selected as the pictorial representation for the UK. Retailers and manufacturers were approached to support this new representation of balanced eating. It was agreed by the Working Party that we would attempt to place our new healthy eating symbol on foods consistent with the food selection guide illustrated by the tilted plate.

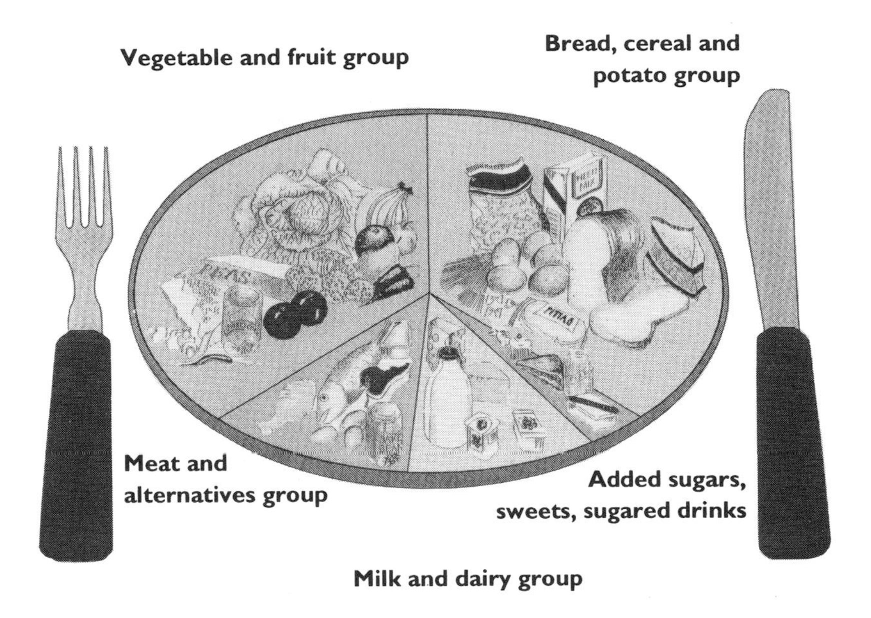

Figure 20.3 Tilted food plate.

One disadvantage regarding the tilted plate was that it referred only to single foods or single food components, rather than multicomponent foods of which we marketed an extremely wide range.

Although assigning the healthy eating symbol to single food components was a relatively simple task, deciding which multicomponent processed foods should display the symbol was more complicated.

A decision tree was therefore devised to determine which composite foods should display the symbol (Fig. 20.4). The decision tree attempted to focus principally on those foods low in fat, and took account of the frequency with which individual foods were consumed on a daily basis. It was essential that foods which carried the symbol were appropriate to avoid consumer criticism. It was also necessary to recognize salt and sugar levels of foods and to embrace foods high in fat that people will use in the normal course of cooking and preparation, such as oils and spreads.

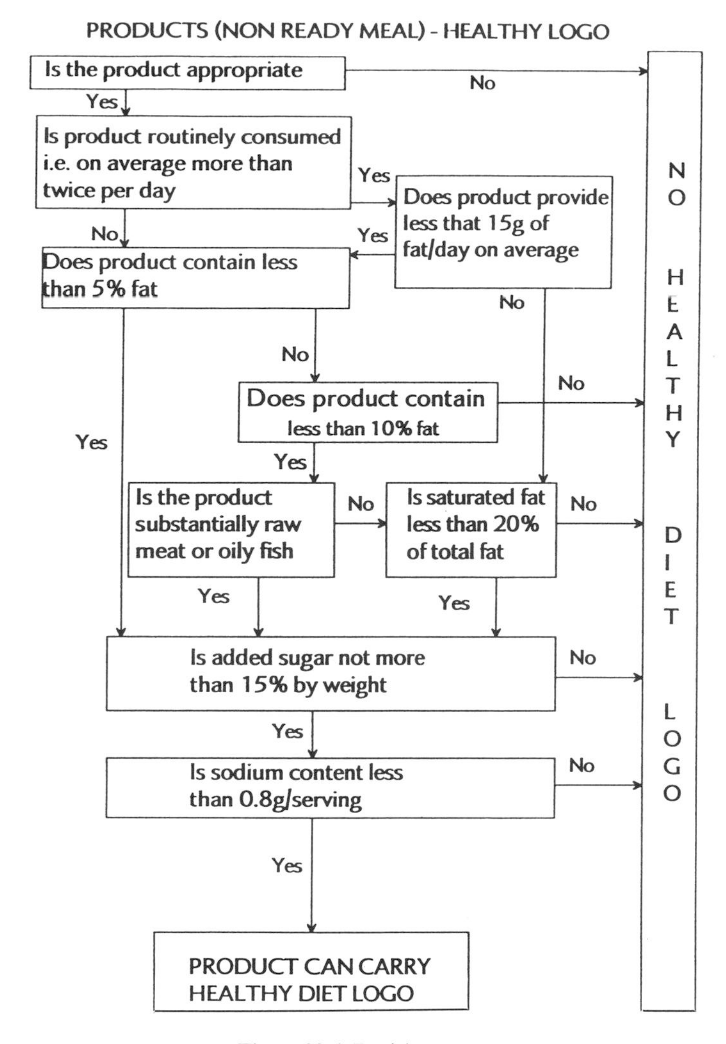

Figure 20.4 Decision tree.

It was decided that the symbol should be applied to the range of foods that are good food sources, generally low in fats, especially saturated fats, which possess intrinsic properties such as providers of protein, starch, minerals, vitamins or fibre, which help the attainment of a balanced diet. The symbol was also to be applied to a limited range of high-fat foods consumed regularly in the normal diet, such as vegetable oil, spreads and vegetable cooking oils to guide customers to the best alternatives.

Products to carry the symbol, therefore, fell into six groups:

- All fruits and vegetables, whether fresh, frozen, canned or dried;
- starch-based products, such as rice, pasta, oats and bread;
- lean red meat products, most poultry, all fish;
- dairy products generally low in fat, such as yogurts, cottage cheese, fromage frais;
- selected convenience foods, such as sandwiches, breakfast cereals and ready meals;
- selected spreads and culinary oils.

In all, over 2000 own-brand Sainsbury products qualified to carry the healthy eating symbol, which provided encouragement that a whole-diet approach that portrayed healthy eating as enjoyable, convenient and affordable, was achievable.

20.1.3 Enhanced labelling

In compliance with the market research, it was decided to highlight the two key components of a balanced diet identified by our customers, viz. calories and fats, by providing a highlighted box at the base of the existing nutritional panel, in the same colour as the healthy eating symbol, to provide calories and fat in grams per serving of food (Fig. 20.5).

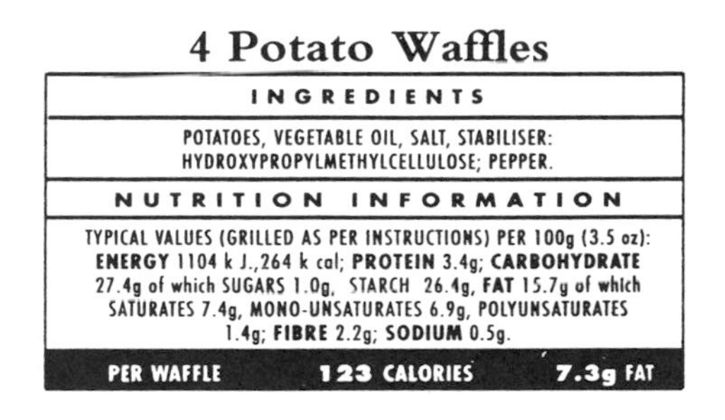

Figure 20.5 Nutritional panel.

This highlighted nutritional information box was incorporated on the packaging of all foods and drinks produced under own label by Sainsbury's, irrespective of whether the individual products carried the healthy eating symbol or not. In this way, all foods – even those products regarded as self-indulgent – could be considered within the context of a balanced diet.

20.1.4 Benchmarks

In response to our market research, information to customers was provided on how much fat and calories could be consumed on a daily basis by the average person in compliance with the 'healthy eating' guidelines. This information was calculated from the COMA Report and is summarized in Table 20.1. Clearly, these figures relate to the average man or woman and allowances need to be made for different individuals.

Table 20.1 Amount of fat and calories recommended by the guidelines

Woman		Man	
cal/day	fat (g/day)	cal/day	fat (g/day)
2000	70	2500	90

20.2 Customer communication programme

Having developed a strategy that would enable our customers to make a more informed choice, a customer information programme was developed to communicate this strategy. It was recognized that communication of issues such as 'healthy eating' is difficult, as it is a complex issue. It was, therefore, agreed to convey our 'healthy eating' strategy as enjoyable, convenient and affordable.

20.2.1 Customer leaflets

Customer leaflets are probably the most common form of conveying information to our customers. Four leaflets were therefore developed to communicate the key points of our strategy. The leaflets were attractively presented, with high-quality illustrations. Messages were simple, with clear product focus.

- *Balanced Diets for Hectic Lifestyles* – explained the overall strategy, the meaning of the symbol, introducing the tilted plate concept in support of the Department of Health, and guidance on how to achieve a balanced diet, by using the enhanced nutritional information per serving, and the fat and calories benchmarks.
- *Cutting Down on Fats* – easy tips on how to reduce overall fat consumption.
- *Take 5! Healthy Eating with Fruits and Vegetables* – introduced the 5-a-Day concept, serving sizes, and encouraged customers to explore the range of fruit and vegetables on offer.
- *Healthy Eating with Meat* – explained the role of meat in the concept of a balanced diet.

In all, over 1 million leaflets were produced and the success of these leaflets, which were available free of charge from our stores, is illustrated by the fact that they required reprinting twice within 9 months of the launch of the strategy.

20.2.2 Recipes

To respond to customer requirements for recipes, ideas and serving suggestions, a range of recipes was specially produced by the Home Economics Department which presented healthy eating as enjoyable, convenient and affordable. The recipes demonstrated how a balanced meal could be provided by careful selection of ingredients. For these recipes, and for all subsequent recipes produced by Sainsbury's in any form and for any purpose, the recipe cards, also available free from within the store, carried the highlighted calorie and fat per serving information. The recipes featured are listed in Table 20.2 with the associated calorie and fat per serving information.

Table 20.2 Recipes featured in the customer communication programme

	calories/serving	g fat/serving
Golden shepherds pie	382	11
Chicken casserole	227	7
Tuna and pasta bake	356	12
Autumn fruit fool	109	0.64
Turkey stir fry	217	9
Citrus bread and butter pudding	324	8

20.2.3 Advertising

The customer communication programme was supported by press advertising. Figure 20.6 shows an example which featured in all the major newspapers and women's magazines. In addition, at this time, Sainsbury's had developed a very successful national television advertising campaign based upon recipes presented by well-known celebrities. A special healthy eating recipe was developed – turkey and apricot bake – which was presented by Sue Barker, a former professional tennis player.

20.3 Assistance for special dietary groups

Serving 9 million customers/week, it is inevitable that many of our customers have special dietary requirements, such as pregnant women, diabetics, coeliacs and those suffering from food allergies which are rightly receiving increasing publicity and attention.

In order to ensure we discharged our responsibility to help all our customers eat more healthily, a strategy for special dietary groups was

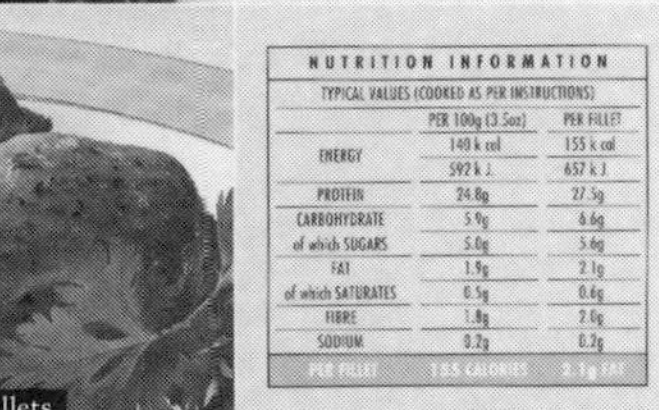

At Sainsbury's we won't starve you of information either.
They look good enough to eat don't they?
But are they good for you?
Are they crammed with calories, or full of fat?
If you love your food but want to keep a healthy balanced diet, the secret is to eat a wide variety of foods and watch your fat intake.
So that you know what is in the food you are eating, we have added a new panel at the bottom of our nutrition tables (like the examples shown on the page opposite).
You'll see at a glance not only the total nutrient content but even more importantly the calorie and fat content per serving.
And to help you identify those foods which are generally low in fat, we suggest that you look for the Sainsbury's healthy eating symbol on our packs.
In the next few months it will be introduced on more than a thousand everyday foods at Sainsbury's.
So, bon appetit.
SAINSBURY'S Where good food costs less
Sainsbury's Chilli Con Carne for one.
NUTRITION INFORMATION
TYPICAL VALUES (COOKED AS PER INSTRUCTIONS)
PER 100g (3.5oz) PER PACK
ENERGY 96 k cal 290 k cal
405 k J. 1216 k J.
PROTEIN 4.6g 12.8g
CARBOHYDRATE 12.5g 37.5g
of which SUGARS 1.7g 4.8g
STARCH 10.8g 32.7g
FAT 3.1g 9.3g
of which SATURATES 1.0g 3.0g
MONO-UNSATURATES 1.5g 4.5g
POLYUNSATURATES 0.6g 1.8g
FIBRE 1.0g 3.0g
SODIUM 0.2g 0.5g
Sainsbury's Fruit on the Bottom Bio Yogurt.
NUTRITION INFORMATION
STRAWBERRY AND REDCURRANT
TYPICAL VALUES PER 100g (3.5 oz): ENERGY 108 k cal, 455 k J.; PROTEIN 4.3g; CARBOHYDRATE 16.6g of which SUGARS 15.8g, STARCH 0.8g; FAT 2.7g of which SATURATES 1.7g; FIBRE 0.1g; SODIUM less than 0.1g.
Sainsbury's Orange and Yogurt Chicken Fillets.
NUTRITION INFORMATION
TYPICAL VALUES (COOKED AS PER INSTRUCTIONS)
PER 100g (3.5oz) PER FILLET
ENERGY 140 k cal 155 k cal
592 k J. 657 k J.
PROTEIN 24.8g 27.5g
CARBOHYDRATE 5.9g 6.6g
of which SUGARS 5.0g 5.6g
FAT 1.9g 2.1g
of which SATURATES 0.5g 0.6g
FIBRE 1.8g 2.0g
SODIUM 0.2g 0.2g
Sainsbury's Red Salmon with Cucumber Sandwich.
NUTRITION INFORMATION
TYPICAL VALUES PER 100g (3.5 oz): ENERGY 166 k cal, 700 k J.; PROTEIN 10.5g; CARBOHYDRATE 19.4g of which SUGARS 0.3g, STARCH 19.1g; FAT 5.2g of which SATURATES 0.9g, MONO-UNSATURATES 2.6g, POLYUNSATURATES 1.4g; FIBRE 3.0g; SODIUM 0.5g.
TYPICAL VALUES PER PACK: ENERGY 235 k cal, 990 k J.; PROTEIN 14.9g; CARBOHYDRATE 27.4g of which SUGARS 0.4g, STARCH 27.0g; FAT 7.3g of which SATURATES 1.3g, MONO-UNSATURATES 3.7g, POLYUNSATURATES 1.9g; FIBRE 4.3g; SODIUM 0.7g.

Figure 20.6 Press advertisement.

developed. A range of customer information brochures was produced to cover the following groups:

- *A Diet that's Nut Free*
- *A Diet that's Egg Free*
- *A Diet for Coeliacs*
- *A Diet for Diabetics*
- *A Diet that's Shellfish Free*
- *A Diet for Pregnant Women*
- *A Diet that's Milk Free*
- *A Diet that's Soya Free*

The brochure contained information regarding how customers who had special dietary requirements could obtain expert guidance; how foods were specially labelled for certain groups, e.g. a gluten-free symbol to appear on foods suitable for coeliacs; and, for those suffering from food allergies, Sainsbury's made available lists of foods free of specific allergenic components. These detailed product lists could be obtained free of charge from our Customer Services Department.

20.4 Endorsement

It was agreed that, in order for our initiative to have greatest impact, it would be essential for it to be endorsed by as wide a range of nutrition experts and organizations as possible. Many organizations and individuals had assisted in the formulation of the initiative.

Endorsements were sought, and were forthcoming, from the following organizations:

- Department of Health – including a message of support from the Under Secretary of State
- Ministry of Agriculture
- Dunn Nutrition Centre
- British Dietetic Association
- Coronary Prevention Group
- British Heart Foundation
- British Nutrition Foundation
- Imperial Cancer Research Fund

Room does not permit these endorsements to be printed in full, but the quotation of Dame Barbara Clayton, Chairman of the Nutrition Task Force is reproduced as an example:

> We all need a healthy, balanced diet, which is also enjoyable. Consumers require consistent and clear information to understand

that all foods can have a place in our diet. A good diet is about getting the balance right. It is not about banning foods The informative leaflets, clear labelling and recipes, which are available from Sainsbury's stores, will help us all achieve a balanced diet.

20.5 Staff briefing

Although our strategy was devised to help our customers, it would have been totally inconsistent with our company philosophy if we had not involved our staff in the quest to improve the nutritional status of our customers. Sainsbury's as a company employs almost 100 000 staff within the UK and that in itself is a significant proportion of the population. Staff briefings were, therefore, conducted to explain the links between diet and disease and the key components of the Sainsbury's strategy. Briefings were conducted reaching 2000 management personnel. Staff briefing packs were also developed for the branch staff.

Staff throughout the company were encouraged to develop healthy eating initiatives in restaurants and canteens to ensure that our own workforce benefited from this customer-oriented initiative. One of the most encouraging responses came from the management of the Sainsbury's Company Training Centre at Fanhams Hall, who developed the Fanhams Hall Healthy Eating Charter (Fig. 20.7) which is on display in the restaurant.

20.6 Launch

The initiative was launched at a specially convened press conference in September 1994, chaired by the Chairman of Sainsbury's, Mr David Sainsbury. The launch was opened by Dame Barbara Clayton, who explained to the conference the need for company-based healthy eating strategies based upon the *Health of the Nation* white paper. This was followed by an explanation of the Sainsbury's initiative by myself, which was then strongly endorsed by Dr Roger Whitehead, Director of the Dunn Nutrition Centre, and Chairman of the COMA Panel. Significantly, Dr Whitehead emphasized the need for responsible reporting to ensure that consumers received balanced and consistent messages on healthy eating. The conference was well attended by journalists and media representatives, as well as representatives of the key nutritional organizations. The launch was well reported in national and local newspapers, and generated sufficient interest for the initiative to be reported through a range of radio networks. In the main, the call for a responsible press was heeded.

HEALTHY EATING POLICY

FANHAMS HALL

SERVICE

- Half fat milk is always available
- Skimmed milk is available on request
- Flora is offered as an alternative to butter
- Deep fat frying is kept to a minimum
- Skin is removed from poultry
- Fresh fruit is always available
- Low fat dressings are offered
- Yogurt is always available as an alternative to cream
- Only high fibre white and brown bread are served

COOKING

- Half fat milk is always used
- Vegetable oil is always used
- Minimum amounts of salt are added
- Wholemeal flour is used in baking

Douglas Goodall MHCIMA
General Manager
Fanhams Hall

Figure 20.7 Fanhams Hall Healthy Eating Charter.

20.7 One year on

As we approach the first anniversary of the launch it is appropriate to reflect what has has been achieved through this initiative.

It should be remembered that our purpose was not to achieve a significant increase in sales. This was an exercise designed to inform those who required information, and demonstrate to the food industry that it was possible for one major company to contribute significantly to the objectives of the Nutrition Task Force.

Detailed market research needs to be undertaken to determine to what extent we have influenced our customers in their buying decisions, and how our initiative has helped them understand the perceived complexity of eating healthily.

However, two points are clear:

- whenever we have sought customer opinion, the response has been very positive;
- in addition, our initiative has generated interest within the food industry with some companies already following, or intending to follow, our lead.

Finally, it must be emphasized that the initiative was never an end in itself. We have, in many ways, only built a platform from which other initiatives can be launched – and these are under consideration.

The links between diet and disease are becoming more clearly established. There will be an undoubted future emphasis on diet as a means of disease prevention. The Sainsbury's Healthy Eating Initiative has given this culture change a hefty push – and we will continue to devise strategies that encourage and allow our customers to reap the benefits of greater scientific understanding.

21 The Heinz approach to improving public health by means of good food

NIGEL DICKIE

21.1 Introduction

Improving a nation's diet is a difficult and complex task. It involves all sections of society, but has to be based on individual choice. The food industry has an important role in translating current scientific knowledge into food production and marketing. It therefore has a great impact on the diets of those in developed and developing countries. Improving national diets has opposite meanings in these situations. In the former, it means controlling dietary excesses to minimize the risk of chronic diseases. On the other hand, in developing countries it means providing sufficient food and nutrients to sustain life and normal physical activity, and for children growth and development as well.

The food industry has an important responsibility in helping to improve national diets. In both the developed and developing countries producing and marketing the desired 'healthy' foods that taste good and are culturally appropriate makes good business sense. It is also good business sense for the industry to educate consumers on how these products may be used as part of a healthy, balanced diet and to find ways to promote the science of nutrition.

21.2 Improving the diet in developed nations

A healthy diet is part and parcel of a healthy life. The right approach to improving the health of the nation is not through sensational headlines, or more legislation or exhortation, but by working as a team. The UK government initiative of *The Health of the Nation* (Department of Health, 1992) has enabled a proper collaboration to take place between government, industry, expert bodies, educators, caterers and retailers.

Implementing Dietary Guidelines for Healthy Eating. Edited by Verner Wheelock. Published in 1997 by Blackie A&P, an imprint of Chapman & Hall, London. ISBN 0 7514 0304 0

21.3 Heinz philosophy and approach

Heinz is a worldwide producer of food products. Heinz varieties now number more than 4000 and its business extends to loyal consumers in more than 200 countries and territories. The company's two strongest global brands are Heinz and Weight Watchers, which in the United States are joined by brand names such as Ore-Ida, StarKist, 9-Lives and many others.

In the UK, although the association with 57 varieties is still a feature on Heinz labels today, the company now has a portfolio of over 400 products. This extends from the traditional ever-popular varieties of baked beans and ready-to-serve soups to salad cream and ketchup. There is also a range of prepared baby food, under both Heinz and Farley's brand names, which extends to more than 100 individual varieties, as well as a range of well over 100 Weight Watchers from Heinz products.

Heinz has always made it its business to take nutrition seriously. A commitment to producing good food from quality ingredients without the use of artificial colours or preservatives, whenever possible, is part of the company's philosophy. This dates back to company founder, Henry J. Heinz, who was a leading figure in the US campaign for pure food laws.

Principles of good nutrition have been a long-standing part of the company's quality policy. This clearly states:

> Heinz products shall be formulated and packaged with due consideration to current dietary recommendations and in conformity with legal requirements.
>
> Heinz will at all times comply with the law. It will be normal practice to comply with Government guidelines and relevant codes of practice in labelling and advertising.
>
> Heinz is committed to formulating products with the minimal use of additives.
>
> A list of additives will be maintained, listing their use for specific products.
>
> Board approval will be required for the use of any additive which is not on the approved list, or where an existing additive is used in another range of products.
>
> Detailed nutrition and dietetic information shall be made available to Health Professionals and interested consumers.
>
> The labels of all Heinz Branded products shall bear Nutritional Information.

21.4 Heinz sugar and salt reduction programme

In the early 1980s, conscious of the increasing weight of evidence of the health effects of excessive salt and sugar (NACNE, 1983; DHSS, 1984; British Medical Association, 1986), Heinz set out to reduce the levels of these ingredients in standard Heinz varieties. Although the levels of added salt and sugar in Heinz products do not make a major impact on intakes, the aim was to make significant reductions in these ingredients in the best-selling Heinz products, since this could do most to contribute toward improving public health. The use of salt or sugar substitutes was not considered as part of the programme.

This pioneering company initiative to reduce added salt and sugar levels is not transitory, but is in fact, part of an on-going Heinz Nutrition Policy. Heinz has made no secret of this. Comprehensive nutritional information, introduced across all products in 1986 and showing values for energy, protein, carbohydrate and fat as well as sugars, saturates, fibre and sodium, has referred to it. So too has widely distributed consumer literature. However, this unobtrusive policy of 'doing good by stealth' has never been promoted and the initiative was quite separate from the launch in 1985 of Weight Watchers from Heinz products.

21.4.1 Research and development of sugar and salt levels

In 1984 a large-scale project began to examine the levels of salt and sugar in over 100 Heinz varieties. The aim was to make recommendations as to potential reductions in their use, particularly where recipes contained both ingredients, possibly producing a counter-balancing effect. The project involved key product categories from soups and pasta to beans and sponge puddings. Of overriding concern was the need to ensure that proposed changes would not impact negatively on acceptability, or indeed would be preferred. Evidence from Heinz consumer research showed that many consumers may articulate a desire for healthier products but they are not prepared to trade off taste preference to achieve this.

Considerable research effort was needed in developing special batches of products with measured reductions of salt and sugar at a variety of levels. Tastings were first conducted in-house before commissioning extensive market research, including detailed trials with large samples of Heinz consumers up and down the country.

On such important issues as a possible recipe change the company had to be as certain as possible about the validity of the results. To this end statistically robust discrimination tests (repeat preference testing) enabled Heinz to check, first, whether consumers could genuinely tell the difference between two different recipes, and if they could, whether they had a preference between them and in what direction the preference lay.

At each stage in the research once a lower level of salt or sugar could be achieved in a recipe without being detected or impacting negatively on acceptability, more work was put in hand with the aim of reducing the level further. Reductions were made up to the point where research showed that the threshold of acceptability had been crossed and consumers not only showed statistically significant levels of discrimination, but they also demonstrated a clear preference for the original, higher-level product.

To take Heinz Ready-to-Serve Soup as an example, an initial study showed a reduction in the added sugar content from 3.9% to 3.4% – a reduction of 12.8% of the sugar – could be made without it being detected or impacting negatively on acceptability. Further work was then put in hand to take the reduction down by an additional 14%, in other words, to reduce the added sugar content by a quarter from the original. In doing so, the research showed that the company had crossed the threshold of acceptability. Not only did consumers show statistically significant levels of discrimination but they also demonstrated a clear preference for the original, higher-level product.

21.4.2 Reductions achieved

In 1986 reductions in the levels of added salt and sugar were made to most Heinz core products. Continuing to pursue a policy of striving to reduce sugar and salt levels, Heinz made a further round of changes in 1990. Thus over time, by means of a gradual weaning process and reflecting changes in consumer tastes, Heinz has been able to make reductions in salt and sugar levels of up to 25%. Examples of the changes are shown in Table 21.1.

Table 21.1 Examples of Heinz salt and sugar reduction programme

Heinz variety	Percentage added salt reduction	Percentage added sugar reduction		
	1986	1986	1990	Sugar reduction from pre-1986 level
Baked beans	14	12	10	20
Spaghetti in tomato sauce	10	8	15	24
Noodle Doodles	2	10	10	18
Ready-to-Serve tomato soup	17	13	5	17
Ravioli in beef and tomato sauce	18	100	–	100
Macaroni cheese	24	100	–	100

The nutritional modifications made to Heinz varieties involved around 70% of the company's sales volume. In adopting this policy the aim is to make a significant contribution towards improving public health. In the process, Heinz has built up a considerable bank of data from the tests conducted so as to be able to judge with a considerable degree of confidence what consumers are looking for in a particular product and how best to deliver that.

Heinz baby foods also benefited from a parallel programme of sugar reduction. Although savoury varieties do not contain sugar as an ingredient, in 1982 a maximum of 10% added sugar was adopted for desserts, which involved reducing added sugar in seven varieties – the greatest reduction being from 13.5%. In 1983, a maximum of 7.5% added sugar was adopted which involved reducing sugar in 21 varieties. In 1988 the level of added sugar was reduced to a maximum of 5% and in some instances to 'no added' sugar. Of 48 Heinz baby food desserts only 14 contain added sugar, and this is kept to within a low maximum of 5% in order to achieve an acceptable flavour. A policy of gradual reduction was adopted rather than a massive reduction from 13.5 to 5% overnight.

21.5 Heinz Light

Most Heinz products are naturally low in fat and saturates, such as beans and spaghetti in tomato sauce. However, the company's 'Light' initiative, launched in 1994, has looked at ways of reducing levels of fat in those products where fat is a significant component.

Examples that have been brought to market include Salad Cream with the taste and texture of the classic standard Heinz counterpart but with 25% less fat and 50% less saturates. Another introduction has been Heinz Light Mayonnaise which provides around 50% less fat and a 70% reduction in saturates.

21.6 Weight Watchers from Heinz

21.6.1 Meeting the needs for a healthy balanced diet

In affluent societies, chronic diseases such as coronary heart disease, hypertension and cancer are the major causes of death. These problems are largely related to lifestyle, a major part of which is dietary. Being overweight and consuming diets that are high in energy, fat, saturated fats and sodium and low in complex carbohydrates are conducive to these chronic diseases, the treatment of which is costing a large proportion of the national economies. A recent Office of Health Economics study (West, 1994) estimated that the financial burden of obesity on the UK National Health Service was almost £30 million in direct costs with a further £165 million in costs linked to diseases where obesity is a risk factor, such as non-insulin-dependent diabetes mellitus.

Health authorities in affluent societies recognize the importance of achieving and maintaining a healthy body weight through healthy eating and physical activity. *The Health of the Nation* (Department of Health, 1992) set a target to reduce the percentage of men and women aged 16–64 who are obese by at least 25% for men and 33% for women by 2005 (from 8% for men and 12% for women in 1986/87 to no more than 6% and 8%, respectively). Data for 1993 (Department of Health, 1995) continue to show that the trend is away from the target, with 13% of men and 16% of women aged 16–64 who are classified as obese.

In the United States, the nutritional goal by the year 2000 is to reduce overweight to a prevalence of no more than 20% of people (a 23% decrease) and to reduce dietary fat intake to an average of 30% of calories (a 17% decrease). Included in these dietary goals is increasing the availability of low-fat food products. Weight control is emphasized since obesity has a significant negative impact on the risk of coronary heart disease, hypertension and certain types of cancer. Controlling fat intake is the major dietary concern since excessive fat intake contributes to obesity as well as the chronic diseases.

Eating 'healthy' was considered a lifestyle. With the promotion of the health goals for the year 2000, it is now a way of life. Therefore marketing foods that are 'healthy' and tasty is good business sense. The food industry has risen to meet the challenge of providing 'healthy' foods. Since the 1990s there has been a proliferation of low-calorie and/or low-fat products in all food categories.

The production of low-calorie and low-fat foods is achieved through reformulation and portion-control, aided by the use, where possible, of substitutes for fat and sugar. Each year about 15–20% of new products launched in the United States are low-calorie and/or 'healthy' foods. In 1991, 1200 new products claiming to be low fat or non-fat were introduced on US grocery store shelves.

Acquired in 1978, Weight Watchers is the gold standard for weight loss in the United States and elsewhere. Each week more than 1million people attend Weight Watchers meetings. In addition, Heinz markets an array of Weight Watchers brand food products in the United States, Europe and Australia.

The Weight Watchers Company has launched about 150 new products in the US since 1991, the newest of which are called 'Smart Ones' – a range of frozen ready meals that contain 200 calories and only 1 g of fat. Today the company has a product line of about 400 foods. These products can be part of the 7-day menu plan that conforms to the healthy eating concept and delivers all the essential nutrients to satisfy 100% of the recommended daily allowances of nutrients.

A national survey in America conducted in 1991 by the Calorie Control Council showed that two-thirds of adult Americans were using reduced-fat foods and beverages. The most popular low-fat products were low-fat dairy products, including cheese, ice-cream, yogurt and sour cream. Low-fat dips and snack foods were consumed by one-third of the survey population. One quarter of adults consumed low-fat cakes, breads and other baked goods.

The primary reason for the Americans in the survey to use low-calorie or low-fat foods was to stay in better overall health. More than two-thirds of these consumers were not on a diet. Maintaining current weight and an attractive appearance were the second and third reasons.

The use of these low-calorie and low-fat foods will increase as the industry continues to improve products that meet the high expectations of consumers. While the number of 'healthy' foods is increasing, there is also an increase in services, to assist individuals to achieve and maintain a healthy body weight through proper eating and physical activity. A good example is the Weight Waters International classroom programmes which are personalized to help the members achieve and maintain healthy body weight. In addition, Weight Watchers in 1990 launched Health Watch 2000 which is a comprehensive education programme to help Americans outside the Weight Watchers classroom situation to achieve the goals set by Healthy People 2000.

There are now both products and services that are aimed at helping individuals to assume a healthy lifestyle. This is an initiative of the food industry that assists the improvement of the national diet. This is not isolated in America but exists in most industrialized countries. The UK is no exception.

Marketed under the Weight Watchers from Heinz brand in the UK and launched in 1985 the range offers a more direct approach to healthy eating. It is now the country's largest 'healthy packaged grocery' brand (AGB, 1995). The guiding philosophy behind the brand is to provide 'Great tasting, everyday foods which are lower in fat, sugar and calories to help maintain a healthy lifestyle and stay in shape'. The products must deliver on taste in order to gain mainstream acceptance, since Weight Watchers from Heinz products are normal, everyday foods – not marginalized meal replacements or food substitutes. This can be technically challenging where fat or salt content is critical to a product's performance in terms of taste, flavour or mouthfeel.

The Weight Watchers from Heinz range in the UK now includes around 120 products across 19 market sectors (Table 21.2).

Table 21.2 Examples of the Weight Watchers from Heinz range

Ambient	Frozen
Canned soup	Ready meals
Instant soup	Ice-cream
Baked beans	Desserts
Canned pasta	
Salad dressing	
Jam	
Breakfast cereal	
Rice pudding	
Cookies	Chilled
Potato toppers	Low-fat spread
Cooking sauces	Cheese

21.6.2 Weight Watchers from Heinz nutritional criteria

So as to offer a lower calorie alternative by providing reduced levels of fat or sugar, or both, the Weight Watchers from Heinz brand has adopted clear criteria as a central part of a comprehensive nutritional policy. Depending on the individual product category, the aim is to provide a nutritional profile with a 25% reduction in calories through fat and or sugar reduction, or through recipe modification. A reduced sodium level is also a stated aim where appropriate and achievable, remembering always that the product has to taste as good as the 'standard' equivalent, or indeed better.

Taking frozen ready meals as an example category, the target value for fat is that it should provide no more than 30% of food energy, saturates should provide no more than 10%, while the level of sodium should be no more than a maximum of 1 g/serving.

The Weight Watchers from Heinz range of Cookies contain at least 40% less fat and provide the additional benefit of portion control since the Cookies are sold in a box containing individually wrapped portions of two Cookies.

One of the latest additions to the Weight Watchers from Heinz range is a vanilla and chocolate chip gateau of vanilla ice-cream, called Dolcetta. It is a reduced-fat dessert providing 45% less fat than the current brand-leading product in this market.

21.6.3 Product development

Product development is often particularly challenging. Driven by the organoleptic requirements, the self-imposed nutritional criteria, legal and technical constraints, the challenge is to develop a recipe that provides a good tasting product without taste compromise (Fig. 21.1). Reduced energy and fat generally means lower fat and total solids content. This can result in loss of quality during shelf-life unless a 'total' recipe is developed. The scope for driving fat and saturates down further has to be balanced by constraints over the choice of fat and, for some foods, compositional standards. For example, ice-cream is currently controlled by the Ice Cream Regulations 1967, which give a definition of ice-cream and lay down the requirement for a minimum fat content of 5%. A definition is likely to remain in some form, requiring the presence of fat, but deregulation may mean the removal of the requirement for a minimum 5%.

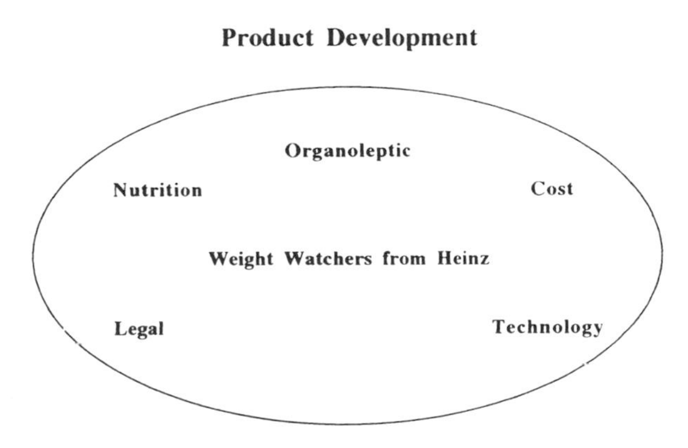
Product Development
Organoleptic
Nutrition
Cost
Weight Watchers from Heinz
Legal
Technology
• Good tasting product - no taste compromise
• Meets nutrition criteria
• At the right price - price parity with full calorie product

Figure 21.1 Weight Watchers from Heinz product development considerations.

Innovation by ingredient suppliers has created opportunities to substantially reduce product fat levels without impairing taste or texture quality, but there is no universal 'magic' ingredient to service all requirements. The challenge is to use systems of ingredients and processes developed specifically for individual products. Successful application requires substantial development and technical input. Furthermore, it must be at the right price, since Heinz does not believe consumers should have to pay more to choose a healthier alternative. Products in the Weight Watchers from Heinz range should be priced at parity with their full-calorie counterparts.

In developing such products taste remains of paramount importance since Heinz research shows that consumers are not prepared to sacrifice taste in order to achieve their healthy eating goals. There is a substantial investment cost in developing 'healthy eating' products in terms of ingredient cost and development resource but there are substantial further opportunities in areas where there are high-fat contributors to the normal diet.

21.7 Consumer education

The company's commitment to the provision of information to consumers on nutritional matters has continued over many years. As well as an established range of literature on healthy eating, food safety and nutritional labelling with a total of more than 1 million pieces in distribution, Heinz has supported a number of school teaching aids which have received wide acclaim. All teaching materials have been prepared in close collaboration with a team of educationalists and teachers to ensure the resources are appropriate for National Curriculum requirements.

A survey commissioned by Weight Watchers from Heinz and undertaken by Gallup (1992) highlighted one of the underlying problems in implementing healthy eating. While 75% of the population recognized the key elements to a healthy lifestyle, the survey also found that 14% were trying to include more saturated fat in their diet and only 27% were trying to include more carbohydrate foods in their diet. Although people knew what they could be doing to improve the balance of their diet, seemingly few knew how to achieve it.

The survey also pointed to the fact that 75% of people surveyed felt that dietary guidance would help them to achieve a better balance to their diet. In response, Weight Watchers from Heinz took an initiative to offer personalized dietary guidance as part of a nationwide competition – the Health Sense Challenge. Six 'finalists' of up to four people were given the opportunity of receiving tailored practical healthy eating advice.

21.8 Improving diets in developing countries

In developing countries, the struggle remains in providing enough food and nutrients to sustain everyday life. Hunger afflicts most severely older infants and young children. FAO and WHO have estimated that 1 billion people in over 100 countries suffer from blindness caused by vitamin A deficiency; mental and physical retardation from iodine deficiency; and impaired motor development and behaviour from iron deficiency. At the World Summit for Children in 1990, 71 heads of state and senior policy-makers from 80 other countries endorsed the goals and planned action to:

- virtually eliminate iodine deficiency disorders as a public health problem;
- virtually eliminate vitamin A deficiency and its consequences, including blindness;
- reduce by one-third the 1990 levels of iron deficiency anaemia among women of child-bearing age, by the year 2000.

In industrialized countries through food fortification and nutritional education, iodine and vitamin A deficiency are virtually eliminated and iron deficiency is under control. If the same results are to be achieved in developing countries, fortification of culturally appropriate foods and effective nutritional education must take place.

21.9 Heinz initiative in China

In 1983, Heinz was invited to China to assess the opportunity of establishing a business in baby foods that were lacking in a country in which the birth rate was 20 million per year. Production of nutritious baby foods was listed as a priority of the Chinese government.

Heinz assessed the feasibility of building a baby food factory in Guangzhou in southern China and identified the type and nutritional quality of the baby foods. Nutrition was given top priority in the project. The immediate task was to seek out the distinguished paediatricians, nutritionists and public health administrators and to find out as much as possible about what the Chinese infants were fed and how well they were fed. The Chinese 'experts' contacted were in Guangzhou and in the Academy of Preventive Medicine in Beijing.

The understanding in 1984 was that during the first 3–4 months of life, infants were similar in size or slightly bigger than US infants, but thereafter they tended to grow at a significantly slower rate. The infants were, by and large, breast-fed and were weaned by 3–4 months of life. The weaning food consisted of rice water to start, followed by congee (or rice gruel) and soft rice. Some egg yolk or whole egg, meat or fish might be added. In most instances the amount of protein-rich foods was small. Seasonal fruit was occasionally given to infants but vegetables were uncommon. By about 1 year of age the infants were fed table foods.

Locally produced baby foods were mostly rice flour and baby cakes made from rice flour. They were not fortified and were of little nutritional value. Imported infant cereals were scarce and expensive. It was therefore not surprising that the major nutritional problems among infants were sub-optimal growth, iron deficiency anaemia, and vitamin D deficiency rickets. Dietary deficiencies of calcium, riboflavin and thiamin were also considered prevalent.

With this knowledge it was recommended that the first product that Heinz should produce be rice based, the staple of most of China, which would be for infants starting from 3 – 4 months. A high-protein soy product should be produced for older infants. These products would be fortified with iron, calcium, thiamin, and riboflavin at 100% of the Chinese recommended daily allowances per serving of 25 g.

Wet baby foods in jars were not possible because of the lack of meat, vegetables and fruit that would meet specifications and the high cost of glass jars. A condition Heinz placed was that the baby foods had to be affordable, which meant that all the ingredients had to be locally produced.

Since 1986 when the first Heinz baby foods were launched in China, the capacity of the factory has been expanded twice to meet demand and the product line has increased. Furthermore, fortification with zinc, and vitamins A and D is now included. Feedback from health professionals and research indicates that the products are meeting the nutritional needs of the infants and alleviating deficiency of the micronutrients.

During early visits to China in 1984, it appeared that nutritional science was weak. One of the main reasons was that during the Cultural Revolution, which started in 1966, nutrition was considered reactionary. Human nutritional education and research were stopped. Although nutrition was reinstituted in the universities in the late 1970s a whole generation of nutritionists was lost. It was clear that China needed assistance in re-establishing nutritional sciences.

For this purpose, the Heinz Institute of Nutritional Sciences (HINS) was created in 1986 as an entity that was at arm's length to the local food company. HINS has since:

- organized an annual international symposium on maternal and infant nutrition;
- published the proceedings of the symposia;
- published and circulated free-of-charge to health professionals a quarterly newsletter on maternal and child nutrition;
- supported small research projects, the results of which have been published in local and international journals;
- facilitated academic exchanges between universities in China and North America;
- developed educational materials for educators and consumers.

Thus far, HINS is meeting its objective of facilitating the development of nutritional sciences in China.

The success of HINS in China makes it a good model to emulate. Today, the HINS model is being applied in Thailand, Russia and Hungary. It will be expanded as Heinz expands its horizon in the baby food business. In the industrialized countries such as Australia, Canada, Italy, UK and US, similar Heinz nutritional programmes that promote the advancement of nutritional sciences are already in existence.

21.10 The future

In both the developed and developing countries producing and marketing the desired 'healthy' foods that taste good and are culturally appropriate makes good business sense. It is also good business sense for the industry to educate consumers on the proper use for these products and to find ways to promote the science of nutrition.

The Heinz policy of acceptable change through a careful programme of gradual salt and sugar reduction rather than a massive reduction 'overnight' will continue. The round of changes introduced in 1990 will be reviewed and reassessed for opportunities that could lead to further nutritional modification. At the same time, Weight Watchers from Heinz will continue to expand its range of products within existing categories as well as developing a presence in new sectors offering lower-calorie alternatives with reduced levels of fat and/or sugar.

As a responsible and responsive company, Heinz is committed to the objectives of *The Health of the Nation* white paper (Department of Health, 1992) and aims to continue to contribute towards improving public health by means of good food. From its earliest days Heinz led industry in many key areas of nutrition. Heinz is committed to continuing this policy into the future.

Improving the national diets so as to markedly reduce obesity and nutrition-related chronic diseases on the one hand, and to eliminate micronutrient deficiencies on the other by the year 2000 can be achieved. The food industry is able and willing to be a full partner in this endeavour.

References

AGB Superpanel (1995) MAT March.

British Medical Association (1986) *Diet, Nutrition and Health*, Report of the Board of Science and Education, BMA, London.

Department of Health (1992) *The Health of the Nation: A Strategy for Health in England*, HMSO, London.

Department of Health (1995) *Fit for the Future*, Second Progress Report on the Health of the Nation, HMSO, London.

DHSS, (Department of Health and Social Security) (1984) *Diet and Cardiovascular Disease*, Report on Health and Social Subjects 28, COMA, HMSO, London.

Gallup (1992) *Survey of Knowledge and Attitudes about Diet and Lifestyle*, commissioned by H.J. Heinz Co. Ltd.
NACNE (1983) *A Discussion Paper for Nutritional Guidelines for Health Education in Britain*, The Health Education Council, London.
West, R. (1994) *Obesity*, Office of Health Economics, London.

22 Food industry responses to government dietary guidelines

JOHANNA M. HIGNETT

Over half a century before the science of modern nutrition was formally recognized, Henri Nestlé started the infant nutrition industry with the invention of his famous 'Farine Lactée', a milk-based infant cereal. As such the Nestlé company has been consciously and actively aware of the importance of the nutritional value of food products ever since it was founded in 1866. Nestlé is now the largest food company in the world, selling 15 000 products in every market in the world, and employing some 200 000 people in over 60 countries.

The year the company was founded, the population of the world was less than 1 billion, by the year 2000 it is expected to have increased to 6 billion. Medicine, hygiene, better housing and working conditions have played a part in this population explosion, but so has food. People are living longer now than ever before and the importance of good food cannot be overstated.

Malnutrition can be subdivided into undernutrition and overnutrition. The former is still a major problem in developing parts of the world where problems such as iron, iodine and vitamin A deficiencies are prevalent. However, the problems of overnutrition are becoming ever more apparent in the developed world. These problems have stimulated governments to issue healthy eating guidelines. Both qualitative guidelines and quantitative targets have been issued. These have provided benchmarks enabling the food industry to work together to determine strategies to respond to the recommendations.

22.1 Background

In many of the countries of the developed world diseases of affluence far outnumber other health problems that predominate in underdeveloped countries. Coronary heart disease, stroke, cancers and obesity are among those conditions that are recognized as being causes of premature or avoidable ill health and where effective interventions should be possible.

Implementing Dietary Guidelines for Healthy Eating. Edited by Verner Wheelock. Published in 1997 by Blackie A&P, an imprint of Chapman & Hall, London. ISBN 0 7514 0304 0

Significant reductions in both morbidity and mortality statistics are expected following adoption of the recommendations. Obviously, diet is only one factor implicated in development of such conditions and a number of other life-style factors are also involved. These include smoking, stress and physical exercise.

A number of governments in the developed world have studied the links between diet and disease and have issued recommendations for the diets of the populations in those countries. These countries include the United States of America, Sweden, Norway, Canada, the United Kingdom and Australia.The UK government's *Health of the Nation* white paper (1992) (Department of Health, 1992, 1994) and the Committee on Medical Aspects of Food Policy (COMA) Reports including the Report of the Cardiovascular Review Group (1994) (Committee on Medical Aspects of Food Policy 1991, 1994) are the most recent dietary guidelines in the UK. Both of these contain quantified dietary targets with the aim of improving the health of the UK population.

The recommendations from these two reports and the role the food industry plays in assisting the population to achieve these guidelines will be discussed in more detail. In addition, examples of initiatives taken by other Nestlé businesses throughout the world will be explored.

22.2 Dietary targets

In the past 10 years in the UK a number of dietary recommendations have been issued and endorsed by the UK government, the Health Education Authority and COMA (Committee on Medical Aspects of Food Policy, 1991, 1994; Department of Health, 1992, 1994). All reports have had a common thread, being the recommendation to reduce the average fat intake of the population and, in particular, the average intake of saturated fatty acids. This common thread is seen through all the sets of dietary recommendations issued throughout the developed world. The COMA Report

Table 22.1 *The Health of the Nation* and COMA recommendations

Health of the Nation (1992)	COMA (1994)
<35% energy from total fat	<35% energy from total fat
<19% energy from saturates	<10% energy from saturates
	No increase in total PUFA intakes
	Increase *n*-3 PUFA to 0.2 g/day
	Intakes of *trans* remain at 2% of energy
	Cholesterol intakes should not rise
	50% energy from carbohydrate
	6 g salt/day
	Increase potassium to 3.5 g/day

PUFA, polyunsaturated fatty acids.

(1994) is unique in that it is the first report that includes recommendations on the types of foods that could be included in a diet that meets the recommendations. *The Health of the Nation* (1992) and COMA (1994) recommendations are in Tables 22.1 and 22.2.

Table 22.2 COMA (1994) food recommendations

Eat two portions of fish, one of which should be oily, weekly
Use reduced fat spreads and dairy products instead of full fat
Replace fats rich in saturated fatty acids with those low in saturates and rich in monounsaturates
Increase consumption of vegetables, fruit, potatoes and bread by at least 50%

22.3 Current intakes

The proportion of fat in the UK diet has increased steadily throughout the twentieth century (Table 22.3). Although recent evidence suggests that this increase has ceased and is beginning to reverse, there are still changes to be made. Alongside these trends is a marked reduction in levels of energy expenditure. Although energy intakes in the UK are declining, this decline is not as steep as that for energy expenditure. The obvious consequence is a net increase in the levels of obesity.

Table 22.3 UK dietary intakes of energy and fat over previous years

Year	Energy intakes	% Energy from fat	g of fat/day
1900s	2760	32	98
1955	2640	36	106
1981	2210	42	103

22.4 Dietary surveys

Recent dietary surveys (Dietary Survey of British Adults (Gregory *et al.*, 1990), and National Food Survey (Ministry of Agriculture, Fisheries and Food, 1992, 1995)) indicate that the average consumption of fat and saturates represent 40% and 15%, respectively, of total energy intake. In gram terms for an average 2000 kcal diet this translates to 89 g fat of which 33 g is saturates. At the desired levels of 35% energy from fat and 10% energy from saturates this equates to 78 g of fat of which 22 g is saturates per day at this energy intake. Therefore, in practical terms, achieving the government targets for fat means an average reduction in fat intakes of 11–14 g/day.

An additional analysis of the Dietary Survey of British Adults (Ministry of Agriculture, Fisheries and Food, 1994) has investigated the proportion of individuals actually meeting the targets currently. In practice, the majority of the population does not achieve the targets set. However, certain subgroups can be identified who meet certain targets. Ten per cent of the adult population had less than 35% energy from fat, 2.8% met the target for saturates and 12.6% met the target for non-milk extrinsic sugars (<10% energy from sugars added to products). Less than 1% of the population met a combination of these. Many studies have illustrated that fat and sugar intakes are inversely related in the diet of free-living individuals. As the fat level in the diet is reduced, the sugar is seen to increase, when expressed as a percentage of total energy intakes. This phenomenon is commonly known as the sugar–fat see-saw. Clearly, care needs to be exercised when giving health messages and dietary recommendations to ensure that the final result is both achievable and provides real benefit in health terms.

Changes in fat, carbohydrate and sugar contents of diets cannot be discussed in isolation from the foods that contain them. We eat foods, not proteins, fats, carbohydrates, vitamins and minerals. It is in translating government recommendations from health professionals into foods that food industry professionals are able to use their knowledge and experience to develop tasty, competitive products that the public will enjoy. Providing a variety of products and suitable educational methods are two important parts of promoting healthy eating.

22.5 Achieving the healthy eating targets

Achievement of the UK government targets for fat consumption involves a reduction of an average of 11–14 g of fat/day. When expressed in this manner it seems a target that is perfectly achievable. Based on average consumption figures from the UK National Food Survey, the following daily dietary changes would more than achieve these goals: changing all milk to skimmed milk, a saving of 11.9 g of fat; changing all butter and margarine to low-fat spread, a saving of 13.3 g of fat; changing all hard cheese to cottage cheese, a saving of 4.5 g. The total fat saving would be approximately 29.7 g of fat, an amount that would more than meet the targets set by the government. These could be straightforward dietary changes, but, in practice, would probably not be acceptable to the majority of the population. However, changing milk to semi-skimmed milk and cheese to reduced-fat cheese would be more acceptable changes as the resulting product is not too dissimilar to the full-fat standard. Fats are important in foods for organoleptic and functional reasons as well as nutritional.

22.6 Why do we eat fat?

In nutritional and physiological terms fat supplies energy and when fat levels are reduced, energy levels are reduced. This could pose a problem for young children who have high energy requirements relative to their size. Fat-reduced products, especially milks, are not recommended for children under 5 years of age by the UK government. Fat is the carrier of the fat-soluble vitamins (vitamins A, D, E and K) and reducing fat levels in foods automatically reduces the levels of these vitamins. Intakes of micronutrients are largely adequate in the UK, but certain subgroups could need special surveillance. Importantly, certain fats, principally polyunsaturated vegetable fats, provide the essential fatty acids.

Fat plays a key role in developing the palatability of foods. A fat-free diet would consist mainly of carbohydrate foods. It would be largely unpalatable, very bulky and, for many people, would be considered unpleasant to eat.

Fat is a major flavour carrier in foods and when fat levels are reduced the taste of the product can also be affected. Fat plays a key role in texture, helping develop the short texture in biscuits. It also helps develop mouthfeel, examples being the creamy mouthfeel of whole milk, whole milk yoghurt and cream. Fats and oils play a very important role in development of texture in fried foods. Fats can be heated to high temperatures and used to give crispy textures to fried foods. Low-fat spreads are not suitable for cooking, baking or frying due to their high water content and therefore do not mimic the properties of full-fat margarines or butter (Gurr, 1992).

It is clear that fat reductions are technically feasible, but in many cases the results do not meet the qualities of the original product or the consumers' expectations in terms of taste and functionality. In order for reduced fat products to be accepted by consumers they need to deliver various attributes to meet consumer needs and expectations. They need to be correctly targeted and marketed, they need to reach consumers' demands in terms of taste, functionality and price, and once these have been met the product has a chance of survival in the increasingly competitive marketplace. Where a product does not deliver on any one of these characteristics, its likelihood of competing in the marketplace is reduced.

22.7 Input from the UK food industry

Developing products that assist the public to achieve reduced levels of fat in their diets is not a straightforward procedure of removal of fat. This can have many consequences in nutritional and sensory terms, as detailed above. However, the food industry can, and does, use its technical expertise in providing products with reduced levels of fats and saturates to meet consumer demands.

Following publication of the UK government's *Health of the Nation* document a number of working groups were established to examine opportunities to implement the recommendations in various sectors. The Nutrition Task Force commissioned four working groups to look at four distinct areas of food provision. These covered catering, education, the National Health Service and the food chain (Department of Health, 1994). The latter group was most concerned with the production, distribution and marketing of foods to consumers. The Food Chain Working Group looked at opportunities for the food industry to contribute to the target for reducing fat intakes. They identified two steps to be undertaken, firstly a 'fat audit' assessing the sources and types of fat in a product, and secondly the potential for fat reductions, both marginal and more substantial.

22.7.1 Fat audit

The food industry is encouraged to undertake a fat audit of all its key products. This will identify the quantity and quality of fat in products and can be used to identify options for changing the amount and types of fat in accordance with the *Health of the Nation* and COMA guidelines. The procedures involved in a fat audit are outlined in Table 22.4. First, the level of fat in a product is determined. The ingredients that contribute to this fat and the proportions in which they do so are identified. The potential for reducing fat levels by reducing levels of the ingredients that contribute to the level of fat is elucidated. In products such as milk or margarine it is easy to identify the sources of fat; however, in a more complex product such as lasagne the ingredients that contribute to the total level of fat will be numerous. Proposed modifications are prepared on a small scale, and sensory analysis must follow to ensure that any changes that are made to the product do not compromise the taste or functionality of that product. Finally, if all steps have been undertaken, the modified recipe can be introduced.

Table 22.4 Considerations in reducing fat levels

Qualitative and quantitative analysis of fat in a product
Potential for marginal and more substantial fat reductions
Effects on taste and functionality
Legal constraints
Labelling and claims

The use of claims on products to identify those foods that have reduced levels of fat is a subject of debate. One school of thought suggests that use of a lowered fat claim on a product could prejudice the expectations of that product, perhaps encouraging some to purchase, and discouraging others. As there are a number of low- and reduced-fat products on the market, consumers are likely to have preformed ideas about the taste delivery of these products. There is a clear need for more research into expectations and education about the roles of reduced-fat foods.

22.7.2 Fat reductions

The food industry is encouraged to use the fat audit to identify the potential for reducing fat levels in products. In the past, product development to reduce fat levels has been undertaken to meet legislative targets so claims could be made, 'low' meaning 50% less and 'reduced' 25% less. This has restricted fat reductions in some products and has, in some cases, resulted in products which lose taste and/or functionality. It must be remembered that all nutrients, including fat, do play an important role in food functionally as well as nutritionally. The Health of the Nation's Nutrition Task Force proposes that the food industry assess the possibility for marginal fat reductions (5–25%) across a wide number of products. These changes are unlikely to have significant effects on technical functionality or on consumer acceptability. To date many of the initiatives to reduce fat levels in foods have been limited to certain sectors of the food industry. The proposal to undertake marginal fat reductions is relevant to most, if not all sectors of the industry. The cumulative effect of these smaller reductions in fat levels across a wider range of foods could be significant in achieving the targets set by the government. Opportunities for more substantial reductions in fat content are also identified through the fat audit, and for changes in the balance of saturates, monounsaturates and polyunsaturates. To date the response of the food industry has demonstrated willingness and technical expertise to achieve the recommendations.

22.7.3 Intakes of starchy foods, fruits and vegetables

If the targets for reductions in fat intakes are to be met, there will be a net reduction in the total energy content of the diet. This drop in energy can be replaced by an increased consumption of carbohydrate-containing foods, namely pasta, bread, potatoes, rice and other cereals and grains. This confers a number of added benefits, including increased bulk, increased fibre intakes, increased satiety and decreased energy density of the diet.

In addition, people should, and are being advised to, increase their intakes of fruits and vegetables, ideally to approximately five or six servings per day. Fruits and vegetables are the principal sources of anti-oxidant nutrients (namely beta-carotene, vitamin C and vitamin E). Compelling scientific evidence indicates that these three major anti-oxidants play important roles in preventing or delaying the onset of major degenerative diseases. Fruit and vegetable intake in the UK is notoriously low when compared with the Mediterranean countries. The food industry is now playing a major role in increasing the use of fruits and vegetables in products and promoting increased consumption of these. Achieving increased intakes of fruits, vegetables and starchy carbohydrates can be translated into a public message that is straightforward and easy to understand for a number of reasons. These include the fact that people are familiar with these foods and how to use them, they are relatively cheap and, for the most part, readily available. The target expressed in servings per day is clear and easy to interpret, as opposed to being in grams or percentage of a recommended intake for instance.

Last and by no means least, we are giving a positive message. Health messages do tend to be negative, advising avoidance or reduction of foods or nutrients. Positive messages are more likely to be well received as people are being advised to eat more!

22.7.4 Communicating nutrition

The food manufacturing industry, along with health educators and retailers can, and do, play key roles in educating the consumer about the basic principles of healthy eating. Nestlé continue to monitor consumer interest and understanding of nutrition and to identify opportunities to improve nutritional education through informative labelling and promotions on food products.

Consumer research in the UK suggests that the interest shown in food, ingredients and nutrition has risen over the past 10 years and is expected to continue to do so. The UK Ministry of Agriculture, Fisheries and Food commissioned a study to assess the usage and understanding of food labels (Research Services Limited, 1995). A nationally representative sample of 1000 individuals who were all involved in selection and purchasing of food for a household were questioned. The results showed that 59% of respondents consult nutritional information on packs, of these 51% take the information into account when purchasing foods. Sixty-eight per cent of the respondents checked the fat content of products, and 49% checked for energy or calories. Information expressed per serving was seen to be the most useful, with 65% of respondents preferring this, whereas only 21% preferred 'per 100 g' information.

An increasing number of products now carry nutritional information, and this is now becoming easier to understand as it is presented in a standard format in accordance with the EC Nutrition Labelling Directive (1990). This states that where information is provided it is done so on a per 100 g basis and optionally per serving. It is clear from research that has been undertaken that per serving information is more useful to consumers than per 100 g. Both fat and energy levels are the two pieces of information checked most often (National Health Survey, 1993; Research Services Limited, 1995).

Many manufacturers already include full nutritional labels on their products and should be encouraged to continue this. Where space permits additional information showing nutrient values per serving should be included. However, although most consumers have a reasonable idea of the number of calories they require daily, they have little, if any, idea of what the targets for fat mean in quantitative terms (i.e. g/day). A number of retailers and manufacturers have explored options for explaining the nutritional information in different ways, such as graphically, with varying degrees of success. Any scheme to illustrate nutritional information must be meaningful, clear, concise and not mislead the consumer. It is important that foods are not singled out as being good or bad, but that a balanced intake is promoted.

Consumers could be educated to count up the contribution to calorie or fat intake of the various servings of food consumed in a day. Recommended intakes would enable them to compare this total amount with an average daily target, given in grams or calories. This could be a simple way of encouraging consumers to be aware of the amount of fat they are eating and the foods that contribute the most fat to their diets.

22.8 Nestlé healthy eating initiatives

Nestlé is a large, multinational company that is well known by its brand names. Brands such as Nescafé, Findus, Stouffers, Maggi, Libby's, Rowntree, Crosse and Blackwell, Carnation and Buitoni are but a few of those in the Nestlé portfolio. Good food and nutrition are essential to life, to health and to well-being. Nestlé has always recognized this, and has also recognized that nutrition *per se* is of no use unless the food is eaten and for this it has to have appetite appeal. Pleasure, taste, fun and convenience are thus an integral part of Nestlé product strategy.

Findus Lean Cuisine is the flagship nutritionally modified product in the United Kingdom, and in many other major markets in the Western world. It offers customers a calorie-counted, low-fat and tasty frozen ready meal. However, healthy eating does not just involve specific ranges of products, it relates to every product in the Nestlé portfolio. Sound nutrition is about balance and variety in all things. Findus products, Nestlé Ice Cream, Nescafé coffees, Buitoni pasta, Crosse and Blackwell and Maggi culinary products, Rowntree confectionery, Libby's juices and Nestlé breakfast cereals all play a role in a healthy diet.

The Nestlé operating companies worldwide have long been active in informing the consumer on food and nutrition. To ensure the flow of information, the Nestlé Nutrition Centre has been newly created in Switzerland (Nestlé Publications, 1995). It will work closely with the business units, the headquarters, the operating companies and the research and development units. The development of this unit strengthens the Nestlé commitment to nutrition and will act as a link between all the different markets.

In selecting a diet a number of factors influence the foods we choose for our own diets. These include cultural background, health, age, gender and social status. Two additional factors that can often be overlooked, especially when discussing healthy eating, are that all food must taste good and be enjoyed. The repeated purchase and use of a product by a consumer is largely based on the fact that it tastes good. If the taste delivery of a product is poor when first tried, the chance that a consumer will try that product for a second time is very small. Guaranteeing and monitoring a high taste quality in all products is an important part of product development and manufacture for Nestlé.

The development of healthy eating initiatives in any market will always centre around objectives that are physically and technically feasible, are within the local legal constraints and promote balanced, varied, tasty and enjoyable eating. Here we take the opportunity to explore some of the initiatives taken in various Nestlé markets in the Western world.

22.9 Nestlé UK

Dietary guidelines from the UK government impact the business in three major ways. They relate to our products, our customers and our people. Each of these areas will be discussed in detail below.

22.9.1 Products

Initiatives in relation to products and product developments, such as fat audits and marginal fat reductions have been formulated in response to the UK government's *Health of the Nation* dietary targets. These principles have already been applied to a number of products within the Nestlé portfolio, and further opportunities are continually being sought. Products with low or reduced levels of calories or fat have been developed in certain sectors in response to consumer demand. Low-calorie hot chocolate drink, low-fat coffee whitener and low-calorie salad dressings are all established products on the UK market. In recent years there has been a great deal of product development and promotional activity in the areas of reduced- and low-fat products and low-calorie foods. Many new products have been launched in response to consumer demands for these products and this trend is likely to continue. In all cases where a product is developed to be nutritionally modified the overriding factor in the development process is that the product must taste good throughout its shelf-life (Richardson, Hignett and Inman, 1994).

22.9.2 Customers

The key links with customers for Nestlé are the provision of information about the products sold and education about nutrition and healthy eating. We play a role in informing consumers about the content of the foods they purchase, both in nutritional and ingredient terms. Nutritional information on the 'Big 8' (energy, protein, carbohydrate, sugars, fat, saturates, fibre and sodium) is provided on over 80% of Nestlé UK products and details of the 'Big 4' nutrients (energy, protein, carbohydrate and fat) are included on many products where space is a restriction. In accordance with the EC Nutrition Labelling Directive information is provided on a per 100 g basis. Where space permits information showing nutrients per serving is also included. Claims, such as low fat, low calorie and high fibre are used on products to promote certain aspects of that product to consumers and to highlight a specific feature. In addition, support literature such as Lean Cuisine Lean Plans, recipe leaflets with nutritional information included, and product leaflets are available, providing background information on nutrition and giving ideas to introduce healthy eating to the family's diet.

The development of consumer carelines is another method of communicating with our customers. A low-cost phone line is dedicated to a specific brand and promoted on the packaging of the products. Customers are able to discuss any aspect of the product such as its nutrition value, suitability for certain diets, recommended cooking instructions and recipes, and history of the brand with trained operators. A careline provides a direct means of communication for both the customers and Nestlé and can also be used by the company to provide feedback on the usage and perceptions of a product. Nestlé UK has shown its commitment to the use of carelines with the development of such for Crosse and Blackwell and Buitoni.

22.9.3 People

Staff restaurant. All office and factory sites within Nestlé UK have a staff restaurant for use of the employees. Each provides an ideal opportunity to promote healthy eating to the staff. At head office, in particular, nutritional information is provided on the range of sandwiches and salads that are routinely available. The information is presented on an eye-catching background and provides customers with information about the dishes available, enabling them to make an informed choice. In addition, a colourful promotional sheet is provided advising customers to enjoy more fruit in their diets and to inform them of the benefits of doing so. It is hoped that by promoting healthy eating in a positive and practical manner staff will retain the key messages and will take the messages away to reach a wider audience of family and friends.

Fitness centres. Exercise is clearly a key part of a healthy life style. The latest indication from UK statistics is that, as a nation, our energy expenditure is decreasing and we are becoming more sedentary. The promotion of healthy eating and exercise together is essential to reverse the trend for a rising level of obesity.

Nestlé UK has taken the initiative to promote increased levels of exercise amongst its employees by providing fully equipped and staffed fitness centres for use of employees at the two major locations. A healthy eating initiative has been developed to support the work of the fitness centres, providing fairly detailed information on nutrients and their role in a healthy diet. The promotion is intended to highlight the importance of both exercise and nutrition in a healthy life style. Posters providing information in a light-hearted, yet informative manner are displayed throughout the fitness centres. All information is positioned for exercisers to read while they complete their workout. This promotion work with the fitness centre fits neatly with the objectives of the government's *Health of the Nation* white paper, which recommends a reduction in intakes of fat and saturates, alongside a national target to reduce the incidence of obesity.

22.9.4 Nutritional initiatives in Foodservice

In the UK, as in many other countries in the developed world, the popularity of eating out is on the increase. There has been a steady increase in the number and variety of establishments catering for customers outside the home. These now range from traditional restaurants to fast food outlets, takeaways, canteens, pubs, snackbars and coffee shops. In the United Kingdom the variety of cuisines offered ranges from the more well-known Mexican, Chinese and Indian, to Thai, Mongolian and Russian. As the proportion of our food intake eaten outside the home increases, there is both an increasing opportunity and responsibility to work with catering outlets to provide suitable foods and to promote healthy eating.

Nestlé Foodservice is a major player in the foodservice market in the UK. A number of projects to introduce and promote healthy eating through menus in catering establishments have been developed covering a wide spectrum of outlets and customers. All the initiatives are the results of requests from our customers, the caterers, to meet the needs of their customers, the consumers.

In addition to seeing an increase in eating out of home, the trends in customers are changing too, and this fact has been acknowledged by many of those who provide food in catering establishments. Eating out is becoming more family and group oriented and establishments need to provide dishes that suit people with very different requirements, such as children, teenagers, elderly, slimmers and very active people. One key project has been initiated with a public house chain that also provides a comprehensive catering service. A need was identified to feature 'healthy eating' dishes on menus in response to the needs of customers. It was decided that the healthy eating option must be an integral part of the menu rather than a separate section. This mirrors trends seen in the UK where healthy eating is now seen as mainstream, and not a trend followed by only a small number of the population. Criteria were established so that dishes meeting the standards could be identified by a flag on the menu. Dishes meeting the criteria must be less than 500 calories, have a lowered level of fat when compared with a standard dish and be tasty, colourful and appealing. Rather than developing completely new dishes, existing dishes on the menus were modified to reduce levels of fat and provide more carbohydrate, fruit and vegetables. The importance of the taste and appearance of the dish was a critical consideration in its development.

In this instance, the skills and product knowledge of the chefs in the Foodservice division, and the expertise of marketing and communications staff worked together to identify opportunities and to provide solutions. Healthy eating was promoted in a simple and straightforward manner without distancing it from the other dishes on the menu. In essence, customers are given the choice and are able to select a healthier option if desired, without compromising the taste of their selected dish.

22.10 Healthy eating through Nestlé USA

Fat free, low fat, cholesterol free, high fibre and low calorie are all claims that are abundant on food products in the USA. They may well be at the forefront of many Americans' minds when shopping, and represent targets and marketing tools for the food industry. America is clearly the king of healthy eating trends and nowhere else in the developed world is the knowledge of diet and its links to disease as well developed in customers' minds as it is in the USA. Whether the beliefs and desires are correct scientifically seems to be irrelevant in some areas. There has been a strong thrust in the US for many years for claims on packs, and claims relating to fat are in abundancc. The claim proliferation and resultant consumer confusion is what prompted the American Congress to pass the Nutrition Labelling and Education Act (NLEA) in 1990, requiring nutritional labelling and defining nutrient content claims. The food industry worked closely with the Food and Drugs Association (FDA) and the United States Department of Agriculture (USDA) in writing the regulations and implementing the Act. Since the NLEA became effective in 1994 there has been an even greater introduction of new fat-modified products aimed at assisting consumers in choosing healthy diets. Many of the activities have also involved industry and educational bodies, producing educational materials to teach consumers about health and nutrition.

Nestlé USA has long been involved in the development and marketing of low-fat, calorie-counted products, the most well known of which is Stouffer's Lean Cuisine. Trends in healthy eating can be seen in the United States and the food industry is well positioned to respond to these consumer demands. The following is a quote from the Lean Cuisine consumer leaflet, identifying how these consumer trends have changed and the moves that Nestlé USA has made.

> When introduced in 1981, Stouffer's Lean Cuisine line of products was welcomed enthusiastically by weight conscious consumers who were searching for easy to prepare, flavourful, reduced calorie meals. In short order, the brand became a household name and set new standards in the prepared foods freezer case.
>
> As the decade progressed, however, concern over 'diet for appearance sake' evolved into the desire for a well-balanced, healthier lifestyle. Responding to its customers, the brand introduced a second generation of Lean Cuisine that contained reduced amounts of fat, sodium and cholesterol. New products, including meatless and ethnic varieties continue to be developed each year.
>
> For the many consumers who want to eat a healthier diet without sacrificing the food taste that is a trademark of Stouffer's, Lean Cuisine provides a good for you alternative that is both flavourful and satisfying.

While offering a calorie-counted diet suitable for a slimming diet, Lean Cuisine has also moved with consumer trends to capitalize on the whole 'well-being' issue encompassing good eating habits, regular exercise and enjoyable eating and drinking.

It is interesting to note that, although the food industry has developed a wealth of products and educational material in response to the healthy eating recommendations issued by the government and in response to consumer demand, as a population the Americans are not getting any less overweight. Reduced-fat products are indeed popular, but clearly people still want to indulge, so there is a simultaneous trend toward foods that 'throw caution to the wind'.

22.11 Labelling initiatives in Sweden

In 1989, the Swedish National Food Administration developed a symbol that could easily identify products that were low in fat or high in fibre. The symbol, a green keyhole (see Chapter 14) is free to use and its application is supervised by the local public health administration. The symbol is used on a number of foods that meet specific criteria for different product categories, as follows: milk <0.5% fat, fermented milk <1.5% fat, hard cheese <17% fat, margarines <40% fat. For soft cheeses and mixed meat products there is a variation of limits, depending on the product. In the case of cereal products flours need to be wholegrain (>11% dietary fibre) and breads must contain >7% dietary fibre. The labelling has now been extended to prepared food and restaurant meals containing <30% energy from fat or <17 g fat/serving. The keyhole symbol used is a white keyhole shape on a green or black background.

The ability to include the keyhole symbol is seen as an important marketing advantage. Svenska Nestlé see the keyhole symbol as an essential part of product development and the criteria are considered from the very early beginnings of development of a new product. For most products the fat content is monitored to ensure that the criteria for lower-fat products are met. In developing recipe dishes it is not possible to use full-fat cheese, cream or high-fat meats in the same recipe, so great care is taken in the initial choices of ingredients. A recent development for the Foodservice market has shown the opportunities to increase the fibre content of bread by adding wheat bran, beet fibre, potato fibre and wholegrain flour.

The keyhole symbol has been well received and is understood by consumers, with about half of all consumers looking for the keyhole on products while shopping for food. From an industry point of view it represents a focus for product developments and an opportunity to be proactive and to promote healthy eating.

22.12 Summary

Nestlé, together with many other members of the food industry, have initiated a great number of activities in response to healthy eating guidelines issued by governments throughout the developed world. These have been wide ranging and far reaching. However, although mortality and morbidity statistics are improving in many areas there is no excuse for complacency. The food industry, together with the government, health professionals and health educators have important roles to play in promoting further the principles of healthy life styles.

A number of guiding principles are in place throughout Nestlé that apply in all cases where healthy eating is discussed. In developing initiatives to promote healthy eating the approach must always be positive and realistic. The emphasis must be on the promotion of healthy life styles. The combination of enjoyable eating and drinking within the framework of an active life style is the central focus. The reduction in levels of fat in food products, both marginally and more substantially is only one of the priority areas. Major attention should also be paid to encouraging the increased consumption of fruits and vegetables and foods containing a good supply of anti-oxidant nutrients, including those to which nutrients have been added. Alongside these activities the taste of the product must always be a principal factor in product development. Nestlé is well positioned to use all the products in its portfolio to promote a healthy, balanced, varied and tasty diet.

In addition to product developments, there is still a great deal of scope for educational developments. Educational efforts should focus on promotion of healthy life styles that are to be enjoyed by everyone. Specifically, consumers should be encouraged to be aware of the kinds of foods that contribute fat to the diet and the amount of fat in grams in typical servings and in relation to a daily target.

In conclusion, we should remember that good eating habits and regular exercise are essential for a healthy life style. Eating is a pleasure which, with a little guidance and general knowledge, can be tasty and healthy too.

References

Committee on Medical Aspects of Food Policy (1991) *Dietary Reference Values for Food Energy and Nutrients for the United Kingdom*, Department of Health Report on Health and Social Subjects No. 41, HMSO, London.

Committee on Medical Aspects of Food Policy (1994) *Nutritional Aspects of Cardiovascular Disease*, Department of Health Report on Health and Social Subjects No. 46, HMSO, London.

Department of Health (1992) *Health of the Nation: A Strategy for Health in England*, HMSO, London.

Department of Health (1994) *Eat Well! An Action Plan from the Nutrition Task Force to achieve the Health of the Nation targets on diet and nutrition*, HMSO, London.

European Community (1990) Nutrition Labelling for Foodstuffs (90/496/EEC). *Off. J. Eur. Comm.*, 6/10/90.

Gregory, J., Foster, K., Tuler, H. and Wiseman, M. (1990) *The Dietary Survey of British Adults*, HMSO, London.

Gurr, M.I. (1992) The importance of fat in the diet, in *Role of Fats in Food and Nutrition*, 2nd edn., Elsevier Science Publishers, London.

Ministry of Agriculture, Fisheries and Food (1992) *Household Food Consumption and Expenditure*, Annual Report of the National Food Survey Committee, HMSO, London.

Ministry of Agriculture, Fisheries and Food (1994) *The Dietary and Nutritional Survey of British Adults – Further Analysis*, HMSO, London.

Ministry of Agriculture, Fisheries and Food (1995) *Food Survey Directorate Information 1995–6*, MAFF, London.

National Health Survey (1993) Jones Rhodes Associates Market Research, Nottingham, England.

Nestlé Publications (1995) *Nestlé Nutrition Centre*, Lausanne, Switzerland.

Research Services Limited (1995) *Nutrition Labelling Study Report – Prepared for the Ministry of Agriculture Fisheries and Food*, RSL, Harrow, Middlesex.

Richardson, D.P., Hignett, J.M. and Inman, J. (1994) Food industry responses to the Health of the Nation. *Nutrition and Food Science*, No. 4, 13–14.

23 Implementing dietary guidelines – implications for the meat industry

M. J. WATSON

23.1 Introduction

In earlier times, nutrition was a concept of health that was strongly influenced by shortages and deficiency diseases in less affluent societies. According to that model, animal products such as meat and dairy foods, being nutrient dense, were valued as excellent sources of a range of essential nutrients. When these foods were rationed in the United Kingdom during wartime to ensure a more equitable distribution, the nutritional status of the population improved. The increasing incidence of diet-related disease in the 1960s and 1970s and influential studies such as the Seven Countries Study (Keys, 1980) with its focus on the role of saturated fatty acids in the diet, resulted in a review of this earlier paradigm. With the recognition that diet is an aetiological factor in chronic disease morbidity and mortality there has been a shift in emphasis in public health nutritional advice from nutrient deficiency to overconsumption of certain nutrients. A particular emphasis has been saturated fat, with the assumption that animal products are implicated. This has increasingly focused attention on the role of animal products in the diet and the implication for lean meat production is evident in many publications (National Research Council, 1988; Thomas, 1991). More recently the health care costs associated with consumption of meat have been estimated in the US (Barnard, Nicholson and Howard, 1995).

This chapter analyses the effect of changing emphasis in dietary guidelines and public health nutritional advice on the red meat industry, and describes some of many linkages in the production and consumption of lean meat. Experiences in Australia are primarily discussed, but much of this is relevant to the food supply in other countries.

23.2 Background

The most recent dietary guidelines from Australia, USA and the United Kingdom generally advise on increased consumption of foods of plant

Implementing Dietary Guidelines for Healthy Eating. Edited by Verner Wheelock. Published in 1997 by Blackie A&P, an imprint of Chapman & Hall, London. ISBN 0 7514 0304 0

origin, namely breads and cereals and vegetables and fruits. This emphasis on plant food fits with the focus on lower fat consumption. In the United Kingdom, the report of the Cardiovascular Review Group Committee on Medical Aspects of Food Policy (COMA) (Department of Health, 1994) recommended an increase of 50% in consumption of vegetables, fruit, potatoes and bread. The advisory committee in submitting its recommendations for revising the Dietary Guidelines for Americans (released in January 1996) again agreed with the 1990 Dietary Guidelines that Americans need to increase their intake of fruits and vegetables. The recommendation 'choose a diet with plenty of grain products, vegetables and fruits' moved to third on the list of seven guidelines, to increase the focus on plant foods. While the Australian guideline in 1992 (NHMRC, 1992) to 'eat plenty of breads and cereals and vegetables and fruits' was modified from the earlier (1981) 'eat more breads and cereals and vegetables and fruits', it was also elevated from sixth to the second guideline.

Although unfortunately insignificant in the overall scale of food advertising, ongoing nutritional education and health promotion programmes have focused on increasing the consumption of plant foods. The role of anti-oxidant nutrients found in plant foods (vitamin C, carotene, vitamin E and selenium), while not yet explicit in the dietary guidelines is evident in the scientific literature, more recently implicit in background information on which dietary guidelines are based and increasingly in the popular media. The effect of anti-oxidants, together with a possible influence of other substances in plant food (see, for example, American Dietetic Association, 1995) which may also protect against certain chronic diseases including cardiovascular disease and cancer, are presently of great interest and further increase the emphasis for the consumption of plant foods. While individual dietary guidelines are not intended to be used in isolation or to be applied to single food items, it is axiomatic that in well-fed populations current messages will lead to an increasing debate on the role of meat in the diet and consideration of a possible reduced intake.

As animal products usually contain higher proportions of saturated fatty acids than plant foods, it is not unexpected that the role of red meat has been questioned. However, an undue negative focus on red meat and 'animal fat' in the diet–health debate may not always be justifiable. Meat is frequently an important source of fat in the diet, but it is by no means dominant, red meat contributing slightly less than 10% and processed meat slightly more than 10% of the total saturated fat in the Australian diet (CSIRO Division of Human Nutrition, 1993). Presumably it has frequently been cited as a food to avoid because most of the fat in red meat is visible, in contrast to other sources of 'hidden' fat in the diet. This simplistic message can be criticized as it fails to recognize the influence of food choice in the context of an overall diet. If meat (or any other food) in the diet is replaced by other foods, any impact will be determined by the basal diet and any replacement food substituted for meat in a diet. A population-based study in the United States of young adults (Hampl and Betts, 1995) compared the sources of fat in low- and high-fat diets. In males consuming

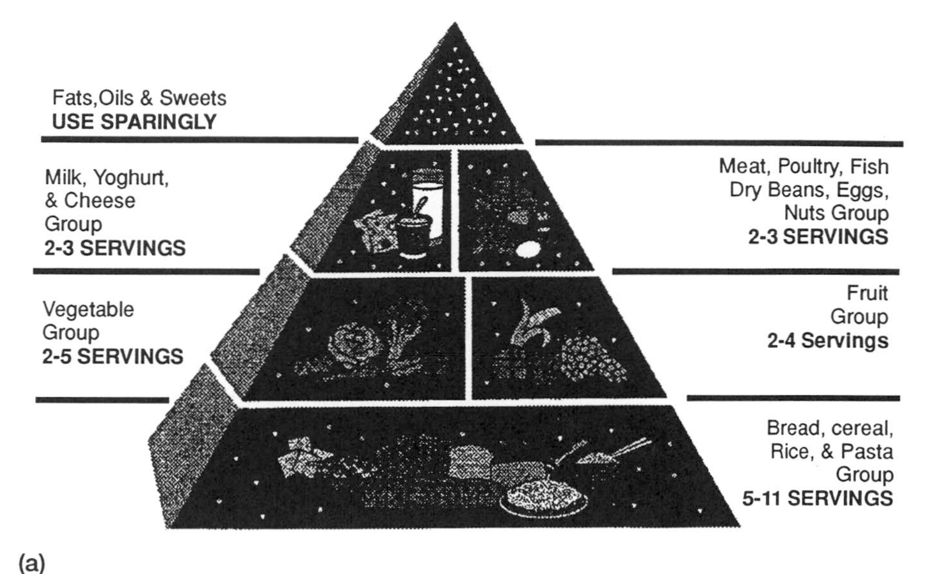

(a)

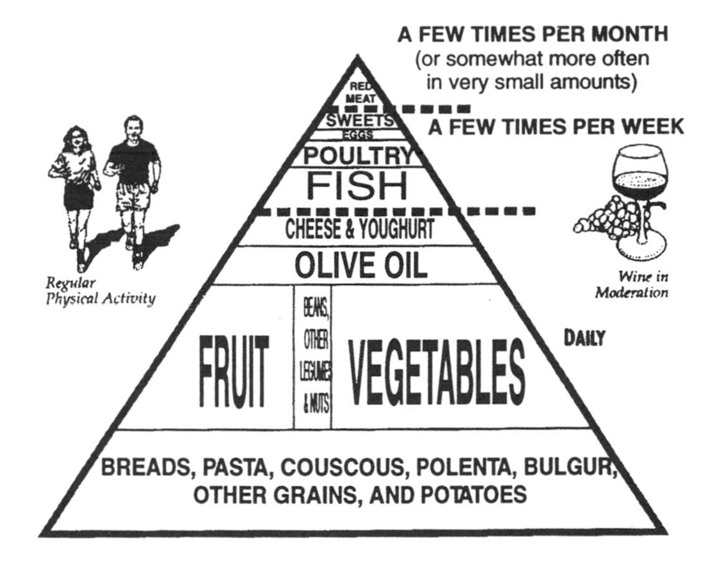

(b)

Figure 23.1 (a) The 1992 US Department of Agriculture food guide pyramid (UDSA, 1992) and (b) the Mediterranean diet pyramid (copyright Oldways Preservation and Exchange Trust).

more than 30% of energy from fat, ground beef was the highest-ranked food group, with beef, pork and poultry ranked 2, 8 and 9 respectively. In males consuming less than 30% of energy from fat, ground beef was the highest-ranked food group, but intake was approximately half (102 g/day v. 205 g/day), and other meat and poultry sources were ranked lower than in the higher-fat diet. Relative consumption patterns in women for these food groups in the two dietary patterns were comparable to the men. In contrast to the higher ground beef consumption in the high-fat diet, intake of fruit (including juice) and rice were higher in the low-fat diet. The impact of these differences in food choices on nutrient intakes were confounded by differing consumption of alcoholic beverages (higher in the low-fat diet). While vitamin A (women only), vitamin C (men only) and folate were higher in the low-fat diet, calcium, zinc (women only) and vitamin E were lower. Because of the potential benefits of nutrients which lean meat can contribute (discussed below) the role of lean meat in the diet has been generally accepted by health professionals, with consumption of 1 or 2 servings per day being commonly recommended. However, more recently red meat has been challenged by the proponents of the Mediterranean diet pyramid which proposes a very much reduced intake of red meat (but not poultry) compared to other food guides (Fig. 23.1). This pyramid, which has been profoundly influenced by studies conducted by the Harvard University School of Public Health, has been given some credence by international agencies (WHO and FAO), but has to date received no national endorsement. The rationale for this radical revision of current guidelines was thoroughly explored in a supplement to the *American Journal of Clinical Nutrition* (Kushi, Lenart and Willett, 1995). The ramifications of this radical change to both meat production and the formulation of dietary guidelines are potentially profound, and are discussed later.

23.3 Role of lean meat in the diet

Meat, principally beef, lamb and pork, makes a significant contribution to the diet in many Western countries, and the consumption of meat and poultry has markedly increased in many developing countries. Meat is an important dietary source of high-quality protein and essential nutrients, such as iron and zinc, in a highly bioavailable form, and B-group vitamins such as riboflavin, niacin and vitamin B_{12}. Although these nutrients can be obtained by the consumption of foods of plant origin, in the absence of due care there is potential for these nutrients to be marginal. The Dietary Guidelines for Australians (NHMRC, 1992) contains specific recommendations for foods containing iron, particularly for groups at risk (girls, women, vegetarians and athletes).

23.4 Trends in meat consumption and the fat content of meat

23.4.1 Meat consumption

In Australia, total meat and poultry consumption has been high but stable over the past 30 years, although the proportion of red meat in all meat and poultry has declined. The changes in the consumption of individual red meats and poultry in Australia are shown in Fig. 23.2. In Australia these changes have been very marked; 30 years ago pork and poultry comprised a little more than 10% of meat consumed, but now currently accounts for about 46% of the total. The growth in demand for poultry is especially pronounced. In 1975 poultry consumption exceeded pork, in 1986 it exceeded sheep meat. In part this probably relates to the historically high beef and lamb consumption in Australia and to changing food consumption habits associated with migration and altering life styles, as well as the increasing availability of poultry. The increase in food preparation outside the household has had different outcomes with respect to the various products, being positive with respect to poultry and negative with respect to lamb. While it seems that beef consumption has stabilized, lamb consumption in Australia continues to decline.

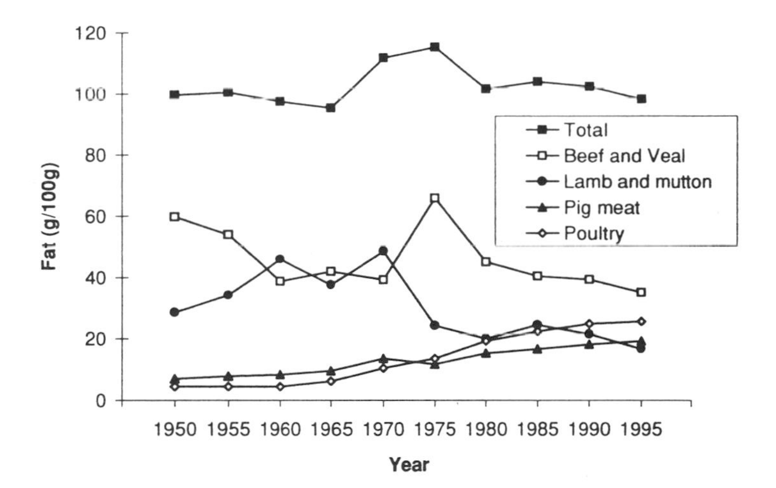

Figure 23.2 The consumption (kg/year) of beef and veal, lamb and mutton, pig meat and poultry and total meat consumption in Australia.

In contrast, in the USA, 30 years ago consumption of meat and poultry was less than in Australia (by about 10 kg) but is now higher (by about 10 kg). While meat consumption in the UK is low, this is atypical for the European Community; for instance meat consumption in France is slightly higher than in Australia. In Japan, and in many developing countries there has been a dramatic increase in meat consumption in recent years. For example in China, consumption of meat products more than doubled between 1975 and 1990 and the diet in large and medium-sized cities has become 'Westernized' at a greater rate, with dietary fat now contributing 30% of total energy (Chen and Ge, 1995).

23.4.2 *Fat content of meat*

Red meat. Red meat is a heterogeneous food, particularly with respect to variation in the fat content both between and within retail cuts. Establishing any temporal changes in the fat content of meat is important as a potential influence on the nutrient composition of the diet. It is also very relevant to the meat industry to determine how well it has addressed consumer preference for leaner cuts of meat, especially in view of the emphasis given to lean meat in its promotional campaigns. There have been some long-term reductions in the fat content of meat, e.g. in the USA and the UK, which have resulted in the adjustment of nutrient databases. The fat content of more than 2900 samples of untrimmed retail beef and lamb cuts as sold to consumers was determined in a long-term public health nutrition project at Deakin University, with the objective of testing the possibility of improving public health by producing dietary change passively through changing the composition of the food supply. The major focus was on sources of saturated fat in the diet, with emphasis on red meat. Details of the results of these meat analyses are given in Watson *et al.* (1992a,b). The current values for the fat content in Australian meat in *Composition of Foods, Australia* (COFA) (CDCSH, 1989), were derived from samples collected

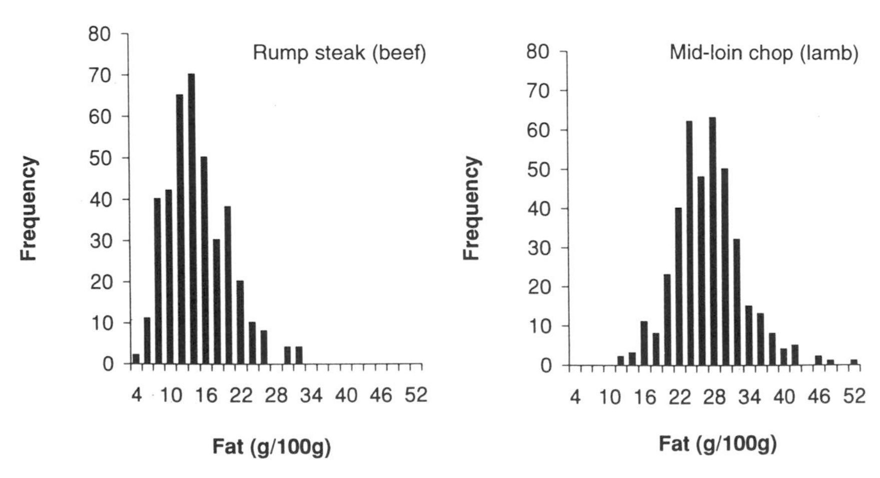

Figure 23.3 The variation in the fat content of untrimmed beef rump steak and lamb mid-loin chops.

between 1983 and 1986. The results of the more recent analyses indicated that the mean values for fat content of beef and lamb are comparable to the earlier published data, suggesting that there has been little recent shift towards leaner red meat in the retail supply. While previously it was recognized that there was considerable variation in the fat content between individual cuts, also of significance, these analyses showed that the fat content of retail meat is extremely variable within individual cuts. Figure 23.3 illustrates the variability in the fat content of retail cuts of beef and lamb.

The results indicate that the variation in fat content is extreme; in the case of rump steak it was greater than sevenfold – with less than one-fifth of the samples having less than 10% fat. The optimistic interpretation is that a leaner beef supply is possible, since lean beef is available; however, at present it represents only a small fraction of the total market. Less than 30% were above the current COFA value, but a large reduction in average fat level is required to achieve a value of 10% fat or less. The range in fat content of mid-loin chops was fourfold. As with the rump steak samples, there is evidence that there has been a reduction in fat content, with less than 15% exceeding the published COFA value; however, this cut remains very fatty.

The reality of the current red meat supply is in contrast to the image promoted by the meat industry, which emphasizes the image of lean meat alone, ignoring the high fat content of a large part of the supply. The small downward trend in the fat content of untrimmed retail cuts of meat is unlikely to have a significant impact on the potential contribution of red meat to saturated fat intake. Clearly, trimming of visible fat would be required to reduce the fat content to less than 10% which is the level recommended for approval as low-fat meat.

Pork. Associated with strong market signals, i.e. discrimination against fat carcasses, there has been a marked reduction in fat content of Australian pigs in spite of increasing carcass weight (Taverner and Ransley, 1994). There have been similar influences and comparable changes in the fat content of pig meat and pig carcasses in other countries (Blanchard, 1995). A study conducted in 1991 comparing the fat content of conventional and new-fashioned pork cuts in Geelong retail outlets, Mann *et al.* (1992) found the fat content of both conventional and new-fashioned pork cuts considerably lower (approximately 60% and 45% respectively) than the values given in the COFA. This is in contrast to beef and lamb and reflects the success of the Australian pig industry in producing leaner meat.

Trimming practices. An increasing proportion of all meat and poultry is trimmed at the retail outlet, although there are unfortunately insufficient longitudinal data to quantify this. It is probable that the rate of increase in trimmed cuts is not uniform between the individual meats, and it is likely that the relatively higher proportion of trimmed pork cuts has been an impetus for both beef and lamb to be trimmed. Should the trimmed fat be reincorporated in other foods, then any supposed gains from trimming may be illusory with respect to overall food supply nutrients, although there may be different sequelae with respect to individuals and groups who consume, for example, more processed meats. In Australia, and presumably in other countries, the production of leaner pigs has reduced the surplus of fat for incorporation into processed pig meat. Concern has been expressed at the re-entry of trimmed carcass fat into the food supply, and there is unquestionably a momentum to incorporate trimmed carcass fat into processed meats and other processed foods. However, it has to be acknowledged that the food industry is likely to use fat from alternative sources if this is not available, as tropically derived oils, e.g. palm oil, are cheap and abundant. It might be noted that wide acceptance of reduced-fat milk and the decline in butter consumption have resulted in fundamental changes in the prices paid for the fat and non-fat components of milk solids, but the dairy industry remains with a relatively larger burden of fat compared to the meat industry. The fate of this fat is a more critical issue for the food supply as dairy products contribute a large proportion of saturated fat intake; greater than one-third in the case of the Australian diet (CSIRO, 1993).

As noted above, trimming of visible fat would be required to reduce the fat content to less than 10% and this may be achieved in the kitchen or dining room as well as in the meat market. The proportion of respondents (approximately 80% in 1990) in Australia who claim to be trimming visible fat is also increasing, being marginally higher in women than men (CSIRO, 1993). Aside from the potential for response bias, the amount of visible fat trimmed may be overestimated by such data as it will include cases where only partial trimming takes place.

It is of interest to consider why there has been a difference in the ease with which the sectors of the meat industry have been able to produce leaner meat.

23.5 Primary production systems

With beef and lamb production systems based on grazed pasture, subject to the vagaries of seasonal variation, there are significant obstacles to the production of a uniform product when compared with pig and poultry systems. Beef and lamb production units are often relatively small businesses, and often lack investment and are unwilling to innovate. By contrast, pig and poultry production is usually large scale and increasingly vertically integrates management of all aspects of the production system, including breeding, feeding, environmental control and processing and marketing. Also, beef and lamb production is commonly only part of the farm operation, so that there are competing demands from other enterprises, e.g. grain production. Furthermore in Australia, meat production from sheep is frequently a by-product of wool production. The long generation interval in cattle and sheep slows the rate at which changes in the production system can be introduced. Efficiency of utilization of food energy for meat production needs to consider the cost of maintaining the breeding population as well as the slaughter generation (Webster, 1989). In prolific species such as pigs and poultry, the majority of food is consumed by the slaughter generation, and so the relative significance of the parent population is much less than for beef and lamb production systems. In pigs and poultry, emphasis can be directed towards important traits for meat production such as carcass quality and food conversion efficiency. In addition to the more ready application of quantitative genetics and sophisticated nutritional management, with respect to meat production, the ability to introduce any benefits of biotechnology to the pig industry is much higher than in the grazing industries. Porcine somatotrophin (PST) has been approved and recently introduced in commercial production in the Australian pig industry. Increasingly there is also the possibility that healthy and fertile transgenic pigs in which the gene for PST is controllable will be available (Campbell, 1995). These developments have the potential to accelerate further the disparity between the fat content of retail cuts of pork and beef and lamb.

23.6 Trends in meat and poultry prices

With the changes in the relative biological and technical efficiency with which the various meat products can be produced, it is not surprising that the relative increase in prices of beef and lamb have been greater than those of pork and poultry, especially when allowance is made for the change in fat content of pork. In Australia between 1980 and 1981 and 1991 and 1992, relative to other household commodities and services, the retail price of meat and seafood decreased by 43%, considerably more than the 12% decrease for all food (Lester, 1994). When considering individual meats, the decreases in the prices of beef and veal, lamb and mutton, pork and poultry were 27, 42, 44 and 80% respectively. Comparable analysis of the retail price of these foods in the United Kingdom (Thomas, 1991) indicates similar trends.

23.7 Conditions required for lean meat production

If the production of lean meat is to be successful, it is essential to ensure that the lean meat is consistently of high quality, preferably with a minimum price differential to alternatives. Establishing good meat quality is dependent on the end use, which can be highly variable. The role of the market is to sort carcasses and traditionally it has been easiest to use the price mechanism to focus more on unacceptable carcasses, e.g. dark cutting beef. Consumer demand for leaner meat, together with supermarket and other speciality retailing which emphasizes the visual presentation, has increased the importance of leanness. This market influence is likely to continue and possibly become even stronger in the future.

Pork is no longer considered to be expensive and fatty. The industry is characterized by a high degree of technical efficiency in nutritional management together with direct consignment to abattoirs with payment based on specified criteria and including assessment of saleable yield of meat coupled with substantial penalties for overfatness. This has had a substantial impact, such that the largest pig production company in Australia (producing approximately 900 000 pigs/annum), now imports pork fat for its smallgoods operation. In contrast, price differentials for overfatness are small for cattle and sheep, because many different factors affect the profitability of beef and lamb production on pasture. Matching the production system with what the market wants will inevitably demand compromises. For example, in the event of favourable seasonal conditions and abundant feed, producers are prepared to retain livestock to heavier weights because any penalty for excess fat is almost invariably less than the overall increase in price paid per head. This applies particularly to lambs which have a shorter growth period so that overfatness can occur in a few weeks, and high processing costs restrict opportunities for trimming. In addition, the increasing value of the skin (due to additional wool production) is a further countervailing influence.

The seasonality of production has major implications for the meat processing sector because of the high investment in plant and other fixed costs. In order to maintain a constant throughput, which is critical to profitability, processors are prepared to be more flexible in their requirements for particular specifications in times of undersupply of livestock (Read and Malcolm, 1994). Thus for beef and lamb, with less quality control than pig meat, there is a tendency to relax specifications for weight range and fatness so that the relationship between buying price, selling price and margin is preserved. This strategy helps avoid scarcity which could result if excessively demanding specifications are set, thereby increasing prices (Kempster, 1989). Because of these factors, price signals to beef and lamb producers are generally less direct, especially compared with pork and poultry where precise forward scheduling for slaughter is possible. In New Zealand, where scheduling of export lamb is common and there are severe financial penalties for excessive fatness, there has been a profound impact on carcass fatness (Purchas, Butler-Hogg and Davies, 1989).

23.8 Production and processing influences on lean meat production

There is a multitude of both production and processing factors which can potentially impact both pre- and post-farm gate on the quality of lean meat produced. Many of these also interact and there is a voluminous literature on this complex area (Watson, 1994). There is no universal inflexible predetermined blueprint which can be invoked as a protocol for production of quality lean meat, but it is vital that the various sectors of the industry develop an environment in which they can address constraints to lean meat production. Recognition that this is a multidimensional problem requiring a collective approach to co-ordinate production from farm to fork is essential. The wider acceptance and implementation of 'Hazard Analysis Critical Control Point' (HACCP) principles beyond its fundamental role in modern meat hygiene, has the potential to provide a quality assurance framework for the more consistent production of high-quality lean meat. None the less, there are obviously limits to which control can be invoked, e.g. in the domestic kitchen, and given that biological variation will occur in a natural product that is derived from the interaction of an animal with its environment.

While the production characteristics are critical with respect to composition, their impact on eating quality is of generally less importance than how the animal is handled during the slaughter phase and up to and including cooking. All sectors of the industry need to recognize that leaner cattle are more predisposed to adverse effects if pre-slaughter (farm to lairage), and post-slaughter (stunning to retail sale) animal, carcass or meat-handling practices are inadequate. Both welfare and economic efficiency criteria should encourage this approach. These factors can only be addressed by quality assurance and total quality management throughout the meat production chain. To date the distribution system has been reluctant to invest in quality assurance because of the variable supply and the higher demands of processing leaner carcasses. In the current environment processors prefer fatter beef and lamb carcasses as this is considered more 'fail safe' and, unlike pork carcasses, the penalties are not great for fat carcasses. This expedient option to slaughter at a level of fatness which is less liable to cause problems if animal handling and slaughter practices are haphazard, leads to lost opportunities to produce leaner meat and the need to discount carcass value to defray for disposal of fat. Also, fat deposition is inefficient in terms of feed conversion, because of its high energy and low moisture content compared to muscle deposition.

23.9 Other requirements for the production of lean meat

The introduction of larger price differentials based on carcass fatness in the pork industry has underpinned the decrease in fatness. Estimation of saleable yield in pork carcasses is easier because of the greater influence of subcutaneous fat compared to beef and lamb carcasses. In Australia, there has been some progress in the estimation of saleable yield of beef carcasses with the development of technology based on video image analysis (Jones, Richmond and Robertson, 1995). Used in combination with adequate animal identification this has the potential for greater price transparency (i.e. pricing accurately reflecting market demands) to be realized. This would be facilitated by direct selling rather than saleyard selling, a strategy which also has other benefits (welfare and meat quality) in addition to aiding objective description. If a practical means to determine the tenderness of beef carcasses objectively could be introduced, meat processors and their clients would be better able to trade directly on the basis of this important criterion, rather than rely on poorly related surrogate measures as at present. The development of this technology for the measurement of these carcass and meat quality attributes is probably a necessary precondition to facilitate quality control and provide greater transparency in the production–marketing chain. The culture of the meat industry has generally been to maximize throughput, with little consideration of quality assurance except to maintain hygiene standards. A transition from a commodity-based system to a marketing framework based on objective description requires mechanisms to protect individuals and provide adequate rewards for the production of quality. In the current environment, 'cutting corners' has long-term implications for the industry, but careful individual operators outside the norm are at financial risk. The evidence is compelling that the existing marketing system for beef and lamb presently has insufficient discrimination to provide incentives for production of lean carcasses with high-quality meat. Unless the returns for producing leaner stock are financially worth while, the supply of suitable lean carcasses will be limited. Pricing mechanisms based on group selling on live weight or per head basis with averaging of both inferior and superior animals within the pen have inadequate transfer of information on saleable meat yield and quality. Producers need to be more aware of the penalties of averaging, and accept that in direct selling, any premiums offered for quality must be associated with countervailing discounts for poor quality. Equally, processors need to foster their relationship with producers, preferably with price schedules which reward and penalize carcasses fairly according to the market's preference.

There is evidence that many, although not all, meat producers are cognisant of the need for a more market-oriented view of their farm enterprise. These should reinforce existing trends in production systems, e.g. new breeds, cross-breeding systems and objective means for live assessment of animals; at the same time devaluing factors of lesser importance. The continuing structural readjustment in primary production should ensure that this process continues, provided the market becomes more transparent.

Given that the production, processing and meat selling sectors are largely financially independent, they are competing for any potential margins. Each sector needs to appreciate that the meat industry is part of the whole food supply and is vulnerable to consumer disaffection. It is thus in their long-term interests to work together as an integrated industry to find solutions to structural inefficiencies rather than seek short-term advantage. The Meat and Livestock Commission's Blueprint programmes in the UK represent an attempt to co-ordinate the interest groups to improve quality assurance throughout the meat production chain (Harrington, 1995). Given the realities of the marketplace, and the competition between individual meat products for market share, such relationships will inevitably be uneasy. A further complication in Australia, at least with respect to meeting any domestic requirement for leaner meat, is the dominance of the export market in the beef industry, with more than 60% of beef produced exported, compared to about 5% in the USA. While much of this beef is specifically targeted for particular export markets, the requirements for heavier and fatter carcasses do complicate the production of leaner meat for the domestic market.

23.10 Justification for the Mediterranean diet pyramid

As noted in section 23.2, the Mediterranean diet pyramid recommends that consumption of red meat be restricted to 'a few times a month or somewhat more often in very small amounts'. Previously emphasis was on how leaner meat can play an important part in the reduction of fat intake, recognizing that this needs to be in concert with decreases in other foods and not necessarily from a reduction in meat intake *per se* (Department of Health, 1994). Detailed critical review of this complex area is beyond the scope of this analysis, but because of its importance an overview is provided.

23.10.1 Meat intake and cardiovascular disease

There has at times been an undue emphasis on 'animal fat' and the importance of serum cholesterol in the aetiology of heart disease. While atherosclerosis is significant in the initiation of coronary disease, there is a need to recognize that atherosclerosis is not solely a direct function of saturated fat intake. In addition to non-modifiable risk factors, including age, genetic predisposition and gender, important modifiable life-style characteristics, such as smoking status and physical activity patterns, and other significant dietary factors, including the composition of individual fatty acids in the total fat intake, as well as their isomeric form and the oxidative status of lipid membranes and particles, are all important in the atherogenic process. Other factors impinging on cardiovascular risk status which have a strong diet-related component include, obesity (particularly central obesity), insulin sensitivity, hypertension and dyslipidaemia (raised triglycerides and low high-density-lipoprotein cholesterol).

There has also been an increasing realization that thrombosis is often critical to the onset of a coronary disease event, and that other dietary factors are involved in this process. Epidemiological studies, ranging from ecological comparisons to intervention studies, are strongly suggestive of the importance of the long-chain polyunsaturated fatty acids, in particular the presence of *n*-3 fatty acids of marine origin and their ratio with *n*-6 polyunsaturated fatty acids which influence platelet aggregation and bleeding time. It is believed that diets rich in saturated fatty acids also increase platelet aggregation and, as is the case with the impact of individual saturated fatty acids on plasma cholesterol, there are also differences with respect to platelet behaviour. However, whereas stearic acid, which occurs in significant amounts in meat lipids, is not considered to be hypercholesterolaemic, it is viewed as likely to increase platelet aggregation (Department of Health, 1994). It is conceivable that any influence of stearic acid in red meat fat on platelet function is counterbalanced by lower amounts of *n*-6 polyunsaturated fatty acids and higher amounts of long-chain *n*-3 polyunsaturated fatty acids compared to poultry. The Department of Health (1994) report recommended further investigation of the impact of dietary fat and fatty acids on thrombosis. Even in the light of new knowledge it can be safely anticipated that prediction of the impact of dietary changes such as change in meat intake will remain difficult to predict precisely, even on a population group basis. The proponents of the Mediterranean diet pyramid suggest that a lower incidence of cardiovascular disease can be anticipated mainly on the basis of prospective studies in the USA on Seventh-day Adventists.

Although these studies were large and well conducted (Fraser *et al.*, 1992) and are suggestive of an increased risk of heart disease associated with beef consumption, the generalizability may be influenced by the otherwise healthy behaviour of the study population compared to the population at large. Another possible influence of meat on cardiovascular disease is potentially via an effect on iron stores. A recent interest in iron stores followed the report that a high stored iron level, as assessed by elevated serum ferritin concentration, is a risk factor for cardiovascular disease (Salonen *et al.*, 1992). While other prospective population-based studies have not confirmed this finding, an association between haem iron intake, but not non-haem iron intake, and cardiovascular disease has been shown (Ascherio *et al.*, 1994). The implications of high iron stores to health and to the meat industry were reviewed by Watson, Sinclair and O'Dea (1993). Poultry has approximately half the concentration of total iron of red meat (higher in beef, lower in chicken, intermediate in pork, turkey and lamb) and the proportion of haem iron of total iron is higher in red meat (Carpenter and Clark, 1995).

23.10.2 Meat intake and cancer

Kushi, Lenart and Willett (1995) reviewed in detail the associations between meat intake and cancer. This is an important question in public health nutrition especially in view of the declining rates of cardiovascular disease and ageing populations in many Western countries; circumstances in which the prevalence of cancer can be expected to increase. The evidence is reasonably strong for a positive association between meat intake for colon and prostate cancer incidence, but not breast cancer. The key question with respect to lean meat is the extent to which dietary factors other than fat might contribute to cancer initiation and promotion. While a heavily browned meat surface as a result of cooking at high temperatures is associated with an increased risk of colon cancer (Gerhardsonn de Verdier *et al.*, 1991), it should be appreciated that the proportion of disease attributable to this single cause would be small. In the studies in Europe a positive association between meat intake for colon cancer has only been established for processed meat (higher fat content) whereas in the US both consumption of processed meat and meat cuts indicate positive associations (Kushi, Lenart and Willett, 1995). The negative association of poultry consumption with colon cancer observed in the landmark study of Willett *et al.* (1990) may be an artefact, as poultry consumption was inversely correlated with red meat intake. While fibre is generally believed to be protective of large bowel cancer, the evidence is equivocal, possibly related to methodological difficulties. Higher consumption of fibre may attenuate any impact of meat on colon cancer incidence.

23.11 Conclusion

The Mediterranean diet pyramid represents a significant shift in dietary guidelines. The rationale in the Mediterranean diet pyramid for the proscription of red meat but inclusion of poultry a few times a week is questionable if the poultry includes skin. Further clarification in the future of the role of meat and poultry in the diet and influence of iron stores as a pro-oxidant can be expected from current large prospective dietary studies which have been established in an attempt to establish the role of diet in the aetiology of chronic diseases. In establishing the effects of exposure to meat, it will be necessary to differentiate between the lean and fat components in order that the influence of these two entities can be distinguished, and preferably to discriminate at least between red meat and poultry. Estimation of exposure in this way does present difficulties, but is necessary for interpretation of the differential effects of these two components. It would also have the advantage that translation of findings to health education messages would be simplified. It is essential that such studies include both male and female subjects and for blood samples to be collected. This will facilitate investigation of both nutrients and foods as potential risk factors for chronic diseases in both sexes, but the limitations of such studies need to be recognized. Frequently extrapolation may be inappropriate, as there are potentially serious problems in generalizing too widely beyond the particular cultural settings of individual studies.

Should the involvement of red meat in the aetiology of chronic disease be substantiated more universally, it clearly has importance as a public health nutritional issue in relation to iron in the diet. Some groups (e.g. pregnant women and, indeed, all women in their reproductive years) have higher requirements than others (e.g. men and post-menopausal women) and may be at increased risk of iron deficiency if intake of meat is restricted. A survey of iron status in the Australian population in 1989 established that approximately 8% of women had depleted iron stores (Cobiac and Baghurst, 1993). Many foods and vitamin supplements are fortified with iron, and careful consideration of their role is needed, together with that of foods with significant amounts of naturally occurring iron.

The absence of absolute certainty with respect to the potential impact of dietary changes on diet-related non-communicable diseases is no reason for inaction with respect to public health nutritional advice in Western countries where the high prevalence of these diseases imposes a large burden and where a change in dietary patterns is likely to reduce their incidence. Also, increasingly this needs to be seen as a global problem as most of the world's population rapidly undergoes a nutritional transition to a higher fat diet (Popkin, 1994) and in many situations health service systems are unlikely to be able to deliver adequate treatment for an emerging epidemic of chronic disease.

Sensible public health nutritional policy requires a consensus, and there are particular problems in nutritional epidemiology, because we are all exposed to some foods (Stein, 1995). The Mediterranean diet pyramid is undoubtedly healthy, but as proposed is revolutionary rather than evolutionary and potentially likely to cause disaffection amongst those who might benefit from dietary modification. It would seem prudent to reserve judgement until there are more intercountry comparisons of the influence of lean meat in the diet and, in the meantime, proceed with more conventional guidelines. If the population is to move towards a more healthy diet it is probable that this can be more easily achieved with a series of small incremental changes to a number of foods, as described by the UK Department of Health (1994). The meat industry can make a significant contribution to this change. Self-interest should encourage a greater regard for health concerns associated with red meat, as the industry also needs to contend with other intractable problems including doubts about production and processing methods and welfare practices. As stated by Harrington

(1995), 'the marketing of foods of animal origin – particularly meat – must surely be the ultimate challenge for the meat industry as it approaches the 21st century'.

Acknowledgement

The author acknowledges the former association with colleagues in the School of Nutrition and Public Health at Deakin University and the financial support of the Public Health Research and Development Committee of the National Health and Medical Research Council and the National Health Advancement Program.

References

American Dietetic Association (1995) Position of the American Dietetic Association: Phytochemicals and functional foods. *Journal of the American Dietetic Association*, **95**, (4), 493–6.

Ascherio, A., Willett, W.C., Rimm, E.B. *et al.* (1994) Dietary iron intake and risk of coronary disease in men. *Circulation*, **89**, (3), 969–74.

Barnard, N.B., Nicholson, A. and Howard, J.L. (1995) The medical costs attributable to meat consumption. *Preventive Medicine*, **24**, 646–55.

Blanchard, P. (1995) How can the eating quality of pork be influenced by management on the farm? 1: Fatness. *Meat Focus International*, **4**, (8), 329–33.

Campbell, R.G. (1995) The role of biotechnology in improving animal agriculture and the quantity and quality of food for consumers. *Proceedings of the Nutrition Society of Australia*, **19**, 67–72.

Carpenter, C.E. and Clark, E. (1995) Evaluation of methods used in meat iron analysis and iron content of raw and cooked meats. *Journal of Agriculture and Food Chemistry*, **43**, (7), 1824–7.

CDCSH (Commonwealth Department of Community Services and Health) (1989) *Composition of Foods, Australia. Vol. 1, Meat, fruit and vegetables, snack and take-away foods*, Australian Government Publishing Service, Canberra.

Chen, X.S. and Ge, K.Y. (1995) Nutrition transition in China: the growth of affluent diseases with the alleviation of undernutrition. *Asia Pacific Journal of Clinical Nutrition*, **4**, (3), 287–93.

Cobiac, L. and Baghurst, K.I. (1993) Iron status and dietary iron intakes of Australians. *Food Australia*, **45**, (4), (Suppl.), S1–S23.

CSIRO Division of Human Nutrition (1993) *What are Australians eating?* Results from the 1985 and 1990 nutrition surveys, Deakin University Food and Nutrition Program, Victoria.

Department of Health (1994) *Nutritional Aspects of Cardiovascular Disease*, Report on Health and Social Subjects 46, Report of the Cardiovascular Review Group Committee on Medical Aspects of Food Policy, HMSO, London.

Fraser, G.E.E., Sabate, J., Beeson, W.L. and Strahan, T.M. (1992) A possible protective effect of nut consumption on risk of coronary heart disease. *Archives of Internal Medicine*, **152**, (7), 1416–24.

Gerhardsonn de Verdier, M., Hagman, U., Peters, R.K. *et al.* (1991) Meat, cooking methods and colorectal cancer: a case-referent study in Stockholm. *International Journal of Cancer*, **49**, (4), 520–5.

Hampl, J.S. and Betts, N.M. (1995) Comparisons of dietary intake and sources of fat in low- and high-fat diets of 18–24-year-olds. *Journal of the American Dietetic Association*, **95**, (8), 893–7.

Harrington, G. (1995) Look at it this way. *Outlook on Agriculture*, **24**, (1), 3–5.

Jones, S.D.M., Richmond, R.J. and Robertson, W.M. (1995) Instrument beef grading. *Meat Focus International*, **4**, (2), 59–62.

Kempster, A.J. (1989) Carcass and meat quality research to meet market needs. *Animal Production*, **48**, (3), 483–96.

Keys, A. (1980) *Seven Countries: A Multivariate Analysis of Death and Coronary Heart Disease*, Harvard University Press, Cambridge, MA.

Kushi, L.H., Lenart, E.B. and Willett, W.C. (1995) Health implications of Mediterranean diets in light of contemporary knowledge. 2. Meat, fats, and oils. *American Journal of Clinical Nutrition*, **61**, (6S), 1416S–27S.

Lester, I.H. (1994) *Australia's Food and Nutrition*, Australian Government Publishing Service, Canberra.

Mann, N.J., Gazenbeek, J.E., Warick, G. *et al.* (1992) Composition of Australian pork: Results of 1991 retail study. *Food Australia*, **44**, (11), 508–10.

National Research Council (1988) *Designing Foods: Animal product Options in the Marketplace*, Prepared by the Committee on Technological Options to Improve the Nutritional Attributes of Animal Products, National Academy Press, Washington DC.

NHMRC (National Health and Medical Research Council) (1992) *Dietary Guidelines for Australians*, Australian Government Publishing Service, Canberra.

Popkin, B.M. (1994) The nutrition transition in low-income countries: an emerging crisis. *Nutrition Reviews*, **52**, (9), 285–98.

Purchas, R.W., Butler-Hogg, B.W. and Davies, A.S. (eds) (1989) *Meat Production and Processing*, Occasional Publication No. 11, New Zealand Society of Animal Production, Hamilton, New Zealand.

Read, M. and Malcolm, L.W. (1994) *The Changing Victorian Meat Processing Industry*. Paper presented to the 38th Annual Conference of the Australian Agricultural Economics Society, Wellington, New Zealand, February 1994.

Salonen, J.T., Nyyssonen, K., Korpela, H. *et al.* (1992) High stored iron levels are associated with excess risk of myocardial infarction in Eastern Finnish Men. *Circulation*, **86**, (3), 803–11.

Stein, A.D. (1995) Cause and noncause – nutritional epidemiology and public health nutrition. *American Journal of Public Health*, **85**, (5), 618–20.

Taverner, M.R. and Ransley, R.M. (1994) Food production and human nutrition: The impact of health messages primary production perspective – the pig industry experience. *Proceedings of the Nutrition Society of Australia*, **18**, 133–40.

Thomas, B. (1991) *Meat Diet and Health: A Report on Red Meat Today*, The Meat and Livestock Commission with the Health Education Authority, Milton Keynes, UK.

USDA (US Department of Agriculture) (1992) *The Food Guide Pyramid*, Publication HG252, Human Nutrition Information Service, Hyattsville, MD.

Watson, M.J. (1994) Fostering leaner red meat in the food supply. *British Food Journal*, **96**, (8), 24–32.

Watson, M.J., Sinclair, A.J. and O'Dea, K. (1993) Heart disease: Are high iron stores associated with increased risk of coronary heart disease? *Meat Focus International*, **2**, (8), 359–62.

Watson, M.J., Mann, N.J., Sinclair, A.J. and O'Dea, K. (1992a) Fat content of untrimmed retail beef and lamb cuts 1. *Food Australia*, **44**, (11), 511–14.

Watson, M.J., Mann, N.J., Sinclair, A.J. and O'Dea, K. (1992b) Fat content of untrimmed retail beef and lamb cuts 2. Influence of outlet and neighbourhood over a year. *Food Australia*, **44**, (11), 516–18.

Webster, A.J.F. (1989) Bioenergetics, bioengineering and growth. *Animal Production*, **48**, (2), 249–69.

Willett, W.C., Stampfer, M.J., Colditz, G.A. *et al.* (1990) Relation of meat, fat, and fiber intake to the risk of colon cancer in a prospective study in women. *New England Journal of Medicine*, **323**, 1664–72.

24 Quorn mycoprotein: a new food for better nutrition

TERRY SHARP

Mycoprotein, produced by Marlow Foods under the brand name 'Quorn', is now so much a part of the British food scene that it is worth while retracing its stages of development. It is a model of how a new food can be used to bring wide-ranging benefits to the nutritional status of the average consumer.

24.1 The need for a new food

We have to go back to the 1950s for the beginning of this story. At that time, the memories of the Second World War and its aftermath of food shortages in Europe were still fresh. The worry for the future was that population growth would outstrip the ability of conventional methods of agriculture to supply enough food. In other words, there would be a 'protein gap', even in the relatively affluent countries of western Europe.

This gloomy prediction was the stimulus for much official and scientific activity focused on the investigation of new, sometimes unconventional, sources of supply of protein-based foods. In 1955, the Protein Advisory Group of the World Health Organization was set up to advise the United Nations Food and Agriculture Organization on how to establish guidelines for the safety, nutrition and palatability of new protein foods for human consumption. In 1968, the United Nations produced a report *International Action to Avert Impending Protein Crisis*, which considered how the protein gap might be met by the use of microbial protein.

The 1960s saw much commercial activity directed towards the development of 'single-cell proteins', which were, in reality, microbial cells containing large amounts of protein. Many research projects were started but only a few edged towards commercialization. Two partial successes were BP's Toprinao, produced by growing yeast on crude oil residues, and Pruteen, an animal feed from fermentation of methanol by ICI. Both reached large-scale production but were denied commercial viability for a

Implementing Dietary Guidelines for Healthy Eating. Edited by Verner Wheelock. Published in 1997 by Blackie A&P, an imprint of Chapman & Hall, London. ISBN 0 7514 0304 0

number of reasons, not least of which was the world oil crisis which greatly increased the cost of the feedstock in both projects.

The exception to this pattern was the research project on mycoprotein, which was started by Rank Hovis McDougall in 1964. This was different since the objective was to produce a new food for human consumption, based on edible feedstocks.

24.2 The idea

Lord Rank, of Rank Hovis McDougall (RHM), briefed his scientists to find the modern equivalent of the philosopher's stone, an agent that reputedly turned lead into gold. Translated into food, he wanted to find the means of changing starch, a cheap and plentiful low-grade food component, into protein, which was seen to be in ever shorter supply and, therefore, more valuable.

The vision went further. If the original idea was difficult, further constraints were added, which would make the project near impossible. Ironically, it was these same rules that would guarantee both the continuing development and ultimate success of the project, because they required a sustained focus on both consumer and product benefits, rather than the cleverness of the technology employed.

24.3 The search for a new ingredient

What could be found to change starch into protein? In trying to answer this question, RHM's scientists leaned heavily on tradition. For thousands of years, both mushrooms and fermented products have been widely accepted as substantial foods, sometimes even used as alternatives to meats. RHM decided to try to put these two elements together, and to attempt to produce a food from fermented edible fungi.

To do this, to begin the search, they needed to follow certain basic rules:

- Consumer acceptance – whatever the technical merits of a food, its ingredients ultimately had to be acceptable to the consumer.
- Safety – of paramount importance was the need to demonstrate the safety of the new food. This had to include tolerance by all sectors of the population.
- Nutritional value – once safety is assured, the next question for a new food is one of nutritional value. It has to satisfy all normal needs for growth and maintenance of health, while supplying necessary macro- and micronutrients. There could be no reduction of the overall nutritional quality of food intake when a new food was to be introduced to the diet.

- Quality – all aspects of quality demanded by the consumer had to be satisfied. The taste, texture, appearance and ease of use had to be, at least, up to the standards of the rest of the food supply.
- Economic viability – ingredients, processes and yields had to combine to give costs similar to other comparable foods.

All of these major constraints, although independent of each other, had to be considered at all times. For instance, it would have been pointless to conduct a major programme of safety testing, only to find that the ingredients chosen were either too expensive, or did not give the required quality.

The starting point was a 3-year programme, which screened over 3000 samples of microfungi collected from all parts of the world. Of these, 30 were subjected to further testing and, finally, one emerged as the candidate for further development. This was *Fusarium graminearum* (Schwabe), a filament-type fungus which was found just beneath the surface of a field in Marlow, Buckinghamshire, just 8 km from the RHM research site.

24.4 The development of production

It was necessary to develop the means for small-scale production to enable sufficient food to be produced for use in safety testing – in total, approximately 100 tonnes was used.

Continuous liquid culture fermentation was chosen as the method, which would ensure relatively low capital and running costs, high yields and stable conditions for culture growth. Productivity was estimated to be five times greater than for a batch process, with the added benefit of ease of increasing the scale of production.

The ingredients chosen for the process were:

- *Fusarium graminearum* (Schwabe) – the culture;
- glucose syrup – hydrolysed pure syrup obtained from wheat starch;
- minerals, biotin – nutrients to help culture growth;
- oxygen, nitrogen sources – essential for growth in biological systems.

The conversion rates of carbohydrate to protein, in comparison to other sources of food protein, are shown in Table 24.1. It is clear from these data, that the fermentation process is very much more efficient than the other methods of protein production.

Table 24.1 Conversion rates of carbohydrate to protein

Species	g Protein from 1 kg carbohydrate
Fusarium graminearum	136
Chicken	49
Pig	41
Cattle	14

To enable growth of the pure and stable culture, it is necessary to sterilize all other ingredients before combining them, and, further, to maintain a contamination-free environment in the fermenter.

The process route was established at an early stage of development, and has changed very little through scale-up. Process conditions were agreed with the UK Regulatory Authorities and may only be changed with their permission. The process for mycoprotein production is shown in Fig. 24.1.

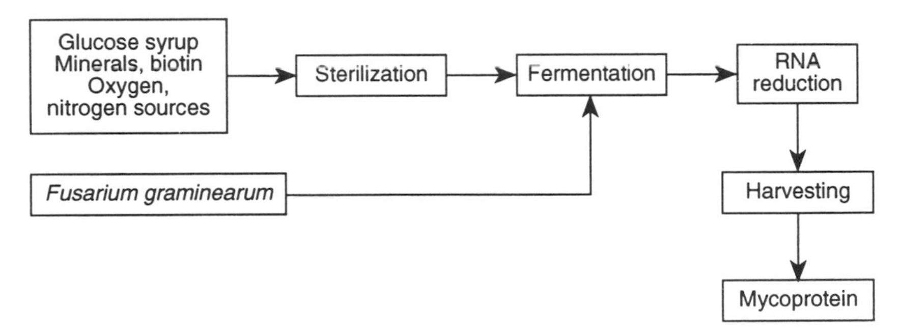

Figure 24.1 The process for mycoprotein production.

24.5 Safety testing, nutritional value and approval

It is essential that any new food is safe, wholesome and nutritious. Extensive testing over 13 years showed that *Fusarium graminearum* (Schwabe) and mycoprotein were non-toxic to all living species, including crops and plants. Feeding trials using 100 tonnes of mycoprotein were carried out on 11 species of animal, within and between generations, and no evidence of a toxicological response was found. Later, large-scale studies with 4000 consumers confirmed that there were no immunological responses to mycoprotein, an important and necessary result for a new food.

The test data, accumulated in a 26-volume, 2 million word report, were submitted to the UK Ministry of Agriculture, Fisheries and Food (MAFF), who set up a new committee specifically to evaluate this information.

The protocols developed for both the feeding trials and their evaluation were so successful, that they have been used as the basis for the testing of other new foods and ingredients.

In 1984, MAFF gave approval for the unconditional sale of mycoprotein in food products in the UK. Further approvals, based on this evidence, were granted by The Netherlands, The Republic of Ireland and Denmark. Similarly, Belgium, France and Germany allowed the sale of mycoprotein.

Since the commercial launch, there has been continuous monitoring of the impact of mycoprotein, although under free-living conditions it would be extremely difficult to link cause and effect. It is clear though, because of

Marlow Foods' close relationship with health and regulatory authorities, as well as its customers, that should there be any pattern of an adverse reaction, it would become apparent. There has been no evidence of any such pattern.

The nutritional quality of mycoprotein has also been thoroughly investigated (Table 24.2). Protein and energy studies showed good availability, and growth trials with chickens, which have well-defined nutritional requirements and are sensitive to dietary changes, showed normal weight gains compared to control diets. Table 24.3 shows the net protein utilization of various foods, including mycoprotein.

Table 24.2 Protein quality, mycoprotein v.s. milk in humans

	Mycoprotein	Milk
Digestibility	78	95
Biological value	84	85
Net protein utilization	65	80

Table 24.3 Comparison of net protein utilization in protein foods

Food	NPU
Egg	100
Skimmed-milk protein	85
Fish	83
Beef	80
Cow's milk	80
Mycoprotein	65
Wheat flour	52
Beans	47

Mineral availability studies in both rats and humans have shown that the fibre in mycoprotein does not adversely affect the absorption of minerals.

The composition of mycoprotein was also well researched, and there are no unusual components. The amino acid and fatty acid profiles are similar to other foods, the fibre is mainly β-glucans, with some chitin, found also in mushrooms (Garrow, 1992). Vitamins and minerals are present in reasonable quantities, thus giving a good balance of macro- and micronutrients.

In fact, it has been demonstrated subsequently that the composition of mycoprotein offers many benefits, detailed later in the chapter.

24.6 The product, 'Quorn'

The information given so far has been about mycoprotein, the unique, new, food ingredient, which is fermented on food starch. Parallel developments were taking place, not only to ensure that adequate quantities could be produced, but also with regard to the type of food products which would be most acceptable.

Mycoprotein has a soft texture, which is similar to uncooked pastry. It is rather bland with a slight taste of mushrooms, and alone has insufficient organoleptic properties to be an exciting food.

Food technology harnessed the meat-like fibrous structure of mycoprotein and generated texture and succulence in a series of simple operations, in which egg albumen, water and seasonings were added. This process is shown in Fig. 24.2. The product made in this way has the brand name 'Quorn'.

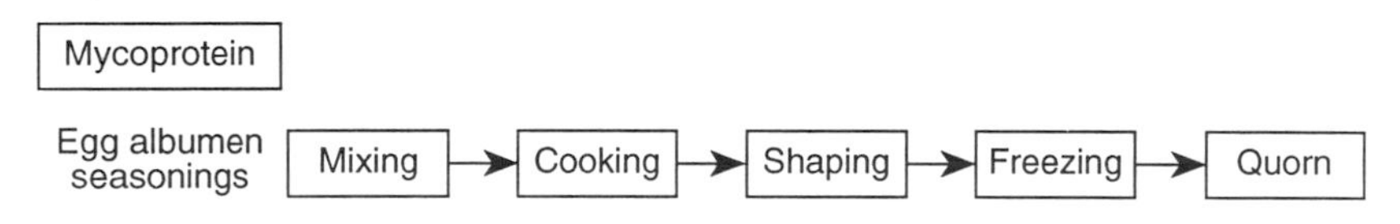

Figure 24.2 The production process for Quorn.

The usual high standards of the UK food industry are applied in production, including quality control, quality assurance systems, and on-line process monitoring and control. The factors affecting quality are well understood and product quality targets can, therefore, be met consistently.

24.7 Market development – the need for Quorn now

By 1985, RHM had completed its major development programme, and had realized its vision of being able to supply a protein food produced from starch-based ingredients. Quorn had arrived. Unfortunately, the protein gap did not! In the 20 years it had taken to develop Quorn, western European population growth had slowed and the availability of food protein dramatically increased, mainly due to more intensive agricultural techniques.

Where then was there to be a market for the new protein food? The answer was in the new trends. Since people were eating more of everything and, at the same time, generally leading more sedentary lives, there started to be a new imbalance. Diets contained too many calories, too much fat, not enough fibre, and were thought by experts to be leading to various (avoidable) diseases and conditions. First the nutritional experts, then governments set 'official' targets for food intakes, backed up with advice on how to achieve them through food choice.

In parallel, European consumer trends led to the growth of new demands. In the 1980s and 1990s, to be attractive, food must satisfy certain needs: convenience, quality, nutritional balance and versatility. Also, with different emphasis from country to country, there has been an increased awareness of ethical issues, including animal welfare, the environment, perceived risks from animal-derived products (bovine spongiform encephalopathy (BSE), salmonella, etc.) and a reluctance to accept new husbandry techniques such as the use of growth hormones.

Although these trends began for different reasons, a common theme has emerged. Driven by different motives, and guided by media pressure regarding 'healthier' eating, there has been a reduction and change in the balance of meat consumption. So, to a greater or lesser extent, consumers in western Europe have switched from red to white meat or have gone further, in omitting meat from their diets altogether.

The overall effect has been for large numbers of European consumers to seek 'healthier' alternatives to meat. Quorn is one of these alternative foods.

24.8 The resources for development

To develop an idea into a project and then to commercial reality over more than a quarter of a century, requires considerable resources. In the early days, RHM assembled its team of scientists and this was to become the core of the Group Research and Development Centre, eventually increasing to a staff of 200, many of whom were engaged in mycoprotein research. Safety and nutritional testing was conducted independently by external facilities and the cost of this alone has been estimated at over £10 million.

At two more key stages of development, there was a need for substantial resources in the shape of both know-how and finance. First, in the early 1980s, when it appeared likely that mycoprotein was going to be approved for sale, RHM turned its attention to the scale-up of production. The Group, for all its knowledge of cereals, cultures and fermentation science, had no experience of production-scale fermentation and so began to investigate strategic partnerships with other companies which would be able to bring engineering and production experience of continuous fermentation processes.

At this point, Pruteen, the animal feed protein developed by Imperial Chemical Industries (ICI) becomes relevant. In its development, there were similar challenges and problems to be overcome – fermenter scale-up, the engineering of sterile systems, ingredients handling and continuous production. It seemed natural then that ICI should join RHM in a joint venture to take the project forward to commercial reality, and a partnership formed in 1984. The company formed to produce mycoprotein and sell Quorn products was called Marlow Foods. In this way, a great deal of experience gained from the development of Pruteen was transferred to Marlow Foods. The various scales of production, and uses for the output are shown in Table 24.4.

Table 24.4 Scales of production for mycoprotein

	Fermenter type	Volume (m^3)	Output (tonnes/annum)	Use of output
1975–84	CSTR[a]	1.3	25	Product safety testing
1984–93	Airlift	40	1000	Market development, UK Non-UK market trials
1994	Airlift	200 (× 2)	14 000	Full UK trading Market development, Europe

[a]CSTR, continuous stirred tank reactor.

That a second, major, input was going to be necessary became increasingly clear from 1985 onwards. It is not enough for a company to believe that it has a good product. It must be clearly aware of the benefits that its products offer and how they fit with consumer needs. Further, it must work hard at raising consumer awareness to its products.

To achieve these objectives requires a major investment in market research, advertising and selling in each potential market for the products. The need for this further investment, together with the capital requirement for production scale-up, led RHM to rethink its long-term strategy. Consequently, in 1990, ICI acquired 100% ownership of Marlow Foods.

Although difficult to estimate, the total costs of development until 1994 have been in excess of £100 million.

24.9 UK diet trends

The UK, amongst a few other European countries, has been at the leading edge of nutritional research for many years. As early as 1978, the government recognized the need for better nutritional education advice, and the UK Department of Health and Social Security consequently established the National Advisory Committee on Nutrition Education (NACNE, 1983).

Five years later, NACNE published its report, which recommended changes to the average British diet. These guidelines gave not only general advice, but backed them up with actual target figures for change. Table 24.5 shows official advice on UK diets.

Table 24.5 Official advice on UK diets, 1983; some NACNE guidelines for the diet

General advice	Target	
	From	To[a]
Reduced total and saturated fat consumption	38 (%E)	34 (%E)
Increase ratio of polyunsaturates to saturates	0.24	0.32
Reduce sugar consumption	14 (%E)	12 (%E)
Increase fibre consumption	20 (g)	25 (g)
Reduce salt consumption	12 (g)	11 (g)

[a]These were short-term targets on the way to greater changes.

At about the same time, another official body, COMA (Committee on Medical Aspects of Food Policy), published its report, which gave very similar guidelines. The COMA report concentrated on the relationship between diet and cardiovascular disease, but, in any case, its recommendations were essentially similar to the NACNE report (COMA, 1984).

These two reports were instrumental in raising awareness of the need for 'healthier' eating. In the 1980s, the media took up the cause and have continuously presented evidence for diet-related medical problems. As a result, public awareness of the need to eat the right foods in the correct amounts has grown, although it is probably true to say that understanding at both lay and expert levels is inconsistent and far from complete.

By the early 1990s, the UK government had clearly identified the advantages of the population consuming a better diet, and it decided to enshrine nutritional understanding in a white paper *The Health of the Nation* (Department of Health, 1992):

- it recognized that priorities should be set, based on the seriousness of a particular disease or condition, and the potential to achieve improvements;
- it spelled out the need for more disease prevention rather than cure;
- it set dietary and health targets and agreed the importance of monitoring progress towards them.

The significance of the white paper is that it has full government support and has, therefore, become official national policy, to be followed and implemented by all government departments and ministers.

COMA itself continued throughout this period to assess research data, and in late 1994, published a new report, *Nutritional Aspects of Cardiovascular Disease* (COMA, 1994). Its conclusions reinforced previous advice, while also discussing broader factors such as the need to change patterns of food choice and consumption and research proposals to increase understanding of nutrition and health.

The relevant points from *The Health of the Nation* are shown in Table 24.6.

Table 24.6 *Health of the Nation* – some targets

40%	reduction of mortality from coronary heart disease and stroke (1990–2000)
12%	reduction in energy contributed by fat in the diet (1990–2005)
35%	reduction in energy contributed by saturated fat in the diet (1990–2005)

The question of how far such advice is acted upon by the UK population can be answered, in part, by reference to average food consumption data. For over 50 years, the UK authorities have collected information about what kinds of food are eaten in the home, and in what quantities. The National Food Survey, as it is called, is published quarterly and has become a useful guide to long-term trends and shifts in consumption. Table 24.7 shows average UK consumption across a 20-year period. It is clear that any changes in the diet take place slowly, and that there is still a significant gap between actual and target dietary intake and balance.

Table 24.7 Twenty-year trend in UK dietary balance[a] (source: MAFF, 1990a)

% Energy	1970	1980	1990
From carbohydrate	47	45	44
From fat	42	43	42.5
From protein	11	12	13.5

[a]It should be noted that the proportion of food consumed in the home has gradually decreased as external catering has become more popular. In 1990, approximately 30% of all food consumption was away from the home

Consumers have two choices if they wish to move towards recommended targets. The first is to change the amounts of various foods in their current diet, for instance, reducing the proportion of fried foods or increasing the proportion of brown and wholemeal breads. The second is to switch to perceived or actual 'healthier' alternatives, some examples of which are shown in Table 24.8.

Table 24.8 Alternative 'healthier' choices

From	To
Full-fat dairy products	Reduced-fat versions, e.g. milk, cheese
Butter	Spreads high in mono/polyunsaturated fats
Crisps/snacks	Reduced-fat versions
Red meats	White meats
Animal-derived products	Non-animal-based alternatives

24.10 Quorn and today's diet

These health and dietary trends have created today's need for Quorn. The spectre of a food protein gap in western Europe has long disappeared and has been replaced with the problem of an oversupply and overconsumption of food. Quorn mycoprotein fits into the demands for 'healthier' alternatives by offering a wide range of benefits at different levels. Although the focus will be on nutritional quality and its relevance, other benefits are shown in Table 24.9.

Table 24.9 Overall benefits of Quorn

Issue	What Quorn offers
Life style changing demographics and eating patterns	Wide availability Versatility Ease of use Quality
Cultural environmental, social and ethical	Efficiency of production Vegetable in origin No artificial processing or additives
Health foods, diets and ease of change	Nutritional composition Actual health benefits Ease of use to improve dietary balance

Table 24.10 Composition of Quorn and other foods

Per 100 g	Quorn	Mycoprotein	Skinless chicken	Stewing steak
Energy (kJ/kcal)	355/85	355/85	621/148	932/223
Protein (g)	12.3	12.1	24.8	30.9
Carbohydrate (g)	1.8	1.7	0	0
Fat (g)	3.2	3.4	5.4	11.0
Dietary fibre (g)	4.8	6.0	0	0
Cholesterol (mg)	0	0	76	82

From official sources for cooked foods.

The composition of Quorn (and mycoprotein) is shown compared to equivalent alternatives in Table 24.10. The overall balance of macronutrients is particularly interesting, since Quorn offers low fat, high fibre, no cholesterol, and a low calorific value. Micronutrients are shown in Table 24.11. The protein level is sufficiently high to make it a viable alternative to meat when used as the main ingredient for a wide range of recipes. It is used in exactly the same way as chicken or minced beef would be, and it is sold, usually through supermarkets, in various forms.

Most popular is Quorn for home cooking, sold either minced or in pieces, and this has a tender texture and a mild savoury flavour, which complements the herbs, spices and sauces it can be cooked with. Popular recipes for home preparation include casseroles, curries and stir fries, bolognese, lasagne and Chinese dishes, e.g. in a sweet and sour sauce.

Table 24.11 Quorn micronutrients

Dietary component		Amount in 100g Quorn
Vitamin	B_1 (mg)	36
	B_2 (mg)	0.15
	B_3 (mg)	0.30
	B_5 (mg)	0.14
	B_6 (μg)	2.0
	B_{12} (μg)	0.25
	Biotin (μg)	9.0
Sodium (mg)		240
Potassium (mg)		111
Calcium (mg)		21
Magnesium (mg)		38
Phosphorus (mg)		240
Iron (mg)		0.7
Copper (mg)		0.6
Zinc (mg)		7

In the UK, in addition, there are approximately 30 ready-prepared Quorn-based products on sale, including ready-to-cook meals such as curries, filled pasta dishes, crisp-coated vegetable escalopes and vegetarian burgers and sausages, which contain substantially less fat than the meat-based equivalents.

Although many meat-based products are a valuable source of important nutrients, very often the Quorn-based equivalent is seen as a 'healthier' alternative. This is not to say that meat or its products are bad, but rather that using Quorn as an alternative will help to move the nutritional intake closer to official targets.

The impact upon the nutritional balance of the average UK diet has been studied using UK government statistics for food intakes. Various assumptions were made regarding the frequency of Quorn product consumption, as well as which types of products would be replaced by their Quorn equivalents. A short list is given in Table 24.12.

Table 24.12 Some commercial meat-based products and Quorn equivalents

Meat products	Quorn products
Beefburgers	Quorn cutlets and burgers
Chicken casserole	Quorn 'harvest' casserole
Chicken pie	Quorn 'savoury' pie
Pork sweet and sour	Quorn sweet and sour
Bolognese sauce	Bolognese sauce and minced Quorn

In the calculations, it was assumed that Quorn-based products would partially replace red and white meat used in products such as burgers, ready meals and pies, and also chicken and beef, which might be used as the basis for meat-containing meals. Steaks, or whole-muscle meats, were not included.

Overall, the results show a significant improvement in the balance of macronutrients and a shift towards official dietary targets. Intakes of energy, fat and dietary cholesterol and protein were reduced, whereas the polyunsaturated/saturated fat (P/S) ratio and dietary fibre intake increased. A summary is given in Table 24.13.

Table 24.13 Changes to dietary balance with Quorn-based products

Dietary component	National Household Diet[a]	Average NACNE target[b]	Diet with Quorn products
Energy (kcal)	1970	1970	1914
Protein (g)	70.9	49.3	65.9
Fat (g)	89.0	74.4	84.7
Polyunsaturates (g)	12.7	10.9	13.0
Saturates (g)	36.2	32.8	33.9
P/S ratio	0.35	0.45	0.38
Carbohydrates (g)	236	263	237
Dietary fibre (g)	18.4	23.3	20.4
Dietary cholesterol (g)	259	–	226

[a]Source, MAFF (1990b).
[b]Source, NACNE (1983).

For micronutrients, Quorn supplies mainly B vitamins together with useful amounts of iron and zinc, and the study showed that the micronutrient status was not compromised with the Quorn-based diet. Indeed, there is evidence that Quorn may be the most important non-animal-derived source of iron and zinc, and may make a significant contribution to the diets of those who no longer eat meat.

24.11 Beyond today's diet

It is clear from the evidence shown that Quorn makes a positive contribution to better diets. It is also clear that changing the balance of food intake can achieve a similar effect. (It can be argued, of course, that if changing food intake was easy, with clear targets and so much advice readily available, consumers should now have diets closer to official targets. Surveys show that this change is extremely gradual.)

This possibility encouraged the Quorn development team to identify further nutritional and health benefits, which might be uniquely associated with Quorn. In the late 1980s, a major external research programme was set up with mainly UK-based centres of excellence which monitored, with volunteer subjects, the effects of eating Quorn on blood cholesterol, appetite and weight change. A summary of research projects, results and subsequent publications and presentations is shown in Table 24.14.

Table 24.14 Quorn nutrition and health research projects

Study	By/at	Published	Presented
Cholesterol lowering – metabolic	Dr Leeds, King's College, London	Turnbull, Leeds and Edwards (1990)	14th International Congress of Nutrition, Korea 1989
Cholesterol lowering – free living	Dr Leeds, King's College London	Turnbull, Leeds and Edwards (1992)	International Conference on Fibre, Hungary 1991
Mycoprotein digestion	Dr Cummings, Dunn, Cambridge	Cummings (1990)	6th European Conference on Nutrition, Greece 1991
Effect of mycoprotein on hunger, satiety and food consumption	Dr Turnbull, King's College London	Turnbull, Walton and Leeds (1993)	3rd European Conference on Obesity, France 1991
The contribution of Quorn mycoprotein to the UK diet	Dr Sharp, Marlow Foods	Sharp (1991)	2nd European Conference on Food and Nutrition Policy, Holland 1992
Influence of Quorn mycoprotein on appetite	Dr Blundell, Leeds University, Leeds	Burley, Paul and Blundell (1993)	4th European Conference on Obesity, Holland 1992
Effect of repeated administration of Quorn mycoprotein on satiety and appetite control	Dr Blundell, Leeds University, Leeds	Burley, Paul and Blundell (1993)	
Use of Quorn in the management of obesity	Prof. Garrow, St Bartholomew's Hospital, London	Garrow (1992)	
3-month cross-over study on the effect of Quorn on weight control in obese children and adults	Prof. Biro, National Institute of Food Hygiene and Nutrition, Hungary	Biro (1994)	

The effects on blood cholesterol are now well documented (Turnbull, Leeds and Edwards, 1990, 1992). Original research at the Massachussets Institute of Technology (MIT) during safety testing, showed that serum cholesterol in rats was reduced during regular Quorn consumption. Much later, studies at King's College, London, with human subjects, confirmed that in highly controlled conditions over 3 weeks (metabolic study) total cholesterol reduced by 13% (low-density-lipoprotein cholesterol, 9%) for those on the Quorn diet, whereas in an 8-week free-living study, the introduction of Quorn reduced total cholesterol by 16%. Although a direct link cannot be made between blood cholesterol levels and the incidence of coronary heart disease, it is considered to be one of the risk factors and, in many countries, official advice is to 'Know your number' (i.e. cholesterol count) and to find ways to reduce it. These studies show that Quorn can help.

The effects on satiety and food intakes have also been thoroughly investigated (Burley, 1993; Turnbull, Walton and Leeds, 1993). This work was started because, over the years of development, there was circumstantial evidence that Quorn was particularly satisfying to eat, even though it was lower in calories than many other foods. Because it is not an energy-dense food, if it has a satiety value proportionately 'higher' than its calorific value, it should help the control of appetite, food intake and, therefore, body weight control.

Investigations by J. Blundell at Leeds University, UK, studied the effects of eating Quorn on satiety and subsequent food intakes over (1) 24 hours, and (2) a 5-day period. After lunches with identical energy values, but containing either Quorn or chicken, the onset of hunger was delayed after the test meal with Quorn. At the evening meal on the same day, food intakes of the test group were on average 18% lower than for the controls.

In the second study over 5 days, the effect was repeated and proven to be sustainable. The conclusions from these separate studies were that, certainly between 1 and 5 days, Quorn is more satisfying to eat than chicken and leads to a reduction of overall food intake.

These encouraging results laid the foundation for a much more extensive study, which monitored physiological changes in children and adults eating Quorn or meat-based diets over a period of 3 months. Measurements, including serum cholesterol, vitamin and mineral status, blood sugar, appetite, food intake, weight changes, total body fat and Body Mass Index (BMI) were taken. This study was conducted in Hungary by the National Institute of Food, Hygiene and Nutrition, Budapest (Biro, 1994).

The results available mid-1995 confirm the net beneficial effects of Quorn-based diets in maintaining key physiological variables, but also, most importantly, that they allow the use of reduced energy diets over an extended period, which leads to weight loss.

As part of a consultation process with top scientists, the researchers who conducted these studies have published results in respected journals and presented their results at international conferences. This has allowed for informed comments and guidance at each step in the nutritional research programme.

24.12 The future for Quorn

Experience of over 30 years' development has provided many lessons in how to bring a new food to the market, while meeting the requirements of the many interested sectors of the community, from regulators and safety experts, through manufacturing distribution and retailing, to both the needs and preferences of consumers.

Over such an extended period, the world has changed considerably, and a key factor in the success of Quorn has been the ability of the development team to adapt to changing conditions and requirements. This has been equally true of the team itself, who, in the early days, were mainly scientists, followed by development technologists and commercial and production personnel.

The success of Quorn, in the final analysis, is due to the fact that it meets the needs of the populations of many countries, which are striving to adjust the balance of food intakes. As people slowly come to terms with the need to change their eating habits, and make new and informed choices, only food that makes it easier is going to be highly acceptable.

Quorn will have a bright future in any country that is taking steps to improve the nutritional status of the average diet.

References

Biro, E. (1994) *3-Month Crossover Study on the Effect of Quorn on Weight Control in Obese Children and Adults*, National Institute of Food Hygiene and Nutrition, Hungary, Final Report.

Burley, V.J., Paul, A.W. and Blundell, J.E. (1993) Influence of a high fibre food (myco-protein) on appetite. *European Journal of Clinical Nutrition*, **42**, 409–18.

COMA (Committee on Medical Aspects of Food Policy) (1984) *Diet and Cardiovascular Disease*, Report on Health and Social Subjects No. 28, HMSO, London.

COMA (Committee on Medical Aspects of Food Policy) (1994) *Nutritional Aspects of Cardiovascular Disease*, Report of the Cardiovascular Review Group No. 46, HMSO, London.

Cummings, J.H. (1990) *The Effect of Myco-Protein on Digestion in Human Subjects*, The Dunn Nutrition Centre, Cambridge, Final Report.

Department of Health (1992) *Health of the Nation: A Strategy for Health in England*, HMSO, London.

Garrow, J. (1992) *The Influence of Myco-protein on Food Intakes and Weight Control in Obese Subjects*, St Bartholomew's Hospital, London, Final Report.

MAFF (Ministry of Agriculture, Fisheries and Food) (1990a) *Fifty Years of the National Food Survey 1940–1990* (ed. J.M. Slater). Proceedings of a symposium, December 1990, London.

MAFF (Ministry of Agriculture, Fisheries and Food) (1990b) *The Dietary and National Survey of British Adults*, OPCS, HMSO, London.

NACNE (National Advisory Committee on Nutrition Education) (1983) *Proposals for Nutritional Guidelines for Health Education in Britain*, The Health Education Council (NACNE), London.

Sharp, T.M. (1991) *The Contribution of Quorn to the UK Diet*, Royal College of General Practitioners Members Reference Book, London.

Turnbull, W.H., Leeds, A.R. and Edwards, D.G. (1990) Effect of myco-protein on blood lipids. *American Journal of Clinical Nutrition*, **52**, 646–50.
Turnbull, W.H., Leeds, A.R. and Edwards, D.G. (1992) Myco-protein reduces blood lipids in free-living subjects. *American Journal of Clinical Nutrition*, **55**, 415–19.
Turnbull, W.H., Walton, J. and Leeds, A.R. (1993) Acute effects of myco-protein on subsequent energy intake and appetite variables. *American Journal of Clinical Nutrition*, **58**, 507–12.

Part Five

Public/Private Policy Initiatives

25 *The National 5 a Day – for Better Health! Program:* an American nutrition and cancer prevention initiative

SUSAN B. FOERSTER,
JERIANNE HEIMENDINGER,
LORELEI K. DiSOGRA and ELIZABETH PIVONKA

The National 5 a Day – for Better Health! Program is a large-scale, public/private partnership which aims to reduce the incidence of cancer and other diet-related chronic diseases through dietary improvement. Its goal is to increase average fruit and vegetable consumption as part of a low-fat, high-fibre diet from an estimated 3.4 servings in 1991 (Subar *et al.*, 1992) to five servings or more by the year 2000. Increasing fruit and vegetable consumption to this level was established as one of the nation's prevention objectives in 1990 (USDHHS, 1990).

One of the Program's objectives is to increase public awareness of the need to eat five servings or more of fruit/vegetables daily from a baseline level of 8% (Subar *et al.*, 1992). A second objective aims to provide consumer skills information and increase social support for acting upon the new information. Simultaneously, the National Program is organized to promote environmental, organizational and policy changes to establish social norms supportive of long-term maintenance of the new behaviour.

The Program is led by the National Cancer Institute (NCI), a division of the National Institutes of Health of the US Department of Health and Human Services, in co-operation with the Produce for Better Health Foundation (PBH). The PBH is a non-profit consumer education foundation established by the produce industry for the purpose of working with NCI on this programme. Since establishment of the national programme in 1991, 52 of the 56 American state and territorial health departments and over 1200 food industry organizations (representing about 35 000 supermarkets nationwide) have become licensed to participate. All partners participate at their own expense, as there are no earmarked federal funds for state or industry implementation. The Program is directed to the entire adult US population of more than 200 million persons.

This chapter will describe for the international reader the policy and scientific environments that contributed to the establishment and operation

Implementing Dietary Guidelines for Healthy Eating. Edited by Verner Wheelock. Published in 1997 by Blackie A&P, an imprint of Chapman & Hall, London. ISBN 0 7514 0304 0

of this initiative; development of the prototype campaign in California; the subsequent establishment and implementation of a nationwide programme, including its research and evaluation components; and examples of specific industry and state initiatives. A brief discussion of issues that affect achievement of the Program's objectives will conclude the chapter. Citations will assist interested readers in locating more detailed information.

25.1 Policy underpinnings

The strong link between diet and cancer first compiled in the early 1980s was incorporated shortly thereafter in American health policy (Doll and Peto, 1981; NRC, 1982; NCI, 1984, 1986). The National Cancer Institute issued *Diet, Nutrition and Cancer Prevention: A Guide to Food Choices* (NCI, 1984) for consumers first, followed by *Cancer Control Objectives for the Nation: 1985–2000*, a policy report (NCI, 1986). In the latter document, the NCI concurred with estimates by Doll and Peto (1981) and the National Research Council that 35% of all cancer deaths are diet related. NCI went on to project that by the year 2000, 30 000 lives could be saved annually through modification of dietary habits, and it noted that the same dietary changes would also reduce the occurrence of heart disease, the nation's leading cause of death. The estimate that at least 35% of cancer deaths are diet related has been affirmed more recently and by others (NRC, 1989; Doll, 1992; Ames *et al.*, 1995).

The 1986 NCI objectives were significant because they cited dietary change as a fundamental component of the nation's cancer prevention strategy. They estimated that by the year 2000, cancer mortality could be reduced by 8% through diet and by 8 to 15% through tobacco control. In comparison, 3% could be reduced through early detection, and 10 to 26% by the improved application of cancer treatments. These projections therefore showed primary prevention to be as quantitatively significant as medical approaches, and, for the first time, nutrition was rated as important as tobacco control.

NCI's control objectives for the American population called for the per capita consumption of fat not to exceed 30% of calories and for the daily consumption of high-fibre foods, including certain fruits and vegetables, to increase. Fruits, vegetables and juices high in vitamins A and C, along with cruciferous vegetables, were singled out as being particularly beneficial. NCI did not cite a specific quantity of fruits and vegetables to eat every day, nor did it include baseline estimates of per capita fruit and vegetable intake.

Against this backdrop of interest in cancer prevention, NCI issued a new type of grant solicitation. In 1985 it invited state and large county health departments to develop technical capacity for conducting large-scale cancer prevention initiatives. The technical capacities of interest were situational analysis, epidemiology, coalition development, marketing and evaluation. Nine awards were made, of which the states of California, Connecticut, Massachusetts and Minnesota each proposed to conduct nutritional interventions. The California Department of Health Services was the only grantee to focus its entire effort on developing methods to secure dietary change in the general population (Meisner, Bergner and Marconi, 1992). The project was funded at about $300 000 (US) annually for a 5-year period (1986–91).

25.2 Foundations of the national programme: California's 5 a Day – for Better Health! Campaign

The scientific literature of the mid 1980s contained neither theoretical models nor examples of large-scale dietary initiatives for chronic disease prevention. Therefore, in its proposal to NCI, California derived a three-pronged, systems approach model for securing dietary change in a population then estimated at 19 million adults. The three intervention components were mass media and public education, population surveys leading to organizational mobilization, and incremental food system change. The first two components were selected because of the success attributed to them in smaller community heart disease prevention trials conducted in Finland, California (US) and Minnesota (US), while the theoretical model of Fallows and Wheelock (England) was attractive because of its pragmatic economic approach (Fallows and Wheelock, 1982; Blackburn *et al.*, 1984; Farquhar, 1985; Puska *et al.*, 1985). The California project planned to address a variety of dietary factors associated with diet-related chronic diseases, not solely those associated with cancer.

The application of NCI's specific technical capacities to California's model resulted in the development by 1988 of the California 5 a Day – for Better Health! Campaign, a statewide initiative to promote fruit and vegetable consumption. The decision to focus on fruits and vegetables as part of a low-fat, high-fibre diet, rather than on all foods or nutrients in the diet, was based on situational analysis conducted early in the project period that yielded critical new information.

The most significant finding was that average fruit and vegetable (f/v) intake in California was far lower than expected, a potentially very important public health problem. The low consumption was especially surprising because marketplace availability was not a major barrier. California grows slightly over half of all fruits and vegetables in the US, and stores carry a wide variety of produce all year. These factors suggested that other, possibly modifiable, factors were at play. It also appeared that consumption could be even lower in other regions of the country where availability was more limited.

The other reasons for focusing on fruits and vegetables were more pragmatic. First, intervening in f/v consumption would fill a void, because no other health authorities had ever singled out fruits and vegetables for promotion. Secondly, in California alone the f/v industry was made up of hundreds of independent companies, boards and commissions. With a large number of potential partners, a coalition approach would be feasible. This contrasted markedly with other sectors of the food supply which are more concentrated, with decision-making occurring in headquarters located elsewhere in the US or in Europe. Thirdly, unlike some other food groups and nutrients, f/v consumption could be measured comparatively quickly and inexpensively by telephone surveys, meaning that progress toward achieving the goal could be monitored regularly over time, a critical feature of any initiative. Finally, it was felt that becoming experienced with f/v would lay the groundwork for the health department to tackle more complex dietary interventions, such as fat lowering, in the future.

Once the decision to focus on fruits and vegetables was made, it was still undetermined where to start, with whom to work, what an intervention would look like and how it would be operated. The state agriculture department suggested approaching the quasi-governmental commodity marketing boards and commissions. The leaders they suggested contacting were recognized by their peers as visionaries and problem solvers. They represented the iceberg lettuce, prune, table grape, tomato and tree fruit (peaches, nectarines, plums and pears) industries. The marketing leaders recommended working in the larger industry environment by using a specific, time-limited campaign approach and developing a marketing plan in which industry groups could participate. To do this would require that the state health department set a campaign goal and establish the identifying features of the campaign, most especially the logo, slogan and standards. The marketing board leaders agreed to work with the department on a public/private marketing campaign.

The department set the goal of five servings of fruits and vegetables daily using several parameters. First, it defined eligible items as consisting of fruits and vegetables in any form, whether fresh, frozen, canned, dried or juiced, as long as they were without fat, added salt or sugar. It did not single out those with more favourable nutrient or cancer-preventing properties, reasoning that the major challenge was to increase the total amount of f/v in the diet, not the share of certain items within the f/v category. Avocados, coconuts and olives were excluded because of their high fat content.

The number of daily servings to be recommended also had to meet several criteria. The amount had to be a significant increase over then-current levels; it had to be biologically important; it had to be clear, actionable and memorable for consumers; it had to be large enough to reasonably include choices from the cruciferous family, f/v high in vitamins C and A and in fibre; and it had to be small enough to be perceived by consumers as achievable. Five servings fit those requirements.

Similarly, the definition of a serving needed to be understandable to consumers, consistent with common household portions and perceived as a reasonable amount. The serving sizes used in American dietary guidance were chosen as the base. These are: a whole fruit or vegetable, like an orange or baked potato; a half cup of cut fruit or vegetable; a one-cup serving of raw salad greens; a 6-ounce glass of 100% juice, and a ¼ cup of dried fruit, such as raisins. These sizes tend to be somewhat smaller than those recently established by the US Food and Drug Administration for nutritional labels.

While acting under the authority of the state health department, it was essential that the many different partners be consistent and accurate in all forms of consumer communications, including to portray fruits and vegetables as part of a low-fat, high-fibre eating style. Therefore, standards for Campaign recipes, photography and advertising text were established by the department. The standards provided industry partners with the specificity and latitude they needed to use their expertise and resources to market the message independently and fully.

The key to operation of the Campaign standards was establishing and then controlling the use of the logo and slogan (Fig. 25.1). The logo and slogan were officially registered with state and federal trademark authorities to ensure that the marks would be used as intended in commercial settings. Partners could use the logo and slogan only if they signed a license agreement to follow the programme standards. The logo was designed to depict an array of identifiable and popular fruits and vegetables against a backdrop of California sunshine. The slogan was intended to be behavioural, specific and upbeat: Eat 5 a Day – for Better Health!

Figure 25.1 Licensed partners use the logo and slogan of the National 5 A Day – for Better Health Program extensively. It appears on labels, packaging, advertisements, photography and consumer materials of all sorts. Service mark protection helps ensure that fruits and vegetables when shown with the logo are depicted as part of a high-fibre low-fat eating style.

25.3 Campaign implementation and evaluation

Mass media and supermarkets were selected as channels that would reach the maximum number of consumers. The concept was to introduce the 5 a Day messages through broadcast and print media and then reinforce them and provide cues to action at point of sale. The target audience was defined broadly, as those persons who spoke and read English at the tenth grade level or higher. Since consumers would be at different levels of awareness, knowledge, belief and skill, Campaign communications addressed all four constructs.

In August 1988 the Campaign was kicked off by the state health director at press conferences in San Francisco and Los Angeles, the state's largest media markets. Media tours by project staff followed in three other media markets. The launch received heavy media coverage, which resulted in requests by six of the state's then 18 major supermarket chains to be part of the initiative. The health department was not prepared to handle the high level of response.

Over the next year, the health department convened a structured strategic planning process with an industry Steering Committee to plan the balance of the Campaign. Two critical decisions were made. First, the industry secured a commitment from the health department to support establishing a national campaign once the California project period ended. In return, they would support a series of four, California-only theme-related promotions through early 1991.

The components of each promotion evolved over time into a formula that worked. The health department identified a theme, secured the maximum amount of media coverage possible, offered the public appealing printed information, and helped the retail partners reinforce the message at point of sale. Themes were selected based on hard news such as survey results (whenever possible) and a seasonal food 'hook' that could be developed further by food writers and produce managers. A companion consumer brochure was created with informational, skill-building and interactive content, such as a reference table, idea list or self-assessment. Press kits were distributed to journalists in print and broadcast media in the news, food, feature, and community service departments. If there was hard news, press conferences were held in a photogenic setting convenient to the media outlets. If a media tour was conducted, a public relations agency was used to secure the best bookings. In each case, the brochure was offered free through NCI's Cancer Information Service toll-free telephone number, a feature that also increased pick-up of press releases. The supermarket partners were provided with theme-related camera-ready advertising copy, line art, signage, tip sheets, the consumer brochure and script for radio tags or in-store audio. For the more costly items like four-colour brochures, partners could either purchase supplies from the Program or obtain film to do their own printing.

The news hooks and companion promotional themes were: launch of the first phase of supermarket participation with a convenience theme (*Fast and Easy: Fruits and Vegetables for Better Health!*) in April 1989; results of the 1989 California Dietary Practices Survey with a summer salad theme (*Eat More Salads for Better Health!*) in July 1990; and a holiday theme (*Easy Entertaining with Fruits and Vegetables*) in November/December 1990. The theme of the final promotion in March 1991 was *5 a Day Week*, the concept being to encourage consumers to establish one new fruit and vegetable habit each day of the week, Monday through Friday. This promotional wave was the first to recruit local community groups suchas health maintenance organizations, health departments and dietetic associations. An estimated 60 organizations and 1750 of the state's 2000 supermarkets participated.

Since it lacked an experimental design, impact evaluation of the Campaign is not possible. However, in addition to the favourable process measures of media coverage and industry participation, statewide population surveys suggest that the Campaign had a positive effect. Between 1989 and 1991, fruit and vegetable consumption rose by 0.3 servings in both White and Black adults, groups that were likely to be exposed repeatedly to the Campaign message. This was about four times the expected secular increase of about 1% per year, which would have been less than 0.1 servings in 2 years. Other Campaign-related consumer variables that precede behaviour change also increased significantly during this period.

More details about California's prototype programme and subsequent population trends have been reported (Foerster and Hudcs, 1994; Foerster *et al.*, 1995).

25.4 Establishment of the National 5 a Day Program

Coverage by the trade press and presentations at professional meetings over the years had resulted in considerable interest in the Campaign outside California. For example, a prominent New England retailer persuaded the state health department in Vermont to enter into a franchise agreement with California to conduct a counterpart campaign in partnership with local industry organizations. Negotiations initiated by several other states also were under way. However, as the project period drew to an end, industry leaders and the California team met with principals at NCI to request it to adopt the Campaign as a nationwide initiative. The complementary roles that the federal government and industry would play were major discussion points. In a spontaneous and dramatic move at the meeting's end, all 20 industry representatives raised their hands in a unanimous show of commitment to work with NCI on a programme modelled after California's. This was the moment of conception of the National 5 a Day Program.

The Produce Marketing Association, a trade organization with over 2000 produce business members, took the lead on industry's behalf. It established a new, non-profit entity, the Produce for Better Health Foundation (PBH), to create a single industry partner for NCI. PBH established a board of directors, began raising funds, sponsored a national baseline survey and scheduled the launch of the new initiative for their convention in October 1991. California negotiated an agreement turning over legal rights to the logo, slogan and programme standards to NCI for an initial 10-year period. The NCI began laying the scientific foundations for sponsoring a very atypical programme in an organization whose primary mandate is research, although it did fit the less utilized mission of applying tax-supported research to benefit the American public.

The agreement between the NCI and PBH lays out complementary roles for the public and private sectors. NCI serves as the Program's scientific voice to the public, sets all health-related standards, secures other health and government partners, conducts evaluation and advances intervention research. PBH's role is to facilitate implementation in the food industry, work with NCI on overall programme direction, help develop guidelines for partners, license industry partners, ensure industry compliance with programme standards and assist with evaluation. In an initial structured strategic planning process sponsored by PBH, the two partners laid out a specific mission, values, vision, key result areas, objectives, strategies, action steps and benchmarks for the first 3-year period. The organizations set up a four-person Coordinating Committee of representatives from NCI and PBH to provide co-ordination between the public and private sectors. The National Program was officially announced to the industry at its annual meeting in Boston in October 1991, just 9 months after the first meeting in Washington.

25.5 National Program implementation and evaluation

The PBH set out immediately to recruit and license partners, raise funds and roll out supermarket promotions. A glossy promotional flyer with testimonials by the US Secretary of Health and Human Services, NCI officials and industry leaders was widely distributed in the f/v and supermarket industries. Donor categories were set at defined levels, from $500 to $100 000 (US), with contributors of $20 000 or more being entitled to a seat on the PBH board of directors, In conjunction with NCI, the California materials were adapted for national use, and a nationwide materials distribution system was set up. Industry members signed licenses pledging to abide by the standards of the programme, sponsor at least two promotions a year and participate in state or community publicity events. They paid an annual $100 fee and received starter materials with theme-specific advertising copy, line art, camera-ready materials, posters, signage and brochures for their company's participation in the Program.

To tie partners together across the country, the PBH published periodic newsletters which showcased the National Program's major accomplishments, highlighted innovations by partners and listed the dates of future Program promotions. For the first *National 5 a Day Week* in September 1993, a handbook for organizating a wider array of promotional and community activities was provided to all partners, and the services of a public relations company were secured to obtain media coverage and publicise the Program on Capitol Hill and with state governors across the US.

Meanwhile, the NCI helped to analyse a large national telephone survey of Americans' f/v consumption, began developing licensing standards for health departments and other channels, and initiated the nation's first-ever research programme solely to develop dietary change methods in defined community channels (Subar *et al.*, 1992, 1995; Krebs-Smith *et al.*, 1995). Over 75 organizations competed to conduct 4-year research grants. The nine winning institutions represent a second generation of community-based research which uses community channels as the unit of randomization, a strategy that provides more statistical power than the larger community-wide, non-randomized designs have provided. The purpose of these grants is to implement and evaluate interventions to increase f/v consumption among specific population segments using specific community channels. The channels of interest are schools (four projects), worksites (three projects), the Women, Infant and Children's Supplemental Food Program (w/c) (one project) and African-American churches (one project). The projects, which will be completed in 1997, are described elsewhere (Havas *et al.*, 1995).

Since the National 5 a Day Program is a social marketing initiative, maintaining contact with consumers is critical. In 1991, the NCI's Office of Cancer Communications conducted the first formative research with consumers. Its purpose was to narrow the Program's target audience and design tailored messages that would specifically reach the large fraction of consumers who are currently eating two to three servings of f/v per day and are expected to be most receptive to change.

The services of a public relations agency were secured to develop ongoing media relations with major print and broadcast outlets. A glossy news magazine with computer graphics, camera-ready art and feature stories was produced periodically for media. Events throughout the year were designed to involve broadcast media, nationally prominent spokespersons and paid media events. Licensed states are encouraged to use these as 'hooks' for their own state-based interventions.

For example, for the 1995 *National 5 a Day Week theme*, 'Take the 5 a Day Challenge', celebrity astronauts issued a national challenge to the public using contemporary communications technology, in this case a video

Figure 25.2 The *National 5 a Day Program* provides newspaper-quality graphics that motivate and inform. Media outlets and licensed partners receive the theme-related figures and charts for each promotional wave. Graphics are provided in a variety of computer formats, allowing for maximum reuse in newsletters, reports, slides and consumer education materials.

news release down-linked by a satellite to television outlets across the nation (Fig. 25.2). The promotion featured a new consumer brochure, *Take Time for Five*, and media outreach by the NCI's nationwide network of Cancer Information Service offices. States were encouraged to use state or local opinion leaders, such as athletes, disk jockeys, politicians and other celebrities, who would also challenge each other in the spirit of fun by eating five servings each day for a week. Thus the national template for media attention could be localized and amplified in each state.

State health departments agree in their license with NCI to act as the designated state health authority for the Program and to serve as a forum for statewide intervention activities. The states agree to sponsor or participate in at least one major publicity event every year, to implement 5 a Day activities and policy within state programmes and to monitor conformity with programme standards among all partners in the state. More than half the states have established 5 a Day coalitions as a means of organizing statewide activities, and many states sublicense local health departments to provide local leadership. The coalitions typically include representatives from other units of state and local government, such as the education and agriculture departments, local health departments, produce and supermarket industry groups, farmers' markets, professional societies and voluntary organizations such as the American Cancer Society. The structure and composition of the coalitions are left to the discretion of the state as to what works best in their setting. The Program Guidelines provide a template for action by all partners.

State health departments set priorities and develop innovative interventions for specific channels. Several have conducted statewide f/v consumption surveys. For example, the states of Alabama, Hawaii, Illinois,

Indiana, Michigan, New Jersey, North Carolina, South Dakota, Virginia and Vermont have developed 5 a Day educational content for the WIC Program, several of which are done in conjunction with the US Department of Agriculture's *WIC Farmers' Market Nutrition Program*. At least 18 states have worked with their state education departments to develop 5 a Day school initiatives for classroom and/or cafeteria implementation. Arizona has developed a manual for preschools with foodservice, parent and activity components. Worksites have been targeted by Alaska, Alabama, Indiana, Massachusetts and South Carolina. Hawaii, Massachusetts, Rhode Island and Vermont have targeted restaurateurs and/or non-commercial foodservice. Alaska, Indiana, South Carolina and Utah have targeted churches. Four states are principals in the 5 a Day research projects. Virtually all states conduct mass media, supermarket, community and policy activities.

As part of their contribution, industry licensees have developed a variety of 5 a Day initiatives. The California Tree Fruit Agreement has provided an estimated 6.5 million ripening bags which communicate the 5 a Day message while teaching consumers how to hold their fruit until it reaches maximum flavour, an important skill since the fruit is shipped long distances. In their seasonal radio co-operative advertising buys, the California Table Grape Commission, Sunkist Growers and the Chilean Fresh Fruit Association offer retailers the chance to include 5 a Day public service announcements and the NCI tag. In its school foodservice programme, the Florida Citrus Commission has offered 5 a Day promotional materials, such as California's new *Power Play! School Idea and Resource Kit*. The Washington Apple Commission and the International Apple Institute have developed an elementary school curriculum which is available free to teachers. The Kroger and Dominick's supermarket chains have sponsored *5 a Day Kids' Clubs* that expose children to new fruits and vegetables through tastings, coupons and engaging activities such as poster contests and competitions. As often as possible, the state and industry activities are accomplished in a collaborative manner.

In 1994, the US Centers for Disease Control and Prevention (CDC) and NCI agreed to work together to provide state health departments with ongoing training via teleconference. In addition, CDC offered to assist states with 1-year grants averaging $40 000. In that year, 25 of the 30+ funded states and Indian tribal nations chose to use their 1-year grant for 5 a Day interventions; in 1995 additional states selected 5 a Day as their priority chronic disease nutrition intervention. In the same 2 years, NCI for the first time offered 1-year evaluation grants of up to $90 000 for state licensees. Results of the first group of four evaluation grantees will be available in 1996.

Evaluation of the National Program consists of process and outcome measures. All licensees provide regular reports of their activities, policy initiatives and the approximate dollar value of their contributions at least annually. Clipping services track media coverage. The NCI will conduct nationwide follow-up telephone surveys in 1996 and 2001. Those surveys are designed to detect change not only in self-reported f/v consumption information but also in intermediate consumer measures that are related to specific theoretical constructs of the Program. The most robust outcome measures will be provided by the nine NCI grants which have randomized designs. In addition, several of the surveys conducted as part of the National Nutrition Monitoring System will have f/v questions added. For example, the Behavioral Risk Factor Surveillance System, a computer-assisted telephone survey which is centrally administered by the CDC and operated by state health departments, included a module of f/v questions which was used by 16 states in 1990 (Serdula *et al.*, 1995). In 1996 and the year 2000, the f/v questions will be asked nationwide.

25.6 Scientific, theoretical and structural underpinnings of the National Program

Programmes at NCI follow five progressive steps from research to application, starting with basic biomedical investigation and ending with the nationwide application of prevention and health services programmes (Greenwald, Cullen and McKenna, 1987). Therefore, a strong science base and creation of an intervention research programme that included methods development, controlled intervention trials, defined population studies and demonstration and implementation projects were fundamental requirements for NCI participation.

By late 1990, a number of major reports and studies documenting the cancer prevention benefits of f/v had been published or were known to be nearing completion (US Public Health Service, 1988; NRC, 1989; Trock, Lanza and Greenwald, 1990; Willett, 1990; Negri *et al.*, 1991; Steinmetz and Potter, 1991a, b; Weisburger, 1991; Ziegler, 1991; Block, Patterson and Subar, 1992; Ziegler *et al.*, 1992). Among the most powerful of these was a meta-analysis of the available world's literature. In 128 of 156 retrospective and prospective dietary studies that calculated relative risk, an inverse association between f/v consumption and the occurrence of cancers in 13 different sites was found (Block, Patterson and Subar, 1992). These studies associated many different f/v with lower cancer risk, including dark green, yellow and orange vegetables and fruits, cruciferous vegetables, dried fruits, tomatoes, citrus fruits, berries and melons. Of all the dietary factors postulated to be related to cancer, the epidemiological evidence was most consistent for f/v.

Adding to the weight of epidemiological evidence were the existence of plausible biochemical mechanisms to explain the protective effects of f/v. The proposed mechanisms involved a variety of dietary components which are provided primarily or exclusively by f/v. These include: vitamins A, C, E and folate, fibre, carotenoids and other anti-oxidants, and other phytochemicals such as dithiolthiones, flavonoids, glucosinolates, indoles, isothiocyanates, phenols, limonene and allium compounds.

Relative to behavioural change, it was essential that intervention activities of the National Program be organized based on strong behavioural theory, that their methods reflect proven community approaches, and that new research be designed to test the application of specific theoretical models in defined community channels. It was widely agreed, based on heart disease risk reduction research in Finland, California, Minnesota and Pawtucket (US), that awareness, knowledge, motivation, skills development and environmental modification were constructs essential to securing behavioural change in communities (Mittlemark *et al.*, 1986; Lefebvre *et al.*, 1987; Nissinen, Tuomilehgo and Puska, 1988; Kottler and Roberto, 1989; Farquhar, 1990). Specific theories explaining these constructs were the health belief model, consumer information processing, and social learning. More pragmatically, NCI itself had found that public confidence in messages from a credible health agency, when actively promoted by the food industry using customary marketing practices, could generate consumer purchases of the desired foods on a nationwide scale (Levy and Stokes, 1987). The theoretical basis of the National Program is described more extensively elsewhere (Heimendinger *et al.*, 1996).

The newer transtheoretical model being used in other areas of cancer control provided a useful overarching framework for the new programme (Prochaska and DiClemente, 1992). This model views behavioural change as a stage-based process in which people are at any one of five sequential points in their readiness to change. Some people will be unaware of the message or aware but not ready to act (Precontemplation), others will be aware and thinking about change (Contemplation), others will be testing out a few new behaviours and otherwise actively getting ready to change (Preparation), others will be trying or have recently changed their behaviour (Action), and as time goes on, an increasing number will be trying to establish the new 5 a Day behaviour permanently but occasionally regressing to old habits (Maintenance). With large population segments being in each of the five stages of change, the Program's objective is to shift increasingly large proportions toward the Action and Maintenance stages.

To unify the science into a national programme, it was recognized that social marketing approaches could provide both the undergirding discipline for applying the theoretical constructs in intervention work and also a natural fit for industry partners. For example, social marketing is consumer-driven and user-friendly, it uses mass communications heavily, and it works through existing channels and institutions to sell its product, rather than creating new systems (Manoff, 1985; Kottler and Roberto, 1989; Rice and Atkin, 1989).

With a largely national food supply and marketing system, the positional advantage of health authorities could be combined with the natural strength of partners in business to reach the public when they were making food purchasing decisions. By working with partners in many different channels, the Program would be able to provide consistent information and increased access to f/v by every major segment of the population. Since organizations in each channel have centralized decision-making and similar operations, working through such partners also offered efficiency in leveraging the available human and material resources and a valuable organizing tool for community interventions. As open systems that interface with the larger community at multiple points, channels also provide opportunities for changing social norms. In addition, the social marketing features of using mass communications, being consumer-driven and attending to the user needs of intermediaries were especially appealing to all partners.

The following case studies demonstrate how these principles are implemented in practice.

25.7 Dole Foods *5 a Day Adventures*: a company-sponsored children's campaign

The Dole Food Company was involved early in the 5 a Day Program. It first participated in the *California 5 a Day – for Better Health! Campaign* through the state's original Steering Committee (1989–91), and in 1991 became a founding member of the *National 5 a Day Program*. Dole Food company, based in Westlake Village, California, is one of the world's largest producers and marketers of high-quality, fresh fruit and vegetables, juices, packaged fruit and nuts. Believing that the *National 5 a Day Program* would significantly improve the nation's health, as well as be an incredible opportunity for the produce and supermarket industry, Dole became a produce industry leader in the National Program.

In order to play a vital leadership role, Dole established a Nutrition and Health Program in 1991. To maximize limited national resources and avoid duplication of efforts with NCI and PBH, Dole's Nutrition Program strategically selected children between the ages of 5 and 10 years (kindergarten through third grades) as the focus of its nutritional education efforts. The goal of all of Dole's nutrition education programmes is to encourage children and their parents to eat at least five servings of fruits and vegetables a day to reach the National 5 a Day Program goal.

To achieve behavioural change, Dole's nutrition programmes are driven by fundamental principles of: integrity, leadership, partnership, collaboration with NCI and PBH, interactivity and cutting-edge technology. Dole utilizes multiple communication channels to teach children about 5 a Day and motivate changes in their eating behaviour. These channels are:

- Television – a television public service announcement (PSA) reaching children on Saturday mornings.
- Supermarkets – supermarket *5 a Day Tours* programme for local elementary schools.
- Schools – *5 a Day Adventures*, the first nutritional education CD-ROM program.
- Homes – availability of its 'edutainment' CD-ROM to consumers.
- The information superhighway – an e-mail address for kids to communicate with fruit and vegetable characters via the Internet and a 5 *a Day Home Page* on the worldwide web.

25.7.1 Using TV to educate children about 5 a Day

In June 1991, the Center for Science in the Public Interest (CSPI) reported that more than 90% of children's television advertisements on a typical Saturday morning promoted foods of low nutritional value. In support of CSPI's concerns, Representative Ron Wyden (D-OR) urged government officials to support a voluntary agreement from broadcasters and advertisers to air more public service announcements (PSAs) and programming encouraging children to build their diets around fruit, vegetables, grains, lean meats and low-fat milk. In July, the American Academy of Pediatrics recommended the elimination of all television food advertising aimed at children.

In March 1992, the Dole Food Company responded to this 'call to action' by introducing the first component of their national nutrition education programme aimed at children. A 5 a Day PSA, sponsored by the American Academy of Pediatrics and funded by Dole, began airing nationwide on all the major television networks during Saturday morning cartoons. The PSA was targeted to children aged 5–10, and encouraged them to eat five servings of fruits, vegetables and juices each day. The *Fruits and Vegetables Jumps* 5 a Day PSA reached millions of children across the country and is still airing today – 4 years after its introduction.

25.7.2 Interactive educational materials

In 1992, Dole also developed several educational pieces designed to give children the hands-on knowledge and experience required to change their eating habits, and incorporate five servings of fruits and vegetables into their daily diet. ***Fun With Fruits and Vegetables Kids Cookbook*** – a children's cookbook featuring whimsical fruit and vegetable characters – is designed to excite children about making and eating fruit and vegetable recipes. The cookbook includes easy-to-follow directions and illustrations that demonstrate how to prepare and incorporate fruits and vegetables into their diets. Over 4 million cookbooks have been distributed to date, and the demand is consistently high.

How'd You Do Your 5 Today? – a refrigerator chart with 36 reusable, fruit and vegetable character stickers – is intended for children to keep track of the fruits and vegetables they eat every day and to encourage them visually to eat 5 a Day. Currently, 1.5 million charts are in circulation, and their popularity grows daily.

25.7.3 5 a Day supermarket tours

In 1992, Dole met with supermarket leaders around the country to discuss their vision for 5 a Day. Virtually every supermarket expressed interest in the same four objectives: to develop partnerships with schools, provide educational programmes for children, make 5 a Day come alive in their stores and attract local media attention for the national programme.

Dole created the *5 a Day Supermarket Tours* and *Adopt-A-School Programs*, with an ***Activity Guide for Retailers***, designed to educate schoolchildren about fruits and vegetables via supermarket 5 a Day tours. During the 1994–95 school year, over 1 million students toured their supermarket's produce department, learning about 5 a Day and the nutritional value of fruits and vegetables. Today, thousands of supermarkets nationwide offer 5 a Day Tours to local schools. Dole's goal for the 1995–96 school year is to have more than 1.5 million schoolchildren participate in the tours.

25.7.4 Teaching nutrition that's fun in school

In 1990, only 12 states required nutritional education as part of their curriculum for pre-school through high-school-age children. *Healthy People 2000*, the nation's prevention objectives, calls for 'an increase to at least 75% in the number of schools that provide nutrition education for preschool through 12th grade' by the end of the decade.

Research into existing nutrition education materials available to schools revealed that these materials were not frequently used by teachers. Meanwhile, educators were moving towards computer technology in schools. Computer software programs were being developed for maths, science and social studies, but none existed for nutrition education. The emergence of interactive multimedia technology provided Dole with an opportunity to develop a CD-ROM program for elementary schools that would combine education and entertainment – 'edutainment' – to teach children about 5 a Day.

In partnership with the Society for Nutrition Education, Dole developed *5 a Day Adventures*, the first nutritional education CD-ROM program for children. *5 a Day Adventures* brings to life 36 animated fruit and vegetable characters from the *Land of 5 a Day*. Characters like Bobby Banana,

Barney Broccoli and Pamela Pineapple, with their own distinctive voices and personalities, speak to children about the 'cool' way to eat 5 a Day. In the fall of 1993, *5 a Day Adventures* was evaluated by more than 100 third grade classes in five cities: Atlanta, San Francisco, Dallas, Minneapolis and New York. The program was highly praised by educators for its ability to deliver the 5 a Day message while captivating students' attention.

Since February 1994, Dole has made the CD-ROM available free to schools nationwide. The CD-ROM program has been revised several times to incorporate feedback from educators and government and to ensure that the information it contains remains up to date. *5 a Day Adventures* is currently in its third version. Some of the exciting features on the CD-ROM include: ten original 5 a Day Top Tunes, two e-mail addresses for students and teachers, an educational module on the new FDA Food Label, and a copy centre. To enhance the program's interactive capabilities, *5 a Day Adventures* now includes components on the information superhighway. A worldwide web site and an e-mail address allow students to learn about nutrition by using cutting-edge technology.

To date, over 18 000 schools nationwide are using the *5 a Day Adventures* program to teach children to eat five servings of fruits and vegetables a day. Dole currently receives nearly 300 requests for the CD-ROM from teachers each week. Teachers who order the CD-ROM program automatically receive the *5 a Day Aventures Newsletter* which updates them on exciting 5 a Day news and upcoming *5 a Day virtual classroom* activities on the worldwide web site.

25.7.5 'Edutaining' children at home

The explosive growth in the area of multimedia hardware products for the home resulted in an invitation by Apple computers to bundle the *5 a Day Adventures* CD-ROM with their Macintosh Performa 630 CD and 638 CD series. Within a year, this partnership has resulted in 270 000 *5 a Day Adventures* CD-ROMs being used by children at home. This venture marked the entry of Dole's CD-ROM program into the home market.

Today, approximately 30 million American homes have CD-ROM computers. By the end of the decade, there will be more than 42 million multimedia computers in homes across America. Parents today are looking for 'edutainment' software products for their kids.

To achieve widespread distribution of its *5 a Day Adventures* CD-ROM, Dole developed a partnership with Future Vision Multimedia in early 1995. Future Vision made the *5 a Day Adventures* CD-ROM available to consumers for $14.95 through their toll-free order line, and through multimedia software retailers nationwide. In late 1995, Future Vision was acquired by SoftKey International which continues to distribute the *5 a Day Adventures* CD-ROM. Consumers also can buy the CD-ROM in produce departments. To date, thousands of consumers have purchased the CD-ROM program.

25.7.6 5 a Day over the Information Superhighway

Today, more and more children are actively 'surfing the net' for fun and information. According to ***Education 2000*** goals, every school in America will be connected to the Internet by the end of the decade. As a result, Dole was encouraged by the US Department of Education to use the Internet to support the *5 a Day Adventures* program.

Dole sees the Internet as an important communication channel to reach children and, throughout 1995, it has conducted several innovative educational on-line activities. One of the exciting communications vehicles is an e-mail address for children to learn about 5 a Day via the Internet. By writing to fiveaday@bev.net, hundreds of children communicate directly with 36 fruit and vegetable characters, such as Bobby Banana and Barney Broccoli, who e-mail them back with fun tips on how to reach their 5 a Day goal. Committed to maintaining a two-way dialogue, Dole listens to children and responds to their requests and recommendations. To enable teachers to share how they're teaching 5 a Day in the classroom, an e-mail address for teachers, dole.nutrition@bnt.com, was established and is widely used.

In May 1995, Dole rolled out the electronic welcome mat to its 5 a Day worldwide web site at http://www.dole5aday.com. The Dole 5 a Day home page includes: background materials and news about the national 5 a Day program, information about the *5 a Day Adventures* CD-ROM, a fruit and vegetable nutrition centre, 5 a Day information for schools, an easy-to-use e-mail form for children, the character caravan tour schedule, a newsroom, information about Dole, and much more.

During *National 5 a Day Week*, 11–15 September 1995, the first 5 a Day virtual classroom was conducted on the 5 a Day home page. Students in schools from 23 states logged on to talk about the importance of eating five servings of fruits and vegetables a day. The 5 a Day virtual classroom will become an umbrella for a variety of interactive on-line educational activities for students during the year. Increased participation from schools in these events is anticipated due to government efforts to get more schools connected to the internet.

To further enhance the educational value of the 5 a Day home page, several new features will be added in 1996. Enhancements will include a 'Learn About' series which will feature different fruits and vegetables each month. As an adjunct to the e-mail, children can now learn more about the fruit or vegetable that is writing to them. In response to a recommendation from a student who e-mailed the Salad Sisters, the web site will include a tour of a Dole salad factory. A 'Teachers Lounge' will also be added to encourage two-way communication between educators who want to share how they are teaching 5 a Day in their classrooms. Technology and the Internet will play an even larger role as Dole further enhances the 5 a Day home page and develops new programs for reaching children via new and innovative technology applications.

Dole is committed to developing 5 a Day programs that use cutting-edge technology, are fun, interactive and effective.

25.8 The California 5 a Day – for Better Health! Campaign: state-sponsored targeted initiatives

Starting in 1992 the California Department of Health Services allocated $300 000 annually from its federal Prevention Block Grant funds to resume activities of the *California 5 a Day – for Better Health! Campaign*. The original 13 industry partners and other interested organizations were invited to a meeting to explore possible partnership initiatives with the department. They agreed on a five-point strategic plan. Its priorities were: children, Spanish-language dominant adults, the general population, commercial foodservice and community-level coalitions. Each targeted initiative had a clear rationale, and it was felt that together this combination would enable the state to reach the 5 a Day consumption goal by the year 2000.

25.8.1 The California Children's 5 a Day–Power Play! Campaign

Children and their parents were selected as the first priority because of the interest among prospective partners, continuing requests from parents and media to 'do something for kids', and the suspicion that f/v consumption was low and possibly even dropping among young people. In addition, the state education department wanted help from public health to augment their existing school-based child nutrition initiatives. The state's 900 000 children between 9 and 11 years of age (fourth and fifth grade) were selected because at this age they are beginning to make independent food choices and fixing more of their own meals and snacks, they are still interested in health, and they have not yet begun their adolescent decline in healthy eating (Nicklas, 1995).

The Children's Campaign was intended to be consumer-driven. Eight focus groups with boys and girls separately were conducted to determine the messages, spokespersons, elements and creative design of the Campaign. Two weekdays of parent-assisted food records were collected by mail from 400 households participating in market research; these data were weighted to reflect the state's demographics for households with children. This survey found that even in stable households, children's daily consumption was lower than that of adults – only 3.4 servings – but that eating school meals daily or having had nutrition lessons in school correlated positively with f/v consumption (Briggs and Beall, 1994).

The theoretical frameworks adopted for the Campaign were reciprocal determinism and resilience theory, a model being used successfully with adolescents to prevent substance abuse (California Department of Education, 1991; Perry, Baranowski and Parcel, 1990; Domel *et al.*, 1993). the resilience theory constructs of Skills, Norms, Bonding and Rewards/ Recognition seemed likely to add powerful dimensions beyond those of other behavioural change theories. The California Department of Education and the American Cancer Society, California Division, became the Children's Campaign principal co-sponsors. At least two dozen other organizations helped by co-funding co-operative projects, such as the Campaign materials described below.

The Campaign was designed to provide an overarching communications programme delivered through five channels that reach children and their parents: mass media (TV for children, print for parents), schools (classroom and cafeteria), community youth organizations, supermarkets and farmers' markets. The elements of the Campaign were:

- A new logo, slogan and 5 a Day kids spokespersons (Fig. 25.3) – new graphics were needed to better communicate with children. The focus groups found that children this age still preferred 'cool' cartoon characters over real children, but details such as clothing, hair, sports equipment and activities were critical. A Hollywood creative firm was selected to give the Campaign an appealing look and sound.

Figure 25.3 *The Children's 5 a Day–Power Play! Campaign* logo features five 'cool' kids from four major ethnic groups. As the Campaign spokespersons, the 5 a Day Kids appear graphically on all Campaign materials, and they come alive through animation and song in the TV PSAs and the 5 a Day Rap.

- The 5 a Day Rap – a rap song featuring f/v in multiple forms was created as the Campaign jingle by a Hollywood sound studio.
- *Help Kids Eat More Fruits and Vegetables – Tips for Parents of Pre-teens* – a brochure was created for English- and Spanish-speaking parents.
- Four 'idea and resource kits' for schools, community youth organizations, farmers' markets and supermarkets, and a 'community youth organization mini-kit'. The 65-activity *School Idea & Resource Kit* serves as the centrepiece for all the kits, with activities for the other channels designed to complement those for school. The activities are user-friendly for teachers, with cross-references for the required curricular courses (language, arts, social studies, mathematics, etc.), and they include activities that can be done with individual students, the entire class, in the cafeteria, with parents, schoolwide or in the community.
- Four television PSAs – each 30 seconds in length, featuring the 5 a Day Kids and the 5 a Day Rap interacting with children's celebrities.
- Four full-colour editorials – these were full-colour food pages provided free to food editors that featured campaign messages, recipes and tips for parents.
- Point-of-sale materials – these include full-colour posters and small signs, clip art, advertising copy and script for radio PSAs or in-store audio.
- ***Kids ... Get Cookin'!*** – children said that having their own f/v cookbook would be cool, so a laminated cookbook featuring the 5 a Day Kids, celebrities and 22 f/v recipes in English and Spanish was created.

As *Power Play!* was pilot tested in each channel, the feedback from adult intermediaries and parents was very positive. For example, teachers reported that following *Power Play!* activities, children brought f/v snacks from home and substituted f/v for the usual sweet and salty snacks brought for class parties. A Girl Scout Council developed a *Power Play!* Patch programme which required girls to complete activities from the community youth organization idea and resource kit, and their week-long summer *Power Play! Day Camp* was overenrolled. Partners in farmers' markets went into the classroom with *Power Play!* activities and also featured signage and activities on market days.

25.8.2 Power Play! evaluation

In 1994, the NCI and CDC awarded California a 1-year evaluation grant. The study hypothesized that when *Power Play!* was conducted in the school channel alone over a 10-week period, reported f/v consumption would increase by 0.4 serving/day. If all five channels were used (the public health approach), it was expected that consumption would increase by 0.65 serving over that of the control. Three 'school communities' in separate media markets participated from March through May 1995. Nearly 60 schools and over 2600 students ultimately returned matched pre- and post-intervention surveys. Dietary intake was measured using a specially designed children's food diary that was administered in class by trained teachers.

Preliminary results were surprising. First, f/v consumption at baseline was only about 2.9 servings in all three 'school communities', even lower than expected. Secondly, instead of the anticipated seasonal increase, the Control school community unexpectedly dropped by 0.3 serving over the study period. In the School-only community intervention, reported consumption rose by 0.2 serving, while in the School + community study site, consumption rose by 0.4 serving. Both increases were lower than expected, but they were statistically significantly higher than the control, though not from one another. Adverse conditions, namely severe storms and floods, resulting in low availability and high costs of f/v and possibly parental unemployment, are likely to have negatively impacted children's diets in the Control and School + community study sites, both of which are major agriculture centres in California.

The only published school-based f/v intervention for children found that the 300 fourth and fifth grade subjects reported a rise in consumption of 0.3 servings in both the Control and the Intervention classes (Domel *et al.*, 1993). Recent US Department of Agriculture data indicate that f/v are the most under-consumed of the five food groups, with average consumption of children 5–14 years of age being about 3.45 servings daily (Kennedy and Goldberg, 1995; Kennedy *et al.*, 1995). Clearly, the challenge for California will be to find ways of securing widespread participation in the *Power Play! Campaign.*

25.8.3 The California Latino 5 a Day Campaign

The 1991 California Dietary Practices Survey of Adults found a dramatic 18% drop in consumption among Latino adults which persisted through 1993, a marked contrast to the 8% increase found in Caucasian adults between 1989 and 1991. Starting in 1993, the department provided the *California 5 a Day Campaign* an additional $230 000 annually over 3 years to conduct the research, development and feasibility testing for a Spanish-language campaign targeting the state's estimated 4 million Spanish-language dominant adults and 7 million children. The great majority of California Latinos are of Mexican heritage.

The Campaign approach was to develop culturally relevant 5 a Day messages, materials and activities for use in the *Power Play! Campaign* and the *National 5 a Day Program*. Rather than simply translating from English, all Campaign messages are adapted to Mexican–American cultural traditions and speak to the interests, wants and needs of this segment. For

Figure 25.4 For the *Latino 5 a Day Campaign*, a three-generation family group invites the Spanish-speaking consumer to enjoy fruits and vegetables. They remind the reader that family and good health go hand in hand. The logo's design mirrors that of the English-language logo, while displaying an array of culturally popular produce items.

example, if a National Program theme involved football players, the Latino Campaign would use soccer players, a more popular sport with Latinos. Focus groups of men and women separately were conducted to identify the campaign slogan, messages, creative design and elements. Subsequently, elements similar to those of *Power Play!* were developed. These included a special logo and slogan (Fig. 25.4), brochure, power, two taped radio PSAs, one TV PSA and recipes. The logo depicts three generations of Latinos with popular Mexican and American produce items, and the printed materials invite (rather than direct) Latinos to maintain the healthy food tradition of using plenty of f/v because health and family go hand in hand. Emphasis was placed on the disease prevention benefits of f/v in an effort to reduce the marked disparities in knowledge that exist between Latino and other white adults.

The delivery of the Latino Campaign occurs primarily in conjunction with the state's major two promotions, *National 5 a Day Month* every September and the *Power Play!* promotion in March/April. Specific interventions include Spanish-language press kits to ethnic media, radio and TV PSAs, and tag lines with industry partners, 'live remote' radio station broadcasts from cultural events or supermarket parking lots and placements of Spanish-speaking spokespersons on TV and radio. Outcome evaluation is conducted by including a Latino oversample in the statewide California Dietary Practices Surveys every 2 years.

25.8.4 The National 5 a Day Program

The supermarket channel is the most powerful point of sale location for reaching the public, and supermarket partners agree in their licenses to conduct two promotions annually. With the National Program being headquartered 3000 miles away, however, state-specific media and publicity activities are critical for obtaining media pick-up and supermarket participation. Therefore, the California Campaign has developed collateral materials for supermarkets to offer the general adult market, Spanish-speaking adults and parents at store level and in their advertising twice a year. Every September, the California Campaign develops its own 'hooks' to enhance *National 5 a Day Week* and in addition sponsors a month-long spring promotion focusing on children. This new approach offers a platform for virtually all partners to work together and gain maximum benefit from available resources. The challenge is having enough lead time and staff for planning and co-ordinating the efforts of so many organizations.

25.8.5 Additional targeted campaigns

All three state surveys had shown significantly lower f/v consumption when people ate one or more meals away from home (Foerster and Hudes, 1994). The difference was greatest for people who ate in fast-food restaurants. With completion by the National Program of licence standards for restaurants and non-commercial foodservice, the California Campaign is piloting and will launch a statewide restaurant initiative in late 1996. It will focus on medium-priced family chain restaurants, with opinion leader chefs from fine dining establishments providing glamour and media appeal.

Finally, the California Campaign needs to complete its three-level infrastructure by partnering with local organizations that can facilitate regional activities among the channels at the community level, as well as work in each of the state's nine distinct media markets. To date, funds have been insufficient for this function, but it remains the fifth major strategy in the state's long-term plan.

25.9 Epilogue: advances in science and nutritional policy

Since the *5 a Day Campaign* began in 1988, many advances in science and policy have occurred. First, the importance of fruit and vegetable intake to human health has become better understood. Epidemiological data show that the upper quintile of f/v intake which correlates with lower cancer risk also corresponds to eating five servings a day, suggesting that, while higher consumption is likely to lower risk even more, achieving the 5 a Day goal will significantly reduce cancer rates in the general population. Higher consumption of f/v also correlates with lower risk of heart attack, stroke and certain infections (Gey *et al.*, 1993; Gillman *et al.*, 1995; Khaw and Woodhouse, 1995; Verschuren *et al.*, 1995), suggesting that the benefits of higher f/v intake extend to other leading causes of death. National nutritional monitoring data show that Americans who eat more f/v tend to eat less fat, suggesting that 5 a Day may be an important strategy for achieving another national nutritional objective, that of lowering intake of fat to ≤30% of total calories.

Secondly, dietary guidance policy has advanced significantly. Five to nine servings of f/v became official US dietary guidance policy in 1990 (NRC, 1989; USDAHHS, 1990; USDHHS, 1990), replacing the basic four food groups which had recommended only four servings. With the US Department of Agriculture's Food Guide Pyramid becoming the dominant dietary guidance tool used by nutritional educators and the food industry, the 5 a Day recommendation is embedded in virtually all nutrition education materials. This should help raise public awareness of the need to eat at least five servings every day, a principal objective of the *National 5 a Day Program*.

Thirdly, a model for nationwide dietary change now exists. *The National Action Plan to Improve the American Diet* recommends a three-pronged approach of public/private partnerships, improved communications and marketing, and targeted initiatives (Trumpfheller, Foerster and Palombo, 1993). The *National Action Plan* was developed using consensus techniques by opinion leaders in the food industry, voluntary agencies and government. Its framework closely parallels the design being used by the *National 5 a Day Program*. This suggests that since the National Program is using approaches recommended by some of the best thinkers in the food business, it has a good likelihood of continuing to be accepted by them, expanding and increasing in effectiveness.

25.10 Issues for the future

The strength of the evidence linking the typical American diet with excess chronic disease prevalence has grown steadily since the American Heart Association's pioneering call for dietary change in 1961. Poor diet and physical inactivity have recently been blamed for 14% of all premature deaths in the US, second only to tobacco and far outdistancing alcohol, which occupies third place (McGinnis and Foege, 1993). It is estimated that cancer will soon overtake heart disease as the leading cause of death, perhaps by the year 2000. With at least 70–80% of all Americans failing to meet even minimal levels of dietary quality for chronic disease prevention (Kennedy *et al.*, 1995), as compared to half being sedentary and one-quarter still smoking, dietary improvement may be the most prevalent of all unhealthy life-style factors.

On a population basis, dietary change occurs very slowly (Byers, 1993), and interventions take time to achieve results. Based on trends among adults and the readiness of most Americans to change (Kristal *et al.*, 1990;

Glanz *et al.*, 1994; Laforge, Greene and Prochaska, 1994; Patterson *et al.*, 1995), the target date for achieving the national goals of ≤30% of total calories from fat and at least five servings of fruits and vegetables is likely to slip well past the year 2000. For children and young adults where the quality of dietary intake appears poorer than that of adults, the delay in securing improvements may be even longer (Cross, Babicz and Cushman, 1994; Crockett and Sims, 1995; Kennedy and Goldberg, 1995; Kirby *et al.*, 1995; Lytle and Achterberg, 1995; McPherson, Montgomery and Nichaman, 1995). Clearly, it is urgent that large-scale interventions be implemented without further delay.

As outlined above, the *National 5 a Day Program* provides an important opportunity for American public health. Indeed, preliminary data from the *National 5 a Day Program* and the *California 5 a Day Campaign* suggest that intermediate variables associated with consumption are improving. For example, the proportion of persons thinking that five servings is the amount to eat every day has increased, a variable highly correlated with consumption. In California significant proportions of the population have moved from the Precontemplation to Contemplation stage of change. The question for the future is, 'What challenges must the *National 5 a Day Program* anticipate, and what policy decisions are required?'

From a scientific perspective, it will be necessary to more fully understand the determinants of f/v intake. Demographics such as age, gender, ethnicity and education have been associated with only 10% of the variability of f/v intake, while up to 25% has been explained by a rather limited list of psychosocial factors, namely Attitude, Belief, Habit, Confidence, Taste and eating f/v since Childhood (Dittus, Hillers and Beerman, 1995; Krebs-Smith *et al.*, 1995). What are the other modifiable factors and how much do they contribute to variability? These might include eating out, skipping or eating incomplete meals (meals that contain no f/v), cost, convenience and family acceptability. Further, eating is a complicated activity consisting of innumerable behaviour chains that are mediated by motivations consisting of reinforcements (with immediate, frequent and especially obvious reinforcements exerting the strongest influence), self-efficacy and the setting of personal goals (Ewart, 1989). There may be opportunities to impact these variables by focusing messages on near-term benefits such as flavour, style and satiety (Heimendinger and Van Duyn, 1995).

Secondly, are the current models for large-scale change likely to be strong enough? Recent questions have been raised about the efficacy of community models used in cardiovascular disease prevention (Luepker *et al.*, 1994; Fortmann *et al.*, 1995; Goodman, Wheeler and Lee, 1995; Susser, 1995). In the field of tobacco control, it was found that when there are powerful industry interests at play, information and education are not powerful enough interventions. Even with a US ban on television advertising of tobacco products starting in the 1970s, it has been necessary to mobilize a more powerful combination of tactics that include counter-advertising, advocacy and community mobilization to denormalize tobacco use in society at large and to secure policy changes such as clean indoor air ordinances and constraints on minor access (Brownson *et al.*, 1995). It seems likely that the *National 5 a Day Program* will need to make better use of social marketing techniques, especially mass media, combined with development of stronger consumer demand and advocacy at the grass roots, possibly through local community organizing and initiatives to change the food environment in locations such as restaurants, worksites and schools (Wallack and Dorfman, 1992; Glanz *et al.*, 1995; McAlister, 1995).

Thirdly, marketplace economics cannot be ignored. The US food supply is national, rather than local or regional, and it is becoming more concentrated (Gallo, 1995). An estimated $35 billion is spent on promotion every year, food is the single largest advertising segment of the economy, and only a small proportion of advertising promotes basic foods such as f/v (Story and Faulkner, 1990; Taras and Gage, 1995). Competition is keen. For the 3700 calories per capita produced by American agriculture, only 2500 calories are consumed. Share of market comes from price and, increasingly, non-price competition, which includes new offerings, brand loyalty and trade incentives. Perishable and undifferentiated commodities such as fruits and vegetables have special competitive challenges. When farmers have a specific crop to sell in a short window of time, there are few incentives for generic marketing. In the f/v industry, the greatest growth has been in value-added, fresh processed, brand differentiation, and niche markets, rather than promoting fruits and vegetables as a category.

In the food industry, nutrition is often viewed as a long-term strategy which does not contribute to short-term profits, and companies often develop and promote multiple-product categories. Profit margins may be higher when products are made with less expensive and highly stable ingredients, such as sugar, fat, salt or water. Increasingly, factors other than supply and demand mediate what is promoted and available to consumers. When the structure of an industry permits vertical integration and concentration, marketing practices other than consumer preference can dominate. For example, if the *5 a Day Program* wants to promote f/v as snacks, then a major competitor could be the salty snack industry, which is heavily and persuasively advertised and which pays slotting fees as high as $40 000 per shelf foot, thereby ensuring multiple and prominent locations throughout the store (Frank, 1995). In addition, some agricultural economists maintain that a shift to diets which meet the *Healthy People 2000* targets could require major – albeit largely positive – modifications in American agriculture (O'Brien, 1995).

Fourthly, nutrition messages sent to the public will continue to be problematic. While the media rightly cover the release of new studies and researchers promote the latest finding as a critical breakthrough, often the public is provided with little context that reinforces healthy eating. Many studies emphasize nutrients rather than foods, and pharmaceutical industry marketing departments stand ready to support supplementation 'when you cannot always eat a healthy diet'. Further, consensus messages used in dietary guidance, such as balance, variety and moderation, or slogans such as 'all foods fit', give little specific direction as to what to eat or avoid on a daily basis (Nestle, 1995). Indeed, the media thrive on novelty, conflict and controversy, all factors that do not necessarily characterize the 5 a Day message.

25.11 Conclusion

It is significant that the National Cancer Institute has pioneered an effort that translates scientific evidence into action. To do so has required confidence in the soundness of the scientific base and the building of an intervention model. Achieving population behavioural change requires the application of the scientific method to human behaviour, integrating findings from the fields of behavioural science, communications and organizational behaviour. The *5 a Day – for Better Health! Program* has been built on sound science and has incorporated all the known, appropriate elements for success. Only adequate penetration and intensity may be lacking. Most of the activities at the state and local levels receive no consistent funding and are therefore sporadic.

To succeed in its mission, the National Program needs: a broader commitment from industry and government, a more vigorous media component, an expansion of its research into effective interventions for channels such as physicians' offices and restaurants, targeted intervention for some ethnic and less literate groups, and innovative ways of expanding the appeal and reach of the message. An elaborate infrastructure and government/industry partnership has been created. They are functioning well. What is necessary for success is a critical mass of activities flowing through the infrastructure.

The National Program can be, and has been, a model for other nations. However, the concept requires tailoring to reflect the health, agricultural and social contexts of each nation. A number of questions need to be asked, such as: 'Are the health problems associated with low fruit and vegetable consumption the prevalent health problems in my country?', 'What is my culture's perspective on the consumption of fruits and vegetables?', 'What do we know about the barriers to increased consumption that our target populations face?', 'Will an increase in fruit and vegetable consumption require increased fruit and vegetable production and/or imports?' 'If so, what impacts will they have on the current ecological balance in the agricultural system, or on the balance between the farmers and the land?' 'If the ecological balance is disturbed, are the risks worth the benefits?'

If it seems that the *5 a Day Program* could be helpful to other nations, the 5 a Day partners are ready to assist in any way possible.

Acknowledgements

The authors would like to acknowledge the contributions of the many partners in the food and produce industry, other units and levels of federal, state and local government, and partners from voluntary, civic, service and professional organizations without whom this Program would not be possible. Most especially we appreciate the continued help and teamwork from our co-workers who provide the glue to make partnering a reality.

References

Ames, B.N., Bold, L.S. and Willett, W.C. (1995) The causes and prevention of cancer. *Proceedings of the National Academy of Science* USA. **92**, 5258-65.
Blackburn, H. *et al.* (1984) The Minnesota Heart Health Program: A research and demonstration project in cardiovascular disease prevention, in *Behavioral Health – A Handbook for Health Enhancement and Disease Prevention*, John Wiley and Sons, New York.
Block, G., Patterson, B. and Subar, A. (1992) Fruit, vegetables and cancer prevention: A review of the epidemiological evidence. *Nutrition and Cancer*, **18**, 1–29.
Briggs, M. and Beall, D.L. (1994) 5 a Day – Power Play! *School Food Service Journal*, January, 44–87.
Brownson, R.C., Koffman, D.M., Novotny, T.E. *et al.* (1995) Environmental and policy interventions to control tobacco use and prevent cardiovascular disease. *Health Education Quarterly*, **22**, (4), 478–98.
Byers, T. (1993) Dietary trends in the United States. *Cancer Suppl.* **72**, (3), 1015–18.
California Department of Education, Office of Healthy Kids, Healthy California (1991) *Not Schools Alone – Guidelines for Schools and Communities to Prevent the Use of Tobacco, Alcohol, and Other Drugs among Children and Youth*, California Department of Education, Sacramento, California.
Crockett, S.J. and Sims, L.S. (1995) Environmental influences on children's eating. *Journal of Nutritional Education*, **27**, (5), 235–49.
Cross, A.T., Babicz, D. and Cushman, L.F. (1994) Snacking patterns among 1,800 adults and children. *Journal of the American Dietetic Association*, **94**, (12), 1398–1403.
Dittus, K.L., Hilles, V.N. and Beerman, K.A. (1995) Benefits and barriers to fruit and vegetable intake: Relationship between attitudes and consumption. *Journal of Nutrition Education*, **26**, (3), 120–6.
Doll, R. (1992) The lessons of life: Keynote address to the Nutrition and Cancer Conference.

Cancer Research (Suppl.) **52**, (7), 2024S–29S.

Doll, R. and Peto, R. (1981) The causes of cancer: Quantitative estimates of avoidable risks of cancer in the United States today. *Journal of the National Cancer Institute*, **66**, (6), 1191–308.

Domel, S.B., Baranowski, T., Davis, H. *et al.* (1993) Development and evaluation of a school intervention to increase fruit and vegetable consumption among 4th and 5th grade students. *Journal of Nutrition Education*, **25**, (6), 345–9.

Ewart, C.K. (1989) Changing dietary behavior: A Social Action Theory approach. *Clinical Nutrition*, **8**, (1), 9–16.

Fallows, S.J. and Wheelock, J.V. (1982) The means to dietary change – the example of fat. *Journal of the Royal College of Physicians*, **103**, (5), 186.

Farquhar, J.W. (1985) The Stanford Five-City Project: Design and methods. *American Journal of Epidemiology*, **122**, (2), 323–34.

Farquhar, J.W. *et al.* (9190) Effects of community-wide education on cardiovascular disease risk factors. *Journal of the American Medical Association*, **264**, 359–85.

Foerster, S.B. and Hudes, M. (1994) *California Dietary Practices Survey: Focus on Fruits and Vegetables – Trends among Adults, 1898–1993*, California Department of Health Services and the California Public Health Foundation, Sacramento, California.

Foerster, S.B., Kizer, K.W., DiSogra, L.K. *et al.* (1995) California's '5 a Day - for Better Health!' Campaign: An innovative population-based effort to effect large scale dietary change. *American Journal of Preventive Medicine*, **11**, (2), 124–31.

Fortmann, S.P. *et al.* (1995) Community intervention trials: reflections on the Stanford Five-City Project experience. *American Journal of Epidemiology*, **142**, (6), 576–86.

Frank, R. (1995) Frito-Lay devours snack-food business. *Wall Street Journal*, B1, 27 October, 4.

Gallo, A.E. (1995) *The Food Marketing System in 1994*, Agriculture Information Bulletin No. 717, US Department of Agriculture, Washington DC, pp. 1–17.

Gey, K.F., Moser, U.K., Jordan, P. *et al.* (1993) Increased risk of cardiovascular disease at sub-optimal plasma concentrations of essential antioxidants: An epidemiologic update with special attention to carotene and vitamin C. *American Journal of Clinical Nutrition*, **57**, (Suppl.), 787S–97S.

Gillman, M.W., Cupples, L.A., Gagnon, D. *et al.* (1995) Protective effects of fruits and vegetables on development of stroke in men. *Journal of the American Medical Association*, **273**, (14), 1113–17.

Glanz, K., Patterson, R.E., Kristal, A.R. *et al.* (1994) Stages of change in adopting healthy diets: fat, fiber, and correlates of nutrient intake. *Health Education Quarterly*, **21**, (4), 499–519.

Glanz, K., Lankenau, B., Foerster, S.B. *et al.* (1995) Environmental policy approaches to cardiovascular disease prevention through nutrition: issues and opportunities. *Health Education Quarterly*, **22**, (4), 512–27.

Goodman, R.M., Wheeler, F.C., and Lee, P.R. (1995) Evaluation of the Heart to Heart Project: lessons from a community-based chronic disease prevention project. *American Journal of Health Promotion*, **9**, (6), 443–55.

Greenwald, P., Cullen, J.W. and McKenna, J.W. (1987) Cancer prevention and control: from research through applications. *Journal of the National Cancer Institute*, **79**, (2), 389–400.

Havas, S., Heimendinger, J., Damron, D. *et al.* (1995) 5 A Day for Better Health – nine community research projects to increase fruit and vegetable consumption. *Public Health Reports*, **110**, (1), 68–79.

Heimendinger, J. and Van Duyn, M.A. (1995) Dietary behaviour change: the challenge of recasting the role of fruit and vegetables in the American diet. *American Journal of Clinical Nutrition*, **61**, (Suppl.), 1397S–1401S.

Heimendinger, J., Van Duyn, M.A., Chapelsky, D. *et al.* (1996) The National 5 A Day – for Better Health Program: a large-scale nutrition intervention. *Journal of Public Health Management and Practice*, **2**(2), 27–35.

Kennedy, E. and Goldberg, J. (1995) What are American children eating? Implications for public policy. *Nutrition Reviews*, **53**, (5), 111–25.

Kennedy, E.T., Ohls, J., Carlson, S. *et al.* (1995) The healthy eating index:design and applica-

tions. *Journal of the American Dietetic Association,* **95**, (10), 1103–8.
Khaw, K. and Woodhouse, P. (1995) Interrelation of vitamin C, infection, hemostatic factors, and cardiovascular disease. *British Medical Journal*, **310**, 1559–63.
Kirby, S.D., Baranowski, T., Reynolds, K.D. *et al.* (1995) Children's fruit and vegetable intake: socioeconomic, adult–child, regional, and urban–rural influences. *Journal of Nutrition Education*, **27**, (5), 261–71.
Kottler, P. and Roberto, E.L. (1989) *Social Marketing: Strategies for Changing Public Behavior*, The Free Press, New York.
Krebs-Smith, S.M., Heimendinger, J., Patterson, B.H. *et al.* (1995) Psychosocial factors associated with fruit and vegetable consumption. *American Journal of Health Promotion*, **10**, (2), 98–104.
Kristal, A.R., Bowen, K.J., Curry, S.J. *et al.* (1990) Nutrition knowledge, attitudes and perceived norms as correlates of selecting low-fat diets. *Health Education Research*, **5**, (4), 467–77.
Laforge, R.G., Greene, G.W. and Prochaska, J.O. (1994) Psychosocial factors influencing low fruit and vegetable consumption. *Journal of Behavioral Medicine*, **17**, (4), 361–75.
Lefebvre, R.C. *et al.* (1987) Theory and delivery of health programming in the community: the Pawtucket Heart Health Program. *Preventive Medicine*, **16**, 80–95.
Levy, A.S. and Stokes, R.C. (1987) Effects of a health promotion advertising campaign on sales of ready-to-eat cereals. *Public Health Reports*, **102**, 398-403.
Luepker, R.V. *et al.* (1994) Community education for cardiovascular disease prevention: Risk factor changes in the Minnesota Heart Health Program. *American Journal of Public Health*, **84**, 1383-93.
Lytle, L. and Achterberg, C. (1995) Changing the diet of America's children: What works and why? *Journal of Nutrition Education*, **27**, (5), 250-60.
McAlister, A. (1995) Behavioral journalism: beyond the marketing model for health communication. *American Journal of Health Promotion*, **9**, (6), 417-20.
McGinnis, J.M. and Foege, W.H (1993) Actual causes of death in the United States. *Journal of the American Medical Association*, **270**,(18), 2207–12.
McPherson, R.S., Montgomery, D.H. and Nichaman, M.Z. (1995) Nutritional status of children: what do we know? *Journal of Nutrition Education*, **27**, (5), 225–34.
Manoff, R.K. (1985) *Social Marketing: New Imperative for Public Health*, Prager Publishers, New York.
Meisner, H., Bergner, L. and Marconi, K.M. (1992) Developing cancer control capacity in state and local public health agencies. *Public Health Reports*, **107**, (1), 15–24.
Mittlemark, M. *et al.* (1986) Community-wide prevention and cardiovascular disease: Education strategies of the Minnesota Heart Health Program. *Preventive Medicine*, **15**, 1–17.
NCI (National Cancer Institute) (1984) *Diet, Nutrition and Cancer Prevention: A Guide to Food Choices*, US Department of Health and Human Services, Public Health Service, National Institutes of Health NIH Publication No. 85–2711.
NCI (National Cancer Institute) (1986) *Cancer Control Objectives for the Nation: 1985–2000* (ed P. Greenwald and E. Sondik), National Cancer Institute Monographs No. 2, Rockville, MD.
Negri, E. *et al.* (1991) Vegetable and fruit consumption and cancer risk. *International Journal of Cancer*, **48**, 350–4.
Nestle, M. (1995) Viewpoint: Dietary guidance for the 21st century. *Journal of Nutrition Education*, **27**, (5), 272-5.
Nicklas, T.A. (1995) Dietary studies of children: The Bogalusa Heart Study experience. *Journal of the American Dietetic Association*, **94**, (10), 1127-33.
Nissinen, A., Tuomilehgo, J. and Puska, P. (1988) From pilot project to national implementation: Experiences from the North Karelia Project. *Scandinavian Journal of Primary Health Care*, Suppl. **1**, 49–56.
NRC (National Research Council Committee on Diet, Nutrition and Cancer) (1982) *Diet, Nutrition and Cancer*, National Academy Press, Washington DC.
NRC (National Research Council (US) Committee on Diet and Health) (1989) *Diet and Health: Implications for Reducing Chronic Disease Risk*, National Academy Press, Washington DC.
O'Brien, P. (1995) Dietary shifts and implications for U.S. agriculture. *American Journal of*

Clinical Nutrition, **61**, (Suppl.), 1390S–6S.

Patterson, R.W., Kristal, A.R., Lynch, *et al.* (1995) Diet-cancer related beliefs, knowledge, norms, and their relationship to healthful diets. *Journal of Nutrition Education*, **27**, (2), 86–92.

Perry, C.L., Baranowski, T. and Parcel, G.S. (1990) How individual, environments, and health behavior interact: social learning theory, in *Health Behavior and Health Education: Theory, Research and Practice* (eds K. Glanz, F.M. Lewis and B.K. Rimer), Josey-Bass Publishers, San Francisco, California.

Prochaska, J.O. and DiClemente, C.C. (1992) Stages of change in the modification of problem behaviors, in *Progress in Behavior Modification* (eds M. Hersen, R.M. Eisler and P.M. Millers), vol. 28, pp. 184–218, Sage Publications, Thousand Oaks, California.

Puska, P. *et al.* (1985) The community-based strategy to prevent coronary heart disease: conclusions from ten years of the North Karelia Project. *American Review of Public Health*, **6**, 147–93.

Rice, R.E. and Atkin, C.K. (eds) (1989) *Public Communications Campaigns*, 2nd edn, Sage Publications, Newbury Park, California.

Serdula, M.K., Coates, R.J., Byers, T. *et al.* (1995) Fruit and vegetable intake among adults in 16 states: results of a brief telephone survey. *American Journal of Public Health*, **85**, (2), 236–9.

Steinmetz, K.A. and Potter, J.D. (1991a) Vegetables, fruit and cancer. I. Epidemiology. *Cancer Causes and Control*, **2**, 324–7.

Steinmetz, K.A. and Potter, J.D. (1991b) Vegetables, fruit and cancer. II. Mechanisms. *Cancer Causes and Control*, **2**, 427–41.

Story, M. and Faulkner, P. (1990) The prime time diet: a content analysis of eating behavior and food messages in television program content and commercials. *American Journal of Public Health*, 80, 738–40.

Subar, A.S., Heimendinger, J., Krebs-Smith, S.M. *et al.* (1992) *5 A Day for Better Health: A Baseline Study of Americans' Fruit and Vegetable Consumption*, National Cancer Institute, Rockville, Maryland.

Subar, A.F., Heimendinger, J., Patterson, B.H. *et al.* (1995) Fruit and vegetable intake in the U.S.: the baseline survey of the 5 a Day – for Better Health Program. *American Journal of Health Promotion*, **9** (5), 352–60.

Susser, M. (1995) Editorial: The tribulations of trials – intervention in communities. *American Journal of Public Health*, **85**, (2), 156–8.

Taras, H.L. and Gage, M. (1995) Advertised foods on children's television. *Archives of Pediatric and Adolescent Medicine*, **149**, 649–52.

Trock, B., Lanza, E. and Greenwald, P. (1990) Dietary fiber, vegetables and colon cancer: critical review and meta-analysis of the epidemiologic evidence. *Journal of the National Cancer Institute*, **82**, (8), 50–66.

Trumpfheller, W., Foerster, S.B. and Palombo, R. (eds) (1993) *The National Action Plan to Improve the American Diet: A Public/Private Partnership*, Panel to Develop a National Strategic Plan to Prevent Diet-Related Chronic Diseases, Association of State and Territorial Health Officials, Washington DC.

USDAHHS (US Departments of Agriculture and Health and Human Services) (1990) Nutrition and your health: dietary guidelines for Americans. *Home and Garden Bulletin, No. 232*, USDA, Washington DC.

USDHHS (US Department of Health and Human Services, Public Health Service) (1990) *Healthy People 2000: National Health Promotion and Disease Prevention Objectives*, DHHS Publication No. (PHS) 91-50213, US Government Printing Office, Washington DC.

US Public Health Service, Office of the Surgeon General (1988) *The Surgeon General's Report on Nutrition and Health*, DHHS Publication No. PHS 88-50210, US Government Printing Office, Washington DC.

Verschuren, S.M.M., Jacobs, D.R., Bloemberg, B.P.M. *et al.* (1995) serum total cholesterol and long-term coronary heart disease mortality in different cultures. *Journal of the American Medical Association*, **274, (2)**, 131–6.

Wallack, L. and Dorfman, L. (1992) Health messages on television commercials. *American Journal of Health Promotion*, **6**, 190–6.

Weisburger, J.H. (1991) Nutritional approach to cancer prevention with emphasis on vitamins, antioxidants, and carotenoids. *American Journal of Clinical Nutrition*, **53**, 226S-37S.

Ziegler, R.G. (1991) Vegetables, fruits, and carotenoids and the risk of cancer. *American Journal of Clinical Nutrition*, **53**, 251S–9S.

Ziegler, R.G. *et al.* (1992) Does beta-carotene explain why reduced cancer risk is associated with fruit and vegetable intake? *Cancer Research*, **52**, 2060S–2066S.

Index